Published by: Travel Publishing Ltd, 64-66 Ebrington Street,
Plymouth, Devon PL4 9AQ

ISBN13 9781904434703

© Travel Publishing Ltd

First published 1997, second edition 2001,
third edition 2004, fourth edition 2006,
fifth edition 2008

Printing by: Ashford Colour Press, Gosport

Maps by: ©Maps in Minutes ™ (2007) All rights reserved.
©Collins Bartholomews 2007 All rights reserved.

Editor: David Gerrard

Cover Design: Lines and Words, Aldermaston

Cover Photograph: Cwmbran, Gwynedd
© David Noble Photography/Alamy

Text Photographs: © www.picturesofbritain.co.uk
and © Bob Brooks, Weston super Mare
www.britainhistoricsites.co.uk

Foreword

This is the 5th edition of the *Hidden Places of Wales* which has been fully updated. In this respect we would like to thank the Tourist Information Centres in Wales for helping us update the editorial content. The guide is packed with information on many interesting places to visit in a country often referred to as the "Red Dragon". You will find comprehensive details of places of interest as well as advertisers of places to stay, eat and drink included under each village, town or city.

Wales is a country blessed with some of the most dramatic landscapes in Britain. To the north lies Snowdonia, a land of awe-inspiring mountains, wild moorlands and enchanting lakes whilst further south the land is abundant with deep valleys and vast forests. To the west the country has a spectacularly varied coastline of cliffs, coves and sandy beaches. Wales also has a rich cultural heritage full of myths and legends founded on Celtic ancestry but has an equally strong industrial past. We are sure that you will enjoy your visit!

The *Hidden Places* series is a collection of easy to use local and national travel guides taking you on a relaxed but informative tour of Britain and Ireland. Our books contain a wealth of interesting information on the history, the countryside, the towns and villages and the more established places of interest. But they also promote the more secluded and little known visitor attractions and places to stay, eat and drink many of which are easy to miss unless you know exactly where you are going.

We include hotels, inns, restaurants, public houses, teashops, various types of accommodation, historic houses, museums, gardens, and many other attractions all of which are comprehensively indexed. Most places are accompanied by an attractive photograph and are easily located by using the map at the beginning of each chapter. We do not award merit marks or rankings but concentrate on describing the more interesting, unusual or unique features of each place with the aim of making the reader's stay in the local area an enjoyable and stimulating experience.

Whether you are visiting Wales for business or pleasure or are a local inhabitant, we do hope that you enjoy reading and using this book. We are always interested in what readers think of places covered (or not covered) in our guides so please do not hesitate to use the reader reaction form provided to give us your considered comments. We also welcome any general comments which will help us improve the guides themselves. Finally if you are planning to visit any other corner of the British Isles we would like to refer you to the order form for other *Hidden Places* titles to be found at the rear of the book and to the Travel Publishing website at **www.travelpublishing.co.uk**.

Did you know that you can also search our website for details of thousands of places to see, stay, eat or drink throughout Britain and Ireland? Our site has become increasingly popular and now receives over **500,000** visits annually. Try it!

website: www.travelpublishing.co.uk

Location Map

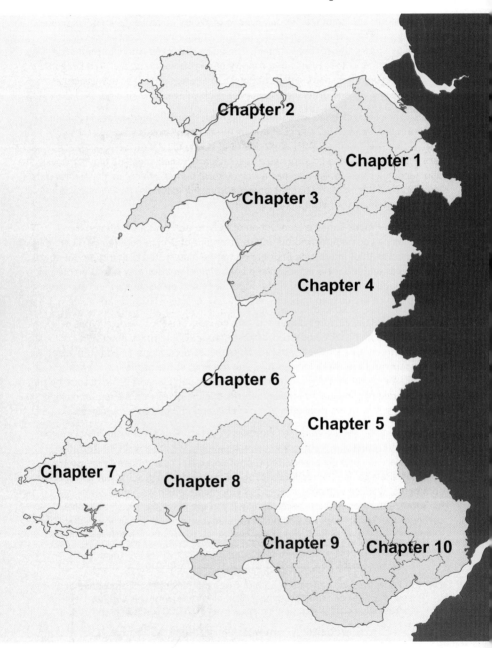

Contents

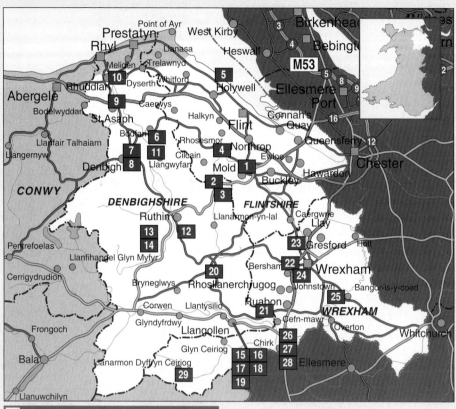

North Wales Borderlands

This area of Wales, the North Wales Borderlands, can easily be overlooked by visitors to the country as they speed westwards, but it is a mistake not to stop and explore the towns, villages and countryside, as they are rich in history and scenic beauty. Each of the different areas has its own special character and scenery: the Clwydian Hills, a 22-mile designated Area of Outstanding Natural Beauty; the Dee estuary; the broad, gentle sweep of the Vale of Clwyd with historic towns like Ruthin, St Asaph and Denbigh; Wrexham, the largest town in North Wales, and its surrounds; The Maelor, where the Cheshire Plains transform into the Welsh Hills; Chirk and the beautiful Ceiriog Valley. The Romans certainly forayed into the area from their major town of Chester and there is also evidence of Celtic settlements.

However, it was during the 13th century that Edward I, after his successful campaign against the Welsh, set about building his ambitious Iron Ring of huge fortresses along the Dee estuary and the North Wales coast. Each was built a day's march from the last and the first stronghold was begun at Flint in 1277. Though the great fortresses are now in ruins, the remains of this massive project - the largest seen in Europe - are still very much in evidence today.

The land around the Dee estuary is home to a great number of waders and wildfowl which feed on the mudflats left by the retreating tides. Between the estuary and the Clwydian Range lie small, compact villages as well as the market towns of Mold and Holywell, a place of pilgrimage that became known as the Lourdes of Wales. The range, a grassy line of hills above the Vale of Clwyd, offers fabulous views and exhilarating walks; it is one of the five designated Areas of Outstanding Natural Beauty in Wales

View of Moel Famau from Foel Fenlli

(see Anglesey, the Gower Peninsula, the Llyn Peninsula and The Wye Valley in their respective chapters).

Further south lie Llangollen and the Dee Valley. Llangollen is a delightful old town in a picturesque riverside setting which is not only a charming place to visit but is also the home of the annual International Music Eisteddfod (not the same as the National Eisteddfod). An eisteddfod was originally a meeting of bards where prizes were awarded for poetry reading and singing. The event at Llangollen has a true international flavour with such eminent figures as Luciano Pavarotti having graced its stage.

Though this northern gateway to the country is not a particularly large area, it boasts all but one of the Seven Wonders of Wales, wonders which while not quite as spectacular as the more familiar Seven Wonders of the World are nonetheless all interesting in their own right and well worth a visit. They are listed in the famous 19th century rhyme:

Pistyll Rhaeadr and Wrexham Steeple,
Snowdon's Mountain without its people,
Overton Yew Trees, St Winefride's Well,
Llangollen Bridge and Gresford Bells.

1 DROVERS ARMS

Mold

Popular hostelry close to town centre serving appetising home-made food and only keg ales.

🍴 see page 231

•

Another son of Mold was Richard Wilson, an 18th century landscape painter who spent his childhood in the town and who, after studying abroad, returned to his native Wales to concentrate on the dramatic scenes of mountainous Welsh countryside which became his trademark. Although he was a co-founder of the Royal Academy, his work was not valued in his lifetime and he died penniless. Wilson's memorial can be found near the north entrance to the parish church.

•

2 LOGGERHEADS COUNTRY PARK

Loggerheads

A popular visitor attraction where the beauty of the area, together with its abundant wildlife, can be enjoyed.

  see page 231

4

MOLD

The county town of Flintshire, Mold is a pleasant little town with a bustling street market every Wednesday and Saturday. The town's finest building is **St Mary's Church** which was built by Margaret Beaufort, the mother of Henry VII, to celebrate her son's victory over Richard III at Bosworth in 1485. It has some interesting stained glass windows as well as some fine architectural ornamentation. A light and airy building, the church was constructed on the site of an earlier church whose original oak roof, carved with Tudor roses, has been retained in part.

The church stands at the foot of **Bailey Hill**, the site of a Norman motte and bailey fortification which was built at this strategic point overlooking the River Alyn by Robert de Montalt. First captured by the Welsh in 1157 and then again by Llywelyn the Great in 1199, ownership of the castle passed through many hands and today, not surprisingly, nothing remains of the fortress; its site is now marked by a bowling green. Montalt gave the town its English name - a straightforward translation of its Welsh name, Yr Wyddgrug, meaning 'The Mound'.

Mold's most famous son is Daniel Owen, the first Welsh novelist of any note. He was born here in 1836 and died here in 1895. Writing only in Welsh, it was Owen's honest accounts of ordinary life that were to make him one of the greatest 19th century novelists and also to gain him the title the 'Welsh Dickens'. His statue stands outside the town library which is also the home of Mold's **Museum** (free), where a room is dedicated to Owen's memory.

On the outskirts of Mold lies **Clwyd Theatre Cymru**, which offers a wide range of entertainment including theatre, music and frequent exhibitions of art, sculpture and photography. It has a bar, coffee shop, bookshop, free covered parking and disabled access.

The composer Felix Mendelssohn was said to have been inspired by the town's surroundings when writing his opus *Rivulet*. The nearby limestone crags provide panoramic views over the surrounding countryside.

One such scenic area lies three miles west of Mold on the A494 - **Loggerheads Country Park** which is situated on the edge of the Clwydian Range. Classified as an Area of Outstanding Natural Beauty, this large park is an ideal environment for all the family, especially younger members, as there are various trails which are each about one and a half miles long. The trails all start near the late-18th century mill building that used water from the River Alyn to drive a water wheel and two sets of stones to grind corn from the local farms.

Around 200 years ago, Loggerheads was part of the lead mining industry, which was founded in this area of ore-bearing limestone. Many relics of those days remain and can still be seen within the quiet woodland. There is a fine selection of local arts, crafts and souvenirs on display in the Craft Shop at the **Loggerheads Countryside Centre**, where there is also a tea room.

AROUND MOLD

RHOSESMOR

3 miles N of Mold on the B5123

Moel Y Gaer, near this small village, was considered to be a fine example of an Iron Age hill fort until archaeological digs unearthed evidence that suggested this site had been inhabited from as far back as 3500 BC.

To the west of the Rhosesmor lie the remains of a short section of **Wat's Dyke**, a much shorter dyke than Offa's which is thought to have been built by the Mercian King Aethelbald in the 8th century.

Just under 40 miles long, the dyke ran southwards from the Dee estuary to Oswestry.

HALKYN

4½ miles N of Mold on the B5123

The village lies close to the long ridge of the **Halkyn Mountains**, which rise to some 964 feet at their highest point and are scarred by the remnants of ancient lead mines and quarries, some of which date back to Roman times.

FLINT

5 miles N of Mold on the A5119

A small and modest town that was once the port for Chester, Flint can boast two historical firsts: it was the first associated borough in Wales to receive a charter (in 1284) and it was also the site of the first of Edward I's Iron Ring fortresses. Dotted along the North Wales coast, a day's march apart, Edward I's ring of massive fortresses represented Europe's most

3 THE MINERS ARMS

Maeshafn

Picturesque early 18th century hostelry serving delicious home-cooked food and real ales.

see page 232

4 THE ANTELOPE HOTEL

Rhydymwyn

Charming 200-year-old inn with excellent cuisine, real ales and comfortable en suite accommodation.

see page 233

Wat's Dyke, Rhosesmor

ambitious and concentrated medieval building project. Started after the Treaty of Aberconwy in 1277 and completed in 1284 by James of St George, **Flint Castle**, now in ruins, stands on a low rock overlooking the coastal marshes of the Dee estuary towards the Wirral peninsula. Originally surrounded by a water-filled moat, the remains of the Great Tower, or Donjon, are an impressive sight. Set apart from the main part of the castle, this tower, which is unique among British castles, was intended as a last retreat and, to this end, it was fully self-sufficient, even having its own well.

Flint Castle featured in the downfall of Richard II, when he was lured here in 1399 from the relative safety of Conwy Castle and was captured by Henry Bolingbroke, the Duke of Lancaster and future Henry IV. The imprisonment of Richard here is remembered in Shakespeare's *Richard II*, where, in response to Bolingbroke's, "My gracious Lord, I come but for mine own," the defeated Richard replies, "Your own is yours, and I am yours, and all." At this point even the King's faithful greyhound is said to have deserted him.

During the Civil War, the town and castle remained in Royalist hands, under the leadership of Sir Roger Mostyn, until 1647, when both were taken by General Mytton, who was also responsible for dismantling the castle into the ruins we see today.

HOLYWELL

7 miles N of Mold on the A5026

In the town lies one of the Seven Wonders of Wales, **St Winefride's Well**, which was once such a place of pilgrimage it was described as the "Lourdes of Wales". According to tradition, Winefride, the niece of St Beuno, was beheaded by Prince Caradoc after refusing his advances. A well bubbled up at the spot where her head fell. Caradoc was struck dead by lightning instantly

St Winefride's Well, Holywell

but Winefride was restored to life after her uncle replaced her head. Winefride (Gwenfrewi in Welsh) went on to become an abbess at Gwytherin Convent near Llanrwst. After her death in 1138, her remains were given to Shrewsbury Cathedral. Thought to have healing qualities, the well has been visited by pilgrims since the 7th century and still is, particularly on St Winefride's Day, the nearest Saturday to 22 June. The well, and the Vale of Clwyd, was beloved of the poet Gerard Manley Hopkins. He trained as a priest at St Beuno's College, Tremeirchion, and St Winefride's Well inspired him to write a verse tragedy, which contains many beautiful, evocative lines:

The dry dene, now no longer dry nor
dumb, but moist and musical.
With the uproll and downcarol of day
and night delivering water.

On Wales in general he was equally lyrical:

Lovely the woods, water, meadows,
combes, vales,
All the air things wear that build this
world of Wales.

St Winefride's Chapel was built by Margaret Beaufort (the mother of Henry VII) in around 1500 to enclose three sides of the well. The Victorian statue of St Winifride has a thin line round the neck showing where her head was cut off. Also here is the **Church of St James**, the local parish church which was built in 1770. It is thought that it stands on the site of the original chapel which was constructed by St Beuno in the 7th century.

Linking Holywell with the ruins of Basingwerk Abbey is the **Greenfield Valley Heritage Park**, a 70-acre area of pleasant woodland and lakeside walks with a wealth of monuments and agricultural and industrial history. There are animals to feed, an adventure playground and picnic areas. In the 18th and 19th centuries this was a busy industrial area which concentrated on the newly established production processes for textiles, copper and brass. Several of the copper works and cotton mills have been restored.

The trail through the park leads down towards the coast and to the ruins of **Basingwerk Abbey** (free). Built by Cistercian monks in 1132, the abbey functioned as a self-sufficient community - the Cistercians placed great emphasis upon agricultural labour. Although this was an English house, Basingwerk absorbed Welsh culture and the Welsh bard, Gutun Owain, was associated with the abbey where he wrote *The Chronicle of Princes*, which is also known as the *Black Book of Basingwerk*.

The Visitor Centre at the abbey provides access to the **Museum of Buildings and Farm**, a collection of reconstructed buildings from across North Wales, including a Victorian school. Other buildings have been grouped to create a working farm where visitors can feed the animals.

EWLOE

4 miles E of Mold on the B5125

Hidden in a steeply wooded glen area are the remains of **Ewloe**

5 GREENFIELD VALLEY HERITAGE PARK

Greenfield, Holywell

An enjoyable day out for all the family with delightful walks, displays and exhibits.

 see page 234

•

The parish church in Hawarden, as well as having stained glass windows by Burne-Jones, also contains the Gladstone Memorial Chapel, where marble effigies of the distinguished statesman and his wife, who are buried in Westminster Abbey, can be seen. The village's connections with Gladstone continue to this day as the former Prime Minister donated his collection of books to the famous St Deiniol's Residential Library, which stands adjacent to the church. The library also houses a small Gladstone Exhibition.

•

Castle, a fortification which was originally an English stronghold until it fell into the hands of the Welsh in around 1146. Owain Gwynedd set about strengthening the fortress as an ambush castle ready to surprise the soldiers of Edward I on their march through Wales when the battle of Ewloe took place in 1157. Some 150 years later, a tower, two wards protected by a curtain wall and an outer ditch were added. But the castle failed to live up to expectations, particularly after the construction of nearby Flint Castle, and by the late 13th century it ceased to have any military significance.

HAWARDEN

5 miles E of Mold on the A550

Mentioned in the *Domesday Book*, this small village close to the English border has two castles, one a ruin dating from the 13th century and another that was once the home of the Victorian Prime Minister, William Gladstone. He lived at **Hawarden Castle** (private) for some 60 years after his marriage to the daughter of Sir Stephen Glynne in 1839. The house was built in 1750 and enlarged and castellated by Sir Stephen in 1809. The remains of the older castle, chiefly the circular keep and the hall, still stand in **Castle Park**.

CAERGWRLE

6 miles SE of Mold on the A541

Once occupied by the Romans as an outpost station for nearby Chester, **Caergwrle Castle**, which

stands on a high ridge, probably started life as a Bronze Age hill fort. It was Dafydd, brother of Llewelyn the Last, who constructed the fortification more or less in its present form and it was from here, in 1282, that Dafydd launched his last, and fatal, Welsh attack on the English King Edward I.

CILCAIN

3½ miles W of Mold off the A541

This charming hamlet in the heart of the Clwydian Range has a medieval church with a double nave, a hammerbeam roof and stained glass. To the south lies **Moel Famau** (The Mother of Mountains); a path leads from Cilcain to the summit which at 1,820 feet is the range's highest peak. It is well worth the climb to the summit as not only are there the remains of a **Jubilee Tower**, started in 1810 to commemorate George III's Golden Jubilee (later blown down in a storm in 1860) but the panoramic views are breathtaking. Westwards lies the Vale of Clwyd with the river stretching down to the Irish Sea, while to the east the land rolls gently down to the Dee estuary.

CAERWYS

8½ miles NW of Mold on the B5122

Originally a Roman station, Caerwys grew to become a village of such significance that it received a charter from Henry III. Once an important market town, Caerwys is credited with being the place where, in around 1100, Gruffydd ap Cynan called the first Eisteddfod. This cultural feast was revived in the 16th century following the intervention of Elizabeth I, who gave permission for a competitive festival of Welsh music and poetry to be held here in 1568.

AFONWEN

8 miles NW of Mold on the A541

Another small village in the Clwydian Range, Afonwen is home to one of the largest craft and antique centres in north Wales. **Afonwen Craft and Antique Centre** not only has a whole host of crafts, accessories and gifts for sale, including furniture, crystal, china and silver, but also holds regular exhibitions and demonstrations.

WHITFORD

10 miles NW of Mold off the A5026

Close to the village of Whitford can be found a curious monument, **Maen Achwyfaen** (The Stone of Lamentation). This Celtic cross, sculpted in the shape of a wheel, is said to have been erected in about 1000 and is the tallest such cross in Britain. The person or event it commemorates is unknown. The renowned 18th century travel writer Thomas Pennant is buried in the graveyard adjacent to the grand 19th century church. Born in 1726, he is best known for his book *A Tour in Wales*. Though he travelled constantly throughout the country, he could speak no Welsh and relied on others to translate for him.

DENBIGH

Recorded as a small border town in the 11th century, Denbigh, whose Welsh name 'Dinbych' means a small fortified place, grew to become a residence for Welsh princes and a leading centre of Welsh power. Today, it still retains a charm that is enhanced by buildings dating from the 16th century onwards, and most of the centre is now a conservation area. The old town is concentrated around the castle that was built on the site of a Roman settlement and commands good views over the Vale of Clwyd.

Denbigh Castle was one of the biggest and most imposing fortifications in Wales and its ruins are still an impressive sight as they crown the top of a steep hill above the town. It was originally a stronghold of the Welsh prince Dafydd ap Gruffydd, brother of Llewelyn the Last, but when the Earl of Lincoln was given Denbigh by Edward I he began construction of a new castle in 1282. De Lacy removed all traces of the older Welsh fortification and, at the same time, created a new English borough protected by town walls. More than 3,000 labourers worked on the castle and the walls. The walled town was completed by 1311 but it was subject to sporadic attacks during its occupation. In 1402, Owain Glyndwr laid siege to the town and it suffered again during the Wars of the Roses, when the old town was burnt to the ground. In 1645, during the Civil War, Charles I stayed at the

6   DENBIGH CASTLE

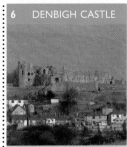

Denbigh

Denbigh Castle, crowning a steep hill above the town, enjoys commanding views of the pastoral Vale of Clwyd.

 see page 234

7 THE FORUM TEA ROOMS & RESTAURANT

Denbigh

Quality tea room and restaurant housed in a striking Grade II listed building in town centre.

🍴 see page 234

8 THE PLOUGH INN

Denbigh

Traditional hostelry serving wholesome home-cooked lunches and draught beers; regular live entertainment.

🍴 see page 235

•

Denbigh developed gradually round its market place and town square, and by the time of the first Elizabethan era it was one of the largest and richest towns in North Wales, and also a centre of culture. Of particular interest is Back Row, where part of Denbigh's original medieval street pattern still exists and where several 15th century buildings, including the Golden Lion Inn, still give a flavour of those times.

•

Denbigh Castle

castle, which was held for him by Sir William Salusbury (nicknamed Old Blue Stockings because of his flashy taste in hosiery); it later endured a six-month siege before falling, in October 1646, to Parliament forces, after which the castle and the walls gradually fell into disrepair. But an impressive triple-towered Gatehouse and a large stretch of the **Town Walls** still exist and can be walked today. The walk opens up a splendid historic view of the town, particularly the section that includes Countess Tower and the Goblin Tower.

Throughout the centuries Denbigh has been the home to many famous characters including the physician, musician, antiquarian and Member of Parliament, **Humphrey Llwyd,** who, in the 16th century, made the first accurate maps of Wales; they were published in an atlas of 1573. He is sometimes known as the Father of Modern Geography.

Born in 1739, **Thomas Edwards** was another noted native of the town, who went on to become an actor and playwright, under the name of Twm o'r Nant, and was given the nickname the Welsh Shakespeare. After a full, colourful and eventful life, Edwards lived out his last days peacefully in Denbigh and he now lies buried in the churchyard of the splendid 14th century St Marcella's Church.

One of the few towns in Wales approved of by Dr Samuel Johnson during his travels through the Principality, Denbigh was also the birthplace of **Henry Morton Stanley.** He was born John Rowlands in 1841, the illegitimate son of John Rowlands and Elizabeth Parry, and grew up partly in the care of relatives and partly in the workhouse in St Asaph. In his late teens he sailed from Liverpool to New Orleans as a cabin boy. There he was befriended by a merchant, Henry Hope Stanley, whose first and last names he took - the Morton came later. He spent the next few years as a soldier, sailor and journalist, and his several commissions for the *New York Herald* culminated in a quest to find the explorer David Livingstone, who had set out for Africa to search for the source of the Nile. At the head of an American-financed expedition, and keeping his intentions hidden from the British, he set out from Zanzibar and struggled to Ujiji, where in 1871 he found the explorer and addressed him with the immortal words "Dr Livingstone, I presume". The two became firm friends, and Livingstone continued his quest after being restocked with provisions. He died a year later. Stanley wrote about his expedition and returned to Africa to take up the exploration where Livingstone left off. He was involved in numerous adventures and enterprises, mainly with Belgian backing, and was instrumental in paving the way for the creation of the Congo Free State. On his return to Britain, he married, spent some years as a Member of Parliament and was knighted by Queen Victoria. He died in London in 1904 and was buried in the churchyard of St Michael in Pirbright; his rough granite headstone bears the one-word inscription "Africa".

Another child of Denbigh was the Elizabethan beauty **Catherine of Berain**, a distant relation of Elizabeth I who married four times and produced so many descendants that she was known as 'Mam Cymru' ('Mother of Wales').

AROUND DENBIGH

BODFARI

3 miles NE of Denbigh on the B5429

Situated in the heart of the Vale of Clwyd, at the foot of the Clwydian Range, Bodfari marks the abrupt change in landscape from arable fields to heath and moorland. Thought to have been the site of a Roman station, the village is famous for **St Deifar's Holy Well**, which can be found at the inn next to St Stephen's Church.

TREMEIRCHION

6 miles NE of Denbigh on the B5429

This small village contains several buildings of interest. The 14th century Church of Corpus Christi is the only church in Britain with that dedication. Inside, there's a 14th century tomb-niche containing the effigy of a vested priest while, in the chancel, a tablet commemorates Hester Lynch Piozzi who is better known as Dr Johnson's friend, **Mrs Thrale**. In 1774, Mrs Thrale inherited a house in Tremeirchion she had known in her childhood which was dilapidated and in need of great repair. Following her marriage to the Italian musician, Gabriel Piozzi, the couple rebuilt the house, living there happily until Piozzi's death.

ST ASAPH

6 miles N of Denbigh on the A525

This small town on a ridge between the River Clwyd and Elwy has city status because of its cathedral. Standing on a hill and constructed

•

In 1567, Sir Richard Clough, a wealthy merchant, built a house which he named Bachegraig near the village of Tremeirchion. Though the house is now demolished, Bachegraig Gatehouse still stands. Its unusual architectural style so shocked the local inhabitants that they thought the devil must have been the architect and had also supplied the bricks. The local story has it that the devil baked the bricks in the fires of hell; to this day, a nearby stream is known as Nant y Cythraul or the Devil's Brook.

•

9	ST ASAPH CAFÉ

St Asaph

Popular town centre café serving appetising food at value-for-money prices. Excellent Sunday roasts.

🍴 see page 235

In the centre of St Asaph is Elwy Bridge, which is believed to date from the 17th century although it was the fine renovation work by Joseph Turner in 1777 that allows it to carry today's heavy traffic. The River Elwy is linked with a particularly fishy tale about Bishop Asaph, after whom the town is named. One day, Queen Nest, the wife of Maelgwn Gwynedd, King of North Wales, lost a precious ring - the ancient and sacred ring of the Queens of the North - while bathing in the river. Upset and fearing her husband's anger, the Queen went to St Asaph to ask for his help in retrieving the ring. Comforting the lady, St Asaph invited the royal couple to dine with him the following evening where he told Maelgwn about the loss of the ring. The king's terrible rage could only just be restrained by St Asaph and he suggested they begin their meal. As the king cut into the locally-caught salmon that started the feast, the sacred ring fell out on to his plate.

on the site of a Norman building, **St Asaph's Cathedral** is not only the country's smallest cathedral, it has also had to endure a particularly stormy past. It was founded in AD 560 by St Kentigern (also known as St Mungo), who left his small church in AD 573 in the hands of his favourite pupil, Asaph, while he returned to Scotland. The cathedral was sacked by Henry III's forces in 1245 and then destroyed during Edward I's conquest of Wales some 37 years later. Edward wished to rebuild at nearby Rhuddlan but Bishop Anian II insisted that the new cathedral remain at St Asaph. The building still standing today was begun by Anian and completed by his two successors.

In 1402 the woodwork was burnt during Owain Glyndwr's rebellion (it was subsequently restored by Bishop Redman) and by the 17th century matters were so desperate that many of the possessions were sold and the Bishop's Palace became a tavern. However, St Asaph's Cathedral has survived and today it holds several treasures including a first edition of the William Morgan Welsh Bible (dating from 1588) that was used at the Investiture of Charles as the Prince of Wales in 1969.

Bishop of St Asaph from 1601 to 1604, **William Morgan** began his mammoth task of translating the Bible into Welsh while he was a rector. During his ministry over the parish of Llanrhaeadr ym Mochnant his congregation grew so upset with his neglect of his pastoral duties for his translation work that he had to be escorted by armed guards to the church. Not only was the finished work of importance to the Welsh churches, each one of which received a copy, but it also set a standard for the Welsh language, which, without being codified, could have been lost forever. Only 19 copies have survived, one of which is on display. A special monument, the **Translator's Memorial**, commemorates and names those who, under Morgan's guidance, assisted him in translating the Bible.

In the 1870s, major restoration work on the cathedral was entrusted to Sir George Gilbert Scott, who also worked on the restoration of the cathedrals at Bangor and St David's as well as building many churches and houses throughout the United Kingdom. (The Scott dynasty takes a bit of sorting out: Sir George Gilbert Scott (1811-1878), the most prolific builder and restorer, had two architect sons, George Gilbert Scott Jr (1839-1897) and John Oldrid Scott (1842-1913). John Oldrid's son Sir Giles Gilbert Scott (1880-1960) was responsible for Liverpool Cathedral.)

RHUDDLAN

8 miles N of Denbigh on the A525

Rhuddlan is the site of an early Norman stronghold known as Twt Hill, which today is marked by a prominent earthen mound. Rhuddlan is now overshadowed by its impressive castle ruins. One of the Iron Ring of fortresses built by

Edward I, **Rhuddlan Castle**, as one of the most massive and impenetrable of his defences, was the king's headquarters during his campaign. It was from here, in March 1284, that Edward issued the Statute of Rhuddlan that united the Principality of Wales with the Kingdom of England. He also gave the town a Royal Charter when his sovereignty was confirmed. The statute, which lasted until the Act of Union in 1536, was enacted on the site now occupied by Parliament House which bears a commemorative tablet on the wall which is said to be from the original building. Although the castle, like many, was partially destroyed during the Civil War, the town is still sometimes referred to as the Cradle of Wales.

Rhuddlan Castle, nr Rhyl

While the castle in its heyday was a magnificent example of medieval defensive building, the most impressive engineering feat in the area was the canalisation of the River Clwyd to give the castle access by ship to the sea some three miles away. The remains of the dockgate, **Gillot's Tower**, can still be seen - this was built by James of St George, who was also responsible for the interesting concentric plan of the castle which allowed archers, stationed on both the inner and outer walls, to fire their arrows simultaneously.

DYSERTH

10 miles N of Denbigh on the A5151

Lying in the foothills of the Clwydian Range, below Craig Fawr's slopes, this village in the scenic Vale of Clwyd boasts a 60-foot waterfall as well as a charming parish church which dates from the 13th century.

Just to the west of the village stands **Bodrhyddan Hall**, the 17th century manor house of the Conwy family who have had their home here since the early 15th century. The hall houses the Charter of Rhuddlan, and visitors can also see, around the fireplaces in the white drawing room, panels that came from the chapel of a ship of the Spanish Armada that foundered off the coast of Anglesey. Other notable items include Hepplewhite chairs, suits of armour and ancient weapons, a family portrait by Sir Joshua Reynolds and an Egyptian mummy. The **Gardens** here too are of interest, the main feature being a box-edged Victorian parterre designed by William Andrews Nesfield, father of the famous William Eden Nesfield, who remodelled the house in 1875. William E had a very varied life, being a soldier and a watercolour

10 RHUDDLAN CASTLE

Rhuddlan, nr Rhyl

Rhuddlan was one of the 'iron ring' of fortresses built by Edward I during the English king's late 13th century campaigns against the Welsh.

🏛 see page 235

**11 THE KINMEL ARMS
TAVERN**

Llandyrnog

16th century hostelry
offering outstanding food
and hospitality; spacious
beer garden and play area.

🍴 see page 236

painter before taking up garden design when he was over 40. He worked on well over 200 estates, among the most notable being the Royal Botanic Gardens at Kew. A much older part of the garden at Bodrhyddan is centred around a well house (bearing the inscription 'Inigo Jones 1612') containing a spring, St Mary's Well, that may once have had pagan significance.

BODELWYDDAN

8 miles N of Denbigh off the A55

The village church, known as the **Marble Church**, was built between 1856 and 1860 by Lady Willoughby de Broke as a memorial to her husband. The landmark white spire is of local limestone, while inside is an arcade made of 14 different types of marble.

Opposite the eye-catching church stands **Bodelwyddan Castle**, a Victorian country house and estate which occupies the site of a 15th century house. The castle is the Welsh home of the National Portrait Gallery, and as well as the wonderful collection of Victorian portraits on display, visitors can see beautiful furniture on loan from the Victoria and Albert Museum and sculptures from the Royal Academy. Anyone tiring of the glorious pieces exhibited here can relax and play one of several hands-on Victorian games and inventions in the gallery, while outside are picnic tables, an adventure playground, maze, terrace café and secret woodland walk. A hands-on science centre is the latest attraction.

18th and 19th century landscaped parkland surrounds the castle and here, too, is an Arts and Crafts walled garden originally planted by TH Mawson, with some redesign work being undertaken by H Moggridge in 1980.

LLANRHAEADR-YNG-NGHINMEIRCH

3 miles SE of Denbigh on the A525

This pretty little village with its whitewashed Georgian almshouses attracted pilgrims in their thousands in medieval times. They came to drink from the Holy Well where a 6th century hermit had invested a waterfall with healing powers capable of curing "scabs and the itch" and even smallpox. St Dyfnog would do penance by standing under the waterfall in his hair shirt, thus transferring his virtues to the water. As late as the 1700s his "mighty spring was still much resorted to" and it was then that the 'bath' was paved with marble which is still in place.

The nearby **Church of St Dyfnog** is entered by a striking timber porch richly adorned with carving from about 1530 but its chief treasure is a marvellous Tree of Jesse window. The Tree of Jesse, most often seen depicted in church windows, details the family tree of Christ down from Jesse, the father of King David. This superb window, made in 1553, was saved from destruction during the Civil War by being buried in a dug-out chest, which can also be seen in the church.

RUTHIN

7 miles SE of Denbigh on the A525

This old market town lies in the Vale of Clwyd, more or less surrounded by a ring of hills, with a layout that appears to have changed little from medieval days. In fact, a description of Ruthin written in Elizabethan times, extols it as "the grandest market town in all the Vale, full of inhabitants and well replenished with buildings". Remarkably, this is as true today as it was then. **St Peter's Square** is a good place from which to view the town; it was here in 1679 that a Catholic priest was hung, drawn and quartered. Situated behind a magnificent set of 18th century wrought iron gates stands the town's splendid **St Peter's Church**. Founded in the late 13th century as a collegiate church, its notable features include an early 16th century oak roof that consists of 408 carved panels while behind the church there are some beautiful buildings in the collegiate close: 14th century cloisters, the Old Grammar School of 1284 and 16th century almshouses.

St Peter's Square itself is edged with many lovely buildings, including the particularly eye-catching 15th century **Myddleton Arms** with its unusual Dutch style of architecture and its seven dormer windows that have been dubbed the 'Eyes of Ruthin'. At one time there were around 60 inns and pubs in Ruthin - one for every 10 men in the town - and nine of these were to be found around the

Old Courthouse, Ruthin

square. On the south side of St Peter's Square stands the impressive wattle and daub **Old Courthouse** which dates from 1401 and was a temporary resting place for prisoners, who were kept in the cells below the magnificent beamed court room. The building is now occupied by the National Westminster Bank but the beam once used as a gibbet still projects from the north-west wall.

Also in the square is Maen Huail, a stone which according to legend marks the place where Huail was beheaded by King Arthur because of their rivalry in love.

In Castle Street can be found one the oldest town houses in North Wales. **Nant Clwyd House** is a fine example of Elizabethan architecture although the present 16th century building shows traces of an earlier house. During the reign of Elizabeth

On Clwyd Street in Ruthin is Ruthin Gaol through whose gates thousands of prisoners - men, women and children, the guilty and the innocent - passed between 1654 and 1916. Visitors can see how prisoners lived their daily lives: what they ate, how they worked, the punishments they suffered. The cells, including the punishment, 'dark' and condemned cells, can be explored, and there are hands-on activities for children.

15

12 THREE PIGEONS INN

Graig-fechan

Traditional rural Welsh hostelry serving real ales and wholesome home-made food.

see page 237

13 PARADISE COTTAGE

Clocaenog

Characterful 15th century cottage offering 4-star self-catering accommodation close to Clocaenog Forest.

see page 237

14 GLAN LLYN INN

Clawddnewydd

Welcoming village hostelry with conservatory restaurant, bar snacks and real ales.

see page 235

It it was the home of Dr Gabriel Goodman, an influential man who was the Dean of Westminster for 40 years. He established Ruthin School in 1595 and built the town's almshouses. Work is under way to open the house to the public in the near future.

Ruthin Castle, begun in 1277 by Edward I, was the home of Lord de Grey of Ruthin who, having proclaimed Owain Glyndwr a traitor to Henry IV was given a large area of land originally held by the Welshman. After Glyndwr crowned himself Prince of Wales, de Grey was the first to suffer when Ruthin was attacked in 1400. Though the town was all but destroyed, the castle held out and survived the onslaught. During the Civil War, the castle again came under siege, this time surviving for 11 weeks in 1646 before eventually falling to General Mytton. He then had the building destroyed. Partially restored and then owned by the Cornwallis-West family, Ruthin Castle played host, before and during World War I, to many famous and influential Edwardians including the Prince of Wales (later Edward VII), the actress Mrs Patrick Campbell and Lady Randolph Churchill, the mother of Winston Churchill. Today, the castle, with its charming grounds and roaming peacocks, is a hotel specialising in medieval banquets.

LLANARMON-YN IÂL

11 miles SE of Denbigh on the B5431

The capital of the upland Iâl region and occupying an attractive position on the banks of the River Alun, this small village boasts one of Denbighshire's most notable churches. Standing in a spacious churchyard rather like a village green, it is dedicated to **St Garmon**, a 5th century warrior bishop who won a great victory in AD 429 against an invading army of pagan Picts and Saxons. The church at Llanarmon became a shrine to the saint thus generating the funds that enabled the building of the double nave. It has a fine timber roof, a well-preserved effigy of a 14th century knight, two old parish chests and a magnificent 18-branched chandelier made in Bruges around 1500. The church was extensively restored during the 1730s and the Georgian influence is apparent in the large round-topped windows, the Classical-style porch and the elegant Georgian font.

LLANFIHANGEL GLYN MYFYR

11 miles SW of Denbigh on the B5103

This sleepy village lies in the fertile vale through which the River Alwen runs. Just to the north lies the **Clocaenog Forest**, Wales' second largest commercial plantation, which covers much of the southern moorland between the vales of Clwyd and Conwy. Managed by the Forestry Commission, it has well-marked forest trails of varying lengths that lead walkers through the mixed plantation of larch, spruce, pine, beech, oak and ash.

On the edge of the forest lies **Llyn Brenig**, a massive man-made reservoir that was completed in 1976 to accompany the smaller **Llyn Alwen**, which dates from the early 1900s. Close to the dam, and reached along the B4501, is a Visitor Centre which explains the local history and ecology of this tranquil Welsh valley as well as acting as a starting point for lakeside walks. By the lake, depending on the time of year, butterflies such as Orange Tip and Tortoiseshell can be seen. Along with the water sports on the lake, fishing is also available.

CERRIGYDRUDION

12½ miles SW of Denbigh on the B4501

This village's name, often misspelt as 'druidion', means 'Place of the Brave' and has absolutely no connection with Druids. There are many tales of fairy cattle to be found in Wales, creatures that are thought to have descended from the aurochs, the wild cattle that roamed Britain in prehistoric times. Cerrigydrudion has it own cow, Y Fuwch Frech (the freckled cow), which lived on nearby Hiraethog mountain. For years she supplied the area with milk and would always fill any receptacle brought to her. One day, a witch began to milk her into a sieve and continued until the cow went insane and drowned herself in Llyn Dau Ychen.

GWAENYNOG BACH

1½ miles W of Denbigh on the A543

During the 19th century Beatrix Potter was a frequent visitor to the beautifully situated estate of Gwaenynog Hall, which was owned by her uncle, Fred Burton. It is thought that her sketches of the kitchen garden (which has now been restored) were the basis for *The Tale of the Flopsy Bunnies* and also the working environment of the fictional Mr McGregor the gardener, who wanted to bake Peter Rabbit in a pie.

LLANGOLLEN

A busy and picturesque town set on low hills beside the River Dee, Llangollen is known worldwide for its annual **International Musical Eisteddfod** which has been held here since 1947. For six days at the beginning of July musicians, choirs, folk singers and dancers from all over the world, and many performing in their national costumes, converge on the town to take part in this wonderful cultural event that is centred around the **Royal International Pavilion,** a modern cultural complex which hosts concerts, exhibitions, film shows and craft events throughout the rest of the year. The International Eisteddfod should not be confused with the **National Eisteddfod**, the annual Welsh language cultural festival whose venue alternates between the north and south of the country. The first recorded eisteddfod was held at Cardigan Castle in 1176, and the modern eisteddfod began as a competition between bards at the Owain Glyndwr hotel in Corwen in 1789. It became a truly national event at Llangollen in 1858, when thousands of people came to

15   GALES OF LLANGOLLEN

Llangollen

Town centre hotel offering outstanding food, a superb choice of wines and luxurious accommodation.

⊨ ¶ *see page 238*

16   POPLAR HOUSE

Llangollen

Former coaching inn in town centre offering B&B or self-catering accommodation, disabled facilities and a hot tub.

⊨ *see page 239*

17   THE SMITHFIELD ARMS

Llangollen

Lively town centre hostelry with good home cooking, regular entertainment and accommodation.

¶ ⊨ *see page 240*

River Dee, Llangollen

Llangollen

Llangollen Railway has restored part of the former cross-country line that once served the town of Llangollen.

 see page 240

Llangollen from all over the country. Music, prose, drama and art are included in the festival, which culminates in the chairing and investiture of the winning poet.

The focal point of the town is the fine old **Bridge** over the Dee which is mentioned as one of the 'Seven Wonders of Wales' in the famous poem. Originally built in 1347 with an 8ft breadth by Dr Trevor, who later became Bishop of St Asaph, the four-arched

structure was partly rebuilt in 1656, and again in 1863 to allow access to the new railway to pass beneath it. The bridge is still used by today's traffic.

Llangollen's history goes back to the late 6th and early 7th century when St Collen, after whom the town is named, founded a church here. The church is still standing but has been much restored and refurbished over the years.

On the north side of the river is **Llangollen Station**, home of the Llangollen Railway Society. Since taking over the disused line in 1975, the Society has restored 8 miles of the railway track and journeys along the banks of the River Dee can be taken on this delightful steam railway. The station houses a museum with a collection of engines, coaches and rail memorabilia. Also along the banks of the Dee lies **Llangollen Wharf**, from where pleasure cruises have started since 1884. Some trips are horse-drawn, while others cross the **Pontcysyllte Aqueduct** in the narrow boat *Thomas Telford* whose name pays homage to the architect of this impressive structure. Eighteen massive columns 126ft high support the huge cast iron trough, 11ft 10in wide and 1007ft long. Those who have a head for heights can walk along the towpath where only a lip a few inches high stands between the walker and the river. Opened in 1805, the aqueduct has been recently nominated as a World Heritage Site.

Overlooking the town are the dramatic remains of **Castell Dinas**

Bran. Originally an Iron Age hill fort, the site was used by Prince Gruffudd ap Madoc to build a castle in 1260. The remains are not extensive, but the climb is well worth the effort as the view over the town and the Vale of Llangollen is quite breathtaking.

In the early 19th century Llangollen became famous as the home for 50 years of the "Ladies of Llangollen", Lady Eleanor Butler and Miss Sarah Ponsonby. These two eccentric Irish women ran away from their families in Ireland and set up home together in 1780 in a cottage above the town. As well as devoting their lives to "friendship, celibacy and the knitting of blue stockings", the ladies also undertook a great deal of improvements and alterations that turned a small, unpretentious cottage into the splendid house - **Plas Newydd** - that is seen today. The marvellous 'gothicisation' of the house was completed in 1814 . Some of the elaborate oak panels

Pontcysyllte Aqueduct, Llangollen

and the glorious stained glass windows were donated to the couple by their famous visitors. These included Sir Walter Scott, William Wordsworth, the Duke of Gloucester and the Duke of Wellington. The ladies were both buried in the churchyard of St Collen, sharing a grave with their friend and housekeeper, Mary Caryll.

19 GREENBANK HOTEL & RESTAURANT

Llangollen

A fine restaurant with rooms, serving excellent cuisine throughout the day.

⊨ ‖   *see page 241*

Plas Newydd, Llangollen

The **Gardens** at Plas Newydd are interesting and, while the formal layout to the front of the house was created after the ladies had died and the terraces have been altered since they lived here, they still reflect the peace and quiet the couple were seeking as well as containing more interesting curios from those early Regency days.

The main route north out of Llangollen passes the impressive ruins of **Valle Crucis Abbey**. Situated in green fields and overshadowed by the surrounding steep-sided mountains, this was an ideal place for a remote ecclesiastical house, the perfect spot for the Cistercians, medieval monks who always sought out lonely, secluded places. This abbey was founded in 1201 by Madog ap Gruffyd, the Prince of Powys, and was a very suitable location for the monks of this austere order. Despite a fire, the tower collapsing and the Dissolution in 1535, the ruins are in good condition and visitors can gain a real feel for how the monks lived and worked here. Notable surviving original features include the west front with its richly carved doorway and rose window, the east end of the abbey and the chapter house with its superb fan-vaulted roof. Also to be seen are some mutilated tombs which are thought to include that of Iolo Goch, a bard of Owain Glyndwr. Valle Crucis means 'Valley of the Cross' and refers to **Eliseg's Pillar**, which stands about half a mile from the abbey and was erected in the early 9th century.

The inscription on this Christian memorial cross is now badly weather-beaten but fortunately a record was made in 1696 of the words. It was erected in memory of Eliseg, who annexed Powys from the Saxons, by his great-grandson Concenn. The pillar was broken by Cromwell's men and not re-erected until the 18th century.

A little further northwards along this road lies the spectacular **Horseshoe Pass** which affords remarkable views of the surrounding countryside. From the top of the pass can be seen the Vale of Clwyd and the ridge of Eglwyseg Rocks where Offa's Dyke path runs.

AROUND LLANGOLLEN

JOHNSTOWN

6 miles NE of Llangollen on the B5605

On the B5605 between Johnstown and Rhosllanerchrugog lies **Stryt Las Park**, a predominantly wetland area with a large lake and three small ponds. This Site of Special Scientific Interest is home to one of Europe's largest colonies of the Great Crested Newt. The park is open daily, the visitor centre daily in summer, weekends only in winter. In Rhosllanerchrugog, the Stiwt is a forum for Welsh language choirs, stage performances and crafts.

BERSHAM

7½ miles NE of Llangollen off the A483

Bersham lies in part of the **Clywedog Valley and Trail** that skirts around the south and west of

Wrexham and includes several places of industrial interest. The village was established around 1670 and was the home of the Davis brothers. The fine workmanship of these two famous iron masters can be seen in the beautiful gates at Chirk Park and at St Giles' Church in Wrexham.

The master and owner of **Bersham Ironworks** from 1762, John 'Iron Mad' Wilkinson, was himself famous for the cannons he bored for use in the American War of Independence and for the cylinders he produced at the ironworks for James Watt's steam engines. The remains of the ironworks are open in the summer, the **Heritage Centre** all year round. The Clywedog Trail passes through Plas Power and Nant Mill, woods that stretch along the River Clywedog between Bersham and Coedpoeth. A well-preserved section of Offa's Dyke cuts through Plas Power.

WREXHAM

9½ miles NE of Llangollen on the A483

The largest town in North Wales, Wrexham has been extensively 'refurbished' in recent years. Its pedestrianised town centre now offers a good mix of small independent shops and boutiques as well as the regular high street names. Wrexham's origins as a market town are reflected in its three indoor markets - the People's, Butcher's and General - the monthly Farmer's Market and the occasional French and Continental Markets. There's also an open air market every Monday in Queen's Square.

For those wishing to find out more about the town and its social, industrial and local history then **Wrexham Museum** (free), housed in the County Buildings that were originally constructed as the militia barracks in 1857, is a very good place to start. The discovery of a skeleton nearby - it became known as Brymbo Man - traces the town's history back as far as the Bronze Age while the Romans are also known to have settled in the Wrexham area. Both Roundhead and Cavalier troops were garrisoned in the town during the Civil War and, in more peaceful times, in the late 19th century, Britain's first lager brewery was built in Wrexham in 1882. The suburb of Acton was the birthplace of Judge Jeffreys, the notoriously harsh lawman who was nicknamed 'Bloody' for his lack of compassion and his belief in swift justice. More recently, Wrexham was central to the early development of football in wales and the museum houses the Welsh Football Collection.

Perhaps Wrexham's best known building, and one that's a particular favourite of American tourists, is the **Church of St Giles** that dominates the town's skyline. It is famous for being the burial place of Elihu Yale, the benefactor of Yale University, who was laid to rest here on his death in 1721. His father had emigrated from Wrexham to North America in 1637 and Elihu was born soon afterwards in Boston. In 1691 Elihu

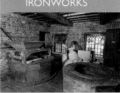

22 BERSHAM HERITAGE CENTRE & IRONWORKS

Bersham

Discover the industrial heritage of Wrexham where the remains of an 18th century iron works can be seen.

 see page 243

•

In 2005, a study of 258 cities and towns revealed that Wrexham is the car lovers' capital of Europe. Apparently, 93% of Wrexhamite commuters travel by car, about the same as in Detroit and Los Angeles. It's not just a Welsh thing, however. Of the top 20 car-mad cities, 15 were in England.

•

Church of St Giles, Wrexham

23   QUEENS HEAD

Bradley

Lively hostelry serving a good selection of food and beverages, including 2 real ales, and offering a wide range of entertainment.

 see page 244

24   ERDIGG

Erdigg, nr Wrexham

Two miles south of Wrexham, in a glorious 2,000-acre estate and country park, Erddig is one of the most fascinating houses in Britain

 see page 243

sent a cargo of books and Indian goods from Fort Madras where he was Governor. The sale of the books enabled him to initiate the University of Yale in 1692. The memorial quadrangle at Yale has a Wrexham Tower. Yale's tomb in St Giles was restored in 1968 by members of Yale University to mark the 250th anniversary of the benefaction. It can be found in the churchyard to the west of the tower.

The church itself is also well worth taking the time to look over; its 136 feet pinnacle tower is one of the Seven Wonders of Wales. Begun in 1506 and much restored, this Gothic tower still bears some of the original medieval carvings, in particular those of St Giles, which are recognisable by his attributes of an arrow and a deer. Elsewhere in the church are a colourful ceiling of flying musical angels, two very early eagle lecterns, a Burne Jones window and the Royal Welsh Fusiliers chapel.

Just to the south of Wrexham and found in a glorious 2,000-acre estate and Country Park, is **Erddig**, one of the most fascinating houses in Britain. Construction on the late-17th century mansion was begun by Joshua Edisbury, the High Sheriff of Denbighshire, who later fled to avoid his creditors. The house passed into the hands of the Yorke family and their descendants, until finally it came into the ownership of the National Trust. Its fabulous state rooms have been restored to their original glory whilst, below stairs, visitors can see the living and working conditions of the many servants a house of this size required. The Servants' Hall is particularly remarkable for its array of portraits of the servants commissioned by the owner. Within the exquisite grounds are restored outbuildings, walled gardens, a yew walk, woodland trails and the National Ivy Collection.

Along with Erddig, which lies within the Clywedog Valley and Trail, is **King's Mill**, a restored mill that dates from 1769 although an older mill has been on the site since 1315.

GRESFORD

13 miles NE of Llangollen on the B5445

This former coal mining town was the site of a mine explosion in 1934 that killed 266 men. The colliery closed in 1973 but the wheel remains in memory of those who lost their lives in this terrible disaster. The town's **All Saints' Church** is one of the finest in Wales, with notable medieval screens, stained glass, font and misericords, and a memorial to the mining disaster. It is also home to the famous **Gresford Bells**, one of the Seven Wonders of Wales, which are still rung every Tuesday evening and on Sundays.

HOLT

15 miles NE of Llangollen on the B5102

The River Dee, which marks the boundary between Wales and England, runs through this village and its importance as a crossing point can be seen in the attractive 15th century bridge. The village of Holt was also the site of a Roman pottery and tile factory that provided material for the fort at nearby Chester.

BANGOR-IS-Y-COED

11 miles E of Llangollen on the B5069

Bangor-is-y-coed, also known as Bangor-on-Dee, is in the area called the Maelor, where the Cheshire Plains turn into the Welsh Hills. The village is well known to race-goers as it is home to a picturesque **Racecourse**, situated on the banks of the River Dee, that stages several National Hunt meetings annually. The village itself has a charming 17th century bridge said to have been built by Inigo Jones. Across the bridge, the **Plassey Craft and Retail Centre** occupies some attractively converted Edwardian farm buildings surrounded by the beautiful scenery of the Dee Valley. There's a wide choice of traditional hand-made crafts on sale, along with a working blacksmith, an equestrian supplier, restaurant and coffee shop.

Bangor was the site of a Celtic monastery founded in around AD 180, which was destroyed in AD 607 by Ethelfrid of Northumbria in what turned out to be the last victory by the Saxons over Celtic Christianity. Apparently, 1,200 monks were laid to the sword as Ethelfrid considered praying against him was tantamount to fighting against him. Those fortunate enough to have survived are thought to have travelled to Bardsey Island. Local legend also suggests that Owain Glyndwr married Margaret Hanmer in the hamlet of Hanmer, just four miles away.

OVERTON

10 miles E of Llangollen on the A539

This substantial border village is home to another of the Seven Wonders of Wales - the **Overton Yew Trees**, 21 trees that stand in the churchyard of the village Church of St Mary. Dating from medieval times, these tall, dark and handsome trees have a preservation order placed upon them. Within the church itself there are some interesting artefacts from the 13th century.

CHIRK

5½ miles SE of Llangollen on the B5070

This attractive border town's origins lie in the 11th century castle of which, unfortunately, little remains except a small motte close to the town's 15th century church. Today, Chirk is perhaps better known for **Chirk Castle** (National Trust) which lies half a mile west of the

25 BUCK HOUSE HOTEL

Bangor-on-Dee

Small, family-run hotel with quality cuisine, en suite rooms and games room.

 see page 245

26 CHIRK CASTLE

Chirk, Wrexham

An impressive fortress originating in the 13th century, the castle is still inhabited and many of the rooms and the garden are a delight to wander around.

see page 246

27 THE HAND HOTEL

Chirk

Historic 17th century coaching inn offering excellent cuisine and quality en suite accommodation.

see page 247

Chirk Castle

28 COFFEE SHOP

Chirk

Long-established café serving wholesome home-made food at very reasonable prices.

see page 246

village. Begun in the late 1200s on land granted to Roger de Mortimer by Edward I, this still magnificent fortress - with a massive drum tower at each corner - has been rebuilt on several occasions but has managed to remain as impressive today as it must have been centuries ago. The castle is still lived in today by the Myddleton family whose antecedent, Sir Thomas Myddleton, Lord Mayor of London, purchased the castle in 1595 for £5,000. Visitors to the castle see the elegant state rooms, some fine Adam-style furniture, tapestries and portraits. By contrast, the castle's dramatic dungeons indicate that life here was not always so peaceful and genteel.

The early 15th century Welsh hero, Owain Glyndwr, was brought up initially at Chirk Castle before attending the English court of Richard II. Educated as a lawyer, the charismatic Glyndwr rebelled against the English in middle age. Along with uniting the Welsh, he came close to overrunning the English. Finally defeated in 1409, he mysteriously disappeared in 1415 and his death has never been documented.

The parkland surrounding the castle and gardens is very impressive and the estate is entered through a magnificent set of wrought iron gates that were made by the Davies brothers of Bersham Ironworks. Chirk Castle Gardens are also well worth taking the time to look around. Much of their layout is based on designs by William Emes that date from the 1760s. Along with the topiary yews, roses and flowering shrubs, the gardens contain a picturesque hawk house.

Just south of Chirk are two splendid constructions spanning the Ceiriog valley: the first, an aqueduct built in 1801 by Thomas Telford, carries the Llangollen branch of the Shropshire Union Canal, while the other is a viaduct built in 1848 to carry the then new Chester to Shrewsbury railway line over the River Ceiriog.

GLYN CEIRIOG

2½ miles S of Llangollen off the B4500

This former slate mining village is home to the **Chwarel Wynne Mine Museum** which, as well as telling the story of the slate industry that used to support the village, offers visitors a guided tour of the caverns. There is also a nature trail around the surrounding countryside. A narrow gauge tramway, the Glyn Valley Railway, once linked the Shropshire Union Canal at Gledrid with the quarries and mines at Glyn Ceiriog. Opened in 1873 and originally horse-drawn, it was later converted to steam and diverted through Chirk Castle estate to meet the Great Western Railway at Chirk station. It carried slate, silica, chinastone and dolerite downstream and returned with coal, flour and other commodities. It also carried passengers, and though it closed in 1935, the bed of the tramway can still be seen here and there. The Glyn Valley Tramway Group was founded in 1974 to conserve evidence of the GVR. The Group has small museums in the Glyn Valley Hotel at Glyn Ceiriog and the former waiting room at Pontafog station, and a GVR Museum and Visitor Centre is to be established in the old locomotive shed and yard at Glyn Ceiriog.

The village lies in the secluded Vale of Ceiriog. Just to the west is the beautiful **Ceiriog Forest** which offers surprisingly pastoral views and vistas along with forest walks and trails.

LLANARMON DYFFRYN CEIRIOG

6½ miles SW of Llangollen on the B4500

This small and peaceful village in the heart of the Vale of Ceiriog was the birthplace of the famous Welsh bard, Ceiriog, whose real name was John Hughes. The 14-mile Upper Ceiriog Trail for walkers, mountain bikers and horse riders passes his home, Pen-y-Bryn. In the churchyard at Llanarmon DC are two yew trees certified as over 1000 years old.

LLANTYSILIO

1 mile W of Llangollen off the A5

The **Church of St Tysilio** occupies an idyllic setting surrounded by steep wooded hills. The church dates back to the 1400s and its notable features include a fine medieval roof, a rare oak eagle lectern, a sculpted font and an east window in the pre-Raphaelite style. The poet Robert Browning worshipped here in 1866, an event marked by a brass plaque placed here by Lady Martin, also known as the actress Helena Faucit. She lived in the house next to the church and is remembered at the church by a chapel that was built following her death in 1898.

Below the sloping churchyard, the River Dee cascades over the picturesque Horseshoe Falls and a short distance away is Thomas Telford's **Horseshoe Weir** which was built in 1806 to supply water to the Llangollen Canal.

GLYNDYFRDWY

4 miles W of Llangollen on the A5

Once the estate of Owain Glyndwr, this village lies on the historic and important A5 and between the Berwyn and Llantysilio mountains. A mound by the road, known as **Owain Glyndwr's Mound**, was once part of an impressive earthwork fortress that was later incorporated into part of the Welsh hero's manor house and estate. Much more recently, Glyndyfrdwy has become known as the home of the Original Butterfly man, Eos Griffiths, who is known worldwide for creating the bright and colourful ornamental butterflies that can be seen adorning homes from Scandinavia to Australia.

CORWEN

9 miles W of Llangollen on the A5

This market town, in a pleasant

29 THE WEST ARMS HOTEL

Llanarmon Dyffryn Ceirog

Exceptional 300-year-old country hotel with outstanding cuisine and offering top quality accommodation.

see page 248

Rug Chapel, Corwen

Owain Glyndwr Hotel in 1789 in Corwen that a local man, Thomas Jones, organised a bardic festival that laid the foundations for the modern eisteddfod. Across the River Dee from the town lies **Caer Derwyn**, a stone rampart around a hill that dates from Roman times.

To the west of Corwen and set in pretty, landscaped grounds is the simple, stone built **Rug Chapel**. A rare example of a private chapel that has changed little over the years, Rug ('*heather*' in Welsh) was founded in the 17th century by 'Old Blue Stockings', Colonel William Salusbury, in collaboration with Bishop William Morgan, the first translator of the Bible into Welsh. The chapel's plain exterior gives no clues to its exquisitely decorated interior. Best described as a 'painted chapel', few parts of the building have been left unadorned. As well as the beautifully carved rood screen, the ceiling beams are painted with rose motifs. However, not all the decoration here is exuberant; there is also a sombre wall painting of a skeleton as a reminder of mortality. The architect Sir Edwin Lutyens acknowledged that his work was influenced by this beautiful chapel and evidence can be seen of this in his most elaborate commission, the Viceroy's House, New Delhi, which was completed in 1930.

Another interesting religious building can be found just to the south of Rug, in the direction of Llandrillo. **Llangar Church**, overlooking the confluence of the Rivers Dee and Alwen, is older

One of Corwen's most impressive buildings is Corwen Manor which was built in 1840 as the workhouse for seven local parishes. It could house up to 150 paupers with men and women in separate wings. It is now a craft shop and café. There's more unconventional accommodation at the Old Police Station where bed & breakfast guests, if they so wish, can sleep in cells complete with the original doors.

setting between the Berwyn Mountains and the River Dee, has, for many years, been known as the 'Crossroads of North Wales'. The town's origins can be traced back to the 6th century when the Breton-Welsh saints, Mael and Sulien, founded a religious community here - Corwen's 13th century church still bears their dedication.

Corwen was also once the headquarters of Owain Glyndwr, who gathered his forces here before entering into his various campaigns. A steel statue of him stands in the centre of the town. The church at Corwen has an incised dagger in a lintel of the doorway that is known as **Glyndwr's Sword**. The mark was reputedly made by Glyndwr when he threw a dagger from the hill above the church in a fit of rage against the townsfolk. However, the dagger mark actually dates from the 7th to 9th centuries and there is another such mark on a 12th century cross outside the southwest corner of the church. It was in the

than its near neighbour - it is medieval - and, though it was superseded in the 19th century, this small place still retains many of its original features. In particular, there are some extensive 15th century wall paintings and a minstrels' gallery. Both Rug Chapel and Llangar Church are now cared for by CADW - Welsh Historic Monuments.

LLANDRILLO

12 miles SW of Llangollen on the B4401

The road to Llandrillo from the north follows the Vale of Edeirion and the River Dee as it weaves its way below the northwest slopes of the **Berwyn Mountains**, another mountain range that is popular with walkers and visitors. This small village is a good starting point for walks in the Berwyns and footpaths from the village lead towards Craig Berwyn, whose summit is more than 2100 feet above sea level.

BRYNEGLWYS

5 miles NW of Llangollen off the A5104

Standing on the slopes of Llantysilio Mountain, the large 15th century Church of St Tysilio, in the heart of the village is, surprisingly, connected with the family who helped to found Yale University in the United States. Close to the village lies **Plas-Yn-Yale**, the former home of the Yale family and the birthplace of Elihu Yale's father. Elihu himself was born in 1647 in Boston, Massachusetts, and went on to become a governor of India before coming to England. Known for his philanthropy, Elihu was approached by an American College who, after receiving generous help, named their new college in Newhaven after him. In 1745, 24 years after his death, the whole establishment was named Yale University. Elihu Yale is buried in the Church of St Giles in Wrexham.

27

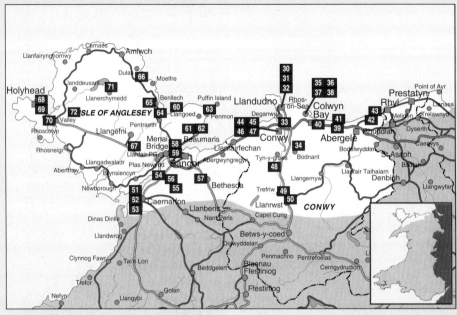

North Wales Coast & Isle of Anglesey

The coast of North Wales is a perennially popular stretch of British coastline that attracts visitors in their thousands to its holiday resorts.

This very traditional region, where Welsh is often still spoken on a daily basis, has many treasures, both man-made and natural, to discover. Before the coming of the railways, the coastline from Prestatyn to Bangor was sprinkled with small fishing villages. As the hours of mill workers from the industrial towns of Lancashire and others working in the factories of the Midlands were reduced, the concept of an annual holiday, albeit in some cases just the odd day at the seaside, became widespread. Served by the newly built railway network, the fishing villages expanded to accommodate the visitors. Boarding houses and hotels were built for the society visitors coming to take the sea air, and amusements and entertainment were soon a regular feature. Llandudno, always considered 'a cut above', still retains much of its Victorian and Edwardian charm, while other resorts, such as Rhyl, have endeavoured to counter the unsettled British summer weather by the creation of indoor complexes.

Prestatyn, to the east, lies at one end of Offa's Dyke. Built more as a line of demarcation rather than a fortification, the dyke runs from the coast southwards to Chepstow. Still substantially marking the border with England, many sections of the ancient earthwork are visible and can be seen from the waymarked footpath that runs the length of the dyke.

It was also along this coast that Edward I built his Iron Ring of castles. While many are now in ruins, two in particular are exceptional. Conwy Castle, now a World Heritage Site, was built in such a position that the surrounding land provides suitable protection from attack. Caernarfon Castle, as much a royal residence as a fortress, was the place where Edward created the first Prince of Wales when he crowned his own son. Centuries later, in 1969, it was in the grounds of the splendid castle ruins that Queen Elizabeth invested the same title on her eldest son, Prince Charles.

Caernarfon and Bangor lie at opposite ends of the Menai Strait, the channel of water that separates mainland Wales from the Isle of Anglesey. It was not until the 19th century that a bridge was constructed across the strait. Thomas Telford's magnificent Menai Suspension Bridge of the 1820s was joined some 30 years late, by Stephenson's Britannia Bridge.

The Isle of Anglesey, with its rolling hills, fertile farmland and miles of wild and craggy coastline, has attracted settlers from the Stone Age onwards and is littered with evidence of Neolithic, Bronze Age and Iron Age people. Anglesey has its own impressive castle, Beaumaris, built by Edward I to repel invasion from its neighbours. Today's invaders are largely tourists and holidaymakers, attracted by the elegant seaside resorts, the fishing, sailing and walking.

30 WINCHMORE HOTEL

Llandudno

Superbly located seafront hotel with licensed restaurant and en suite Accommodation.

see page 249

31 CAFÉ MONET

Llandudno

Attractively designed café serving a wide range of appetising hot and cold meals.

see page 250

32 OASIS HOTEL

Llandudno

Superbly located on the Central Promenade, the Oasis Hotel offers quality en suite accommodation.

see page 249

LLANDUDNO

Llandudno enjoys a glorious setting overlooking a gently curving bay between the headlands of the Great Orme and the Little Orme, with a second sweep of beach on West Shore which commands glorious views of Snowdonia and Anglesey across the Conwy Estuary.

The largest and one of the most popular of the North Wales coast resorts, Llandudno was developed in the 1850s by the Liverpool surveyor, Owen Williams, and the town still retains an abundance of Victorian features. There's a splendid **Promenade** lined with renovated, redecorated and elegant hotels; a magnificent Pier built in 1878 and the longest in Wales which fortunately survived an attempt in 1914 by Suffragettes to burn it down; a Victorian tramway that still uses the original carriages, and a cable car (Britain's longest) that transports visitors to the top of Great Orme. Opposite the entrance to the Pier, **Codmans Punch and Judy Show,** established in 1860 and still run by the same family, operates from Easter to mid-September. Nearby is a statue of the White Rabbit from Lewis Carroll's much loved story *Alice In Wonderland*. The tribute is to the real Alice - Alice Liddell - who came here on holiday with her family; it was also at Llandudno that her parents spent their honeymoon. Among the visitors to Dean Liddell's holiday home were such notable characters of the day as William Gladstone and Matthew Arnold as well as Lewis Carroll. Though little is known today of Carroll's stay with the family, visitors can be certain that it was on the broad, sandy beaches at Llandudno that the Walrus and the Carpenter "wept like anything to see such quantities of sand" and it was the White Knight who considered "boiling it in wine" to prevent the Menai Bridge from rusting. **The Alice in Wonderland Centre** presents an interesting exhibition dedicated to Alice and her time in Wonderland.

Off the Promenade towards the Little Orme by the fields, **Bodafon Farm Park** is a working farm and also home to the North Wales Bird Trust. Farm attractions include sheep shearing, ploughing, harvesting and collecting eggs. The Trust houses 1000 birds, including eagle owls and falcons.

Although Llandudno is very much a product of the Victorian age, it earlier played host to Bronze Age miners and the Romans and, in the 6th century, St Tudno chose Great Orme as the site of the cell from where he preached. At **Llandudno Museum** visitors are taken through the town's history, from ancient times to the present day, by a collection of interesting exhibits: a child's footprint imprinted on a tile from the Roman fort of Canovium (Caerhun) and objets d'art collected from all over the world by Francis Chardon.

As well as being the home of Llandudno's roots, the massive limestone headland of **Great Orme** still dominates the resort today and also separates the town's two beaches. Two miles long, one mile wide and 679 feet high, its name, Orme, is thought to have originated from an old Norse word for sea monster. In what is now a country park, there are prehistoric sites in the form of stone circles and burial sites, the remains of the Bronze Age mines and **St Tudno's Church**, a 15th century building constructed on the site of the saint's original cell from the 6th century. The summit can be reached by the **Great Orme Tramway**, a magnificent monument to Victorian engineering constructed in 1902 that is Britain's only cable hauled, public road tramway. The **Great Orme Copper Mine** is the only Bronze Age copper mine in the world open to the public. Visitors can explore the 3,500-year-old passages, see the great opencast mine workings, peer into the 470ft shaft and discover how our ancestors turned rock into metal. The Visitor Centre is open to non-mine visitors, and also at the site are

a tea room serving Welsh cream teas and a shop selling a wide variety of books, minerals, fossils and other souvenirs. Outside, look out for the herd of wild goats descended from a pair presented to Queen Victoria by the Shah of Persia.

AROUND LLANDUDNO

GLAN CONWY

3 miles SE of Llandudno off the A470

In Garth Road at Glan Conwy, **Felin Isaf** has two working watermills and a museum describing the history of the site and the various uses and types of mills.

DEGANWY

1 mile S of Llandudno off the A546

Just south of Llandudno lies Deganwy, a once thriving fishing village that shares the same stretch of coastline though it has now been taken over by its larger neighbour. Often mentioned in Welsh history,

33 CAFÉ T'AIR

Deganwy

Delightful Victorian-style tea room with bow-tied staff and outstanding home-made food.

see page 251

Great Orme Copper Mine, Llandudno

34 BODNANT GARDEN

Tal-y-Cafn

One of the most beautiful gardens in the UK, Bodnant has something to interest everyone with plants from around the world.

 see page 252

35 PENRHYN OLD HALL

Penrhyn Bay

Popular pub, restaurant and function venue in delightful cluster of buildings with Grade I listed building status.

 see page 253

36 THE QUEENS HEAD

Glanwydden

Delightful village hostelry with outstanding food and wine; charming self-catering cottage available.

 see page 254

Deganwy was a strategically important stronghold and its castle was the seat of Maelgwn Gwynedd as early as the 6th century. The first medieval castle was probably built here by Lupus, Earl of Chester, shortly after the Norman Conquest. The remains seen today are, however, of a castle built by one of the earl's successors in 1211. Henry II was besieged here by the Welsh and Deganwy was finally destroyed by Llewelyn ap Gruffyd (Llewelyn the Last) in 1263.

BODNANT

6 miles S of Llandudno off the A470

Situated above the River Conwy and covering some 80 acres are the famous Edwardian **Bodnant Gardens** (National Trust) laid out in 1875 by the 2nd Lord Aberconwy and still managed by his descendant. Designed in two parts, the upper garden around the house is terraced and the lower, known as The Dell, is formed around the River Hiraethlyn, a tributary of the River Conwy. The pretty Garden House was built in Gloucestershire in the 1730s and was later used as a Pin Mill before being brought to Bodnant in 1938.

RHOS-ON-SEA

3½ miles E of Llandudno on the B5115

Sitting on the western end of Colwyn Bay, Rhos is a delightful little boat haven with plenty of shops and cafés, an award-winning

Bodnant Gardens

beach 2 miles long, and excellent launch facilities for visiting day sailors. It was from Rhos that Prince Madoc set sail in 1170 and is believed to have landed on the north American continent, some 325 years before Columbus made his historic voyage to the New World.

Along the promenade is the small **Chapel of St Trillo**, thought to be the smallest church in Britain with seating for just 6 people. It is dedicated to a 6th century Celtic saint who built his cell here. It stands on the site of an ancient well which provided St Trillo with his drinking water - the well can still be seen in front of the altar. For centuries it supplied the water for baptisms. The chapel is the only surviving building of an abbey that stood here in the 12th century.

COLWYN BAY

5 miles SE of Llandudno on the A55

A more genteel place than the resorts found to the east, Colwyn Bay was built largely during the 19th century to fill the gap along the coast between Rhos-on-Sea and the village of Old Colwyn. As a result, there are many fine Victorian buildings to be seen, and the beach is served by a promenade along which most of the town's attractions can be found. Colwyn Bay includes among its famous sons ex-Monty Python Terry Jones and a former James Bond, Timothy Dalton. The philosopher Bertrand Russell (1872-1970) was cremated with no ceremony at Colwyn Bay crematorium and his ashes scattered in the sea.

Although Colwyn Bay lies on the coast it is also home to the

37 RHOS FYNACH

Rhos-on-Sea

Delightful old hostelry on the seafront with history going back to AD 1181.

¶ *see page 255*

38 BARNABY'S BISTRO

Rhos-on-Sea

Stylish eating place with cuisine based on locally caught fish and local meats. The huge scones must not be missed!

¶ *see page 255*

39 ZANZIBAR COFFEE SHOP

Colwyn Bay

Stylish coffee shop offering extensive menu, all based on locally sourced fresh products.

¶ *see page 256*

Victoria Pier, Colwyn Bay

40 THE MARINE HOTEL

Old Colwyn

Former coaching inn noted for its home-made cooking, and offering real ales and en suite accommodation.

¶ ⊨ see page 256

41 DULAS ARMS

Llanddulas

Hostelry with sea views offering good home cooking, real ales and accommodation.

¶ ⊨ see page 257

42 JAKES

Towyn

Welcoming family-run hostelry serving a wide range of appetising food throughout the day.

¶ see page 257

43 THE MORTON ARMS

Towyn

Outstanding hostelry offering the very best in food, drink, accommodation, entertainment and hospitality.

¶ ⊨ see page 258

Welsh Mountain Zoo, a conservation centre for rare and endangered species that is best known for the Chimp Encounter, its collection of British wildlife and its feeding of the sea lions. The zoo's gardens, laid out by TH Mawson at the end of the 19th century, incorporate both formal terraces and informal woodlands with paths offering superb views of Snowdonia as well as the Conwy estuary and the North Wales coast. The Tarzan Trail Adventure Playground is a surefire winner with young visitors.

Also popular with children - and some parents - is the Harlequin Puppet Theatre which is the only permanent traditional marionette theatre in Britain. It stages daily performances during all the main school holidays.

ABERGELE

10½ miles SE of Llandudno on the A548

Along with **Pensarn**, its neighbour on the coast, Abergele is a joint resort which, though more modest than such places as Rhyl, Prestatyn and Colwyn Bay, popular with those looking for a quieter seaside holiday.

Situated on higher ground behind the castle are the natural caverns of **Cefn-Yr-Ogo** whose summit commands magnificent views of the surrounding coastline.

RHYL

14 miles E of Llandudno on the A548

Between them, Rhyl and its neighbour Prestatyn have 4 beaches covering 7 miles of sand. In 2005, two of the beaches were granted the Seaside award for cleanliness and water quality. During the summer months a team of lifeguards patrol the beaches equipped with quad bikes, 4x4s and a rib boat. A more traditional presence on the beaches is the team of donkeys which is owned by a family business now in its 6th generation.

Part of the town's Victorian heritage is **Marine Lake,** a huge artificial lake first opened in 1895 for bathing and boating. Canoeing, water-skiing and windsurfing have since been introduced along with a 15-inch railway which is the oldest in Britain - it opened in 1911 - and one of the oldest anywhere in the world. Visitors can still ride on Joan, the very same train that first arrived here in 1920. The building of a new station, museum and workshop was completed in 2007 and now offers a selection of engines to take you around the 1-mile long track.

As well as the full range of amusement arcades and seaside attractions, Rhyl is home to three large 'fun' complexes. The **Sun Centre** is one of the first all-weather leisure attractions in the country, with indoor surfing and daredevil water slides and flumes. At **SeaQuarium** visitors can enjoy a seabed stroll surrounded by sharks, rays and other ocean creatures. The **Ocean Beach Amusement Park** is the largest funfair in North Wales with a huge variety of rides and other amusements.

Smaller attractions include the Children's Village - for younger children - and Terror Tombs where macabre surprises elicit squeals and screams.

PRESTATYN

16½ miles E of Llandudno on the A548

With three great beaches - Ffrith Beach, Central Beach and Barkby Beach - Prestatyn has proved a popular holiday destination over the years. As you would expect, all types of entertainment are available, making the town an ideal centre for family holidays. Although the town undoubtedly expanded with the opening of the Chester to Holyhead railway line in 1848, people were flocking here 50 years before, lured by descriptions of the air being like wine and honey and with the abundant sunshine being deemed excellent for the relief of arthritic conditions and nervous disorders.

However, Prestatyn's origins go back to prehistoric times, as excavated artefacts have shown. While the Roman 20th legion was stationed at Chester, it is thought that an auxiliary unit was based at a fort on what is now Princes Avenue. The discovery in 1984 of a Roman bath house in Melyd Avenue would certainly seem to support this assumption.

The settlement is mentioned in the *Domesday Book* as Prestetone, from the Anglo Saxon Preosta Tun (meaning a settlement in which two or more priests reside). It was Lord Robert Banastre who was responsible for building the Norman Prestatyn Castle; it was of a typical motte and bailey design, but all that remains of the fortification today is one stone pillar on the top of a raised mound that can be found close to Bodnant bridge.

Prestatyn lies at one end of the massive 8th century earthwork **Offa's Dyke**. Although the true origins of the dyke have been lost in the mists of time, it is thought that the construction of this border defence between England and Wales was instigated by King Offa, one of the most powerful of the early Anglo-Saxon kings. From AD 757 until his death in AD 796 he ruled Mercia, which covers roughly the area of the West Midlands. He seized power in the period of civil strife that followed the murder of his cousin King Aethelbald and, ruthlessly suppressing many of the smaller kingdoms and princedoms, created a single settled state that covered most of England south of Yorkshire. His lasting memorial is the dyke, which he had built between Mercia and the Welsh lands. With an earthwork bank of anything up to 50 feet in height and a 12ft ditch on the Welsh side, much of this massive feat of engineering is still visible today. The northern end of **Offa's Dyke National Trail** leads up the High Street, climbs the dramatic Prestatyn hillside and wanders through the Clwydian Range. This long-distance footpath of some 180 miles crosses the English-Welsh border ten times and takes in some extraordinarily beautiful

●

Rhyl's most distinctive landmark is the Sky Tower, also known as the "Eye in the Sky". Standing 240ft high, the slender tower dominates the seafront. Its glass bubble, which can accommodate up to 30 people, rises at a rather alarming speed and is not for the faint-hearted. Once at the top, the bubble revolves twice to unveil a glorious panorama which on a clear day stretches as far as Blackpool Tower. The whole experience lasts about 5 minutes.
The tower stands at the end of the newly built Drift Park - a series of walkways through wooded areas and flowerbeds linking a brand new children's playground, a new paddling pool with water features, fountains and changing areas. There's also an outdoor amphitheatre where daytime entertainment is provided throughout the summer months. A new crazy golf course and a skate park have also been installed.

●

In the churchyard of St Digain's Church in Llangernyw stands the Llangernyw Yew. The oldest known tree in Wales, and one of the oldest living things in the world, the yew is estimated to be more than 4,000 years old.

countryside. Most people walk the trail in sections; hardier souls take about 12 days to complete it in one go.

A less demanding walk, starting at the southern end of the town, follows the trackbed of the former Prestatyn and Dyserth Railway which closed in 1973.

LLANASA

20 miles E of Llandudno off the A548

Close by the village, whose church has stained glass windows taken from Basingwerk Abbey, stands **Gyrn Castle** which originates from the 1700s and was castellated in the 1820s. It now contains a large picture gallery, and its grounds offer some pleasant woodland walks.

TRELAWNYD

19 miles E of Llandudno on the A5151

Sometimes called Newmarket, this village is well known for its Bronze Age cairn, **Gop Hill**, the biggest prehistoric monument in Wales, which marks the place where, traditionally, Offa's Dyke began, although the town of Prestatyn also claims this honour.

MELIDEN

17 miles E of Llandudno on the A547

Just to the south of Meliden lies **Craig Fawr**, a limestone hill that supports a wide variety of flowers and butterflies, including the Brown Argus, a rare sight in North Wales, whose larvae feed on the Common Rockrose. Nature trails have been laid around the site that not only take in the myriad of wildlife and

plants but also an old quarry where the exposed limestone reveals a wealth of fossils deposited here more than 300 million years ago. The short walk to the summit is well worth the effort as there are panoramic views from the top over the Vale of Clwyd, the coastline and beyond to Snowdonia.

POINT OF AYR

21½ miles E of Llandudno off the A548

Marking the western tip of the Dee estuary and with views across the river mouth to Hilbre Island and the Wirral, this designated RSPB viewing point is an excellent place to observe the numerous birds that come to feed on the sands and mudflats left by the retreating tide.

LLANGERNYW

10½ miles SE of Llandudno on the A548

This quiet Denbighshire village was the birthplace in 1852 of Sir Henry Jones who became known as 'the cobbler philosopher'. Born the son of a local shoemaker, Henry Jones left school at the age of 12 to become apprenticed to his father but, after the long working day, Henry continued his studies well into the evenings. His hard work paid off and he won a scholarship to train as a teacher and then went on to study philosophy before eventually becoming Professor of Moral Philosophy at Glasgow University. A well-known and highly regarded academic and a widely acclaimed lecturer on social affairs and liberalism, Henry received his knighthood in 1912, and was made a Companion of

Honour in 1922. He died in the same year. Though Sir Henry is buried in Glasgow, this village has not forgotten its local hero. In 1934, Jones' childhood home, Y Cwm, was purchased by a fund set up to honour his memory and his work. Today, at the **Amgueddfa Syr Henry Jones** (Sir Henry Jones Museum) visitors can explore the family house including the tiny kitchen and bedroom where the family lived and the shoemaker's workshop where Henry and his father worked.

CONWY

At Conwy, one of the most magnificent medieval castles ever built towers over one of the world's most complete medieval walled towns. Designated a World Heritage Site, the whole town is in a remarkable state of preservation. Within the walls, the old town is a delight with its tangle of streets and varied shops, pubs and restaurants. A tunnel opened in 1991 carries the A55 under the Conwy estuary and has provided some relief from the heavy traffic that once clogged the town - until then, all traffic had to pass through narrow arches in the city walls.

Conwy Castle is situated on a rock which overlooks the River Conwy and its estuary, and commands wonderful views of the whole area. Begun in 1283, the castle's construction was largely finished by the autumn of 1287. Compared with other of Edward I's castles, Conwy is of a relatively

simple design which relies on its position rather than anything else to provide a defence against attack. The town was walled at the same time and they still encircle the vast majority of Conwy, stretching for three quarters of a mile and including 22 towers and three gateways. The castle was also built to be a suitable royal residence. It was used twice by Edward I: once on his way to Caernarfon where his son, the first English Prince of Wales, was born, and again in 1294, when trying to put down the rebellion of Madoc ap Llewelyn.

In 1399, Richard II stayed at the castle before being lured out and ambushed by the Earl of Northumberland's men on behalf of Henry Bolingbroke, the Duke of Lancaster, who later became Henry IV.

As with other castles further east, Conwy was embroiled in the Civil War. A Conwy man, John Williams, became Archbishop of York and, as a Royalist, sought refuge in his home town. Repairing

44 FISHERMAN'S CHIP SHOP

Conwy

Sample Britain's national dish at its very best at this town centre restaurant and takeaway.

‖ see page 259

45 THE BRIDGE INN CONWY

Conwy

Fine old traditional hostelry opposite Conwy Castle offering quality food, real ales and en suite rooms.

‖ ⊨ see page 259

Conwy Castle

46 YE OLDE MAILCOACH

Conwy

Lively town centre hostelry with good traditional food, real ales and accommodation.

see page 260

the crumbling fortifications at his own expense, Archbishop Williams finally changed sides after shabby treatment by Royalist leaders and helped the Parliamentary forces lay siege to the town and castle, which eventually fell to them in late 1646.

The town developed within the shadows of its now defunct fortress, and slate and coal extracted from the surrounding area, were shipped up and down the coast from Conwy. Later, as Conwy's trade and links grew with the outside world, the town fathers approached Thomas Telford who planned a causeway and bridge. Built in 1826, the elegant **Suspension Bridge** (National Trust) replaced the ferry that previously had been the only means of crossing the river so close to its estuary. At the entrance to the bridge, the Toll House has been restored and furnished as it would have been a century ago. The bridge continued in use until 1958 and is now a pedestrian crossing. The Suspension Bridge was soon followed by the construction of railways. By the side of Telford's bridge stands the tubular rail bridge of 1846 designed by Robert Stephenson. Both builders breached the town walls in styles that complemented the town's architecture and the two structures are still admired today.

Bridges, however, are not the only architectural gems Conwy has to offer. **Plas Mawr**, an Elizabethan town house on the High Street, is one of the best preserved buildings from that period in Britain. Built for the influential merchant Robert Wynn between 1576 and 1585, the house has an interesting stone façade and more than 50 windows. Plas Mawr (the name means Great Hall) is particularly noted for its fine and elaborate plasterwork, seen to striking effect in the glorious decorated ceilings and friezes and in the overmantel in the hall. The authentic period atmosphere is further enhanced by furnishings based on an inventory of the contents in 1665. The house came into the possession of the Mostyn family during the 18th century and in 1991 was given by Lord Mostyn to the nation. Close by is **Aberconwy House** (National Trust), a delightful medieval merchant's home that dates from about 1300 and is the oldest house in Conwy. The rooms have been decorated and furnished to reflect various periods in the house's history. The collection of rural furniture on display is on loan from the Museum of Wales.

Just behind Plas Mawr and occupying a converted chapel is the **Royal Cambrian Academy Art** Gallery (free). The Academy was formed to encourage art in Wales and most of the artists featured are Welsh or working in Wales.

Occupying part of the site of a 12th century Cistercian Abbey that was moved to Maenan by Edward I is **St Mary's Church**. This abbey church became the parish church of the borough created by Edward and some interesting features still remain from that time though there have been many additions over the centuries.

Conwy's **Teapot Museum and Shop**, on Castle Street, is an interesting and unusual attraction where visitors can see a unique collection of antique, novelty and humorous teapots that date from the mid-1700s to the present day. Many of the pieces on show have taken their place in the annals of teapot history, including the celebrated Worcester 'aesthetic' teapot of 1880, the Wedgwood cauliflower pot of 1775 and the Clarice Cliffe tepee-shaped pot of 1930. The museum shop is also a must for tea enthusiasts as it not only sells a wide variety of teas but also a mass of tea paraphernalia.

It is not surprising that the town and the surrounding area have strong links with the sea and Conwy, like many seaside towns has a traditional mermaid story. Washed ashore by a violent storm in Conwy Bay, a mermaid begged the local fishermen who found her to carry her back to the sea. The fishermen refused even though she could not survive out of the water. Before she died, the mermaid cursed the people of the town, swearing that they would always be poor. In the 5th century, Conwy suffered a fish famine that caused many to believe that the curse was fulfilled.

Another fish famine story involves St Brigid. Walking by the riverside carrying some rushes, she threw the rushes upon the water. A few days later the rushes had turned into fish and ever since they have been known as sparlings or, in Welsh, brwyniaid - both meaning rush-like. On the quayside the fishermen still land their catches, and from here pleasure boat trips can be taken. Nearby, in between terraced housing, can be found what is claimed to be **Britain's Smallest House**, measuring 10 feet by 6 feet; it seems that its last tenant was a fisherman who was 6 feet 3 inches tall - he was presumably also a contortionist!

Conwy was once a famous pearl fishing centre and had a thriving mussel industry, whose history is told in the **Conwy Mussel Centre**, Not on display is the dazzling pearl found in a Conwy mussel in the 1600s - it now forms part of the Crown Jewels.

AROUND CONWY

ROWEN

4 miles S of Conwy off the B5106

From this very pretty, quiet village a track, which was once a Roman road, skirts by the foot of **Tal-y-fan**, which climbs to 2000 feet at its peak. Roughly six miles in length, the path passes by Maen-y-Bardd, an ancient burial chamber, and eventually drops down towards the coast at Aber. Another, circular, walk of about five miles, one of several in the Conwy Valley devised by Active Snowdonia, passes many impressive cromlechs and standing stones. The route also takes in Caer Bach, where there are traces of a neolithic settlement, the wonderfully unspoilt 14th century St Celynin's Church and the Woodland Trust's Parc Mawr woods.

47 ABERCONWY HOUSE

Conwy

14th Century Merchant's House

🏛 see page 257

In Bodlondeb Park, just 300 yards from Conwy quay, Conwy Butterfly Jungle brings tropical warmth and colour to the town. In the jungle garden here, visitors can see some of the largest and most beautiful tropical butterflies in free flight.

48 THE LODGE HOTEL

Tal-y-bont

Rural, family-run hotel with excellent restaurant and wide choice of quality accommodation.

see page 260

49 FAIRY FALLS HOTEL

Trefriw

Hotel with chalet accommodation, restaurant, function room and regular live entertainment.

see page 261

TREFRIW

8 miles S of Conwy on the B5106

This village, nestling into the forested edge of Snowdonia in the beautiful Conwy valley, was once one of the homes of Llywelyn the Great. He is said to have built a church here to please his wife who refused to climb to the nearest church, which was at Llanrhychyrn.

Once the biggest inland port in Wales, the village today has two main attractions: **Trefriw Woollen Mills** and the local chalybeate springs. The woollen mill has been in operation since the 1830s and it is still owned by descendants of Thomas Williams who purchased it in 1859. It is run by hydro-electric power generated from the two lakes - Crafnant and Geirionydd - which lie to the west of the village. While the source of power is modern, the tapestries and tweeds produced here from raw wool are very traditional.

A footpath above the woollen mill leads to **Fairy Falls** where, in the early 19th century, a forge was founded to make hammers and chisels for use in the slate quarries. It closed at the beginning of the 20th century. Sometime between AD 100 and AD 250, while prospecting for minerals in this area, the Romans opened up a cave where they found a spring rich in iron (chalybeate). Covered in later years by a landslide, it was not until the 18th century that the spring was uncovered by Lord Willoughby de Eresby, owner of nearby Gwydir Castle. He went on to build a stone bathhouse. Taking the waters became so popular that by 1874 the original bathhouse was replaced with a pump house and bath, and the bottled water was exported worldwide. Following a decline during much of the 20th century, interest in the natural spring waters has been rekindled. Visitors can take the waters, view the museum artefacts in the tea room and browse in the spa beauty shop.

Lake Geirionydd was the birthplace in the 6th century of the great bard Taliesin to whom in 1850 Lord Willoughby erected a monument. In 1863, a local poet, Gwilym Cowlyd, being dissatisfied with the National Eisteddfod, started an arwest, a poetical and musical event that was held in the shadow of the monument every year until 1922. The monument fell down in a storm in 1976 but was restored in 1994. It lies on one of Active Snowdonia's Conwy Valley walks, which also passes Fairy Falls and old mine workings; it skirts Lake Crafnant and provides memorable views at many points along its route.

LLANRWST

10 miles S of Conwy on the A470

The market centre for the central Conwy Valley owes both its name and the dedication of its church to St Grwst (Restitutus), a 6th century missionary who was active in this area. The town lies in the middle of the Conwy Valley between rich agricultural hills to the east and the imposing crags of Snowdonia to the west. Famous for its livestock fairs and the manufacture of grandfather clocks and Welsh harps, it was also known for its woollen yarn and its sail-making industry. The **Church of St Grwst** with its fine rood screen dates from 1470, though the tower and north aisle are 19th century. It replaced a thatched building from 1170 that was destroyed in the fighting of 1468.

Next to the church lies **Gwydir Chapel**, famous for its richly carved Renaissance interior. This was the private chapel of the Wynn family and among its treasures is an imposing stone sarcophagus of the Welsh prince Llewelyn the Great. This chapel should not be confused with **Gwydir Uchaf Chapel** which lies on the opposite bank of the river Conwy and is particularly noted for its ceiling covered with paintings of angels.

Below the chapel lies **Gwydir Castle**, the Wynn family's lovely Tudor mansion. The dining room is especially fine with its richly carved oak panels, Baroque door-case and fireplace, and rampant gilded Spanish leather. In the grounds are some fine Cedars of Lebanon planted in 1625 in celebration of the marriage of Charles I to Henrietta Maria of France. A short distance from the house is the **Gwydyr Uchaf Chapel** (free), austere on the outside, flamboyantly baroque inside with a jaw-dropping painted ceiling depicting the Creation, the Trinity and the Day of Judgement.

A walk west from the town takes in these historic buildings, the remains of an old crushing mill and the site of the old Hafna Galena Mine.

Back in town, the **Old Bridge** is thought to have been designed by Inigo Jones; it was built in 1636 by Sir Richard Wynn. Next to it stands **Tu Hwnt i'r Bont** (the House over the Bridge), a 16th century courthouse which has since been divided into two cottages and is now a National Trust tea room.

Gwydir Chapel, Llanrwst

CAPEL CURIG

9 miles S of Conwy on the A5

Situated at the junction of the mountain roads to Beddgelert, Llyn Ogwen and Betws-y-Coed, Capel Curig is primarily dedicated to the needs of hikers and climbers who also use the village as a base. A walk south of the village passes by lonely Llyn y Foel and climbs the steep ridge of Daiar Ddu to the top of Mount Siabod; the reward for this expenditure of energy is the most spectacular panoramic view of many of Snowdonia's great peaks. **Plas-y-Brenin,** the National Mountain Centre, is located just to the southwest of the town and provides excellent facilities and training courses for climbing, canoeing, dry slope skiing and orienteering.

50 MEADOWSWEET HOTEL

Llanrwst

Outstanding hotel offering fine cuisine and en suite accommodation in lovely scenic location.

⊨ ‖ see page 262

41

BANGOR

A cathedral and university city, Bangor incorporates a wide variety of architectural styles that remind the visitor that this is not only an interesting and stimulating place but also one with a long history. A monastic community was founded here as early as AD 525 by St Deiniol. The town's name is derived from the wattle fence which surrounded the saint's primitive enclosure - the term 'bangori' is still used in parts of Wales to describe the plaiting of twigs in a hedge.

There were settlers in the area long before St Deiniol, including the Romans at nearby Segontium. The **Gwynedd Museum and Art Gallery** (free) is just the place to discover not only the past 2,000 years of history of this area of Wales but also to see reconstructions of domestic life in days gone by. The Oriel Art Gallery exhibits changing displays of work by mostly Welsh contemporary artists.

The mother church of the oldest bishopric in Britain, Bangor's **Cathedral** dates from the 13th century and has probably been in continuous use for longer than any other cathedral in Britain. During the Middle Ages, the cathedral became a centre of worship for the independent principality of Gwynedd and when Owain Gwynedd was buried here his tomb became a starting point for pilgrims setting out on the arduous journey to Bardsey Island. Restored in 1866, the cathedral also contains a life-size carving of Christ dating from 1518 while, outside, there is a Biblical garden that contains plants which are associated with the Bible.

Until the slate boom of the 19th century, Bangor remained little more than a village, albeit with an impressive church. Its position on the Menai Strait made this the ideal place for nearby Penrhyn Quarry to build their docks and the town soon flourished in its new role as a commercial centre. Its importance

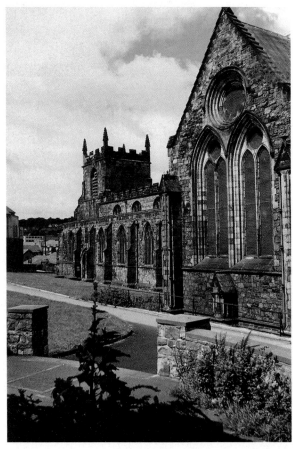

Bangor Cathedral

increased further when **Bangor University** (originally the University College of North Wales) was founded here in 1884. Improvements to the roads and then the coming of the railways to the North Wales coast also saw Bangor grow in both stature and importance. The **Menai Suspension Bridge** was built by Thomas Telford between 1819 and 1826 and was the first permanent crossing of the Menai Strait. Before its completion the crossing had been made by ferry, but cattle on their way to and from market would have had to swim the channel. Not surprisingly there was much opposition to the construction not only from the ferrymen but also from ship-owners worried that the structure would impede the passage of their tall ships. As a result of this concern, the road bridge stands at a height of 100 feet. The **Britannia Bridge**, a mile further southwest from Telford's bridge, is a combined road and rail crossing and was built between 1846 and 1850 by Robert Stephenson. The lions guarding the bridge are by John Thomas, who was responsible for much of the sculpture at the Houses of Parliament. Also jutting out into the Menai Strait from the town is the 1500 feet long **Victorian Pier**, which was built in 1896, almost demolished in 1974 and restored in the early 1980s. It now has original style kiosks and a café at the sea end. As well as being attractive in itself, the pier commands grand

Menai Suspension Bridge

views of the Menai Strait, the Great Orme at Llandudno, Snowdonia, Telford's suspension bridge and Bangor itself. Both pleasure and fishing trips can be taken from the pier head.

AROUND BANGOR

ABERGWYNGREGYN

6 miles E of Bangor off the A55

To the south of the village, reached by taking a footpath through sheltered woodland, are **Rhaeadr Aber Falls** where the drop of the river is said to be among the steepest in Wales.

Above the village is **The Cross,** a group of trees in the shape of a huge cross. Some people claim it was planted as a memorial to the crew of a German bomber that crashed on the hillside. The reality is more mundane - it was planted by scientists from Bangor University in the mid 1950s as an experiment in sheep management.

•

To the west of Bangor and overlooking Beaumaris on the Isle of Anglesey is Penrhyn Castle, a dramatic neo-Norman construction built between 1820 and 1845 by Thomas Hopper with the profits from his slate quarries. It has more than 300 luxuriously appointed rooms and a collection of paintings that was once the largest in Wales. It still contains many fine paintings by artists such as Rembrandt, Canaletto and Gainsborough. Within the grounds is the Industrial Railway Museum displaying rolling stock once used on the estate's own rail link between the slate quarries and the port. There's also a Doll's Museum, Victorian walled garden, licensed tearoom and shop.

•

43

51 GWESTY BRON MENAI

Caernarfon

Recently completely refurbished 1840s house in town centre offering quality B&B en suite accommodation.

see page 263

52 MENAI BANK HOTEL

Caernarfon

Friendly establishment overlooking the Menai Straits; bar, pool room and wonderful breakfasts.

see page 263

PENMAENMAWR

10 miles E of Bangor off the A55

A tiny quarrying village before the arrival of the railway in 1848, this small holiday resort with its sand and shingle beach has changed little since William Gladstone holidayed here in the 19th century, and it still boasts many fine Victorian buildings. Gladstone was a frequent visitor, a fact commemorated by a bust of him on a granite obelisk in Paradise Road. Penmaenmawr has a small industrial heritage park, Parc Plas Mawr.

In the town's steep mountain-backed hinterland can be found many prehistoric sites including one of Wales' best known Bronze Age stone circles, **Cefn Coch**. An urn was uncovered here containing the remains of a child as well as a bronze dagger said to be evidence of a ritual sacrifice that once took place here.

CAERNARFON

If you want to brush up your Welsh, Caernarfon is the place to visit. More than 86% of its 10,000 or so residents could speak Welsh according to the 2001 census. Unsurprisingly, it has also been for many years a base for the Welsh nationalist movement.

Caernarfon's name simply means 'castle in Arfon' - Arfon being simply the region opposite Anglesey. Situated on the right bank of the River Seiont, near the southwest end of the Menai Strait, the town's history goes back to

Roman times when **Segontium Roman Fort** (CADW) was built half a mile from the present town centre. Segontium is the only place in Wales where it is possible to see something of the internal layout of an auxiliary station. Built to defend the Roman Empire against attack from rebellious tribes, the fort dates back to AD 77 when the Roman conquest was finally completed following the capture of Anglesey. Segontium was one of the most important garrisons on the edge of the Roman Empire and was also an administrative centre for northwest Wales. Excavations of the site have revealed coins which show that the fort was garrisoned at least until AD 394. This long occupation can be explained by its strategic position controlling the fertile lands and mineral rights of Anglesey and providing a defence against Irish pirates. The ruins are not impressive, seldom higher than a foot or so, but the displays are informative and the **Museum**, which is run by the National Museum and Galleries of Wales, displays many interesting items, including coins, pottery and weapons which have been uncovered during excavation work.

At the other end of the scale of impressiveness from Segontium is the mighty **Caernarfon Castle** which still dominates the town today. The most famous of Wales' numerous great fortresses, the castle was begun in 1283 by Henry de Elreton, who was also building Beaumaris Castle on the orders of Edward I. Caernarfon took some

40 years to complete, built not just as a fortress but also as a royal palace and a seat of government. The design is based around two oval-shaped courts divided by a wall. The outer defences are strengthened at intervals by towers and are, in places, up to 15 feet thick. Over the years, many attempts were made by the Welsh to destroy the castle but their failure is confirmed by the presence of this magnificent building today. It was here that, in 1284, Edward I crowned his son the first English Prince of Wales. Almost 700 years later, in 1969, the castle once again provided the dramatic setting for the investiture of Prince Charles as Prince of Wales. Also at the castle, and housed in the Queen's Tower, is the **Museum of the Royal Welch Fusiliers**, the country's oldest regiment - 'Welch' is an archaic Anglicisation of 'Welsh'.

The castle sits where the River Seiont meets the Menai Strait, the expanse of water that separates mainland Wales from the Isle of Anglesey. Close by, the old Slate Quay, from where slate was once shipped, is now the place where fishing trips and pleasure cruises depart up the Strait to Beaumaris. Castle Square, on the landward side of the castle, holds markets and here, too, can be found statues of two famous Welshmen: the gesticulating, urging David Lloyd-George, once a member of Parliament for the area, and Sir Hugh Owen, the founder of Further Education in Wales.

The Anglesey Hotel and the

Caernarfon Castle

Hanging Tower stand by the castle walls and were a customs house until 1822. The last hanging to take place in the tower was in 1911 when an Irishman named Murphy was executed for murdering a maid. It is said that when he died the bell clapper in **St Mary's Church** fell off. The church itself was founded in 1307 and, though much of it has since been reconstructed, the arcades of the eastern and southern walls are part of the original 14th century building.

Northgate Street is called in Welsh 'Stryd Pedwar a Chewch' - meaning four and six street. Apparently it originates from the time when sailors flocked to this part of town looking for lodgings: four pence for a hammock and six pence for a bed!

From the town, walkers can enjoy a scenic footpath, the **Lôn Las Menai**, which follows the coastline along the Menai Strait towards the village of Y Felinheli and from which there are views

53 CAERNARFON CASTLE

Caernarfon

This magnificent castle was begun in 1283 as a fortress and a seat of government. Now visitors can explore its many covered passageways and wall walks.

 see page 264

54 HOTEL PLAS DINORWIC

Y Felinheli

Overlooking the Menai Straits, boutique hotel with huge variety of accommodations and many amenities.

see page 265

55 TY MAWR TEAROOMS, RESTAURANT AND B&B

Groeslon Ty Mawr

Licensed restaurant serving excellent home cooking; en suite rooms, in the heart of Snowdonia.

see page 264

56 TY'N RHOS COUNTRY HOUSE

Seion

Beautifully located 5-star establishment awarded rosettes for its food; quality en suite rooms.

see page 266

across the water to the Isle of Anglesey.

Caernarfon is the terminus of the **Welsh Highland Railway,** founded in 1955 and owned and operated by the Ffestiniog Railway. It is the oldest independent railway company in the world and when the two lines are connected will be Britain's longest narrow gauge railway at just over 25 miles. The line currently runs for 12 miles from Caernarfon to the village of Rhyd Ddu on the slopes of Snowdon, but will shortly be extended a few miles further to Beddgelert.

To the southwest of Caernarfon and overlooking Caernarfon Bay is Caernarfon Air World, located on the site of an RAF station that was built in 1940 and which is also the home of the first RAF mountain rescue team. Pleasure flights are available and there is also the Aviation Museum, housed in one of the great hangars which displays more than 400 model aircraft, has various planes and helicopters on show and also provides visitors with the opportunity to take the controls in a flight trainer.

AROUND CAERNARFON

Y FELINHELI

4 miles NE of Caernarfon off the A487

Situated on the other side of the main road from this village is **Greenwood Forest Park,** a forest heritage and adventure park with something for all ages. Opened in the early 1990s, this centre concentrates on exploring and explaining man's relationship with trees and how, using conservation techniques, the loss of species of trees from the countryside can be halted whether in the equatorial rain forests or ancient temperate forests of Europe. The skills of ancient carpenters and joiners are also on show, particularly in the Great Hall, a building that was constructed entirely using medieval skills and knowledge and is held together by 500 oak pegs.

A couple of miles further east off the A487 and bordering the Menai Strait, Glan Faenol (National Trust) comprises parkland and farmland around Vaynol Hall, once one of the largest estates in North Wales. This is an important habitat for wildlife, and there's a pleasant walk leading to the sea and two viewing platforms. The estate has tracts of ancient woodland and several follies, including one built to rival the Marquess Column on Anglesey. The views of Snowdonia and across the strait are memorably depicted in one of Rex Whistler murals at Plas Newydd.

BETHESDA

9 miles E of Caernarfon on the A5

This old quarry town takes its name from the Nonconformist chapel that was built here and served many of the 2,300 men (and their families) who worked in the quarry at its peak in 1875. The gouged rock of the **Penrhyn Slate Quarries** forms a huge hillside amphitheatre. It was the largest open cast slate mine in the world and still produces high-quality slate 250 years after it was first worked.

From the town, the main road travels through the beautiful **Nant Ffrancon Pass** which runs straight through and up the valley of the River Ogwen and into the Snowdonia National Park. Five miles south of Bethesda on the A5, Llyn Idwal is one of several lakes on the National Trust's Carneddau estate. In 1954 it was declared the first National Nature Reserve in Wales.

ISLE OF ANGLESEY

MENAI BRIDGE

Acting as a gateway to Anglesey, this largely Victorian town developed after the construction of Thomas Telford's **Menai Suspension Bridge**, which connects the island to mainland Wales. Opened in 1826, this was the world's first large iron suspension bridge, stretching 580 feet between its piers and soaring 100 feet above the water to allow large ships to pass beneath. Almost a quarter of a century later, Robert Stepehenson's Britannia Tubular Bridge was built to carry both trains and road traffic across the strait. In 1970 it burnt down and only the limestone piers survived. These now support the double-decker A5/A55 road and rail bridge.

The waterfront at Menai Bridge is a popular place for anglers and for people watching the annual Regatta on the Menai Strait held every August. The promenade here is known as the Belgian Promenade because it was built by refugees from Belgium who sought shelter here during World War I.

On **Church Island**, reached by a causeway from the town, there is a small 14th century church built on the site of a foundation by St Tysilio in AD 630. The site is thought to have been visited by Archbishop Baldwin and Giraldus when they may have landed here in 1188.

For a place with a difference, **Pili Palas (Butterfly Palace)** is an interesting and unusual attraction that will delight everyone. The vast collection of exotic butterflies and birds from all over the world are seen in tropical environments with some wonderful tropical plants. There is also a Tropical Hide, an amazing Ant Avenue and a Snake House as well as a café and adventure play area.

AROUND MENAI BRIDGE

BEAUMARIS

4 miles NE of Menai Bridge of the A545

An attractive and elegant town, Beaumaris was granted a charter by Edward I in 1294 and adopted the Norman name 'beau marais' which translates as 'beautiful marsh'. The lawned seafront with its elegant Georgian and Victorian terraces was once a marsh that protected the approaches to **Beaumaris Castle** (CADW). Often cited as the most technically perfect medieval

57 LLANGOLLEN VAULTS

Bethesda

Traditional hostelry with good food and real ales; poker and karaoke evenings and pub quiz.

see page 267

58 THE LIVERPOOL ARMS

Menai Bridge

Charming old hostelry noted for its well-kept real ales and its quality cuisine.

see page 267

59 THE BRIDGE INN (TAFARN Y BONT)

Menai Bridge

Splendidly located inn beside the Menai Suspension Bridge serving excellent food.

see page 268

Beaumaris Village looking across the Menai Straits

60 WERN Y WYLAN COURT/COURTS RESTAURANT & BAR

Beaumaris

Quality self-catering accommodation in area of outstanding natural beauty. Restaurant/bar in listed building serving food daily.

see page 267

61 THE BOLD ARMS HOTEL

Beaumaris

Lively, attractive town centre establishment offering good food in summer, real ales, pool table and 42-inch plasma TVs.

see page 268

In later years, the town briefly enjoyed notoriety as a haven for pirates, as well as being a busy trading port. With the advent of steam ships and paddle boats, the resort developed during Victorian times as visitors from Liverpool and elsewhere took the sea trip down to Beaumaris. The town is now a popular place with the yachting fraternity due to its facilities and involvement in the annual Menai Strait Regatta.

While having connections with both sea trade and developing as a holiday resort, Beaumaris was at one time also an administrative and legal centre for the island. The **Courthouse**, dating from 1614, is the oldest active court in Britain. It is open to the public during the summer and although it was renovated in the 19th century much of its original Jacobean interior remains. It was here, in 1773, that Mary Hughes stood in the dock and was sentenced to transportation for seven years after she had been found guilty of stealing a bed gown valued at six pence (2½p)!

Close by is **Beaumaris Gaol** which was designed as a model prison by Hansom in 1829. In this monument to Victorian law and order, the last man to hang was Richard Rowlands who cursed the church clock opposite as he climbed to the scaffold in 1862. Today's visitors can relive those days of harsh punishment, view the cells, the stone-breaking yard and the tread-wheel, and follow the route taken by the condemned men to their rendezvous with the hangman.

castle in Britain, Beaumaris Castle was the last of Edward I's Iron Ring of fortresses built to stamp his authority on the Welsh. Begun in 1295 and designed by the king's military architect, James of St George, this was to be his largest and most ambitious project. Regarded as a pinnacle of military architecture of the time, with a concentric defence rather than the traditional keep and bailey, the outer walls contained 16 towers while the inner walls were 43 feet high and up to 16 feet thick in places. It looks as if it would be impregnable to any medieval army, but in fact it was seized in 1403 by Owain Glyndwr who held it for 2 years. Now a World Heritage listed site, Beaumaris Castle is still virtually surrounded by its original moat; there was also a tidal dock here for ships coming in through a channel in the marshes - an iron ring where vessels of up to 40 tons once docked still hangs from the wall.

An equally interesting place for all the family to visit is the **Museum of Childhood Memories** a treasure house of nostalgia with a collection of more than 2000 items, all collected over 40 years by one man. There are nine different rooms, each with its own theme, such as entertainment, pottery and glass, and clockwork tin plate toys. The amazing variety of toys vividly illustrate the changing fashions in toys from the 1840s to around 1970.

A popular excursion from Beaumarais is the boat trip around (but not on to) Puffin Island (see below) - trips can be booked at the kiosk at the foot of the truncated pier.

LLANFAES

5 miles NE of Menai Bridge off the B5109

Now a quiet and sedate place, Llanfaes was a busy commercial village long before the establishment of Beaumaris as one of the island's major centres, and travellers from the mainland arrived here after crossing the Menai Strait from Aber and the Lavan Sands.

In 1237, Llywelyn the Great founded a monastery in the village over the tomb of Joan, his wife and the daughter of King John. The tomb can now be seen in St Mary's Church, Beaumaris, where it was moved at the time of the Dissolution. In 1295 Edward I moved the inhabitants of Llanfaes to Newborough so that he could use the stone in the town to build Beaumaris Castle. During World War Two, flying boats were built at the factory on the edge of the village.

LLANGOED

6 miles NE of Menai Bridge on the B5109

In Edwardian times, this historic village was a popular resort with the lower middle classes who came here to stay in boarding houses by the sea. A walk downstream, alongside the river, leads to **Castell Aberlleiniog**, standing in the midst of trees. This was originally a timber castle, built in around 1090 by Hugh Lupus, Earl of Chester, who, along with Hugh the Proud, Earl of Shrewsbury, displayed great cruelty to the Welsh. Lupus was later killed during an attack on the castle by Magnus, King of Norway, when he was struck in the eye by an arrow. The ruins of the bailey, which was constructed later, are still visible. Close by is the site of a battle where, in AD 809, the Saxons were, albeit briefly, victorious over the defending Welsh.

In Llangoed itself, **Haulfre Stables** is a small equestrian museum housed in a historic stable block and contains a collection of Victorian harnesses and saddlery, carts and carriages. There's also a garden shop selling fresh local produce.

PENMON

7 miles NE of Menai Bridge off the B5109

On the eastern tip of Anglesey, this is a beauty spot whose lovely views across the Menai Strait go some way to explaining why it was chosen, centuries earlier, as a religious site. **Penmon Priory** (CADW) was established by St Seiriol in the 6th century. In 1237

62 WHITE LION HOTEL

Beaumaris

Town centre hotel serving good food during the season, and real ales all year. En suite rooms available.

¶ ⊨ see page 269

63 PILOT HOUSE CAFÉ

Penmon

Former lighthouse pilots' cottages in stunning seashore location, now a popular café.

¶ see page 269

Dovecote, Penmon

A nearby **Dovecote**, built in around 1600 by Sir Richard Bulkeley, contains nearly 1,000 nesting places. A path, beginning across the road, leads up to **St Seiriol's Well**, which was probably the site of the original 6th century priory. Although the upper part of the building covering the well appears to date from the 18th century, the lower portion is much older and could indeed incorporate something from the priory's original chapel.

PUFFIN ISLAND

8½ miles NE of Menai Bridge off the B5109

Once known as Priestholm and now often called **Ynys Seiriol**, this island is the home of the remains of St Seiriol's sanctuary and is thought once to have been connected to the mainland. The remains of monastic buildings dating back to the 6th century can still be seen here. The island was so named because of the large puffin colonies that nested here. However, the numbers of the nesting birds declined in the 19th century partly due to rats on the island and also because the young birds were considered a delicacy when pickled. Today, the island is again a nesting site for puffins, guillemots and razorbills and thee are regular boat trips around it from Beaumaris.

Llywelyn the Great gave the monastery and its estates to the prior of Puffin Island. **St Seiriol's Church**, now the parish church, was rebuilt in the 12th century and contains wonderful examples of Norman architecture. A carved cross, recently moved to the church from the fields nearby, shows influences from both Scandinavia and Ireland. The ruins of the priory's domestic buildings include a 13th century wing with a refectory on the ground floor where traces of the seat used by the monk who read aloud during meals can still be seen.

PENTRAETH

4 miles N of Menai Bridge on the A5025

Before land reclamation this sleepy village stood on the edge of Red Wharf Bay, where at low tide the almost 15 square miles of sand supported a flourishing cockling industry. It's now a popular place for a holiday even though it is not ideal for swimming because of the strong tidal currents experienced around this part of the Anglesey coast.

BENLLECH

6½ miles N of Menai Bridge on the A5025

With its excellent beach, Benllech is probably the most popular resort on Anglesey, but those coming here should take care as there are strong tidal currents and the sands can be treacherous. This resort has another claim to fame, as the birthplace of the poet Goronwy Owen.

Traces of a hill fort, **Castell Mawr**, can be found on the west side of Red Wharf Bay, near Benllech. On the evidence of coins found here, the site could once have been occupied by the Romans.

MOELFRE

9 miles N of Menai Bridge on the A5108

This is a charming coastal village with a sheltered, pebbled beach, attractive cottages and sandy beaches to both the north and the south. Fame came to Moelfre in an unfortunate and bizarre way via its lifeboat which, over the years, has been involved in many rescues. Two of them are specially worthy of mention. Returning to Liverpool from Australia in October 1859, laden with cargo and passengers, including gold prospectors coming home after making their fortunes in the Australian Gold Rush, the *Royal Charter* sank. A rigged iron vessel

and the pride of the merchant fleet, the ship was all set to make the long passage in record time but, while sheltering from a hurricane in Moelfre Bay, she foundered with the loss of 450 passengers and crew. Only 39 passengers and crew survived and many believe that the gold still lies with the wreck out in the bay. Efforts have been made to recover the lost fortune with varying but not overwhelming degrees of success. It has been said that the larger houses around Moelfre were paid for with gold washed ashore from the wreck. This is despite Customs Officers swamping the village in an attempt to ensure that any salvaged gold ended in the Exchequer rather than in the hands of the locals. Charles Dickens visited the site on New Year's Eve, 1859, and based a story on the disaster in *The Uncommercial Traveller.*

One hundred years later, almost to the day, in October 1959, the coaster *Hindlea*, struggling in foul weather, had eight crew members rescued by the Moelfre Lifeboat. The rescue earned Richard Evans, the lifeboat's coxswain, his second RNLI gold medal for gallantry.

Beyond the station is a small outcrop of rocks, **Ynys Moelfre**, a favourite spot for seabirds. Occasionally, porpoises can also be seen in the bay. About a mile inland from the village, off the narrow road, is the impressive **Lligwy Burial Chamber**, a Bronze Age tomb which has a huge 28-ton

51

Din Lligwy Hut Group, Moelfre

67 TAFARN Y GORS

Pentre Berw

Family-run smart bar and restaurant with spacious beer garden and adjacent caravan site.

🍴 🛏 *see page 271*

capstone supported by stone uprights. It lies half hidden in a pit dug out of the rock. Close by is **Din Lligwy Hut Group (CASW),** the remains of a Romano-British settlement that covers over half an acre. Certainly occupied around the 4th century AD, after the Roman garrison on Anglesey had been vacated, some of the stone walls of the buildings can still be seen. Excavations of the site have unearthed pottery, coins and evidence of metal working from that period. Nearby are the ruins of the 14th century Capel Lligwy.

LLANDDYFNAN

5 miles NW of Menai Bridge on the B5109

To the west of the village lies **Stone Science**, a most unusual attraction that tells the story of the earth from its beginning to the present - a journey spanning 650 million years. The museum illustrates the science with displays of fossils, crystals and artefacts, and there are numerous and varied items for sale in the Stone Science shop.

LLANGEFNI

6 miles NW of Menai Bridge on the B5420

The island's main market and administrative centre, Llangefni is also the home of **Oriel Ynys Môn** (the **Anglesey Heritage Centre**), an attractive art gallery and heritage centre, built in 1991, which gives an insight into the history of Anglesey. From prehistoric times to the present day, the permanent exhibition covers a series of themes including Stone Age Hunters, Druids, Medieval Society and Legends.

   Llyn Cefni Reservoir to the northwest of the town is an important wildlife habitat and nature reserve overlooked by a hide; it also provides a pleasant picnic area. On the northwest edge of town by the River Cefni, **The Dingle** is a local nature reserve with footpaths through mature woodland. The A5114, which connects Llangefni to the A5, is the shortest A road in the British Isles at less than 2 miles in length.

LLANFAIR PG

1 mile W of Menai Bridge off the A5

Llanfairpwllgwyngyll, often called Llanfair PG, is better known as the village with the world's longest place name. The full, tongue-twisting name is: Llanfairpwllgwyngyllgogerychwyrndrobwyllllantysiliogogogh and the translation is even longer - St Mary's Church in a hollow of white hazel near to a rapid whirlpool and St Tysilio's Church near the red cave. The name is said to have been invented, in humorous reference to the burgeoning tourist trade, by a local man. Whether this is true or not, it has certainly done the trick, as many visitors stop by initially out of curiosity at the name.

The village, overlooking the Menai Strait, is where the Britannia Bridge crosses to the mainland. The **Marquess of Anglesey Column**, 91 feet high, looks out from here over to Snowdonia and the quite splendid views from the top of the column are available to anyone wishing to negotiate the spiral staircase of some 115 steps. The column was finished two years after the battle of Waterloo, but the statue was not added until 1860, following the death of Henry Paget, Earl of Uxbridge and 1st Marquess of Anglesey, whom it commemorates. Paget fought alongside the Duke of Wellington at Waterloo where he lost a leg to one of the last shots of the battle. He lived to be 85, having twice been Lord-Lieutenant of Ireland after his military career (see also under Plas Newydd).

The last public toll house, designed by Thomas Telford when he was working on the London-Holyhead road in the 1820s, stands in the village. It still displays the tolls charged in 1895, the year the toll house closed.

However, the most famous building in Llanfair PG is undoubtedly its railway station - the often filmed station whose platform has the longest station sign and where the longest platform ticket in Britain was purchased. Today, visitors can see a replica of the

Railway Station, Llanfair PG

Victorian ticket office, examine some rare miniature steam trains and wander around the numerous craft and souvenir shops that have sprung up here.

ABERFFRAW

12½ miles W of Menai Bridge on the A4080

Though this was the capital of Gwynedd between the 7th and 13th centuries, there remains little trace of those times, although a Norman arch, set into St Beuno's Church, is said to be from the palace of the ruling princes. However, the **Llys Llywelyn Museum**, although modest, has exhibitions recounting the area's fascinating history.

Inland, the **Din Dryfol Burial Chamber** provides further evidence of Iron Age life on the island while, to the north of Aberffraw, on the cliff tops above Porth Trecastell, is the **Barclodiad y Gawres Burial Chamber** (CADW). Considered to be one of the finest of its kind, this burial chamber, along with Bryn Celli Ddu, contains some notable murals.

•
To the west of Aberffraw, Llangwyran Church occupies a spectacular setting on a small island off the coast, linked to the mainland only by a narrow causeway. The single cell church is believed to be 12th century in origin with a north aisle added in the 1500s. It was made redundant in 1871.
•

In the village of Brynsiencyn and found down the small road leading to the shore is Foel Farm Park, a real working farm which offers visitors the opportunity to bottle feed lambs and baby calves, cuddle rabbits, see and help with milking and enjoy the homemade ice cream. There are also covered areas for rainy days which include an adventure play den and an indoor picnic room. Visitors can also watch expert chocolatiers creating a wonderful variety of hand-crafted chocolates, including novelties such as the range of beautifully moulded animals.

PLAS NEWYDD

2 miles SW of Menai Bridge off the A4080

Although it is now owned by the National Trust, **Plas Newydd** is still the home of the Marquesses of Anglesey, for the first of whom this splendid mansion was built in the late 1700s. The designers, James Wyatt and Joseph Potter, transformed a 16th century manor house into a flamboyantly Gothic building. Inside, there's a fine Gothic Hall with a fan-vaulted ceiling, a wealth of paintings - mostly family and royal portraits - and a gorgeously decorated Music Room. A former kitchen celebrates the work of Rex Whistler who was a regular visitor to the house. There's a dazzling example of his work in the Rex Whistler Room where a 58 feet long mural incorporates places such as Windsor Castle, Portmeirion and Snowdonia in an imaginary seascape seen from a promenade. Whistler included himself twice - once as a gondolier and again as a

gardener. A nearby room houses the Cavalry Museum which contains the world's first prosthetic limb which was made for the 1st marquess who had his leg shot off during the Battle of Waterloo.

Plas Newydd is surrounded by gardens and parkland laid out in the 18th century by Humphry Repton. They command fabulous views over the Menai Strait and also contain a woodland walk, an Australian arboretum and a formal Italian style garden terrace.

BRYNSIENCYN

5 miles SW of Menai Bridge on the A4080

Just to the west of the village is **Caer Leb**, an Iron Age earthwork consisting of a pentagonal enclosure 200 feet by 160 feet encircled by banks and ditches, while, just a short distance away is **Bodowyr Burial Chamber**, a massive stone that is, seemingly, delicately perched upon three upright stones. To the south of the burial chamber, and just a mile west of Brynsiencyn, are the earthwork remains of **Castell Bryn Gwyn**, a site which has been excavated and shows traces of having been used from as far back as the New Stone Age through to the time of the Roman occupation of Britain.

Also overlooking the Menai Strait is the fascinating **Anglesey Sea Zoo**, an award-winning attraction that takes visitors beneath the waves and into the underwater world of a wide variety of sea creatures. The imaginative and innovative displays allow visitors a unique view of these interesting

Castell Bryn Gwyn, Brynsiencyn

beasts, which include sea horses, oysters, conger eels and rays.

DWYRAN

8 miles SW of Menai Bridge off the A4080

Just outside the village lies **Bird World**, a popular family attraction set in extensive parkland with views over to the Snowdonia mountain range. Visitors can admire the wide variety of birds on display - more than 1000 of them from all over the world - and picnic in the beautiful surroundings of the lake. There's a Bird of Prey Centre and several ponds that are home to a large collection of waterfowl, swans, rheas and poultry. On site facilities include a refreshment room and, for the children, indoor and outdoor play areas.

NEWBOROUGH

9 miles SW of Menai Bridge on the A4080

Founded in 1303 by the former inhabitants of Llanfaes who had been moved here by Edward I, the village stands on the edge of a National Nature Reserve that covers 1566 acres of dunes, coast and forest. Among the many footpaths through the reserve, there are several forest trails that show how the Forestry Commission is constantly trying to stabilise the dunes. **Newborough Warren** is so called because, before myxomatosis, about 80,000 rabbits were trapped here annually. There is a route through the warren to **Abermenai Point**, but the way can be dangerous and advice concerning tidal conditions should be sought before considering the walk.

Llanddwyn Island is also accessible on foot but again tidal conditions should be carefully studied before setting out. Until the 1920s, marram grass, which has been grown for conservation purposes from Elizabethan times, was also a mainstay of the area, helping to sustain a cottage industry in the production of ropes, baskets, matting and thatching materials. A high embankment was built here in the 18th century by Thomas Telford as a defence against the sea which had previously almost cut the island into two.

Charles Tunnicliffe, the renowned wildlife artist, had a studio on the island for more than 30 years. Anglesey Council has purchased a collection of his marvellous work which can be seen at the Oriel (Gallery) Ynys Môn in Llangefni. On the A4080 signposted from Newborough, Newborough Forest is a pine forest with rides, glades and miles of walks.

HOLYHEAD

Holyhead Mountain (Mynydd Twr) rises to 720 feet behind this town, which is the largest on Anglesey and is itself on an island - Holy Island. A busy rail and ferry terminal, especially for travellers to and from Ireland, Holyhead has all the facilities needed to cater for visitors passing through although it is also, despite being something of an industrial and commercial centre, a seaside resort. Parts of **St Cybi's Parish Church** date from

Situated between Newborough and Dwyran lies Anglesey Model Village and Gardens, a delightful place where visitors can wander through the attractive landscaped gardens and see many of the island's many landmarks - all built to one twelfth scale. There is a children's ride-on train, as well as the garden railway, and the gardens themselves are particularly beautiful with many water features and a good collection of plants and trees.

68 THE SEVENTY NINE

Holyhead

Popular town centre pub with good, home-cooked food, real ales and regular pub quiz.

see page 272

St Cybi's Parish Church, Holyhead

69 JWMPIN JAC'S CAFÉ BAR

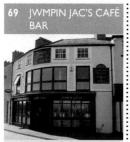

Holyhead

Stylish eatery serving a superb range of coffees and a menu with a distinct Mediterranean element

🍴 see page 271

the 14th to the 17th century and it is situated within the partially surviving walls of the small Roman fort, Caer Gybi (the source of Holyhead's name in Welsh) and on the site of a 6th century chapel. Close to the church is a smaller church, **Egylwys Bedd**, which reputedly contains the tomb of Seregri, an Irish warrior who was repelled by the Welsh chief, Caswallon Lawhir. The town's triumphal arches, built in 1821, commemorate George IV's visit here as well as the end of the A5, the major road from London.

The interesting **Canolfan Ucheldre Centre**, housed in a former convent chapel, is a complete arts centre for northwest Wales. Opened in 1991, it presents film, music and drama events as well as holding all manner of art and craft exhibitions and workshops.

Holyhead itself has little to detain the visitor but a popular amenity just northwest of the town

is **Breakwater Quarry Country Park** which incorporates Britain's largest breakwater. Designed by James Meadow and started in 1845, the structure took 28 years to build and shields an area of 667 acres. From the country park there are many walks along the coast, including a route to **South Stack**. This is a reserve of cliffs and heath teeming with birdlife such as puffins, guillemots and razorbills. The RSPB visitor centre is open daily, the café daily in summer, and the lighthouse is open daily in summer for guided tours. The lighthouse, one of the most impressive in Wales, was built in 1809 and stands on a beautiful but dangerous site reached by a steep stone stairway of more than 400 steps. Above the harbour and breakwater is a memorial in tribute to Captain Skinner who drowned when his packet boat, *Escape*, was lost in 1832.

At the summit of Holyhead Mountain, from where, on a clear day, Snowdonia, the Isle of Man and the Mourne Mountains in Ireland can be seen, the remains of **Caer y Twr**, a hill fort, are visible. Close by is **Cytiau'r Gwyddelod**, a hut settlement from the 2nd century.

Between South Stack and North Stack lies **Gogarth Bay**, where the RSPB sea bird centre includes a cavern, known as Parliament House Cave, which is used by a profusion of sea birds such as puffins, guillemots and even falcons. Visitors here can also watch the thousands of cliff nesting birds via live television pictures and enjoy the bracing cliff top walks. **Ellin's Tower Seabird Centre** is another spot favoured by ornithologists with anything up to 3000 birds nesting in the cliffs. The tower was erected by William Stanley in memory of his wife. It was Stanley who did most of the excavation on the Neolithic hut circles, Cytiau'r Gwyddelod, just across the road from the Seabird Centre car park.

AROUND HOLYHEAD

VALLEY

3½ miles SE of Holyhead on the A5

Valley was thought to have gained its name while Thomas Telford was cutting his road through the small hill here. Centuries earlier this was the home of Iron Age man whose weapons and horse trappings found in the area are now on display in the National Museum of Wales.

Valley is perhaps better known today for the nearby airfield established here during World War II as a fighter pilot base. In 1943, the American Air Force expanded the base's capability for use as an Atlantic terminal and now the RAF uses it for training flights and for Air/Sea rescue.

RHOSNEIGR

7½ miles SE of Holyhead on the A4080

This small resort is situated in a quiet spot, close to the sandy beaches and rocky outcrops of **Cymyran Bay**. The beach is popular with wind surfers. The

River Crigyll, which runs into the sea by the town, was the haunt in the 18th century of the 'Wreckers of Crigyll' who were famous for luring ships on to the rocks. After being caught and tried at Beaumaris in 1741, the group of desperate men were found guilty and hanged. They became the subject of a ballad, *The Hanging of the Thieves of Crigyll*.

The 1400 acres of gorse and dunes at **Tywyn Trewan Common** are a paradise for botanists and ornithologists.

RHOSCOLYN

4½ miles S of Holyhead off the B4545

With a wide sandy beach that is excellent for swimming and fishing, this scattered but pleasant village was once home to a thriving oyster industry that is now, sadly, in decline. China clay was also once quarried here, while the local marble was used in the construction of Worcester, Bristol and Peterborough Cathedrals.

St Gwenfaen founded a church here in the 6th century and her Well, on **Rhoscolyn Head**, was said to have properties that cured, in particular, mental illness. The headland is a superb place for cliff walking and there are splendid views northwards over Trearddur Bay and, southwards, over Cymyran Bay. At **Bwa Gwyn** (White Arch) is a memorial to Tyger, a remarkable dog who, in 1817, led to safety the four-man crew from a sinking ketch. After dragging the cabin boy ashore and returning for the ship's captain, the dog collapsed and died from exhaustion.

Aqua diving, windsurfing, water skiing and fishing are some of the many attractions of Trearddur Bay, a popular part of Anglesey's extensive coastline that lies just to the southwest of Holyhead. With large sandy beaches, clear water and safe bathing, it is naturally popular. The Georgian house, Towyn Lodge, on the south side of the bay, played host to Thomas Telford while he was working on what is now the A5 road in the 19th century.

70 TY MAWR

Valley

Comfortable farmhouse B&B on working farm with uninterrupted views of the Snowdonia mountain range.

see page 273

LLANFAIRYNGHORNWY

7 miles NE of Holyhead off the A5025

This village, on the approach to **Carmel Head**, has two claims to fame. It was here, in the 19th century, that Frances Williams founded the Anglesey Association for the Preservation of Life from Shipwreck. Along with her husband, who was the local rector, Frances raised funds for lifeboats on the island and through her efforts the first lifeboat station in the area was established.

Lying two miles offshore from the point at Carmel Head are **The Skerries**, a group of windswept islets whose Welsh name, Ynysoedd y Moelrhoniaid, means Island of Porpoises. On the islets stands the last **Lighthouse** to be privately owned - ships had to pay a toll as they passed. When braziers fuelled the light during the 18th century they burnt approximately 10 tons of coal a night! Now automated and owned by Trinity House, its beam is rated 4-million candles.

CEMAES

11 miles NE of Holyhead off the A5025

Boasting two glorious, safe, sandy beaches, **Cemaes Bay** is a popular place on the island that was also once a favourite with smugglers. The most northerly village in Wales, Cemaes is flanked by the elderly Wylfa Nuclear Power Station and a wind farm. Yet it remains picturesque with its small tidal harbour, wonderful walks and abundant wildlife.

The Visitor Centre at **Wylfa Nuclear Power Station** is the starting point for a guided tour of the station and also contains a mass of information about the nature trail surrounding the plant.

Ogof y March Glas - the cave of the blue horse - on Cemaes Bay was named after an incident that took place more than 200 years ago. Following a family dispute, a young man furiously galloped away from his house near the bay on his dappled grey horse. Blinded by rage, he galloped headlong over the cliff; only his hat was ever seen again, although the carcass of his horse was found washed up in the cave.

AMLWCH

14 miles NE of Holyhead on the A5025

South of this seaside town lies the pock-marked **Parys Mountain** which has provided copper for prospectors from as early as Roman times. In 1768 a copper boom helped make Anglesey the copper

Porth Amlwch

centre of the world but by 1820 the rush was over as prices fell and the mineral deposits became exhausted. Amlwch had fed off this wealth and swollen in size to become the second largest town in Wales. The harbour, which was built during those more prosperous times, is now used mainly by pleasure craft. In its heyday Amlwch had 6000 inhabitants and 1000 ale houses. The **Amlwch Industrial Heritage Centre** (free) tells the story of the town's rise and fall and distributes a free Heritage Trail leaflet. An oddity worth a look is the church of Our Lady Star of the Sea. It was built of reinforced concrete in the 1930s and its strange design ("like a giant toast rack" according to one visitor) is supposed to represent an upturned boat - with portholes!

DULAS

15 miles NE of Holyhead off the A5025

A once thriving village, Dulas was, in the early 19th century, home to both a brickworks and a shipbuilding industry. Standing at the head of the Dulas River, which runs into the bay, the village overlooks **Ynys Dulas**, a small island which lies a mile or so offshore and is the haunt of grey seals. On the island itself is a 19th century tower built as a beacon and a refuge for sailors; the lady of Llysdulas manor house once had food left there for stranded mariners.

LLANERCHYMEDD

11 miles E of Holyhead on the B5112

To the north of the village lies **Llyn Alaw**, Anglesey's largest lake, well known for its fine trout fishing as well as the abundant wildlife found around its shores. Covering some 770 acres, the lake is actually man-made by flooding of marshland. It supplies most of the island's industrial and domestic needs.

LLANDDEUSANT

6½ miles E of Holyhead off the A5025

Llanddeusant is home to Anglesey's only stone tower working windmill, built in 1775-76 at a total cost of £529.11s.0d. Four storeys high, with a boat-shaped cap, it ceased milling by wind power in 1924 but was restored and opened to the public in 1984. **Llynnon Mill** not only mills stone-ground flour for sale (wind and conditions willing) but also has an attractive craft shop and a popular tea room.

Tradition has it that the green mound, **Bedd Branwen**, near the River Alaw, is the grave of Branwen, the heroine of the Welsh epic, *Mabinogion*. When the mound was excavated in 1813, it revealed a rough baked clay urn containing fragments of burnt bone and ashes. Since the discovery of more funeral urns in 1967, the site has become even more significant.

71 THE BULL INN

Llanerchymedd

Traditional village inn with bar snacks at lunchtimes and evenings, real ales, pool room and regular entertainment.

see page 273

72 TY CRISTION HOLIDAY COTTAGES

Bodedern

Four charming self-catering cottages set in 9 acres of grounds and surrounded by scenic countryside.

see page 273

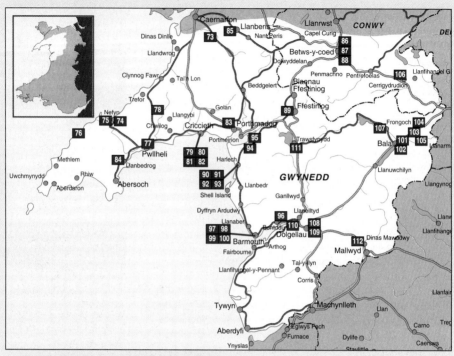

Snowdonia Coast & Inland

To the south of Anglesey lies the Llyn (Lleyn) Peninsula, which forms the great curve of Caernarfon Bay. This is one of the most secluded and most beautiful parts of Wales with more than 100 miles of its shoreline designated Areas of Outstanding Natural Beauty. During the Middle Ages, Bardsey Island, lying off the western tip of the peninsula, was a place of pilgrimage, and the ancient route to Aberdaron, from where the pilgrims sailed to their destination, can still in parts be followed. Reminders of the area's early Christian past can be found throughout Llyn, along with more ancient monuments such as hill forts.

The attractive Victorian resorts along the southern shore of the peninsula are sheltered and provide plenty of scope for sailing, swimming and fishing. The birthplace of one of the country's greatest statesmen, David Lloyd George, is a popular place to visit, but the whole region is filled with splendid attractions to see and exciting things to do. Perhaps the most visited of all is the fantasy village of Portmeirion, built from the 1920s to the 1970s by Sir Clough Williams-Ellis.

There are three National Parks in Wales, and Snowdonia, at some 840 square miles, is the largest and certainly the most dramatic scenically. There are several routes up to the summit of Snowdon beginning at various points around its base. Some call for more energy than others, but the least arduous ascent is by the Snowdon Mountain Railway that runs from Llanberis. The most popular walk follows the railway. In and around nearby Betws-y-Coed, the walking is gentler and includes surviving tracts of the vast forests that once covered much of Wales. From the earliest times, this region was mined for its minerals. Gold was mined here long before the Romans arrived, and as recently as the 19th century there were mini-gold rushes in a belt that stretched from Bontddu along the line of the River Mawddach. Copper, lead and slate were also mined up until the start of the 20th century, and the scars left by those industries can still be seen today. Several of the mines have found new roles as visitor attractions, along with the little railways that once carried the minerals from the mines and quarries to the coast.

In the middle of the 19th century, the coastal villages and towns, many of them obscure, quiet fishing communities, were put on the map and changed radically in character with the arrival of the main railway network. As the fashion for sea air grew and communications were made easier, they became popular seaside resorts, and today many of them still retain Victorian and Edwardian buildings constructed to cater for holidaymakers. The scenery throughout the region is truly inspirational, and few would disagree with the verdict of the 19th century traveller and writer George Borrow:

"Perhaps in all the world there is no region more picturesquely beautiful."

Waunfawr

Idyllically located riverside tavern with good home cooked food, real ale, and its own micro-brewery; also small campsite.

Nefyn

Stylish family-run town centre hotel offering quality cuisine and comfortable en suite rooms.

Edern

Child-friendly hotel set in beautiful grounds with excellent cuisine and quality en suite accommodation

THE LLYN PENINSULA

DINAS DINLLE

3 miles S of Caernarfon off the A499

A seaside village at the mouth of the Menai Strait. With a shingle beach and cliffs overlooking Caernarfon Bay, there are many pleasant spots to picnic and enjoy the views down the Llyn Peninsula or across the bay to Anglesey. At the beach's northerly tip lies **Fort Belan**, which was built in the 18th century along with neighbouring **Fort Williamsburg**. It was constructed by the 1st Lord Newborough who felt concern over the threat of invasion by Napoleon; his lordship also raised and equipped his own private army, The Royal Caernarfonshire Grenadiers, which, by the time of his death in 1807, had cost him a quarter of his fortune.

LLANDWROG

4 miles S of Caernarfon off the A499

Llandwrog was built to serve the estate of Lord Newborough at Glynllifon Park, and memorials to the Newborough family may be seen in the mid-Victorian church.

CLYNNOG FAWR

10 miles SW of Caernarfon on the A499

This typical Llyn Peninsula village on the Heritage Coast is famous for its remarkably large and beautiful church - **St Beuno's Church** - which stands on the site of the chapel founded by the saint around AD 616. One of the sons of the royal family of Morgannwg, St Beuno had great influence in North Wales and he built his chapel on land which was presented to him by Cadwallon, King of Gwynedd. St Beuno's burial place and his shrine can be seen in this early 16th century building, which lies on the Pilgrims' Route to Bardsey Island. For many years, his tomb was thought to have curative powers.

Nearby is **St Beuno's Well**, whose waters were also thought to cure all manner of illness and conditions, especially if the sufferer had first visited the church. Close by, and virtually on the seafront, stands the capstone and three uprights of **Bachwen**, a neolithic burial chamber.

TREFOR

3½ miles SW of Clynnog Fawr off the A499

This coastal village is dominated by **Yr Eifl** (The Forks) which lies to the southwest and affords stunning views from its 1850 feet summit out over Caernarfon Bay to Anglesey and across the Llyn Peninsula. On the south-eastern slopes of the hill is **Tre'r Ceiri** (Town of Giants), one of the finest Iron Age forts in the country. A stone wall surrounds this once heavily populated circle of 150 huts.

NEFYN

9 miles SW of Clynnog Fawr on the A497

Once a herring fishing village, this resort was granted a charter in 1355, along with Pwllheli, by the Black Prince. It was here in 1284 that Edward I celebrated his conquest over Wales. Housed in St

Penarth Fawr, Pwllheli

Mary's church, whose tower supports a sailing ship weathervane, is the **Maritime Museum**, an excellent place to visit to find out more about this interesting and beautiful part of Wales.

PWLLHELI

Pwllheli is the chief town of the Llyn Peninsula and is often referred to as the 'Jewel' in the Welsh scenic crown. Like Nefyn, it was granted a charter in 1355; a gift by the Black Prince to Nigel de Loryng, who had helped the Prince win the Battle of Poitiers. A popular holiday resort with all the usual amusements, this is also still a market town - it is held each Wednesday. Pwllheli' once busy port, where wine was imported from the Continent, is now home to pleasure craft with a 420-berth marina and an annual sailing regatta. Boat trips are available during the summer to Bardsey Island.

As well as being an ancient town, Pwllheli has played its part in the more recent history of Wales. During the National Eisteddfod in 1925, three members of the Army of Welsh Home Rulers met with three members of the Welsh Movement at the town's Temperance Hotel and joined forces to form the political party, Plaid Cymru. The hotel, on the market square, is now a pet shop but a plaque commemorates the meeting.

Just to the east of the town is **Hafan y Mor,** a family-oriented holiday resort that also encourages day visitors to use its wealth of children's amusements. In complete contrast, just a mile inland from the resort is **Penarth Fawr,** an interesting 15th century manor house with an unusual aisle truss hall.

AROUND PWLLHELI

CHWILOG

4½ miles NE of Pwllheli on the B4354

Close to the village lies **Talhenbont Hall,** an early 17th century manor house that was once the home of William Vaughan. A place of history with its fair share of ghosts, the hall was used, during the Civil War, as a garrison for Parliamentary soldiers.

| 76 | THE LION HOTEL |

Tudweilog

Delightful family-run country inn close to beach offering quality food, real ales and en suite rooms.

see page 275

| 77 | ORIEL FACH TEA ROOMS & LICENSED CAFÉ |

Abersoch

Bright and modern tea rooms and café serving delicious range of home-made treats.

see page 277

78 GLASFRYN COTTAGES

Glasfryn

Top quality self-catering accommodation in delightful properties set within a 500-acre park.

 see page 278

79 CRICCIETH CASTLE

Criccieth

Criccieth Castle is on a commanding headland overlooking Tremadog Bay

see page 277

LLANGYBI

5 miles NE of Pwllheli off the B4354

Just to the north of the village is **St Cybi's Well** and, behind it, the Iron Age fort of **Garn Pentyrch**. The well was established in the 6th century when St Cybi was in the process of setting up religious cells and a monastery in Holyhead. Sheltered by an unusual building with beehive vaulting which is thought to be unique in Wales, the well had a reputation for curing blindness and warts among many other ailments.

LLANYSTUMDWY

6½ miles E of Pwllheli on the A497

This peaceful little coastal village is best known as being the home of David Lloyd George, the Member of Parliament for Caernarfon for 55 years and the Prime Minister who, at the beginning of the 20th century, was responsible for social reform as well as seeing the country through the Armistice at the end of World War I. Lloyd George's childhood home, Highgate, is now just as it would have been when the great statesman lived here for the first 18 years of his life. It forms part of the **Lloyd George Museum** which also features a Victorian schoolroom and an exhibition recalling the life of this reforming Liberal politician. When he died in 1945, he won this tribute in Parliament from Winston Churchill: "As a man of action, resource and creative energy he stood, when at his zenith, without a rival. His name is a household word throughout our Commonwealth of Nations. He was the greatest Welshman which that unconquerable race has produced since the age of the Tudors. Much of his work abides, some of it will grow greatly in the future, and those who come after us will find the pillars of his life's toil upstanding, massive and indestructible." The museum is open from Easter to October, and at other times by appointment. David Lloyd George, 1st Earl Lloyd-George of Dwyfor, is buried in the village church, in a tomb designed by Clough Williams-Ellis, architect of Portmeirion. Opposite his grave is a set of **Memorial Gates** presented to the village by Pwllheli in 1952. They feature an elephant and a castle - elephants are part of the town's coat of arms.

CRICCIETH

8 miles E of Pwllheli on the A497

This small family resort lies near the northeast corner of Cardigan Bay and enjoys fine views down the Llyn coastline and northeastwards to Snowdonia. Unlike many of the other resorts on the peninsula, Criccieth is more reminiscent of a south coast seaside town rather than one set in North Wales.

An attractive Victorian town, Criccieth is dominated by **Criccieth Castle**, which stands on a rocky outcrop with commanding views over the sea. Built in the early 13th century by Llywelyn the Great as a stronghold of the native Welsh princes, it was captured in 1283 and extended by Edward I; but the core

East Beach, Criccieth

of the structure - the powerful twin towered gatehouse - still exists from the original fortification. Despite Edward's strengthening of the defences, in 1404 the castle was taken by Owain Glyndwr and put to the torch. The castle walls still bear the scorch marks One of the best preserved of the 13th century castles that litter the North Wales countryside, the romantic ruins of Criccieth Castle have inspired many artists down the centuries including JMW Turner, who used it as the backdrop for a famous painting of storm-wrecked sailors. The annual **Criccieth Festival,** held in the third week of June, is renowned for its showcasing of young local, national and international talent.

GOLAN
9 miles NE of Pwllheli on the A487

Between the entrances to two wonderful valleys, Cwm Pennant and Cwm Ystradllyn, and a mile off the A487 Porthmadog-Caernarfon road, is **Brynkir Woollen Mill.**

Originally a corn mill, it was converted over 150 years ago for woollen cloth production. The waterwheel still turns although the River Henwy is used to generate electricity. Visitors can still see the various machines that are used in the production process: Tenterhook Willey, carders, spinning mules, doubling and hanking machines, cheese and bobbin winder, warping mill and looms. A wide variety of woollen products made at the mill can be bought. The mill is open Monday to Friday; admission is free, and there's ample parking.

TREMADOG
12 miles E of Pwllheli on the A487

This village, developed, like its close neighbour Porthmadog, by William Alexander Madocks, is a wonderful example of early 19th century town planning and contains many fine Regency buildings. Madocks, who was the MP for Boston in Lincolnshire, bought the land in 1798 and built Tremadog on

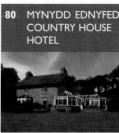

80 MYNYDD EDNYFED COUNTRY HOUSE HOTEL

Criccieth

400-year-old country home offering both comfort and contemporary style in a stunning location

⊨ ¶ *see page 279*

81 TIR A MÔR RESTAURANT

Criccieth

Leading eating place in the area for the discerning diner; French chef specialises in fish dishes

¶ *see page 279*

82 PROS KAIRON GUEST HOUSE

Criccieth

Family-run guest house close to Criccieth Castle with en suite rooms, superb sea views.

⊨ *see page 280*

the reclaimed land in classical style, with broad streets and a handsome market square with a backdrop of cliffs. He hoped that the town would be a key point on the intended main route from the south of England to Ireland, but his rivals in Parliament preferred the North Wales route, with Holyhead becoming the principal port for Ireland. The little town of Tremadog, with its well-planned streets and fine buildings, remains as a memorial to Madocks who died in Paris in 1828; he is buried in the Père Lachaise cemetery (see also Porthmadog). The soldier and author TE Lawrence (of Arabia) was born at Snowdon House - now a back-packers' hostel - in 1888 and the poet Shelley is known to have visited on several occasions.

PORTMEIRION

13½ miles E of Pwllheli off the A487

This extraordinary village in a wonderful setting on a wooded peninsula overlooking Traeth Bay

Portmeirion

was conceived and created by the Welsh architect Sir Clough Williams-Ellis between 1925 and 1972. An inveterate campaigner against the spoiling of Britain's landscape, he set out to illustrate that building in a beautiful location did not mean spoiling the environment. In looks, this is the least Welsh place in Wales: the 50 or so buildings, some of which consist only of a façade, were inspired by a visit Williams-Ellis made to Sorrento and Portofino in Italy and they are mainly either part of the hotel or pastel cottages. In the 1960s the village provided some exotic settings for the cult TV series, *The Prisoner*. Each year, devotees of that series gather at Portmeirion to act out their favourite scenes.

The **Portmeirion Pottery** was established in 1960 by Clough's daughter Susan Williams-Ellis and her husband Euan. Susan had studied under Henry Moore and Graham Sutherland, and her classic designs include Botanic Garden (1972) and the recently relaunched Totem from the 1960s. Williams-Ellis' ancestral home, **Plâs Brondanw**, lies some five miles away, up the A4085 northeast of **Garreg**, and the marvellous gardens here make the extra journey well worth while. They are designed to please the eye and also provide some fabulous views over the mountain scenery. Among the splendid plants are charming statues and elegant topiary terraces. Although less well known than the village and gardens at Portmeirion, the gardens at Brondanw are considered by some to be Clough Williams-Ellis' most important creation, and certainly the most beautiful. Sir Clough continued working up until his death at the age of 94 in 1978.

PORTHMADOG

12½ miles E of Pwllheli on the A487

Porthmadog enjoys a stunning setting with Moel y Gest rising almost 800ft as a backdrop and the wide expanse of the Glaslyn estuary stretching to the north and east. A bustling town with many family-run specialist shops and restaurants, and an open air market every Friday from Easter to Christmas, Porthmadog's attractions also include one of the rare cinemas in the area, the Porthmadog Pottery and the Rob Piercy Gallery featuring works by local artists.

Just over 200 years ago, there was nothing but marshland where Porthmadog now stands. Its transformation was the work of one man, William Madocks, who was also responsible for building neighbouring Tremadog. Member of Parliament for Boston in Lincolnshire and a great entrepreneur, Madocks drained the mud flats that made up the estuary to create land for grazing cattle. The embankment, built to keep the tides at bay, enclosed some 7000 acres of land and re-routed the River Glaslyn to produce a deep water channel that was ideal for the docks. Naming Porthmadog after himself (nearby Tremadog was named after his brother), he saw the beginning of

Portmeirion Beach

the blossoming of the town in the 1820s. The history of the town and its waterfront is described in the **Maritime Museum** where the importance of the trade in slate and Porthmadog's shipbuilding industry is also told.

Porthmadog is also home to both the recently extended **Welsh Highland Railway** and the **Ffestiniog Railway,** the world's oldest narrow track passenger carrying railway. It winds its way up to 650ft to the slate mines at Blaenau Ffestiniog, a journey of some 13 miles passing through some stunning scenery. In the late 1800s, the slate mines were producing some 100,000 tons of slate, all of which was transported by the valiant little locomotives.

LLANBEDROG

3½ miles SW of Pwllheli on the A499

This enchanting village boasts a fine beach and one of the oldest public art galleries in Wales, **Plas Glyn y Weddw**. In 1896, this

•
Black Rock Sands, just to the southwest of Porthmadog, is one of the few beaches in Britain where you can step out of your car straight onto the sands which stretch as far as the eye can sea. The surrounding dunes are a site of special scientific interest and provide glorious views across the whole of Cardigan Bay.
•

83   THE UNION INN

Tremadog

Traditional village hostelry in picturesque estate village serving an enticing selection of home-made food.

🍴   see page 281

67

84 GLYN-Y-WEDDW ARMS

Llanbedrog

Outstandingly good food and real ales in the beguiling surroundings of a traditional Welsh hostelry.

see page 282

imposing neo-Gothic mansion was bought by the Cardiff businessman Solomon Andrews who developed it into a centre of the arts, complete with pleasure gardens. Inside, there's an astonishing hallway with galleries, an enormous stained glass window and an impressive hammer beam roof. The exhibitions combine items from the gallery's permanent collection with touring works, usually with a Welsh theme. Another attraction here is the delightful conservatory tea room overlooking the sea.

Down on the National Trust-owned beach, multi-coloured beach huts add to the appeal. From the beach, a steepish path leads to the summit of Myndd Tir-y-Cwmwd and some stunning views. Also surveying the vista is the **Iron Man**, a modern sculpture built locally and made of beachcombed material.

ABERSOCH

6 miles SW of Pwllheli on the A499

A popular family resort with safe beaches, Abersoch lies on each side of the estuary of the River Soch. Its sheltered harbour attracts a wide variety of pleasure craft and it is the major dinghy sailing centre in Wales. Just off the coast lie **St Tudwal's Islands** - so called because the saint founded a religious cell there in the 6th century. Both islands are now privately owned and dedicated as bird sanctuaries.

The site of the 17th century mansion, Castellmarch, was said to be the home of March Amheirchion, one of King Arthur's knights. Reputed to have the ears of a horse, March (the name is Welsh for horse) kept them hidden and killed anyone who saw them - burying the bodies in a nearby reed bed.

RHIW

11 miles SW of Pwllheli off the B4413

This hamlet lies on a miniature pass and overlooks **Porth Neigwl** (Hell's Mouth), a four mile sweep of beach so called because of its reputation for strong currents; it is a favourite spot for surfing.

Sheltered from strong gales by Mynydd Rhiw, **Plas yn Rhiw** is a small, part medieval, part Tudor, part Georgian manor house which was given to the National Trust in 1952 by the unconventional Keating sisters from Nottingham. The three spinsters, Eileen, Lorna and Honora, purchased the property in 1938 and lovingly restored it after the house had lain neglected for some 20 years. This they did with the help of their friend Sir Clough Williams-Ellis, the architect of Portmeirion.

Abersoch Harbour

The house is surrounded by glorious grounds which were also restored by the sisters and provide fabulous views over Porth Neigwl. Visitors can wander through ornamental gardens and, in the spring, the bluebell and snowdrop woodlands. At one time the poet RS Thomas lived in one of the estate cottages where he wrote some of his finest poetry.

ABERDARON

13½ miles SW of Pwllheli on the B4413

Aberdaron, the land's end of the Peninsula, boasts the unusual distinction of being further from a railway station than anywhere else in England and Wales. This small and delightful village features in history books because of a treaty signed here in 1405. The Tripartite Indenture made Wales independent under the rule of Owain Glyndwr. The English later reneged on the deal.

Close to the sea and originally dating from the 6th century, **St Hywyn's Church** is thought to have sheltered the 12th century Prince of Wales, Gryffydd ap Rhys, from marauding Saxons. During the Civil War, the church once again proved a place of sanctuary as Cromwell's soldiers also sought refuge here. The minister at St Hywyn's for many years was the celebrated poet RS Thomas (1913-2000). He wrote many inspired lines about his beloved country, summed up in this extract:

Every mountain and stream, every farm
and little lane announces to the world
that landscape is something different in
Wales.

St Hywyn's Church, Aberdaron

A mile or so from the village lies **Castel Odo**, an Iron Age fort providing evidence that there have been five different occupations of the peninsula dating back to the 4th century BC.

UWCHMYNYDD

15 miles SW of Pwllheli off the B4413

Uwchmynydd stands on the wild and beautiful tip of the Llyn Peninsula, at the point where the first pilgrims set out to Bardsey Island in the Middle Ages. The National Trust is responsible for much of the land towards the tip of the Llyn Peninsula, including the ecologically outstanding coastal heath of **Braich-y-Pwll** where the ruins of St Mary's Church, once used by the pilgrims, can still be seen. This heath is the spring and summer home of a variety of plant life and birds, including fulmars, kittiwakes, cormorants, guillemots and the rare chough. A similar variety of birds populate the tiny islands of Dinas Fawr and Dinas Bach. Five miles east of

Aberdaron, on the south side of the Peninsula, Porth Ysgo and Penarfynnd cover 245 acres of beaches and cliffs, while two miles northwest of the village Mynydd Anelog is an 116-acre area of ancient common land with the remains of prehistoric hut circles. Here, as in the other National Trust stretches of coastland on the Peninsula, is found our friend the chough, a relative of the crow with a distinctive red bill. Apart from here, this rare bird is usually found only in Pembrokeshire and on part of the western coast of Scotland. The curiously named **Porth Oer** (Whistling Sands), located off the B4417 by Methlem, is worth a visit as at certain stages of the tide the sands seem literally to whistle when walked upon. The noise is caused by the rubbing together of minute quartz granules.

BARDSEY ISLAND

17 miles SW of Pwllheli off the B4413

This wild, whale-shaped island in the Irish Sea has inspired many legends: one says that this is King Arthur's Avalon, another that his magician Merlin sleeps here in a glass castle. Settlement of the island is thought to have begun during the Dark Ages, although it was the death of St Dyfrig on Bardsey that saw the beginning of pilgrimages. At one time it was considered that three pilgrimages to this holy island was equivalent to one to Rome. Little remains of the 12th century monastery, and the island is now an important bird and field observatory. Bardsey is best known for its vast numbers of breeding shearwaters. The Bardsey Island Trust runs a boat from Pwllheli most days and if the weather is favourable also picks up from the hidden fishing cove of Porth Meudwy by Aberdaron.

The island's name is Norse in origin; the Welsh name, **Ynys Enlii**, means Island of Currents - a reference to the treacherous waters that separate Bardsey from the mainland.

LLANBERIS

Llanberis is effectively Base Camp for walkers preparing to tackle the 3560ft high bulk of **Snowdon**, the highest peak in Wales and the most climbed mountain in Britain. On a

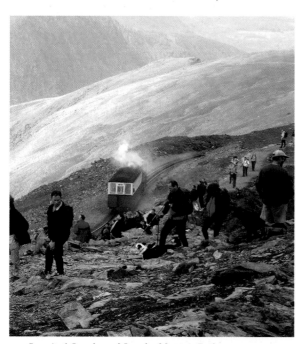

Summit of Snowdon and Snowdon Mountain Railway

clear day, the view from the summit is fantastic, with Ireland sometimes visible. Many reach the summit the easy way, with the help of a 1-hour journey on the **Snowdon Mountain Railway**, Britain's only rack and pinion system which was built in 1896 and has carried millions to the top of the mountain over the years. It is not surprising that this mountainous and inhospitable area is also steeped in legend and mystery. The eagles of Snowdon have long been regarded as oracles of peace and war, triumph and disaster, and Snowdon's peak is said to be a cairn erected over the grave of a giant who was killed by King Arthur.

For those wanting another train ride or are content with a more sedate journey, the **Llanberis Lake Railway** takes a short trip which reveals several different views of the mountain. The railway lies in **Padarn Country Park**, which gives access to 800 acres of Snowdonia's countryside and also includes Llyn (Lake) Padarn. By the side of the lake is Cwm Derwen Woodland and Wildlife Centre with a woodland discovery trail and a time walk exhibition with an audio-visual display. Here, too, is the **Welsh Slate Museum** (free) which tells the story of the slate industry through a variety of exhibitions, a restored slate-carrying incline, a terrace of quarrymen's cottages, audio-visual shows and demonstrations. The De Winton waterwheel is the second largest in Britain and once provided all the power for the mines.

Power on an even greater scale

is to be experienced at **Dinorwig Power Station** where bus tours take visitors deep into the mountain to the tunnels and the machinery rooms that control the vast quantities of water of this major engineering project. In Europe's largest man-made cavern the world's most powerful hydro-electric generators are in action.

In the rugged setting of Snowdonia, where life has always been harsh, it comes as no surprise to find that it is said that the strongest woman ever to have lived came from Llanberis. Born in 1696, Marged Ifan died at the ripe old age of 105. At 70, it was said, she could outwrestle any man in Wales and could also catch as many foxes in one year as the local huntsmen in 10. After receiving many offers of marriage, Marged is said to have chosen the smallest and most effeminate of her suitors. Tradition has it that she only beat her husband twice: after the first beating he married her and after the second he became an ardent churchgoer!

The **Pass of Llanberis** (along the A4086) is one of the most desolate stretches of road in Wales and is dominated by Snowdon to the south and the curiously shaped **Glyder Fawr's** 3279 feet to the north. Sheep graze beside the narrow road, which in some places is almost blocked by boulders and rocks.

Guarding the entrance to the Pass of Llanberis and overlooking Llyn Padarn are the substantial remains of **Dolbadarn Castle**

85 WELSH SLATE MUSEUM

Llanberis

The vast Dinorwig Quarry, carved into the slopes of the "mountain that roofed the world", closed for business in 1969 but its doors remained open as the Welsh Slate Museum

 see page 281

There are several narrow gauge railways in Wales, many of which are in and around Snowdonia, and there are nine members of the narrow-gauge Great Little Trains of Wales (GLTOW):

Bala Lake Railway (Bala)

Brecon Mountain Railway (Merthyr Tydfil)

Ffestiniog Railway (Porthmadog)

Llanberis Lake Railway (Llanberis)

Rheilffordd Eryri (Caernarfon)

Talyllin Railway (Tywyn)

Vale of Rheidol Railway (Aberystwyth)

Welsh Highland Railway (Porthmadog)

Welshpool and Llanfair Railway (Welshpool).

Pass of Llanberis

86 BRYN LLEWELYN GUEST HOUSE

Betws-y-Coed

3-star en suite B&B in picturesque village; self-catering cottage also available.

see page 283

87 THE GWYDYR HOTEL

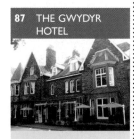

Betws-y-Coed

Village centre hotel with excellent accommodation and cuisine, especially popular with anglers.

see page 284

(CADW; free) which was built by Llywelyn the Great. After the battle of Bryn Derwin, where Llywelyn defeated his two brothers, the victor held Owain ap Gryffydd prisoner here for some 22 years. The last stronghold of the independent princes of Gwynedd, it was from here in 1283 that Dafydd ap Gryffydd fled from the English forces of Edward I. It is a fact known to few that parts of the film *Carry On Up The Khyber* were shot in and around Llanberis.

AROUND LLANBERIS

BETWS-Y-COED

14½ miles E of Llanberis on the A5

A picturesque large village at the confluence of four beautiful forested valleys, Betws-y-Coed lies on the edge of the **Gwydyr Forest Park** as well as in the Snowdonia National Park. The Forest Park offers horse riding, canoeing, mountain biking and over 20 miles of trails through mountain forests. The stone walls in the Park were built by sailors after the defeat of the Spanish Armada to enclose game. The village first came to prominence with the setting up in 1844 of an artists' colony by David Cox and other eminent Victorian countryside painters. Their work inspired others, and the coming of the railway in 1868 brought the tourists to what soon became a busy holiday centre. The Old Church, near the railway station, has been in use since the 14th century and remained the town's major place of worship until the influx of visitors required a larger and more prestigious building.

The town has two small museums. The **Motor Museum** houses a unique collection of vintage and post-vintage cars includes a fabulous Bugatti Type 57. Next to the railway station is the **Conwy Valley Railway Museum** and shop, a popular place to visit in the summer

As the village is close to the point where the Conwy, Lledr and Llugwy rivers meet, it seems natural that these waterways should play an important role in the development, building and beauty of Betws-y-Coed. Thomas Telford's **Waterloo Bridge**, a marvellous iron construction built in 1815, gracefully spans the River Conwy, while the **Pont-y-Pair**, dating from around 1470, crosses the River Llugwy; further downstream, an iron suspension footbridge spans the river by the church. However, the main attractions that draw people to this area are the waterfalls: the spectacular multi-level **Swallow Falls** on the River Llugwy, Conwy Falls, Machno Falls and Fairy Glen Ravine. The village's most famous, and certainly most curious, attraction is **Ty Hyll**, the Ugly House, which stands close by the River Llugwy. Apparently this building, which looks as though it was literally thrown together from rough boulders, is an example of hurried assembly in order to obtain freehold on common land. The house was often used as an overnight stop by Irish drovers taking cattle to English markets.

The scenery around Betws-y-Coed is truly magnificent, and within minutes of leaving the town centre there are numerous well-marked walks lasting anything from an hour to all day and suiting all energy levels.

CAPEL GARMON

15½ miles E of Llanberis off the A5

Close by the village is the **Capel Garmon Burial Chamber**, which dates from around 1500 BC; the remains of a long barrow with three burial chambers, one with its capstone still in position, can be seen.

NANT PERIS

2 miles SE of Llanberis on the A4086

Once known as Old Llanberis, the village lies at the opposite end of Llyn Peris from its larger namesake and at the entrance to the Pass of Llanberis. The **Well of Peris**, which lies just north of the village centre, was, until relatively recently

Ty Hyll, Betws-y-Coed

much visited for its healing powers, as well as for wishing. A successful request was said to be signalled by the appearance of a sacred fish.

DOLWYDDELAN

11 miles SE of Llanberis off the A470

Here can be seen the stark remains of **Dolwyddelan Castle** (CADW) which is unusual among Welsh castles in that it was constructed by a native Welsh prince rather than by the English or the Normans. It was built between 1210 and 1240 by Llywelyn the Great to control a strategic pass through the mountainous region of his kingdom. In 1488, the castle was acquired by Maredudd ap Levan who built the village church that now houses his kneeling brass effigy. After Maredudd's death the castle fell into ruin and the modern roof and battlements seen today were added in the 19th century when the core of the castle underwent restoration. However, the beauty of the castle is very much its lonely setting and from here there are stunning

88 THE WHITE HORSE INN

Capel Garmon

Delightful 18th century hostelry in spectacular Snowdonia serving real ales and quality food.

see page 283

Dolwyddelan Castle, Dolwyddelan

revival of crafts and skills which were used to maintain the estate; among the attractions is a working **Watermill**.

PENMACHNO

14½ miles SE of Llanberis on the B4406

This delightful village of picturesque stone cottages set in a wooded valley lies on the River Machno, from which it takes its name. Surrounded by glorious countryside, Penmachno lies within an area that is a stronghold of Welsh culture.

To the northwest of the village centre and in the secluded Wybrnant valley lies **Ty Mawr Wybrnant (**NT), the birthplace of Bishop William Morgan (1545-1604) who was the first person to translate the Bible into Welsh. Now restored to how it probably appeared in the 16th and 17th centuries, the house contains a display of Welsh Bibles, including Morgan's of 1588. A pleasant one-mile walk starts at the house and takes in woodland and the surrounding fields.

To the northeast of the village and approached by a walk alongside the River Machno, is **Ty'n y Coed Uchaf**, a small farm that gives visitors an insight into the traditional way of life of the Welsh-speaking community in this area.

FFESTINIOG

13½ miles SE of Llanberis on the A470

Situated above the Vale of Ffestiniog, there is a delightful walk, beginning at the village church, to **Cynfal Falls**, just below

mountain views. A walk starting at Dolwyddelan provides a succession of glorious views over the surrounding mountains, particularly Snowdon and Moel Siabod. The last part of the walk is along paths and lanes and across meadows by the River Lledr.

PENTREFOELAS

19½ miles SE of Llanberis on the A5

Once an upland estate village, Pentrefoelas is now becoming a focal point for the continuation and

the village. Above the falls stands a rock, known locally as Pulpud Huw Llwyd, that recalls a local mystic who preached from here. Three miles to the northeast,

Ffestiniog Railway, Blaenau Ffestiniog

Gamallt (NT) is a remote 300-acre moorland that supports a variety of plant life as well as water beetles, sandpipers, ring ousels, wheatears and meadow pipits. Archaeological remains include a large Iron Age settlement, and the important Roman road known as **Sarn Helen** crosses the property.

MAENTWROG

13½ miles SE of Llanberis on the A496

Lying in the Vale of Ffestiniog, this peaceful and attractive village is home to **Plas Tan-y-Bwlch**, where the 19th century terraced gardens provide glorious views of the surrounding area and picturesque walks through woodland. Here, too, among the magnificent trees and rhododendrons, is an oak wood that provides a small reminder of the vast oak forests that once covered much of Wales.

BLAENAU FFESTINIOG

12 miles SE of Llanberis on the A470

This was once the slate capital of the world and the industry still dominates the landscape and economy of this town and the surrounding area. Stretching across

from the feet of Manod towards the Moelwyn Mountains, the legacy of the slate industry is visible everywhere - from the orderly piles of quarried slate waste to the buildings in the town.

At the foot of Manod Bach, beside the waterfall at Bethania, **Pant-yr-ynn Mill** is the oldest surviving slate mill of the Diffwys Casson Quarry. Built in 1846, it later saw service as a school before being converted into a woollen mill in 1881. It worked until 1964, when it was closed down and the machinery scrapped. The original part of the building has been preserved and the waterwheel restored; it is now home to an exhibition dealing with Blaenau - the town, the communities, the landscape and the changes to it made by the 20 quarries in the vicinity. The exhibition includes drawings and paintings by resident artist and industrial archaeologist Falcon D Hildred.

As well as having a main line train service, Blaenau Ffestiniog is the northern terminus of the narrow gauge **Ffestiniog Railway**, which runs through the vale to

Llechwedd Slate Caverns in Blaenau Ffestiniog, the winners of many top tourism awards, takes visitors underground to explore the world of a Victorian slate miner and the man-made caverns of cathedral proportions. The excavations took place on 6 levels and there are 25 miles of tunnels carved out of the hillside. One tour includes a short ride on an underground tramway along a tunnel cut in 1846 to the enormous Cathedral Cave. On the surface, there is a Victorian village depicting the life of the miners and their families in the early 1900s, the era when Llechwedd reached its peak of production. There are a variety of preserved houses and shops, including one selling sweets, toffee and chocolate made to original Victorian recipes. The prices are Victorian too, so you will have to change your money into shillings and pence at the Old Bank. Old style currency is also necessary to buy a drink at the Miners Arms pub.

89 FFESTINIOG RAILWAY

Blaenau Ffestiniog

Steam trains take the visitor through the spectacular scenery of the Snowdonia National Park

 see page 285

Porthmadog. Built to carry slate down to the sea for shipping off around the world, the railway has since been renovated by enthusiasts and volunteers. It now provides a comprehensive service giving passengers the chance to admire the scenery of the vale on their journey to the coast. There are many stopping off points so walkers can take advantage en route of **Tan-y-Blwch County Park** and other beauty spots.

To the southwest of the town, at First Hydro's power station, is the **Ffestiniog Visitor Centre**, the ideal place to discover the wonders of hydro-electricity. Opened in 1963 by the Queen, the station consists of reservoirs and underwater passages constructed inside the mountains and the displays and exhibitions at the centre explain how the electrical power is generated and also the development of electricity over the years.

BEDDGELERT

7½ miles S of Llanberis on the A498

A winner of both National and European Village in Bloom titles, this attractive village is full of flowers in spring and summer. A conservation village, Beddgelert is surrounded by mountains, including the 2566 feet of **Moel Hebog**, and the whole setting is reminiscent of the Swiss Alps. An unlikely spot one might think for shipping to be an important industry. This was thanks to the River Glaslyn being navigable as far as Pont Aberglaslyn, the stone bridge at the narrowest point of the gorge. Shipping remained a major mainstay of life here until the Porthmadog embankment was constructed in the early 19th century.

The **Pass of Aberglaslyn**, through which the racing waters of the salmon river flow, lies to the south of the village; it is a delightful place with steeply wooded slopes and an abundance of rhododendrons.

The village's name translates as **'Gelert's Grave'** and refers to Prince Llewelyn ap Iowerth's

Gelert's Grave, Beddgelert

faithful dog Gelert, which he left to guard his little son. When he returned, he found the dog covered in blood and the child nowhere to be seen. He concluded that Gelert had killed his son, so in his fury he killed the dog. Only then did he realise that his son was alive, saved by Gelert from a wolf, whose body lay nearby. It is said that Llewelyn never again smiled, and he buried Gelert with full honours. The reputed grave of Gelert is in a riverside meadow, just south of the village. The land around the grave was bought in 1987 with grants from the Countryside Commission and the Portmeirion Foundation in memory of Sir Clough Williams-Ellis. Beddgelert has another animal connection: Alfred Bestall, the original illustrator of Rupert Bear for 30 years from 1935, lived here for the latter part of his life. In his memory, the 'Followers of Rupert Bear' have funded the planting of a picnic meadow near the River Glaslyn.

To the northeast of the village, on the road to Capel Curig, lies the **Sygun Copper Mine**, which was abandoned in 1903. The former mine has now been reopened as a remarkable and impressive example of Welsh industrial heritage where visitors can see the maze of underground tunnels and chambers, the massive stalactites and stalagmites and the copper ore veins that also contain traces of gold and silver. Audio commentaries give details of each stage of the mining process, with lighting and sound effects.

Just a short distance further along this road is **Dinas Emrys**, a hill fort that is thought to be associated with the legendary 5th century battle between the two dragons - one red and one white - that was prophesied by the young Merlin. The lake nearby, **Llyn Dinas**, is also associated with the magician and legend claims that the true throne of Britain is in the lake and will only be revealed when a young person stands on a certain stone.

HARLECH

Harlech means Bold Rock and there is no doubting the fact as the town clings to the land at the foot of its spectacularly sited castle, now a World Heritage Site. Another of Edward I's Iron Ring of fortresses, which was begun in 1283, **Harlech Castle** (CADW) is perched on a rocky outcrop for added strength. The castle's situation, close to the sea, has not only proved a great defence but was also useful during its blockade by Madog and his men in 1294, when supplies transported in from Ireland enabled the 37 men inside to hold fast. If the use of power and strength to impress and intimidate an indigenous population was ever aided by architecture then Harlech is a prime example. Situated 200 feet above sea level, its concentric design, with lower outer walls, by the architect James of St George, used the natural defences of its site to emphasise its impregnability. However, in 1404

•

Close to Plas Gwyn, an 18th century Georgian mansion just outside Beddgelert, is the Three Leaps - three stones that commemorate a contest between two rivals for the hand of the same girl. The contest was won by the man who could leap the furthest. In about AD 580, two young men were in contention for the hand of the grand-daughter of the warrior Geraint. On this occasion, the champion was named Hywel, The stones mark his efforts, in possibly what we now know as the triple jump; the loser is said to have died of a broken heart.

•

90 CASTLE RESTAURANT

Harlech

Superb cuisine based on "Welsh recipes with a Mediterranean twist".

|| *see page 283*

91 CEMLYN TEA SHOP

Harlech

Outstanding award-winning tea room serving light lunches and teas, and with glorious views of Harlech Castle.

|| ⊨ *see page 286*

Harlech Castle

92 THE LION HOTEL

Harlech

Handsome 18th century town centre hotel offering good food, real ales and en suite rooms.

see page 287

93 HARLECH CASTLE

Harlech

Harlech Castle is one of the great castles Edward I built to enforce his rule over the Welsh.

 see page 288

Owain Glyndwr managed to capture the castle and held it for five years while using the town of Harlech as his capital.

The song, *Men of Harlech*, has immortalised the siege during the War of the Roses when the castle was held for the Lancastrian side for seven years before it finally became the last stronghold to fall to the Yorkists in 1468. The last time Harlech saw action was 200 years later, during the Civil War, when it again withstood attack and was the last castle in Wales to fall to Cromwell's forces. The panoramic views from the castle's battlements take in both Tremadog Bay and the mountainous scenery behind the town.

Outside the castle stands the monumental equestrian **Statue of the Two Kings** representing Bendigeidfran, King of the British, and his nephew, Gwern, heir to the Irish throne who, along with his father, had been killed in battle. The statue, by Ivor Roberts, depicts a scene from *The Mabinogion*, a 14th / 15th century cycle of Welsh and Irish legends.

Though not as imposing as the castle, **The Lasynys Fawr** is another building worth a visit while in Harlech. The home of Ellis Swynne (1671-1734), one of Wales' most famous prose writers, the house is an excellent example of one of its period - it dates from 1600. Some of the scenes in the early James Bond film *From Russia With Love* were shot in Harlech. The famous Royal St David's golf course is just outside the town.

Just outside Harlech, to the north, lies **Morfa Harlech**, a nature reserve with woodland trails that occupies the flat land between the town and Llanfihangel-y-Thaethau.

BONTDDU

9 miles SE of Harlech on the A496

Looking at this pleasant village it is hard to imagine that just over a century ago. it was a bustling centre of the Welsh gold mining industry. Apparently, there were 24 mines operating in the area around this village and it was one of these mines that provided the gold for royal wedding rings.

Afon Mawddach Estuary, Bontddu

BARMOUTH

9 miles S of Harlech on the A496

Occupying a picturesque location by the mouth of the River Mawddach, Barmouth was once a small port with an equally small shipbuilding industry. As the fashion for seeking out sea air grew in the 18th century, the character of Barmouth changed to accommodate visitors flocking here for the bracing sea air - those suffering from scurvy were even fed seaweed, which is rich in Vitamin C and grew in abundance in the estuary. Barmouth today is, like many other seaside resorts, a product of the railway age and the Victorian architecture is still very much apparent.

From the quay, passenger ferries leave for Fairbourne on the other side of the estuary whenever there are enough passengers, and sea angling and sightseeing boat trips are also available. Also on the quay is the **RNLI Lifeboat Museum** with an exhibition of lifesaving equipment. Nearby, **Ty Gwyn Museum** occupies one of the town's older buildings, dating from the 15th century. The house is now home to a Tudor dynasty exhibition and panels on various local shipwrecks. Ty Gwyn is said to have been built for Henry Tudor, Earl of Richmond, later Henry VII. It was in this house that Jasper Tudor, Henry's uncle, hatched the plot to overthrow Richard III. On the hill behind the museum is **Ty Crwn Roundhouse** which used to be the town's lock-up; it now houses a collection of old photographs of Barmouth.

In late June, the town's harbour is the starting point for the **Three Peaks Race**, a 2-3 day event in which competitors have to sail their

94 TREMEIFION HOTEL

Talsarnau

Vegetarian and vegan hotel with en suite accommodation, superbly located in Snowdonia National Park.

see *page 288*

95 TREGWYLAN

Talsarnau

Quality B&B accommodation with unrivalled views of Snowdonia and the Lleyn Peninsula.

see *page 289*

96 HALFWAY HOUSE

Bontddu

Striking 'black-and-white' building serving traditional home-cooked food and real ales.

see *page 289*

97 THE BELLE VUE HOTEL

Barmouth

Impressive 4-storey Victorian property occupying superb position on the sea front.

see *page 288*

98 BRYN TEG HOTEL

Barmouth

Quality accommodation and appetising food in impressive Victorian house.

see page 290

99 BRYN MELYN GUEST HOUSE

Barmouth

Quality B&B accommodation in 3-star guest house with stunning views of the Mawddach Estuary

see page 290

100 THE ANCHOR RESTAURANT

Barmouth

Quayside restaurant with ravishing views; also an ice cream parlour and self-catering accommodation.

see page 291

monohull yachts to Caernarfon, the English Lake District and Fort William in Scotland. At each point, they then have to run up the highest peak in each country. The current record is 2 days, 14 hours and 22 minutes.

At the junction of the Quay and Church Street, **The Last Haul Sculpture** depicts three fishing generations hauling in a catch. The block of Carrara marble from which it is carved from has an unusual history. Back in 1709 a Genoese galleon with a cargo of the famous marble - the stone that Michelangelo had used - when it sank 5 miles out to sea. About 40 of the 2-ton blocks still lie on the bottom but in the 1980s one block was raised and then carved by local sculptor Frank Cocksey into this striking work of art.

Behind the harbour is **Dinas Oleu**, a small hill that was the first property given to the newly formed National Trust in 1895. It was a gift from the wealthy local

philanthropist, Mrs Fanny Talbot, who was a friend of two of the Trust's founding members. Panorama Walk is a scenic walk created as a tourist attraction at the turn of the 19th century. There are several viewpoints along its route, the best being the one from the promontory at the end of the path. Built more than 125 years ago and half a mile in length, the railway viaduct that spans the river mouth has a walkway on the bridge from where there are magnificent views of the town, coast and estuary.

DYFFRYN ARDUDWY
5 miles S of Harlech on the A496

Neolithic remains, as well as the remnants of Iron and Bronze Age settlements, abound in this area and in this village can be found two burial chambers. Perhaps the most interesting is **Arthur's Quoit**, the capstone of which is said to have been thrown from the summit of Moelfre by King Arthur.

Arthur's Quoit, Dyffryn Ardudwy

SHELL ISLAND

3½ miles S of Harlech off the A496

More correctly described as a peninsula that is cut off at high tide, Shell Island is a treasure trove of seashells and wildlife and the shoreline, a mixture of pebble beaches with rock pools and golden sands, is ideal for children to explore. Seals are often seen close by and there is plenty of birdlife; surprising considering the fairly regular aircraft activity from the nearby Llanbedr airfield.

LLANBEDR

3 miles S of Harlech on the A496

This village is an excellent starting point for walks along the lovely valleys of the Rivers Artro and Nant-col and into the Rhinog Mountains. At 2,360 feet **Rhinog Fawr** may not be the highest local peak, but from its summit it commands superb views over the Coed y Brenin Forest to the Cambrian Mountains.

The parish Church of St Peter (Bedr is Welsh for 'Peter') is worth visiting to see the Llanbedr Stone which was brought down to the church from an Iron Age hut circle above the village. It has an unusual spiral decoration.

LLANFAIR

1½ miles S of Harlech on the A496

Between 1853 and 1906, Llanfair was a prosperous slate mining village and the old, deep quarries, the **Chwarel Hên Llanfair Slate Caverns**, in use until 1906, are now open to the public, who can don miner's helmets and set out on a self-guided tour. During the summer months, there's also a Children's Farm Park with cuddly rabbits, lambs and goats.

BALA

This agreeable town is a good stopping off point when exploring Snowdonia National Park. Roman and Norman remains have been found here, but the modern town was founded around 1310 by Roger de Mortimer, who was looking to tame the rebellious Penllyn district. The town was by Tudor times a small, and by all accounts not very successful, market town. It later became an important centre for the knitted stocking industry that flourished in the 18th century before the inventions and factory systems of the Industrial Revolution put paid to this established cottage industry. Today, though tourism is certainly an important part of the town's economy, it has remained a central meeting point and a market place for the surrounding farming communities. In recent years it has also become a major centre for water sports.

However, it is perhaps as a religious centre that Bala is better remembered. The Reverend Thomas Charles, one of the founders of the Methodist movement in Wales in the 18th century, first visited Bala in 1778 and moved here in 1783 after marrying a local girl. Working for the Methodist denomination,

101 CYNOD CAFÉ & LOCH CAFÉ

Bala

Two superb cafés, one in the town centre, the other on the foreshore of Lake Bala.

see page 292

102 THE SHIP INN (Y LLONG)

Bala

Popular town centre inn offering appetising home-made food and regular entertainment.

see page 293

103 MELIN MELOCH (FORMER WATER MILL)

Bala

Quality bed & breakfast in spectacular converted waterside mill with superb garden.

see page 292

Charles saw the great need for Welsh Bibles and other religious books. He joined forces with a printer from Chester to produce a series of books and pamphlets. The story of Mary Jones, who walked some 25 miles from Llanfihangel-y-Pennant to buy a bible from Charles was the inspiration for the foundation of the Bible Society. Notable sons of Bala include Thomas Edward Ellis, a Liberal Member of Parliament who worked hard for Welsh home rule, and Owen Morgan Edwards, who was a leading light in the Welsh educational system. There are statues to both these worthies in Bala. The son of Owen Morgan Edwards, Sir Ifan ab Owen Edwards, established the Welsh Youth Movement, which has a camp at Bala Lake. To the southwest of the town, **Llyn Tegid** (**Bala Lake**) is the largest natural lake in Wales and feeder of the River Dee. Four miles long, nearly three quarters of a mile wide and up to 150 feet deep, the lake is a popular centre for all manner of watersports. It is also the home of Tegi, the Welsh version of Scotland's Nessie. Formed during the Ice Age, the Lake is an important site ecologically and has been designated a Site of Special Scientific Interest and a Ramsar site (Wetlands of International Importance). Many uncommon wetland plants flourish on its banks, and the birdlife includes coots, mallards, pochards, widgeons and great crested grebes.

The fish life is interesting, too, and Bala is the only lake in Wales which is home to the gwyniad, a white-scaled member of the herring family that feeds on plankton in the depths of the lake.

Along the eastern bank of the lake runs the narrow gauge **Bala Lake Railway**, which provides the perfect opportunity to catch a glimpse of the Tegi.

AROUND BALA

FRONGOCH

2 miles N of Bala on the A4212

Just to the west of the village lies the reservoir **Llyn Celyn** on whose banks is a memorial stone to a group of local Quakers who emigrated to America to escape persecution. The modern chapel close by, **Chapel Celyn**, was built as a reminder of the rural hamlet which was drowned when the reservoir was created in the 1960s. Overlooking Llyn Celyn is **Arenig Fawr**, which has, on its 2800 feet summit, a memorial to the crew of a Flying Fortress that crashed here in 1943.

After the Easter Uprising of 1916 in Ireland, a former German prisoner of war camp near Frongoch was used to hold 1600 Irish prisoners, among them Michael Collins. It earned the nickname of the 'Sinn Fein University' because impromptu lessons on guerilla tactics were given to some of the prisoners. When Lloyd George came to power later that year he closed the camp down.

LLANUWCHLLYN

4 miles S of Bala on the A494

This small village at the southern end of Bala Lake is the terminus of the Bala Lake Railway which follows the lake for four miles with various stops where passengers can alight and enjoy a picnic or a walk. Spreading up from the eastern banks of the lake is the **Penllyn Forest**, which can be reached and passed through via **Cwm Hirnant** on an unclassified road that weaves through the forest to moorland and eventually reaches **Llyn Efyrnwy (Lake Vyrnwy)**.

Llanuwchllyn has long been a stronghold of Welsh tradition, and has statues of two eminent Welshmen, Sir Owen Morgan Edwards and his son Sir Ifan ab Owen Edwards, both closely involved in preserving Welsh language and culture.

DOLGELLAU

Meaning 'meadow of the hazels', Dolgellau is the chief market town for this southern area of Snowdonia and used to be the county town of Merionethshire. Its grey stone buildings are pleasantly situated beside the River Wnion, with Cadair Idris rising in background. The town is very Welsh in custom, language and location, all very evident when the outlying farmers come to town on market day.

Owain Glyndwr held a Welsh parliament here in 1404, later signing an alliance with France's Charles VI. Now, the town's narrow streets can barely evoke those distant times and few early buildings remain. One of the oldest buildings is the seven-arched bridge over the river which dates from the early 1600s.

Before much of Dolgellau was built in an attempt to lure Victorian holidaymakers to the delights of Cadair Idris, there was a small rural Quaker community here. The **Quaker Heritage Centre** in Eldon Square tells the story of this community and also of the persecution that led them to emigrate to Pennsylvania. North of the town, the seven mile **Precipice Walk** offers superb views. The local gold mines provided the gold for the wedding rings of both Queen Elizabeth II (then Princess Elizabeth) and Diana, Princess of Wales.

108 THE STAG INN

Dolgellau

Lively town centre hostelry with good food, real ales, pool, beer garden and petting zoo.

🍴   see page 297

109 UNICORN INN

Dolgellau

Friendly hosts provide a warm welcome, real ales and a very good variety of food at the **Royal Oak**.

🍴   see page 298

Cader Idris, Dolgellau

110 PENMAENUCHAF HALL

Penmaenpool

Immaculate and stylish country house hotel with fine cuisine and luxury accommodation.

⊨ ∬ *see page 298*

Rising to some 2927 feet to the southwest of Dolgellau, **Cader Idris** dominates the local scenery and on a clear day a climb to the summit is rewarded with views that take in the Isle of Man and the Irish coast as well as, closer to home, the Mawddach estuary. Much of the area around the mountain was designated a national nature reserve in 1957. The name Cader Idris means 'chair of Idris' after the great poet and warrior. An old legend asserts that anyone who sleeps on the mountain summit will wake up either mad, or blind, or with the ability to write great poetry.

AROUND DOLGELLAU

LLANELLTYD

2 miles NW of Dolgellau on the A470

This is the point at which the Rivers Wen and Wnion, boosted by other waters further upland, meet to form the Mawddach estuary. Close by, just across the River Wen, stand the serene ruins of **Cymer Abbey** (CADW; free)which was founded by Cistercian monks in 1198. This white-robed order was established in the late 11th century in Burgundy and they arrived in Britain in 1128 to seek out remote places where they could lead their austere lives. Cymer was one of two Cistercian abbeys created in the Snowdonia region during the Middle Ages - the other is Conwy Abbey - and Cymer held substantial lands in this area. Despite their holdings, the abbey was poor and it also suffered badly during the fighting between England and Wales. In fact, by the time of the Dissolution in 1536 the abbey's income was just £51. Visitors to the site can see the remaining parts of the church, refectory and chapter house set in particularly picturesque surroundings.

Cymer Abbey, Llanelltyd

84

LLANFACHRAETH

3 miles N of Dolgellau off the A470

To the south of this beautifully located village is the **Precipice Walk** where two scenic footpaths skirt round a lake. Precipitous they are not, but they do open up some glorious views over the Mawddach river valley, its estuary and out to sea. Nearby is **Nannau Hall**, the ancient seat of the Vaughan family who owned much of the land in this area. It is said that an earlier house on the site belonged to Howel Sele, a cousin of Owain Glyndwr. During a dispute with Glyndwr over Sele's Lancastrian sympathies, the latter shot at but missed his cousin while out hunting. Glyndwr was so enraged that he killed Sele and hid his body in a hollow oak. This hiding place was later to receive a mention in Sir Walter Scott's *Marmion* as "the spirit's blasted tree".

GANLLWYD

5 miles N of Dolgellau on the A470

This hamlet gives its name to the attractive valley in which it is found and which is, in turn, surrounded by the **Coed y Brenin Forest Park**, an area of some 9000 acres around the valleys of the Rivers Mawddach, Eden, Gain and Wen. Originally part of the Nannau Estate, founded by Cadougan, Prince of Powys, in 1100, the forest was acquired by the Forestry Commission in 1922, when extensive planting of conifers took place. Ganllwyd was once a centre for gold mining and, during the 1880s, the nearby mine at

Gwynfynydd was prosperous enough to attract some 250 miners. The mine had produced around 40,000 ounces of gold by the time it closed in 1917; it re-opened from 1981 to 1989. The mine is on the route of one of the four waymarked trails, which also takes in waterfalls, forest nature trails and an old copper works. Orienteering is a good way to explore the park, which also offers some of the best mountain biking in the UK. Bikes can be hired at the Visitor Centre, which has a café, shop and exhibitions. There are also riverside picnic sites and a children's adventure play area.

Broadleaved woodlands once covered the land and some of these woodlands still survive at the National Trust's **Dolmelynllyn** estate. On the slopes of Y Garn, a path through this expanse of heath and oak woodland leads to **Rhaeadr Ddu** (the **Black Waterfall**), one of the most spectacular waterfalls in Wales. Also in the heart of the forest are a series of hundreds of steps, known as the **Roman Steps**, which climb up through the rocks and heather of the wild Rhinog Mountains. In spite of their name they are certainly not Roman; they are thought to have been part of a late medieval trade route between the coastal region around Harlech and England.

TRAWSFYNYDD

10 miles N of Dolgellau off the A470

To the west of the village lies **Llyn Trawsfynydd**, a man-made lake developed in the 1930s as part of a

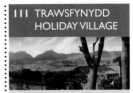

TRAWSFYNYDD HOLIDAY VILLAGE

Bronaber

Quality self-catering accommodation in Norwegian style log cabins overlooking the Rhinog Mountains.

see page 299

85

112 Y LLEW COCH - THE RED LION

Dinas Mawddwy

Centuries-old traditional village inn in picture postcard village offering good value home-cooked food, real ales and en suite rooms.

🍴 🛏 see page 299

hydro-electric scheme. On its northern shore stands the now defunct **Trawsfynydd Nuclear Power Station** which opened in 1965 and was the country's first inland nuclear station, using the lake for cooling purposes.

Down a minor road close to the power station are the remains of a small Roman amphitheatre that also served as a fort. Later used by the Normans as a motte, **Tomen-y-Mur** is associated with the legendary princes of Ardudwy.

In the village centre is a statue in honour of Hedd Wynn, a poet and shepherd who was awarded the bardic chair at the 1917 Eisteddfod six weeks after he had been killed in Flanders.

DINAS MAWDDWY

8½ miles E of Dolgellau on the A470

During the Middle Ages, this now quiet village was a centre of local power but the only surviving building from those days is a packhorse bridge, **Pont Minllyn**. A gateway to the upper Dyfi valley, it was once alive with quarries and mines but all that today's visitors can see of past industry is the traditional weaving of cloth at **Meirion Mill** which is known as the 'Mill in the Mountains'. There is also a visitor centre, café and a shop stocking a wide range of beautifully designed craftware and clothing, including a tremendous selection of woollen items, Portmeirion Pottery and Welsh Royal Crystal.

MALLWYD

9 miles SE of Dolgellau on the A470

This small village's inn, **The Brigand**, recalls the days during the 16th century when this area was menaced by a gang known as the Red Robbers of Mawddwy. Eighty gang members were finally caught and executed in 1554 but the survivors exacted revenge by murdering their prosecutor, Baron Lewis Owen, at the nearby town of Llidiart-y-Barwn.

CORRIS

6 miles S of Dolgellau on the A487

This small former slate-mining village, surrounded by the tree-covered slopes of the Cambrian Mountains, was home to the first narrow-gauge railway in Wales. It was constructed in 1859 as a horse drawn railway, then steam locomotives were introduced in 1878 and passenger service began in 1883. After finally closing in 1948, the Corris Railway Society opened a **Railway Museum** that explains the railway's history and also the special relationship with the slate quarries through displays, exhibits and photographs.

Industry of a different kind can be found at the **Corris Craft Centre**, which is home to a variety of working craftsmen and women. An excellent place to find a unique gift, the craft centre is also home to the fascinating **King Arthur's Labyrinth** - a maze of underground tunnels where visitors are taken by boat to see the spectacular caverns and relive tales of the legendary King Arthur.

The legend of King Arthur is first told in **The Mabinogion**, a collection of stories which evolved over 1000 years. Passed from generation to generation from the 4th century onwards, they were not written down in a surviving manuscript form until the 13th century. The *White Book of Rhydderch* and the *Red Book of Hergest* between them contain 11 stories, five of which centre round the exploits of King Arthur and his contemporaries. In these tales we meet Gwenhwyfar (Guinevere), Cei (Sir Kay), Bedwyr (Sir Bedivere), Myrddin (Merlin) and Gwalchmei (Sir Gawain). In the *History of the Britons*, written by the Welsh cleric Nennius around AD 830, we first read of Arthur's battles, some at least of which took place in Wales, from about AD 515 onwards. The last great battle, against his nephew Mawdred and his Saxon allies, marked the end of a phase of Celtic resistance to the Saxons; this battle has been dated to AD 537 and is located by some historians on the Llyn Peninsula. In Welsh tradition Merlin and the great bard Taliesin took the dying King Arthur to the magical Isle of Avalon, which recent research has identified as Bardsey Island, where St Cadfan established a monastery and where 1000 Welsh saints are buried. The caverns of King Arthur's Labyrinth are the workings of the Braich Goch Slate

Mine, which was operational between 1836 and 1970. At its peak, the mine employed 250 men and produced 7000 tons of roofing slate annually.

TAL-Y-LLYN

5 miles S of Dolgellau on the B4405

This tiny hamlet lies at the southwestern end of the **Tal-y-llyn Lake**, which is overshadowed by the crags of Cadair Idris to the north. The lake is a great favourite with trout fishermen. In the village itself, the 15th century **Church of St Mary's** has an unusual chancel arch painted with alternating red and white roses and studded with some fanciful bosses.

LLANFIHANGEL-Y-PENNANT

7 miles SW of Dolgellau off the B4405

Just to the northeast of this small hamlet lie the ruins of **Mary Jones's Cottage**. After saving for six years for a Welsh Bible in the early 1800s, Mary Jones, the daughter of a weaver, walked to Bala to purchase a copy from Thomas Charles. As Charles had no copies of the Bible available, he gave her his own copy and the episode inspired the founding of the Bible Society. Mary lived to a ripe old age (88 years) and was buried at Bryncrug, while her Bible is preserved in the Society's headquarters in London.

Close by stand the ruins of **Castell y Bere** (CADW), a hill top fortress begun by Llywelyn the Great in 1223. Taken by the Earl of Pembrokeshire on behalf of

Just south of Corris, the Centre for Alternative Technology is Europe's leading Eco-centre. Seven acres of interactive displays demonstrate the power of wind, water and the sun, and the buildings manifest the latest in eco-friendly materials and design. A visit begins with a ride up the sheer 180ft hillside on a unique water-balanced railway from which there are dramatic views of Snowdonia. Organic gardens, a wholefood restaurant and a 'green' shop are among the other attractions, while for youngsters there's a new well-equipped eco-adventure playground, an underground mole-hole and free events during the school holidays.

Castell y Bere, Llanfihangel-y-Pennant

Edward I in 1283, the castle stayed in English hands for two years before being retaken by the Welsh and destroyed.

ARTHOG

6 miles SW of Dolgellau on the A493

Overlooking the Mawddach estuary, this elongated village is a starting point for walks into Cadair Idris. Beginning with a sheltered woodland path, the trail climbs up to the two **Cregennan Lakes** from where there are glorious mountain views. The lakes are fed by streams running off the mountains and they have created a valuable wetland habitat that is now in the care of the National Trust. Down by the river mouth, there is an **RSPB Nature Reserve** protecting the wealth of birdlife and wildlife found here.

FAIRBOURNE

8 miles SW of Dolgellau off the A493

This small holiday resort lies on the opposite side of the Mawddach estuary from Barmouth and was developed in the late 1800s as a country estate for the chairman of McDougall's flour company. From the ferry that carries passengers across the river mouth, runs the **Fairbourne Railway**. Originally a horse-drawn tramway, now steam-hauled, this 12¼ inch gauge railway runs from Fairbourne to the mouth of the Mawddach estuary. Its midway halt was given an invented name that outdoes the 59 letters of LlanfairPG by eight. Translated from the Welsh, it means "Mawddach Station with its dragon's teeth on North

Penrhyn Drive by the golden sands of Cardigan Bay". The dragon's teeth are anything but mystical: they are concrete tank traps left over from the Second World War.

LLWYNGWRIL

10 miles S of Dolgellau on the A493

The village is named after the giant Gwril, who was supreme in this part of the coast. A 'llwyn' is a bush or grove in Welsh, so the name means Gwril's grove. A mile south of the village is the wonderful medieval Church of St Celynin at Llangelynin, more than 600 years old and largely unrestored. Its treasures include wall texts, a rare set of pews named after local families and the grave of Abram Wood, King of the Welsh gypsies.

TYWYN

14 miles SW of Dolgellau on the A493

This coastal town and seaside resort on Cardigan Bay has long sandy beaches, dunes and a promenade, as well as being the start (or the end) of the famous **Talyllyn Railway** which, from 1866 to 1946, was used to haul slate from the inland quarries. The line stretches 7 miles inland and passes at a maximum speed of 15 mph through the lovely wooded Talyllyn Valley. This area inland from Tywyn is also wonderful walking country. The way-marked walks include the

new National Trail that runs between Machynlleth, Welshpool and Knighton. One of the stations on the Talyllyn line is Dolgoch, from which a walk takes in three sets of magnificent waterfalls. Four walks of varying lengths and difficulty start at Nant Gwernol station and provide an opportunity to enjoy the lovely woodlands and to look at the remains of Bryn Eglwys quarry and the tramway that served it.

ABERDOVEY (ABERDYFI)

16 miles SW of Dolgellau on the A493

This resort at the mouth of the River Dovey (or Dyfi) was once one of the most important ports along the Welsh coast. Shipbuilding flourished here alongside the busy port, whose records show on one particular occasion having 180 ships unloading or waiting for a berth. The town has been attracting holiday-makers since Edwardian times. Today Aberdovey has the highest proportion of holiday homes on this coast and also some of the highest prices. It is a gentle, civilised spot, with all the best attributes of a seaside resort and none of the kiss-me-quick tat of many larger places. Aberdovey has given its name to a Victorian ballad called *The Bells of Aberdovey*, recounting the legend that the sea drowned a great kingdom here and how on quiet summer evenings the bells can be heard ringing out from beneath the waves.

89

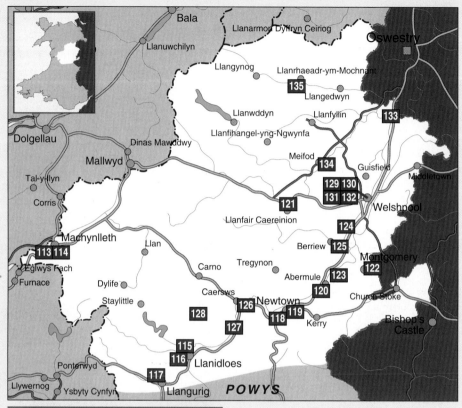

North Powys

Once part of the old county of Montgomeryshire, this northern region of Powys is an area of varied landscape and small towns and villages. Situated between the high, rugged landscape of Snowdonia and the farmland of Shropshire, this is a gentle and pleasant region through which many rivers and streams flow. As well as being home to the highest waterfall outside Scotland, Pistyll Rhaeadr, one of the Seven Wonders of Wales, the region has another landmark in Lake Vyrnwy. Built in the 1880s to supply the expanding city of Liverpool with water, this large reservoir is a splendid feat of Victorian engineering that later found fame as a location for the film *The Dambusters*.

The major settlement here is Welshpool, a town situated on the banks of the River Severn close to the English border Originally known as Pool, the prefix was added to ensure that the dispute regarding its nationality was finalised once and for all. From the town leisurely canal boat trips can be taken along the Montgomery Canal but there is also a narrow gauge steam railway running westwards to Llanfair Caereinion. Near the town stands the splendid Powis Castle, which is famous for the many treasures it houses and also for its magnificent gardens.

Montgomery has a splendidly situated ruined borderland castle and is also close to some of the best preserved sections of Offa's Dyke. Nearby Newtown, which despite its name was founded in the 10th century, is another interesting and historic market town where the famous High Street newsagents, WH Smith, had its first shop. The associated museum tells of the company's growth from its humble beginnings in 1792. Also in Newport is the Robert Owen Memorial Museum commemorating the social reformer and founder of the Co-operative movement.

To the west and beyond the quaint town of Llanidloes lies Machynlleth, the home of Owain Glyndwr's parliament in the 15th century. A visit to the Welsh hero's centre, which is found in the part 15th century parliament house, tells the story of Glyndwr and his struggle against the English.

North Powys is great walking country that takes in some of the finest scenery in Wales. The many marked established trails and walks include a large part of Offa's Dyke Path and Glyndwr's Way, a 123-mile walk that follows a circular route across dramatic landscapes from Welshpool to Knighton by way of Machynlleth.

Lake Vyrnwy

91

113 THE RED LION

Machynlleth

Popular town centre hostelry serving appetising home-made food and real ales.

¶ see page 300

114 MAENLLWYD GUEST HOUSE

Machynlleth

Long-established quality guest house with en suite rooms and spacious garden.

⊨ see page 300

MACHYNLLETH

This small town is a popular but not overcrowded holiday centre in the shadow of the Cambrian Mountains. It was here that Owain Glyndwr held one of his parliaments in around 1404. On the site today, stands **Parliament House**, a part 15th century building occupies the site and contains an exhibition about this legendary hero. Revered as the last native prince of Wales, Glyndwr's aims were independence for Wales, a church independent of Canterbury and the establishing of a Welsh university. After being refused redress when Lord Grey of Ruthin seized some of his land, he laid waste the English settlements in northeast Wales and spent the next few years in skirmishes. He established other parliaments in Dolgellau and Harlech, and sought alliances with the Scots, the Irish and the French. He resisted many assaults by Henry IV's armies, but eventually Henry V seized Aberystwyth and Harlech and Glyndwr soon disappeared from the scene, dying, it is thought, at the home of his daughter Anne Scudamore. It was while presiding over the parliament that Owain was nearly killed by his brother-in-law Dafyd Gam. The plot failed, and Dafyd was captured. He was granted a pardon by Owain and later fought at the Battle of Agincourt.

Opposite the house is the entrance to **Plas Machynlleth**, an elegant mansion built in 1653 for the Marquess of Londonderry. In the 1840s, in order to improve his views, his descendant bought up the surrounding lands, had the houses demolished and re-routed the main road away from his mansion. This space is now filled with attractive gardens open to the

Parliament House, Machynlleth

public and was given to the town by Lord Londonderry.

At the centre of the town is an ornate **Clock Tower** dating from 1872 which was built by public subscription to mark the coming of age of Lord Castlereagh, heir to the Marquess of Londonderry. Machynlleth's Tabernacle Chapel is now the **Museum of Modern Art,** Wales with six different exhibition spaces, including a constantly changing exhibition featuring leading artists from Wales. The complex also contains a 350-seat auditorium ideal for chamber and choral music, drama, lectures and conferences. Every year in late August, the auditorium is the focal point for the week-long **Machynlleth Festival.**

AROUND MACHYNLLETH

CARNO

10 miles E of Machynlleth on the A470

The dress and interior designer Laura Ashley, who was born in Wales, and her husband moved to Machynlleth in 1963 and later settled at Carno, which became the site of the headquarters of the Laura Ashley empire. It was in the churchyard of St John the Baptist, close to the factory, that she was buried after her death due to a fall in 1985.

LLANBRYNMAIR

8½ miles E of Machynlleth on the B4518

Set on the banks of the River Twymyn, this village was the birthplace of Abraham Rees who published an edition of *Ephraim Chambers Cyclopedia* between 1778 and 1788 after having added more than 4500 new pieces of information.

In the former village hall is **Machinations,** a museum of mechanical magic devoted to automota - figures driven by clockwork, electricity, wind or turned by hand. The collection is housed in an open plan café and each model is operated by a token. The models are fascinating and it's possible to take courses on constructing, painting and carving them.

DYLIFE

8½ miles SE of Machynlleth off the B4518

Apart from an inn and a few houses, there is little left of this once prosperous lead mining community which provided employment for some 2000 workers in the mid-1900s. A footpath from the settlement passes close to a grassy mound which was once a Roman fort, built, it is believed, to guard the nearby lead mines. The path continues past more redundant lead mines that were last worked during the late 17th century before it meanders through a woodland, following the banks of River Clywedog, and on towards Staylittle. The final part of the route lies close to Bronze Age tumuli which suggest that mining occurred in the area even before the Roman occupation.

Close to the village is **Glaslyn Nature Reserve**, a 540-acre tract

•

In the hills of Trannon Moor near the village of Machynlleth is the National Wind Power's Centre for Alternative Technology, a former slate quarry containing dozens of turbines that generate enough electricity to meet the needs of many thousand homes. The 200ft plateau on which the farm is located is reached from the car park during the summer months by a cliff railway. The 7-acre site contains displays revealing the incredible power of wind, water and sun, an eco-adventure playground, workshops, games and creative projects - and a vegetarian restaurant. The site access road is located off the A470 at the northern end of Carno village.

•

115 THE RED LION HOTEL

Llanidloes

Traditional town centre hotel serving honest-to-goodness pub grub and real ales; games room and en suite rooms.

🍴 🛏 see page 301

116 THE GREAT OAK CAFÉ

Llanidloes

Popular vegetarian whole food café with wonderful home-made food and excellent service.

🍴 see page 302

117 THE BLUE BELL INN

Llangurig

Charming grade 2 listed building offering quality food, fine wines, real ales and en suite accommodation.

🍴 🛏 see page 303

of heather moorland that is the breeding site for the wheatear, golden plover, ring ousel and red grouse.

STAYLITTLE

11 miles SE of Machynlleth off the B4518

A one-time lead mining village, Staylittle is said to have derived its name from the village's two blacksmiths who shoed horses so rapidly that their forge became known as Stay-a-Little. Situated in a remote area high in the Cambrian Mountains, Staylittle is on the edge of the **Hafren Forest**, which has several waymarked trails through the forest, along the banks of the upper River Severn and up to Plynlimon, which rises to 2500 feet.

LLANIDLOES

16½ miles SE of Machynlleth on the A470

One of the great little market towns and the first town on the River Severn, Llanidloes is an attractive and friendly place with lots of small, family-run shops of character, including Laura Ashley's first fashion shop and a vintage fashion shop. The town is also home to more than a dozen art and craft outlets, including three sculptors, a jeweller working in crystal, and four painters of stained glass windows. There are also four galleries and the **Minerva Arts Centre** which is the home of the Quilt Association and displays a unique collection of antique Welsh quilts.

In front of the town's picturesque black-and-white **Market Hall**, which dates from c. 1612 and stands on wooden stilts is

a stone on which John Wesley stood while preaching here three times in the mid-1700s. The upper floors of the building now house the **Llanidloes Museum**, where there are displays and information on the textile and mining industries that thrived in the area during the 18th and 19th centuries. There is also a natural history exhibition and a red kite centre.

In 1839, the town was a focal point of the bitter Chartist Riots after the Reform Bill of 1832 had failed to meet demands that included universal suffrage and social equality. Cheap labour, cheap wool and efficient new machinery had led to a boom in the wool and flannel trade in Llanidloes, as in Newtown, Machynlleth and Welshpool. Workmen flooded in, and in 1858 the population was more than 4000. But the boom did not last, the factories closed, and unemployment inevitably ensued. Chartist propaganda reached the town and the Llanidloes unions adopted the Charter. The crowds started to gather and to arm, the police moved in, the Chartist leaders were arrested then released by the crowd, the magistrates fled. The Chartists then ruled for a few days: mills were re-opened and the prices of goods fixed. Then the Montgomeryshire Yeomanry came on the scene, 32 arrests were made and the Chartist ringleaders put on trial at Welshpool. Three were transported, the rest served terms of hard labour.

The Severn Way and Glyndwr's Way cross in Llanidloes, and an interesting waymarked 5-mile walk covers sections of each. To the northwest of the town lies **Llyn Clywedog,** a reservoir that developed in the mid-1960s to regulate the flows of the Rivers Severn and Clywedog. Roads go around both sides of the lake, with the B4518 curving round the slopes of the 1580 foot Fan Hill where the chimneys of the now disused **Van Lead Mine** are still visible. It was once one of the most prosperous mines in this area of Wales, producing 6850 tons of lead in 1876. The deserted houses and chapels of the village that grew up around the mine add a sombre, evocative note.

Llyn Clywedog, Llanidloes

NEWTOWN

The name has not been appropriate for centuries since Newtown's origins date from around AD 973. But the town only came to prominence after being granted a market charter by Edward I in 1279. This was a centre for textiles and weaving and by the 19th century, Newtown was the home of the Welsh flannel industry that led it to be referred to as the 'Leeds of Wales'. Some of the brick buildings were built with a third or even fourth storey with large windows to let in light for the looms. **Newtown Textile Museum** is a typical example of an early 19th century weaving shop. It consists of six back-to-back cottages on the ground and first floors, and two rooms on the second and third floors running the whole length of the building. The displays include a re-created weaver's cottage and working area from the 1830s.

The museum gives a very good impression of the working conditions of the people which Newtown's most famous son, Robert Owen, devoted much of his life to changing. Born in Newtown in 1771, Owen grew from a humble background to become a social reformer and the founder of the co-operative movement who lobbied vigorously for an improvement in the working conditions specifically within the textile industry. He is particularly associated with the New Lanark mills in Scotland which he ran and partly owned. The workforce at New Lanark numbered 2000, including 500 children, and Owen provided good housing, cheap goods and the first infants' school

118 WAGGON AND HORSES

Newtown

Fine old traditional hostelry serving excellent food and real ales. Spacious beer garden.

|| see page 302

119 THE GRO GUEST HOUSE

Newtown

Quality en suite B&B accommodation in impressive building, parts of which date back to 1650.

|— see page 305

120 ABERMULE HOTEL

Abermule

Charming village hotel with superb food, real ales, comfortable accommodation, spacious beer garden and camping park.

🍴 🛏 *see page 304*

121 THE GOAT HOTEL

Llanfair Caereinion

Appetising home-cooked food and comfortable B&B accommodation in traditional village hostelry.

🍴 🛏 *see page 305*

122 COTTAGE INN

Montgomery

Popular and friendly town centre hostelry serving delicious home-made food and real ales.

🍴 *see page 306*

in Britain. His remarkable life is told at the intimate **Robert Owen Memorial Museum** (free) which occupies the house where he was born in 1771. Following his death at Newtown in 1858, Owen was buried by the river in the churchyard of St Mary's. His monument depicts the man with his workers and is surrounded by magnificent Art Nouveau iron railings.

Another interesting visit to consider while in Newtown is to the **WH Smith Museum**, where the shop has been restored to its original 1927 layout and devotes much of its space to the history of the booksellers from 1792 onwards.

The people of Newtown must certainly be an enterprising lot as it was here that the first ever mail order company was begun in 1859 by a man called Pryce-Jones. The business started in a small way with Welsh flannel but expanded rapidly, and Pryce-Jones even obtained the Royal seal of approval by having Queen Victoria on his list. Sadly, his successors were not as enterprising and the business was sold in 1935. The huge warehouse it used to occupy is now a lacklustre shopping centre, the **Royal Welsh Warehouse.**

Two miles east of Newtown is **Pwll Penarth Nature Reserve**, a feeding and nesting site for many species of wildfowl. The reserve has a nature walk and two hides, one accessible to wheelchairs.

AROUND NEWTOWN

LLANFAIR CAEREINION

9 miles N of Newtown on the B4385

This village is the western terminus of the **Welshpool and Llanfair Railway**. Passengers at Llanfair can enjoy reliving the days of steam and also relax in the Edwardian style tea rooms at the station. The narrow-gauge railway was originally opened to carry sheep, cattle and goods as well as passengers. It now travels, without the animals and the goods but with happy passengers, along the delightful Banwy Valley, its carriages pulled by scaled-down versions of steam locomotives from Finland, Austria, Sierra Leone, Antigua and Manchester. The railway is one of the nine members of the narrow-gauge **Great Little Trains of Wales** group. The others are: Bala Lake Railway, Brecon Mountain Railway *(Merthyr Tydfil)*; Ffestiniog Railway *(Porthmadog)*; Llanberis Lake Railway; Rheilffordd Eryri *(Caernarfon)*; Talyllin Railway *(Tywyn)*; Vale of Rheidol Railway *(Aberystwyth)*; and the Welsh Highland Railway.

MONTGOMERY

7 miles NE of Newtown on the B4385

An attractive market town with a pleasant Georgian character, and also some surviving Tudor and Jacobean buildings that are worthy of note. Above the town, the ruins of **Montgomery Castle** stand in affirmation of this borderland region's turbulent history. The first castle was built in around 1100 by the Norman, Roger de

Montgomery. Stormed over the years by rebels, it was rebuilt in 1223 as a garrison as Henry III attempted to quell the Welsh, a consequence being that the town received a charter from the king in 1227. During the Civil War, the castle surrendered to Parliamentary forces but was demolished in 1649 in punishment for the then Lord Herbert's Royalist sympathies. The remains of the castle are open at all times and entrance is free; access is up a steep paths from the town or by a level footpath from the car park. The visit is worth it for the views alone. A well-preserved section of Offa's Dyke passes close by and is another reminder of the military significance that this area once held.

Housed in a quaint 16th century inn, the **Old Bell Museum** in Arthur Street has 11 rooms of local history including features on civic and social life, Norman and medieval castles, the workhouse and the Cambrian Railway.

The 13th century **St Nicholas' Church** has some interesting features, including wooden carved angels, carved miserere seats and the magnificent canopied tomb of Richard Herbert, Lord of Montgomery Castle. In the churchyard is the famous Robber's Grave: John Davis, hanged in public in 1821 for murder, proclaimed his innocence and swore that the grass would not grow above his grave for at least 100 years!

To the west of the town the Iron Age hill fort **Fridd Faldwyn**

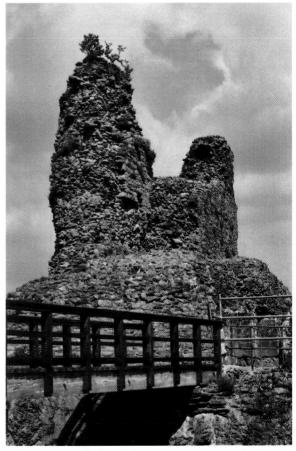

Montgomery Castle, Montgomery

tops a 750-feet hill that also provides stunning views to Cadair Idris and eastwards into England.

BERRIEW

7½ miles NE of Newtown on the B4390

Over the years, this picturesque village of black and white half-timbered houses beside the River Rhiw has been a frequent winner of Best Kept Village awards.

Like a number of other places in Wales, Berriew is associated with

123 UPPER HOUSE INN

Llandyssil

Rural inn in picturesque village serving outstanding food and with an extensive wine list

see page 305

97

124 THE HORSESHOES INN

Berriew

Former coaching inn serving appetising food and real ales.

🍴 see page 306

125 THE LION HOTEL & RESTAURANT

Berriew

Former coaching inn in picturesque village with excellent cuisine and quality en suite rooms.

🛏 🍴 see page 307

St Beuno who apparently heard English voices while communing by the river and warned the villagers of the imposing threat. A large glacial boulder here has been named Maen Beuno after him. Berriew's **Church of St Beuno** contains fine marble effigies of Arthur Price, Sheriff of Montgomeryshire in 1578, and his two wives, Bridget and Jane. The memorial cross of 1933 in the churchyard is by Sir Ninian Comper, whose work can be seen in churches all over Britain.

Close to the bridge, the **Andrew Logan Museum of Sculpture** celebrates the art of popular poetry and metropolitan glamour. Logan's work thrived on the inventive use of whatever was to hand and the flamboyant results make this possibly the most cheerful museum anywhere. It contains examples of Andrew Logan's sculpture, mirrored portraits and jewellery from the mid-sixties to the present day. Logan achieved some notoriety in the 1970s as the instigator of the Alternative Miss World Contest which introduced the world to the late drag queen, Divine. A 'Divine Shrine' is dedicated to her memory and the Alternative Miss World Crown is also on display..

A mile outside the town, the gardens at **Glansevern Hall**, entered from the A483 by the bridge over the River Rhiew, were first laid out in 1801 and now cover 18 acres. Noted in particular for the unusual tree species, they also have lovely lawns, herbaceous beds, a walled garden, rose gardens, a lovely water garden and a rock garden complete with grotto. In the Old Stables are a tea room, a garden shop and a gallery with regular exhibitions of paintings, sculpture and interior design. A wide variety of herbaceous plants, all grown at Glansevern, can be bought. Surrounding a very handsome Greek Revival house, the gardens are themselves set in parkland on the banks of the River Severn. Built for Arthur Davies Owen, Glansevern was the seat of the Owen family from 1800 until after the Second World War.

CHURCH STOKE

10½ miles E of Newtown on the A489

This attractive village lies right on the Welsh-English border; just to the west can be found some very visible and well preserved sections of Offa's Dyke. At Bacheldre, two miles along the A489, **Bacheldre Mill** is a fully restored watermill producing award-winning organic stoneground flour. Visitors can enjoy a guided tour and even mill their own flour.

ABERMULE

4 miles NE of Newtown on the B4386

Across the Montgomery Canal and River Severn from this village, which is also known by its Welsh name Abermiwl, lie the scant remains of **Dolforwyn Castle**, which was built in 1273 by Llywelyn the Last (he was the last native ruler of Wales). This was the last castle to have been built by a native Welsh prince on his own soil. Llywelyn also tried to establish a small town around the castle to rival that of nearby, and much anglicised, Welshpool. However, the castle was only a Welsh stronghold for four years before it was taken by the English and left to decay into the haunting ruins of today.

KERRY

2½ miles SE of Newtown on the A489

Situated on the banks of the River Mule, a tributary of the River Severn, this village lies in the heart of sheep rearing country and has given its name to the Kerry Hills breed of sheep characterised by distinctive black spots on their faces and legs. Small, hornless and usually white apart from the markings, the Kerry Hills have very dense fleeces that are particularly suitable for dyeing in pastel shades for knitting yarns. This breed is one of several variants on the Welsh Mountain Sheep; others include Black Welsh Mountain, Badger-faced Welsh Mountain, Beulah Speckle Face, Lleyn and Llanwenog.

The village church in Kerry has a chained Welsh Bible of 1690. There was, in former times, a custom at the church that the sexton would 'patrol' the congregation during services and would ring a bell if he found anyone asleep.

LLANDINAM

5½ miles SW of Newtown on the A470

This quiet village with its black and white half-timbered houses was the home of David Davies, an industrialist who was instrumental in

founding the docks at Barry in South Wales. Davies' bronze statue, made by the same Sir Alfred Gilbert who was responsible for Eros in Piccadilly, stands in the village.

CAERSWS

4 miles W of Newtown on the A470

The village is built on the site of a 1st century Roman fort that was strategically positioned here by the Rivers Severn and Carno. To the north, the remains of an earthwork fort can still be seen. In more recent times, Caersws was the home for some 20 years of the poet John 'Ceiriog' Hughes, who was then the manager of the local Van Railway. Born at Llan Dyffryn Ceiriog in 1833, he took employment on the railways in Manchester when he was 17. In 1865 he became stationmaster at Llanidloes and six years later took over at Caersws, managing the six-mile railway that ran to the Van lead mines. It is said that many people came to Caersws just for the delight of having a chat to the affable poet. Hughes lies buried in the graveyard at the nearby village of Llanwnog. Near Caersws, signposted off the A470 Machynlleth road, Llyn Mawr Reserve is a 20-acre lake with wetland habitat noted for wetland birds such as the great crested grebe, tufted duck, snipe and curlew.

WELSHPOOL

This bustling market town, which was granted a charter in 1263 by the Prince of Powys, was for a long

126 THE RED LION

Caersws

Cosy traditional pub serving real ales and good food; en suite rooms available.

🍴 🛏 see page 307

127 THE LION HOTEL

Llandinam

Former coaching inn with spacious riverside beer garden, excellent cuisine and en suite accommodation.

🍴 🛏 see page 308

128 THE RED LION

Trefeglwys

Traditional country inn serving home-made food and real ales; beer garden and patio.

🍴 see page 309

99

Montgomery Canal, nr Welshpool

129 POWIS CASTLE

Welshpool

Powis Castle was originally built by Welsh Princes and later became the ancestral home of the Herbert family and then of the Clive family.

 see page 309

time known as Pool - the Welsh prefix was added in 1835 to settle the long running dispute concerning its nationality as it is so close to the border with England. As is typical with many places in the upper Severn Valley, Welshpool has numerous examples of half-timbered buildings among its other interesting architectural features.

Housed in a former warehouse beside the Montgomery Canal is the **Powysland Museum** which was founded in 1874 by Morris Jones. Earlier, many of the artefacts that formed the museum's original collection had been put together by the Powysland Club - a group of Victorian gentlemen who were interested in the history of mid-Wales. The museum covers various aspects of the region: the development of life in

Montgomeryshire from the earliest times to the 20th century; local agriculture and farming equipment; and the building of the first canals and railways in the area. There are also some remains from Strata Marcella, the Cistercian abbey founded around 1170 by Owain Cyfeiliog, Prince of Powys; the abbey was all but destroyed during the Reformation.

Along with the museum, the old warehouse is also home to the **Montgomery Canal Centre** where the story of this waterway is told. Completed in 1821, the canal carried coal and food from Welshpool to the upper reaches of the River Severn. Though, as with other canals, its decline came with the arrival of the railways, the section of the canal around Welshpool is once again open, now for pleasure cruises.

From the town, the narrow gauge **Welshpool and Llanfair Railway** takes passengers on an 8-mile steam train journey through the Powis estates and the delightful Banwy valley to the quiet village of Llanfair Caereinion. Welshpool's original railway station, an impressive listed building, has been ingeniously converted into a shopping centre and restaurant.

The town is also home to two other interesting buildings, the **Cockpit** and **Grace Evans' Cottage.** The only surviving cockpit on its original site in Wales, this venue for the bloodthirsty sport was built in the 18th century and remained in use until the sport was banned in Britain in 1849. Grace Evans is certainly one of the town's

100

best known citizens as she was instrumental in rescuing Lord Nithsdale (who was in disguise as a lady) from the Tower of London in 1716. As Lady Nithsdale's maid, Grace fled with the couple to France but she returned to Welshpool in 1735 and lived at the cottage, which is said to have been given to her by a grateful Lord Nithsdale, until her death three years later.

Just to the southwest of the town lies one of the best known places in the area - the magnificent **Powis Castle** (National Trust) Originally built by the Welsh princes, it later became the home of Edward Clive, son of Clive of India. One of the Clive family's legacies is the superb display of Indian treasures on display in the **Clive Museum**. The castle is renowned for its collections of paintings and furniture. Perhaps the finest room is the magnificent Long Gallery with its family portraits and statuary.

The castle is perched on a rock above splendid terraces with enormous clipped yew trees overlooking the world-famous gardens. Laid out in 1720, these show the clear influence of Italian and French styles of that time. Some striking original features still remain, including the lead statues and urns, an orangery and an aviary. The woodland, which was also landscaped in the 1700s, overlooks the Severn Valley.

A series of tragedies suffered by the Powis family, the last private owners, led to the castle being acquired by the National Trust in 1952. George, the 4th Earl of Powis, lost his elder son Percy at the Battle of the Somme in 1916, his wife died after a car crash in 1929, and his only surviving son Mervyn was killed in a plane crash in 1942. So, before his own death in 1952, the earl ensured that the castle, its treasures and its gardens should be looked after for the future by leaving Powis to the Trust.

Long Mountain stretches four miles along the Welsh side of the border east of Welshpool. It is crossed by Offa's Dyke and on its highest point is an ancient hill fort known as Beacon Ring. It was on Long Mountain that Henry Tudor camped in 1485 before crossing the border, defeating Richard III at Bosworth Field and ascending the throne of England as Henry VII.

AROUND WELSHPOOL

LLANGEDWYN

10½ miles N of Welshpool on the B4396

Just to the northeast of the village and close to the English border, lies one of Wales' most nationalistic shrines, **Sycharth Castle**. A grassy mound is all that remains of one of Owain Glyndwr's principal houses, which was immortalised in a poem by Iolo Goch, which speaks of its nine halls, many guest rooms and a church. The poem appears in a translation by Anthony Conran in the *Penguin Book of Welsh Verse*:

Here are gifts for everyone
No hunger, disgrace or dearth,
Or ever thirst at Sycharth!

130 GREEN DRAGON

Welshpool

Popular town centre pub serving real ales and bar snacks; pool tables, beer garden and regular entertainment

🍴 see page 310

131 WESTWOOD PARK HOTEL

Welshpool

Town centre hotel with superb, brand new restaurant and quality en suite accommodation.

🍴 🛏 see page 312

132 THE RAVEN INN

Welshpool

Outstanding restaurant with extensive menu based 100% on local produce; lovely beer garden.

🍴 see page 311

MIDDLETOWN

5½ miles NE of Welshpool on the A458

To the north of this border village lies **Breidden Hill**, which is thought to have been the venue for a fierce battle between the Welsh and the forces of Edward I in 1292. On the summit stands an obelisk, **Rodney's Pillar**, which commemorates Admiral Rodney's victory over the French off Domenica in 1782. A little way further along the A458 is the remote hamlet of Melverley whose church, perched above the River Vyrnwy, is one of the most delightful in the region, with a 'magpie' exterior, timber-framed walls and a tiny tower.

MEIFOD

5½ miles NW of Welshpool on the A495

This picturesque village in the wooded valley of the River Vyrnwy is remembered in Welsh literature as being the location of the summer residence of the princes of Powys. The village **Church of St Tysilio and St Mary**, which was consecrated in 1155, is home to an interesting 9th century grave slab that bears old Celtic markings as well as a Latin cross and a Greek crucifix. According to legend, in AD 550, when St Gwyddfarch was asked where he would like to build his first church, he is said to have replied, in Welsh, "yma y mae i fod" ('here it is to be'). So the village got its name. The saint is thought to have been buried a short distance from the village. In the 9th century, while the princes of Powys had their main residence close by, Meifod became a religious centre and it is thought that the grave slab is a memorial to one of the princes.

LLANFIHANGEL-YNG-NGWYNFA

10½ miles NW of Welshpool on the B4382

In the small church of this tiny village are some interesting artefacts, a memorial to the Welsh writer, Ann Griffith, and some 15th century graves in the churchyard. Born in 1776 at a farm near Dolanog where she lived most of her short life, Ann only ever travelled as far as Bala, less than 50 miles distant, where she went to hear Thomas Charles preach. However, despite dying at the early age of 29 years, Ann wrote over 70 Welsh hymns, all dictated to a friend. In her home village of Dolanog, about 3 miles down the road, the Ann Griffiths Memorial Chapel was erected in 1903 and there is a 7-mile walk from Pontllogel to Pontrobert dedicated to her memory.

LLANWDDYN

14 miles NW of Welshpool on the B4393

The village lies at the southern end of **Lake Vyrnwy** (Llyn Efyrnwy), a four mile stretch of water that was created in the years following 1881 by the flooding of the entire Vyrnwy Valley to provide the people of Liverpool with an adequate water supply. Close to the dam, which is 390 yards long, 144 feet high and a splendid testament to Victorian engineering, is a monument that marks the

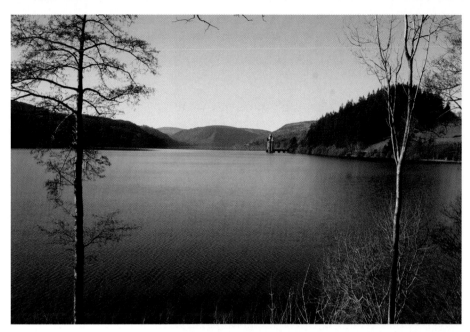

Lake Vyrnwy

beginning of the **Hirnant Tunnel** - the first stage of a 75-mile aqueduct that carries the water to Liverpool. Another striking building is the Gothic tower designed by George Frederick Deacon, engineer to the Liverpool Water Board. On higher ground is an obelisk that is a monument to the 44 men who died during the construction of the reservoir. To construct this, the first of several massive reservoirs in north and mid-Wales, the original village of Llanwddyn, home to some 400 people, was flooded along with the valley. On the hill south of the dam stands the 'new' village and the church, built by Liverpool Corporation in 1887. Photographs in the Lake Vyrnwy Hotel show the original village with its 37 houses, all now along with the church submerged under the Lake's 13,000 million gallons of water. The **Vyrnwy Visitor Centre** tells the story of the construction and is also home to an RSPB centre. There are four RSPB hides at various points around the lake and guided tours can be arranged around the estate for schools and groups. A road circumnavigates the lake but walking around the lake or on any of the nature trails is an ideal way to observe the abundant wild and bird life that live around the shores. Lake Vyrnwy's sculpture park was started in 1997 and has evolved constantly ever since, using local timber and on-site materials. Local artists have worked in partnership with

103

Pistyll Rhaeadr Waterfall

canoeing, climbing and abseiling; the lake is also a favourite spot for anglers. With its lovely scenery and coniferous forests, the lake has doubled in films for Switzerland or Transylvania; it was also used for location shots in *The Dambusters*.

LLANRHAEADR-YM-MOCHNANT

13 miles NW of Welshpool on the B4580

Despite its relative isolation this village attracts many visitors who pass through on their way to **Pistyll Rhaeadr**, which lies up a narrow road to the northwest of the village. This is one of the Seven Wonders of Wales and, with a drop of 240 feet, is the highest waterfall in Britain south of the Scottish Highlands. The English translation of the name is Spout Waterfall, an obvious name as the water drops vertically for 100 feet before running into a cauldron, and on through a natural tunnel in the rock before reappearing.

It was while he was vicar at Llanrhaeadr-ym-Mochnant in the late 16th century that Bishop William Morgan made his famous translation of the Bible into Welsh. He was granted permission to carry out this work by Queen Elizabeth I, her father Henry VIII having banned any official use of the Welsh language. The villagers here maintain a tradition that was once common in the area - the Plygeiniau, a form of Christmas carol service, where groups of men wander from church to church giving unaccompanied performances of Welsh carols.

135 BRON HEULOG

Llanrhaeadr ym Mochnant

Beautiful Victorian house in spectacular countryside offering both quality B&B and self-catering.

see page 313

sculptors from Russia, Estonia, Lithuania and Australia. The local artists have been inspired by species found on the site, while the international artists have drawn inspiration from their homelands. The sculpture park is managed jointly by Severn Trent Water, the RSPB and Forest Enterprise Wales. Bethania Adventure, based at the Boat House, organises activities on and around the lake, including sailing, windsurfing, kayaking,

LLANFYLLIN

9 miles NW of Welshpool on the A490

This charming and peaceful hillside town lies in the valley of the River Cain where it joins the Abel. It was granted its charter as a borough in 1293 by Llewelyn ap Gruffydd ap Gwenwynwyn, Lord of Mechain; Welshpool is the only other Welsh borough to have been granted its charter from a native Welsh ruler. To celebrate the 700th anniversary in 1993 of the granting of the charter, a large tapestry of the town's historic buildings was created. It can be seen in the parish church of St Myllin, a delightful redbrick building dating from 1706. Overlooking the town is the beauty spot of **St Myllin's Well.** From the 6th century onwards water from the well has been thought to cure all manner of ailments. Certainly the view from the well over the town and to the Berwyn Mountains beyond, has restorative powers. St Myllin, a 7th century Celt, is traditionally alluded to as the first cleric to baptise by total immersion in his holy well.

Opposite the church is the brick Council House, which has 13 wall paintings in an upstairs room. These were all done by a Napoleonic prisoner of war, one of several billeted in the town between 1812 and 1814. Ann Griffiths, the famous Welsh hymn writer, was baptised in Pendref Congregational Chapel, one of the oldest Non-Conformist places of worship in Wales, established in 1640; the present building dates from 1829.

Two miles southeast of Llanfyllin, off the A490, **Bryngwyn** is a handsome 18th century house by Robert Mylne, surrounded by 18th century and early 19th century parkland.

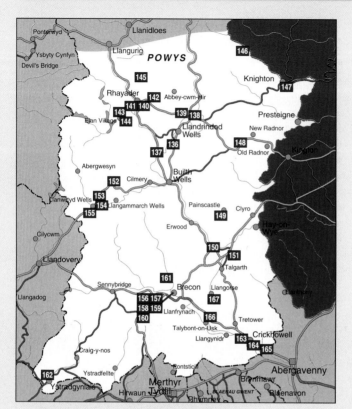

South Powys & Brecon Beacons

This southern region of the large county of Powys is steeped in history and there is evidence aplenty of turbulent times past, from the Romans onwards. The Celtic standing stones and burial chambers and the ruined castles are among the many notable buildings and memorials left by past inhabitants.

In the heart of the county (the northern part of this region) can be found the four spa towns of Llandrindod Wells, Builth Wells, Llangammarch Wells and Llanwrtyd Wells. Still popular tourist centres today, though no longer primarily spas, these places all grew and developed as a result of the arrival of the railways and the Victorians' interest in health. Although the architecture of these towns suggests that they date mainly from the 19th and early 20th centuries, there are the remains of a Roman fort (Castell Collen) close to Llandrindod Wells, and Builth Wells saw much fighting in medieval times. As well as the spa towns, the region also has the border settlements of Knighton and Presteigne, the second-hand book capital of the world Hay-on-Wye and the ancient cathedral city of Brecon, but it is perhaps for its varied countryside that south Powys is better known. Close to Rhayader, in the Cambrian Mountains, are the spectacular reservoirs and

Elan Valley

dams that make up the Elan Valley. Built at the end of the 19th century to supply water to the West Midlands, not only are these a great feat of Victorian engineering but the surrounding countryside is home to one of Britain's rarest and most beautiful birds - the Red Kite.

Further south lies the Brecon Beacons National Park which takes its name from the distinctively shaped sandstone mountains of the Brecon Beacons. To the east of the Brecon Beacons rise the interlocking peaks of the Black Mountains which stretch to the English border, while to the west is Black Mountain, which, though its name is singular, refers to an unpopulated range of barren, smooth-humped peaks.

LLANDRINDOD WELLS

•

Llandrindod's major celebration of the year is its Victorian Festival, held in the last full week of August before the Bank Holiday. Horses and carriages, Victorian shop window displays, and visitors in costume all help create a 19th century atmosphere, and Temple Gardens provides an ideal venue for many different types of free street entertainment. The festivities close with a torchlight procession and a fireworks display over the lake.

•

The most elegant of the spa towns of mid-Wales, Llandrindod Wells has retained much of its Victorian and Edwardian character and architecture. It was only a small hamlet until 1749 when the first hotel was built here. For a time, until that hotel closed in 1787, the town had a reputation as a haunt for gamblers and rakes. Despite its chiefly 19th and early 20th century architecture, Llandrindod Wells has ancient roots. To the northwest of the town lies **Castell Collen**, a Roman fort that was occupied from the 1st century through to the early 4th century and whose earthworks are clearly detectable today. The first castle was built of turf and timber in about AD 75, later versions were made of stone.

It was the Romans who first understood the possible healing powers of Wales' mineral rich waters, but it was with the coming of the railway in 1867 that Llandrindod Wells really developed into a spa town. At its peak, some 80,000 visitors a year would flock to the town to take the waters in an attempt to obtain relief from complaints and ailments ranging from gout, rheumatism and anaemia to diabetes, dyspepsia and liver trouble. Special baths and heat and massage treatments were also available. The most famous of the individual spas in Llandrindod during its heyday, **Rock Park,** is a typically well laid out Victorian park where visitors coming to the town would take a walk between their treatments. With particularly fine tree planting and shrubbery, the park is still a pleasant place today. Here and elsewhere in town, visitors can still take the waters or experience some of the more modern therapies.

Visitors can find out more about the spa's history at the **Radnorshire Museum** where there is a collection of Victorian artefacts along with relics excavated from Castell Collen. A splendid attraction in the Automobile Palace, a distinctive brick garage topped by rows of white lions, is the **National Cycle Collection**, an exhibition that covers more than 100 years of cycling history through an amazing collection of more than 250 bicycles and tricycles. Some date back as far as 1818. The collection displays every development from the hobby horse and bone-shaker to the high-tech machines of today. Also here are old photographs and posters, historic replicas, the Dunlop tyre story and displays on cycling stars.

Castell Collen, Llandrindod Wells

Llandrindod Wells Victorian Festival

Each year in the last full week of August, Llandrindod Wells hosts a **Victorian Festival** which swells the population of the town from its resident 5000 to more than 40,000. Horses and carriages, Victorian window displays, townspeople and visitors in appropriate garb all contribute to the jollity which culminates in a torchlight procession and fireworks display over the lake.

Just outside Llandrindod Wells, off the A44 Rhayader road, there is free access to **Abercamlo Bog**, 12 acres of wet pasture that are home to water-loving plants, breeding birds such as the whinchat and reed bunting, and butterflies. Not far away, at Ithon gorge, is **Bailey Einion**, woodland home to lady fern, golden saxifrage, pied flycatchers, woodpeckers and cardinal beetles.

Wales is famous for its amazing little narrow-gauge railways, but it also has some full-size trains, too.

One of the most popular tourist lines is the **Heart of Wales Line** that runs from Shrewsbury to Swansea, stopping at Llandrindod Wells en route. It promotes itself as 'one line that visits two viaducts, three castles, four spa towns, five counties, six tunnels and seven bridges'.

AROUND LLANDRINDOD WELLS

ABBEY-CWM-HIR

6 miles N of Llandrindod Wells off the A483

Standing rather forlornly in the lonely Clywedog Valley are the ruins of **Cwmhir Abbey**. It was founded in 1143 by the Cistercians who had grandiose plans to build one of the largest churches in Britain with a nave more than 242ft long - only the cathedrals of Durham, Winchester and York have a longer nave. Unfortunately, an

137 NEW INN

Newbridge-on-Wye
Characterful village hostelry with its own butcher's shop offering quality cuisine, B&B and bunkhouse accommodation.

❙ ⊨ *see page 314*

138 THE BUILDERS ARMS

Cross Gates
Family-run, family-friendly inn serving top quality food and offering B&B and self-catering accommodation.

❙ ⊨ *see page 315*

139 GWYSTRE INN

Gwystre
Friendly village hostelry noted for its good food and real ale; also en suite rooms.

❙ ⊨ *see page 316*

109

Rhayader

Quality cuisine and 5-star en suite accommodation in hotel with stunning mountain views.

🍴 🛏 see *page 317*

Rhayader

Former Victorian workhouse transformed into a beautiful family-run hotel.

🛏 🍴 see *page 318*

Llwynbaedd

Quality self-catering holiday lodges in beautiful countryside overlooking the Elan Valley.

🛏 see *page 319*

attack by Henry III in 1231 forced them to abandon their plans. A slab on the altar commemorates Llywelyn ap Gruffydd, the last native prince of Wales, whose headless body is reputed to be buried here. His head had been despatched to London.

RHAYADER

6½ miles NW of Llandrindod Wells on the A44

Often referred to as the Gateway to the Lakeland of Wales, Rhayader lies in a loop of the River Wye at the entrance to the magnificent Elan Valley with its impressive collection of dams and reservoirs. The town's name means 'Waterfall of the Wye' though the waterfall all but disappeared with the construction of a bridge over the river in 1780.

Little except some defensive ditches remains of Rhayader Castle, built here by Rhys ap Gruffyd in about 1177. Over the centuries, the town has been fortunate in avoiding major conflicts although there was some turbulence in the mid-1800s when the **Rebecca Riots** took place. These were protests against road tolls which were painfully expensive for local labourers and itinerant workers. The men dressed up as women to avoid being recognised, their female garb earned them the nickname 'Rebecca's Daughters', and they destroyed toll gates in protest at the high toll charges. The first gate to be destroyed was at Yr Efail Wen where 'Rebecca' proved to be a huge man called Thomas Rees. Many toll gates were demolished by

the protesters until in 1844 the remainder were removed legally.

Welsh Royal Crystal, a manufacturer of hand-crafted lead crystal tableware and gift items, is located in the town and the factory takes visitors on a guided tour to watch the craftsmen at work.

Rhayader is at one end of the beautiful **Wye Valley Walk,** which follows the river valley, criss-crossing the border, through Builth Wells and Hay-on-Wye to Hereford, Monmouth and Chepstow.

The area around Rhayader is still very rural and on the outskirts of the town lies **Gigrin Farm**, where visitors can see red kites at close quarters as they are feeding. Three miles north of the town, **Gilfach Farm Nature Reserve** (free) is operated by the Radnorshire Wildlife Trust which has a visitor and exhibition centre here where twitchers can watch live video footage from nests around the 418 acres of the reserve.

ELAN VILLAGE

8 miles W of Llandrindod Wells off the B4518

The village is close to the beautiful reservoirs of the **Elan Valley** - a string of five dammed lakes that are together around nine miles long and were constructed between 1892 and 1903. Built to supply millions of gallons of water to Birmingham and the West Midlands, the first of the dams was opened in 1904 by Edward VII and Queen Alexandra. The final dam, the Claerwen Dam, was finished in 1952. Dubbed the 'Lakeland of

Wales', the five man-made lakes are surrounded by magnificent scenery and this is a popular area for walkers, cyclists and birdwatchers. The **Elan Valley Visitor Centre** incorporates a tourist information office and also has an exhibition telling the story of the building of the reservoirs together with lots of information about the red kite.

Percy Bysshe Shelley visited his cousin Thomas Grove at Cwm Elan after being expelled from Oxford for writing a treatise supporting atheism. Soon after this visit he eloped with the schoolgirl Harriet Westbrook and married her in Scotland. They returned to Wales and for a brief spell in 1812 stayed at a house in the area called Nant Gwyllt. Like Thomas Grove's house, it is now submerged under

143 RIVERSIDE LODGE GUEST HOUSE

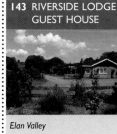

Elan Valley

Guest house in idyllic riverside location offering quality B&B en suite accommodation.

 see *page 318*

144 THE ELAN VALLEY

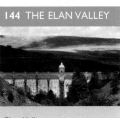

Elan Valley

An area of the Cambrian Mountains with a diverse landscape, rich in wildlife.

 see *page 320*

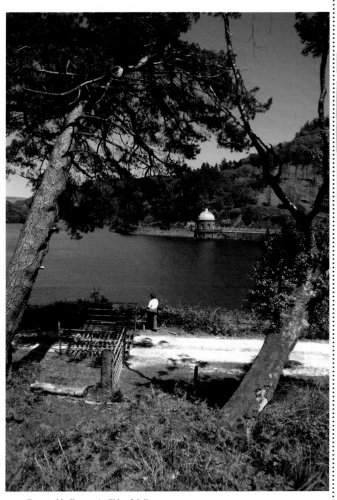

Garreg-ddu Reservoir, Elan Valley

145 MID WALES INN

Pant-y-Dwr

Welcoming inn serving
excellent food and real ales;
en suite rooms available.

 see *page 320*

146 THE RADNORSHIRE ARMS

Beguildy

One of the prettiest pubs in
Wales, serving excellent food
and real ales.

see *page 320*

*To the southwest of the
village of St Harmon lies
Gilfach Nature Reserve,
a Site of Special
Scientific Interest at the
mouth of the Marteg
Valley. Oak woodland,
meadows and upland
moorland support a rich
diversity of wildlife. In
the ancient longhouse at
the heart of the reserve
there are exhibitions on
the building's history and
the surrounding wildlife.*

the waters of **Caben Coch**
reservoir, but when the water level
is low the walls of the garden can
still be seen. In 1814 Shelley left
Harriet for Mary Godwin, and
soon after Harriet drowned herself
in the Serpentine. Shelley married
Mary, who was later to write
Frankenstein. In 1822 Shelley
himself drowned off the Italian
coast.

ST HARMON

8 miles NW of Llandrindod Wells on the B4518

The diarist Francis Kilvert was
vicar here in 1876 and 1877, after
his time at Clyro. Kilvert was born
near Chippenham in 1840 and was
educated at Wadham College,
Oxford. He was curate to his father
in Wiltshire before taking up a post
at Clyro in 1865, where he started
his famous diaries which provide
detailed, vivid and very personal
accounts of life in the remote
Welsh countryside in mid-Victorian
times.

KNIGHTON

Situated in the Teme Valley on the
border of Powys and Shropshire,
Knighton lies on the path of Offa's
Dyke - the Welsh name for the
town is Tref-y-Clawdd which means
'town of the dyke'. Appropriately,
Knighton is home to the **Offa's
Dyke Centre** where there is
information about the long distance
footpath that runs from Prestatyn
to Chepstow. Here, too, visitors
can find out more about the
historic background to the 8th
century dyke and the bloodshed of

the battles that continued in the
borderlands for hundreds of years.

Knighton and its near
neighbour, the border town of
Presteigne, saw many battles
between the Anglo Saxons and the
Celts. "It was customary for the
English to cut off the ears of every
Welshman who was found to the
east of the Dyke (Offa's), and for
the Welsh to hang every
Englishman found to the west of
it", wrote George Borrow in his
19th century book, *Wild Wales*.

Beginning in Knighton,
Glyndwr's Way follows the route
taken by Owain Glyndwr, one of
Wales' favourite sons, as he fought
the English for Welsh
independence in the 1400s. This
scenic and important route travels
southwest to Abbey-cwm-hir,
passing by the ancient abbey ruins,
before heading northwards into the
old county of Montgomeryshire
and the market town of Llanidloes.
The 128 miles of the path takes in
some of the finest scenery in mid-
Wales before reaching Machynlleth,
from where it heads south-
eastwards and finally ends at the
border town of Welshpool.

High on a hill overlooking
Knighton, the **Spaceguard Centre**
occupies the former Powys
Observatory. It was established in
2001 to observe and track comets
and asteroids that might collide
with Earth. Guided tours are
available around the centre which
has a planetarium, solar telescope
and camera obscura.

Beside the banks of the River
Teme is **Pinners Hole**, a natural

112

amphitheatre that is strengthened on one side by a superb section of Offa's Dyke where there is a stone that commemorates the opening of the footpath. Across the river lies **Kinsley Wood**, a sizeable area of native oak woodland. Sited on a hillside, trees of different species were planted to form the letters 'ER' to commemorate the Coronation of Her Majesty Queen Elizabeth II in 1953.

AROUND KNIGHTON

PRESTEIGNE

5 miles S of Knighton on the B4362

Once the county town of Radnorshire, tiny Presteigne remains a charming and unspoilt place on the southern bank of the River Lugg. In recent years it has seen an influx of escapees from urban stress and now has a smattering of craft shops, trendy cafés, antique and second-hand book shops.

A border town distinguished by its handsome black and white half-timbered buildings, Presteigne grew up around a Norman castle that has long since been destroyed; the site is now occupied by a pleasant park. Presteigne's history is as turbulent as that of most of the region: it was captured by the Mercians in the 8th century, besieged by Llywelyn in 1262 and pillaged by Owain Glyndwr in the early 15th century. By Tudor times the town had got its breath back and had become a peaceful market centre, but it was its position on a major mail coach route between London, Cheltenham and Gloucester and Aberystwyth that brought it prosperity and importance.

One of the town's most outstanding buildings is **The Radnorshire Arms** which dates from 1616. Originally built as a house for Sir Christopher Hatton, one of Elizabeth I's courtiers, this superb timber framed building became the property of the Bradshaw family before becoming an inn in 1792. The best known member of this family was John Bradshaw, who was Lord President of the Parliamentary Commission that brought Charles I to trial. He headed the list of signatories to the King's death warrant, refusing to let him speak in his defence. The town also claims the oldest inn in Radnorshire, the **Duke's Arms**, for which records show that an inn on the site was burnt to the ground by Owain Glyndwr in 1401. The rebuilt inn became a local headquarters for the Roundheads during the Civil War and in later centuries was an important coaching inn.

Although the **Judge's Lodging** only dates from 1829, it is another fascinating attraction in Presteigne. Designed by Edward Haycock and built on the site of the county gaol, this was the judicial centre for Radnorshire and the home of the Radnorshire Constabulary. Today, the house, with its adjoining court, has been furnished as it would have appeared in 1870 with many of the original furnishings and furniture. Visitors can explore the world of

147 THE SPACEGUARD CENTRE

Knighton

The Spaceguard Centre is a working astronomical observatory that specialises in Near Earth Objects (NEOs), asteroids and comets that could potentially hit the Earth.

 see page 321

the judges, their servants and the felons. One of the trials conducted here concerned Mary Morgan who gave birth to an illegitimate child that her father urged her to murder. Her crime was detected and she was sentenced to death. Incredibly, her father was among the jury that found her guilty. In the churchyard of St Andrew there are two gravestones recalling the event; the first, erected at the time, is nauseatingly sanctimonious about "the victim of sin and shame"; the second, set up later by chastened townspeople, is inscribed "He that is without sin among you, let him cast the first stone at her".

OLD RADNOR

8½ miles S of Knighton off the A44

Situated on a hill, Old Radnor was once home to King Harold. The motte by the church was the site of his castle, while the church itself contains interesting examples of 14th century building design, as well as a huge font made from a glacial boulder.

NEW RADNOR

8½ miles SW of Knighton off the A44

Once the county town of Radnorshire, the village is overlooked by the remains of its 11th century motte and bailey **Castle**. Like many other strongholds in this border region, New Radnor Castle suffered at various hands: it was destroyed by King John, rebuilt by Henry III and destroyed again by Owain Glyndwr in 1401. New Radnor was the start point in 1187 of a tour of Wales by Archbishop Baldwin, who was accompanied by the scholar and churchman Giraldus Cambrensis. They preached the Third Crusade, and after the tour Baldwin, the first archbishop to visit Wales, made a pilgrimage to the Holy Land, where he died. Baldwin was the Bishop of Worcester before becoming Archbishop of Canterbury, in which capacity he crowned Richard I.

HAY-ON-WYE

This ancient town, tucked between the Black Mountains and the River Wye in the northernmost corner of the Brecon Beacon National Park, grew up around its Hay Motte which still survives across the river from the main town centre today. This castle was replaced by Hay Castle, a stone structure although this was all but destroyed in the early 1400s by Owain Glyndwr. A Jacobean manor house has since been grafted on to part of the remaining walls and, close by, there are traces of a Roman fort.

Historic though this town may be, it is as the second-hand book capital of the world that Hay-on-Wye is best known. Among the town's many buildings can be found a plethora of book, antique, print and craft shops. The first second-hand bookshop was opened here in 1961 by Richard Booth, owner of Hay Castle, and since then they have sprung up all over the town - the old cinema, many houses, shops and even the old castle are now bookshops, at least 35 in all and with a stock of more than a million books. The annual **Festival of Art and Literature**, held every May, draws thousands of visitors to the town.

AROUND HAY-ON-WYE

CLYRO

2 miles NW of Hay on the A438

Although little remains of the Roman station that was here, the ruins of a motte and bailey castle built by the fiendish William de Braose can still be seen. The diarist Francis Kilvert was curate in the village between 1865 and 1872. In his journal, he describes both life in the village and the surrounding area. There are Kilvert memorabilia in his former home, now a modern art gallery.

A little way north of Clyro, **Cwm Byddog** is a 15-acre ancient woodland with pollarded oaks, bluebells in spring, the remains of a motte and bailey castle and a variety of birds, including the blackcap and the garden warbler.

PAINSCASTLE

5 miles NW of Hay on the B4594

Sometimes known as **Castell Paen**, the early motte built in 1130 by Payn FitzJohn was later rebuilt in stone and, by the late 12th century, was in the hands of the notorious William de Braose whose cruelty has earned him a place in Welsh folklore. He was given the nickname the "Ogre of Abergavenny" while his wife Maud is thought to have lived long after his death as a witch. Their names have also been given to several breeds of cattle in Wales including the de Braose Maud and the de Braose David.

In 1198, de Braose's stronghold of Painscastle was attacked by Gwenwynwyn, Prince of Powys, but William and his English army slaughtered more than 3000 of Gwenwynwyn's men and the prince's dreams of a united Wales died along with them. de Braose finally met his match for cruelty in King John who stripped him of his land; de Braose died a pauper. After her husband's death, Maud suggested that John had also killed his nephew Prince Arthur and for this accusation both she and her youngest son were imprisoned in Corfe Castle with little food to keep them alive. Legend has it that when, some 11 days later, the dungeon door was opened, both prisoners were dead. In an attempt to keep herself alive, Maud had half eaten the cheeks of her son.

Close to the castle remains is an altogether more pleasant place to visit, the **Tawny Owl Animal Park and Craft Centre**, which lies in the shelter of beautiful hills. Opened in 1999, the park is named after the wild owls that live in the broad leaved woodlands surrounding the farm. As well as the owls (which are not caged), visitors can also see a whole range of farm animals at close quarters. Along with the animals and the farm trails, there are also traditional country crafts on display and for sale.

149 ROAST OX INN

Painscastle
Traditional country inn serving excellent food and real ales; also en suite rooms.

see page 321

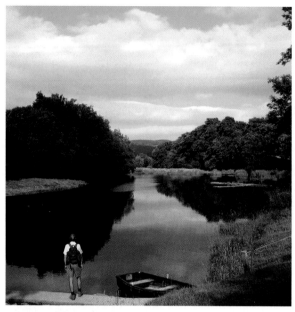

Wye Valley Walk, Builth Wells

150 THE GRIFFIN INN

Llyswen

Picturesque 15th century inn with many original features serving good food, real ales and offering en suite rooms.

 see page 323

BUILTH WELLS

Another spa town , Builth Wells lies on the River Wye, which is spanned at this point by a six-arched bridge. The discovery of the saline springs in 1830 helped Builth Wells develop from a small market town into a fashionable spa that became even more popular with the arrival of the railways towards the end of the 19th century. As a result, many of the town's original narrow streets are dotted with Victorian and Edwardian buildings.

The town grew up around a Norman castle that changed hands many times during the struggles with the English. The inhabitants of Builth Wells earned the nickname 'traitors of Bu-allt' because of their refusal to shelter Llywelyn the Last from the English in 1282. Twenty years later Llywelyn took his revenge by partly destroying the Norman stronghold. At the **Castle Mound** only the earthworks remain of the town's 13th century castle that was built by Edward I on the site of the earlier motte and bailey structure. The earthworks can be reached by a footpath from the town centre.

Since the 1963 opening of the **Royal Welsh Show Ground** at nearby Llanelwedd, the annual Royal Welsh Show, held in July, has gained a reputation as being the premier agricultural show in the country. Builth Wells is regarded as the centre for farming and agriculture in Wales and the show provides an opportunity for the farming communities to come together at what is considered to be one of the finest and most prestigious events of its kind. The showground is also used for monthly flea markets and occasional collector's fairs.

Although spa treatments are no longer available here, Builth Wells remains a popular touring centre and base. As well as the many shops and the weekly market on Mondays, visitors can also enjoy the wide variety of arts and cultural events held at the **Wayside Arts Centre,** housed in the town's Victorian Assembly rooms, or take a pleasant riverside stroll through Groe Park.

On the summit of the nearby mountain, **Cefn Carn Cafall,** is a cairn that is said to have been built by King Arthur. The stone on top

116

of the cairn bears the imprint of a dog's paw that, according to local legend, was left by King Arthur's dog, Cafall, while they were out hunting. Arthur built the cairn, placing the stone on top, and then named the peak. The story continues that if the stone is removed it will always return to this spot.

AROUND BUILTH WELLS

ERWOOD

7 miles SE of Builth Wells on the A470

Pronounced 'Errod', the village's name is actually a corruption of the Welsh Y Rhyd (the ford), a name that harks back to the days when the shallow crossing of the River Wye here was used by drovers. The station at Erwood, closed in 1962, has been turned into a centre for local art and craft and has a resident wood-turner.

CILMERY

3 miles W of Builth Wells on the A483

It was at this village on the banks of the River Irfon, in 1282, that Llywelyn the Last, while escaping after the abortive battle of Builth, was killed by the English. According to legend, the place where Llywelyn fell and died was once covered in broom which then ceased to grow on the site - in mourning for the loss of the last native Prince of Wales. Thirteen trees have been planted here to represent the 13 counties of Wales. The rough hewn stone **Memorial**

to **Llywelyn the Last** describes him as "ein llyw olaf" (our last leader) while the English tablet beside the monument calls him 'our prince'. Following his death, Llywelyn's head was taken to London and paraded victoriously through the city's streets.

LLANWRTYD WELLS

13 miles W of Builth Wells on the A483

The appealing little town of Llanwrtyd Wells is surrounded by rugged mountains, rolling hills and the remote moorland of **Mynydd Epynt**. It was here, in 1792, that a scurvy sufferer discovered the healing properties of the town's sulphur and chalybeate spring waters. The town was soon welcoming a steady stream of afflicted visitors. Today, despite being listed as the smallest town in Britain in the *Guinness Book of Records*, Llanwrtyd Wells is still a popular holiday centre, particularly with those who enjoy bird watching, fishing and walking.

Anyone visiting Llanwrtyd Wells may well be surprised that somewhere so small could host so many events and festivals throughout the year. It is the home of the 'Man versus Horse' race in May, a Folk Weekend in spring and a late autumn Beer Festival. However the most unusual of all the events held here is undoubtedly the annual **World Bog Snorkelling Championship** that takes place each August. Competitors have to swim two lengths of a specially dug 180ft peat bog located a mile from the town. The swimmer's head

151 THE THREE HORSESHOES

Velindre

Charming old village hostelry serving appetising home-made meals and real ales.

see page 324

152 THE TROUT INN

Beulah

Traditional village inn serving quality food and real ales; en suite and dormitory accommodation

see page 324

153 STONECROFT INN

Llanwrtyd Wells

Traditional warm and friendly country pub with delicious food, real ales, and B&B or self-catering accommodation.

see page 325

117

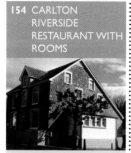
must be submerged, and the use of the arms is forbidden. The latest variation is bog-snorkelling on mountain bikes!

On the outskirts of the town lies the **Cambrian Woollen Mill**, which recalls the rich history of Wales' rural past. The first mill was founded in the 1820s, but its modern form dates from 1918, when it was opened by the Royal British Legion for the benefit of servicemen disabled in the Great War. A tour of the mill allows visitors to see traditional cloths being woven while, in the factory shop, there is a wide choice of beautifully finished items to buy.

On high ground to the northwest of the town is **Llyn Brianne**, the latest of Wales' man-made lakes, which was opened in 1973. The dam that holds the water is the highest of its type in the country - at 300 feet - and the grand scale of the lake has to be seen to be believed.

LLANGAMMARCH WELLS

8 miles W of Builth Wells off the A483

Situated where the Rivers Irfon and Cammarch meet, Llangammarch Wells was the smallest of the Welsh spas and was renowned for its barium chloride carrying waters that were thought to be useful in the treatment of heart and rheumatic complaints. Lloyd George was one of many notables who came to sample the waters. The old well and pump house are contained in the grounds of the Lake Country House Hotel.

ABERGWESYN

12 miles W of Builth Wells off the B4358

Situated in an isolated spot in the Irfon Valley, this riverside hamlet lies on an old drovers' route that twists and climbs through the **Abergwesyn Pass** which is known as the 'roof of Wales'. Tis is a beautiful pathway that centuries ago consisted of nothing more than dirt tracks along which the drovers would shepherd cattle and other livestock from one market town to the next. A number of drovers' routes can still be followed - some in part by car. Many of the roads are narrow and in the south one such route begins at Llandovery and travels across the Epynt mountain to the ford at Erwood.

BRECON

Famous for its ancient cathedral, Georgian architecture and annual Jazz Festival, Brecon lies on the banks of the River Usk at the confluence of the Rivers Honddu and Tarrell on the northern edge of the Brecon Beacons National Park. Established in 1957, the park's 520 square miles of scenic grandeur is dominated by a backbone of the highest mountains in southern Britain. Buzzards and ravens soar over the hills and in the west you can often see Red Kites, a magnificent bird of prey that was almost extinct in Britain a century ago.

The first evidence of a settlement in the area are the remains of the Roman fort **Y Gaer**

Brecon Cathedral

which lie to the west of the town. First built in around AD 75, the fort was rebuilt twice before it was finally abandoned in about AD 290. A garrison for the 2nd Legion and the Vettonian Spanish cavalry, parts of the fort were excavated by Sir Mortimer Wheeler in 1924. Sections of the outer wall - in places 10 feet high - and traces of gates can be seen.

A walk along the promenade beside the River Usk leads to the remains of medieval **Brecon Castle** which can be found partly in the Bishop's Garden and partly at the Castle Hotel. The town grew up around this castle which was built in the late 11th century by

Bernard of Newmarch. It was besieged first by Llywelyn the Last and again during Owain Glyndwr's rebellion in the early 15th century. When the Civil War erupted, the people of Brecon were so determined to protect their thriving cloth-weaving trade that they dismantled the castle and the town walls to ensure that neither side would be interested in seizing Brecon.

Close by stands **Brecon Cathedral**, an impressive and magnificent building that originated from an 11th century cell of the Benedictine monastery at Battle in Sussex. The Priory Church of St John the Evangelist was elevated to the status of a cathedral in 1923. Inside there are many interesting examples of religious artefacts and of the chapels dedicated to craftsmen which once filled the aisle - only that to the corvisors (shoemakers) remains. Housed in a 16th century tithe barn is the cathedral's imaginative Heritage Centre.

Another of the town's old buildings, the elegant former Old Shire Hall, now houses the **Brecknock Museum** where visitors can see the old assize court

156 THE COPPER KETTLE

Brecon

Popular town centre café serving tasty home-made meals and snacks.

🍴 *see page 326*

157 PARIS GUEST HOUSE

Brecon

Town centre premises offering quality en suite accommodation

🛏 *see page 328*

158 CAMDEN ARMS

Brecon

Outstanding cuisine, real ale and quality B&B accommodation in this town centre inn.

🍴 🛏 *see page 327*

159 THE DROVERS ARMS

Llanfaes

The Drovers Arms, Traditional Welsh hostelry serving delicious home-made food and real ales.

🍴 *see page 328*

119

160 BRECKNOCK MUSEUM AND ART GALLERY

Brecon

Visit the Brecknock Museum and learn more about the history, environment and art of the Brecon Beacons area.

🏛 *see page 328*

161 SELAND NEWYDD INN

Pwllgloyw

Former 18th century farmhouse popular for its quality food and real ales; en suite rooms available.

🍴 ⊨ *see page 329*

as well as take in the extensive collection of artefacts and other items from past centuries, including the museum's large collection of Welsh love spoons. The town's second museum is equally fascinating. The **South Wales Borderers Museum** features memorabilia of the regiment's famous defence of Rorke's Drift. More than 300 years of military history are recorded here through various displays that include armoury, uniforms and medals. The regiment has taken part in every major campaign and war and has won 29 Victoria Crosses as well as more than 100 Battle Honours. Though its history is long and stirring, it is the regiment's participation in the Zulu wars that is best remembered and which was immortalised in the film *Zulu* starring Michael Caine. It recalls the heroic defence of Rorke's Drift in 1879, when 141 men from the regiment were attacked by 4000 Zulus; nine VCs were awarded here in a single day.

As well as having the River Usk flowing through the town, Brecon is also home to the **Monmouthshire and Brecon Canal**, a beautiful Welsh waterway which used to bring coal and limestone into the town. There are attractive walks along the canal towpath along with pleasure cruises on both motorised and horse-drawn barges. The canal basin in the town has been reconstructed and is now proving to be an attraction in its own right.

AROUND BRECON

LLANFRYNACH

2 miles S of Brecon on the B4558

Housed in an 18th century warehouse, the **Water Folk Museum** tells the story of life on the canal. Horse-drawn boat trips start from here, and sometimes a blacksmith can be seen at work.

LIBANUS

4 miles SW of Brecon on the A470

To the northwest of this attractive hamlet, on Mynydd Illtyd common, is the **Brecon Beacons Mountain Centre** where visitors can find out about the Brecon Beacons National Park from displays and presentations. There are also some interesting remains to be seen in the area - Twyn y Gaer, a Bronze Age burial chamber, and Bedd Illtyd, a more modest ancient monument said to be the grave of St Illtyd, the founder of the monastery at Llantwit Major. Brecon Beacons are a small part of the National Park. The Beacons, including the sandstone peaks of **Pen y Fan** and **Corn Du**, were given to the National Trust in 1965 and have become one of the most popular parts of the UK with walkers. (At 886 metres, Pen y Fan is the highest point in southern Britain.) The area is also important for sub-alpine plants and is designated a Site of Special Scientific Interest. But the very popularity of the Beacons with walkers has caused great problems, exacerbated by military manoeuvres and the sheep that have grazed here since Tudor times. Erosion is the biggest problem, and the National Trust has put in place an ambitious programme of footpath and erosion repair.

YSTRADFELLTE

12 miles SW of Brecon off the A4059

This small village is a recognised hiking centre and the area of classic limestone countryside around it is one of the most impressive in the British Isles.

The narrow road heading north from the village climbs sharply and squeezes its way along a narrow valley between Fan Llia on the east side and Fan Nedd on the west. The **Maen Madog** is a nine-feet high standing stone with a Latin inscription proclaiming that Dervacus, son of Justus, lies here.

To the south of Ystradfellte is Porth-yr-Ogof, a delightful area with a string of three dramatic waterfalls as the River Melte descends through woodland.

YSTRADGYNLAIS

18½ miles SW of Brecon on the B4599

Situated at the top end of the Tawe Valley, which stretches down to the city of Swansea, and close to the boundary of the Brecon Beacon National park is Ystradgynlais, a former mining community. Iron was produced here as far back as the early 17th century and the legacy of this industrious past can still be seen, although the area surrounding Ystradgynlais is known as waterfall country and is popular with walkers, ramblers and cavers.

Maen Madog, Ystradfellte

CRAIG-Y-NOS

15½ miles SW of Brecon on the A4067

The **Dan-yr-Ogof Showcaves**, the largest complex of caverns in northern Europe, lie to the north of this village. Discovered in 1912, the caverns have taken 315 million years to create and they include both the longest and the largest showcaves in Britain. Prehistoric tribes lived in these impressive caverns - more than 40 human skeletons have been found here.

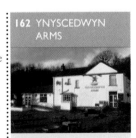

162 YNYSCEDWYN ARMS

Ystradgynlais

Welcoming inn offering fine ales, comfortable en suite rooms and a superb Restaurant.

⫟ ⊨ see page 330

163 THE WHITE HART

Crickhowell

Charmingly traditional tavern offering appetising home-cooked food and real ales.

🍴 see page 329

164 THE DRAGON INN

Crickhowell

Appealing town centre hotel noted for its excellent restaurant and quality en suite accommodation.

⊢ 🍴 see page 331

165 GLANGRWYNEY COURT

Crickhowell

Quality B&B or self-catering accommodation in Grade II listed Georgian building set in extensive grounds.

⊢ see page 332

Exploring these underground caverns is only one aspect of this interesting attraction as there is also an award winning **Dinosaur Park**, where life size replicas of the creatures that roamed the earth during Jurassic times can be seen. The replica **Iron Age Farm** gives a convincing representation of how farmers lived so long ago.

To the east of the village lies **Craig-y-Nos Country Park** where visitors can enjoy the unspoilt countryside and the landscaped country parkland of the upper Tawe Valley. The mansion in the country park, known as **Craig-y-Nos Castle**, was once the home of the 19th century opera singer Madame Adelina Patti. She bought the estate in 1878 as a home for her and her second husband, the tenor Ernesto Nicolini, and lived here for 40 years. She installed an aviary, a little theatre modelled on Drury Lane and a winter garden that was subsequently moved to Swansea's Victoria Park. The castle is now a hotel.

SENNYBRIDGE

7½ miles W of Brecon on the A40

Situated along the southern edge of the Mynydd Epynt and on the northern border of the Brecon Beacons National Park, this village is very much a product of the industrial age. It only began to develop after the railways arrived here in 1872 and Sennybridge became a centre for livestock trading. However, the remains of **Castell Ddu**, just to the west of the village, provides evidence of

life here from an earlier age. Dating from the 14th century and believed to stand on the site of an 11th century manor house, this was the home of Sir Reginald Aubrey, a friend of Bernard of Newmarch.

Two new waymarked walks have been opened on the Sennybridge army training area, beginning at **Disgwylfa Conservation Centre** on the B4519. The centre has an interactive learning centre and military and conservation displays. One of the walks is accessible for disabled visitors.

CRICKHOWELL

Situated in the beautiful valley of the River Usk and in the shadow of the Black Mountains that lie to the north, Crickhowell is a charming little town with a long history. The town takes its name from the Iron Age fort, **Crug Hywell** (Howell's Fort) that lies on the flat-topped hill above the town that is aptly named Table Mountain. The remains of another stronghold, **Crickhowell Castle** - once one of the most important fortresses in this mountainous region of Wales - can be found in the town's large park. Built in the 11th century, only the motte and two shattered towers remain of the Norman fortress that was stormed by Owain Glyndwr and abandoned in the 15th century.

The picturesque and famous **Crickhowell Bridge**, which dates from the 16th century, spans the River Usk in the heart of the town. Still carrying traffic today, the bridge is unique in that it has 13 arches on one side and only 12 on the other! For the rest, this is a pleasant place, with some fine Georgian architecture which, due to its close proximity to the Black Mountains and the National Park, is popular with those looking for outdoor activities including walking. Close by is **Pwll-y-Wrach Nature Reserve** in a steep-sided valley. Owned by the Brecknock Wildlife Trust, this woodland reserve has a waterfall and also a great variety of flora, for which it has been designated a Site of Special Scientific Interest.

AROUND CRICKHOWELL

TRETOWER

2½ miles NW of Crickhowell on the A479

This quiet village in the Usk Valley is the home of two impressive medieval buildings - **Tretower Court and Tretower Castle** (both in the hands of CADW). The elder of these historic sites is the castle where all that remains on the site of the original Norman motte is a stark keep that dates from the 13th century. The castle was built in this valley to discourage Welsh rebellion but, nonetheless, it was besieged by Llywelyn the Last and almost destroyed by Owain Glyndwr in 1403. Adjacent to the bleak castle remains stands the court, a magnificent 15th century fortified manor house that served as a very desirable domestic residence particularly during the less turbulent years following Glyndwr's rebellion.

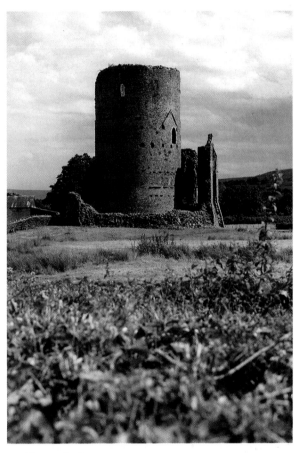

Tretower Castle

While the 15th century woodwork here and the wall walk, with its 17th century roof and windows, are outstanding, it is the court's **Gardens** that are particularly interesting. The original late 15th century layout of the gardens has been re-created in such a manner that the owner of the time, Sir Roger Vaughan, would have recognised them. Among the many delightful features is a tunnel arbour planted with white roses - Sir Roger was a Yorkist - and vines,

123

Talybont-on-Usk

"Welsh Pub of the Year, 2005" offering award-winning food and 4-star accommodation.

 see page 333

Llangorse

Restaurant close to Llangorse Lake serving appetising home-made food.

see page 334

Tretower Court

an enclosed arbour and a chequerboard garden. Tretower Court's Gardens are best seen in the early summer.

TALYBONT-ON-USK

7 miles NW of Crickhowell on the B4558

Just beyond this attractive village, the Monmouthshire and Brecon Canal passes through the 375 yard long Ashford Tunnel while, further south still, lies the **Talybont Reservoir**. In this narrow wooded valley on the south-eastern slopes of the Brecons there are several forest trails starting from the car park at the far end of the reservoir.

LLANGORSE

8 miles NW of Crickhowell on the B4560

To the south of the village lies the largest natural lake in South Wales - **Llangorse Lake** (Llyn Syfaddan). Around four miles in circumference and following its way round a low contour in the Brecon Beacons, the waters of this lake were, in medieval times, thought to have

miraculous properties. Today, the lake attracts numerous visitors looking to enjoy not only the setting but also the wide variety of sporting and leisure activities, such as fishing, horse riding and sailing, that can be found here. There is also a Rope Centre, with climbing, abseiling, potholing, log climbing and a high-level rope course.

TALGARTH

10½ miles N of Crickhowell on the A479

Lying in the foothills of the Black Mountains, Talgarth is an attractive market town with narrow streets that boasts many historic associations as well as some fine architecture. The 15th century parish **Church of St Gwendoline** has strong links with Hywell Harris (1714-73), an influential figure in the establishment of Welsh Methodism. Harris was also instrumental in establishing a religious community, The Connexion, which was organised on both religious and industrial lines.

Although this is now a quiet and charming place, Talgarth once stood against the Norman drive into Wales. Some of the defensive structures can still be seen today - the tower of the church and another tower that is now incorporated into a house. The latter tower has also served time as the jail.

On the outskirts of Talgarth stands **Bronllys Castle** a well-preserved centuries old keep built by the Norman baron Bernard of Newmarch. Originally a motte and bailey castle, it was later replaced with a stone edifice and now it is a lone circular tower standing on a steep mound that is in the hands of CADW - Welsh Historic Monuments.

LLANGYNIDR

4 miles W of Crickhowell on the B4558

Rising to the south of this riverside village on the open moorland of Mynydd Llangynidr, lies the **Chartists' Cave**, where members of the movement stored ammunition during their active years in the mid-19th century.

LLANGATTOCK

1 mile SW of Crickhowell off the A4077

The village church was founded sometime during the early 6th century and is dedicated to St Catwg, one of Wales' most honoured saints. He was born around AD 497 and by the end of his life, in around AD 577, Catwg, had become a Bishop and had taken the name Sophias.

To the southwest of the village, towards the boundary of the Brecon Beacons National Park lies the **Craig-y-Cilau Nature Reserve**. With over 250 plant species and more than 50 kinds of birds breeding within the reserve, this is one of the richest in the National Park.

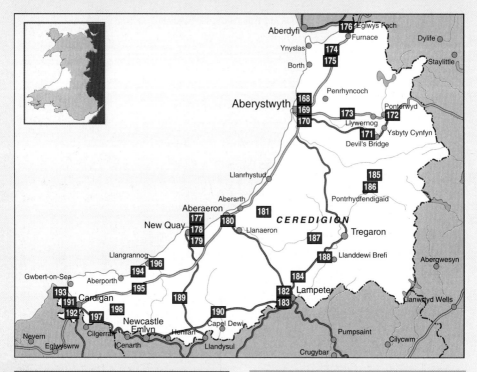

Ceredigion

Ceredigion means the land of Ceredig, son of the Celtic chieftain Cunedda. The area is renowned for its unique brand of Welshness and ancient myths and legends are still vivid in the folk memory. The patron saint of Wales, St David, was born in Ceredigion and many famous Welsh princes are buried in the ruins of Strata Florida Abbey.

For visitors, though, this county is best known for its coastline on the great sweep of Cardigan Bay. Many of the one-time fishing villages have now become genteel resorts but few seem to have attained the great degree of brashness that is associated with other seaside holiday destinations. In the north of the county and close to the mouth of the River Dyfi is the great expanse of sand at Borth while, further south, the coastline gives way to cliffs and coves - once the haunt of smugglers.

Ceredigion's countryside features some of the most beautiful landscapes in Wales in which many rare species of birds, wildlife and plants abound. In particular, it is home to the graceful red kite. Keen birdwatchers are well served by nature reserves around the Teifi and Dyfi estuaries and at Llangranog, New Quay and Cors Caron.

Mountain Road, Tregaron

The region is not as well endowed with castles as the counties further north, but Aberystwyth and Cardigan castles both saw fighting before they were left to ruins, and Cardigan is credited with being the venue for the first recorded Eisteddfod in 1176. This is also an important area of learning. St David's College at Lampeter, a world renowned ecclesiastical establishment, is now, as University College, part of the University of Wales, while Aberystwyth is home not only to the first university in Wales but also to the National Library of Wales.

ABERYSTWYTH

Located on the campus of the University of Wales is one of the most striking buildings in the town, the Aberystwyth Arts Centre. It hosts a busy year-round programme of performances, exhibitions, cinema screenings, events, courses and workshops. Also within the complex are cafés, a theatre bar, a bookshop and a Craft & Design Shop.

168 THE WESTON VAULTS

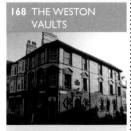

Aberystwyth

Lively town centre pub with traditional amusements, bar food and ales; also rooms with showers.

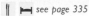 see page 335

169 LA TABERNA - CASA MIGUEL

Aberystwyth

Stylish taberna serving authentic Spanish food with terrific choice of tapas, paellas and house specialities.

see page 334

The largest town in Cardigan Bay, the seat of local government, the home of the University College of Wales and the National Library of Wales, Aberystwyth is not only the unofficial capital of mid-Wales but also a cosmopolitan coastal resort. Its Victorian and Edwardian heyday as a holiday centre has left a pleasing architectural legacy and its status as a university town means that there are plenty of pubs and they stay open later than in most of Wales.

Although there is evidence that the town is older, Aberystwyth as we know it, can certainly be traced back to the late 13th century when, in 1277, Edward I began building **Aberystwyth Castle.** He also granted a charter that made the settlement around the new fortification a free borough with a ditch and wall, a guild of merchants, a market and two fairs. In the early 1400s, Owain Glyndwr used the castle as his base for four years until it was recaptured by Prince Henry, later Henry V. There was more fighting here during the Civil War until it finally fell to Cromwell's soldiers in 1646 and was largely destroyed three years later. Today, the ruins, standing on the rocky headland, remain an impressive sight. Also on Castle Point can be found the town's **War Memorial,** a splendid monument that was commissioned the year after World War I ended; it is the work of the Italian sculptor Mario Rutelli.

In the years following the turmoil of the Civil War, and before the arrival of the railways, Aberystwyth remained essentially a fishing town, but with a growing shipbuilding industry. Although much of this industry has now ceased, **Aberystwyth Harbour and Marina** is still a bustling place that can accommodate more than 100 vessels. All manner of fish and seafood are still landed at the town quay

The arrival of the railways in the 1860s saw the town expand rapidly as first the Victorians and then the Edwardians made their way here to enjoy the sea air and

Aberystwyth Castle

the beauty of the great sweep of Cardigan Bay. The town's 700 feet long **Pier** was constructed in 1864 and the Pavilion at the end was added in 1896 to provide a capacious venue for light entertainment. Just to the north, along the coast from the town centre, lies the longest electric **Cliff Railway** in Britain - another product of the Victorian development which still carries passengers up the cliff face at a sedate four miles an hour. It was originally water-balanced but is now powered by electricity. From the summit there are panoramic views over the bay and inland to the Cambrian Mountains.

Opened nearly 100 years after the railway was constructed, and also on the cliff summit, is the **Great Aberystwyth Camera Obscura**, housed in an octagonal tower. A faithful reconstruction of a popular Victorian amusement, the huge 14 inch lens - the biggest in the world - gives visitors an even better view from this excellent vantage point.

While the town today certainly seems to cater to holidaymakers' every need, Aberystwyth is also a major seat of learning. The very first college of the University of Wales was established at Aberystwyth as was the very first Welsh medium Primary School. The **Old College** was originally built in the 1870s to a design by JP Seddon and was intended to be a hotel designed to accommodate the influx of Victorian visitors. However the venture failed and in

Aberystwyth Sea Front

1872 the high Gothic building was sold, becoming the first university in Wales and now home to the departments of Welsh, Education and Theatre, Film and Television.

The town is also the home of the **National Library of Wales**, one of only six copyright libraries in Great Britain and the keeper of the majority of materials that relate to the Welsh people and their culture. Founded in 1909 and eventually opened in 1937 by George VI, the library holds many early Welsh and Celtic manuscripts among which is the *Black Book of Carmarthen*, a 12th century manuscript that is the oldest in Welsh. Within the complex, the Drwm cinema and auditorium presents a wide range of screenings and performances.

Housed in a beautifully restored Edwardian music hall, right in the centre of the town, is the **Ceredigion Museum** (free). It boasts what has been described as "probably the most beautiful museum interior in Britain". The

170 ABERYSTWYTH CLIFF RAILWAY

Aberystwyth

Aberystwyth Cliff Railway, the only one in Wales, was opened in 1896 and rises 430 feet in its 778 feet of undulating track.

🏛 see page 334

Devil's Bridge, Aberystwyth

The spectacular 300feet
waterfalls can be seen in a
breathtaking woodland
setting.

see page 336

various exhibits tell the history of
Cardiganshire through an
interesting collection of materials:
the history of seafaring, agriculture
and silver and lead mining are all
well chronicled.

St Michael's Church is the
home of the **Welsh Christian
Centre**, with an exhibition and film
about the history of the Christian
faith in Wales.

AROUND ABERYSTWYTH

DEVIL'S BRIDGE

10 miles SE of Aberystwyth on the A4120

The terminus of the **Vale of
Rheidol Railway**, the narrow
gauge steam train railway that runs
for 12 miles from Aberystwyth
through the Rheidol valley. It was
built in 1902 for the valley's lead
mines and continued as part of the
British Rail network until the late
1980s when it was sold to the
private company that now operates
it from April to October.

What draws most people to
Devil's Bridge are the splendid
waterfalls that drop some 300 feet
through a breathtaking gorge.
While the scenery is marvellous,
there are also three interesting
bridges here - dating from the 11th,
18th and 20th centuries - which
were built one on top of the other.
An iron bridge built in 1901
straddles the top of the falls; just
below it is a stone bridge of 1753
while, further down stream again,
the original 11th century **Pont-y-
gwr-Drwg** (Bridge of the Devil)
spans the turbulent river. It was

probably built by the monks of
Strata Florida Abbey although local
legend suggests that the bridge was
built by the Devil and that he
would claim the first soul to cross
to the other side. However, an old
woman, wanting to retrieve her
stray cow, outwitted the Devil by
throwing a crust across the bridge
which her dog chased after. The
Devil had to make do with the soul
of the dog and the old lady safely
retrieved her cow.

Along with the footpaths and
nature trails that descend the 94
steps of Jacob's Ladder to view the
falls, other paths lead to another
vantage point - **The Hafod Arch**.
It was erected in 1810 by Thomas
Johnes, the squire of Hafod, to
honour the Golden Jubilee of
George III, the farmer king; Johnes
also transformed the area with
forestation, planting the
surrounding countryside with more
than four million trees as if in
anticipation of the Forestry
Commission who now own the
land. The Arch, which marks the
highest point on the former Hafod
Estate of the old Aberystwyth-
Rhayader road, is one of many
points of interest on the
Pwllpeiran Trail, a four-mile trail
that affords exciting views over
Hafod and the Upper Ystwyth
Valley and provides information on
the agriculture, forestry, wildlife
and history to be seen along its
route. One section of the walk
joins the Cambrian Way Long
Distance Path through Myherin
Forest; on its way it passes through
Gelmast farmyard, which was

Thomas Johnes' original experimental farm.

YSBYTY CYNFYN

10½ miles E of Aberystwyth on the A4120

Found in the circular wall of the 19th century village church are the remains of a Bronze Age **Stone Circle**. Two of the stones have been moved from their original positions to form the gate posts but many of the other ancient stones remain as they have for centuries.

PONTERWYD

10 miles E of Aberystwyth on the A44

An inn called the Borrow Arms recalls George Borrow who came here to dry out after falling into a peat bog. Norfolk born, Borrow was a noted philologist and linguist who travelled widely overseas, acting for a time as an agent for the British and Foreign Bible Society. Later, he tramped around England and Wales, sometimes with his step-daughter, and in 1862 published his best-known work *Wild Wales*.

Close by is the **Nant yr Arian Visitor Centre**, a Forest Enterprise centre with forest walks and trails, a mountain bike trail, orienteering course, tea room, local crafts, and picnic and play areas. Here, too, is the **Kite Country Centre** and feeding station. Designated the Bird of the Century in 1999, the Red Kite was a fairly common bird in the Middle Ages, seen even in London scavenging in the streets. It was at that time considered useful and was even protected by the Crown, but with the passing of the Enclosures Act in the 16th century this impressive bird was among many species thought to be a threat to agriculture. Persecuted as vermin, they disappeared entirely from England and Scotland, although a few pairs remained in mid-Wales. With care and conservation efforts from individuals and organisations, the numbers gradually increased, so that now there are more than 300 breeding pairs in Wales. At 2 o'clock each afternoon throughout the year the kites swoop down to be fed, joined by other species looking for an easy meal, including crows, buzzards and ravens. Other red kite feeding stations in Wales are at Gigrin Farm near Rhayader, Powys, and Tregaron in Ceredigion, the latter feeding in winter only.

LLYWERNOG

9 miles E of Aberystwyth on the A44

Just to the north of the village lies the **Llywernog Silver-Lead Mine Museum and Caverns**. The museum covers the history of this major rural industry in mid-Wales. Llywernog opened in 1740 and enjoyed its most prosperous period between 1850 and 1879. In the slump that followed most of the mines closed for good, but Llywernog refused to die and was briefly reopened in 1903 as a zinc prospect. It was saved in 1973 by the present owners. Visitors are taken on a 30-minute underground tour of the mine itself and, once outside again, can then pan for 'fool's gold' or try their dowsing skills by searching for veins of galena.

172 THE GEORGE BORROW HOTEL

Ponterwyd
Characterful 18th century inn offering excellent food, real ales and en suite rooms.
❙ ⊨ *see page 336*

173 THE DRUID INN

Goginan
Welcoming village inn with spectacular views, excellent food and real ales.
❙ *see page 337*

174 BLACK LION HOTEL

Talybont
Fine old village hostelry serving delicious home-made food and real ales; en suite accommodation available.

¶ ⊨ see page 338

175 WHITE LION HOTEL

Talybont
Popular village hotel with outstanding cuisine, real ales and comfortable en suite accommodation.

⊨ ¶ see page 339

LLANBADARN FAWR

1 mile E of Aberystwyth on the A44

This village has now become a suburb of Aberystwyth but it was once a town in its own right and the seat of the oldest bishopric in Wales, established in the 6th century. St Padarn established a small monastery here and the huge 13th century church is dedicated to him. It contains his tomb as well as two striking Celtic crosses from the 10th century that are associated with St Samson, Padarn's brother.

TRE TALIESIN

7½ miles NE of Aberystwyth on the A487

This village was the home, in the 6th century, of one of the earliest recorded British poets, Taliesin. He is thought to have been buried here. The standing stone behind the village, **Bedd Taliesin** (Taliesin's Grave), actually dates from the Bronze Age (around 15,000 BC) and while it marks a burial chamber it is unlikely to be that of the poet.

TRE'R-DDOL

8 miles NE of Aberystwyth on the A487

The former medieval deer park, **Lodge Park**, is now managed by Forest Enterprise who have restored this semi-natural woodland and have also preserved the

Celtic Cross, Llanbadarn Fawr

northern boundary of the park that comprised a ditch and bank.

FURNACE

10½ miles NE of Aberystwyth on the A487

Dyfi Furnace (free) is an important early industrial site that has one of the country's best preserved charcoal burning blast furnaces. In the 18th century, this quaint old village was the site of an iron ore smelting foundry. The bellows that pumped the air into the furnace were powered by a huge waterwheel driven by the River Einion. The wheel has been restored to working order and visitors can browse around this industrial heritage site and museum.

The road opposite Dyfi Furnace leads up the **Cwm Einion** - Artists' Valley - which is so called

132

because it's lovely views made it a favourite haunt of 19th century water colourists. Walkers climbing up the valley will find pleasant woodland trails and picturesque picnic spots.

EGLWYS FACH

11 miles NE of Aberystwyth on the A487

Found in the sheltered waters of the Dovey estuary, the **Ynyshir RSPB Nature Reserve** provides sanctuary for a great many species of birds, in particular waders. It has an extensive network of walks, with bird watching hides, where visitors in winter can observe the unique flock of White-fronted Geese from Greenland and also the smaller flock of Barnacle Geese. This is also the most important breeding site in Wales for lapwings and redshanks. The Visitor Centre has copious information on the various species of birds found here and also arranges special interest guided walks on most weekends.

BORTH

5½ miles N of Aberystwyth on the B4353

The original settlement of this now popular seaside resort lies on the slopes of Rhiw Fawr and it is there that some of the older fishermen's and farmer's cottages can still be seen. The growth of the village began with the arrival of the railway linking it with Aberystwyth in the 1860s and its long, safe, sandy beach, along with the spectacular views out over Cardigan Bay and inland to the mountains, have ensured that it is still a popular holiday destination.

At very low tide it is possible to see the remains of a submerged forest that, according to local legend, once formed part of the dynasty of Cantre'r Gwaelod (the Lower Dynasty) which extended out into the bay and was protected by a huge sea wall. One night the gatekeeper is said to have had too much to drink and had forgotten to close the gates against the rising tide that, with the help of a storm, drowned the forest and the dynasty.

To the east of the village lies **Borth Bog** (Cors Fochno), an important area of raised coastal peat mire (one of only two such areas in Europe) that supports an abundance of wildlife.

YNYSLAS

7½ miles N of Aberystwyth off the B4353

Situated at the northern end of Borth beach, Ynyslas - the name means Green Island - extends to the Dovey estuary, where there are broad expanses of sand, particularly at low tide, although the swimming is unsafe. The **Ynyslas Sand Dunes and Visitor Centre** explains the natural beauty of the Dyfi in wildlife displays and slide shows. There is also a conservation shop selling books, stationery and "green" pocket money gifts. From the centre there are glorious views over the river mouth to Aberdovey.

NEW QUAY

This small yet busy resort, whose harbour now boasts more yachts than fishing boats, built its economy on both shipbuilding and

A popular family attraction at Borth is Animalarium, an interesting collection of exotic animals including monkeys, crocodiles, large cats and reptiles. During the summer, pony rides are available.

176 YNYS-HIR RSPB NATURE RESERVE

Derwenlas, nr Machynlleth

Ynys-hir reserve mixes the delights of Welsh oak woodland with wet grassland and estuarine salt marshes.

🏛 see page 338

177 THE DOLAU INN

New Quay

Inn occupying a superb position close to the shore; bar snacks, real ales and occasional entertainment.

🍴 see page 340

133

178 BLACK LION HOTEL

New Quay

Beautifully sited hotel with strong Dylan Thomas connections; en suite accommodation, good food, beer garden and children's play area.

⊨ ∥   see page 342

coastal trading. However, although these traditional ways of life declined in the 19th century as the rail links developed, New Quay has retained much of its maritime charm. The first vessel to be built here was a 36 ton sloop; the subsequent shipping boom brought a great deal of employment to the area and this caused the population to rise to 2000. Hand in hand with the shipbuilding and fishing industry, smuggling was also rife. In 1795 New Quay was described as a place of "infamous notoriety" and the headland was reputedly riddled with a network of caves where contraband was stored.

New Quay's natural surroundings as a port and harbour of refuge led to its being considered, at one time, as a suitable place from which direct communication could be made with Wicklow and Dublin. Today's visitors will find a variety of boat trips leaving from the main pier to cruise the waters of the Ceredigion Marine Heritage Coast. The cruises pass a rugged coastline whose cliffs support a myriad of sea bird colonies and there are regular sightings of bottlenose dolphins, porpoises and grey Atlantic seals.

The **Heritage Centre** has displays on the town's history, including local characters, shipbuilding, smuggling and fishing. It also details what is being done to protect the area's bottlenose dolphins, grey seals and porpoises.

The sands and boating facilities at New Quay have long been an attraction for holidaymakers and the town's **Yacht Club** welcomes all visitors. The north beach leads to the rocky headland, New Quay Head, where an invigorating path follows the line of the sheer cliffs to Bird Rock, the home of many sea birds. Inland, the **Bird and Wildlife Hospital** treats and returns to the wild any birds or mammals needing veterinarian treatment, particularly birds involved in oil spillages.

To the south of New Quay there is a Heritage Coastal path that threads its way along the clifftops down through Cwmtudu to Llangranog and beyond. To the northwest of the town are the long sandy beaches of **Treath Gwyn** (White Beach) and **Cei Bach** (Little Quay) that were once a hive of shipbuilding activity and are now peaceful and secluded places.

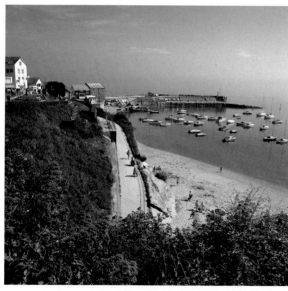

Beach, New Quay

134

Along with Laugharne in Carmarthenshire, New Quay lays claim to being the original Llareggub in Dylan Thomas' *Under Milk Wood*. Thomas and his family lived in New Quay for the last half of World War II and had an ambiguous relationship with the town: it is said that he was disliked in the town not least for his failure to pay his bills. On one occasion while drinking in his favourite watering hole, the Black Lion, Thomas had a row with an ex-commando officer just back from the front. The officer followed him home and shot at his rented bungalow with a machine gun. The officer was later tried for attempted murder but acquitted. Thomas's true opinion of New Quay may be inferred by spelling Llareggub backwards. In the spring of 2007, filming was under way for a movie based on Thomas' life, *The Best Time of Our Lives*. Some scenes were shot on the beach at New Quay with Keira Knightley and Sienna Miller as the stars.

AROUND NEW QUAY

LLANINA

1 mile E of New Quay off the A486

This tiny village, with a long tradition of fishing, is also associated with the legend of King Ina of England. One day, in the early 8th century, a ship was wrecked on the rocks close to the village during a violent storm. A local fisherman, his wife and daughter, having seen the disaster, rowed out to rescue the stricken sailors. Once safe, the family, unable to understand the language spoken by the shipwrecked strangers, sent for a monk who told them that they had saved King Ina. In thanksgiving, the king built a church from which the present church, **Ina's Church**, takes its name. **Cerrig Ina**, Ina's Stones, can be seen offshore and mark the spot where the original church stood.

ABERAERON

4½ miles NE of New Quay on the A487

Situated at the mouth of the River Aeron, this is a delightful small town with charming Georgian houses, particularly around **Alban Square**. These are the result of astute town planning initiated in the early 19th century by the Reverend Alban Gwynne, who was happy to spend his wife's inheritance on dredging the Aeron estuary and creating this new port with its neat streets and elegant terraces. This was instrumental in turning the settlement from a small fishing hamlet into a bustling port that also became famous for its shipbuilding.

On the quayside, the former Sea Aquarium is where you can buy tickets for boat trips around the bay with a fair chance of spotting dolphins en route.

At the southern end of the town, **Clôs Pengarreg** is a craft centre housed in traditional stone buildings where visitors can see the beautiful products being hand-made and have the opportunity to buy a unique reminder of their time in the town.

179 THE HUNGRY TROUT

New Quay

Renowned seafood restaurant in superb location overlooking Cardigan Bay; B&B also available

see *page 341*

180 FRIENDS COFFEE SHOP

Aberaeron

Popular town centre coffee shop serving wholesome fresh light refreshments.

see *page 342*

Just inland from the town of Aberaeron lies Aberaeron Wildlife Park, the home of llamas, red deer, parrots, owls and Jimmy, who is believed to be the world's only albino crow and who starred in the television series Gormenghast. As well as the animals at the park, there are natural trails, a miniature railway and plenty of other activities to keep all the family entertained.

181 RHOS YR HAFOD INN

Cross Inn

Delightful village inn serving appetising food and real ales.

¶ see page 343

ABERARTH

6 miles NE of New Quay on the A487

Although often bypassed because of the charm of its more illustrious neighbour, Aberaeron, Aberarth is a picturesque village overlooked by **St David's Church**. Founded in the 6th century, and originally hidden from the sea, the church was rebuilt in 1860 but it still contains three early Christian inscribed stones from the 9th and 10th centuries.

PENNANT

8 miles E of New Quay on the B4577

In the 19th century, this village was the home of a recluse named Mari Berllan Piter (Mary of Peter's Orchard). Supposedly granted magical powers, her exploits were legendary: when a miller refused to grind her corn she made his mill wheel turn the wrong way, a young girl who stole an apple from Mari's orchard was forced to walk home backwards and sometimes, it is said, that Mari turned herself into a hare. The ruins of Mari's cottage, known locally as The Witch's Cottage, can still be seen surrounded by her now overgrown orchard.

LLANARTH

3 miles SE of New Quay on the A487

A local story tells that one night the Devil tried to steal the bell from **Llanarth Church**. However, he made such a noise that he woke the

Llanarth Church

vicar who, armed with a bell, a book and a candle, climbed up into the belfry to investigate. By solemnly repeating the name of Christ, the vicar managed to drive the Devil to the top of the tower and forced him to jump off. In the graveyard there is a strangely scarred stone that is said to bear the marks made by the Devil when he landed.

CROSS INN

2 miles S of New Quay on the A486

To the south of the village is **New Quay Honey Farm** which is the largest honey farm in Wales and is housed in an old chapel. The farm attracts more than 35,000 visitors a year and has a shop, tea room and live bee exhibition. Travellers from all over the world have witnessed one of nature's most fascinating processes and sampled at first hand a wonderful range of natural hive products. In 1999 a meadery was added to produce some delicious honey wines which can be bought in the shop.

LAMPETER

Lampeter is best known as the home of University College. Founded in 1822 by Bishop Thomas Burgess of St David's, **St David's College**, as it was first known, is a world renowned ecclesiastical and predominantly Welsh speaking college that is the oldest institution in Wales. The main university buildings include CB Cockerell's original stuccoed quadrangle of buildings dating from 1827 which were designed to mimic an Oxbridge College. Underneath these buildings lies the town's old castle motte. Since 1971, the college has been integrated with the University of Wales - hence its new name **University College** - although the campus still retains its own unique atmosphere.

While the students add a certain bohemian flavour to Lampeter during term time, this is essentially a genteel and very Welsh town with a pleasant mixture of Georgian and Victorian buildings. Perhaps the most striking of these is the Black Lion on the High Street, an 18th century coaching inn complete with original stables and coach house. Also of architectural interest is Falcondale Hall which was built in the early 1800s for the local landowning family, the Hartfords. It is now a luxury hotel.

Back in the 1600s, on what is now Maesyfelin Street, stood the home of the Lloyds of Maesyfelin. When the only daughter of the family, Elen, became engaged to a certain Samuel Pritchard, her four brothers, fearing the loss of their inheritance, tied her lover underneath a horse and galloped him from Lampeter to Llandovery. Samuel died of his injuries and the brothers threw his body in nearby River Teifi. On hearing what had happened Elen was driven mad with sorrow and died soon afterwards. Samuel's father, Rhys, put a curse on the family and, just a short while later, their family house caught fire and burnt to the ground; the eldest brother, out of remorse or perhaps due to the curse, killed his brothers and then himself.

AROUND LAMPETER

PONTRHYDFENDIGAID

15 miles NE of Lampeter on the B4343

Just a short distance from the village, and close to the ford of the Blessed Virgin, stands **Strata Florida Abbey** (CADW, free), a Cistercian house founded in 1164. This austere order was renowned for seeking out remote and isolated sites for its religious establishments and Strata Florida - the vale of Flowers - is one such site. Even though the abbey is in ruins today, it is still an evocative place for visitors. Just two years after its foundation the abbey's lands were

185 THE TEIFI INN

Ffair Rhos

Appealing old hostelry dating back to the 12th century, now serving excellent food and real ales.

¶ see page 346

186 RED LION HOTEL

Pontrhydfendigaid

Former coaching inn offering excellent home-cooked food, real ale and en suite accommodation

¶ ⊨ see page 347

Strata Florida Abbey, Pontrhydfendigaid

overrun by Rhys ap Gryffyd but in 1184 he refounded the abbey; most of the buildings now seen in ruins date from this time. During the 12th and 13th centuries, Strata Florida became one of the most important religious centres in Wales. Some of the last native princes and princesses of Wales were buried here, as was Dafydd ap Gwilym, probably the most famous of all Welsh medieval poets. In 1238, the Welsh princes swore their allegiance to Llywelyn the Great's son, Dafydd, at the abbey. This was also the time when the abbey flourished in terms of wealth, mainly through wool from the sheep that grazed on its vast lands.

After the Dissolution in the 16th century, the abbey and its lands passed through various hands and the ruins today consist mainly of the cloister, a monumental Norman west doorway, and the chapter house by the church that now serves as Pontrhydfendigaid's parish church. In the north transept stands a memorial to the poet Dafydd ap Gwilym. The yew tree that stands amidst the abbey's remains is thought to mark his grave. One legend associated with the abbey suggests that the Holy Grail, which was given to the monks at Glastonbury by Joseph of Aramathea, later ended up at Strata Florida. When the abbey, which formed part of the Nanteos estate, was left to fall into ruins, the cup, which had pieces bitten out of its sides by pilgrims convinced of its healing powers, was stored at Nanteos mansion.

TREGARON

9 miles NE of Lampeter on the A485

This small market town - a meeting place for 19th century drovers - still serves the remote farming communities in the Teifi valley. A stronghold of Welsh language and culture, it's an attractive place with a pleasantly old world atmosphere. Handsome Georgian and Victorian houses surround the market place, together with a fine old drover's inn, the Talbot Hotel. In the centre of the square stands a statue of Henry Richard (1812-1888), the Liberal MP and son of Tregaron, who was a vociferous supporter of disarmament and an advocate of arbitration in international disputes; he became known as the "Apostle of Peace".

In one corner of the square is the **Rhiannon Welsh Gold Centre** which stocks an up-market selection of jewellery based on Celtic designs and made partly from Welsh gold.

Housed in the Old National School, which opened in 1873, the **Tregaron Red Kite Centre and Museum** is an interesting and informative place which is dedicated to the red kite. It has the dual aim of providing people with a better understanding of these beautiful birds of prey and with ensuring their survival in this part of mid-Wales. Visitors to the centre can also see the kites being fed daily here during the winter months. Also on display at the museum are artefacts from Ceredigion Museum that relate specifically to Tregaron and the surrounding area.

The land around Tregaron is sheep country and the town was to become famous for its woollen industry and, in particular, hand-knitted woollen socks. Most of the socks were transported to the mining communities of South Wales,

but David Davies, an engineer from Llandinam, found another use for the wool - he used it to form a stable bed on which to lay the railway across **Cors Caron** bog. Lying to the north of the town this ancient bog is home to rare flora and fauna. The land here was originally covered by a glacier which, at the end of the last Ice Age, melted to create a natural lake which filled with sediment and vegetation. The peat surface grew, creating three distinctive domes above the original lake bed level. The **Old Railway Walk** follows the trackbed of the old Manchester-Milford Haven railway, provides visitors with the chance to observe some of the 170 or so species of bird recorded here, including red kites, buzzards and sparrow hawks. The walk starts from the car park near Maesllyn Farm on the B4343, two miles north of Tregaron.

187 THREE HORSE SHOE INN

Llangeitho
Cosy traditional hostelry with superb cuisine, real ales and separate self-catering accommodation.

❙❙ ⊨ see *page 347*

Mountain Road, Tregaron

139

Popular village inn offering excellent home cooking and comfortable accommodation.

 see page 348

Ffostrasol

Recently refurbished former coaching inn offering quality food, real ales and accommodation.

 see page 349

Prengwyn

Friendly village inn noted for its real ales and good food.

see page 348

LLANDDEWI BREFI

7 miles NE of Lampeter on the B4343

The small community of Llanddewi Brefi (population 500) has become famous as the home of Daffyd - "the only gay in the village" in the TV comedy series *Little Britain*. Residents say the rather ducious fame has changed little, although the village shop does sell T-shirts printed with the tag. But shopkeeper Neil Driver observed "I only sell the *Gay Times* to order, and one hasn't been placed with me yet!"

This traditional country village was host in AD 519, to a synod which was attended by St David. The meeting was called to debate the Pelagian heresy, a doctrine advocating freedom of thought rather than the biblical version of original sin that determined the morality of the time. **St David's Church**, in the village, stands on a mound said to have risen up as St David preached during the synod. The church itself dates from the 13th century and, inside, contains some old inscribed stones: one is known as St David's Staff and another has an inscription in the obscure Ogham language thought to commemorate a heretic of the type that St David was denouncing.

Close by are the sites of several hill forts including **Llanfair Clydogau**, where the Romans mined for silver. They sit beside the Sarn Helen - a military road. The road once connected a gold mine in the south, at Dolaucothi, with a fort at Bremia in the north.

CAPEL DEWI

8½ miles SW of Lampeter on the B4459

Close to the village is **Rock Mills Woollen Mill** which was established in 1890 by John Morgan whose descendants still weave here. The machinery is powered by a waterwheel which also drives a small alternator to provide lighting. The mill once provided power to the neighbouring church. From pure new wool, the mill produces all manner of woollen goods, including bedspreads, blankets and rugs, and it is one of the last traditional mills where the entire process, from fleece to fabric, may be viewed.

LLANDYSUL

11 miles SW of Lampeter on the A486

Set in the deep and picturesque valley of the River Teifi, this traditional little Welsh town was another centre of the woollen industry. Today, this tranquil little town is renowned for its outstanding scenic views, fishing and white water canoeing as well as for the delights of its Victorian town centre. The agricultural nature of the area is reflected in the town's fortnightly livestock market.

Just outside the town, the **National Wool Museum** is a flagship museum in this part of Wales. It recently underwent a major redevelopment and now presents a comprehensive history of the Welsh woollen industry. A working mill on the site can be seen in operation and supports the production of fabrics in traditional Welsh patterns. The extensive displays here include the National Textile Collection.

A few miles up the A486, **Ffostrasol** is the setting for the annual Cnapan Folk Festival, the largest Celtic folk music event on the British mainland.

CILIAU AERON
9 miles NW of Lampeter on the A482

Set in the beautiful Aeron valley with extensive estate and parkland walks, **Llanerchaeron** (National Trust) is an 18th century Welsh gentry estate – a rare survival. Designed and built by John Nash, the house has many unaltered features including a service courtyard with dairy, laundry, brewery and salting house. It gives a wonderful insight into how the Welsh gentry and their staff lived some 200 years ago. Also within the estate are two restored walled gardens and a working organic farm.

CARDIGAN

Once the busiest port in Wales, Cardigan is an ancient borough which received its first charter in 1199 and was at that time a power base of Lord Rhys, one of the last Welsh princes to rule an independent principality. The few remains of **Cardigan Castle**, which stand beside the river, conceal a turbulent history: built in the late 11th or early 12th century by Gryffydd ap Rhys, the fortifications were strengthened around 1170

before it passed into the hands of the Earl of Pembroke in 1240. Thought to be the site of the first Eisteddfod in 1176, the castle fell to Parliament in 1645 during the Civil War. Badly neglected over the years, the castle featured in BBC-TV's *Restoration* series but failed to win enough votes to get the funding it needed. However, a vigorous local campaign continues and the castle is now occasionally open to the public.

The River Teifi, which provides Cardigan with its Welsh name Aberteifi, continues to be fished for trout and some anglers still use the traditional coracle. Dating from pre-Christian times, coracles were once common on many of Britain's rivers and have changed little in design over the centuries. The silting up of the Teifi estuary, along with the arrival of the railway, were the main causes of Cardigan's decline as a major port which had, at one time, more than 300 ships registered here.

However, while the river is no longer at the centre of the town's

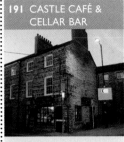

191 CASTLE CAFÉ & CELLAR BAR

Cardigan

Delightfully atmospheric café selling honest-to-goodness food, and Cellar Bar with regular live entertainment.

see page 350

192 THE HIGHBURY GUEST HOUSE & RESTAURANT

Pendre

Splendid late-Victorian villa with 3-star B&B accommodation and excellent restaurant.

see page 352

Teifi Bridge, Cardigan

141

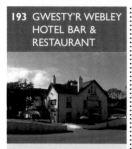
economy it is still a place of charm enhanced by the six-arched **Teifi Bridge** - an ancient structure which was rebuilt in 1726.

Housed in an 18th century warehouse on Teifi Wharf, the **Cardigan Heritage Centre** tells the story of this former county town, from prehistoric times through to the present day. From its origins in the medieval age to its heyday in the 18th and 19th centuries, the port, in particular, is explored through the eyes of those who lived here. In addition to the permanent exhibitions, there is a programme of temporary exhibitions covering a range of topics.

Those looking for performing arts and other cultural events will not be disappointed as the **Theatr Mwldan**, in the town, is one of Wales' leading theatrical venues.

Beside the river, just outside the town, is the **Welsh Wildlife Centre** (free), a nature reserve that provides a variety of habitats, including reed beds, woodland and meadow. As well as an extensive network of footpaths and being home to a surprisingly wide variety of flora and fauna, the reserve also has an excellent modern visitor centre.

AROUND CARDIGAN

ST DOGMAELS

1 mile W of Cardigan on the B4546

Situated on the western banks of the mouth of the River Teifi, it was here that the Lord of the Manor,

St Dogmael's Abbey, St Dogmael's

Robert Martyn, founded **St Dogmael's Abbey** in the 12th century for the monks of the Benedictine order brought over from Tiron in France. An earlier Welsh abbey on the site was sacked by the Vikings. Adjacent to the abbey ruins is a church which features an inscribed Sagranus stone whose markings and Latin inscriptions provided the key to deciphering the ancient Goidelic language. Close to the abbey is **The Mill** (Y Felin), a water-powered flour mill.

GWBERT-ON-SEA

2½ miles N of Cardigan on the B4548

This small resort on the eastern banks of the River Teifi estuary is an excellent place for cliff walking and for looking out over the estuary and observing its wildlife. **Cardigan Island Coastal Farm Park** is an ideal place from which to look out over Cardigan Island from the headland and also to observe the rare choughs that nest on the cliffs. In the caves below, a colony of seals breed and some lucky visitors may also spot Cardigan Bay's bottle-nosed dolphins. The farm is home, too, to friendly farm animals, including goats, sheep, pigs, ponies and ducks, as well as a llama, a wallaby and rare breed cows.

MWNT

3½ miles N of Cardigan off the A487

This beauty spot was on the Pilgrims' Route to Bardsey Island - the burial ground of

over 20,000 Celtic saints - in the north. The tiny **Church of the Holy Cross** dates from around 1400 and stands on the site of a much earlier Celtic church, originally built in a hollow to hide it from view and to protect it from possible raiders coming by sea.

Much of the coastline here, including the cliffs, the rocky headland and the safe family beach, is owned by the National Trust. This area is a geological SSSI (Site of Special Scientific Interest) and is part of the Ceredigion Heritage Coast; it is especially rich in maritime flora. The bay was the site of a battle in 1155, when Fleming invaders were repelled by the local forces.

FELINWYNT

3½ miles NE of Cardigan off the A487

The village is home to the **Felinwynt Rainforest and Butterfly Centre** where, in a large

To the north of the village of Gwbert-on-Sea, and lying some 200 yards offshore, is Cardigan Island, a nature reserve to which there is no unauthorised access and which is inhabited by a flock of wild Soay sheep.

Felinwynt Rainforest and Butterfly Centre, Felinwynt

194 CARTWS CAFÉ

Penbryn Beach

Charming café serving light meals through the day and delicious home-made dishes in the evening.

see page 352

195 EMLYN CAFÉ

Tanygroes

Licensed family-run café offering a wide choice of breakfasts, lunches and light meals.

see page 352

196 THE SHIP INN

Llangrannog

Beautifully sited seaside inn in picturesque village offering outstanding cuisine and real ales.

see page 353

197 CASTELL MALGWYN HOTEL

Llechryd

Classic Georgian mansion in 8 acres of grounds offering first class cuisine, gracious surroundings and en suite rooms.

see page 354

tropical house, visitors are transported to the jungle to see the beautiful free-flying butterflies that live amidst the exotic plants. Sounds recorded in the Peruvian Amazon intensify the tropical atmosphere. There is also a rainforest exhibition, which explains the delicate ecology of this interesting habitat, a tea room and a gift shop.

ABERPORTH

6 miles NE of Cardigan on the B4333

The original village of Aberporth consisted of small, single storeyed cottages with thick mud walls and thatched roofs that reflected the simple and hard lives of those living in this fishing and farming community At one time Aberporth became famous for its herring industry as great shoals of the fish came to feed and spawn in the shallow waters of this sheltered part of the Cardigan Bay coast. Today, the village is a small yet thriving resort that is popular with yachtsmen.

A little way up the coast is the National Trust's beach at **Penbryn**, an SSSI, part of the Ceredigion Heritage Coast, and a good spot for insect, bird and dolphin spotting.

The approach to this popular, sandy beach is by way of Hoffnant Valley from the Trust's car park at Llanborth Farm where a shop, café and WCs are open in season. The valley is known locally as Cwm Lladron, Robbers Valley, probably because of old-time smuggling connections.

TANYGROES

8 miles NE of Cardigan on the A487

Just north of the village**, The Internal Fire Museum of Power** explores the history of the stationary internal combustion engine in industry and agriculture. Exhibits are run daily ranging from small farm engines through to 25-ton diesel engines. One of the oldest diesel engines in the world is on display here.

LLANGRANOG

9½ miles NE of Cardigan on the B4334

Lying in a narrow valley and rather reminiscent of a Cornish fishing village with its narrow streets dropping to the sea, Llangranog is one of the most attractive villages along the Ceredigion coast and its small beach can become crowded in summer. The headland and cliffs to the north of the village (now the property of the National Trust) offer excellent walks and dramatic scenery. The sheltered coves around Llangranog helped to sustain a thriving shipbuilding industry but they also proved perfect landing and hiding places for contraband and the area was rife with smuggling activity.

To the east of the village lies the **Walled Garden at Pigeonsford**, a Georgian walled garden which has been replanted with botanical collections of herbaceous plants and shrubs as well as vegetables and fruits. Maintained as a working garden, the walled garden is set in large and less formal grounds that

144

include shrubbery, woodland and riverside walks.

HENLLAN

11½ miles SE of Cardigan on the B4334

This village is home to the **Teifi Valley Railway**, another of Wales' famous little trains. This narrow gauge railway, which originally served the slate quarries, was created from a section of the Great Western Railway (also known as God's Wonderful Railway) that served the rural areas of West Wales. Today's passengers can enjoy a 40 minute steam train journey through this delightful valley. At the Henllan terminus there are plenty of attractions to keep the whole family amused: woodland walks, crazy golf, the station tearooms and a gift and souvenir shop.

Also at Henllan are the remains of a World War II Italian prisoner of war camp. The church here was built by the Italians and was constructed of anything that was available and would normally be considered as rubbish - tin, hardwood, paper and so on. The results are amazing. The church can be visited by appointment.

198 PENLLWYNDU INN

Llangoedmor

Traditional village inn serving good home-made food and real ales; secluded beer garden.

see page 354

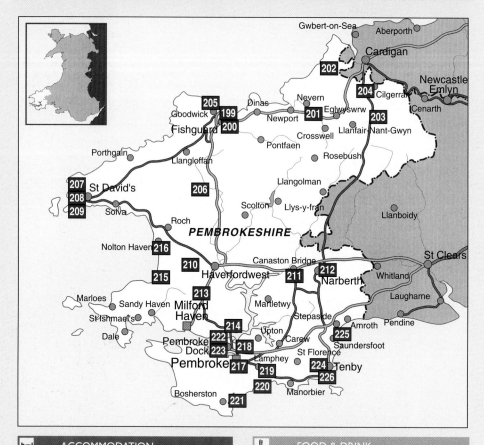

ACCOMMODATION	**FOOD & DRINK**

Pembrokeshire

Pembrokeshire, which is known as Sir Benfro in Welsh, is home to Britain's only coastal national park - the Pembrokeshire Coast National Park. Running right around the ruggedly beautiful south western tip of Wales, around St Brides Bay and up along the north facing coast almost to Cardigan, the Park also includes quiet fishing villages, the huge cliffs at Castlemartin, sweeping golden beaches and small, often busy harbours. Although not strictly on the coast, the labyrinthine Cleddau river system also lies within the Park's boundaries and here there are delightful little villages such as Cresswell and Carew as well as the superb sheltered harbour of Milford Haven.

Offshore there are various islands, including Grassholm, Ramsey, Skokholm and Skomer, which have changed little since they were named by Viking invaders. Many are now bird and wildlife sanctuaries of international importance. Grassholm is home to thousands of gannets, Skokholm has Manx shearwaters, Skomer has shearwaters and puffins. Ramsey harbours such species as choughs and the red-legged crow, and is also the resting place of many Welsh saints. One island, Caldey, has for more than 1500 years

Marloe Sands and Gateholm Island

been the home of a religious community which continues today to live a quiet and austere life. Between their devotions, the monks of Caldey scrape a living from the land and are famous for their range of perfumes and toiletries inspired by the island's wild flowers. Pembrokeshire is the home of the corgi, which was brought to the notice of the Kennel Club by Captain Jack Howell. He presented Princess Elizabeth with her first corgi, and the rest, as they say, is history.

FISHGUARD

Situated at the mouth of the River Gwaun, from which the town takes its Welsh name Abergwaun, the geography of Fishguard can be somewhat confusing to visitors. The picturesque old harbour, a pretty little quayside lined with fishermen's cottages, is Lower Fishguard, which was the location for the fictional seaside town of Llareggub used in the filming in the 1970s of Dylan Thomas' play, *Under Milk Wood*, starring Richard Burton. The new harbour, built at the beginning of the 20th century, lies across the bay at Goodwick and it is from here that the ferries depart for Ireland. On the high ground between the two harbours lies the main town of Upper Fishguard, a bustling place packed with shops, restaurants and pubs.

It was here, in February 1797, that the last invasion of Britain took place when a poorly equipped band of Frenchman landed at Carregwastad Point. Under the command of an American officer, Colonel William Tate (who hoped to start a peasants' rebellion), the 1400 strong French expeditionary force - mostly ex-convicts - stole drinks and looted the local farms. Unchecked by the local militia, the unruly invaders set up headquarters at a nearby farm and, according to local tradition, several local women, dressed in red cloaks, advanced on the French soldiers. The women were led by Jemima Nicholas who carried a pitchfork, and the drunken invaders fled in terror mistaking the ladies for the British army. The French retreated to the beach below Goodwick, where they formally surrendered to Lord Cawdor just two days after landing. Jemima Nicholas, who is said to have captured 12 Frenchmen singlehanded, became famous as the 'General of the Red Army'. She died in 1832 and is buried in St Mary's Church.

In 1997, to mark the bicentenary of this bizarre event, Elizabeth Cramp RWS was commissioned to design **The Last Invasion Embroidered Tapestry** (free). Worked by more than 70 embroiderers, the 100-feet long tapestry is in the style of the famous Bayeux Tapestry and depicts scenes from the invasion. It now has its own gallery in Fishguard's recently renovated Town Hall.

AROUND FISHGUARD

DINAS

3½ miles NE of Fishguard on the A487

The village is situated at the base of **Dinas Island (NT)** which is, in fact, a promontory that culminates in Dinas Head. At the end of the Ice Age it was indeed an island but over the millennia has gradually moved westward to join up with the mainland. The headland is an important nesting site for sea birds, and grey and Atlantic seals can often be seen swimming offshore.

NEWPORT

6½ miles E of Fishguard on the A487

Spread across a hillside that falls gently to the estuary of the Afon Nyfer river, Newtown is an engaging place that is well geared up for tourists with a range of good accommodation, restaurants and pubs. As its name would suggest, Newport was once an important port; it had a brisk wool trade until the time of the great plague, when trade was diverted to Fishguard. Newport was also the capital of the Marcher Lordship of Cemmaes - the only one not to have been abolished by Henry VIII. The people of Newport still elect their mayor annually and each August the mayor leads the ceremony of 'Beating of the Bounds' when he circles the town's boundaries on horseback. The Lords' Castle (private), which was built in the 13th century, has now been incorporated into a mansion house.

Newport's former school now houses the **West Wales Eco Centre** (free) whose aim is the advancement of public education in all aspects of energy conservation and energy use. It hosts various exhibitions and offers advice on aspects of sustainable living.

Newport is an excellent base from which to explore the Preseli Hills to the south. It was from these mountains that the famous bluestones were taken to Stonehenge, an incredible feat of engineering involving transporting 8-tonne stones along rivers and over land to Salisbury Plain. In 1995, a ready-cut bluestone was discovered in the river near Milford haven. It is assumed that the mighty pillar had fallen off the barge during the long journey to Wiltshire some 4000 years ago.

NEVERN

8 miles E of Fishguard on the B4582

Nevern's **Church of St Brynach** is dedicated to the 5th century Irish saint whose cell was on nearby **Carn Ingli** - the Hill of Angels. Inside the church are two interesting carved stones. The Maglocunus Stone, dating from the 5th century, commemorates Maglocunus, the son of Clutor and it bears both Latin and Ogham inscriptions. The Cross Stone is incised with a very early Celtic cross and dates from the 10th century. Outside in the churchyard with its ancient yews stands one of the finest Celtic crosses in Wales - **St Brynach's Cross**. Dating from the 10th or 11th century, the cross stands some 13 feet tall. According

• *Just to the north of Newport is Carreg Coetan Arthur, a burial chamber reputed to hold the remains of King Arthur.* •

201 THE SALUTATION INN

Felindre Farchog

Outstanding hotel in beautiful riverside location offering excellent cuisine and 3-star en suite accommodation.

⊨ ¶ see page 357

Church of St Brynach, Nevern

to tradition, the first cuckoo to be heard each year in Pembrokeshire sings from the top of the cross on St Brynach's Day (7th April). Another curiosity in the churchyard is the 'bleeding yew'. One of the trees exudes a browny-red sap from its bark. Local tradition asserts that it will continue 'bleeding' until Welsh-born lord of the manor rules once again from Nevern Castle whose overgrown and tumbledown ruins stand high above the village to the northwest.

EGLWYSWRW

11½ miles E of Fishguard on the A487

To the west of the village lies **Castell Henllys**, an Iron Age fort that is still being excavated by archaeologists. While the dig is continuing throughout the summer months, visitors to this late prehistoric site can also see the thatched roundhouses and outbuildings created to give as true as possible an insight into the lives of Iron Age man. Events throughout the season help to portray the wide spectrum of Celtic culture, from story-telling and craft demonstrations to the celebration of ancient festivals. A sculpture trail through woodland and the river valley features works inspired by tales from The Mabinogion.

CILGERRAN

15 miles NE of Fishguard off the A478

The substantial remains of **Cilgerran Castle**, one the most picturesque in Wales, can be seen sitting on a rocky promontory overlooking the River Teifi. A tranquil site today, this land was once hotly disputed territory and the castle's defences reflect this - there are almost sheer drops on two sides of the building, while the 13th century twin round towers and curtain walls protect the flank away from the cliff. The building of the castle is thought to have begun around 1093 but it was strengthened by Gerald de Windsor, to whom it was granted by Henry I. Thereafter it changed hands many times, being partially sacked by Rhys ap Gryffydd in 1164, retaken by the Earl of Pembroke in 1204 and finally falling to Llywelyn the Great in 1233.

The castle is forever associated with the legend of Princess Nest, the Welsh Helen of Troy. In 1109 she was abducted by the besotted Owain, son of the Prince of Powys, who also imprisoned her husband, Gerald of Pembroke. Gerald escaped by slithering down a toilet waste chute inside the castle walls.

Cilgerran Castle was one of the earliest major tourist attractions in Wales - in the 18th and 19th centuries it was fashionable to take a river excursion to the ruins from Cardigan. The romantic ruins provided inspiration to artists as distinguished as JMW Turner and Richard Wilson.

From the point where the A478, A484 and A487 meet, brown and white tourist signs lead to the **Welsh Wildlife Centre**, an excellent place for spotting birds and animals, wild flowers and butterflies. Wild footpaths pass through woodland, reed beds, meadows, marsh and riverside, providing the chance to see a vast variety of wildlife in different habitats. More than 130 species of birds have been recorded, and more than 20 mammals, including otter, red deer, voles, badgers and bats.

The River Teifi is one of the few rivers in Britain where fishing from coracles can still be seen. In August, coracle races are held on the river at Cilgerran.

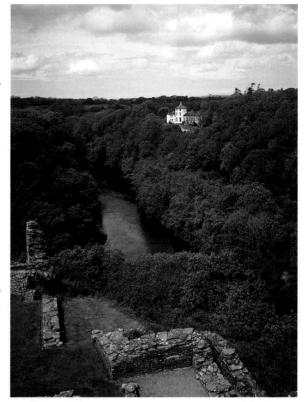

Cilgerran Castle

CROSSWELL

10 miles E of Fishguard on the B4329

This village, on the northern slopes of the Preseli Hills, is home to one of the grandest megalithic remains in Wales, **Pentre Ifan Burial Chamber** (CADW). An ancient chamber with a huge 16-feet capstone, the monument is made of the same Preseli bluestones that somehow found their way to Stonehenge on Salisbury Plain.

PONTFAEN

4½ miles SE of Fishguard off the B4313

The village lies on the western edge of the **Preseli Hills**, whose highest point, **Foel Cwmcerwyn** (1,759ft) lies to the southeast; the views stretch as far as Snowdonia to the north and the Gower Peninsula to the south. These hills have seen many inhabitants come and go and they are littered with prehistoric sites. There are Iron Age hill forts, Bronze Age burial cairns and standing stones scattered along the 'Golden Road', the ancient bridleway across the range.

In the foothills of the Preselis is the **Gwaun Valley**, a truly hidden place that runs from the hills to Fishguard. Some of the locals in this area still celebrate New Year on 12 January, in keeping with the custom that predates the introduction of the Gregorian calendar in 1752.

LLANGOLMAN

11½ miles SE of Fishguard off the A4313

Housed in a renovated 18th century corn mill, **The Slate Workshop** is a place where the art

151

205 GLENDOWER HOTEL

Goodwick

Long-established family-run hotel with a fine restaurant, well-stocked bar and comfortable en suite accommodation.

 see page 360

206 STONE HALL HOTEL & RESTAURANT

Welsh Hook

Historic country house in 10 acres of grounds offering genuine French cuisine and quality en suite rooms.

see page 360

of handcrafting quality Welsh slate items continues. A wide range of articles is made here, including high quality plaques, sundials, clocks and objets d'art. Many illustrate the great skill required to work and carve the slate.

To the south of the village stands another interesting building, **Penrhos Cottage**, which is one of the few lasting examples of an 'overnight' house. If a man, with the help of his friends, could build a dwelling between sunset and sunrise, he was entitled to all the land that lay within, literally, a stone's throw from the door. This particular 'overnight' house dates from the 19th century and still contains the original furnishings.

GOODWICK

1 mile W of Fishguard off the A487

This once small fishing village is now effectively the base for Fishguard harbour which was built here between 1894 and 1906 by the Fishguard and Rosslare Railways and Harbours Company to provide a sea link between southwest Wales and Ireland. Still offering a busy ferry service today, Goodwick is older than it first appears. The settlement was known to ancient inhabitants as Gwlad hud a Lledrith - the Land of Mystery and Enchantment. The surrounding countryside certainly lives up to this name, although the tales told by James Wade, one of Pembrokeshire's best known storytellers, are rather far fetched, but nonetheless delightful. On one occasion Wade, who died in 1887,

recounted that, while he was fishing on Goodwick beach, a great carrion crow swooped out of the sky and carried him in its beak across the sea to Ireland. On reaching land, the crow dropped Wade and he landed in a cannon where he spent the night. As he was waking the next morning, the cannon was fired and Wade was rocketed across St George's Channel and he landed beside his fishing rod in the exact spot from which he had been plucked!

STRUMBLE HEAD

4 miles W of Fishguard off the A487

This huge headland, with its lighthouse warning ships off the cliffs on the approach to Fishguard harbour, offers some spectacular coastal scenery as well as an outlook over the great sweep of Cardigan Bay. Just to the east lies **Carregwastad Point**, a remote headland which was the landing place of the ill-fated French invasion of Britain in the 18th century. Also to the east is **Good Hope** (National Trust), a traditional farmed landscape with an unusually wide variety of plant life.

LLANGLOFFAN

6 miles SW of Fishguard off the A487

This village is home to the **Cheese Centre** where, in the heart of the Pembrokeshire countryside, traditional Welsh farmhouse cheese is made by the Downey family on their farm. The cheese-making process - from milk to the finished cheese - begins at 6am and visitors are welcome to view the process from 10am onwards. Llangloffan cheese is sold in specialist shops around the world but visitors to the centre have the chance to sample the cheese at the farm's tea rooms, as well as to look round the museum and meet the friendly farm animals.

PORTHGAIN

10 miles SW of Fishguard off the A487

As well as being a natural beauty spot, the sheltered harbour at Porthgain has added interest as the harbourside is dominated by the shell of a 19th century brickworks. This monument to the village's industrial heritage stands close to remnants from Porthgain's heyday as a slate and granite exporting port. Many buildings as far afield as London and Liverpool have Porthgain granite in their construction. Nowadays, it is difficult to imagine the hectic scenes of around a century ago when the harbour would have been packed with boats queuing for their cargoes of stone and brick needed for Britain's building boom. The harbour's almost unique personality has led it to being used as a location by film-makers.

ST DAVID'S

16 miles SW of Fishguard off the A487

Although it enjoys the status of a city because of its cathedral, St David's is actually an attractive large village. It was here, in the 6th century, that St David founded a religious order and on this site, in 1176, the magnificent **St David's Cathedral** was completed. It stands

in a deep hollow below the streets so that not even its square 125ft high tower can be seen above the rooftops. The cathedral is approached by way of the medieval Tower Gate, the only one of the original four city gates to have survived. It contains an exhibition about the history of the city. From the Gate, a flight of steps, known as the 39 Steps after the Church of England's 39 Articles of belief, leads to the cathedral entrance. The undoubted highlight of the interior is the oak roof which displays wonderfully ornate carvings by 15th century craftsmen. Other treasures include an intricate 14th century rood screen, the exquisite 16th century fan tracery roof in Bishop Vaughan's Chapel, and some saintly bones which are believed to be those of St Caradoc. In 1120, Pope Calixtus II decreed that two pilgrimages to St David's were equivalent to one to Rome and successive British monarchs, from William the Conqueror to Queen

207 THE CITY INN

St David's

Popular city centre inn offering real ale, peak season food and all year round en suite rooms.

see page 361

208 THE WATERINGS

St David's

4-star en suite accommodation in quiet location just a short walk from the city centre.

see page 361

St David's Bishop's Palace and Cathedral

St David's

Imposing medieval palace
stands in a grassy hollow
next to purple-stoned St
Davids Cathedral.

🏛 *see page 361*

Elizabeth II, have worshipped here. The Queen also has a special seat reserved for her in the cathedral and it was from here that Maundy Money was distributed for the first time in Wales.

On the other side of the river, across from the cathedral and in the same grassy hollow, stand the ruins of **St David's Bishop's Palace**, a once imposing building. Even in its present ruined state, it still conveys the wealth and influence of the Church in medieval times. Most of the Palace's construction was overseen by Bishop Henry de Gower in the mid-1300s and he spared no expense on creating this lavish residence, which he felt befitted a leader of both the Church and State. There were two complete sets of state rooms at the Palace set around a courtyard; de Gower used one for his private business and the other for ceremonial entertaining. The palace fell into disrepair in the 16th century after the incumbent bishop stripped the roof of its lead in order to pay for his five daughters' dowries.

In August 2002, St David's hosted the National Eisteddfod, one of the highlights of which was the induction of the Archbishop-designate of Canterbury, Dr Rowan Williams, into the Gorsedd of Bards, a historic order of Druids. The ceremony was held in a circle of standing stones fashioned, like the stones at Stonehenge, from Pembrokeshire rock. The ceremony involved the singing of Welsh Christian hymns and the Welsh National Anthem, the reading of a citation by the Arch-Druid and the wielding of a giant ceremonial sword - a burdensome task entrusted to Druid Ray Gravell, a former Welsh rugby international. Dr Williams is the third Archbishop of Wales to be a member of the Gorsedd. Speaking Welsh is a prerequisite for consideration for nomination, with one exception - the Queen.

Just outside the city, in a stunningly beautiful spot overlooking the sea, are **St Non's Well** and the ruins of **St Non's Chapel**. The bay, too, is named after St David's mother - St Non - and legend has it that David was born here during a great storm in around AD 520. The waters of St Non's Well are said to have special powers for healing diseases of the eye and it was much visited during the Middle Ages by pilgrims to St David's. David's father was the chieftain Sant, his grandfather Ceredig, king of the region around Cardigan. Little is known about David, save that he received a formal education, gained great authority in the church and moved the seat of ecclesiastical government from Caerleon to Mynyw, now St David's. St David is

St Non's Well, St David's

154

a central figure in one of the many legends concerning how the leek came to be adopted as the national emblem of Wales. The legend states that just before a battle against the Saxons he advised the Britons to wear a leek in their caps to distinguish them from the enemy. St David's Day, March 1st, is the traditional national day of the Welsh, when Welsh people all over the world wear the national emblem, the leek, or the other national emblem, the daffodil. The Welsh words for leek and daffodil are the same (*cenhinen* means leek, *cenhinen pedr* means daffodil), which could explain why both are national emblems.

Another coastal beauty spot, which is also steeped in legend, is **St Justinian's**, a rock-bound harbour that is home to the St David's Lifeboat Station. Justinian was a 6th century hermit who retreated across to **Ramsey Island**, a short distance offshore, to devote himself to God. A strict disciplinarian, he must have been too severe with his followers as they eventually rebelled and cut off his head! Justinian is then said to have walked across the waters of Ramsey Sound, back to the mainland, with his head in his arms. Ramsey is a Norse name, a legacy of the Dark Ages when this part of the coast was terrorised by Viking invaders. Today, the island is an RSPB reserve that is home to an abundance of wildlife. Boat trips round the island offer visitors the chance to observe the numerous sea birds and the colonies of grey seals. Ramsey has the greatest

concentration of grey seals among Pembrokeshire's estimated seal population of 5,000.

SOLVA
16 miles SW of Fishguard on the A487

Situated at the end of a long inlet and well protected from the sometimes stormy waters of St Bride's Bay, Solva harbour is one of the most sheltered in Wales. Green hills roll down to the quayside and this picturesque view was the last sight of Wales for many 19th century emigrants who sailed from Solva to America for 10 shillings - the price of a one way ticket. Now no longer such a busy port, Solva is a charming old seafaring village that boasts a good range of craft shops. **Solva Woollen Mill,** in the beautiful valley of the River Solfach, has been in continuous production since it opened in 1907. It now specialises in carpets and rugs, and visitors can usually see weaving in progress.

HAVERFORDWEST

This old county town, with its pleasant rural surrounding, stands on the banks of the labyrinthine Cleddau river system and is more or less in the centre of Pembrokeshire. Lining the steep streets of this hilly town are some fine Georgian buildings that date back to the days when Haverfordwest was a prosperous port trading largely with Bristol and Ireland.

However, the town predates this trading boom by several centuries and its unusual name is a

In the foothills of the Preselis is the Gwaun Valley, a truly hidden place that runs from the hills to Fishguard. Some of the locals in this area still celebrate New Year on 12 January, in keeping with the custom that predates the introduction of the Gregorian calendar in 1752.

legacy of Viking raids. Set on a hill overlooking the River Cleddau is the striking landmark of **Haverfordwest Castle** which was built around 1120 by Gilbert de Clare. The town grew up around the fortress and throughout the 12th and 13th centuries it saw various noble residents including Gryffydd ap Rhys, Henry II and Edward I.

Haverfordwest also saw fluctuating fortunes during the Civil War as the town changed hands several times before it was finally taken by Parliament's General Laugharne in 1645. He ransacked the castle and the tumbledown remains offer little of interest apart from the former Governor's house which is now home to the town's **Museum and Art Gallery**.

The remains of a **Priory Church**, founded by Augustinian Canons in the early 13th century, can be found by the Western Cleddau river. Excavations of the priory land have revealed that there were gardens here in the cloister and also between the priory buildings and the river. The riverside gardens, which were laid out in the mid-15th century, provide a rare example of the sort of garden that is often seen in medieval manuscripts and the narrow raised beds have been replanted with plant species appropriate to the period.

Close by is a strange, ghostly border that cannot be seen. It is known locally as the **Landsker** (or land scar) it divides the English speaking 'little England beyond Wales' of south Pembrokeshire from the Welsh speaking north. This abrupt division of the county can be traced back to early medieval times when Norman invasions into these parts paved the way for Anglo Saxon and Flemish immigrants.

A line of castles was built from Amroth right across to Roch and, although the Landsker is an invisible border, its significance has been profound in the past. It was unthinkable that a marriage should take place between a man and a woman from different sides of the line even though they may have lived only a short distance apart.

AROUND HAVERFORDWEST

SCOLTON

4½ miles NE of Haverfordwest on the B4329

Scolton Manor House is a small country house dating from around 1840. Its interior provides interesting insights into the lifestyle of a fairly wealthy 19th century family. The house, stable block and exhibition hall form part of the **Pembrokeshire County Museum** and feature a number of displays that illustrate the history of this south-western region of Wales. Outside, there's a Carriage House displaying a collection of local artefacts, including traps. The surrounding **Country Park** has lovely landscaped grounds, nature trails, picnic areas and a play area. There's also an award - winning **Visitor Centre** with an exhibition that looks to the future, highlighting in particular various green issues and the wildlife of the surrounding park.

LLYS-Y-FRAN

7½ miles NE of Haverfordwest off the B4329

The impressive dam built to form **Llys-y-fran Reservoir** in the 1960s has been constructed in sympathy with the surrounding countryside and, when it was officially opened in 1972 by Princess Margaret, the reservoir was able to meet the growing needs of the county's population and of the oil refineries at Milford Haven. Surrounded by the glorious **Country Park**, which lies in the shadow of the Preseli Hills to the north, there is a seven-mile perimeter path around the reservoir that provides an opportunity to possibly see some of the local inhabitants, including foxes, badgers, mink, squirrels and otters. The fishing on the reservoir is some of the best in Wales. It is regularly stocked with rainbow trout and has a steady population of brown trout.

Wilson Castle, Narberth

CANASTON BRIDGE

7 miles E of Haverfordwest on the A40

To the south of the village can be found two very different attractions. **Blackpool Mill**, beside the Eastern Cleddau river, dates from the early 19th century and it is one of the finest examples of a water powered mill in Britain. Further south and hidden among trees is **Oakwood**, Wales' premier theme park. It boasts Europe's longest watercoaster, biggest wooden rollercoaster and largest skycoaster. As well as the outdoor rides there is an all-weather complex with a multitude of games, puzzles and rides and also Playtown, which is aimed at younger children.

NARBERTH

9½ miles E of Haverfordwest on the A478

This agreeable little town set on a steep hill has become something of a magnet for shoppers because of its up-market shops and art galleries. According to The Mabinogion, Arberth (its Welsh name) was where Pwyll, Prince of Dyfed, held his court. **Wilson Castle**, in the southern part of the town, is a successor to the original fortification here. Only a few fragments still stand of the castle rebuilt in 1264 by Sir Andrew Perrot and dismantled following the Civil War.

211 THE BUSH INN

Robeston Wathen

Welcoming family-run hostelry with glowing reputation for its food; also serving real ales.

see page 363

212 THE ANGEL INN

Narberth

Popular town centre inn with excellent food, real ales and en suite rooms.

see page 364

157

213 WINDSOR HOTEL

Johnston

Welcoming family-run hotel with great home cooking and en suite accommodation.

see page 365

214 THE JOLLY SAILOR

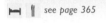
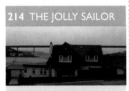

Burton

Riverside inn in sensational location serving real ales and top quality cuisine; spacious garden, children's play area and aviary.

see page 366

The tomb of Sir William Hamilton can be seen in the graveyard of St Katharine's Church in Milford Haven, while inside the church are a bible and prayer book presented by Lord Nelson.

MARLETWY

6 miles SE of Haverfordwest off the A4075

Cwm Deri Vineyard, to the south of Martletwy and set in the Valley of the Oaks, is the ideal place to see vines growing from spring through to the autumn harvest. At the vineyard shop visitors can purchase estate grown vintage wines, fruit wines and liqueurs. For younger members of the family, the vineyard is home to some rescued donkeys and there is also a teddy bears' hideaway.

THE RHOS

3½ miles SE of Haverfordwest off the A40

East of the Cleddau toll bridge lies the tidal estuary formed by the confluence of the Western and Eastern Cleddau rivers, into which also flow the Rivers Cresswell and Carew. Winding a silvery ribbon through the rural landscape, it passes some of the Pembrokeshire Coast National Park's most beautiful scenery. Yet this area is so often overlooked by visitors that is has become known as the Secret Waterway.

The Rhos, the only village in the ancient parish of Slebach, overlooks the Eastern Cleddau and here, close to the river, stands **Picton Castle**, the historic home of the Philipps family. It is still lived in by the direct descendants of Sir John Wogan, who had the castle built in the 13th century. Although the principal rooms were remodelled in the mid-18th century, some medieval features remain. In the 1790s, the 1st Lord Milford

added the wing that now includes the superb dining room and drawing room.

The castle is also home to an **Art Gallery** with a permanent exhibition of paintings by Graham Sutherland. Outside, the gardens are equally impressive and include a walled garden with fish pond, rosebeds, culinary and medicinal herbs and herbaceous borders. In the extensive **Woodland Garden** there is a fine collection of woodland shrubs in among the ancient oaks, beeches, redwoods and other mature trees.

MILFORD HAVEN

6½ miles SW of Haverfordwest on the A40

As well as being the name of the town, Milford Haven is also the name of the huge natural harbour here. Described by Nelson as "the finest port in Christendom", the harbour offers some of the best shelter in the world to large ships as it is some 10 miles long by up to two miles broad. Norsemen used the harbour, as did both Henry II and King John who set sail from here to conquer Ireland, but it was Sir William Hamilton (husband of Lord Nelson's Lady Emma) who, having inherited two nearby manors, saw the potential of the Haven as a major harbour. Hamilton was away in Naples as an Envoy Extraordinary so he appointed his nephew RF Greville to establish the town around the harbour. Greville contracted a Frenchman, J-L Barrallier, to lay out the town and dockyard in a square pattern that can still be seen today. Although the docks, completed in 1888, failed to attract the hoped-for larger ships, the Neyland trawler fleet moved here and by the beginning of the 20th century, Milford Haven had become one of the country's leading fishing ports. During both World Wars, the Haven was busy with Atlantic convoys but after 1945 there was a decline and trawling also began to disappear. However, since the 1960s Milford Haven has developed as a major oil port and is still used by the leading oil companies. New natural gas terminals and storage facilities have been built and work starts soon on a new power station on the north shore of the Milford Haven waterway.

Aptly housed in a former whale oil warehouse that dates from 1797, the **Milford Haven Museum** has a range of displays that follow the fortunes of the town and dockyard including hands-on exhibits tracing the town's history from a whaling port to a premier oil terminal.

SANDY HAVEN

8 miles SW of Haverfordwest off the B4327

The sheltered creek in this lovely village has been described as truly idyllic. Many birds can be seen feeding here., particularly at low tide in the spring and autumn, The picturesque banks of the creek are heavily clad with trees and a path from the village provides walkers with an excellent view of the entrance to Milford Haven harbour.

ST ISHMAEL'S

9 miles SW of Haverfordwest off the B4327

This small village on the Marloes and Dale Peninsula is named after a colleague of the 6th century St Teilo. Close by is evidence of even earlier inhabitants of the area. Just half a mile away stands the **Long Stone**, the tallest standing stone in the Pembrokeshire Coast National Park.

DALE

11 miles SW of Haverfordwest off the B4327

A delightful little sailing and watersports centre, Dale lays claim to being one of the windiest places in Britain - on average, it endures gale force winds on more than 30 days each year. However, on the other side of the climatic coin, Dale is also one of the sunniest places in the country with an annual average of 1800 hours a year - or five hours a day! To the south of the village, on the southern tip of the peninsula, is **St Ann's Head** where a lighthouse and coastguard station keep a close watch over the dangerous rocky shores at the entrance to Milford Haven.

MARLOES

11 miles SW of Haverfordwest off the B4327

This inland village, on the road to **Wooltrack Point**, has a sandy bay to the southwest with **Gateholm Island** at its western extremity. Only a true island at high tide, the name comes from the Norse for Goat Island and there are traces here of a possible monastic settlement.

During the 14th century, Sir Rhys ap Thomas of Carew Castle is said to have promised Richard III that if Henry Tudor passed through Pembroke it would be by riding over his body. When Henry landed at Mill Bay, to salve his conscience, Sir Rhys lay under Mullock Bridge (between St Ishmael's and Marloes) as Henry rode over the river and then Sir Rhys rode quickly to Carew Castle to welcome Henry.

159

Marloe Sands and Gateholm Island

215 THE GALLEON INN

Broad Haven

Traditional pub in idyllic location offering appetising home-cooked food and real ales.

❙❘ see page 365

216 NOLTON HAVEN QUALITY COTTAGES

Nolton Haven

Holiday properties ranging from 5-star cottages to caravans, from farmhouse B&Bs to the local hotel.

⊨ see page 367

160

Right up until the end of the 19th century the ancient custom of hunting the wren, which was supposed to embody the evils of winter, was followed throughout Wales. In Pembrokeshire, the hunting took place on Twelfth Night and the captured bird would be placed in a carved and beribboned 'wren house' and paraded around the village by men singing of the hunt. A particularly fine example of a wren house, from Marloes, can be found in the Welsh Folk Museum, at St Fagans, near Cardiff.

Close by, at Martin's Haven, boats leave for Skomer and Skokholm Islands. Skomer Island National Nature Reserve and Skokholm and Grassholm provide some of the best and most spectacular birdwatching anywhere in Britain.

NOLTON HAVEN

6½ miles W of Haverfordwest off the A487

The village sits at around the centre of St Brides Bay and the coastline here has steep, undulating cliffs and sandy beaches which have remained completely unspoilt despite being within easy reach of Haverfordwest and Milford Haven. As part of the Pembrokeshire Coast National Park, the coastline here is rich in outstanding natural beauty with a wide variety of natural amenities available to the holidaymaker including various short and longer distance footpaths from where an abundance of wildlife, sea birds and wild flowers can be seen. This area is a mecca for walkers, bird watchers, surfers, swimmers and sailors.

ROCH

5½ miles W of Haverfordwest off the A487

Found on a rocky outcrop overlooking the village and the surrounding plain, are the remains of **Roch Castle**, which was originally built in the 13th century by the feudal Lord of Roch, Adam de la Roche. A local story tells that de la Roche was told by a witch that he would be killed by a snake, but that if he could pass a year in safety, then he need never fear her prophecy. Accordingly, de la Roche had the castle built in such a way as to be out of reach of any snake and constructed on this particularly well defended site. His year free from snakes began and de la Roche moved into the top floor of the castle and remained there, in constant fear, for a year. The very last night of his self-enforced imprisonment was bitterly cold and someone sent a basket of firewood to the castle to help Adam pass the night in comfort. The basket was taken to his room and, as de la Roche was putting the logs on the fire, an adder crawled out from among the logs and bit him. The next morning, Adam de la Roche was found dead in front of his hearth.

PEMBROKE

This historic town on the southern side of the Pembroke River is notable for its long and unbroken line of well-preserved medieval town walls, dominated by the mighty fortress of **Pembroke Castle**. The castle was founded in the 11th century by the Montgomerys, who established the first timber castle on a rocky crag above the River Cleddau. The present structure was built between 1189 and 1245 and became the focal point for the control of "Little England Beyond Wales" as this area became known. The famous round keep is nearly 80ft tall with walls 19ft thick and the towers, turrets, oak-beamed halls, tunnels and battlements resound with history. In 1454, the castle and the accompanying earldom passed to Jasper Tudor whose nephew, Henry Tudor, was born in the castle and later became Henry VII.

Just half a mile from the castle, and across Monkton Pill, stood **Monkton Priory** that was founded in 1098 by Arnulf de Montgomery

Roch Castle

for Benedictine monks and was given to St Albans in 1473. The priory church, with its long narrow barrel-vaulted nave and monastic chancel, was rearranged in the 14th century and, after lying in ruins for many years, was restored again in the late 19th century.

AROUND PEMBROKE

UPTON

3 miles NE of Pembroke off the A477

Set in a secluded valley running down to the River Carew, **Upton Castle Gardens** has three raised formal terraces that drop down from the medieval castle. Along

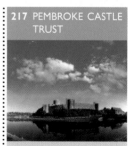

217 PEMBROKE CASTLE TRUST

Pembroke

Dating back to the 12th century, this imposing structure is a magnet for lovers of history.

 see page 368

161

A Great Tournament held at Carew in 1507 was attended by 600 nobles; but the castle also gives an insight into the lives of servants, craftsmen, priests and common soldiers of the time. During the summer months a wide variety of events is held in the castle grounds, including drama, school projects, holiday activities, battle re-enactments, country fairs and concerts.

218 THE BREWERY INN

Cosheston

Picturesque former coaching inn offering exceptional cuisine, real ales and self-catering accommodation.

see page 369

with the rose gardens and herbaceous borders, there are 40 acres of wooded grounds containing some 250 species of trees and shrubs. There's also a medieval chapel from which the walled garden can be seen.

CAREW

4 miles E of Pembroke on the A4075

Located on the shore of the tidal mill pond, **Carew Castle** is one of the few such buildings to display the development from Norman fortification (it was built between 1280 and 1310) to Elizabethan manor house. The site is much older, as archaeological excavations have found remains which go back some 2000 years. Various remarkable individuals have connections with the castle, but the castle displays also give insights into the lives of servants, craftsmen, priests and common soldiers of the time.

Here too can be seen one of only three restored tidal mills in Britain. **Carew Tidal Mill** still retains its original machinery. The Story of Milling exhibition traces the history of milling through the ages and the mill's role in the local community. While touring this lovely four-storey building, visitors are given explanations of each stage of the milling process. As well as the castle and the mill, the Carew site also incorporates a causeway, a medieval bridge and an 11th century **Celtic Cross** that is one of the best examples of its kind in Wales.

MANORBIER

5½ miles SE of Pembroke off the A4139

Manorbier is charmingly situated at the head of a valley that reaches down to the shore in a beautiful bay with a safe bathing beach. The village's name is thought to have been derived from Maenor Pyr (Manor of Pyr) and Pyr is believed to have been the first Celtic abbot of Caldey, living in the 5th century. Overlooking the bay of the same name, **Manorbier Castle** was conceived by Odo de Barri in 1095 when he built a wooden hall within a defensive structure but it was his son, William, who began construction of the stone fortification in the early 12th century. Famous for being the birthplace, in 1146, of Giraldus Cambrensis, Gerald of Wales, a monk and chronicler who wrote the first account of life in medieval Wales, the castle was described by him as being "the pleasantest spot in Wales".

Today, life size wax figures placed at various points, including the impressive great hall, the turrets and the chapel, bring the history of this ancient building to life as atmospheric music captures the castle's spirit. The castle gardens were laid out by JR Cobb in the late 19th century and there is also a late Victorian cottage with appropriate herbaceous borders lining the castle walls.

LAMPHEY

1½ miles SE of Pembroke on the A4139

Just northwest of the village, in the

13th century, the medieval bishops of St David's built the magnificent **Lamphey Bishop's Palace** as a retreat from the affairs of Church and State. Though improved over a period of 200 years, the major building work was undertaken by the dynamic Bishop Henry de Gower between 1328 and 1347 and he was responsible for the splendid great hall. Although now in ruins, this is a peaceful and tranquil site where successive bishops were able to live the life of country gentlemen among the estate's orchards, vegetable gardens and rolling parkland.

ST GOVAN'S HEAD

5 miles S of Pembroke off the B4319

The cliff scenery is at its most spectacular at St Govan's Head where the tiny religious site of the 13th century **St Govan's Chapel** huddles among the rocks almost at sea level. Accessible by climbing down 52 stone steps, this minute chapel was built on the site of a holy well that once attracted pilgrims who believed the well's waters to have miraculous healing powers.

Inside is a vertical cleft in the rock which, according to legend,

St Govan's Chapel, St Govan's Head

219 THE LANTERN LICENSED RESTAURANT AND TEA ROOMS

Lamphey
Outstanding cuisine is served in this stylishly refurbished village restaurant; disabled- and child-friendly establishment.

see page 370

220 FRESHWATER INN

Freshwater East
Inn commanding spectacular coastal views and serving good food and real ales.

see page 371

221 THE STACKPOLE INN

Stackpole
Beautifully located outstanding inn with excellent cuisine, real ales and en suite rooms.

see page 372

222 THE FERRY INN

Pembroke Dock

Superb olde worlde riverside inn serving real ales and quality food.

¶ see page 373

223 PEMBROKE DOCK MUSEUM

Pembroke Dock

Pembroke Dock's Gun Tower Museum, in Front Street was built in 1851 to repel "unwelcome guests".

🏛 see page 373

first opened so that St Govan could hide inside and escape his enemies. Closing behind him, the rock did not reopen until the danger had passed. Accordingly, a wish made while standing in the cleft and facing the rock will come true provided the person making the wish does not change his or her mind before turning round. Although many miracles have been credited to St Govan he remains a mysterious and little known man. Some believe him to have been a disciple of St David while others claim that he was a thief who, having miraculously found the hiding place, became a convert. St Govan is also thought by some to have been a woman named Cofen - the wife of a 5th century chief - who became a recluse.

BOSHERSTON

4½ miles SW of Pembroke off the B4319

To the east of the village and occupying part of the former Stackpole estate of the Earls of Cawdor are **Stackpole Gardens**, which were landscaped in the 18th century. Romantic in style and containing some interesting and well-engineered water features, including an eight arched bridge, these are intriguing gardens to explore. The original manor house has gone but the 19th century terraces, woodland garden and summer house remain, along with a grotto, an ice house and three walled gardens.

Also within the Stackpole Estate are some beautiful woods, two miles of coastline and, at Stackpole Quay, what must be the smallest harbour in the country. It barely has space for two boats side by side.

PEMBROKE DOCK

1½ miles NW of Pembroke on the A477

Once an important naval dockyard, Pembroke Dock stands on the dividing line between the developed and the undeveloped shores of the Milford Haven. Downstream are the large petrochemical plants and oil terminals which take advantage of the Haven's deepwater channels while, upstream, are the enchanting waters of the Cleddau river system.

The town mushroomed in the 19th century when it was chosen as a site for the naval dockyard after Milford Haven, on the other side of the haven, refused to provide a site. The town was constructed on an American-style grid plan with wide streets which are lined with some sturdy Victorian houses. Today, its most visible activity is as the terminal for ferries sailing to Rosslare in Ireland.

Close to the harbour is the **Gun Tower,** reached by a footbridge off Front Street. It is one of several such towers built in 1851 to defend the Royal Naval Dockyard but this is the only one open to the public. Within the 3-storey building, visitors can see how soldiers lived in Victorian times, explore the magazine floor below sea level, go up to the roof where there is a genuine cannon, and browse around exhibits on topics such as the dockyard and the flying boats that operated out of

Pembroke Dock for nearly 30 years. There are models of flying boats, of the Dockyard as it looked in 1855, and models and photographs of Royal Navy ships built at the Pembroke Dockyard.

TENBY

In Wales's National Tourism Awards, 2005, Tenby won top honours as the most popular tourist destination in the principality. The whole place is a real delight, prompting many eulogies such as this from the artist Augustus John: "You may travel the world over, but you will find nothing more beautiful: it is so restful, so colourful and so unspoilt." The artist was born in Tenby at Belgrave House, where a collection of his works, and those of his sister Gwen, can be found.

Tenby's Welsh name, Dinbych y Pysgod, means "Little Fort of the Fishes" and certainly its most photographed scene is the pretty harbour surrounded by pastel coloured Georgian houses. From the dockside arches, fishermen still sell the day's catch. The heart of the town still retains its charming medieval character together with the crooked lanes that are enclosed within its surprisingly well-preserved 13th century town walls. On one particular stretch, **South Parade**, the walls are still at their full height and the two tiers of arrow slits are very much visible; the **Five Arches**, a fortified gateway on the walls, is perhaps the most famous feature. Unfortunately,

the same is not true for **Tenby Castle**, the scant remains of which can be found on a small headland. However, the ruins are well worth a visit for the spectacular views out across Carmarthen Bay and along the Pembrokeshire coast. A statue to Prince Albert can also be found on the headland along with **Tenby Museum,** which began life in 1878. As well as having archaeological and historical material relating to the area, the museum has a fascinating maritime section and an impressive art gallery.

224 HAMMONDS PARK HOTEL

Tenby

A friendly, family run hotel just 500 yards from the beach and equipped with many facilities for keeping kids happy.

see page 374

Tudor Merchant's House, Tenby

•

Perhaps of more interest to younger visitors to the town of Tenby is the Silent World Aquarium and Reptile Collection housed in an attractive 19th century chapel. In these interesting, if somewhat unusual surroundings there is a wide range of exotic fish, amphibians and invertebrates on display as well as fish and other creatures that live around the shores of Pembrokeshire. Upstairs are the reptiles and here visitors can see a fascinating collection of snakes and lizards from around the world. Gifts for all ages, some made by local craftsmen, are on sale in the shop, where grown-ups can enjoy coffee, tea and a snack while the youngsters play with toys, draw, do a brass rubbing or try one of the quizzes.

•

225 THE DECK

Saundersfoot

Appetising home cooking and real ale provide two good reasons for visiting The Deck.

🍴 *see page 375*

Close to the quay stands the **Tudor Merchant's House** (National Trust), a relic of Tenby's prosperous sea-faring days and a fine example of a comfortable townhouse of the 15th century. Narrow and built with three storeys, the house has been furnished to re-create the atmosphere and environment in which a wealthy Tudor family would have lived. The furniture is either genuine 17th or 18th century pieces, or reproduction items made in Tudor style without glue or nails. With a Flemish chimney, early floral frescoes on some of the interior walls and a small herb garden outside, there is plenty at the house to evoke the times of around 600 years ago.

The large and lavish **St Mary's Church** is another testament to the town's prosperous maritime past. The tower was built in the early 1300s and served as a place of sanctuary and as a lookout in times of trouble. The tower is topped by a small spire which is itself more than 500 years old. The whole structure stands 152ft high. The chancel is 13th century and its barrel roof has more than 75 bosses. A plaque commemorates the 16th century mathematician and alchemist, Richard Recorde (1510-1558), who invented the equals (=) sign. After a distinguished career in London, he died a pauper in King's Bench Prison, Southwark.

On the eastern side of the church, Upper Frog Street is notable for its varied craft shops and an arcaded indoor market with craft stalls and gift shops.

AROUND TENBY

SAUNDERSFOOT
2½ miles NE of Tenby on the B4316

This picture postcard perfect fishing village is centred around its harbour, which during the summer months is packed with colourful sailing craft. The harbour was constructed in the 1820s primarily for the export of anthracite which was mined a short distance away and brought to the quay by tramway. Today, however, the industry has all but ceased and this resort, which has an attractive sandy beach, is probably one of the busiest watersports centres in South Wales.

AMROTH
4½ miles NE of Tenby off the A477

Lying at the most south-easterly point of the Pembrokeshire Coast National Park, this quiet village has a lovely beach overlooking Carmarthen Bay. As well as the delightful surroundings, the village is home to the enchanting **Colby Woodland Garden** (NT), an eight acre area of woodland set round a Nash-style house in a secluded valley. The garden contains one of the finest collections of rhododendrons and azaleas in Wales. The carpets of bluebells follow the displays of daffodils in the spring and there is a mass of colour during the summer when the hydrangeas flower, before the garden is taken over by the rich colours of autumn. The garden is part of the Colby Estate, which takes its name from John Colby, a 19th century industrialist.

Amroth is also the eastern terminus of the **Pembrokeshire Coast Path**, the 186-mile route that follows every inlet and rise and fall of the cliffs all the way to St Dogmael's near Cardigan.

STEPASIDE

4 miles N of Tenby off the A477

Between 1849 and 1877 this village, set in a wooded valley, had a thriving colliery and an iron works and, in 1877, the village school opened to provide education for the workers' children. Finally closing in 1992, the school has been reopened as the **Victorian School Museum** and provides today's visitors with the chance to experience a 19th century school day. Sitting at 100-year-old desks with slates and pencils, visitors can relive the austere school world of over a century ago. Outside, the playground has been re-created to match the environment where Victorian children would let off steam. Also at the museum is a display that brings the mining history of the village back to life. Along with the reconstructed mine shaft, visitors can see the hardships of the children as young as six who worked at the colliery until the school opened.

CALDEY ISLAND

2½ miles S of Tenby off the A4139

This peaceful and tranquil island, which along with its sister island of St Margaret's lies just a short distance off the coast from Tenby, has been the home of monks for some 1500 years. Currently, it is a working monastery with a community of 20 monks of the Reformed Cistercian Order. Today's monks live their lives according to the austere Rule of St Benedict which necessitates them attending seven services a day - the first beginning at 3.15am. Between their devotions, the monks of Caldey scrape a living from the land and are famous for their range of perfumes and toiletries inspired by the island's wild flowers. St Illtud's Church, along with the old 13th century priory ruins, can be visited, and a small museum tells the history of this beautiful island.

226 CROSS INN

Penally

Popular free house renowned for good food and real ales, and located in charming seaside village.

see page 375

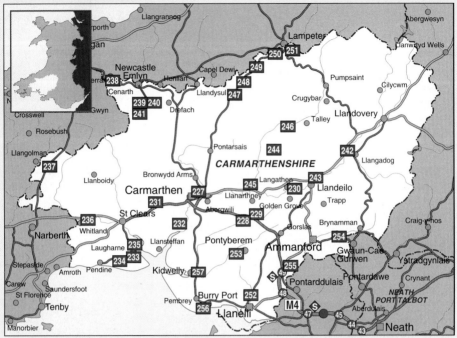

Carmarthenshire

A county of contrasts, Carmarthenshire has a wealth of interesting places and superb countryside to enchant the visitor. There are coastal strongholds at Laugharne and Kidwelly, abbey ruins at Talley and Whitland and the famous rugby and industrial centre of Llanelli. Covering some 1000 square miles, the county also has beautiful clean beaches, seaside towns and villages and rural idylls. A place of myths and legends, Carmarthenshire has remained essentially Welsh in most aspects.

Carreg Cennen Castle, Trapp

The coastline, which is more than 50 miles long, includes the award-winning Pembrey Country Park and beach, once the site of a munitions factory, and Pendine, whose long stretch of sand saw many land speed world records established. Of the seaside villages, Laugharne is certainly the most famous, due mainly to the fact that it is the place where Dylan Thomas lived for the last years of his short life. But the village does not rely solely on its literary links as it also has one of the country's most handsome castles and offers wonderful views over the estuary of the River Taf.

Inland lies Carmarthen, the county town, whose origins lie back in the time of the Romans. The town is a centre for the agricultural communities of West Wales, and to the east is an area associated with the legends and mysteries of Merlin the magician. Also in this part of Carmarthenshire is one the country's most recent important projects - the National Botanic Garden of Wales.

Evidence of the Roman occupation of Carmarthenshire is most striking at the Dolaucothi Goldmines, to the northwest of Llandovery. At Cenarth, visitors can see salmon fishermen on the River Teifi still using the coracle, a tiny round boat whose origins are lost in the mists of time. A fascinating museum tells the story of these distinctive little craft.

227 HUMBLE PIE

Carmarthen

Popular town centre café serving an appealing menu of tasty home-cooked food.

see page 376

If legend is to be believed, Carmarthen was Merlin's city and one particular story associated with the town has, thankfully, so far turned out not to be true. Carmarthen's inhabitants are eternally grateful that, when Merlin's Oak was removed during a road widening scheme, the town remained unharmed and the prophecy, "When Merlin's Oak shall tumble down, then shall fall Carmarthen town" was not realised. According to another tradition, the magician is said still to live in a cave on Merlin's Hill (Bryn Myrddin), just outside Carmarthen, where he is kept in perpetual enchantment by Vivien, the lady to whom he taught all his spells.

CARMARTHEN

One of the oldest Roman towns in Wales, Carmarthen (or Caerfyrddin in Welsh) is now the county town of Carmarthenshire and lies at the centre of the West Wales agricultural community. The historic old part of Carmarthen grew up around **Carmarthen Castle** which was originally built in around 1109 by Henry I. Overlooking the River Tywi, little remains of the castle today except the early 15th century gatehouse. The **Guildhall**, which was built in 1767 to replace the hall of 1583, is in Nott Square - named after Major General Sir William Nott, victor of the First Afghan War in the 1840s and a native of Carmarthen - his father was landlord of the Ivy Bush pub. Now renamed the Ivy Bush Royal Hotel, it also has some notable literary connections. A stained glass window and stone circle commemorate the 1819 Eisteddfodd when Iolo Morganwg introduced the Gorsedd (Society of Bards) to the Eisteddfodd. The essayist and dramatist Sir Richard Steele stayed at the Ivy Bush in the later years of his life. Bad health and pressing debts had forced him to move to Wales, and he died in Carmarthen in 1729. A brass plaque on the wall of St Peter's Church commemorates him.

This church, which dates back to the 12th century, has many interesting features, including an organ thought to have been built in the reign of George III for Windsor Palace, and the impressive tomb of Sir Rhys ap Thomas, who led an army to fight for Henry Tudor at the Battle of Bosworth Field where Richard III was killed and Henry crowned King Henry VII on the battlefield.

The town's Victorian Old Art College has, since 1991, been the home of **Oriel Myrddin** (free), a contemporary craft gallery and regional art venue. Focusing on the present and the future, the work of some of the most innovative and interesting craftspeople in Wales is displayed here and, in the retail area, there is a wide range of crafts for purchase. By contrast, housed in a new development on the banks of the River Tywi is the **Carmarthen Heritage Centre** which, through displays, multi-media and video presentations, tells the story of the town from the time of the Roman occupation in AD 75 through to the present day. At the site of **Caer Maridunum**, the most westerly Roman fort in Britain, the remains of the amphitheatre can still be seen and the Roman town walls were known to have been visible in the 12th century.

Carmarthen has a thriving food market, where one of the local specialities on sale is Carmarthen ham, which is air-dried, sliced and eaten raw, like the Spanish Serrano ham.

AROUND CARMARTHEN

BRONWYDD ARMS

2 miles N of Carmarthen on the A484

From Bronwydd Arms Station (just off the A484 Carmarthen to

Cardigan road) the **Gwili Railway** offers visitors the opportunity to step back in time and take a short steam train journey through the Gwili Valley on part of the old Great Western Railway line. This line originally opened in 1860 and, although it finally closed in 1973, since the late 1970s it has been run by volunteers. Trains run on timetabled days between April and October and in December. The station has a souvenir shop and sells hot and cold refreshments. Visitors can enjoy the train journey through a beautiful wooded valley, and the other end of the line, Llwyfan Cerrig, is the perfect place for a picnic by the river.

PONTARSAIS

5 miles N of Carmarthen on the A485

Pontarsais is best known as the home of the **Gwili Pottery** which has been producing fine hand-thrown and hand-decorated ceramics for more than 25 years. There's a wide variety of different pieces in more than 30 designs, both traditional and contemporary.

DREFACH

12 miles N of Carmarthen off the A484

Many of the water driven mills of this area still continue to produce flour and distinctive woollen goods, and this important part of the region's industrial heritage is explored in the **National Woollen Museum**. One of the most traditional and rural industries, the processes involved in the spinning, weaving and dyeing of wool are explained here, and there are also

demonstrations of cloth making and dyeing carried out on 19th century machinery. As well as trying their hand at spinning, visitors can stroll around the sites of the old woollen mills in the village, which still produce flannel cloth and tweeds, and follow all or part of the Woollen Mill Trail through the scenic Teifi Valley. There are 24 miles of way-marked trails from the Museum, the longer ones taking in the seven so-called flannel villages.

ABERGWILI

1½ miles E of Carmarthen off the A40

The **Carmarthen County Museum** occupies a lovely old house that was once a palace of the bishop of St David's and visitors to the museum can still see the bishop's peaceful private chapel. Concentrating on Carmarthenshire's past, the museum's displays range from Roman gold through to Welsh furniture and there is also a reconstruction of a school room. The palace's grounds, too, are open to the public, and the delightful parkland is ideal for a stroll and a picnic.

LLANARTHNE

7½ miles E of Carmarthen on the B4300

To the southwest of the village lies **Paxton's Tower**, designed by SP Cockerell and built in the early 19th century on the Middleton estate for William Paxton. It was dedicated to Lord Nelson. Constructed so that this Gothic eyecatcher could be seen from the main house, it affords panoramic views from the

•

Found on land that has been farmed for more than 2000 years, the Merlin's Hill Centre at Alltyfyrddin farm near Abergwili explains the history and legends of the surrounding area and its connections with Merlin the magician. As well as listening out for the wizard's wailings - he is supposed to be sleeping beneath the Iron Age hill fort known as Merlin's Hill. Visitors can also explore this dairy farm and learn about farming, past and present.

•

228 THE WHITE HART THATCHED INN & BREWERY

Llanddarog

Famous old hostelry with excellent cuisine, real ales from its own brewery, and beautiful patio garden.

¶ see page 377

Paxton's Tower, Llanarthne

229 THE NATIONAL BOTANIC GARDEN OF WALES

Llanarthne

The botanic gardens boasts the largest single-span glasshouse in the world and is set in more than 500 acres of fantastic, unspoilt, rolling Welsh countryside.

 see page 376

recently restored Double Walled Garden, a Japanese garden, a bee garden with a million residents, lakeside walks and the Physicians of Myddfai, an exhibition that pays tribute to the legendary Welsh healers of the Middle Ages. Tribute is also paid to the Welsh botanist Alfred Russel Wallace, whose theories of natural selection paralleled those of Charles Darwin. This is also very much a garden of the future. In the Energy Zone, there is a biomass furnace using salvaged or coppiced wood for heating the site, and the Living Machine sewage treatment system. Another attraction is Millennium Square, a spacious venue for open air concerts and performances.

tower over the estate and Tywi valley.

To the south of Llanarthne, and set in the 18th century parkland of the former regency estate of Middleton Hall (which no longer exists), is the **National Botanic Garden of Wales** - a Millennium project that covers an amazing 568 acres on the edge of the beautiful Towy Valley. Dedicated to conservation, horticulture, science and education, this national botanic garden, the first to be constructed in Britain for more than 200 years, is centred around a great glasshouse designed by Norman Foster that is the largest single span house of its kind in the world. Among the many delights to be found within this old parkland are one of Europe's longest herbaceous borders, the

LLANGATHEN

11 miles E of Carmarthen off the A40

The village is home to **Aberglasney**, one of the oldest and most interesting gardens in the country. The first recorded description of Aberglasney house and gardens was made by the bard Lewis Glyn Cothi in 1477 when he wrote of "a white painted court, built of dressed stone, surrounded by nine gardens of orchards, vineyards and large oak trees." At the beginning of the 17th century the estate was sold to the Bishop of St David's and it was Bishop Anthony Rudd, whose grand tomb can be found in the village church, who improved both the house and gardens in a manner befitting a bishop's palace. At the heart of the 9 acres is a unique and fully restored Elizabethan/Jacobean cloister garden and a parapet walk, the only surviving example in the UK. Also remarkable is the Yew Tunnel, planted more than 300 years ago. The tunnel is created by training the 5 yew trees over the path and getting them to root on the other side.

GOLDEN GROVE

11 miles E of Carmarthen off the B4300

To the east of the village lies **Gelli Aur Country Park,** part of the estate of the ancestral home of the Vaughan family. It contains remnants of a 17th century deer park (where the deer still roam). The landscaped parkland was laid out in the 18th century and the country park also includes a Victorian arboretum planted by Lord Cawdor. Other attractions include nature trails, a new adventure playground and a cafeteria. The original mansion, now part of an agricultural college, was the work of the architect Joseph Wyatville.

LLANSTEFFAN

7 miles SW of Carmarthen on the B4312

This village, near the mouth of the River Tywi, is dominated by the ruins of **Llansteffan Castle** (free) on a headland above the estuary. The successor to an earlier defensive earthwork, the castle dates from the 12th century and its main remaining feature is the impressive gateway dating from 1280. To the southwest of the castle lies **St Anthony's Well**, the waters of which were thought to cure lovesickness.

Llansteffan, along with Ferryside, its neighbour across the river mouth, is a paradise for walkers as well as sailors and the way-marked walks around the estuary take in some truly breathtaking coastal scenery. The promontory of Wharley Point, in particular, affords stunning views across the Taf and Tywi estuaries to Carmarthen Bay.

LAUGHARNE

9 miles SW of Carmarthen on the A4066

Over the past few years this pretty rural town of Georgian houses on the estuary of the River Taf has become a shrine to the memory of its most famous resident, Dylan Thomas. The poet, together with his wife Caitlin and their three children, spent the last four years of his life living at **The Boathouse,** set on a cliff overlooking the Taf estuary. Discovering this small out-of-the-way place in 1949, Thomas famously "got off the bus and forgot to get on again". Approached by a narrow lane and now renamed the Dylan Thomas Boathouse, it's a remarkably evocative place, partly because of the many artefacts connected with the poet, partly because of the serene views of the estuary and its "heron-priested shore". In the family living room, a vintage wireless is tuned to the poet himself reading his own work. As well as the fascinating memorabilia on display here, there is also an interpretation centre, bookshop and tea room. It was while in Laugharne

230 THE GARDEN CAFÉ

Llangathen

Quality food in charming café with terrace overlooking a lake in the award-winning Aberglasney Gardens.

❙ *see page 378*

231 TAFARN YR HELGWN A'R CADNO / FOX & HOUNDS INN

Banc-y-felin

Ideal family pub with a welsh welcome, serving appetising food and real ales.

❙ *see page 379*

232 TAFARN PANTYDDERWEN

Llangain

Popular village inn noted for its excellent cuisine and real ales.

❙ *see page 378*

233 THE CARPENTERS ARMS

Laugharne

Child-friendly pub with excellent food and comfortable en suite accommodation.

see page 380

234 BROADWAY COUNTRY HOUSE

Laugharne

Impressive restored Victorian country retreat in scenic location offering quality cuisine and en suite accommodation.

see page 380

235 DYLAN THOMAS BOATHOUSE

Laugharne

The former home of Dylan Thomas is now a heritage centre dedicated to the poet.

see page 381

Dylan Thomas Boathouse, Laugharne

that Thomas wrote some of his best works, including the radio play *Under Milk Wood*, a day in the life of his imaginary village of Llareggub (read the name backwards to find why it has this odd name). Thomas, notoriously prone to destructive drinking sprees, died in The White Horse Bar in New York while on a lecture tour in 1953, at only 39 years of age. The parish church of St

Martin, where he is buried, contains a replica of the plaque to his memory which can be seen in Poets' Corner, Westminster Abbey.

Luahgarne is also home to one of the country's most handsome castles, "a castle brown as owls" according to Dylan Thomas. Originally an earth and timber fortress, **Laugharne Castle** (CADW) was rebuilt in stone around the 13th century and some of that fortification still remains, But it is the transformations undertaken by Sir John Perrot in the 16th century that make this a particularly special site. Granted Laugharne by Queen Elizabeth I, Perrot, an illegitimate son of Henry VIII, turned the castle into a comfortable Tudor mansion. In 1591 Perrot was found guilty of high treason and confined to the Tower of London where he died the following year. As soon as word reached Laugharne of his conviction, looters stripped the castle of much of its finery. The devastation continued during the Civil War and an attack in 1644 left the romantic ruins seen today.

However, romantic though the castle ruins are, this is not all Laugharne Castle has to offer as the Victorian garden has been splendidly restored. Both the castle ruins and the superb surroundings have provided inspiration for artists over the centuries and, in particular, they are the subject of a dramatic watercolour by JMW Turner. Writers, too, have found this an inspiring place. Dylan Thomas wrote in a gazebo in the grounds, and Richard Hughes, author of *A High Wind in Jamaica*, stayed at the adjoining Castle House from 1934 to 1942.

PENDINE

13½ miles SW of Carmarthen on the A4066

The vast expanse of sand, six miles long, which makes Pendine a popular place with families for a day out by the sea was used in the 1920s by Sir Malcolm Campbell and others for attempting land speed records. In 1924, Sir Malcolm broke the World Motor Flying Kilometre Record here by averaging 146 miles per hour. He later raised that to 174 mph, and went on to achieve speeds in excess of 300 mph on the salt flats at Bonneville, Utah. In 1927, while attempting to beat Sir Malcolm's record, Welshman JG Parry Thomas was decapitated in an accident on the beach and his car, *Babs,* lay buried in the sand for some 44 years before being unearthed and restored. *Babs* can now be seen in all its gleaming glory at the **Museum of Speed** (free) which explores the history of this stretch of sand where so many records were broken. Not all the record attempts involved land vehicles as it was from these sands in 1933 that the intrepid aviatrix Amy Johnson set off on her solo flight across the Atlantic.

WHITLAND

13 miles W of Carmarthen on the B4328

This small market town and centre of the dairy industry is historically important as the meeting place of the assembly convened by Hywel Dda (Hywel the Good) in the 10th century. Born towards the end of the 9th century, Dda made a pilgrimage to Rome in AD 928 and, some 14 years later, he was ruler of most of Wales. Summoning representatives from each part of Wales to Whitland, Dda laid down a legal system that became known for its wisdom and justice. For its time, the code was remarkably

236 THE FISHERS ARMS

Whitland

Welcoming hostelry offering good food, real ales and camping and caravan site.

see page 381

Whitland Abbey

made. As well as watching chocolate-making demonstrations and touring the factory to see just how the chocolate is produced, visitors can buy gifts and treats for family and friends (and selves) at the farm shop which has the largest selection of chocolates in Wales. And as this is rich dairy country, there are also farmhouse cheeses and other dairy delights at the shop (don't even try to resist the homemade fudge!), along with a wide range of hand roasted coffee beans prepared daily.

237 CAFFI BECA

Efailwen

Popular village café serving an appetising selection of hot and cold meals based on local produce.

see page 381

238 THE THREE HORSESHOES

Cenarth

Fine old hostelry noted for its appetising food and choice of real ales.

see page 383

democratic, including provisions such as the equal division of property between spouses on separation. The code remained in force in Wales up until the Act of Union with England in 1536. This system and its instigator are remembered at the Prince of Wales Design award winning building, the **Hywel Dda Centre**. Here, too, is a **Memorial** in the form of six gardens representing the six separate divisions of the Law: Society and Status, Crime and Tort, Women, Contract, the King, and Property.

Just north of the town lie the remains of the once great **Whitland Abbey**, which was founded in 1140 by Bernard, the first Norman Bishop of St David's.

LLANBOIDY

12 miles NW of Carmarthen off the A40

In old stone farm buildings to the north of the village is a chocoholic's dream - the **Welsh Chocolate Farm**, where chocolates of all shapes, sizes and flavours are

CENARTH

16 miles NW of Carmarthen on the A484

This ancient village was first mentioned by Giraldus Cambrensis in the late 12th century when he passed through on his journey with Archbishop Baldwin. The village is situated on the banks of the River Teifi which at this point is famous for its rapids which are conveniently close to the road. This conservation village is also home to **Cenarth Mill**. Dating from the 18th century, the watermill has two pairs of stones (one for barley, the other for oats) and is powered by the river close to the rapids. Now restored and producing wholemeal flour, the mill complex also houses the **National Coracle Centre** where visitors can see a unique collection of these ancient boats from around the world. Dating back to the Ice Age, these little round boats, once covered in skins, are still used for salmon fishing and at the Centre visitors can see demonstrations of coracles at work.

NEWCASTLE EMLYN

14 miles NW of Carmarthen on the A484

The first settlement here grew up around a loop of the River teifi. At this strategic spot in 1240, Maredudd ap Rhys built **Newcastle Emlyn Castle**, which was to change hands many times over the years and was almost completely destroyed during the Glyndwr rebellion in the early 1400s. Having fallen into disrepair, the castle was granted to Sir Rhys ap Thomas by Henry VII in the late 15th century and became a country residence before being, once again, all but demolished during the Civil War for harbouring Royalist sympathisers. What remains is not particularly exciting but the setting, surrounded by the river on three sides, is pastoral and peaceful.

In medieval times, Newcastle Emlyn was an important farming and droving centre and it still has a cattle market every Friday.

The town has another small claim to fame since it was in Newcastle Emlyn that the first printing press in Wales was set up by Isaac Carter in 1718.

On the B4571 a mile north of Newcastle Emlyn are **Old Cilgwyn Gardens**. This is a 14-acre mixed garden set in 900 acres of parkland that includes a 53-acre Site of Special Scientific Interest.

LLANDOVERY

Visiting in the 19th century, the author George Borrow called Llandovery "the pleasantest little town in which I have halted". This appealing little market town stands at the confluence of the Rivers Bran, Gwennol and Tywi, so its Welsh name, Llanymddyfri (meaning the church amid the waters), seems particularly apt. The Romans came here and built a fort within whose ramparts a church was later built. The Church of St Mary on the Hill still has some Roman tiles within its walls; also of note here are the barrel-vaulted chancel and tie-beam roof.

The town boasts two famous sons: Rhys Pritchard, known as a preacher and as the author of the collection of verses *The Welshman's Candle*, was vicar here from about 1602; in the following century, the renowned Methodist poet and hymn writer William Williams was born in Llandovery. Amongst his many hymns, the best-known in English is *Guide Me, O Thou Great Redeemer*.

Llandovery Castle, the scant remains of which overlook the cattle market, (held every other Tuesday) was the most easterly Norman castle within Carmarthenshire. It was constructed in 1116 by Richard Fitzpons but was captured and destroyed some 42 years later. Although it was repaired in the late 12th century by Henry II, the castle was left to decay after 1403 and only the tumbledown remains are visible today. Henry IV stayed at the castle during his campaign against Owain Glyndwr. The king witnessed the hanging, drawing and

239 THE BUNCH OF GRAPES

Newcastle Emlyn

Popular hostelry known for its fresh home-cooked food, real ales and regular live entertainment.

🍴 see page 382

240 TEIFI TEA ROOMS/ TÉ AR Y TEIFI

Newcastle Emlyn

Top quality tearooms serving home-made cakes, scones and light meals.

🍴 see page 383

241 EMLYN ARMS HOTEL

Newcastle Emlyn

Delightful 300-year-old former coaching inn now providing good food, Welsh ales and en suite accommodation.

🛏 🍴 see page 383

242 THE CASTLE HOTEL

Llangadog

19th century hostelry in pretty village offering good food and well-kept ales.

❚ see page 384

quartering of Llywelyn ap Gruffyd Fychan, a Welsh patriot who is commemorated by an imposing monument on the castle mound.

The history of this town, which has pleased many before and since George Borrow, is told at the **Llandovery Heritage Centre** where the legends surrounding the hero Twm Sion Cati - the Welsh Robin Hood - and the local **Physicians of Myddfai** are also explored. The legend concerning the physicians is that a lady appeared one day from a lake in the Black Mountain. A local farmer's son fell in love with her and she agreed to marry him on condition that he did not hit her three times without cause. Over the years he had given her three light taps for what he thought was poor behaviour and sure enough she returned to the lake. But before disappearing she passed on her herbal healing secrets to her three sons, who became the first of the famous Physicians of Myddfai, a line of healers who practised from the 12th to the 18th centuries.

AROUND LLANDOVERY

CILYCWM

3½ miles N of Llandovery off the A483

The attractive **Dolauhirion Bridge**, spanning the River Tywi, was built in 1173 by William Edwards, and the village's chapel is said to have been the first meeting place of Methodists in Wales. Close by lies **Twm Sion Cati's Cave**, the hideout of the 16th century 'Robin

Hood of Wales'. A poet whose youthful escapades earned him his title, Twm Sion (who died in 1620) curtailed his activities and settled down after marrying the heiress of Ystradffin; he even became a magistrate. He died in 1620.

LLANGADOG

5 miles SW of Llandovery on the A4069

This picturesque village set beneath the great bulk of Black Mountain in the Vale of Towy once boasted a castle, although all that remains today is a mound. The castle was destroyed by its owners in 1277 rather than letting it fall into the hands of the English.

BETHLEHEM

8 miles SW of Llandovery off the A4069

As Christmas approaches the village Post Office at Bethlehem experiences a remarkable upturn in business as people visit to have their mail franked with the evocative name.

To the southwest of Bethlehem lies **Garn Coch**, the largest hill fort in Wales, whose earthworks and stone ramparts cover some 15 acres.

TRAPP

12 miles SW of Llandovery off the A483

Situated on the top of a precipitous limestone crag on the Black Mountain and with a vertical 300ft drop to the River Cennen below, **Carreg Cennen Castle**, to the east of Trapp, enjoys one of the most spectacular locations of any Welsh castle. Although the present castle dates from 1248, some attribute a castle here to Urien, a knight of

Arthur's Round Table. It remained a Welsh stronghold for less than 30 years, falling to Edward I during his first invasion in 1277. During the War of the Roses, the castle became a base for bandit Lancastrians. Taken on behalf of the Yorkists in 1462, the fortress was dismantled on the orders of Edward IV, leaving the romantic ruins seen today. A visit here is well worth the effort to enjoy the impressive views and to appreciate what a daunting task attacking the castle must have been. There is only one way up: a steep, grassy hill protected by a complicated system of defences.

In the converted barns of Llwyndewi Farm is the **Trapp Arts and Crafts Centre** which specialises in crafts from Wales. The shop stocks an interesting range of quality items including stained glass, lovespoons, pottery and jewellery, and the Art Gallery, on the first floor, is devoted to showing the work of local artists. Demonstrations and exhibitions run throughout the summer months and the centre has a coffee shop.

LLANDEILO

11½ miles SW of Llandovery on the A483

The former ancient capital of West Wales, Llandeilo's hilltop position shows off to best advantage this pretty little market town. Pastel coloured Georgian houses line the main road, which curves elegantly up from the **Tywi Bridge** whose central span is said to be the longest in Wales. The road continues to the Church of St Teilo, dedicated to the 6th century

Carreg Cennen Castle, Trapp

saint who gave the town its name.

In recent years the town has been upwardly mobile with an influx of smart shops and galleries, along with delis, cafés, restaurants and a stylishly revamped former coaching inn.

Llandeilo was one of the original founders of the Welsh Rugby Union, and the so-called Lichfield Gospels, the most perfect Welsh Christian manuscripts, were written here.

To the west of the town stands **Dinefwr Castle** (CADW), the former seat of the Princes of Deheubarth, one of the three ancient kingdoms of Wales. The fortress was built on the site of an Iron Age fort and legend has it that Merlin's grave is in the area. The castle ruins are surrounded by **Dinefwr Park**. Extensive areas of parkland were landscaped by Capability Brown in 1775 and incorporated the medieval castle, house, gardens and ancient deer park into one breathtaking

243 THE SALUTATION INN

Llandeilo

Former coaching inn recently refurbished; stylish restaurant and real ales on tap.

❚ *see page 386*

244 FARMERS ARMS

Llanfynydd

300-year-old rural inn serving excellent home cooked meals and real ales. Regular entertainment and B&B accommodation.

❚ ⊨ *see page 385*

245 THE SALUTATION INN

Pontargothi

Excellent cuisine is served at this small village pub; real ales and beer garden with play area.

see page 386

246 BLACK LION INN

Abergorlech

Delightful 17th century inn in idyllic riverside location; excellent home-made food and real ales.

see page 387

247 THE TALARDD ARMS

Llanllwi

Traditional village inn with good home-cooked food, real ales, beer garden and regular pub quiz.

see page 388

panorama. Footpaths through the parkland lead to the castle, bog wood and beech clumps and offer outstanding views of the Tywi valley. The site is one of international importance for wintering birds, including white-fronted geese, shovelers, curlews and lapwings.

Also within the park is **Newton House**, originally built in 1660, provided with a new limestone façade in the 1860s, and restored by the National Trust in 2006. The ground floor and basement are being restored to the Edwardian era and visitors will be taken back to 1912 where they will be able to see, touch and hear about life above and below stairs in the early years of the 20th century.

TALLEY

8½ miles W of Llandovery on the B4302

This village, with its backdrop of rolling hills, takes its name from

Talley Abbey

Tal-y-llychau, meaning Head of the Lakes. Between two lakes lies **Talley Abbey**, founded in the late 12th century by Rhys ap Gryffyd, and the only Welsh outpost of the austere Premonstratensian canons. One of the few remains to have survived is an immense tower which still overshadows the peaceful abbey lawns. The nearby 18th century **Church of St Michael** is something of an oddity: it was built with no aisle and its interior is entirely taken up with box pews.

PUMSAINT

8 miles NW of Llandovery on the A482

Near this hamlet, whose name means Five Saints, are the **Dolaucothi Goldmines** (National Trust), which date back some 2000 years to a time when the open-cast gold workings were secured by the Roman army. Once a likely source of gold bullion for the Imperial mints of Lyons and Rome, the mines are still in a remarkable state of preservation despite being abandoned by the Romans in AD 140; they were reopened for a short time between 1888 and the late 1930s. Visitors to this site in the beautiful Cothi Valley can see both the ancient and modern mine workings, including a number of the horizontal tunnels dug into the hillside for drainage and access. There is also the opportunity to try gold panning, see an exhibition of vintage mining machinery and to tour the surrounding woodland on a waymarked trail. The site also has a shop selling Welsh Gold and a

tearoom serving delicious home-cooked food.

LLANELLI

Best known today for its enormous Felinfoel and Buckley breweries and perhaps even more famous as the home of the Scarlets, one of the most illustrious rugby teams in Wales; the saucepan tipped rugby posts at Stradey Park and the Scarlets' anthem, *Sospan Fach* ('little saucepan'), are both reminders of a time when Llanelli was a major industrial centre with thriving tinplating, steel, chemical and engineering works.

In Stepney Street, the Stepney Wheel was made in the early 20th century; this was an inflated spare tyre on a spokeless rim, to be fixed over a punctured wheel. In India, the term Stepney Wheel is still sometimes applied to any spare tyre.

Housed in a former mansion set in a large civic park with grand sea views, **Parc Howard Museum and Art Gallery** (free) has a collection of local paintings and 19th century Llanelli pottery as well as displays on the history of the town and, curiously, a nightdress and chemise once owned by Queen Victoria.

One of the country's newest attractions, the **Millennium Coastal Park and Cycleway** (free) is located in Llanelli. Providing all manner of leisure activities and peaceful wildlife havens, the park incorporates wetlands, gardens, woodlands, a golf course and both

248 TAFARN BELLE VUE

Llanllwni

Charming old inn dating back to the mid-1700s and serving outstanding cuisine and real ale and cider.

see page 389

249 GLASFRYN GUEST HOUSE

Llanbydder

Quality en suite B&B accommodation in gracious 1890s Vicarage with delightful secluded garden.

see page 390

250 ROBINS ROOST

Lampeter

Top of the range bed & breakfast establishment in 1810 house in secluded location with wonderful views.

see page 390

251 CWMANNE TAVERN

Cwmanne

Former coaching inn offering fine country cooking, real ales, accommodation and regular live entertainment.

see page 392

252 THE HARRY WATKINS

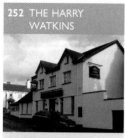

Felinfoel

Welcoming and popular hostelry well known for its mouth-watering food and choice of real ales.

🍴 see page 391

253 THE NEW LODGE INN

Pontyberem

Friendly and atmospheric village hostelry serving good, home-cooked food and real ales.

🍴 see page 392

254 HALF MOON INN

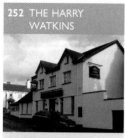

Garnant

Traditional inn serving real ales and bar snacks; en suite accommodation, regular live entertainment and heated patio.

🍴 🛏 see page 392

---

sailing and watersports.

To the east of Llanelli lies the **National Wetlands Centre of Wales** which is one of the eight centres established by the Trust founded by Sir Peter Scott at Slimbridge in 1946. Also a haven for wild plant and animal life throughout the year, the centre's 200-acre salt marsh is home to flocks of curlew, lapwing and redshank which visitors can observe from secluded hides. The Discovery Centre has hands-on activities to help visitors find out about conservation.

AROUND LLANELLI

GORSLAS

9 miles NE of Llanelli on the A476

On **Mynydd Mawr**, a mountain to the north of the village, there was a well that, centuries ago, so legend says, was looked after by a man called Owain. After watering his horses one day, Owain forgot to replace the slab of stone which covered the well and a torrent of water poured down the mountainside. The great rush of water would have drowned the whole area if Owain had not galloped his horse around it and used magic to check the flood. The lake of water which was left is known as Llyn Llech Owain - the lake of Owain's stone slab.

Today, the lake forms part of **Llyn Llech Owain Country Park.** The lake and the peat bog that surround.s it have been designated a Site of Special Scientific Interest within which are a variety of rare

---

plants such as Bogbean, Round Leafed Sundew and Royal Fern. The park's visitor centre has an exhibition that describes both the history and the natural history of the park.

PEMBREY

5 miles W of Llanelli on the A484

This village lies on the flat lands which border Carmarthen Bay and during World War II a Royal Ordnance Factory here produced munitions for the Allied Forces. At the factory's peak, in 1942, it covered some 500 acres and employed 3000 people; it ceased production in 1965. Since then the land has been landscaped, and as **Pembrey Country Park** it offers visitors an unusual mix of pine forests, sand dunes, beaches and such attractions as a dry ski slope, a toboggan run, a miniature railway and an adventure playground. Pembrey Pines Trail is a four-mile walk through dunes and woodland, with splendid views. There's also a visitor centre, and to the east lies Pembrey Saltmarsh, a local nature reserve and a Site of Special Scientific Interest. The park also includes **Cefn Sidan**, one of Europe's best and safest beaches, from which there are glorious views over the Gower coastline.

KIDWELLY

7½ miles NW of Llanelli on the B4308

This historic town, whose charter was granted by Henry I in the 12th century, boasts an ancient church and a 14th century bridge over the River Gwendreath.

Kidwelly Castle

Llanedi

Outstanding village inn serving quality home-made food and with en suite rooms.

see page 393

256 CORNISH ARMS

Burry Port

Outstanding village hostelry with real ales and exceptionally good cuisine; patio garden and regular entertainment.

see page 394

257 THE MASONS ARMS

Kidwelly

Delightful thatched inn dating back to 1350 and offering appetising food, real ales and regular entertainment.

see page 395

However, the most interesting and impressive building is undoubtedly the remarkably well preserved Norman **Kidwelly Castle** (CADW) which stands on a steep bluff overlooking the river. The castle spans four centuries but most of what remains today is attributed to a Bishop of Salisbury who endeavoured to build a home-from-home from Sherbourne Abbey in Dorset. One of Wales' best kept secrets, Kidwelly Castle gives a fascinating insight into the evolution of a medieval castle into a domestic dwelling of more settled times.

For hundreds of years, the ghost of Gwenllian, daughter of the King of Gwynedd and the wife of the Prince of South Wales, was said to haunt the countryside around the castle. During an attack on the Norman castle in 1136 which Gwenllian led, she was decapitated and legend has it that her headless ghost was unable to find rest until a man searched the battlefield and returned her skull to her. Princess Gwenllian was certainly a warrior, and she was perhaps also a writer. Some have attributed parts of *The Mabinogion* to her, and if the attribution is correct, she would be Britain's earliest known woman writer.

On the outskirts of the town, marked by its 164ft redbrick chimney, the **Kidwelly Industrial Museum** (free) is housed in an original tinplate works. Here visitors have a unique opportunity to see how the rolling mills produced the plate as well as learning something of the county's industrial past. The Museum contains Britain's sole surviving pack mill.

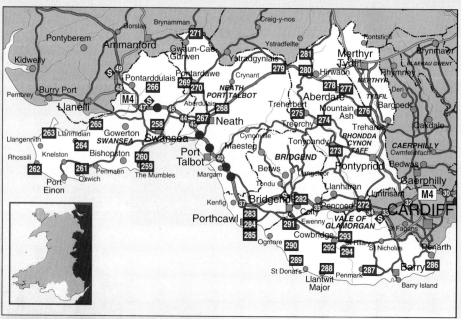

Gower Peninsula and the Heritage Coast

The delightful city of Swansea marks the gateway to the southernmost bulge of Wales, the lovely Gower Peninsula, a region designated an Area of Outstanding Natural Beauty. Much of it is owned by the National Trust. The Gower's southern coastline is made up of a succession of sandy, sheltered bays and along its whole coastline it is dotted with charming and relaxed seaside resorts.

This is also an area rich in natural beauty, with a long history that can be explored not only at the Gower Heritage Centre but also through its various castles, religious sites and ancient monuments. The area has many small family farms that yield some of the finest produce in south Wales; the Gower is known in particular for its cockles and its laverbread (edible seaweed). The peninsula was once the haunt of elephants, bears, rhinoceros and other large beasts whose bones have been found in the many caves on the shoreline.

The Vale of Glamorgan is characterised by gentle rolling hills, genteel towns, pretty villages and a splendid natural coastline. An area of rich farmland, the Vale stands at the foot of the spectacular valleys of south Wales and offers visitors an enticing heritage coastline. This is another area rich in history, where Norman warlords built their castles and where one of the oldest seats of learning was founded at Llantwit Major.

Behind the coastal region lie the valleys of southwest Wales which are known the world over for their coal mining and heavy industry heritage. The best known is the Rhondda Valley, where only one mine survives from the

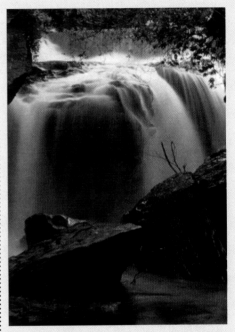

Aberdulais Falls

numerous collieries that once powered not just this country but many parts of the world. Though mining has all but gone from the valleys the heritage remains: the towns and villages with their rows of cottages where life revolved around the colliery, the chapel and the music, especially male voice choirs.

In many cases, nature has reclaimed the hills and vales once scarred by the mining industry and, while the legacy of pride in the industry remains, the various new country parks and nature reserves developed on the sites of the old mines are giving the area a new appeal.

SWANSEA

Swansea, Wales's city by the sea, is an attractive and welcoming place with an appealing blend of traditional and modern. It was founded in the late 10th century by Sweyne Forkbeard, King of Denmark - its English name means 'Sweyne's Ey' - ey being an inlet. **Swansea Castle**, which gained notoriety in the 18th century when the northern block became a debtors' prison, was first built by the Norman Henry de Newburgh in the late 11th century. However, it was all but destroyed by Owain Glyndwr in the early 1400s when he ransacked the town that had grown up around the fortification.

As early as the 14th century, shipbuilding and coalmining were important industries in the area and by 1700 Swansea was the largest port in Wales. Smelters from Cornwall arrived here, attracted by the plentiful supply of coal, and copper works also flourished; Nelson's ships were covered in Swansea copper. At one time 90% of the country's copper was smelted here and, in the heyday of the industry, other metals such as tin, lead, nickel and zinc were imported to the town for smelting and refining. In the 19th century, Swansea porcelain was another famous local product. Much of the traditional industry has disappeared and the old dock area has been transformed into a marina surrounded by stylish waterfront buildings. This **Maritime Quarter** is arguably the most impressive part of the town and is alive with cafés, pubs and restaurants. Here, too is the £33 million project that opened in late 2005, the **National Waterfront Museum.** Its 15 different zones are dedicated to topics such as coal, landscape, energy and genealogy. Inventive interactive technology allows visitors to fly over Swansea or go on a virtual shopping spree in the past. This impressive complex, generally regarded as the best museum in Wales, also contains several shops, a café and a waterfront balcony.

Also in this dockside quarter is the **Swansea Museum**, founded in 1835 and the oldest in Wales. Its displays combine bygone Swansea

Swansea Castle

history and culture with new exhibitions and events. Among the displays are Swansea porcelain, a Cabinet of Curiosities, a Welsh kitchen and the Mummy of Tem-Hor. More artefacts from Egypt can be seen at the **Egyptian Centre** at Swansea University where more than 1000 objects, including impressive painted coffins and everyday household items dating back as far as 3500 BC can be seen. At the Marina Pontoon is the Swansea Museum Services **Historic Vessels Collection** that includes a former Trinity House Gower Coast lightship, a steam tug and a Bristol Channel pilot cutter.

At the **Glynn Vivian Art Gallery** a broad spectrum of the visual arts is on display. Based on the bequest of Richard Glynn Vivian, the gallery houses an international collection of Swansea porcelain and various Old Masters as well as numerous paintings and sculptures by 20th century artists including Hepworth, Nicholas, Nash, Ceri Richards and Augustus John.

No coverage of Swansea would be complete without referring to the town's most famous son, Dylan Thomas, who described the town as viewed from his hillside home:

Ugly, lovely town crawling, sprawling, slummed, unplanned, jerry-villa'd, and smug-suburbed by the side of a long and splendid curving shore......

His former home on steep Cwmdonkin Drive in the Uplands displays a blue plaque with the simple inscription, "Dylan Thomas, Poet, 1914-53. Born in this house". The house can be viewed by appointment. Cwmdonkin Park, close to his home, was much loved by Thomas who featured the park in his poem *The Hunchback in the Park*. The **Dylan Thomas Centre** is dedicated to the poet's life and works, with exhibitions featuring some of his original manuscripts, letters to friends and family, and a moving American documentary about him. The Centre also contains a theatre space, two galleries, bookshops, craft shops and a restaurant. The poet is also honoured at the **Dylan Thomas Theatre** down in the Maritime Quarter which alternates productions of his work with others by local and visiting companies.

For real aficionados of the poet, there are Dylan Thomas Trails to follow - in the City Centre, Uplands, Mumbles and Gower,- and the annual Dylan Thomas Celebration which attracts visitors from around the world.

The city was also the birthplace of other well-known people: Sir Harry Secombe, Catherine Zeta Jones, Michael Heseltine, Archbishop Rowan Williams and the singer Bonnie Tyler.

If Dylan Thomas was Swansea's most famous son, its most famous dog was Jack, a retriever who lived in the city during the 1940s. He was reputed to have saved 27 humans and two dogs from drowning and was awarded the canine Victoria Cross.

> *Swansea has its own Botanical Garden, housed in the walled garden of Singleton Park, and at Plantasia, visitors can wander around a glass pyramid with three climatic zones - tropical, humid, arid - and 5000 exotic plants. The hot house is also home to numerous exotic insects, fish and reptiles, such as leaf cutting ants, and there is a butterfly house where the various colourful species fly freely. Clyne Gardens, at Blackpill off the A4067 Mumbles road, are known in particular for their marvellous rhododendrons, including National Collections, their imposing magnolias and an extensive bog garden. In 2001 the rhododendrons captured 23 awards from the Royal Horticultural Society. These 19th century landscaped gardens were laid out by the Vivian family, who were also responsible for nearby Sketty Hall, a 19th century version of an Italian parterre garden.*

258 THE PLOUGH AND HARROW

Brynhyfryd

Spacious village hostelry noted for its award-winning food and regular live entertainment.

🍴 see page 395

259 G & T'S BISTRO

Mumbles

Facing onto Swansea Bay, quality restaurant serving a wide range of English, European, local seafood dishes and international cuisine.

🍴 see page 396

260 TIDES REACH GUEST HOUSE

Mumbles

4-star accommodation in recently refurbished guest house occupying a prime position overlooking Swansea Bay.

🛏 see page 396

GOWER PENINSULA

MUMBLES

4½ miles SW of Swansea on the A4067

This charming Victorian resort grew up around the old fishing village of Oystermouth, which has its roots in Roman times and where the Normans built a castle to defend their land. Now in ruins, **Oystermouth Castle** was the home of the de Breos family and the gatehouse, chapel and great hall all date from around the 13th to 14th centuries. Surrounded by small but beautiful grounds overlooking the bay, the ruins are now the scene of re-enactments which chart the history of the castle and, in particular, the siege of the fortress by Owain Glyndwr.

Mumbles is now a popular sailing centre, with numerous pubs - the Mumbles Mile is Wales' best known pub crawl - fine restaurants, a restored late-Victorian pier and, on the headland, a lighthouse guarding the entrance into Swansea harbour. The churchyard of All Saints Church at Oystermouth contains the grave of Thomas Bowdler, the literary censor. In 1818 he published an expurgated edition of Shakespeare that omitted all words and expressions which he considered could not with propriety be read aloud by a father to his family. Although sexual references, however fleeting or obscure, were ruthlessly excised,

cruelty and violence remained largely unexpurgated. Bowdler died at Rhydding, near Swansea, in 1825, leaving a bowdlerised version of Gibbon's *Decline and Fall of the Roman Empire*.

An unusual attraction in Mumbles is the **Lovespoon Gallery**, where visitors will find an amazing variety of these unique love tokens. Lovespoons were traditionally carved from wood by young men and presented to their sweethearts as a token of their devotion. The custom dates back many centuries, but in these less romantic days the spoons are often bought simply as souvenirs of Wales. The Gallery is open from 10am to 5.30pm Monday to Saturday.

The **Mumbles Passenger Railway** was the world's first, and from 1807 to its closure in 1960 the five-mile line used in succession horse, sail, steam, battery, petrol, diesel and electricity. On Bank Holidays in the mid-Victorian period it was known to carry up to 40,000 passengers.

Beyond The Mumbles - the unusual name is derived from the French *mamelles* meaning 'breasts' and is a reference to the two islets of the promontory beyond Oystermouth - lies the lovely **Gower Peninsula**, designated an Area of Outstanding Natural Beauty. Gower's southern coast is made up of a succession of sandy, sheltered bays and the first of these, Langland Bay, is just around the headland from the village.

PARKMILL

8 miles SW of Swansea on the A4118

This village is home to the **Gower Heritage Centre** which is itself centred around a historic water mill built in the 12th century by the powerful le Breos family, the Norman rulers of Gower. Originally constructed to supply flour for nearby Pennard Castle, this water mill is a rare survivor in Wales of a rural complex that would once have been found in most villages and hamlets. The Heritage Centre has displays on the history of this beautiful region along with a farming museum. Visitors can also tour the mill, where the restored machinery grinds flour on most days. Younger visitors to the centre can make friends with the farm animals and everyone will enjoy wandering around the craft units and workshops where a wheelwright, a potter, a blacksmith and a mason can be seen plying their trades.

About 1 mile north of the village is **Parc le Breos Burial Chamber,** a Neolithic tomb that was discovered in 1869 and contained the 6000 year old remains of 24 people. Close by is **Cathole Cave** where archaeologists have discovered remains suggesting that there were people in the area around 12,000 years ago.

PENMAEN

7 miles SW of Swansea off the A4118

Tradition has it that a village is buried here beneath the sand dunes. The National Trust owns an area

Parc le Breos Burial Chamber, Parkmill

that includes High Pennard, topped by a prehistoric hill fort, and Three Cliffs Bay, where there are old lime kilns, an ancient burial chamber and a pillow mound - an artificial warren used to farm rabbits. Cut into the rocks is Minchin Hole, a geological Site of Scientific Interest where evidence has been found of mammals and early man.

OXWICH

11 miles SW of Swansea off the A4118

One of Gower's prettiest villages, Oxwich lies huddled along a lane at the western end of a superb three mile long beach. Once a small port exporting limestone and also a haven for smugglers, Oxwich is today a marvellous holiday area with safe bathing, clean beaches, wind surfing and water skiing. The village has some picturesque cottages of the traditional Gower style which include one that was once occupied by John Wesley. The village **Church of St Illtud**, half hidden by trees, is well worth

261 LITTLE HAVEN GUEST HOUSE

Oxwich

Overlooking Oxwich Bay, long-established guest house offering quality en suite accommodation.

see page 397

189

262 THE BAY BISTRO & COFFEE HOUSE

Rhossili

Popular licensed Café Bistro serving appetising food and enjoying superb views over Rhossili Bay.

see page 398

seeking out as its ancient font is believed to have been brought here by St Illtud himself.

Just to the south of the village lies **Oxwich Castle**, which was once a grand Tudor manor house built around a courtyard. The splendid house was established by Sir Rice Mansel in the 1520s and added to by his son, Sir Edward Mansel, whose building work includes the Elizabethan long gallery. The Mansel family's time at this lavish mansion was short lived, and after they left in the 1630s the house fell into disrepair, although the southern wing was used as a farmhouse and the southeast tower still survives to its full height of six storeys.

For walkers there are plenty of footpaths to explore and the walk to **Oxwich Point**, in particular, provides some magnificent views of the Gower Peninsula. Close to the beach lies part of the **Oxwich Nature Reserve**, home to many rare species of orchid as well as other plant life and a variety of birds.

KNELSTON
12½ miles SW of Swansea on the A4118

To the north of this attractive village lies **Arthur's Stone**, a large burial chamber capstone. Traditionally, this is said to be the pebble which King Arthur removed from his shoe while on his way to the Battle of Camlann in the 6th century. According to legend, Arthur threw the stone over his shoulder and the stone lies exactly where it landed. Up until the 19th century, local girls would enact a ritual here to discover whether their lovers were true or not. At midnight and with a full moon, the girls would place a honey cake soaked in milk on the stone and then crawl under it three times. If their lovers were true, they would join them at this point.

RHOSSILI
16 miles SW of Swansea on the B4247

This village, on the westernmost area of the Gower Peninsula, is thought to have been named after St Fili, who is said to have been the son of St Cenydd. Inside the small church is a memorial plaque to a Gower man, Edgar Evans, who is perhaps better known as Petty

Rhossili Bay

Officer Evans, who died in the ill-fated expedition to the Antarctic led by Captain Scott in 1912.

To the west of Rhossili lies **Worm's Head**, an island which is a National Nature Reserve. Reached by a causeway at low tide, there is public access to the island, but those making the crossing should take great care not to be cut off by the tide. Worm's Head marks the southern edge of Rhossili Bay, whose beach can be reached by a steep downhill climb. At low tide, the remains of several wrecks can be seen, most notably the *Helvetia*, which was wrecked in 1887. The area is very popular with fishermen, surfers and bathers. Behind Rhossili Beach stretches **The Warren**, under the sands of which are the remains of old Rhossili village and church.

LLANGENNITH

15 miles W of Swansea off the B4271

This quiet village is home to the largest church on the Gower peninsula. It was built in the 12th century on the site of a priory founded six centuries earlier by St Cenydd and was destroyed some 400 years later by Viking raiders. Inside, there is a curious gravestone thought to mark the resting place of St Cenydd. To the west of the village and marking the northern edge of Rhossili Bay lies **Burry Holms**, another small island which can be reached via a causeway at low tide. On the island are the remains of an Iron Age earthwork and also a monastic chapel dating from the Middle Ages.

LLANRHIDIAN

10½ miles W of Swansea on the B4295

Close to the wild and lonely north coast of the Gower Peninsula, where some of the finest beaches in the country can be found, this village is also close to **Weobley Castle** (CADW). Dating from the early 14th century and built by the de Bere family, Weobley is more a fortified manor house than a castle and stands today as one of the few surviving such houses in Wales. On an isolated site overlooking the eerie expanse of Llanrhidian Marsh, this house has been remarkably well preserved and visitors can gain a real insight into the domestic arrangements of those days and, in particular, the owners' desire for comfort. In the late 15th century the house came into the hands of Sir Rhys ap Thomas, an ally of Henry VII, He made further improvements including the addition of a new porch and an upgrade of the accommodation in the private apartments. The castle also has an exhibition on the Gower Peninsula - its history and other ancient monuments.

LOUGHOR

6½ miles NW of Swansea on the A484

A strategic location on the mouth of the River Loughor gave this village prominence and importance down the centuries. The Romans built their station of Leucarum here in the 1st century, and in the early 12th century a Norman nobleman, Henry de Newburgh, built **Loughor Castle** on the edge of the Roman

263 THE BRITANNIA INN

Llanmadoc

Picturesque village pub/restaurant with internationally experienced chefs; en suite rooms available.

see page 397

264 THE GREYHOUND INN

Llanrhidian

Handsome 19th century roadhouse noted for its appetising home-cooked food and real ales.

see page 399

265 CEDI COTTAGES

Penclawdd

Delightful self-catering cottages renovated from farm outbuildings in scenic country setting.

see page 400

191

Felindre

Outstanding country inn
serving quality home-made
food and offering en suite
rooms.

🍴 🛏 *see page 401*

Skewen

Popular town centre café
serving a huge variety of
wholesome and appetising
home-made food.

🍴 *see page 401*

192

site. Unfortunately, all that is left of
the stronghold, which protected the
confluence of the Burry Inlet and
the River Loughor, is the ruined
13th century square tower.

PORT TALBOT

Well known for its steel industry,
Port Talbot was named after the
Talbot family who were responsible
for the development of the town's
docks in the 19th century. Now
called the Old Docks, this area saw
significant expansion again in the
20th century when a new deep
water harbour was opened by the
Queen in 1970. Today Port Talbot
is home to factories and processing
plants, and also to the solar centre
of **Baglan Bay Energy Park**,
which explains the history of the
area and its power generating
potential.

Coal mining has taken place in
the area around Port Talbot for
centuries and during this time many
superstitions have grown up. In
1890, the miners at Morfa Colliery
reported seeing ghostly images in
and around the colliery. They were
said to be fierce hounds and became
known as the 'Red Dogs of Morfa'.
They would run through the streets
with their appearance being
accompanied by a sweet, rose-like
scent which filled the mine shaft.
Such were the number of eerie
manifestations that on the morning
of 10th March 1890, nearly half the
morning shift failed to report for
work. Later that same day, there was
an explosion at the colliery - 87
miners died in the disaster.

AROUND PORT TALBOT

NEATH

4 miles N of Port Talbot on the A465

While Neath's industrial history
dates back to the late 16th century,
when the first copper smelter in
South Wales was built here by
Cornishmen, the town has its
origins in Roman times. Remains
of Roman Nidum can still be seen
close to the ruins of **Neath
Abbey**, which was founded in the
13th century by Richard de
Granville on land seized from the
Welsh in around 1130. The abbey
buildings were converted into a
mansion for Sir John Herbert in
the 16th century and it was later
used to house copper smelters. It
was also de Granville who built
Neath Castle, in the mid 12th
century, around which the town
grew and whose scant remains can
be found near a town centre car
park.

Housed in the Old Mechanics
Institute, the **Neath Museum
and Art Gallery** has permanent
displays on the history of the
town, including finds from the
time of the Roman occupation, as
well as regularly changing art and
photographic exhibitions. The
museum has many hands-on
activities, including grinding corn,
using a Celtic loom and making a
wattle fence.

Held each September, **Neath
Fair** is the oldest such event in
Wales, founded by Gilbert de Clare
in 1280.

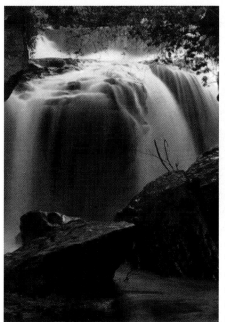

Aberdulais Falls

ABERDULAIS

6 miles N of Port Talbot off the A4109

From as early as 1584 the power generated by the magnificent **Aberdulais Falls** (National Trust) has been harnessed for a number of industries, including copper smelting and tin plating. Every day 160 million litres of dark green water cascade over the shelves and pools of the falls. Some of the environmentally friendly energy is still used via a waterwheel that is the largest in Europe. The Turbine House provides access to a unique fish pass.

CRYNANT

9 miles N of Port Talbot on the A4109

In the beautiful Dulais Valley, **Cefn Coed Colliery Museum** provides a

wonderful opportunity for visitors to discover what life was like for the miners who worked underground in some of the most difficult conditions experienced anywhere in the world. Through photographs, maps and other exhibits, the tradition and legacy of mining are brought to life. The museum also has a well-stocked souvenir and gift shop, with one of the best selections of genuine and reproduction miner's lamps in the region. It is ideal for finding a special present from Wales.

PONT-RHYD-Y-FEN

3½ miles NE of Port Talbot on the B4287

This village was the birthplace of the actor Richard Burton.

CYNONVILLE

6 miles NE of Port Talbot on the A4107

Virtually surrounding the village (to the north, west and south) lies the **Afan Forest Park**, a large area of woodland where there are trails for cycling, walking and pony trekking. At the Park's **Countryside Centre** an exhibition explains, with the aid of hands-on displays, the landscape and history of the Afan Valley. The **South Wales Miners' Museum**, also at the centre, illustrates the social history of the valleys' mining communities.

268 DULAIS ROCK INN

Neath

Outstanding 350-year-old inn adjacent to Aberdulais Falls offering excellent cuisine and en suite rooms.

❚❚ ⊨ see page 402

269 BISHOPS CAFÉ BISTRO

Pontardawe

Very popular eating place with extensive menu to eat in or to take away.

❚❚ see page 403

270 CELTIC LODGE INN

Alltwen

Welcoming inn offering fine ales, comfortable en suite rooms and a self-catering cottage.

❚❚ ⊨ see page 404

271 TREGIB ARMS

Brynamman

Warm and welcoming village inn serving wholesome home-made food and real ales; en suite rooms available.

❚❚ ⊨ see page 403

Margam Abbey Church

also includes various contemporary sculptures by artists as distinguished as Barbara Hepworth and Elizabeth Frink, a visitor centre, waymarked trails, a deer park, bird of prey centre and the **Margam Stones Museum**, where visitors can see a collection of early Christian memorials dating from Roman times through to the 10th and 11th centuries.

PONTYPRIDD

This friendly valley town is justly proud of its past which is revealed in the **Pontypridd Museum** housed in a splendidly ornate former chapel close to Pontypridd's historic stone bridge of 1776 over the River Taff. As well as its industrial heritage, the town has a long tradition of music. In Ynysangharad Park are two statues commemorating Evan James and his son, a song-writing team who were responsible in 1856 for composing the words and music of what was later adopted as the Welsh National Anthem, *Land of my Fathers (Hen Wlad fy Nhadau)*. The museum also has exhibits on the opera stars Sir Geraint Evans and Stewart Burrows, who were born in the same street in nearby Clifynydd, and the durable warbler Tom Jones who was born in Pontypridd itself.

A curiosity in the town is **John Hughes' Grogg Shop** near the strikingly elegant railway station. On sale here is a bizarre collection of sculptural caricatures of rugby stars and other well-known Welsh personalities.

•

Just outside Pontypridd, at Fforest Uchaf Farm, Penycoedcae, is the Pit Pony Sanctuary, where visitors can meet more than 25 horses and ponies, including several retired pit ponies. Also here are pit pony memorabilia and a reconstruction of a typical pony-powered Welsh drift coal mine.

•

272 CROSS INN HOTEL

Cross Inn

Picturesque village inn serving quality lunchtime food and a choice of real ales.

see page 405

MARGAM

3 miles SE of Port Talbot on the A48

To the southeast of the town lies **Margam Country Park** surrounding a mansion built in the 1840s by the Talbot family. The land once belonged to **Margam Abbey**, a Cistercian house which was founded in 1147 by Robert, Earl of Gloucester. Following a violent revolt by the lay brothers, the abbey went on to become one of the wealthiest in Wales but, at the time of the Dissolution of the Monasteries, the estate passed on to Sir Rice Mansel, who built the first mansion on the estate in 1537.

The park today boasts several buildings left by previous owners including **Margam Abbey Church** (all that remains of the abbey), a classical 18th century orangery, recently restored monastic gardens, a unique fuchsia collection and a restored Japanese garden from the 1920s. This huge recreational area - the park covers some 800 acres -

194

AROUND PONTYPRIDD

LLANTRISANT

4 miles SW of Pontypridd on the B4595

This old town stands between two hills rising sharply from the valley of the rivers Ely and Clun. It takes its name, Three Saints, from Saints Illtud, Gwyno and Dyfod, to whom the parish church is dedicated. All that remains of 13th century **Llantrisant Castle** is part of a round tower known as the Raven Tower. It was probably to this castle, in 1326, that Edward II and Hugh Despenser were brought after falling into the hands of Queen Isabella.

One of several interesting features in Llantrisant parish church is the east window, which was the work of Burne Jones and depicts an unbearded Christ, one of only three known such windows.

Though some of the traditional heavy industry still remains, Llantrisant is best known nowadays for being the home of the **Royal Mint**, which transferred here from Tower Hill, London in 1967. At the **Model Centre**, a craft and design gallery, there is a permanent Royal Mint display along with a shop, café and a programme of events and exhibitions.

Standing in the town centre is a statue of a figure dressed in a fox skin head-dress. This is the town's memorial to Dr William Price, an amazing and eccentric character who lived from 1800 to 1893. Espousing many causes, some of which scandalised straight-laced Victorian Britain, Price was a vegetarian who believed in free love, nudism and radical politics. His most famous deed, considered infamous at the time, was his cremation of his illegitimate son Iesu Grist (Jesus Christ) who had died in infancy. He burnt the small body in an oil drum on Llantrisant Common in January 1884. As a result of the controversy, and the ensuing court case, cremation became legal in Britain. The statue was donated by the Cremation Society. To commemorate his centenary, the Council constructed a heather garden which can be seen as one enters the town.

TREHAFOD

1½ miles NW of Pontypridd off the A4058

While this area was associated with heavy industry and, in particular, coal mining, the Rhondda and Cynon valleys of today are very different and the only working deep mine left in South Wales is **Tower Colliery**. In the Rhondda Valley alone there were once 53 working mines in just 16 square miles but, although they have now gone, the traditions of the colliery still live on.

When the Lewis Merthyr Colliery closed in 1983, it re-opened as the **Rhondda Heritage Park**, a fascinating place where former miners guide visitors around the restored mining buildings. As well as seeing the conditions in which the miners worked and hearing stories from miners whose families worked in

273 MISKIN HOTEL

Trealaw

Long-established family-run hotel offering good, wholesome food, en suite rooms and regular entertainment.

see page 405

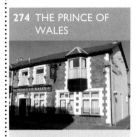

274 THE PRINCE OF WALES

Treorchy

Lively and popular hostelry with quality pub grub, draught ales and regular live entertainment.

see page 406

275 THE DUNRAVEN HOTEL

Treherbert

Village hostelry with country house character offering good food and en suite rooms; also beer garden.

see page 407

195

276 JEFFREYS ARMS HOTEL

Mountain Ash

Welcoming family-owned and run hostelry serving wholesome food and real ale.

🍴 see page 406

277 PEPPERS RESTAURANT

Aberdare

Popular family-run town centre licensed restaurant offering delicious home-cooked food.

🍴 see page 408

278 WELSH HARP INN

Trecynon

Gourmet dining and wining at family-run restaurant in village inn.

🍴 see page 409

Rhondda Valley Landscape

the mines for generations, visitors can also see exhibitions on the role of the women in a mining village, the dramatic history of the 1920s strikes for a minimum wage and the tragedy of mining disasters. Between 1868 and 1919 in Rhondda one miner was killed every six hours and one injured every two minutes. The cultural and social history of a mining community, through brass bands, choirs and the chapel, is explored and visitors also have the opportunity to put on a hard hat and travel down the mine shaft in a cage.

ABERDARE

9 miles NW of Pontypridd on the A4233

Situated at the northern end of the Cynon valley, Aberdare, like other valley towns, is famous for its strong music tradition - particularly male voice choirs. In **Victoria Square** is a statue of the baton waving choir conductor, Griffith Rhys Jones (1834-1897).

The valley's other tradition, coal mining, is celebrated at the excellent **Cynon Valley Museum** which is housed in the town's former tram depot. Various exhibits portray the social and working conditions of the mid-19th century, along with displays of the 1926 General Strike and the Miners Strike of 1984-85. On a lighter note, there are also exhibits on teenage life through the centuries, miners' jazz bands and Victorian lantern slides.

The landscape of Aberdare was once shaped by coal mines and heavy industry, but with the closure of the mines the countryside is, through ambitious land reclamation and environmental improvement schemes, returning to its pre-industrial green and lush natural state. Just a short distance from the busy town centre is the beautiful **Dare Valley Country Park** which was opened in 1973 on former colliery land and where trails tell of the natural and industrial history of the area.

MERTHYR TYDFIL

The main road in this area of Wales, the A645, acts as a dividing line: to the south are the historic valleys once dominated by coal mining and the iron and steel industries, while, to the north, lie the unspoilt southern uplands of the Brecon Beacons National Park. This rigidly observed divide is explained by geology, as the coal bearing rocks of the valleys end here and give way to the limestone and old red sandstone rocks of the Brecon Beacons. The close proximity of the two different types of rock also explains the nature and growth of industry in this particular area of South Wales as the iron smelting process required not just coal but also limestone. The iron ore was locally available too. These ingredients all came together in the most productive way at Merthyr Tydfil and this former iron and steel capital of the world was once the largest town in Wales. In 1831 its population of 60,000 exceeded that of Cardiff, Newport and Swansea combined. The town took its name from the martyr St Tydfil, the daughter of the Welsh chieftain Brychan (after whom Brecon is named). She was martyred by the Irish for her Christian beliefs in AD 480.

Described as 'the most impressive monument of the Industrial Iron Age in Southern Wales', **Cyfarthfa Castle** is a grand mansion situated in beautiful and

279 THE OLD WHITE HORSE

Pontneddfechan

Fine old hostelry noted for its excellent food and well-kept ales; bunkhouse accommodation available.

🍴 ➡ see page 408

280 TY NEWYDD COUNTRY HOTEL

Hirwaun

Quality country house hotel within the National Park offering quality cuisine, en suite accommodation and lovely grounds.

🍴 see page 410

281 THE RED LION INN

Penderyn

Popular hostelry at the heart of village life, offering up to 12 cask ales and a selection of snacks.

🍴 see page 411

Cyfarthfa Castle, Merthyr Tydfil

well laid out parkland. The castle was commissioned in the 1820s by the ironmaster William Crawshay, who constructed the grand house to overlook the family's ironworks, which at the time were the largest in the world. Today, this mansion is home to a **Museum and Art Gallery** which not only covers the social and industrial history of Merthyr Tydfil and the surrounding area but also has an extensive collection of fine and decorative art. The parkland, too, is well worth exploring, and the Visitor Centre has copious information on the park's amenities and natural history.

Joseph Parry's Birthplace in Chapel Row provides a contrasting view of life in Merthyr Tydfil during its heyday. A superb example of a skilled ironworker's home, the cottage gives an interesting insight into the living conditions of those days. It was here that Joseph Parry, the 19th century composer famous for writing the haunting hymn *Myfanwy*, was born; on the first floor is an exhibition of his life and work.

Another of the town's claims

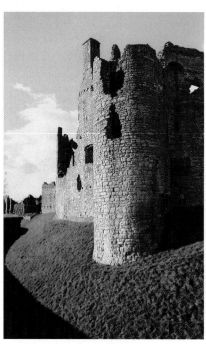

Newcastle Castle, Bridgend

to fame lies in the political sphere: it was the first constituency in Britain to return a socialist Member of Parliament when Kier Hardie was elected to Westminster in 1900.

AROUND MERTHYR TYDFIL

PONTSTICILL

3 miles N of Merthyr Tydfil off the A465

From here the **Brecon Mountain Railway** travels a 2-mile scenic route up to Pontsticill Reservoir in the Brecon Beacons National Park. The charming vintage steam trains follow the tracks of the old Merthyr Tydfil to Brecon line, which has been re-opened by railway enthusiasts.

BRIDGEND

Known in Welsh as Pen-y-Bont Ar Ogwr (meaning 'the crossing of the River Ogmore'), this bustling market town lies at the confluence of the Rivers Ogmore, Garw and Llynfi and was once regarded as so vital a route that it had two castles, one on either side of the River Ogmore. The sparse remains of 12th century **Newcastle Castle** lie on the west riverside while the more extensive ruins of 14th century **Coity Castle** (CADW; free) stand guard on the other. Originally built by the Norman Payn de Turberville and strengthened over the following three centuries, Coity Castle was finally abandoned in the late-16th century. Its late-Norman decorated gateway is the only surviving feature of interest.

Bridgend's distinction as a market town dates back as far as the early 16th century and down the ages there have been tanneries, a woollen factory and local potteries in the area. Today, the Rhiw shopping centre, the new covered market and, on the northern outskirts, the giant McArthur Glen Designer Outlet with almost 100 stores, have made Bridgend something of a shopper's paradise.

AROUND BRIDGEND

TONDU

3½ miles N of Bridgend on the A4063

The nationally important Tondu Ironworks have now been incorporated into the **Tondu Heritage Park**, while the site of an old colliery and open cast coal workings has been developed into the **Parc Slip Nature Reserve**. The reserve's network of paths lead visitors through the various different wildlife habitats, such as grassland, woodland and wetland, where a wide variety of plants, birds and animals have made their homes.

BETWS

5 miles N of Bridgend off the A4063

Just south of the village lies **Bryngarw Country Park**, which throughout the year presents a variety of enchanting landscapes including woodland, grassland, water features and formal gardens. A visitor centre provides information on the country park and on the many species of plants and birds to be found here. Perhaps the most interesting feature of the park is the exotic Japanese Garden, which was laid out in 1910 and where there are not only a series of interlinked ponds and an oriental tea garden pavilion, but also superb azaleas, rhododendrons, magnolias and cherry trees.

The house at the centre of the estate, **Bryngarw House**, was built in 1834 by Morgan Popkin Treherne as a 'small but elegant dwelling'; it has been restored and is now a bistro and conference centre.

MAESTEG

8 miles N of Bridgend on the A4063

This ancient market town with its broad main street, reputedly the widest in Wales, was the centre of iron making in the 1820s, but the last great furnace was 'blown out' in 1886; one of the ironworks is now a sports centre. Maesteg was once linked to the coast at Porthcawl by a tramway, traces of which can be seen at Porthcawl. The Tabor chapel in Maesteg was where *Land of My Fathers* was first sung in public in 1856. The Welsh words were written by Evan James, the music by his son James James. For 112 years, Talbot Street was the only alcohol-free high street in Britain, so covenanted in the will of the teetotal spinster after whom the street was named. In the summer of 2002, a restaurant owner challenged the covenant, and the magistrates ruled in his favour.

282 SIX BELLS

Coity

Welcoming family-run inn noted for its excellent food and real ales.

❙ see page 412

LLANGEINOR

5 miles N of Bridgend on the A4064

This pretty village has a handsome medieval church on a mountainside which was built over the foundations of a religious site dating back to the 6th century. The church, which is dedicated to St Ceinwyr, has a fine 15th century nave, a 16th century tower and a Norman font.

HOEL-Y-CYW

4 miles NE of Bridgend off the B4280

To the northeast of the village lies **Mynydd y Gaer**, a wonderful local landmark which, from its near 1000 foot high summit, provides spectacular views across the valleys to the north and the Bristol Channel to the south.

MERTHYR MAWR

2 miles SW of Bridgend off the A48

Situated down river from Bridgend, this delightful village of thatched cottages bordered by meadows and woodland lies on the edge of **Merthyr Mawr Warren**, one of the largest areas of sand dunes in Europe. Parts of David Lean's *Lawrence of Arabia* were filmed in the dunes. Now a Site of Special Scientific Interest, the dunes offer the perfect habitat for a wide variety of plants and animals.

Surrounded by the dune system are the remains of **Candleston Castle**, a 15th century fortified manor house that was, until the 19th century, the home of the powerful Cantelupe family. Local children believe the house to be

New Inn Bridge, Merthyr Mawr

haunted but the biggest mystery of Candleston is the fate of the village of Treganllaw (meaning 'the town of a hundred hands') which is thought to have been engulfed by the dunes.

On the road approaching the village is the 15th century **New Inn Bridge** which has some interesting holes in its parapet through which in the old days sheep were pushed into the river for their annual dip!

NEWTON

4½ miles W of Bridgend off the A4106

Dating back to the 12th century, the village was founded as a 'new town' and by the 17th century was a thriving port from where grain and knitted stockings were exported. The imposing limestone church was originally built for the Knights of the Order of St John of Jerusalem in the late 12th or early 13th century. On the nearby green is St John's Well where pilgrims would take refreshment from its supposedly healing waters.

PORTHCAWL

6 miles W of Bridgend on the A4229

Porthcawl is one of the region's most popular resorts, with clean sandy beaches at Sandy Bay, Trecco Bay and the quieter Rest Bay which boasts a European Blue Flag. Coney Beach Pleasure Park provides a wide variety of rides, from white knuckle roller coasters to more gentle carousels. This is also a haven for surfers, sailors and fishing enthusiasts, while the headlands above Rest Bay are the

site of the famous Royal Porthcawl Golf Club.

The more dignified side of Porthcawl centres around the Edwardian promenade, a legacy of the prosperous days when this was a port exporting coal and iron. A good way of orienting yourself is to take a trip on the Promenade Princess, a road train that leaves from Coney Beach park. It passes the working harbour where, during the summer months, the veteran steamship *Balmoral* departs for cruises along the Bristol channel and across to Lundy Island. The RNLI has a base at the harbour and nearby there's a white-painted cast iron lighthouse built in 1866. On the edge of the harbour is the **Jennings Building** of 1830, one of the oldest harbour buildings in Wales and now a Skating Centre. On its southeastern wall is a brass plug marking the highest recorded tide of 52ft. The road train continues along the promenade to Rest Bay, passing en route the **Grand Pavilion,** a wonderful Art Deco building of 1932 that plays host to all manner of live shows, cinema and private parties.

The history of the town can be discovered at **Porthcawl Museum**, where there is a fascinating collection of artefacts, costumes and memorabilia on display.

KENFIG

6½ miles W of Bridgend off the B4283

This village was originally founded in the 12th century by Robert, Earl of Gloucester, who also built **Kenfig Castle** here. However,

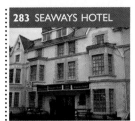

283 SEAWAYS HOTEL

Porthcawl

Impressive town centre hotel offering en suite accommodation, wholesome home-cooked food and real ale.

see page 413

284 SALTHOUSE ON THE SQUARE

Porthcawl

Seafront restaurant offering quality food all day and gourmet dining in the evenings.

see page 414

285 THE PIER CAFÉ

Porthcawl

Quality tea room and café in superb position looking out to sea.

see page 415

286 COMESTON
MEDIEVAL VILLAGE

Penarth

The reconstructed 14th
Century village is on its
original site and consists of
medieval buildings. gardens,
rare breeds and a small yet
fascinating museum.

 see page 415

some 400 years later the sands of
Kenfig Burrows had swamped the
settlement and the medieval town
lies buried in the dunes although
the remains of the castle keep are
still visible. The legend of Kenfig
Pool has it that on a quiet day when
the water is clear, the houses of the
buried town can be seen at the
bottom of the lake and the bells of
the old church can be heard ringing
before a storm.

Today, this marvellous area of
dunes to the northwest of the
present village is the **Kenfig
National Nature Reserve**. With
more than 600 species of flowering
plants, including orchids, a
freshwater lake and numerous
birds, this is a haven for all
naturalists as well as ramblers.

Just up the road from the
Nature Reserve is the **Prince of
Wales pub** which was originally
built in 1605 as a replacement for
the Town Hall which had
disappeared beneath the
encroaching sands. The pub is
notable for having experienced an
unusual number of documented
paranormal events.

PENARTH AND THE VALE OF GLAMORGAN

Often described as the 'garden by
the sea', Penarth (the name means
'bear's head' in Welsh) is a popular
and unspoilt seaside resort which
developed in Victorian and
Edwardian times. Built for the
wealthy industrialists of Cardiff's

shipyards, this once fashionable
town has lost none of its late 19th
and early 20th century elegance and
style typified by the splendidly
restored pier, the sweeping
Esplanade, the abundant flowerbeds and the formal sea view
gardens. Built in 1894, the **Pier**
extends 685ft out into the channel
and is a regular berthing point
during the summer for the cruise
ships *Balmoral* and *Waverley* - the
latter being the last sea-going
paddle steamer in the world. From
the Marina, a water bus sails across
the freshwater lake to Cardiff's
recently developed Bay area with its
chic shops, restaurants, Welsh
Assembly building and award-
winning visitor centre.

Long before the town became
popular as a resort, Penarth's
picturesque setting had inspired
many artists, amongst them JMW
Turner who is commemorated in
the **Turner House Gallery,** part
of the National Museum of Wales,
in the centre of the town.

A famous resident of the town
was Dr Joseph Parry who
composed the much-loved *Myfanwy*.
He is buried in the churchyard of
St Augustine's Church, a building
regarded by many as one of the
finest Victorian churches in Britain.

If the town seems to have
been lost in a time warp, a visit to
the **Washington Gallery**, housed
in a wonderful Art Deco cinema,
will dispel this view through its
exciting collection of modern and
contemporary art.

From Penarth's Esplanade, a
spectacular coastal path leads out to

Lavernock Point. It was from here in 1897 that Guglielmo Marconi sent the very first radio transmission over water to the offshore island of **Flat Holm** some 3 miles distant. The transmission was brief - just the three words "Are you ready?" A tiny island with a wealth of wildlife, Flat Holm has a history that dates back to the Dark Ages, when it was used by monks as a retreat. Vikings, Anglo-Saxons, smugglers and cholera victims are known to have sought refuge on the island, which was also fortified twice, once by the Victorians and again in World War II. Today, it is a Site of Special Scientific Interest, with a local nature reserve that is home to the largest colony of gulls in Wales.

To the south of Penarth lies a **Medieval Village** that grew up around a manor house belonging to the Constantin family (some of the first Norman invaders in Wales) in the 12th century. However, in the mid-14th century the Black Death reached Cosmeston village, killing around one third of the population. Following a period of decline it was left to decay. Today, several of the village's buildings have been reconstructed, allowing visitors, with the help of costumed characters, to gain a real insight into life in a medieval village.

The Medieval Village is in **Cosmeston Country Park**, an area of lakes, woodlands and meadows created from a disused limestone quarry. A peaceful and tranquil habitat for many birds and animals, with a wide range of plant life, the country park has a visitor centre, picnic areas and a café

AROUND PENARTH

BARRY ISLAND & BARRY

5 miles SW of Penarth on the A4055

Barry Island is not an island but a peninsula, facing Barry, whose natural, sheltered harbour has been used since Roman times; **Cold Knap Roman Buildings**, to the west of this seaside resort, are all that remains from those days. A popular place for holidaymakers for generations, Barry Island offers its

287 THE SIX BELLS

Penmark

Spacious and convivial recently refurbished village inn serving real ales.

see page 416

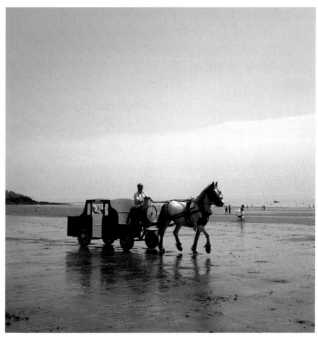

Pony and Cart on Barry Island Beach

288 THE BEACH CAFÉ

Llantwit Major

Long-established family run beachside café serving quality home-cooked food every day of the year except Christmas Day.

see page 416

visitors all the traditional seaside resort trappings, from sandy beaches to a funfair, as well as views across the Bristol Channel to the Somerset coast. Quieter souls will no doubt prefer either **The Knap** with its gardens and lake, or **Porthkerry Country Park** with some 220 acres of parkland, woods and meadows leading down to the sea.

The sands of **Whitmore Bay** are perfect for volleyball - there are volleyball courts on the beach throughout the summer and in August the island hosts the **British Beach Volleyball Championship**. For younger visitors, Triassic Towers offers the ultimate adventure experience with spiral climbs, hanging snakes, wavy stairs and crawl nets.

The latest all-weather attraction is the **Barry Island Railway Heritage Centre**, which has opened its extended line from Barry Island into the neighbouring Waterfront Dock Development.

To the north of the resort is the **Welsh Hawking Centre**, where 200 birds of prey have their homes and provide regular flying demonstrations.

Over recent years, Barry town's Waterfront development has inspired an ambitious multi-million pound regeneration programme, restoring key buildings and adding modern homes and commercial buildings. But perhaps the most impressive building in town is the 1899 **Dock Office Building**. Designed in neo-baroque Renaissance style, the building has a calendar theme: 365 windows, 52

marble fireplaces; 12 panels in the impressive porch; 7 lights in the window above the original doors, 4 floors for the seasons and 2 circular windows in the entrance hall representing the sun and moon.

LLANTWIT MAJOR

14 miles W of Penarth off the B4265

The centre of this delightful town with its narrow streets, quaint stone cottages, olde worlde shops and ancient inns is perhaps the Vale of Glamorgan's most historic settlement. It was here, in AD 500, that St Illtud founded a church and school. One of the great Celtic saints who travelled in Britain, Ireland and Brittany, St Illtud was the tutor of both St David and St Patrick. The latter was abducted from the monastery by Irish pirates and taken to Ireland where he later became the country's patron saint. Although little is known of St Illtud, he does feature in the book *The Life of St Samson of Dol* which was written around 100 years after his death. The church and school he founded here are believed to be the oldest learning centres in the country. The only remains of his original church to have survived are the dedication stones, but the imposing **Church of St Illtud** seen today is a combination of two buildings, one an early Norman structure and the other dating from the late 13th century. John Wesley, visiting in 1777, described the church as "the most beautiful as well as the most spacious church in Wales". Inside can be seen a fine collection of Celtic crosses which includes St Illtud's or St Samson's cross, which was found buried in the church grounds on top of two skeletons.

There are more ancient buildings in the town square. The **Old White Hart** public house was built as a private dwelling for a Robert Raglan around 1440; twenty-five years later, he built another new house which has survived as the **Old School** and is used by community groups.

ST DONAT'S

15 miles W of Penarth off the B4265

Close to the village stands **St Donat's Castle** which dates from around 1300 and was once owned by the American newspaper magnate William Randolph Hearst. Hearst, whose life was fictionalised in the classic Orson Welles film *Citizen Kane*, spent huge sums of money restoring and furnishing this historic building in mock-Gothic style. Here he entertained film stars and other figures on the world's stage. The castle is now the international Atlantic College. Within its grounds is the **St Donat's Arts Centre**, the largest arts venue in the Vale of Glamorgan, which offers a full programme of exhibitions, cinema, dance, theatre and musical events. The centre also hosts the **Beyond the Border Storytelling Festival** in July, and the **Vale of Glamorgan Festival** in September.

To the west of the village lies **Nash Point,** a headland with two lighthouses and the remnants of an Iron Age fort. This area of the

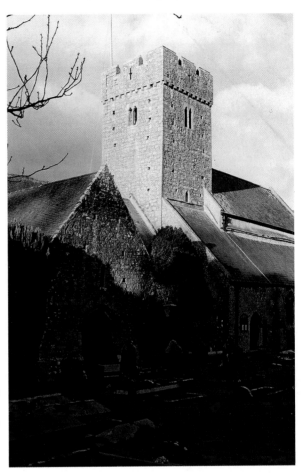

Church of St Illtud, Llantwit Major

coast is overlooked by limestone cliffs which through wind erosion have begun to resemble giant building blocks.

SOUTHERNDOWN

19 miles W of Penarth on the B4265

This popular holiday centre overlooking beautiful Dunraven Bay is home to the **Glamorgan Heritage Coast Centre** which has displays and information about the

289 THE PLOUGH AND HARROW

Monknash

Superb olde worlde village inn offering excellent cuisine and a choice of 9 cask ales.

see page 417

205

290 FOX AND HOUNDS

St Bride's Major

Popular family-run village pub with quality menu and serving real ales.

see page 417

291 EWENNY FARM GUEST HOUSE

Ewenny

Family-run Guest House offering top of the range 4-star accommodation in a friendly relaxed atmosphere.

see page 418

292 THE CROSS INN

Llanblethian

Fine old traditional village hostelry serving good wholesome food and real ales.

see page 419

14-mile long stretch of wild and beautiful coastline which begins in the west at Newton and was the first in Britain to be designated a Heritage Coast.

OGMORE

19 miles W of Penarth on the B4265

Lying at the mouth of the River Ogmore, this pretty village is also close to a ford across the River Ewenny where the impressive ruins of **Ogmore Castle** (private) can be seen. Built in the early 12th century by William de Londres, this was once the foremost stronghold in the area although all that can be seen today are the remains of a three storey keep and the dry moat. This is a great picnic spot with caves, rock pools and stepping stones across the river to Merthyr Mawr.

EWENNY

17½ miles W of Penarth on the B4265

This charming rural village is home to **Ewenny Priory**, which was founded in 1141 by Maurice de Londres, the son of William de Londres of Ogmore Castle. This is one of the finest fortified religious houses in Britain and, while its precinct walls, towers and gateways give the priory a military air, it is believed that they were built for reasons of prestige rather than defence.

Close by is 400-year-old **Ewenny Pottery**, still worked by the same family that founded it and said to be the oldest working pottery in Wales.

COWBRIDGE

12½ miles W of Penarth off the A48

This handsome and prosperous town, with the reputation of being the wealthiest in Wales, has been the principal market town of the Vale of Glamorgan since medieval times and is today noted for its quality shops, crafts and restaurants. The work of local artists and craftspeople can be seen at the **Old Wool Barn Craft Centre** which has studio workshops set around an attractive courtyard. The original Norman grid layout of the town is visible to this day, particularly in the mile-long main street. Parts of Cowbridge's 14th century town walls and one gatehouse, South Gate, still stand.

Close to South Gate is the Grammar School, founded in 1608 and rebuilt in the 1850s in Gothic style. Its most eminent alumnus is the actor Sir Anthony Hopkins.

Across from the Grammar School, in the walled garden of Old Hall, is **Cowbridge Physic Garden.** Opened in 2006, the garden is designed to create awareness of the curative properties of plants.

The history of the town can be explored at **Cowbridge Museum** which is housed in two blocks of cells beneath a sturdy building that began as House of Correction before becoming the Town Hall in 1830. It's an elegant building with a clock tower, cupola and weathervane.

On the outskirts of the town is **Llanerch Vineyard,** the largest vineyard in Wales producing estate-bottled wines which are marketed under the Cariad label.

ST NICHOLAS

6 miles NW of Penarth on the A48

To the south of the village lie **Dyffryn Gardens** which, as part of the Dyffryn estate, were landscaped in the 19th century. One of the finest surviving

Thomas Mawson gardens in Britain, Dyffryn offers a series of broad sweeping lawns, Italianate terraces, a paved court, a physick garden and a rose garden as well as a vine walk and arboretum. Perhaps the most impressive features are the Pompeian Garden and the Theatre Garden where open air plays and concerts are held.

293 FARMERS ARMS

Aberthin

Welcoming village inn serving appetising home-made food and real ales; beer garden beside a stream.

see page 420

294 THE BUSH

St Hilary

Picturesque thatched village inn serving excellent cuisine based on fresh Welsh produce.

see page 421

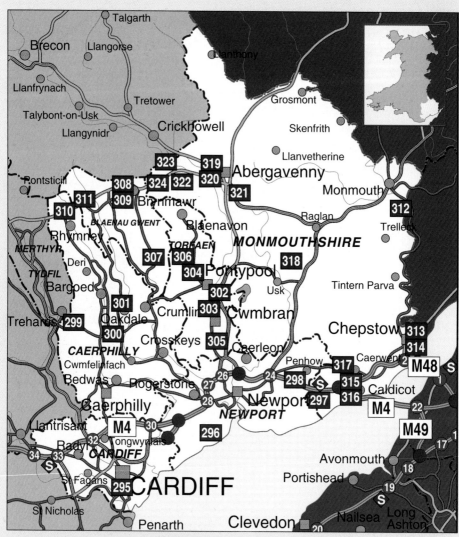

Cardiff and Monmouthshire

istory, ancient and modern, abounds in this region of South Wales, with the distinguished ruins of Norman fortifications and the remains of the industrial past of the valleys. The valleys of the Wye and Usk offer some truly glorious scenery as well as the equally breathtaking sight of Tintern Abbey. An inspiration for both poets and artists, this abbey was at one time one of the richest in the country and the magnificent ruins beside the River Wye are still a stirring sight.

This area, too, is one that saw much contest between the Welsh and the English, so not surprisingly there are numerous fortifications to be seen and explored.

Along this stretch of coastline lies Cardiff, the capital city of Wales and a place which is successfully blending the ancient with the modern. The Romans occupied various sites in this area, but it was heavy industry and the influence of the Bute family that made Cardiff such a powerful port. The home of Welsh rugby,

Harold's Stones, Trelleck

the superb Millennium Stadium and a recently rejuvenated waterfront, Cardiff is a city that vibrates with life, energy and enthusiasm.

To the north lie the valleys that provided so much wealth until the decline of coal mining and the iron industry. Much of the land that was once an industrial wasteland has been reclaimed by nature, with the help of sensitive human intervention, but there are still some monuments to the great industrial age remaining, chiefly at the Big Pit Mine and Blaenavon Ironworks.

209

CARDIFF

The capital city of Wales is a fascinating place with an unexpected beauty, a long history, a sporting tradition and an exciting rejuvenated waterfront that is attracting visitors in their thousands. The Cardiff area was first settled by the Romans in the 1st century, but from their departure a few centuries later to the arrival of the Normans in the 11th century little was recorded of

Cardiff Castle

life around what is now Cardiff. In 1091, Robert FitzHamon built a primitive fortress on what remained of the Roman fortification and this was, over the years, upgraded to a stone castle around which the town began to develop. Overrun by Owain Glyndwr in the early 15th century, the town and its castle came into the hands first of the Tudors and then of the Herbert family and their descendants the Marquesses of Bute.

However, Cardiff is very much a product of the Industrial Revolution and its story is intertwined with that of the Marquesses of Bute. They controlled the docklands and, as the town began to thrive as a coal exporting port, the family made a vast fortune. Cardiff became the biggest coal-exporting port in the world, and at its peak in 1913 more than 13 million tons of coal were exported from the docks. Some of this wealth was poured back into the rebuilding of **Cardiff Castle**. A no-expense-spared project initiated by the 3rd Marquess, the castle is an extravagant and opulent Victorian version of a castle of the Middle Ages. It was designed by the eccentric architect William Burges who allowed his flamboyant imagination to run riot, Burges created magnificent rooms rich in murals, stained glass and marble which really do have to be seen to be believed. While this building is very much a flight of wealthy Victorian fancy, outside in the grounds can be seen the well preserved medieval castle keep and stonework dating from Roman times. Visitors to the castle today also have the opportunity to look around the **Welsh Regiment Museum** and look out over Cardiff from the top of the Norman keep.

As might be expected in a capital city, Cardiff is home to many of the national treasures of Wales. At the superb **National Museum and Gallery of Wales** there is a vast collection of archaeology, natural history (including 55,000 live leaf-cutter ants!) and ceramics as well as permanent exhibitions on the Evolution of Wales, and Man and the Environment. The art gallery boasts a fine collection that includes the largest body of Impressionist paintings outside Paris and the best of Welsh art. The museum and gallery, along with the City Hall, are located in **Cathays Park**, where there are other civic buildings and also various departments of the University of Wales.

The area once known as Tiger Bay - Cardiff's historic dockland and the birthplace of Dame Shirley Bassey - is one of the country's most exciting and imaginative regeneration developments. Now called **Cardiff Bay**, this revived waterfront is home to the new **National Assembly**, the impressive **Pierhead Building** which was built in 1896 for the Bute Docks Company and the **Cardiff Bay Visitor Centre**. At this award-winning tubular building, visitors can see a futuristic

exhibition which lays out the full vision of the complete development which, among other aims, is reuniting the city with its dockland. The **Wales Millennium Centre** is an arts and cultural centre of world importance. Perhaps the single most important part in the revival of the Bay is the massive Cardiff Bay Barrage, a barrier that stretches for a kilometre across the mouth of the Bay. Of particular interest to children at Cardiff Bay is **Techniquest**, the country's leading science discovery centre, where visitors can explore many aspects of science and technology through a range of interactive exhibits.

The former church for Norwegian sailors, which is where the author Roald Dahl was baptised, is now the **Norwegian Church Arts Centre** which maintains the links which have grown up over the years between the two nations.

Although Cardiff's famous Arms Park, the home of rugby football for so many years, has gone, its replacement, the **Millennium Stadium**, is set to become an equally revered shrine to the Welsh national game and is already proving a highly successful replacement for Wembley. The stadium's dazzling debut was to host the last great sporting event of the 20th century, the Rugby World Cup Final in November 1999, Visitors to the stadium can see the hallowed turf and learn how the pitch was laid, find out how the 8000 ton roof opens and closes,

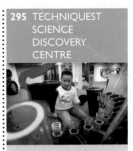

295 TECHNIQUEST SCIENCE DISCOVERY CENTRE

Cardiff

Techniquest Science Discovery Centre located in Cardiff Bay has over 150 hands on interactive exhibits, covering all aspects of science.

 see page 419

A mile or so from Cardiff city centre stands Llandaff Cathedral, a beautiful building set in a grassy hollow beside the River Taff. The cathedral suffered severe bomb damage during World War II and part of its restoration programme included a controversial Epstein sculpture, **Christin Majesty,** *which dominates the interior. Inside, visitors will also find some delightful medieval masonry, a marvellous modern timber roof and some works of art by members of the Pre-Raphaelite movement.*

and walk from the Welsh players' dressing room, through the tunnel and on to the pitch.

Two miles north of the city centre, **Roath Park** is a 19th century urban park with handsome trees, formal flower beds, a wild area and a memorial to Scott of the Antarctic.

AROUND CARDIFF

ST FAGANS

4 miles W of Cardiff off the A48

On the outskirts of Cardiff, this picturesque village is home to the outstanding **St Fagans National History Museum** (free) in the extensive grounds of St Fagans Castle, a splendid Elizabethan mansion. Founded in 1946, this is a museum unlike most others as it

contains an assortment of buildings collected from all over Wales which have been re-erected in these glorious surroundings. Within the 50-acre site you'll find a 17th century farmhouse from Gower, a tiny whitewashed chapel of 1777 from Dyfed, a Victorian schoolroom from Lampeter, a pre-war grocery, a terrace of iron-workers' cottages from Merthyr Tydfil, and a toll house of 1772 from Aberystwyth. There's also a pottery, tannery, bakery, smithy and three mills, most of them with workers demonstrating the original methods employed. Each of the 40 or so buildings has been furnished to reflect a period in its history. The museum also holds demonstrations on traditional craft skills and visitors can enjoy a delightful stroll round the formal gardens, the Italian Garden, the modern knot garden and the terraces that descend to a series of fishponds. There's a restaurant and coffee shop, a traditional bakehouse selling organic bread and cakes, a play area for under-12s, and a gift shop with products relating to the museum's collections.

TONGWYNLAIS

3 miles NW of Cardiff on the A470

Situated in the Taff Valley and hidden by trees, **Castell Coch** (CADW) appears to be a fairytale castle of the Middle Ages, yet it only dates from the 19th century. Built on the site of a 13th century castle, Castell Coch was designed by the eccentric architect William Burges for the 3rd Marquess of

Castell Coch, Tongwynlais

Bute as a companion piece to Cardiff Castle. As the Marquess was reputed to be the wealthiest man in the world - the family owned the thriving Cardiff docks - money was no object. While the medieval illusion of the place is maintained by the working portcullis and drawbridge, the interior decoration is perhaps even more astonishing. Perfectly preserved, each room is a masterpiece, with eye-catching details such as paintings of butterflies on the domed ceiling of the drawing room, scenes from Aesop's Fables and Greek mythology on the walls, and bird and animal mouldings around the doors.

The Marquess planted a vineyard in the castle grounds which, it is said, produced the only commercially made wine in Britain between 1875 and 1914. There are now more than a dozen commercial vineyards in Wales alone.

NEWPORT

With a population of about 120,000, Newport is the third largest city in Wales. It achieved city status in 2002 to mark the Queen's Golden Jubilee.

The town's **St Woolos Cathedral Church**, splendidly situated on the hilltop, is just the latest building on a site which has been a place of worship since the 6th century. The present structure is a medley of architectural styles that includes a magnificent Norman doorway and columns that are

believed to have come from the Roman fort at Caerleon. The church was founded by St Gwynllyw (Woolos is the English version of his name), who before his conversion was a cruel and wicked man. He is said to have had a dream one night that he would go to a hill and find there a white ox with a black spot. This Gwynllyw did the next day and, finding the said ox, saw it as a sign from God and became a devout Christian. In the graveyard of St Woolos are the graves of some of the soldiers of the Welsh Regiment who were killed in the Battle of Rorke's Drift during the Zulu Wars of South Africa.

Just down the road from the cathedral, **Stow Hill** is notable for its Georgian and Victorian town houses, something of a rarity in Newport.

The city grew up around the docks at the mouth of the river Usk and from a population of 1000 in 1801 rocketed to 70,000 by the early 1900s.

The history of Newport's docks and the city itself is explored at the **Newport Museum and Art Gallery** with a range of displays on the city's origins, including a Roman mosaic floor which was excavated close by. Not to be missed here are the John Wait teapot display with some 300 weird and wonderful pieces, and the Fox collection of decorative art. Just to the north of the museum, on the river bank, is another striking art work, Peter Fink's enormous red sculpture, **Steel Wave** of 1991, which

296 CHURCH HOUSE INN

St Brides Wentllooge
Child-friendly village inn with outstanding food, real ales and beer garden.

see page 422

represents steel and sea trades which have played such important roles in Newport's development. The sculpture is part of the city's Public Art Trail which also features an extraordinary **Kinetic Clock** which delivers a repertoire of shudders, spits and shakes on the hour, and a massive **Chartist Mural** depicting the Chartist uprising of 1839 when 22 protesters were killed by soldiers hiding in the Westgate Hotel. Both these works can be found in the pedestrianised John Frost Square. Westgate Hotel itself is a wonderfully ornate Victorian structure fronted by pillars from its predecessor which still bear the bullet pocks from the shooting.

Dominating the cityscape and an impressive reminder of Newport's more recent past is the massive **Transporter Bridge** across the River Usk. Specially designed in 1906 by Ferdinand Arnodin to allow traffic to cross the river without disrupting the movement of shipping, the bridge is one of very few of its kind: one is in Middlesbrough, two others are in France.

Newport was the home of the poet WH Davies, who penned the famous lines:

What is this life if, full of care,
We have no time to stand and stare...

To the west of the town is **Tredegar House and Park**, one of the finest examples of Restoration architecture in Wales and the home of the influential Morgan family for more than 500 years. Visitors can tour the rooms and discover just what life was like here, both above and below stairs, as well as finding out something of this great Welsh family. Its more colourful and famous members include Sir Henry Morgan, the notorious pirate, Godfrey, the 2nd Lord Tredegar, who survived the Charge of the Light Brigade and whose horse is buried in the grounds, and Viscount Evan, whose menagerie included a boxing kangaroo. The park that surrounds the house is equally impressive, with early 18th century walled formal gardens, an orangery with restored parterres, and craft workshops. Carriage drives through the parkland are available and children have their own adventure playground. There's a tea room and gift shop, and a suite of rooms is available for corporate events.

Tredegar House, Newport

AROUND NEWPORT

CAERLEON

2½ miles NE of Newport on the B4236

Despite its close proximity to Newport, Caerleon has managed to maintain the air of a rural town, but its chief attraction is the remarkable Roman remains. Caerleon is one of the largest and most significant surviving Roman military sites in Europe. It was established in AD 75 by the 2nd Augustinian Legion and originally called Isca. A substantial Roman town grew up around the military base and among the remains to be seen at **Caerleon Roman Fortress and Baths** are a large amphitheatre where thousands watched the gladiators, the only surviving Roman barracks to be seen in Europe and a complex system of Roman baths which were the equivalent of today's sports and leisure centres. Finds excavated from the remains are on show at the **Legionary Museum**, where, along with the weapons, mosaics and models, visitors can see one of the largest collections of engraved gem stones.

Caerleon has more to offer than Roman remains - impressive though they are - and the town has some fine examples of timbered buildings. Also well worth a visit is the seemingly unpronounceable **Ffwrrwm Art & Craft Centre** (free) which is set inside an 18th century walled garden. The courtyard here contains several craft shops, a tea room, an art gallery and a sculpture garden. Sculpture is something of a Caerleon speciality.

In midsummer it hosts a two week Arts Festival and International Sculpture Symposium which attracts sculptors from all over the world. The sculptors work in public so that visitors can see the works of art emerging from the raw materials, mostly wood.

Many people believe that Caerleon has links with King Arthur, asserting that the Roman amphitheatre was actually the site of the Round Table. Alfred, Lord Tennyson appears to have given this story some credit since he visited Caerleon, staying at the riverside Hanbury Arms, while seeking inspiration for his Arthurian epic, *Idylls of the King*.

PENHOW

7 miles E of Newport off the A48

This hamlet is home to Wales' oldest lived-in fortress, **Penhow Castle** which still has its stout Norman keep and an impressive 15th century Great Hall complete with minstrels' gallery. Visitors to the castle are invited to guide themselves through the various rooms using a recorded commentary on the 850-year history of the building. The castle was at one time owned by the family of Jane Seymour, Henry VIII's third wife, who died soon after giving birth to a son who became Edward VI.

CAERPHILLY

Despite being surrounded by shops, offices and houses, **Caerphilly Castle** completely dominates the

297 THE WHEATSHEAF INN

Magor

Completely refurbished in Autumn 2007, the Wheatsheaf offers excellent cuisine, real ales, beer garden and en suite rooms.

see page 423

298 THE OLD BARN COUNTRY INN & RESTAURANT

Llanmartin

Outstanding, gastronome's delight of a restaurant; also 4-star en suite accommodation.

see page 424

Nelson

Charming stone-built hostelry offering good food, real ales and B&B accommodation.

 see *page 425*

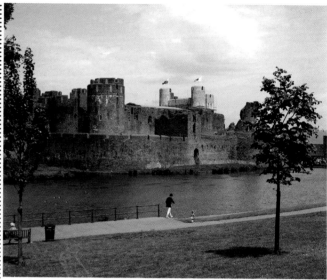

Caerphilly Castle

town. A 'sleeping giant' of a castle, the fortress sprawls over some 30 acres making it the largest castle in Wales. In the whole of Britain it is only exceeded in size by Dover and Windsor.

It is also one of the finest surviving examples of medieval military architecture in Europe. This great moated fortress was built largely in the late 13th century by the Norman Lord Gilbert de Clare. Along with the 'wall within walls' defence system, he also employed a mighty water defensive arrangement that included lakes and three artificial islands. The castle was restored in the 19th century by the Marquess of Bute, but nothing seems to be able to restore the castle's famous leaning tower which manages to out-lean even the better known Leaning Tower of Pisa. Today the castle is home to an intriguing display of full size working replica siege engines.

The town's **Visitor Centre**, as well as providing tourist information, has an exhibition on local history and culture, a display of Welsh crafts and a fine Welsh food shop. Caerphilly is famous for its distinctive white crumbly cheese, first made in 1831. It originated in the farms surrounding the town but during World War II and for a few years after, cheese-making was prohibited. It was only recently that production started up again and it is now possible to get locally made cheese once again.

AROUND CAERPHILLY

DERI

9 miles N of Caerphilly off the A469

To the north of Deri, in beautiful Darran Valley, lies **Parc Cwm**

216

Darran, a glorious country park which, along with the adventure playground and informative Visitor Centre, also has a six-acre coarse fishery.

PONTLLANFRAITH

6 miles NE of Caerphilly on the A4048

Close to this town stands **Gelligroes Mill**, a 17th century water mill restored to full working order. In the early 20th century the mill was owned by Arthur Moore, a radio enthusiast, who on the night of 11th April 1912 claimed to have heard distress signals from the sinking *Titanic*. No one believed Arthur until two days later when confirmation of the disaster reached England

CWMFELINFACH

3½ miles NE of Caerphilly on the A4048

Covering some 1000 acres of both woodland and farmland, the **Sirhowy Valley Country Park** provides the ideal opportunity to walk, cycle or ride along the park's numerous trails. The Full Moon Visitor Centre has all the details of the park's natural history and of other activities here while in the heart of the country park is **Ynys Hywel Centre**, a converted 17th century farmhouse which has conference facilities and a weekend coffee shop.

CWMCARN

6 miles NE of Caerphilly on the B4591

Just to the west of the town lies **Cwmcarn Forest Drive**, a seven-mile stretch of high forest road that provides some of the most

magnificent panoramic views of the South Wales countryside and the Bristol Channel beyond. Another attraction is the **Mabinogion Sculpture Trail**, which depicts characters from the Celtic folklore tales of the *Mabinogion*. The drive's visitor centre has details of the route and what can be seen at various points and also a coffee shop and a gift shop selling local handicrafts. Also here are a campsite and a mountain bike trail.

RISCA

5½ miles NE of Caerphilly on the B4591

To the south of Risca, at High Cross on the Monmouthshire Canal, is the **Fourteen Locks Canal Centre**. This complicated systems of locks was constructed to raise and lower barges some 168 feet in just half a mile with only the minimal wastage of water. There are several walks from the centre which take in the locks, ponds, channels, tunnels and weirs, as well as the countryside in which the centre is sited. Open from Easter to September, the visitor centre has a display that follows the opening (in 1796), the growth and the heyday of the Monmouthshire Canal and the decline that started when the railways began to take trade off the water.

NELSON

5½ miles NW of Caerphilly on the A472

As well as boasting an open-air handball court dating from the 1860s (and still in use), this village is home to **Llancaiach Fawr Manor**, a handsome Elizabethan manor

300 THE HALFWAY HOUSE

Pontllanfraith

Superb country pub oozing with tradition and style; outstanding cuisine and newly refurbished en suite rooms.

🍴 see page 426

301 THE ROCK TAVERN

Blackwood

Recently completely refurbished, The Rock offers excellent food, real ales and en suite rooms.

🍴 🛏 see page 427

302 OPEN HEARTH INN

Sebastopal

Family-run friendly hostelry beside canal; quality home-cooked food and real ales.

🍽 see page 428

303 THE CROSS KEYS INN

Pontnewydd

Popular canalside hostelry noted for its appetising and reasonably priced food; accommodation also available.

🍽 🛏 see page 428

304 THE LITTLE CROWN INN

Wainfelin

Recently refurbished traditional village inn serving honest-to-goodness home cooking and real ales.

🍽 see page 429

house which has been lovingly restored to the year 1645 and the time of the Civil War. During this turbulent time, the Pritchard family lived here and visitors to this living history museum can meet members of the family and their servants, all in authentic costumes, as they carry on with their daily lives. As well as preparing meals, gardening and exchanging gossip of the day, a number of events popular at that time, such as archery and falconry, are staged. This is a wonderfully entertaining and informative living history museum where visitors also get the chance to meet some of the eight resident ghosts on the special ghost tours.

PONTYPOOL

Known to have been in existence before the time of the Normans, Pontypool is credited with being the home of the Welsh iron industry. The first forge here is believed to have been in operation as early as 1425, and the first ironworks opened in 1577. It is said that the first iron working forge in America was started by emigrants from Pontypool in the mid-1600s. This valley also prides itself on being the earliest place in Britain to have successfully produced tin plate, in 1720. The town's industrial heritage can be explored at the **Pontypool Valley Inheritance Centre** where both the industrial and social history of the town and surrounding Torfaen valley is detailed. The centre is located in the late-Georgian stables of Pontypool Park, once the home of the Hanbury family, who were, appropriately, owners of a local ironworks.

Pontypool Park is a 19th century landscaped park whose main attractions include a shell grotto and a unique double-chambered ice house. The formal Italian gardens have recently been restored with the help of Heritage Lottery funding.

The canals, too, have played an important part in the development of Pontypool and this particular legacy is recalled at **Junction Cottage**, a tollkeeper's cottage of 1814 lying at the junction of the Monmouthshire and Brecon Canal and the River Lwyd.

Industry seems worlds away at **Llandegfedd Reservoir**, to the east of Pontypool, where the lake and surrounding countryside provide numerous opportunities for fishing, sailing, walking and bird watching.

AROUND PONTYPOOL

CWMBRAN

3 miles SW of Pontypool on the A4051

This new town in the old industrial valleys of South Wales was founded in 1949 and was once itself dominated by heavy industry. Today, the mines and large works have gone and major environmental improvement schemes, including planting forests, have taken away many of the old eyesores. Not far from the town are some interesting and historic places including the **Llanyrafon Mill and Farm Museum** and the **Llamtarnam Grange Arts Centre**.

Greenmeadow Community Farm, set within the town's planned green belt, is home to all manner of farm animals. Farm trails, a children's adventure playground and an unusual dragon sculpture are among the other attractions which go to provide a popular and entertaining day out.

If you'd rather go shopping, the **Cwmbran Shopping Centre** claims to be the largest undercover shopping complex in Wales.

BLAENAVON

6 miles NW of Pontypool on the B4246

Despite once having been associated with the heavy industries of coal mining and iron working, Blaenavon is set in surprisingly pleasant countryside which can be further explored by taking the **Pontypool and Blaenavon Railway**, the highest standard gauge track to have survived in Wales. Half the site lies within the Brecon Beacons National Park.

The oldest colliery in Wales, Big Pit Mine, closed in 1980, but has been reopened as the **Big Pit National Mining Museum.** This monument to the past employs former miners and engineers from the site to give guided tours accompanied by plenty of anecdotes. Visitors (children must be at least 5 years old and a metre tall), armed with helmet, lamp and battery pack, can travel down a 90 metre shaft in a pit cage and walk through the underground roadways, air doors, stables and engine houses. On the surface at this site, designated Britain's 18th World Heritage Site by UNESCO, there are more buildings to explore, including the winding engine-house, the blacksmith's workshop and the pithead baths.

The other side of the town's industry, iron working, can be discovered at the **Blaenavon Ironworks**, a marvellous site that not only represents an important aspect of the Industrial Revolution but is also one of Europe's best preserved 18th century ironworks. Built against a cliff-face in the 1780s and then at the cutting edge of technology, the steam-powered ironworks became the second largest in Wales. Visitors to the ironworks and the Cordell Museum can see the whole process of production, including the row of blast furnaces and ingenious water balance tower by which the material was transported. Here, too, the human element of the vast ironworks is covered, as a small terrace of workers' cottages, built between 1789 and 1792, has been preserved.

Other buildings of interest in Blaenavon include the wonderfully ornate **Working Men's Hall** in the town centre where miners paid a halfpenny (1.2p) a week to use the library, and the **Church of St Peter,** built to look like an engine house and with tomb covers, font and pillars all made of iron.

EBBW VALE

15 miles NW of Pontypool on the A4048

This old steelmaking town, whose member of Parliament was once the formidable orator and social

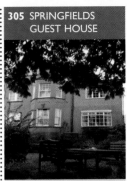

308 THE BRIDGEND INN

Brynmawr

Cosy and welcoming
hostelry serving varied and
appetising food.

🍴 see page 430

309 THE TALISMAN

Brynmawr

Popular traditional town
centre inn noted for its
outstanding food.

🍴 see page 431

310 PRINCE OF WALES INN

Princetown

Superb country hostelry
noted for its excellent
restaurant; en suite rooms
available.

🍴 ⊨ see page 431

311 CROWN INN

Ashvale

Traditional country pub,
formerly a coaching inn,
serving quality food;
peaceful beer garden

🍴 see page 432

reformer Aneurin Bevan, was
transformed by the 1992 Garden
Festival. Following the festival, the
site was developed into **Festival
Park** with houses, shops and a
range of leisure activities. Within
the 70 acres of parkland and
woodland are ornamental gardens, a
lake, owl sanctuary, woodland craft
centre and, in summer, a Japanese
Pavilion selling teas.

A monument to Aneurin Bevan
stands on the outskirts of the town
which still has a number of fine
houses which were built by the
wealthy steel and coal magnates of
the area. The town itself lies in a
crowded valley but just to the north
stretch the moor lands of the lower
Brecon Beacons and some
spectacular country.

TREDEGAR

1½ miles W of Ebbw Vale on the B4256

This pretty town was the birthplace
of Aneurin Bevan, founder of the
National Health Service and
Member of Parliament for Ebbw
Vale. The ashes of Bevan, in 1960,
and of his wife Jennie Lee, in 1988,
were scattered in the hills above
Tredegar.

It was in Tredegar that the
novelist AJ Cronin worked as a
doctor and where he collected
information for his book, *The
Citadel*, which was later made into a
film starring Robert Donat and a
television series with Ben Cross.

Brown and white tourist signs
lead to the **Elliot Colliery
Winding House**, now a museum
of a colliery that once employed
more than 2000 people.

Close by lies **Bryn Bach
Country Park**, a 600-acre area of
grass and woodland, with a 16-acre
man-made lake, an abundance of
wildlife, a visitor centre and
opportunities for walking, fishing,
canoeing, climbing and abseiling.

MONMOUTH

This prosperous and charming old
market town grew up at the
confluence of three rivers - the
Wye, Monnow and Trothy - which
are all noted for their fishing. The
River Wye is crossed by a five
arched bridge built in 1617 but the
Monnow boasts the most
impressive of the town's bridges.
Monnow Bridge is one of
Monmouth's real gems, and its
sturdy fortified gatehouse, dating
from the 13th century, is the only
one of its kind in Britain.

Long before the bridge was
constructed, the Normans built
Monmouth Castle here in around
1068. Later rebuilt by John of
Gaunt in the late 1300s, the castle
was the birthplace in 1387 of his
grandson, later Henry V. It is
believed he was born in the Great
Tower, substantial parts of which
still stand.

Much later, in the 17th century,
Great Castle House was built by
the 3rd Marquess of Worcester
from the ruins of the castle and he
lived here while his other homes,
Badminton and Troy House, were
being rebuilt. Today, the castle
houses both the **Castle Museum**
and the **Regimental Museum**
where the histories of the castle

and the Royal Monmouthshire Royal Engineers are explored. The **King's Garden** is a re-creation of a small medieval courtyard garden, planted with herbs that would have been common around the time of Henry V.

Another interesting building in the town is the 14th century **St Mary's Church** whose eight bells are said to have been recast from a peal which Henry V brought back from France after his victory at Agincourt. The story goes that as Henry was leaving Calais, the ringing of bells was heard and he was told that the French were celebrating his departure. He immediately turned back and took the bells to give as a present to his native town.

One of the graves in the churchyard is that of an obscure house-painter called John Renie who died in 1832 at the age of 33. His headstone is an acrostic of 285 letters that reads "Here lies John Renie". This epitaph can be read over and over again, upwards, downwards, backwards and forwards, and if doglegs and zigzags are also included, it is apparently possible to read "Here lies John Renie" in 45,760 different ways. The memorial also records the deaths of his two sons, one at the age of one year and nine months, the other at the age of 83.

An earlier Monmouth man, Geoffrey of Monmouth, was the Prior at St Mary's before becoming Bishop of St Asaph in North Wales. It was probably in Monmouth that Geoffrey wrote his

Monnow Bridge, Monmouth

massive work, *A History of the Kings of Britain*, with its legends of King Arthur and Merlin.

Also in the town is the **Nelson Museum**, where a fascinating collection of material and artefacts about the great Admiral can be seen. This interesting collection of memorabilia was accumulated by Lady Llangattock, the mother of Charles Stuart Rolls, and generously donated to Monmouth. The history of the town is illustrated in displays in the same building as the Nelson Museum. The exploits of the Hon Charles Rolls in cars, balloons and aeroplanes are also featured here. One of the most evocative pictures

221

is of Rolls in the basket of his
'Midget' balloon at Monmouth
Gasworks in about 1908. Some five
miles from the town is the Rolls
estate where Charles grew up and
developed an early interest in
engineering and motoring that led
to his forming the Rolls-Royce
company. Charles died in an air
accident in 1910 and his statue,
along with a monument to Henry
V, can be seen in the town's main
Agincourt Square. He is buried in
the churchyard of St Cadoc's, at
Llangattock-vibon-Avel, not far
from Monmouth.

Just to the west of the town,
and practically on the border with
England, rises **The Kymin**, a
National Trust owned hill
overlooking the River Wye. From
here there are spectacular views
across the picturesque landscape.
The **Round House**, also found
here, was erected by the Kymin
Club in 1794. The members of this
club were local worthies who liked
to hold open-air lunch parties on
the Kymin. They decided to

construct a building so that they
could picnic inside in bad weather.
The result is the Round House -
round so that the views could be
enjoyed from every part of the
house. Offa's Dyke footpath runs
through the land. Nearby is the
Naval Temple, built to
commemorate the Battle of the
Nile and opened in the early 19th
century.

AROUND MONMOUTH

TRELLECK

4½ miles S of Monmouth on the B4293

This village's name means 'Three
Stones' and these large prehistoric
monoliths can be found to the
southwest of Trelleck. For reasons
unknown they are called **Harold's
Stones**. They do not represent all
the historical interest here as, close
to the Church of St Nicholas, is a
mound known as **The Tump**,
which is all that remains of a
Norman motte and bailey.

TINTERN PARVA

7½ miles S of Monmouth off the A466

This riverside village, which nestles
among the wooded slopes of the
lovely Wye Valley, is a most
beautiful place and the whole of
the valley, between Monmouth and
Chepstow, is designated an Area of
Outstanding Natural Beauty. Here
are found the enchanting ruins of
Tintern Abbey (CADW), which
stand beside the river. The abbey
was founded by Cistercian monks
in 1131 and largely rebuilt in the

Harold's Stones, Trelleck

13th century by Roger Bigod, the Lord of Chepstow Castle. The monks farmed the rich agricultural land as well as remaining dedicated to their rigorous regime of religious devotions right up until the time of the Dissolution. A rich and powerful abbey in its day, Tintern is now a majestic ruin with much delicate tracery and great soaring archways still intact in a glorious setting that has inspired painters and poets such as Turner and Wordsworth.

A mile from the abbey, along the A466 Chepstow-Monmouth road, is the Victorian **Old Station** which now acts as a visitor centre for the Wye Valley. Here, too, are a countryside exhibition, a collection of signal boxes, a gift shop and a model railway.

CHEPSTOW

12½ miles S of Monmouth on the A48

This splendid old market town, which lies on the border with England, takes its name from the Old English 'chepe stow', meaning 'market place'. It occupies a strategic crossing on the River Wye - an important crossing between England and Wales. An elegant 5-arched cast iron bridge built in 1816 is still in full use. The Wye here is tidal and the difference between high and low tide is an extraordinary 49ft - only the Bay of Fundy on the Canadian/US border has an even higher difference.

Situated on a crag overlooking the river are the well-preserved ruins of **Chepstow Castle** which William Fitzosbern began building

in 1067 as a base for the Norman conquest of south east Wales. Its importance can be judged from the fact that it was built of stone; most Norman fortresses of the time were in motte and bailey form, built of earth and wood. Chepstow Castle began life as a keep, and towers, walls, fortifications and gatehouses were added to prepare it for the Welsh wars, in which, as it happened, it played no part. The castle is open for visits throughout the year. A major exhibition ' A Castle at War' relates the history of the castle. A group of local people have come together to form the Chepstow Garrison; dressing up and re-enacting scenes from Chepstow's past, they have become a popular attraction for both local residents and tourists.

Built at the same time as the castle keep, and by the same William Fitzosbern, is the Parish and Priory **Church of St Mary,** which suffered considerable damage after the suppression of the Priory in 1536. The vast three-storey original nave gives some idea of the grand scale on which it was built. The church contains some imposing and interesting monuments, including the Jacobean tomb of Margaret Cleyton with her two husbands and 12 children. This lady paid for the town's gatehouse to be rebuilt in 1609. Also entombed here is Henry Marten, friend of Oliver Cromwell and signatory to the death warrant of Charles I. Marten spent many years imprisoned in Chepstow Castle in the tower that now bears his name.

313 CHEPSTOW CASTLE

Chepstow

Chepstow Castle is set high upon cliffs above the River Wye, where it guarded the main river crossing from Southern England into Wales.

🏛 see page 432

314 THE BRIDGE INN

Chepstow

Picturesquely sited traditional town hostelry with excellent restaurant, real ales and riverside beer garden.

🍴 see page 434

223

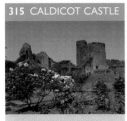

William Fitzosbern also founded the Abbey at Cormeilles in Normandy, with which Chepstow is twinned.

Opposite the castle is **Chepstow Museum** (free) where the rich and varied history of this border town is revealed. Housed in an elegant 18th century building that once belonged to a wealthy Chepstow merchant family, the museum has displays on the town's many industries, including shipbuilding, fishing and the wine trade. Chepstow was at one time an important centre for shipbuilding, and one of the many photographs in the exhibition shows the closing stages in the building of *War Genius* in National Shipyard No1 in 1920. Ships were built here well into the 1920s, and the tradition was revived during World War II with the construction of tank landing craft.

Throughout the town itself, the medieval street pattern is still much in evidence, along with surviving sections of the town wall, called the Port Wall, and the impressive **Town Gate**. But Chepstow is also a thriving modern town, and its attractions include an excellent racecourse offering both Flat and National Hunt racing - the highlight of the jumping season is the valuable and prestigious Welsh Grand National. The racecourse lies within the grounds of historic Piercefield Park. Piercefield Picturesque Walk was created in the 1750s by Valentine Morris the Younger and follows the Wye river cliff up to the Eagle's Nest.

Chepstow is at one end of

Offa's Dyke, the 8th century defensive ditch and bank built by the King of Mercia. It is also the starting point for the long-distance Wye Valley and Gloucestershire Way walks.

CALDICOT
15 miles S of Monmouth on the B4245

Caldicot Castle dates from Norman times and was restored for use as a family house in the 1880s. Of particular note here is the sturdy round keep and the gatehouse dating from the 14th century. Inside, there's an interesting collection of furniture from the 17th to the 19th centuries. The castle, which is set within 55 acres of beautiful parkland, hosts occasional medieval banquets.

CAERWENT
14 miles SW of Monmouth off the A48

Close to the Wentwood Forest, this town - which is now more of a village - was the site of **Venta Silurum**, a walled Roman town built by the invaders for the local Celtic Silures tribe. Sections of the Roman defences still remain and are some of the best preserved in Britain, while inside the walls can be seen the remains of the forum basilica and the Romano-Celtic temple. Venta Silurum is thought to have been the largest centre of civilian population in Roman-occupied Wales.

Much of the present village is built of stone taken from the Roman site, including the Parish Church of St Stephen which was built in medieval times.

RAGLAN

6½ miles SW of Monmouth off the A40

To the north of this pretty village stands **Raglan Castle**, one of the finest late medieval fortresses in Britain. Built towards the end of the Middle Ages, and thus in relatively peaceful times, the castle was also constructed with comfort in mind and it represents wealth and social aspirations as much as military might. Started by Sir William ap Thomas in 1435, the castle was continued in the same lavish manner by his son William Herbert who was responsible for the addition of the formal state apartments and the magnificent gatehouse. Despite being more a palace than a fortress, Raglan Castle withstood an 11-week siege by General Fairfax during the Civil War.

To the west lies **Clytha Castle**, a folly designed by John Nash for an owner of the Clytha Park estate in memory of his wife.

USK

11½ miles SW of Monmouth on the A472

This delightful small town, which takes its name from the river beside which it sits, was founded by the Romans in AD 75. Well known for its excellent local fishing - the River Usk is a fine salmon river - the town attracts fishermen from far and wide. The heart of the town is picturesque Twyn Square with its restored clock tower and 13th century gatehouse. Also noted for its floral displays and historic buildings, Usk is home to the

Gwent Rural Life Museum, housed in an 18th century malt barn, which tells the story of life in this Welsh border region from Victorian times up until the end of World War II. Amassed over many decades by hundreds of local residents, the collection is huge and includes many vintage agricultural implements along with re-creations of a dairy, brewery, carpenter's, a laundry and a thatcher's. Adjacent barns contain collections of stage coaches and farm carts, and an exhibit on the Great Western Railway.

ABERGAVENNY

12½ miles W of Monmouth on the A465

A particularly pleasant and thriving market town, Abergavenny dates back to Roman times when the modest fort of Gobannium was established. Here, too, are the modest remains of the Norman **Abergavenny Castle** where in 1175 the fearsome Norman lord, William de Braose, invited the Welsh lords to dine and then murdered the lot while they were disarmed at his table. Not very much remains, as King Charles I ordered it to be destroyed. Today, the rebuilt keep and a Regency hunting lodge within the castle grounds are home to the **Abergavenny Museum** where exhibits from prehistoric times to the present day detail the history of the town and surrounding area. Displays include re-creations of a Victorian kitchen and a saddler's workshop.

318 THE HALL INN

Gwehelog

Delightful olde worlde inn serving excellent cuisine and real ales; en suite rooms available.

🍴 🛏 *see page 437*

319 THE SOMERSET ARMS

Abergavenny

Popular town centre hostelry with unusual evening menu.

🍴 🛏 *see page 436*

320 CRUMBS CAFÉ

Abergavenny

Town centre café serving good old-fashioned home cooking.

🍴 *see page 436*

321 THE HARDWICK

Abergavenny

Family-owned and run pub/restaurant that is a gastronome's delight.

🍴 🛏 *see page 438*

322 THE LION INN

Govilon

Delightful village inn serving quality home-cooked food and real ales; beer garden, regular entertainment and standard guest rooms.

 see page 439

323 THE NAVIGATION INN

Gilwern

Canalside pub with beer garden offering good food, real ale and regular entertainment.

see page 440

324 ROCK & FOUNTAIN HOTEL

Clydach North

Picturesque inn in beautiful location serving excellent food and real ale; en suite rooms available.

see page 440

Notable treasures in **St Mary's Church** include medieval choir stalls, fine altar tombs and an imposing double life-size wooden figure of Jesse, father of King David. There are also effigies of members of the de Braose family and of Sir William ap Thomas, founder of Raglan Castle.

One of the most accessible gateways to the Brecon Beacons National Park, Abergavenny is a popular place during the summer. Surrounded by glorious countryside, it is a place from where all manner of activities, including walking, pony trekking and canal cruising, can be enjoyed.

A rather bizarre one-time resident of Abergavenny was Deputy Fuhrer Rudolf Hess who crash-landed his plane in Scotland in 1941and was detained in the town's mental asylum. He was permitted a weekly walk in the surrounding hills and was said to have conceived a love of the Welsh countryside.

A popular walk from the town is to the summit of **Sugar Loaf** (1955ft) which rises to the northwest of the town and commands grand views of the Black Mountain foothills.

LLANTHONY

10 miles S of Hay off the B4423

In the beautiful Vale of Ewyas, also known as Llanthony Valley, **Llanthony Priory** was built on a spot which has links with the beginnings of Christianity in Wales, and in the 6th century was chosen by St David for a cell. Much less visited than Tintern Abbey,

Vale of Ewyas

Llanthony has a more spiritual and evocative atmosphere and remains much as it has been for 800 years. The Priory was founded by the Norman William de Lacy in the 11th century when he established a hermitage that evolved into the priory whose wonderful ruins can be seen today.

The beauty and tranquillity of the location have inspired many: Eric Gill and Walter Savage Landor are among those who made their homes here. For many years the site was in a state of near decay, but the Welsh Office graded it as an Ancient Monument and so ensured its survival.

LLANVETHERINE

9 miles NW of Monmouth on the B4521

To the south of the village lies one of the Three Castles, **White Castle**, which is so called because when it was built the masonry was rendered with gleaming white plaster, patches of which can still be seen. Starting life as a simple earthwork not long after the Norman Conquest, White Castle was rebuilt in stone during the late 12th and 13th centuries to provide, along with Skenfrith and Grosmont castles, a triangle of fortresses to control this strategic entry point into Wales. Situated in a beautiful and isolated place, the ruins conjure up the romance of the Middle Ages. Much later, during World War II, Hitler's deputy, Rudolf Hess, fed the swans on the castle's moat while held at Abergavenny's mental hospital following his mysterious flight from Nazi Germany.

GROSMONT

9½ miles NW of Monmouth on the B4347

This village takes its name from the French, 'gros mont', meaning 'big hill'; it is the site of **Grosmont Castle**, the most northerly of the Three Castles. Now in ruins, Grosmont started life as a steep earthen mound but, after having been replaced by a stone fortification, it was unsuccessfully besieged by both Llywelyn the Great and Owain Glyndwr. During exploration of the ruins, an Arabic 'faience jar' was found here - undoubtedly a relic from the Crusades.

SKENFRITH

5½ miles NW of Monmouth on the B4521

At this point the Monnow Valley forms something of a gap in the natural defences of the Welsh Marches and it was here that the Normans built **Skenfrith Castle**, the last of the Three Castles - the others being White and Grosmont. Situated beside the river, Skenfrith Castle was built in the 13th century by Hubert de Burgh and is noted for its fine round tower keep and its well-preserved curtain wall. Once the troubled domain of medieval warlords, this border region is today peaceful and undisturbed.

Skenfrith Castle

Accommodation, Food & Drink and Places of Interest

The establishments featured in this section includes hotels, inns, guest houses, bed & breakfasts, restaurants, cafes, tea and coffee shops, tourist attractions and places to visit. Each establishment has an entry number which can be used to identify its location at the beginning of the relevant chapter or its position in this section.

In addition full details of all these establishments and many others can be found on the Travel Publishing website - **www.travelpublishing.co.uk**. This website has a comprehensive database covering the whole of Britain and Ireland.

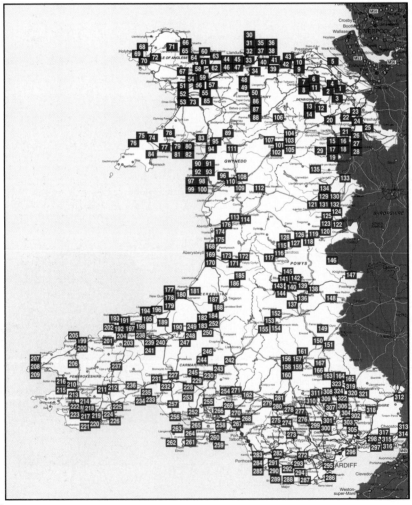

ACCOMMODATION

4   The Antelope Hotel, Rhydymwyn
13   Paradise Cottage, Clocaenog
15   Gales of Llangollen, Llangollen
16   Poplar House B&B and Self-Catering, Llangollen
17   The Smithfield Arms, Llangollen
19   Greenbank Hotel & Restaurant, Llangollen
25   Buck House Hotel, Bangor on Dee
27   The Hand Hotel, Chirk
29   The West Arms Hotel, Llanarmon Dyffryn Ceiriog
30   Winchmore Hotel, Llandudno
32   Oasis Hotel, Llandudno
36   The Queens Head, Glanwydden
40   The Marine Hotel, Old Colwyn
41   Dulas Arms, Llanddulas
43   The Morton Arms, Towyn
45   The Bridge Inn Conwy, Conwy
46   Ye Olde Mailcoach, Conwy
48   The Lodge Hotel, Tal-y-Bont
49   Fairy Falls Hotel, Trefriw
50   Meadowsweet Hotel, Llanrwst
51   Gwesty Bron Menai, Caernarfon
52   Menai Bank Hotel, Caernarfon
54   Hotel Plas Dinorwic, Y Felinheli
55   Ty Mawr Tearooms, Restaurant and B&B, Llanddeiniolen,
56   Ty'n Rhos Country House and Restaurant, Llanddeiniolen
60   Wern Y Wylan Court (Courts Restaurant and Bar), Llanddona
62   White Lion Hotel, Beaumaris
66   Minffordd Self Catering, Minffordd
67   Tafarn Y Gors, Pentre Berw
70   Ty Mawr, Valley
71   The Bull Inn, Llanerchymedd
72   Ty Cristion Holiday Cottages, Ty Cristion
73   Tafarn Snowdonia Parc Brew Pub, Waunfawr
74   Nanhoron Arms Hotel, Nefyn
75   Woodlands Hall Hotel, Edern
76   The Lion Hotel, Tudweilog
78   Glasfryn Cottages, Glasfryn
80   Mynydd Ednyfed Country House Hotel, Criccieth
82   Pros Kairon Guest House, Criccieth
86   Bryn Llewelyn Guest House, Betws-y-Coed
87   The Gwydyr Hotel, Betws-y-Coed
88   The White Horse Inn, Capel Garmon
91   Cemlyn Tea Shop, Harlech
92   The Lion Hotel, Harlech
94   Tremeifion Hotel, Talsarnau
95   Tregwylan, Talsarnau
97   The Belle Vue Hotel, Barmouth
98   Bryn Teg Hotel, Barmouth
99   Bryn Melyn Guest House, Barmouth
100   The Anchor Restaurant, Barmouth
103   Melin Meloch (Former Water Mill), Bala
104   Cwm Hwylfod, Cefnddwysarn
105   The Bryntirion Inn, Llanderfel
106   White Lion Hotel, Cerrigydrudion
107   Cysgod Y Garn, Frongoch
110   Penmaenuchaf Hall, Penmaenpool
111   Trawsfynydd Holiday Village, Bronaber
112   Y Llew Coch - The Red Lion, Dinas Mawddwy
114   Maenllwyd Guest House, Machynlleth
115   The Red Lion Hotel, Llanidloes
117   The Blue Bell Inn, Llangurig
119   The Gro Guest House, Newtown
120   Abermule Hotel, Abermule
121   The Goat Hotel, Llanfair Caereinion
125   The Lion Hotel & Restaurant, Berriew
126   The Red Lion, Caersws
127   The Lion Hotel, Llandinam
131   Westwood Park Hotel, Welshpool
133   The Golden Lion Hotel, Four Crosses
134   Kings Head, Meifod
135   Bron Heulog, Llanrhaeadr ym Mochnant

136   Highland Moors Guest House, Llandrindod Wells
137   New Inn, Newbridge-on-Wye
138   The Builders Arms, Cross Gates
139   Gwystre Inn, Gwystre
140   The Elan Hotel, Rhayader
141   Brynafon, Rhayader
142   Oak Wood Lodges, Llwynbanedd
143   Riverside Lodge Guest House, Elan Valley
145   Mid Wales Inn, Pant -Y-Dwr
148   The Red Lion Inn, Llanfihangel-nant-Melan
149   Roast Ox Inn, Painscastle
150   The Griffin Inn, Llyswen
152   The Trout Inn, Beulah
153   Stonecroft Inn, Llanwrtyd Wells
154   Carlton Riverside Restaurant with Rooms, Llanwrtyd Wells
155   Cerdyn Villa, Llanwrtyd Wells
157   Paris Guest House, Brecon
158   Camden Arms, Brecon
161   Seland Newydd Inn, Pwllgloyw
162   Ynyscedwyn Arms, Ystradgynlais
164   The Dragon Inn, Crickhowell
165   Glangrwyney Court, Crickhowell
166   The Usk Inn, Talybont-on-Usk
168   The Weston Vaults, Aberystwyth
172   The George Borrow Hotel, Ponterwyd
174   Black Lion Hotel, Talybont
175   White Lion Hotel, Talybont
178   Black Lion Hotel, New Quay
182   Black Lion Hotel, Lampeter
183   The Castle Hotel, Lampeter
184   Ardwyn Country House, Llangybi
186   Red Lion Hotel, Pontrhydfendigaid
187   Three Horse Shoe Inn, Llangeitho
188   The New Inn, Llanddewi-Brefi
189   Tafarn Ffostrasol Arms, Ffastrasol
192   The Highbury Guest House & Restaurant, Pendre
193   Gwesty'r Webley Hotel Bar & Restaurant, Poppit Sands
197   Castell Malgwyn Hotel, Llechryd
199   The Tara Hotel & Restaurant, Fishguard
201   Salutation Inn, Felindre Farchog
202   Swn y Nant B & B, Moylegrove
205   Glendower Hotel, Goodwick
206   Stone Hall Hotel & Restaurant, Welsh Hook
207   The City Inn, St David's
208   The Waterings, St David's
210   East Hook Farmhouse, Haverfordwest
212   The Angel Inn, Narberth
213   Windsor Hotel, Johnston
216   Nolton Haven Quality Cottages, Nolton Haven
218   The Brewery Inn, Cosheston
221   The Stackpole Inn, Jason's Corner
224   Hammonds Park Hotel, Tenby
233   The Carpenters Arms, Laugharne
234   Broadway Country House, Laugharne
236   The Fishers Arms, Whitland
241   Emlyn Arms Hotel, Newcastle Emlyn
244   Farmers Arms, Llanfynydd
246   Black Lion Inn, Abergorlech
249   Glasfryn Guest House, Llanybydder
250   Robins Roost, Cwmann
254   Half Moon Inn, Garnant
255   Tafarn-y-Deri, Llanedi
260   Tides Reach Guest House, Mumbles
261   Little Haven Guest House, Oxwich
263   The Britannia Inn, Llanmadoc
265   Cedi Cottages, Penclawdd
266   Shepherds Country Inn, Felindre
268   Dulais Rock Inn, Neath
270   Celtic Lodge Inn, Alltwen
271   Tregib Arms, Brynamman
275   The Dunraven Hotel, Treherbert
280   Ty Newydd Country Hotel, Hirwaun
283   Seaways Hotel, Porthcawl
291   Ewenny Farm Guest House, Ewenny
297   The Wheatsheaf Inn, Magor
298   The Old Barn Country Inn & Restaurant, Llanmartin

299   The Lord Nelson Inn, Nelson
301   The Rock Tavern, Blackwood
303   The Cross Keys Inn, Pontnewydd
305   Springfields Guest House, Llantarnam
307   Mynydd Lodge Guest House, Cwmtillery
310   Prince of Wales Inn, Princetown
318   The Hall Inn, Gwehelog
319   The Somerset Arms, Abergavenny
321   The Hardwick, Abergavenny
322   The Lion Inn, Govilon
324   Rock & Fountain Hotel, Abergavenny

FOOD & DRINK

1   Drovers Arms, Mold
3   The Miners Arms, Maeshafn
4   The Antelope Hotel, Rhydymwyn
7   The Forum Tea Rooms & Restaurant, Denbigh
8   The Plough Inn, Denbigh
9   St Asaph Cafe, St Asaph
11   The Kinmel Arms Tavern, Llandyrnog
12   Three Pigeons Inn
14   Glan Llyn Inn, Clawddnewydd
15   Gales of Llangollen, Llangollen
17   The Smithfield Arms, Llangollen
19   Greenbank Hotel & Restaurant, Llangollen
20   Ponderosa Cafe, Horseshoe Pass
21   The Telford Inn & Restaurant, Trevor
23   Queens Head, Bradley
25   Buck House Hotel, Bangor on Dee
27   The Hand Hotel, Chirk
28   Coffee Shop, Chirk
29   The West Arms Hotel, Llanarmon Dyffryn Ceiriog
30   Winchmore Hotel, Llandudno
31   Café Monet, Llandudno
33   Café T'Air, Deganwy
35   Penrhyn Old Hall, Penrhyn Bay
36   The Queens Head, Glanwydden
37   Rhos Fynach, Rhos-on-Sea
38   Barnaby's Bistro, Rhos-on-Sea
39   Zanzibar Coffee Shop, Colwyn Bay
40   The Marine Hotel, Old Colwyn
41   Dulas Arms, Llanddulas
42   Jakes, Towyn
43   The Morton Arms, Towyn
44   Fisherman's Chip Shop, Conwy
45   The Bridge Inn Conwy, Conwy
46   Ye Olde Mailcoach, Conwy
48   The Lodge Hotel, Tal-y-Bont
49   Fairy Falls Hotel, Trefriw
50   Meadowsweet Hotel, Llanrwst
51   Gwesty Bron Menai, Caernarfon
52   Menai Bank Hotel, Caernarfon
54   Hotel Plas Dinorwic, Y Felinheli
55   Ty Mawr Tearooms, Restaurant and B&B, Llanddeiniolen,
56   Ty'n Rhos Country House and Restaurant, Llanddeiniolen
57   Llangollen Vaults, Bethesda
58   The Liverpool Arms, Menai Bridge
59   The Bridge Inn (Tafarn y Bont), Menai Bridge
60   Wern Y Wylan Court (Courts Restaurant and Bar), Llanddona
61   The Bold Arms Hotel, Beaumaris
62   White Lion Hotel, Beaumaris
63   Pilot House Café, Penmon
64   The Old Boathouse, Red Wharf Bay
65   Caffi Gwenno, Benllech
67   Tafarn Y Gors, Pentre Berw
68   The Seventy Nine, Holyhead
69   Jwmpin Jac's Cafe Bar, Holyhead
71   The Bull Inn, Llanerchymedd
73   Tafarn Snowdonia Parc Brew Pub, Waunfawr
74   Nanhoron Arms Hotel, Nefyn
75   Woodlands Hall Hotel, Edern
76   The Lion Hotel, Tudweilog
77   Oriel Fach Tea Rooms & Licensed Café, Abersoch

🍴 FOOD & DRINK

- 80 Mynydd Ednyfed Country House Hotel, Criccieth
- 81 Tir a Mor Restaurant, Criccieth
- 83 The Union Inn, Tremadog
- 84 Glyn-y-Weddw Arms, Llanbedrog
- 87 The Gwydyr Hotel, Betws-y-Coed
- 88 The White Horse Inn, Capel Garmon
- 90 Castle Restaurant, Harlech
- 91 Cemlyn Tea Shop, Harlech
- 92 The Lion Hotel, Harlech
- 94 Tremeifion Hotel, Talsarnau
- 96 Halfway House, Bontddu
- 98 Bryn Teg Hotel, Barmouth
- 100 The Anchor Restaurant, Barmouth
- 101 Cyfnod Café & Loch Café, Bala
- 102 The Ship Inn (Y Llong), Bala
- 105 The Bryntirion Inn, Llandderfel
- 106 White Lion Hotel, Cerrigydrudion
- 108 The Stag Inn, Dolgellau
- 109 Unicorn Inn, Dolgellau
- 110 Penmaenuchaf Hall, Penmaenpool
- 112 Y Llew Coch - The Red Lion, Dinas Mawddwy
- 113 The Red Lion, Machynlleth
- 115 The Red Lion Hotel, Llanidloes
- 116 The Great Oak Café, Llanidloes
- 117 The Blue Bell Inn, Llangurig
- 118 Waggon & Horses, Newtown
- 120 Abermule Hotel, Abermule
- 121 The Goat Hotel, Llanfair Caereinion
- 122 Cottage Inn, Montgomery
- 123 Upper House Inn, Llandyssil
- 124 The Horseshoes Inn, Berriew
- 125 The Lion Hotel & Restaurant, Berriew
- 126 The Red Lion, Caersws
- 127 The Lion Hotel, Llandinam
- 128 The Red Lion, Trefeglwys
- 130 Green Dragon, Welshpool
- 131 Westwood Park Hotel, Welshpool
- 132 The Raven Inn, Welshpool
- 133 The Golden Lion Hotel, Four Crosses
- 134 Kings Head, Meifod
- 137 New Inn, Newbridge-on-Wye
- 138 The Builders Arms, Cross Gates
- 139 Gwystre Inn, Gwystre
- 140 The Elan Hotel, Rhayader
- 141 Brynafon, Rhayader
- 145 Mid Wales Inn, Pant -Y-Dwr
- 146 The Radnorshire Arms, Beguildy
- 148 The Red Lion Inn, Llanfihangel-nant-Melan
- 149 Roast Ox Inn, Painscastle
- 150 The Griffin Inn, Llyswen
- 151 The Three Horseshoes, Velindre
- 152 The Trout Inn, Beulah
- 153 Stonecroft Inn, Llanwrtyd Wells
- 154 Carlton Riverside Restaurant with Rooms, Llanwrtyd Wells
- 156 The Copper Kettle, Brecon
- 158 Camden Arms, Brecon
- 159 The Drovers Arms, Llanfaes
- 161 Seland Newydd Inn, Pwllgloyw
- 162 Ynyscedwyn Arms, Ystradgynlais
- 163 The White Hart, Crickhowell
- 164 The Dragon Inn, Crickhowell
- 166 The Usk Inn, Talybont-on-Usk
- 167 Lakeside Restaurant, Brecon
- 168 The Weston Vaults, Aberystwyth
- 169 La Taberna - Casa Miguel, Aberystwyth
- 172 The George Borrow Hotel, Ponterwyd
- 173 The Druid Inn, Goginan
- 174 Black Lion Hotel, Talybont
- 175 White Lion Hotel, Talybont
- 177 The Dolau Inn, New Quay
- 178 Black Lion Hotel, New Quay
- 179 Hungry Trout, New Quay
- 180 Friends Coffee Shop, Aberaeron
- 181 Rhos Yr Hafod Inn, Cross Inn
- 182 Black Lion Hotel, Lampeter
- 183 The Castle Hotel, Lampeter
- 185 The Teifi Inn, Ystrad Meurig

- 186 Red Lion Hotel, Pontrhydfendigaid
- 187 Three Horse Shoe Inn, Llangeitho
- 188 The New Inn, Llanddewi-Brefi
- 189 Tafarn Ffostrasol Arms, Ffastrasol
- 190 The Gwarcefel Arms, Prengwyn
- 191 Castle Café & Cellar Bar, Cardigan
- 192 The Highbury Guest House & Restaurant, Pendre
- 193 Gwesty'r Webley Hotel Bar & Restaurant, Poppit Sands
- 194 Cartws Café, Penbryn Beach
- 195 Emlyn Café, Tanygroes
- 196 The Ship Inn, Llangrannog
- 197 Castell Malgwyn Hotel, Llechryd
- 198 Penllwyndu Inn, Llangoedmor
- 199 The Tara Hotel & Restaurant, Fishguard
- 200 The Royal Oak Inn, Fishguard
- 201 Salutation Inn, Felindre Farchog
- 203 Boncath Inn, Boncath
- 204 The Pendre Inn, Cilgerran
- 205 Glendower Hotel, Goodwick
- 206 Stone Hall Hotel & Restaurant, Welsh Hook
- 207 The City Inn, St David's
- 211 The Bush Inn, Robeston Wathen
- 212 The Angel Inn, Narberth
- 213 Windsor Hotel, Johnston
- 214 The Jolly Sailor, Burton
- 215 The Galleon Inn, Broad Haven
- 218 The Brewery Inn, Cosheston
- 219 The Lantern Restaurant and Tea Rooms, Lamphey
- 220 Freshwater Inn, Freshwater East
- 221 The Stackpole Inn, Jason's Corner
- 222 The Ferry Inn, Pembroke Ferry
- 225 The Deck, Saundersfoot
- 226 Cross Inn, Penally
- 227 The Humble Pie, Carmarthen
- 228 The White Hart Thatched Inn & Brewery, Llanddarog
- 230 The Garden Cafe, Aberglasney Gardens
- 231 Tafarn yr Helgwn A'r Cadno (Fox & Hounds Inn), Banc-y- Felin
- 232 Tafarn Pantydderwen, Llangain
- 233 The Carpenters Arms, Laugharne
- 234 Broadway Country House, Laughharne
- 236 The Fishers Arms, Whitland
- 237 Caffi Beca, Efailwen
- 238 The Three Horseshoes, Cenarth
- 239 The Bunch of Grapes, Newcastle Emlyn
- 240 Teifi Tearooms/Té ar y Teifi, Newcastle Emlyn
- 241 Emlyn Arms Inn, Newcastle Emlyn
- 242 The Castle Hotel, Llangadog
- 243 The Salutation Inn, Llandeilo
- 244 Farmers Arms, Llanfynydd
- 245 The Salutation Inn, Pontargothi
- 246 Black Lion Inn, Abergorlech
- 247 The Talardd Arms, Llanllwni
- 248 Tafarn Belle Vue, Llanybydder
- 251 Cwmanne Tavern, Cwmanne
- 252 The Harry Watkins, Felinfoel
- 253 The New Lodge Inn, Pontyberem
- 254 Half Moon Inn, Garnant
- 255 Tafarn-y-Deri, Llanedi
- 256 Cornish Arms, Burry Port
- 257 The Masons Arms, Kidwelly
- 258 The Plough & Harrow, Brynhyfryd
- 259 G & T's Bistro, Mumbles
- 262 The Bay Bistro & Coffee House, Rhossili
- 263 The Britannia Inn, Llanmadoc
- 264 The Greyhound Inn, Oldwalls
- 266 Shepherds Country Inn, Felindre
- 267 La Cucina, Skewen
- 268 Dulais Rock Inn, Neath
- 269 Bishop's Café Bistro, Pontardawe
- 270 Celtic Lodge Inn, Alltwen
- 271 Tregib Arms, Brynamman
- 272 Cross Inn Hotel, Cross Inn
- 273 Miskin Hotel, Trealaw
- 274 The Prince of Wales, Treorchy
- 275 The Dunraven Hotel, Treherbert
- 276 Jeffreys Arms Hotel, Caegarw
- 277 Peppers Restaurant, Aberdare

- 278 Welsh Harp Inn, Trecynon
- 279 The Old White Horse Inn, Pontneddfechan
- 280 Ty Newydd Country Hotel, Hirwaun
- 281 The Red Lion Inn, Penderyn
- 282 Six Bells, Coity
- 283 Seaways Hotel, Porthcawl
- 284 Salthouse On The Square, Porthcawl
- 285 Pier Café, Porthcawl
- 287 The Six Bells, Penmark
- 288 The Beach Café, Llantwit Major
- 289 The Plough & Harrow, Monknash
- 290 Fox & Hounds, St Brides Major
- 292 The Cross Inn, Llanblethian
- 293 Farmer's Arms, Aberthin
- 294 The Bush, St Hilary
- 296 Church House Inn, St Brides Wentllooge
- 297 The Wheatsheaf Inn, Magor
- 298 The Old Barn Country Inn & Restaurant, Llanmartin
- 299 The Lord Nelson Inn, Nelson
- 300 The Halfway House, Pontllanfraith
- 301 The Rock Tavern, Blackwood
- 302 Open Hearth Inn, Sebastopol
- 303 The Cross Keys Inn, Pontnewydd
- 304 The Little Crown Inn, Wainfelin
- 306 The British Constitution Inn, Talywain
- 308 The Bridgend Inn, Brynmawr
- 309 The Talisman, Brynmawr
- 310 Prince of Wales Inn, Princetown
- 311 Crown Inn, Ashvale
- 312 The Boat Inn, Penallt
- 314 The Bridge Inn, Chepstow
- 316 The Castle Inn, Caldicot
- 317 The Northgate Inn, Caerwent
- 318 The Hall Inn, Gwehelog
- 319 The Somerset Arms, Abergavenny
- 320 Crumb's Cafe, Abergavenny
- 321 The Hardwick, Abergavenny
- 322 The Lion Inn, Govilon
- 323 The Navigation Inn, Gilwern
- 324 Rock & Fountain Hotel, Abergavenny

🏛 PLACES OF INTEREST

- 2 Loggerheads Country Park, Nr Mold
- 5 Greenfield Valley Heritage Park, Holywell
- 6 Denbigh Castle, Denbigh
- 10 Rhuddlan Castle, Rhuddlan
- 18 Llangollen Railway, Abbey Road
- 22 Bersham Heritage Centre and Ironworks, Bersham
- 24 Erdigg, Nr Wrexham
- 26 Chirk Castle, Chirk
- 34 Bodnant Garden, Nr Colwyn Bay
- 47 Aberconwy House, Conwy
- 53 Caernarfon Castle, Caernarfon
- 79 Criccieth Castle, Criccieth
- 85 Welsh Slate Museum, Llanberis
- 89 Ffestiniog Railway, Porthmadog
- 93 Harlech Castle, Harlech
- 129 Powis Castle, Welshpool
- 144 The Elan Valley, Elan Valley
- 147 The Spaceguard Centre, Knighton
- 160 Brecknock Museum and Art Gallery, Brecon
- 170 Aberystwyth Cliff Railway, Aberystwyth
- 171 Devil's Bridge Falls, Aberystwyth
- 176 Ynys-Hir RSPB Nature Reserve, Machynlleth
- 209 Bishop's Palace, St Davids
- 217 Pembroke Castle, Pembroke
- 223 Pembroke Dock Museum, Pembroke Dock
- 229 The National Botanic Garden of Wales, Llanarthne
- 235 Dylan Thomas Boathouse, Laugharne
- 286 Comeston Medieval Village, Penarth
- 295 Techniquest Science Discovery Centre, Cardiff
- 313 Chepstow Castle, Chepstow
- 315 Caldicot Castle, Caldicot

HIDDEN PLACES GUIDES

Explore Britain and Ireland with *Hidden Places* guides - a fascinating series of national and local travel guides.

Packed with easy to read information on hundreds of places of interest as well as places to stay, eat and drink.

Available from both high street and internet booksellers

For more information on the full range of *Hidden Places* guides and other titles published by Travel Publishing visit our website on

www.travelpublishing.co.uk or ask for our leaflet by phoning **01752 276660** or emailing **info@travelpublishing.co.uk**

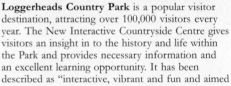

I   DROVERS ARMS   ¶¶

Denbigh Road, Mold, Flintshire CH7 1BP
☎ 01352 753824   Fax: 01352 751299
e-mail: mwilliams89@btinternet.com

Located just a short walk from the town centre, the **Drovers Arms** was built in 1966 on the site of an earlier pub of the same name. Martyn, a chef for more than 30 years, and his wife Sharon, arrived here in the summer of 2006 and have quickly established a glowing reputation for the appetising food and the keg ales on offer. The inn is also very popular for its entertainment: a Pub Quiz on Fridays; karaoke or live music on Saturday, and an organist and singers on Sunday evenings.

---

2   LOGGERHEADS COUNTRY PARK   🏛

Loggerheads, Nr Mold, Denbighshire CH5 5LH
☎ 01352 810586
🌐 www.denbighshire.gov.uk or www.loggerheads.biz or www.fresh-air.info

Loggerheads Country Park is a popular visitor destination, attracting over 100,000 visitors every year. The New Interactive Countryside Centre gives visitors an insight in to the history and life within the Park and provides necessary information and an excellent learning opportunity. It has been described as "interactive, vibrant and fun and aimed at people of all ages, especially families."

This is an established Rural Country Park set in a limestone valley in the Clwydian Range Area of Outstanding Natural Beauty and encompasses a mining and tourism history. The Park is also managed for conservation, with SSSI (Site of Special Scientific Interest) designation and rich and varied natural habitats. A Discovery Trail gets visitors out and about in the park. They can see evidence of the history for themselves, along with abundant wildlife. Visitors also get the chance to become a Trail Detective and collect the secret symbols. New and improved bridges, signs, welcome board, and free events all year round, add to the experience, providing a fantastic day out for all the family.

231

Village Road, Maeshafn,
Denbighshire CH7 5LR
☎ 01352 810464

Managed by Gilly and John Walker, **The Miners Arms** is a picturesque old inn dating from the early 1700s which stands alongside an old drovers road and was originally a row of miners' cottages. It is located in the village of Maeshafn which lies three miles from Mold, one mile from the A494 and is accessed from either Llanferres or Gwernymynydd. Set in an attractive upland wooded area in the Clwydian range, an area of outstanding natural beauty close to Loggerheads Country Park,

Maeshafn was formerly a mining and quarrying community.

During the summer months the front of the inn is adorned with colourful hanging baskets, while the interior is delightfully cosy with a log fire for those chilly autumn and winter days. There are two comfortable bars and a dining area that seats thirty. Children are welcome. The menu is based on fresh local produce wherever possible and includes dishes such as Salmon Fishcakes with lemon mayonnaise amongst the starters; Duck Breast with redcurrant sauce, steaks and Rag Pudding as main dishes. Vegetarian choices include Pea & Parmesan Risotto and Sopa Seca de tortillas; desserts are listed on the blackboard. A selection of wines is available by the glass or bottle. Such is the popularity of the restaurant, it is advisable to book in advance at weekends. Groups and small private events can be catered for.

The bars sell a great range of drinks, from the 3 real ales, (Theakston's Bitter, Old Peculier and a rotating guest ale); beers and wines to spirits and soft drinks. There are occasional folk nights and on the first Sunday in August the inn hosts a music festival. A popular amenity here during the summer months is the spacious beer garden framed by trees. All major credit cards are accepted and there is good disabled access throughout.

4 THE ANTELOPE HOTEL

Denbigh Road, Rhydymwyn, nr Mold,
Flintshire CH7 5HE
☎ 01352 741247 Fax: 01352 741933
e-mail: theantelopeinn@btconnect.com
🌐 www.antelopehotelmold.co.uk

At Rhydymwyn, just a couple of miles northwest of Mold, is **The Antelope**, a charming old inn that dates back more than 200 years. It's run by Kath and Paul who took over here in the spring of 2007 and have quickly made their mark. Kath was brought up in the licensing trade but this is the first time she and Paul have run their own business.

Good food is one of their major priorities. Professional chefs create an enticing selection of dishes based on ingredients that have been sourced within Wales. Amongst their specialities are home-cooked Steak & Ale Pie; Pork & Mushroom Stroganoff and home-made lasagne, but the menu also offers a good selection of fish, chicken and vegetarian dishes. Steaks, home-cooked ham and salads provide further options. Children have their own menu but can also be

served a smaller portion of dishes from the main menu. For those with smaller appetites, there's also a choice of sandwiches, toasties, baguettes, jacket potatoes and home-made soup. In addition to the regular menu, there are always daily specials listed on the board. Food is served from noon until 2pm, and from 6pm to 9pm, Monday to Friday; and from noon until 9pm on Saturday and Sunday. Amongst the comprehensive range of beverages to accompany your meal are 2 real ales, Thwaites Original and Bombardier. With plenty of outdoor seating for fine weather, and the warm and friendly interior for cooler days and the winter, this is a lovely pub that is sure to go from strength to strength.

Entertainment at The Antelope includes a disco or karaoke on Friday and Saturday evenings from 9pm with a late bar, and a pub quiz on Sunday evening from 9pm. A rather unusual but popular amenity of the inn is its courtesy bus. It seats 14 and for private parties, the inn will pick you up and take you home.

The Antelope also offers comfortable accommodation in 10 rooms of various sizes, all with en suite facilities. All major credit cards are accepted apart from American Express and Diners; there is good disabled access for the bar areas.

5 GREENFIELD VALLEY HERITAGE PARK 🏛

Greenfield, Holywell, Flintshire CH8 7GH
☎ 01352 714172 Fax: 01352 714791
🌐 www.greenfieldvalley.com

Referred to as the Borderlands best kept secret, the **Greenfield Valley Heritage Park** is one and a half miles of woodlands, reservoirs, ancient monuments and industrial history. The park is freely accessible year round attracting over 100,000 visitors per year. Within the Park is a Farm and Museum Complex with an attractive collection of original and reconstructed local buildings. A 16th century farmhouse, early 19th century cottage, blacksmith's forge, Victorian schoolroom and farm buildings provide an atmospheric backdrop to agricultural displays and exhibits. The museum holds events most weekends throughout the season. The whole site is a fascinating insight into times past.

There are farm animals to see and feed, an adventure playground and an indoor activity area. Facilities include a Visitor Centre, Environment Centre, free coach and car parking, toilets, café and gift shop. The museum and associated facilities are open from the beginning of April to the end of October.

6 DENBIGH CASTLE 🏛

Bodfari, Denbigh, Clwyd LL16 4HT
☎ 01745 813385
🌐 www.cadw.wales.gov.uk

Denbigh Castle, crowning a steep hill above the town, enjoys commanding views of the pastoral Vale of Clwyd. The castle, built as part of Edward1's 13th century campaigns against the Welsh, was put up by Henry de Lacy, one of the King's chief commanders. Along with the castle, de Lacy established a new English borough at Denbigh protected by town walls. Following a Welsh rising in 1294, the castle's construction proceeded on an even

grander scale, culminating in the mighty triple-towered great gatehouse, its finest feature.

7 THE FORUM TEA ROOMS & RESTAURANT 🍴

27/29 High Street, Denbigh LL16 3HY
☎ 01745 813449
e-mail: cardenliz@yahoo.co.uk

Located in the heart of the town, **The Forum Tea Rooms & Restaurant** are housed in a striking Grade II listed building. The business is owned and run by the brother and sister team of Liz Carden and Nick Campbell who arrived here in the spring of 2007. Nick has been a chef for more than 18 years and his extensive menu is based on fresh local produce. From 10am until 6pm, lunches, light meals and afternoon teas are served, while from 6pm until 10pm there's a choice of either an à la carte or table d'hôte menu.

Typical dishes include a melt-in-the mouth poached salmon, steaks and a vegetarian broccoli & cheese pasta bake.

8 THE PLOUGH INN

Bridge Street, Denbigh LL16 3TF
☎ 01745 812961

Located in the centre of the town, **The Plough Inn**, or 'Ye Arad' in Welsh, is a traditional hostelry where locals and visitors alike are assured of a friendly welcome from mine host Christine Carruthers. The inn serves wholesome home-cooked lunches and offers a good well-kept draught beer and a guest beer.

Meals are served in the bar and on a warm day refreshments can also be enjoyed at the rear of the pub  where picnic tables shaded by parasols are available. The Plough hosts karaoke on Thursday and alternate Saturdays, on the other Saturday the inn resounds to the strains of live music.

9 ST ASAPH CAFÉ

Lower Shop, High Street, St Asaph, Denbighshire LL17 0RF
☎ 01745 584613
e-mail: lin280158@aol.com

Situated on the town's main street, the **St Asaph Café** offers a wide variety of appetising food at remarkable value-for-money prices. You can choose from the printed menu or from the blackboard specials or, if what you fancy isn't there, just ask owner Linda Walker or her daughter Amanda and, provided they have the ingredients, they will cook it for you. The regular menu provides a  choice of all day breakfasts, hot and cold sandwiches, and main courses such as Lamb Hot Pot, burgers and salads. The café is open from 8am to 3.30pm, (Monday, Tuesday, Thursday Friday); 8am to 2pm (Wednesday, Saturday) and from 10am to 3.30pn on Sundays when succulent roasts are served.

10 RHUDDLAN CASTLE

Castle Gate, Castle Street, Rhuddlan, Rhyl, Clwyd LL18 5AT
☎ 01745 590777

Rhuddlan was one of the 'iron ring'of fortresses built by Edward I during the English King's late 13th century campaigns against the Welsh. Its massive twin-towered west gatehouse – heralding the inner core of a characteristic concentric 'walls within walls' system of defences – immediately catches the eye. But possibly the most impressive engineering achievement here is the way in which access for ships to the castle from the sea – almost 3 miles away- was made by canalising the River Clwyd, a mammoth task involving 1,800 ditchers. Remains of a defended river gate can still be seen in the outer ring of walls, overlooked by the towers of the powerful diamond-shaped inner ward.

14 GLAN LLYN INN

Clawddnewydd, Ruthin LL15 2NA
☎ 01824 750754
e-mail: nigel.cooper@onetel.net

Overlooking the village pond, the **Glan Llyn Inn** is a spacious and tasteful hostelry with a good mix of traditional and modern features. Owner Nigel Cooper has more than eight years experience in the trade and has been welcoming customers to this Free House since 2003. Real ales can be enjoyed along with an appetising variety of bar snacks available at lunch and in the evenings, supplemented by daily specials. In the conservatory restaurant, which seats 50, the excellent menu offers a wealth of tempting meat, fish and vegetarian dishes. The Sunday roasts are well worth the journey. Food is available from noon until 9pm, Wednesday to Saturday, and from noon until 8pm on Sundays.

235

11 THE KINMEL ARMS TAVERN

Llandyrnog, nr Denbigh LL16 4HN
☎ 01824 790291

The Kinmel Arms Tavern is the very model of what a traditional village inn should be. Dating back to the 16th century this fine old hostelry stands just outside the village of Llandyrnog, on the B5429 about 3 miles east of Denbigh. Alan and Sue Tubby took over here in the summer of 2005 and quickly established a glowing reputation for outstanding food and hospitality.

Sue is responsible for the excellent cuisine and is particularly renowned for her home-made Steak & Ale Pies, made to her own recipe, and her Sunday roasts. Fish dishes are also very popular – not surprising if you've ever tasted Sue's Arctic char fillet, oven baked on fennel seeds and topped with rosemary. Meat lovers are also well looked after. There are steaks ranging from an 8oz Sirloin to a mighty 28oz T-Bone – this must be ordered at least 2 days in advance. Venison and Field mushrooms in a rich red wine sauce; succulent breast of chicken filled with Stilton or Garlic; various curries and a tasty Lasagne Verdi are also on the menu. Vegetarian choices include a Broccoli & Cream Cheese Bake, and a Brie & Broccoli Pilhivier. Round off your meal with one of the outstanding desserts or a savoury cheese board. Food is served every day from noon until 2.30pm and from 6pm to 9pm – later if the restaurant is busy. Booking is advisable for Friday and Saturday evenings, and essential for Sunday lunches. Meals are taken in the 40-seater restaurant and refreshments can also be enjoyed in the large and peaceful beer garden to the rear where there's also a secure children's play area.

To accompany your meal, the tavern offers a good selection of traditional ales, including 2 real ales – Greene King IPA and a rotating guest ale. The Kinmel Arms is happy to cater for private functions and celebrations; children are welcome and all major credit cards are accepted.

12 THREE PIGEONS INN

Graig-fechan, Ruthin, Denbighshire LL15 2EU
☎ 01824 703178

The village of Graig-fechan is located a few miles south of Ruthin on the B5429 and it's here that you will find the **Three Pigeons Inn,** a traditional rural Welsh 17th Century Drovers Inn with some lovely countryside views from the terrace at the rear. James and Amelia Short took over here in the autumn of 2007 and have been busy upgrading the inn's amenities. James has been in the licensing trade for more than 20 years and is

an enthusiast for real ales. At the Three Pigeons you'll find 4 of them to choose from during the summer months, and 3 brews during the off season period. Hancocks HB and Rev. James are the regular ales, the others are guest brews. Food is served all day Monday to Saturday and lunch time on Sundays during the summer season with shorter hours during the off season. Four menu's are available - Lite Bite, Main, Juniors and Sunday Lunch - specials are also a feature.There's a separate restaurant seating 40, but you can also dine in the lounge bar or outside. Children are welcome - a play area for them should be ready by the spring of 2008, and dogs are welcome in the bar area.

13 PARADISE COTTAGE

Paradwys, Clocaenog, Ruthin,
Denbighshire LL15 2AT
☎ 01824 750330
e-mail: naisby@paradisecottage.co.uk
⊕ www.paradisecottage.co.uk

Located on the edge of a small hamlet in open countryside, **Paradwys Cottage** offers quality self-catering accommodation with a 4-star rating. It is a self-contained wing of a Welsh long house dating back to 1450 which is believed to have been a pilgrim's inn for those travelling to St David's. Ideal for families, the cottage is full of character, has a patio and private lawn, both with garden furniture, and is set in a large enclosed garden where children can play safely.

The cottage has a large well-equipped kitchen with dining area and the amenities include an electric stove with grill and oven, microwave, fridge/freezer and Bosch

washing machine. There's a comfortable living room with beamed ceiling which is equipped with TV, video, radio cassette and information about the area. On the first floor are 2 double bedrooms, one with a super-king size bed, the other with two single beds. A cot and high chair are available. The cottage provides a good centre for exploring Snowdonia and all North Wales. It is close to Clocaenog Forest in ideal walking country, and the Clwyd Hills are just a few miles away.

15 GALES OF LLANGOLLEN

18, Bridge Street, Llangollen LL20 8PF
☎ 01978 860089 Fax: 01978 861313
e-mail: richard@galesofllangollen.co.uk
🌐 www.galesofllangollen.co.uk

Outstanding food, a superb choice of wines and luxurious accommodation – **Gales of Llangollen** offers all this along with friendly and efficient service. Located right in the heart of this historic town, Gales is owned and run by Richard and Gillie Gale who, since they opened their doors in 1977, have gained an enviable reputation for providing value for money in warm, welcoming surroundings. They are also noted for the very high quality of their cuisine, a wonderful feast of imaginative, freshly prepared dishes from a regularly changing menu. They also pride themselves on the contents of their cellar. Occupying an 18th century town house (the adjacent annexe dates back even further to 1676) Gales Wine Bar offers a choice of some 85 different wines.

The accommodation at Gales comprises 15 beautifully appointed guest bedrooms, all with en suite facilities. Each of the 15 rooms has been sympathetically restored and renovated in keeping with the historic character of the premises. Brass beds, inglenook fireplaces and original beams feature in most of the rooms, all of which are equipped with colour televisions, hair dryers, direct-dial telephones and beverage facilities.

The 17th century wing has 7 rooms, one of which is a suite with a comfortable lounge area, which can be used for meetings or simply relaxing. They also have a newly appointed meeting room, which is suitable for up to 20 people and is fully equipped with all necessary technology.. So for those who can't get away from work, why not bring it with you?

Gales is ideal for small business conferences or meetings to allow you to get away from the office and from the large hotel atmosphere offering a variety of options to the business user. Ask for a conference pack to discover all the details. And you can enjoy a virtual reality view of the premises on the hotel's excellent website.

The hotel is now totally non-smoking in line with new regulations in England and Wales. They have provided a sheltered patio area outside to cater for the smokers among their guests.

Set beside the salmon-rich River Dee, Llangollen offers plenty of interest for visitors and if you enjoy the outdoors life there are facilities within easy reach for a huge range of activities including white water rafting, windsurfing, 4x4 go-carting, canoeing, falconry, kayaking, mountain biking, archery, clay pigeon shooting, horse-riding, climbing, sailing, fly fishing and abseiling. Any of these activities can usually be arranged for you by the hotel for the same or next day.

39-41 Regent Street,
Llangollen LL20 8HN
☎ 01978 861772

Located close to the centre of Llangollen, **Poplar House** is an impressive building dating from the early 1700s which, for much of its lifetime served as a Coaching Inn. It's now the home of Ginny Leon who has furnished and decorated the house throughout with great style and taste. In the main house there are 3 spacious guest bedrooms, all provided with TVs and DVD players, and two bathrooms which are comprehensively equipped and meticulously maintained. The rooms enjoy a two star rating from the Welsh Tourist Board.

More accommodation is available in the converted Coach House at the rear of the house. Here, one of the two units has been fully equipped for disabled guests with wide doors, a low bath and a drive-in shower. The other is furnished in traditional cottage style and can be used on either a self-catering or B&B basis. These two units can also be interlinked making them ideal for a family with someone who is disabled. (Poplar House is the only premises in this area providing accommodation

with full disabled facilities). Guests can enjoy either a Continental breakfast or a full English 4-course breakfast – Ginny is renowned for her superb omelettes with a choice of fillings. Vegetarians are also well catered for.

A recent addition to the amenities at Poplar House is proving very popular. In the courtyard at the rear of the house Ginny has installed a hot tub, decorated with a Roman theme, which can seat 6-7 people and is available to all guests. Also, as we go to press, work is being considered to install a Sauna and Steam Room. Ginny is now offering Spa Parties available by prior booking. The parties, held between 11.30am and 1.30pm, will include use of the hot tub, along with a full brunch of Buck's Fizz, smoked salmon and scrambled egg, traditional breakfast or you can of course choose one of Ginny's magnificent omelettes.

17 THE SMITHFIELD ARMS 🍴 🛏

Berwyn Street, Llangollen,
Denbighshire LL20 8NF
☎ 01978 861189
e-mail: mervynedwards@btconnect.com

Located in the heart of Llangollen, adjacent
to the main A5, The **Smithfield Arms** is a
former coaching and posting inn built around
1810. Home cooking using local produce is
the order of the day here with a good choice
available from the regular menu and daily
specials. During the summer, breakfasts are
available from 7am-10am. Food is served
from noon until 8pm, daily except Mondays.
This lively pub hosts bingo on Monday; a
quiz on Tuesday evening; live music on
Friday; karaoke
evening on
Saturday and Sky
Sports live all week.
The inn also offers
recently
refurbished
accommodation in
9 upstairs room,
one of which has
en suite facilities.

20 PONDEROSA CAFÉ 🍴

Horseshoe Pass, nr Llangollen,
North Wales LL20 8DR
☎ 01978 790307
e-mail: info@ponderosacafe.co.uk
🌐 www.ponderosacafe.co.uk

Located on the famous Horseshoe Pass
between Llangollen and Ruthin, the
Ponderosa Café is not just a café but also a
licensed restaurant and gift shop. Owned and
personally run by the Clemence family since
1984, the Ponderosa stands in 14 acres of its
own grounds surrounded by thousands of
acres of scenic countryside. The self service
café offers everything from toast to main
meals, all cooked to order and with at least
50% of the produce sourced locally. There's
seating for 60 people inside, and a further
200 outside. Adjacent to the café, the gift
shop has
items both
local and
from all
around
the world.

18 LLANGOLLEN RAILWAY 🏛

The Station, Abbey Road, Llangollen,
Clwyd LL20 8SN
☎ 01978 860979
e-mail:Llangollen.railway@btinternet.com

Llangollen in North Wales is famous for hosting
the International Eisteddfod at the beginning of
July each year but is also
renowned for the
Llangollen Railway
that has restored part of the former cross-country line that once served
the town. The railway was closed by British Railways in the 1960s but
by 1975 the first signs of a revival could be seen. In 1981 the
dedication of enthusiasts was rewarded and the first passenger train left
Llangollen Station to make the short ¾ mile journey as far as Pentrefelin.

Since that time the work of restoring the railway has continued and
trains now run for 7½ miles up the Dee Valley. Llangollen Station,
where many passengers start
their journey, is situated in
the centre of the town and
easily accessible from the A5
Trunk Road. There are
intermediate stations at
Berwyn and Glyndyfrdwy before the train reaches the
current western terminus at Carrog. The village and
River Dee are a few minutes walk from the Station.
Beyond Carrog the old trackbed stretches into the
distance and work is currently in progress to reinstate
the remaining 2½ miles to Corwen.

Victoria Square, Llangollen,
Denbighshire LL20 8EU

☎ 01978 861835   Fax: 01978 860775
e-mail: info@thegreenbankhotel.com
⊕ www.thegreenbankhotel.com

Greenbank Hotel and Restaurant occupies an impressive 3-storey gabled Victorian Town House. Built in 1887 it is located in the town centre and on an elevated site with a magnificent view of Dinas Bran (Crow Castle) with the Eglwsyg Mountains as its backdrop. It has only recently been taken over by Rich Lovejoy and Chris Ainsworth. Their energy is already showing in the changes happening to the hotel. Richard is a native Australian and brings with him some wonderful dessert and sweet ideas to compliment your dining experience, while Chris is the perfect host who is always on hand to see that you enjoy your Greenbank experience.

During the summer season, the restaurant opens for breakfast from 8.00 weekdays and 8.30 on weekends. Call in any time for coffee and cakes. Lunch is from midday and dinner is available from 6pm. The restaurant can seat up to 60 people, with additional seating in the courtyard. The Greenbank combines good service and friendly atmosphere with excellent food accompanied by a fine selection of beers and wines, all at a reasonable price. Everything is cooked on the premises and there are separate menus for lunch and dinner. Non-residents should book for dinner to avoid disappointment.

Accommodation at Greenbank comprises 12 rooms of various sizes. As we go to press, they are all being refurbished. All rooms are en suite and equipped with televisions and a hospitality tray. All should be completed by the summer of 2008. Most of the rooms are housed within the main building as well as 2 cottages attached with their own private entry. The premises have been awarded 3 stars by Visit Wales and have Premier Suites with at least one four-poster bed available. Wireless access is complimentary to both residents and those using the restaurant.

Llangollen itself offers a huge variety of things to do and see. You could take a relaxing cruise on the Llangollen canal in a horse-drawn barge or stroll 127 feet up across Thomas Telford's stupendous viaduct. The Steam Railway provides trips through the beautiful Dee Valley. The town's major event is the famous International Musical Eisteddfod, supplemented by the Balloon Festival and Jazz Festival. Other attractions include the Motor Museum, Valle Crucis Abbey, Dinas Bran and Plas Newydd, home of the famous 'Ladies of Llangollen'.

21 THE TELFORD INN & RESTAURANT

Station Road, Trevor, Llangollen,
Clwyd LL20 7TT
☎ 01978 820469
e-mail: barking_mad@btconnect.com

Named after the famous civil engineer
Thomas Telford, **The Telford Inn &
Restaurant** stands close to one of Telford's
greatest achievements – the soaring
Pontcysyllte aqueduct that carries the
Llangollen Canal 126 feet above the river Dee.

The inn itself was built around the same
time, the early 1800s and is very popular with
boat people and canal lovers. Mine hosts, Rob
and Sarah, who have been here since 2002,
provide a warm welcome to all their visitors.
Rob and Sarah are also chefs and their menu
offers a good selection of traditional
favourites such as haddock and chips, home-
cooked ham, eggs and chips, along with dishes
such as Mexican chilli con carne and their
home-made sizzling Cajun chicken. Also on
the menu are salads and sandwiches and their
tour de force, the wonderful Steak Pie. They
try to ensure that most of their ingredients are

sourced locally and are of top quality.
Food is served from noon until
2.30pm and from 6pm to 9.30pm,
Monday to Friday plus all day
Saturday and Sunday during the
winter, and from 11am until 10pm
everyday during Spring and Summer.
A wide selection of beverages to
accompany your meal is available,
including one real ale on a rotating
guest ale basis. The pub has seating
for 58 customers inside, and a further
80 outside overlooking the canal
basin. There's also a private function
room available which can cater for up
to 100 guests and has a fully licensed
bar open until midnight.

22 BERSHAM HERITAGE CENTRE & IRONWORKS

Bersham, Wrexham LL14 4HT
☎ 01978 261529
e-mail: bershamheritge@wrexham.co.uk
🌐 www.wrexham.gov.uk/heritage

Hidden in the Clywedog Valley, two miles west of Wrexham can be found the real beginnings of the Industrial Revolution. Bersham's old Victorian school is now the centre for discovering the industrial heritage of Wrexham. Permanent displays feature the history behind John Wilkinson's ironworks and the later steel industry of Brymbo. Some

of the most innovative ideas of the Industrial Revolution were conceived here in Bersham by John "Iron Mad" Wilkinson.

The remains of John Wilkinson's 18th century blast furnace and associated buildings can be seen at **Bersham Ironworks**. It is hard to believe a place so unsung in the history books could have been so important. Industry comes alive in the Heritage Centre when the working forge is used by local students and blacksmiths. The centre hosts a lively programme of temporary exhibitions and events to appeal to all the family.

24 ERDIGG

Nr Wrexham LL13 0YT
☎ 01978 355314
Info Line: 01978 315151

Two miles south of Wrexham, in a glorious 2,000-acre estate and country park, **Erddig** is one of the most fascinating houses in Britain, not least because of the unusually close relationship that existed between the owners and their servants. This is movingly illustrated by the extraordinarily detailed exhibition of family memorabilia collected by the servants and on show to visitors. The late 17th century mansion was begun by Joshua Edisbury, the High Sheriff of Denbighshire, who subsequently fled, unable to meet his debts. The house passed into the hands of the Meller family and to their descendants until finally coming under the ownership of the National Trust. The stunning state rooms display most of their original 18th and 19th century furniture and furnishings, including some exquisite Chinese wallpaper.

The outbuildings have been restored, including kitchen, laundry, bakehouse, stables, sawmill, smithy and joiner's shop, and visitors can wander around the country park and the dairy farm. The large walled garden has been restored to its 18th century formal design and incorporates Victorian additions, notably a parterre and yew walk, as well as a canal garden and fish pool; it also contains the National Ivy Collection, and a narcissus collection. Erddig is open to the public between late March and early November except Thursday and Friday. It has a plant sales area, a shop and a licensed restaurant. Video presentations are available, and conducted tours by prior arrangement.

Glan Llyn Road, Bradley,
Wrexham LL11 4BA

☎ 01978 758151   Fax: 01978 758151
e-mail: info@queensheadbradley.co.uk
website: www.queensheadbradley.co.uk

Located in the village of Bradley, just off the B5425, the **Queens Head** is a lively hostelry serving a good selection of food and beverages, including 2 real ales, and offering a wide range of entertainment. Mine hosts, Nick and Sue, are a friendly and welcoming couple who have been here since the summer of 2006. Amongst their customers are two regulars who actually built the pub back in the mid-1960s.

Nick has been in the hospitality business since 1988 and as well as being a licensee he is also a DJ and can turn his hand to catering. But it is Sue who is in charge of the kitchen where she prepares a good range of dishes based on local produce wherever possible. All the old pub favourites are there – Cottage Pie, Steak & Ale Pie, Sausage and Mash, Chicken Curry and Fish & Chips, all at very reasonable prices. There's also a home-made soup of the day and a choice of great desserts including a home-made apple pie and jam roly-poly. Children have their own menu and for those with a lighter appetite, a selection of bar snacks such as hot and cold baguettes and garlic bread with cheese. On Sundays, Sue cooks a traditional roast with a choice of meats – these are very popular so it is wise to make a booking. Food is available from 2pm to 7pm on Fridays, and from noon until 7pm on Saturday and Sunday. The pub itself is open evenings only, Monday to Thursday, and all day Friday to Sunday. All major credit cards are accepted.

The Queens Head provides a remarkable range of entertainments. In addition to live sport on the large Sky Sports screen, the pub hosts free pool on Mondays and prize Bingo on Wednesdays from 7.30pm. Thursday is Film Night when feature films are shown on the large screen TV, and on Friday and Saturday evenings there's either live entertainment or karaoke. Sunday winds up the week with a poker league session.

As well as successfully running the Queens Head, Nick and Sue are also tenants of the King William Inn at Summerhill near Wrexham. The emphasis here is on entertainment and drinking with 2 real ales – Speckled Hen and a guest ale – always on tap.

25 BUCK HOUSE HOTEL

High Street, Bangor-on-Dee (Bangor-is-y-Coed), nr Wrexham, Clwyd LL13 0BU

☎ 01978 780336 Fax: 01978 781101

e-mail: buckhousehotel@aol.com

🌐 www.buckhousehotel.co.uk

Buck House Hotel is a small, family-run establishment of great character set in the riverside village of Bangor-on-Dee. Over recent years, the hotel has had careful renovation and extensive refurbishment and has become the hub

of the village. Most of the village clubs hold their meetings here, including the Pony Club, numerous sports teams and the British Legion.

The hotel has been owned and run since 1989 by Allan and Kath Hayes, together with their daughter and son-in-law Karen and Kevin Jones. Good food is a priority here and is available every day from 11.30am to 9.30pm. The menu changes with the season and is based predominantly on fresh local produce. Typical dishes include home-made soup or Mushrooms topped with bacon and Stilton crust amongst the starters; as main courses, a

Roast of the Day, Trio of Welsh Lamb on a bed of creamy mash with red wine and mint jus, and Steamed Fillet of fresh salmon with a cucumber and prawn sauce – fish dishes are extremely popular here. Salads and vegetarian dishes are also available. There's also a Light Bites/Snacks menu which includes burgers, home-cooked ham, egg and chips; jacket potatoes, sandwiches, toasties and baguettes. Meals are served in one of the two lounges or a full à la carte menu is available in the restaurant. It is essential to book for Thursday to Sunday evening. The elegant and spacious restaurant seats a maximum of 60 people and is available for private parties or weddings. It can be expanded with a marquee to hold up to

100 guests. To accompany your meal, the hotel offers a good selection of beers, wines and spirits. While waiting for your meal, browse amongst the pictures on the wall which give fascinating views of Bangor years ago.

Accommodation comprises 6 bedrooms, all with shower en suite, colour TV, radio/alarm, direct dial telephone, hospitality tray and full central heating. The hotel also has a well-equipped games room where you can enjoy a game of pool, darts or dominoes. From time to time, the hotel hosts live entertainment.

Bangor itself is perhaps most widely known for its picturesque Racecourse which sits beside the River Dee, known for its good fishing.

26 CHIRK CASTLE

Chirk, Wrexham LL14 5AF
☎ 01691 777701
e-mail: gcwmsn@smtp.ntrust.org.uk

Chirk Castle, a magnificent Marcher fortress, was begun in the late 13th century on land granted by Edward I to Roger de Mortimer. Rectangular, with a massive drum tower at each corner, the Castle has been extensively rebuilt and altered from time to time down the centuries but remains a truly impressive sight. It was bought in 1595 by Sir Thomas Myddleton, Lord Mayor of London, and part of it is still lived in by the Myddleton family. Visitors can see the elegant state rooms, some fine Adam-style furniture, tapestries and portraits. By contrast, the dramatic dungeon is a reminder of the Castle's turbulent history, and that for some, life was not always so peaceful and genteel.

The estate is entered through a superb set of wrought-iron gates that were made by the famous Davis brothers of Bersham Ironworks. The Castle, whose walls are now partly covered in climbing plants, stands in an 18th century landscaped

park whose layout is based on designs by William Emes. The grounds include six acres of trees and flowering shrubs, many of them planted by Lady Margaret Myddleton. There are handsome clipped yews in the formal garden, and a fine rose garden. Among other features are an avenue of lime trees, some 19th century topiary, a rockery and an old hawk house. One mile north of Chirk village and 9 miles south of Wrexham, the Castle is open to visitors from late March to early November, closed Monday and Tuesday except Bank Holidays.

28 COFFEE SHOP

Church Street, Chirk,
Wrexham LL14 5HA
☎ 01691 777646

Located in the heart of the historic small town of Chirk, the **Coffee Shop** has been providing wholesome fare to its customers since it started life in the late 1950s as a Milk Bar. Today it is owned and run by Chris and Keeley, a hospitable couple who have made their business popular with both locals and visitors alike. Customers can choose either from the printed menu or from the specials board. The All Day Breakfasts are especially popular, as are the fresh home-made scones

and Bara Brith cakes and Banana Loaf. There's a good selection of hot snacks, including fish and chips, Steak Pie and filled jacket potatoes, and kids have their own selection of meals. Locally sourced produce is used wherever possible, portions are generous and prices very reasonable. You can enjoy your refreshments either inside the café or at tables on the pavement outside where you can watch the world go by. Food is served from 10am to 4pm, daily; payment is by cash only. The Coffee Shop is located on the B5070, just a short drive from the main A5.

27 THE HAND HOTEL

The Hand Hotel, Church Street, Chirk,
Wrexham LL14 5EY

☎ 01691 773472 Fax: 01691 772479

e-mail: reception@handhotelchirk.com

🌐 www.handhotelchirk.com

Dating back to 1610, during the reign of James I of England, **The Hand Hotel**, in the centre of Chirk, was a coaching inn on the main route between Shrewsbury and Betws-y-Coed, a stretch of the much longer and important London to Holyhead road. Still retaining its original front

façade, this glorious, historic building continues its tradition of hospitality. Mine hosts, Darren and Janice Coles, and their team offer travellers and visitors alike a warm welcome and excellent facilities.

The hotel's cosy bar is open daily and here customers can enjoy a drink from the vast range that are kept in tiptop condition. Here, as elsewhere in the hotel, the décor is light and bright but does not overshadow the hotel's many original features, including its several large fireplaces. The hotel's Regency Restaurant, which is open to non-residents, is a particularly stylish and elegant room. Here customers can

enjoy a wonderful à la carte meal prepared by the hotel's chef, Stephen Southworth. The menu changes constantly and it includes such delights as Pork Steak cooked in a creamy Stilton and red wine sauce, traditional fish and chips, steaks and a vegetable and pasta bake. The desserts are equally imaginative and interesting and, finished with coffee and mints, a meal here is certainly one to savour.

The hotel's 16 en suite guest rooms are the domain of housekeeper, Gill, and she ensures that all guests feel at home in these charming and well appointed rooms. There is even a room with a four-poster bed that is ideal for a special occasion. There are also family rooms and The Hand Hotel is an

excellent place for a family break as not only is there plenty of interest in the surrounding area but, out in the hotel's Beer Garden, there is a special children's play area.

The Hand Hotel is a popular venue for weddings and not only can a reception be easily accommodated in the hotel's function room (which opens out into the garden) but it also holds a license for civil marriage ceremonies. Likewise, businesses have made this hotel their first choice as a conference venue as not only can The Hand Hotel accommodate up to 180 delegates in comfort, but the staff also show a high level of professionalism.

29 THE WEST ARMS HOTEL

Llanarmon Dyffryn Ceiriog, nr Llangollen,
Denbighshire North Wales LL20 7LD
☎ 01691 600665 Fax: 01691 600622
e-mail: gowestarms@aol.com
🌐 www.thewestarms.co.uk

Nestling in the foothills of the Berwyn Mountains, **The West Arms Hotel** has been dispensing hospitality ever since it became a hotel way back in 1670. At that time, the village of Llanarmon Dyffryn Ceiriog stood at the convergence of three tracks used by drovers. They would congregate here before continuing their journey – sometimes to markets as far away as London. More than 300 years later, the hotel is host to visitors from all over the world who relish the unique pleasure of this outstanding establishment.

The West Arms positively oozes warmth and character with ancient timberwork, period furniture and blazing inglenook fires all adding to the charm. In good weather, there are some delightful riverside gardens to explore.

A highlight of any stay at the West Arms is having dinner here. Head chef Grant Williams has worked in kitchens around the world, even as far afield as New Zealand. He has appeared on several TV programmes and even cooked for Prince Charles. His menu offers a superb choice featuring fresh, local produce prepared to the very highest standards. The menu changes regularly, reflecting the seasons, but typically will include dishes such as Medallions of Welsh Beef served with a spinach and wild mushroom roulade drizzled in a Burgundy sauce. If you prefer fish – and the restaurant was runner-up in the Seafish Best Seafood Pub in the UK awards for 2007 – the hotel takes delivery of fresh fish daily. Other awards earned by the hotel include 2 AA Rosettes, AA Best Seafood Pub of the Year and AA Courtesy & Care Awards.

The accommodation at the West Arms maintains the same elevated standards evident throughout the hotel. The superb rooms and suites are particularly spacious, many of them with the ancient beams still in place, and hold a AA 3 Star 87% grading – the highest in Wales.

Mornings begin with a generous Continental or full Welsh breakfast and then there's a huge choice of things to see or do. Chirk Castle, Rhaeadr Waterfall, Llangollen town and Plas Newydd Hall are all within easy reach, or you might prefer a walk through the surrounding hills. If angling is your passion, the hotel has the fishing rights for a 1.5 miles stretch of the River Ceiriog (free to guests), while the nearby River Dee provides salmon and trout fishing all the season.

The West Arms is licensed for civil marriages and offers full facilities and support for weddings and other functions..

248

30 WINCHMORE HOTEL 🛏 🍴

7 Mostyn Crescent, Central Promenade,
Llandudno LL30 1AR
☎ 01492 877458
e-mail: gwnshldn@aol.com
🌐 www.winchmore-hotel-llandudno.co.uk

An impressive Victorian Grade II listed building, the **Winchmore Hotel** occupies a superb position looking out across the promenade to the sea. The premises may be grand but owners Gwen and Terry Sheldon make sure that their guests find their hotel more like a home from home. It has a cosy bar with a wide choice of drinks, and a spacious restaurant where evening meals are available if you are staying on the dinner, B&B tariff. The 30 guest bedrooms are all individually designed, all with en suite facilities, colour TV and hospitality tray, and some have glorious sea views. There's a lift to the upper floors and level access from the hotel's car park.

32 OASIS HOTEL 🛏

4, Neville Crescent, Central Promenade,
Llandudno LL30 1AT
☎ 01492 877822
e-mail: ann@oasis-hotel.co.uk
🌐 www.oasis-hotel.co.uk

Commanding an enviable location on the Central Promenade and enjoying outstanding views of the famous Great Orme and the Little Orme, **The Oasis Hotel** is renowned for its convivial atmosphere and the friendly personal service provided by your hosts, Ann and David Blanchard.

The hotel's front entrance is approached by a beautifully maintained garden and, inside, on the ground floor is a tastefully decorated residents' lounge where guests can relax and unwind. The bar is open every day in high season from noon until midnight – or later! Bar snacks are available throughout the day.

There are 16 spacious and delightfully appointed en suite bedrooms, of which three are on the ground floor. The rooms at the front enjoy captivating views of Llandudno Bay and all rooms are

equipped with colour TV, radio/alarm clock and hospitality tray. Wireless connection is available. Children under 14 years stay for half price; those under 3, stay for free. Breakfast is served between 8am and 9.30am – special dietary requirements can be catered for with prior notice. If you are staying on a dinner, B&B basis, the evening meal is served between 6pm and 7pm. Packed lunches are available on request.

31 CAFÉ MONET

2 Vaughan Street, Llandudno LL30 1AB
☎ 01492 877377
e-mail: la.monet@btconnect.com

Café Monet has an attractive lavender and black frontage with the famous artist's signature dominating the awning. The interior is equally attractive with exposed brick walls and beams, and wooden flooring and furniture. Enid and Russ Daniels took over here in 2004 after running a guest house in Llandudno for three years before that.

Their menu offers a huge choice of hot and cold food, including an All Day Mega Breakfast and a variety of filled breakfast rolls. Light bites include a home-made soup of the day, hot garlic baguette with cheese or simply a scone with butter. Other options include jacket potatoes, omelettes, pasta dishes, toasties, hot ciabatta and foccacia sandwiches and some delicious desserts. Wherever possible, everything on the menu is based on local Welsh produce and offered at value for money prices. In addition to the regular menu, daily specials are listed on the blackboard and might include dishes such as hot bacon with melted Brie and cranberry on a large roll.

The café seats 30 inside and 12 more at tables on the pavement, and also offers a takeaway service. It is open from 8.30am to around 4pm, Monday to Saturday. Children are welcome; payment is by cash or cheque only.

33 CAFÉ T'AIR

135 Station Road, Deganwy,
Conwy LL31 9EJ
☎ 01492 582281

If you cross the road from the railway station at Deganwy and enter **Café T'Air,** it's like stepping back into the Victorian era. This superb establishment with its iron, station-style awning and bow windows is an absolute delight. The interior is furnished in the style of a Victorian drawing room, complete with vintage fireplace and lots of ornaments and knick-knacks. Owners Bryan Hughes and Keith Hallowes have been here since 1995 and have established a glowing reputation for their home cooking and hospitality. Smartly dressed in white shirts and black bow ties, they intensify the sense of visiting an earlier age. Keith is the chef and his menu is deeply enticing. Who could resist the full Afternoon Tea, replete with cucumber sandwiches, Welsh tea bread, and scone with jam and cream? Then there are the wonderful cakes – Lemon Stem Ginger, perhaps, or Coffee & Walnut – and more than half a dozen different kinds of scone, freshly baked each day.

In addition to the teatime treats, the menu also offers a good selection of light lunches, salads, a home-made soup, hot dishes of the day, and toasted or regular sandwiches. On Wednesdays and Saturdays, Keith also adds his famous Steak & Mushroom Pie to the list. The dessert selection offers a memorable apple pie with apricot and sultanas in almond pastry with cream or ice cream. Or you could sample the delicious Plas Farm Ices of Anglesey.

Such is the popularity of this charming tearoom which has just 26 places, it is advisable to book ahead to avoid disappointment. The café is open from 10am to 4.30pm, Tuesday to Saturday. Mature children are welcome; only cash and cheques are accepted.

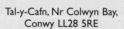

Tal-y-Cafn, Nr Colwyn Bay,
Conwy LL28 5RE
☎ 01492 650460
e-mail: office@bodnant-garden.co.uk
🌐 www.bodnantgarden.co.uk

Situated above the River Conwy, with spectacular views of the Snowdonia range, the National Trust's **Bodnant Garden** is one of the finest in the Britain.

The gardens were laid out by the 2nd Lord Aberconway in 1875 and were presented to the National Trust in 1949. The rhododendrons, camellias and magnolias are a truly magnificent sight in the spring, followed by herbaceous borders, roses and water lilies in the summer and glorious colours in the autumn.

Bodnant has many other attractions, including a laburnum arch, a lily terrace and a stepped pergola; in the Dell, formed round a little tributary of the Conwy, is the tallest redwood in the country. The pretty Garden House was built in Gloucestershire in the 1730s and was later used as a Pin Mill before being brought to Bodnant in 1938. The garden has a shop (not National Trust) and a refreshment pavilion. Bodnant, which is open from mid-March to early November, is located off the A470 eight miles south of Colwyn Bay and Llandudno.

Penrhyn Bay, Llandudno,
Conwy LL30 3EE
☎ 01492 549888

Located just off the coast road (B5115) between Llandudno and Colwyn Bay, **Penrhyn Old Hall** is a delightful cluster of buildings with a medieval manor house at their heart. The Hall enjoys a tranquil, picturesque setting surrounded by woods threaded by well-signed footpaths. At the same time, it is virtually a suburb of Llandudno so the attractions of town, country and coast are all close by. Behind its imposing façade the Hall functions as pub, restaurant and as a unique venue for parties and special occasions. The public rooms are warm, inviting and convivial with a wealth of historic and olde worlde appeal.

The Tudor Bar and Restaurant, open every day, are atmospheric places in which to enjoy a drink or a meal. Fresh, home-cooked food is served from daily changing menus, and include lunches every day, a traditional Sunday lunch and an extensive à la carte choice in the evenings from Wednesday to Saturday. Dishes are based on local produce and the menu

offers a choice of up to 16 main courses to choose from. The restaurant is open from noon until 2.30pm, and in the evenings from 5.30pm to 11.30pm. Children are welcome and Mastercard and Visa credit cards are accepted.

It is said by some that Roderick, grandson of the last King of the Britons, built a palace on this site in the 8th century. Nothing, of course, of that building survives but a few parts of the medieval hall are still to be seen. Designated a Grade I listed building, the whole place is full of architectural and historic interest with some

fascinating features including old fireplaces, remarkable frescoes, carvings and stained glass. The Marsh family, Ann and George, acquired the property in 1963 and set about major restoration work and the construction of sympathetic extensions. They retired in 1988, leaving their children Kim and Guy, and Guy's wife Anne, to run the business. One of the extensions houses the night club which can be hired for functions, with room for up to 200 guests. Popular skittles nights are held in the Baronial Hall which is at other times available for private parties. Places of interest in the vicinity include the resorts of Llandudno and Colwyn Bay, and the massive limestone headland of Great Orme.

253

36 THE QUEENS HEAD

Glanwydden, Conwy LL31 9JP
☎ 01492 546570 Fax: 01492 546487
e-mail: enquiries@queensheadglanwydden.co.uk
⊕ www.queensheadglanwydden.co.uk

One of the finest and best-known inns in Wales, **The Queen's Head** in Glanwydden offers excellent food, wine and a warm welcome to all guests. Professional chefs who have a passion for local produce prepare and present an impressive range of delicious dishes, such the fresh dressed Conwy crab. They have earned the inn a place in guides

such as AA's *Britain's Best Country Pubs for Food Lovers* and the Michelin guide to *Eating Out in Pubs*. As one enthusiastic customer put it, "the Queen's Head is without doubt the warmest and most wonderful place to eat and relax in peace." The bar, too, has a relaxed atmosphere and a roaring log fire – just the place to enjoy a pre-dinner drink. Lunch is served from noon until 2pm, Monday to Saturday; evening meals from 6pm to 9pm, Monday to Saturday; and on Sunday from noon until 9pm. The bar is open from 11.30pm to 3pm; and from 6pm to 11pm on weekdays; and from 11.30am to 10.30pm on Sunday. A recent addition to the inn's amenities is a well designed patio area bordered by colourful shrubs and flowers.

The Queen's Head does not have guest rooms but the owners have a charming little property, Storehouse Cottage, which stands opposite the windmill in the village. It dates back to the early 1700s and was once the original storehouse of the Llangwstennin Parish. The charming lounge has a real flame, wrought iron, open gas fire, colour TV, music centre, and snug and cosy armchairs to curl up in. The well-equipped kitchen with its beamed

roof is provided with thoughtful

extras such as Champagne buckets and cafetière. The galleried bedroom has a romantic 6ft king size bed fitted with pure Egyptian cotton sheets, goose down pillows and duvet. It has an adjoining dressing room. The immaculate bathroom has floor to ceiling mosaic tiling, bath, shower, heated towel rail and fluffy white luxurious towels and robes to feel at home in. Outside, there's a totally private garden with a raised side courtyard where you can settle down with afternoon tea or while away the day in the gentle sunshine.

254

Rhos Promenade, Rhos-on-Sea, Colwyn Bay,
Conwy LL28 4NE
☎ 01492 548185

From the outside, **Rhos Fynach** looks very appealing with its old stone walls covered with creepers and its dormer windows with small latticed panes. The interior is equally charming - old oak beams, exposed stone walls, tiled floors and a huge fireplace which was the entrance to tunnels used by the notorious smuggler Captain Morgan whose home this once was. The pub's history goes back even farther. The original building, reputed to be the oldest in Colwyn, dates back to 1181 when it was a monastery for Cistercian monks who made their living by fishing in the weir. Today, after being sympathetically restored between 1990 and 1992, it is an outstanding pub and restaurant. Owner Robert Skelley, who has been in the hospitality business for some 36 years, offers a choice of 4 real ales and fine home-cooked food based on local ingredients served

daily in the bar and lounge area. Fresh grilled local plaice, individual joints of lamb

Henry Morgan and home-made steak & ale pie feature on the regular menu which is supplemented by an extensive range of daily specials. Upstairs is the charming Monk's Restaurant and conservatory, ideal for any special occasion.

7, Colwyn Avenue, Rhos-on-Sea,
Conwy LL28 4RB
☎ 01492 546980

Barnaby's Bistro is a stylish eating place owned and run by Geraldine Reid. Her specialities include delicious home-made soups and dishes based on locally caught fish. Geraldine is also renowned for her wonderful scones which are as large as a small loaf, come in several varieties and will fill the largest gap. Geraldine uses as much local produce as she can, including fresh fish

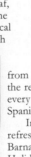

from Rhos itself and locally reared meats. In addition to the regular menu, there's a specials board which changes every fortnight. On it you might find dishes such as Spanish style Tapa, fresh grilled trout or minted diced lamb.

In good weather customers can enjoy their refreshments at sheltered pavement tables outside. Barnaby's is open from Tuesday to Sunday, and on Bank Holiday Mondays, from 9am to 4pm. Children are welcome; all major credit cards are accepted, and there is full wheelchair access throughout the bistro.

39 ZANZIBAR COFFEE SHOP

15 Penrhyn Road, Colwyn Bay LL29 8LE
☎ 01492 534144
e-mail: lyn@zanzibarcoffeeshop.co.uk
🌐 www.zanzibarcoffeeshop.co.uk

Lyn Lyon opened her **Zanzibar Coffee Shop** in 2004. Why Zanzibar? Well, Lyn reasoned, Zanzibar is an exotic island in the Indian Ocean, the ideal place for a getaway to chill and relax. Her coffee shop would be the ideal place to find a haven of tranquillity in a busy world. And so it is. Pictures of those faraway places are displayed around the walls and it seems warmer already. Another major element in the success of this little gem is the excellent quality of the locally sourced fresh products they use and also to the well-cooked, well-presented, and well-served food.

The extensive menu offers everything from Main Meals such as Steak Haché to Nibble and Starters like the Nachos and dips. There are light meals such as Zanzibar's home-made mackerel pâté, jacket

potatoes, salads, sandwiches, toasties, baguettes, paninis, and Zanzibar's own home-made soup. Round off your feast with one of the cakes or home-made scones. Zanzibar is open from 9.30pm to 4pm, Monday to Saturday. Zanzibar also offers an outside catering service, for buffets and business lunches. Recognizing that there is a need for a small venue for meetings, presentations, and training sessions, Zanzibar offers a suite ('The Venue') with full facilities.

40 THE MARINE HOTEL

Old Colwyn, Colwyn Bay,
Conwy LL29 9YH
☎ 01492 515020 Fax: 01492 512710
e-mail: wendymarine@aol.com
🌐 www.marinehoteloldcolwyn.co.uk

Conveniently located close to junction 22 of the main A55 North Wales Coast Road, **The Marine Hotel** is an impressive 3-storey building dating back to the 1840s. In those days it served as a posting house on the Chester to Holyhead stage coach route. Licensee Wendy has been here for 19 years and was joined by her partner Brian 6 years ago. Both are very experienced in the hospitality business and dedicated to making your visit a happy and enjoyable one.

A major attraction here is the excellent food based on local produce. Choose from the printed menu or specials board. Home-made dishes are a speciality – lasagne in particular but the steak dishes are also very popular as is the

superb Sunday lunch. Food is served from noon until 2.30pm, and from 5.30pm to 8.30pm, (9pm on Friday and Saturday).

On Sundays, the hours are from noon until 3pm, and there's no food on Mondays unless it is a Bank Holiday. The hotel is open all day, every day, for drinks, amongst which are 2 or 3 real ales. The hotel has 9 guest bedrooms, 8 of which are en suite. Children are welcome and all major credit cards are accepted.

256

Abergele Road, Llanddulas,
Conwy LL22 8HP
☎ 01492 515747
e-mail: joan494@hotmail.com
⊕ www.dulasarms.co.uk

Conveniently located close to Junction 23 of the A55, **The Dulas Arms** occupies a fine position with views of the Irish Sea from the rear garden. Originally known as the Railway Hotel, the inn was built around 1880 and today is run by Dave and Joan Spencer. They have been in the hospitality business for more than 30 years but when they took over here in the summer of 2006 this was their first venture as landlords. Good food is one of their priorities with specialities of the house including steaks and Steak, Ale & Mushroom Pies. Everything is based on fresh local produce and cooked on the premises. Food is served from noon to 3pm, and from 5pm to 7.30 or 8pm.

To accompany your meal the bar offers 2 cask ales – JW Lees Bitter and a Lees seasonal guest ale – along with a wide choice of other beverages. Children are welcome and there's a well-equipped play area in the spacious beer garden at the rear. For the grown-ups there's a pool room and regular live entertainment. The Dulas Arms also offers accommodation with a choice of single, double, twin and family rooms.

Whitehouse Leisure Park, Towyn Road,
Towyn LL22 9EY
☎ 01745 827333

Conveniently located beside the main A548 coastal road at Towyn, **Jakes** is a welcoming family-run hostelry which has recently been refurbished to a very high standard. Jakes is well-known for its excellent food service which starts at 9am with a selection of breakfasts.

From 11am to 5.30pm, a wide choice of Light Bites is available, and then from 5.30pm

until 9pm an extensive range of appetising dishes is served. In addition to the regular menu, daily specials are also available. On Sundays, there's a separate menu of roast dishes with a vegetarian alternative.

Castle Street, Conwy LL32 8AY
☎ 01492 592246
⊕ www.nationaltrust.org.uk

This is the only medieval merchant's house in Conwy to have survived the turbulent history of the walled town over nearly six centuries. Furnished rooms and an audio-visual presentation show daily life from different periods in its history.

43 THE MORTON ARMS

Sandbank Road, Towyn LL22 9LB
☎ 01745 330211 Fax: 01745 330211
e-mail: laverychris1@aol.com

Located just off the main A458 in the centre of Towyn, close to the seashore, **The Morton Arms** is an outstanding hostelry offering the very best in food, drink, accommodation, entertainment and hospitality. The main building dates back to the 1970s and stands in almost 2 acres of its own grounds. Mine hosts Chris and Lorraine have owned and run the inn since 2002 and have made it a must-visit place for both locals and visitors alike. A major attraction is the excellent food served here with both English and Chinese cuisine on the menu. There's a good variety of dishes, all home cooked and in generous portions. Food is served in the main bar every lunchtime and evening in the season, and also in the elegant main restaurant which specialises in Chinese dishes. The restaurant is also open every lunchtime and evening during the season, and also in the evenings out of season.

The bar offers a comprehensive choice of beverages, including Tetley and Worthington's keg draught ales, and Chris and Lorraine are planning to introduce real ales in the future. Most weekends, The Morton Arms hosts excellent live entertainment with professional artists, which is also presented on some weekdays during the season.

The inn also offers comfortable accommodation in chalet-style buildings within its grounds.

The 20 chalets are available for 7½ months of the year and guests can stay on either a B&B or self-catering basis. Each chalet has its own off road parking area.

As we go to press, plans are far advanced for a new separate café adjacent to the main building which will open in 2008 and from 8am to 11.30pm during the season will serve all types of snacks, hot meals and beverages.

The Morton Arms welcomes children; accepts all major credit cards; has off-road car parking and good disabled access in the bar and restaurant.

3 Castle Street, Conwy LL32 8AY
☎ 01492 593792

If you want to sample Britain's national dish at its very best, a visit to The **Fisherman's Chip Shop** in the town centre of Conwy is strongly recommended. Owners Peter and Tracy Nolan have been here since 1985 and they are kept extremely busy all year round. It's both a sit-down restaurant and a takeaway, offering a full range of fish dishes, burgers (including a veggie burger), and chicken dishes, all at value-for-money prices. In season, mussels are also added to the menu.

There's seating for more than 50 diners, spread over three floors and such is the popularity of the restaurant, it's advisable to book at all times, especially during the summer months. The Fisherman's Chip Shop is open every day

during the summer season from 11.30am to 8pm. In winter, it is open at lunchtimes daily and all day on Saturday and Sunday. Payment is by cash or cheque only.

Rose Hill Street, Conwy LL32 8LD
☎ 01492 573482
e-mail: info@bridge-conwy.com
🌐 www.bridge-conwy.com

As you enter the historic walled town of Conwy from the A55, you will see the magnificent medieval castle on your left and, across the road, **The Bridge Inn** on your right. This is a fine old traditional hostelry where mine hosts, Jenny and Keith, offer a genuinely warm welcome. Keith is very proud of his range

of real cask ales which are kept in tip-top condition. There are 5 in all, with Jennings Cocker Hoop, Marston's Pedigree and Bass as the permanent brews, supplemented by 2 rotating guest ales. The bar

also stocks an excellent collection of single malt whiskeys. Jenny and Keith are also proud of the quality food served here, prepared by professional chefs using locally sourced ingredients wherever possible. The regular menu offers a wide selection to suit every palate and there's also a choice of daily specials. On Sundays, roasts are added to the menu and booking ahead for this is strongly recommended. The Bridge Inn also has excellent accommodation in 5 upstairs rooms, all attractively furnished and decorated and with en suite facilities. The rooms range in size from single to family room.

259

46 YE OLDE MAILCOACH

High Street, Conwy LL32 8DE
☎ 01492 593043
🌐 www.conwymailcoach.co.uk

Ye Olde Mailcoach is a striking building with its black and white decorated upper storeys and bow window. Dating back in parts to the late 1700s, this lively hostelry is located right in the heart of this historic walled town. Mine hosts, David and Alison Fare, have been running the pub since 2003 but took over as tenants in May 2006. David is the cook and his menu offers an appetising choice of freshly cooked traditional dishes. Steaks are something of a speciality and there are special steak nights on some Fridays. Food is served from noon until 4pm, and from 7pm to 9pm on Friday evenings. The pub is also well-known for the quality of its ales which include 2 real ales, one of which always comes from the local Conwy Brewery.

Ye Olde Mailcoach is popular with football fans as it screens matches from the English Premier League, the European Champions

League, and UEFA Cup matches. For those who enjoy pub quizzes, the pub holds two each week, on Monday and Wednesday evenings from 9pm – all are welcome.

If you are planning to stay in this appealing town, Ye Olde Mailcoach has 4 quality guest rooms which by the time you read this should all have been provided with en suite facilities.

48 THE LODGE HOTEL

Tal-y-bont, Conwy LL32 8YX
☎ 01492 660766 Fax: 01492 660534
e-mail: enquiries@thelodgehotelconwy.co.uk
🌐 www.thelodgehotelconwy.co.uk

Located in the peaceful rural village of Tal-y-bont in the heart of the spectacular Conwy Valley, **The Lodge Hotel** was built in 1974 on the site of a small-holding. Owners Diane and Neil Bradshaw, who took over here in the spring of 2005, have made it into a happy and welcoming hotel. The hotel's fully licensed restaurant attracts many plaudits and offers a good choice of appetising food with steaks and fresh fish dishes as specialities of the house. There's a table d'hôte menu which changes every day for those staying on a dinner, bed & breakfast basis, and also an à la carte alternative.

The Lodge offers an excellent choice of bedrooms. The "Classic" rooms offer en suite king size double or twin accommodation while the

"Premier" rooms are extra large rooms with a sitting area, additional settee bed and a private external patio. Also available are cottage suites which have 2 bedrooms which can be arranged as doubles/ twins. These also have a double sofa bed and a private outside patio. All the rooms enjoy views of the attractive and productive gardens.

260

Conwy Road, Trefriw, Conwy LL27 0JH
☎ 01492 642304 Fax: 01492 641665
e-mail: gwestyfairyfallshotel.googlemail.com
🌐 www.fairyfallshoteltrefriw.co.uk

Fairy Falls Hotel takes its name from the local attraction reached via a footpath from Trefriw Woollen Mill which has been in operation since the 1830s. The hotel is also a very popular village inn where extremely friendly locals gather throughout the year. The bar stocks a large selection of ever-changing wines and cask ales, along with a vast choice of draft lagers, ales and ciders.

This is also a good place to eat with an extensive choice of snacks and bar meals available in the lounge area of the cottage inn. Food is served from noon until 9pm, 7 days a week during peak times. Adjacent to the lounge area is the cottage bar restaurant with seating for up to 40 people. A choice of grill, table d'hôte and à la carte menus is available during the afternoon and evening. To accompany your meal, a large selection of wines from around the world is available. Head chef Philip O'Connor is a forward looking man who regularly reviews the menu and welcomes feedback from customers.

Accommodation at the Fairy Falls comprises 6 chalets detached from the main public house and set alongside the river with fantastic views of the Conwy Valley. The rooms are spacious, furnished to a very high standard, and equipped with en suite facilities, TV and hospitality tray. Each chalet has its own balcony with a seating area. At breakfast time, guests can have their meal delivered to the chalet or take it in the restaurant.

The hotel is run by business partners Philip Evans and Dylan Cernyw. Dylan's name will be familiar to lovers of Welsh harp music. He has won in the National Eisteddfod and is a well-known concert entertainer throughout Wales. He has also performed alongside some of the biggest stars such as Bryn Terfel, Katherine Jenkins, Hayley Westenra and many others. So it's no surprise to find that the hotel hosts regular entertainment ranging from top Welsh bands Sara mai a'r moniars, Allistar James, and locally based band Cellar Dwellars.

Another popular amenity at the hotel is the Geirionydd Restaurant and Function Suite which can cater for up to 120 guests. It has the benefits of a music and dance licence and a large dance floor. The hotel also caters for Sunday lunch which has proved so popular that booking ahead is essential.

261

50 MEADOWSWEET HOTEL

Station Road, Llanrwst, Conwy LL26 0DS
☎ 01492 642111 Fax: 01492 642733
e-mail: info@meadowsweethotel.com
🌐 www.meadowsweethotel.com

Enjoying a lovely scenic location on the edge of Snowdonia National Park, the **Meadowsweet Hotel** lies on the outskirts of Llanrwst and from many of its rooms there are glorious views out across the Gwydyr Forest. It is very much a family-run hotel with Nelson and Mary Haerr and their daughter Morgan all involved in the enterprise they took over in February 2007. Nelson used to be a New York City fireman and met Mary when she visited the city on a shopping spree.

They eventually married and lived in the USA but when on holiday in Mary's home town of Llanrwst discovered that the hotel was on the market and decided to buy it.

The hotel has 10 charming and spacious en suite 3-star guest rooms with a choice of family, double, twin or single occupancy. Each room is beautifully decorated and furnished to a very high standard and they all provide the perfect environment for a peaceful night's sleep. There is also a suite with a 4-poster bed for that romantic break away and many guests choose to stay on a dinner, bed & breakfast basis as the hotel is also highly regarded for its cuisine.

The restaurant, which is called Lle Hari (Harry's Place), is open to non-residents and offers a delicious menu of dishes that are all prepared from the freshest local ingredients by a professional chef. A typical menu might include enticing appetisers such as the Welsh version of Maryland crab cakes and a home-made soup of the day. As main courses, how about a local Welsh lamb steak, or a Beef Wellington with a fillet of Welsh beef, or the Dolydd's famous St David's Chicken? A full wine list provides the perfect accompaniment to the excellent fare. The restaurant seats 30 so booking ahead is strongly recommended. Less formal dining can be enjoyed in the cosy bar where a log fire adds to the warm and inviting ambience. There's also a recently created outdoor patio area.

Many guests, once they have found this outstanding hotel, return time and time again and there is plenty to see and do in the surrounding area. Along with the Snowdonia National Park and the nearby Forest Park with its countless lakes and endless walks, there are several golf courses close by, riding and guided walks can be arranged from the hotel, and the coast is just a short drive away.

North Road, Caernarfon,
Gwynedd LL55 1BA
☎ 01286 675589 Fax: 01286 673689
e-mail: enquiries@bronmenai.co.uk
⊕ www.bronmenai.co.uk

When Alan and Val Ashcroft bought **Gwesty Bron Menai** in December 2001, the property was in a semi-derelict state. Over the next nine months they completely refurbished the grand 1840s building to provide high quality accommodation. It now enjoys a 4-star Bed & Breakfast rating from the Welsh Tourist Board. Currently, Alan and Val are just offering bed & breakfast accommodation but are planning to add a fully licensed bar and restaurant.

There are 9 guest bedrooms, all of which are en suite and are provided with colour television and tea and coffee-making facilities. One room is on the ground floor and the mixture of rooms includes family size – children over 10 years are welcome. The tariff includes a hearty breakfast, normally served between 8am and 9am but can be served earlier by arrangement. Evening meals can also be arranged with prior notice – the premises are licensed for guests. You can stay at Gwesty Bron Menai on a bed & breakfast, or dinner, bed & breakfast basis. The house can be found just off the A487 towards the centre of the town and it's just a 2-minute walk to the Menai Straits. It has private parking for one car per room.

North Road, Caernarfon,
Gwynedd LL55 1BD
☎ 01286 673297
e-mail: info@menaibankhotel.co.uk
⊕ www.menaibankhotel.co.uk

Guests arriving at the **Menai Bank Hotel** always receive a warm welcome from owners Patrick and Rachel Coyne. This friendly establishment overlooking the Menai Straits offers comfortable accommodation in individually furnished and decorated rooms, many of which enjoy sea views. Breakfast is a generous buffet including cereals, fruit, bacon, eggs and sausages. A recently acquired (and very expensive) "coffee bean to cup" machine ensures a really fresh cup of coffee. The hotel is licensed and also open for morning coffee and afternoon tea. Other amenities include a pool room, bar and a meeting room.

HIDDEN PLACES GUIDES

Explore Britain and Ireland with *Hidden Places* guides - a fascinating series of national and local travel guides.

Packed with easy to read information on hundreds of places of interest as well as places to stay, eat and drink.

Available from both high street and internet booksellers

For more information on the full range of *Hidden Places* guides and other titles published by Travel Publishing visit our website on

www.travelpublishing.co.uk
or ask for our leaflet by phoning
01752 276660 or emailing
info@travelpublishing.co.uk

263

53 CAERNARFON CASTLE

Caernarfon, Gwynedd LL55 2AY
☎ 01286 677617

Mighty Caernarfon is possibly the most famous of Wales' many castles. Its sheer scale and commanding presence easily set it apart from the rest and, to this day, still trumpet in no uncertain terms the intentions of its builder, Edward 1. Begun in 1283 as the definitive chapter in his conquest of Wales, Caernarfon was constructed not only as a military stronghold but also as a seat of government and royal palace.

The castle's majestic persona is no architectural accident: it was designed to echo the walls of Constantinople, the imperial power of Rome and the dream castle, "the fairest that ever man saw", of Welsh myth and legend. After all these years, Caernarfon's immense strength remains undimmed. Standing at the mouth of the Seiont river, the fortress (with its unique polygonal towers, intimidating battlements and colour banded masonry) dominates the walled town also founded by Edward. Caernarfon's symbolic status was emphasised when Edward made sure that his son, the first English Prince of Wales, was born here in 1284. In 1969, the castle gained worldwide fame as the setting for the investiture of Prince Charles as Prince of Wales.

History comes alive at Caernarfon in so many ways - along the lofty wall walks, beneath the towered gatehouse and with imaginative exhibitions located within the towers.

55 TY MAWR TEAROOMS, RESTAURANT AND B&B

Groeslon Ty Mawr, Llanddeiniolen, nr Caernarfon, Gwynedd LL55 3AW
☎ 01248 352791
e-mail: ruth@tymawrbb.wanadoo.co.uk
🌐 www.tymawr-bandb.co.uk

Offering the very best in bed & breakfast, **Ty Mawr Tearooms, Restaurant & Bed and Breakfast** also offers excellent food, set in the heart of Snowdonia with picturesque views from all the bedrooms and restaurant.

In the licensed restaurant, customers enjoy Ruth and Mark Higgin's wonderful home cooking and a menu that has something for every palate. The B&B accommodation comprises of 5 guest bedrooms (4 ensuite). 2 are on the ground floor and residents lounge - open all year round. A ground floor room for disabled use is being built this year.

Menai Marina, Y Felinheli,
Gwynedd LL56 4XA
☎ 01248 671010 Fax: 01248 670300
e-mail: plasdinorwic@btconnect.com
⊕ www.hotelplasdinorwic.com

Affectionately know as "The Pink Palace" (or
"Palas Pinc") because of its pastel-coloured
exterior, the boutique Hotel Plas Dinorwic is
one of the best-known hotels in the area. It is
beautifully sited above the Menai Straits and
is perfectly located for exploring the
Snowdonia National Park. Among the hotel's
many regular clients are major TV and film
companies, including one of the Welsh language soap operas which was filmed here.

The magnificently furnished and decorated public rooms include the Quiet Room, or lounge,
which has its own real log fire. Other amenities include a fully licensed bar, an indoor heated
swimming pool, sauna and launderette. There is also a function/conference room ideal for weddings
which can cater for 50 people sitting down in the day and 150 in the evening. There's also a slipway
for launching boats.

The hotel offers a huge variety of
accommodation, ranging from single rooms
to suites catering for 6 people – and all at
affordable prices. There's a typical Welsh style
cottage which can sleep up to 4. Other
options include twin-bedded rooms; double
bedded rooms; multi bedded (family) rooms;
a selection of suites and penthouses with
panoramic views of the Menai Straits; Sea
View apartments and detached stone built
cottages. All accommodations are en suite
with tea and coffee making facilities, and
some rooms are specially designed to be
disabled friendly.

Perhaps the most unique accommodation
is to be found in the Tower which offers
luxurious waterfront apartments where you can see the boats entering and leaving the gate-locked
marina. Enjoy feeding the swans and watching the
herons and cormorants fishing. One of the
apartments comprises the second floor and the roof
area of the Tower and has a sun deck / terrace with
barbecue. The upper room comprises the second
bedroom to this two bedroom apartment.

Visitors will find plenty to see and do in the
area. You could climb Snowdon on foot or take the
mountain railway. Caernarfon Castle, the site of
Prince Charles's Investiture has a magnificent
regimental museum (not forgetting the castle itself
of course!) Other attractions include the Menai
Bridge, the world famous suspension bridge
designed by Thomas Telford, and the walled, world
heritage town of Conway with its own unique castle.

View from the Penthouse Apartment

265

56   TY'N RHOS COUNTRY HOUSE AND RESTAURANT

Seion, Llanddeniolen, Caernarfon LL55 3AE
☎ 01248 670489 Fax: 01248 671772
e-mail: enquiries@tynrhos.co.uk
🌐 www.tynrhos.co.uk

Set in a beautiful location on the wide open lush plain between Snowdonia and the sea, **Ty'n Rhos Country House** is an outstanding 5-star establishment with rosette awards for its food. A former farmhouse, it was well known as a leading

farm guest house and restaurant until the autumn of 2006 when Martin and Janet James bought the property and embarked on a major programme of upgrading its facilities. It has a large, restful lounge furnished with many antiques, the dining room and conservatory overlook the gardens and the isle of Anglesey, and there's even a cosy bar.

Quality furnishings and fittings are standard for the bedrooms. All 10 rooms are individual in design and provided with en suite facilities, colour television and hospitality tray. There are 2 king/twin rooms on the ground floor which

have patio doors opening onto the garden. There's also a single room on the ground floor. Other bedrooms are on the first floor with a mixture of king/doubles, twins and a single. Renovated farm byres house 3 spacious bedrooms, one especially designed for the less abled. Also available are 2 self-catering cottages.

Good food is an important priority at Ty'n Rhos. Martin is a talented chef and he and his team of chefs take great care and pride in the dishes that leave the kitchen. They rely on local farmers and butchers, freshly caught local fish and, in the summer, vegetables and herbs straight from the hotel garden. A daily fixed price menu is available Monday to Saturday and changed regularly with a choice of three or more dishes per course. On Sunday there is an excellent 2 or 3-course lunch and a 3-course set dinner. Light lunches are served in the conservatory. Breakfasts are a memorable affair - home-made rolls, preserves and yoghurt, freshly squeezed orange juice, kedgeree and kippers. Or you could sample the Welsh Breakfast with Menai oysters and laver bread.

During the day, guests can relax in the superb garden with its grand views or perhaps play a game of croquet. Beyond the 50 acres of grounds is a colourful patchwork landscape of fields with sheep and cattle grazing while ducks, coots and moorhens busy themselves around the hotel's two lakes. There's also a helicopter landing field beyond the garden.

57 LLANGOLLEN VAULTS

31 High Street, Bethesda,
Gwynedd LL57 3AN
☎ 01248 600491

Very much at the heart of the village, both in location and socially, **Llangollen Vaults** is a satisfyingly traditional hostelry run by Bob and Esther Morris. Esther is the cook and offers a varied menu every day except Tuesday. Her Sunday roasts are particularly popular. To accompany your meal, there's a choice of 2 real ales with Abbot Ale as the regular brew. Payment is by cash or cheque only. This lively

pub hosts a Poker Night on Mondays, and a karaoke evening on Fridays. In the winter months there's also a Pub Quiz on Tuesday evenings.

60 WERN Y WYLAN COURT/ COURTS RESTAURANT & BAR

Llanddona, Beaumaris, Isle of Anglesey LL58 8TR
☎ 01248 810964
e-mail: enquiries@wylan.co.uk
🌐 www.wylan.co.uk

Wern Y Wylan Court stands in an area of outstanding natural beauty, in spacious grounds overlooking Red Wharf Bay, only half a mile from

the blue flag sandy beach at Llanddona. It offers a choice of 7 self-contained, fully furnished and equipped Self-Catering apartments, the smallest sleeping 3 and the largest upto 10 people.

Courts Restaurant and Bar at **17 Church Street, Beaumaris** serves food with an Italian influence and is open daily from 10.30am. Last food orders are taken around 9.30/10pm. It has seating for 60 inside and weather permitting, room for a further 60 outside in the courtyard. The Restaurant is fully licenced and occasionally has real ales available.

58 THE LIVERPOOL ARMS

St George's Pier, Menai Bridge,
Isle of Anglesey LL59 5EY
☎ 01248 712453

Standing close to St George's Pier and just a hundred yards or so from the centre of Menai Bridge, **The Liverpool Arms** is a charming old hostelry which was originally built in 1843. It is a typical former Ferry Inn with lots of small, individually themed rooms adorned with bygone memorabilia. The inn is well-known and recommended for its well-kept real ales – there's usually a choice of 3 with Flowers IPA as the regular brew. It is also highly regarded for the quality of the food on offer which is

served either in the bistro dining area which seats 30, or in the conservatory which can accommodate a further 30 diners. A speciality of the house is its fresh fish dishes which are available

everyday of the week. But the menu also offers a good choice of meat, poultry and vegetarian dishes. Food is available every lunchtime from 12 noon to 3pm, and every evening from 6pm to 9pm. Such is the popularity of the food here, it is wise to book on Friday and Saturday evenings. Children are welcome and all major credit cards are accepted.

59 THE BRIDGE INN (TAFARN Y BONT)

Menai Bridge, Isle of Anglesey
☎ 01248 716888
e-mail: tafarnybont@fsmail.net
⊕ www.boathouse-restaurant.co.uk

Set beside the historic Menai Suspension Bridge on the old road between Anglesey and Bangor, **The Bridge Inn** (Tafarn y Bont) enjoys a prime view of one of the most spectacular examples of engineering not only in Wales, but in the whole world. Built in 1826 by Thomas Telford, the Bridge was the longest suspension bridge in the world. The bridge is illuminated at night and provides a beautiful backdrop for an evening meal or a drink.

Owner Sarah Owen and her family have been here since 2004 and have established a glowing reputation for serving excellent food with a distinct Mediterranean flavour. There are different menus for lunchtime and evening meals – at lunchtime the main dishes are supplemented by a wide choice of sandwiches, filled baked potatoes, paninis and light bites. Fresh local produce is used wherever possible with dishes such as Welsh Black Beef Fillet and locally caught grilled sea bass fillets featuring on the evening menu. The menus are changed every three months or so and roast dinners are added to the choice on Sunday lunchtimes. Meals can be enjoyed throughout the inn, in the bar, Conservatory and restaurant, and are served from noon until 2.30pm, and from 6pm to 9.30pm.

61 THE BOLD ARMS HOTEL

6 Church Street, Beaumaris,
Isle of Anglesey LL58 8AA
☎ 01248 810313
e-mail: theboldarms@tiscali.co.uk
⊕ www.boldarms.co.uk

The Bold Arms Hotel is a lively, attractive establishment in the beautiful old town of Beaumaris, right on the Menai Straits. It is owned by Nick Beguley and managed by his daughter Hannah who places great emphasis on high standards of service, value-for-money prices, and an atmosphere that is friendly and welcoming. During the season, from May to September, the hotel serves good, wholesome food, including many dishes prepared from local produce. Food is served from noon until 3pm. In the bar you'll find 2/3 real ales on tap including Marston's Pedigree plus 2 guest ales.

There's also a pool table and two 42-inch plasma screens for sporting occasions. If you are keen on golf or fishing, Hannah is happy to arrange it for you. And if you are staying

in this appealing old town, the hotel has 3 large en suite upstairs guest rooms. Children are welcome and all major credit cards are accepted. The hotel is located in the centre of Beaumaris which has much to offer the visitor. It is one of the "five walled towns", has a castle that is considered the most technically perfect medieval castle in Britain, and also boasts 2 golf courses as well as offering boat trips from the pier to Puffin Island.

Castle Square, Beaumaris,
Isle of Anglesey LL58 8DA
☎ 01248 810589
e-mail: mail@whitelionhotel.plus.com
⊕ www.whitelionhotelbeaumaris.co.uk

The sister hotel of the Bold Arms Hotel, the **White Lion Hotel** is an impressive 3-storey building with a quaint tower and, appropriately, whitewashed. Like its sister hotel, the White Lion serves food during the summer season, every day from noon until 3pm. In the evenings its restaurant, the Welsh Black Steak House is open from 6pm to 10pm from Wednesday to Saturday. The fare is based predominantly on local produce and, naturally, the speciality of the house is its Welsh Black Steaks.

In the bar you'll find 2/3 real ales on tap including Marston's Pedigree. Children are welcome and all major credit cards are accepted. The hotel also has 10 guest bedrooms, all with en suite facilities and all upstairs.

Black Point, Penmon,
Isle of Anglesey LL58 8RP
☎ 01248 490140
Mobile: 07776 006804

Pilot House Café occupies a stunning position looking out towards Puffin Island. The long, low, whitewashed building was originally home to three lighthouse pilots and their families. Wonderfully isolated, the café is particularly popular with walkers, tourists and fishermen to whom it offers a fine selection of hot and cold food and drinks, all at affordable prices. The menu includes soups, jacket potatoes, home baking and children's favourites such as milk shakes. Especially popular are the delicious scones and cakes.

The café is owned and run by Julie and Bob Andrews who have also put together a goodly array of interesting

local crafts for purchase, along with other souvenirs and gifts. The café is open from 10am to 5pm daily from March 1st to the end of October; at other times it is open only at weekends – "plus any sunny days in the week". On these days, customers can enjoy both the good weather and their refreshments at tables on the terrace where there is seating for up to 60 people. Children are welcome; payment by cash or cheque only.

64 THE OLD BOATHOUSE ¶

Red Wharf Bay, Isle of Anglesey LL75 8RJ
☎ 01248 852731

Overlooking Red Wharf Bay, **The Old Boathouse** has been owned and run by Sarah Owen's family for more than 40 years and is widely regarded as one of the best places to eat in Anglesey. You can eat either in the ground floor restaurant, for which bookings are not

taken, or in the first floor Quarterdeck Restaurant for which bookings are essential. Seafood is a speciality but the extensive menu also offers a wide choice of meat, poultry and vegetarian dishes. During the summer months, customers can dine al fresco in the peaceful garden.

65 CAFFI GWENNO ¶

Benllech, Tyn-y-Gonel, Isle of Anglesey LL74 8TE
☎ 01248 851147

The popular resort of Benllech is well known for its extensive beach but from spring of 2007 there has been another good reason to visit the town. It was then that two local ladies, Gwenllian and Llinos, opened their **Caffi Gwenno**. They offer a superb choice of home-made dishes, all cooked on the premises using fresh local produce. The

choice includes everything from cooked breakfasts to lunch, main meals and afternoon tea. But most popular of all are the wonderful cakes and scones. In addition to the menu – printed in both English and Welsh, there's a daily specials board and freshly prepared lunches are available to take away.

66 MINFFORDD SELF-CATERING ⊟

Minffordd, Dulas, Isle of Anglesey LL70 9HU
☎ 01248 410678 Fax: 01248 410378
e-mail: enq@minffordd-holidays.com
🌐 www.minffordd-holidays.com

Located just one mile from Ligwy Beach, **Minffordd Self-Catering** offers the choice of holidaying in luxurious 5-star holiday cottages or in spacious luxury modern caravans. The four cottages have all been awarded the Welsh Tourist Board's highest rating of 5 stars. 'Fron Ligwy' is a lovely refurbished family home with 4 bedrooms, 2 bathrooms and a glorious conservatory. The other 3 cottages each have 2 bedrooms. 'Minffordd Cottage' is a recent traditionally built character cottage with access through an archway off the courtyard, adjacent to the owner's own property with shared garden and patio facilities, complete with barbecue. 'Sea View' has a ground floor twin bedroom suitable for disabled use with an alarm installed. 'Mountain View' has a ground floor open lounge connecting with an oak-floored conservatory with a

lovely west-facing garden and rural views. The house is equipped with a very comfortable 'day bed' for disabled use if required and is also fully disabled friendly.

If you prefer a caravanning holiday, Minffordd Caravan Park is a well-planned small garden park of only 10 caravans of various sizes surrounded by trees and flowers with ample space between the vans. The site is sheltered, peaceful and ideal for family holidays.

Pentre Berw, Gaerwen,
Isle of Anglesey LL60 6HU
☎ 01248 422155 Fax: 01248 422104
e-mail: enquiries@tafarnygors.co.uk
🌐 www.tafarnygors.co.uk

Tafarn y Gors stands within an 18-acre caravan and camping park although it is quite separate. Until 2005 the building was a private members club but it is now a smart bar and restaurant. Owners Moi and Heulwen Jones and their sons Andrew, Alvan and Daniel are all involved in the running of this popular venue. The bar offers a real ale, Greene King IPA, along with an extensive selection of other beers, lagers and spirits.

In the separate restaurant the menu provides a good choice of steaks and other meat dishes, poultry, fish dishes, salads and vegetarian options such as Leek & Spinach Cakes. Home-cooked dishes include Steak & Ale Pie, Beef Lasagne and Chicken Curry. And if there is

nothing on the menu that takes your fancy, just ask a member of staff. In good weather, customers can enjoy their repast on the large lawn at the front.

As we go to press, plans are under way for an extension to Tafarn y Gors which will include a new Public Bar housing Big Screen live sports, pool, darts and a juke box. If you are caravanning or camping, the well-equipped adjacent site is open from March to the end of October.

20 Marine Square, Holyhead,
Isle of Anglesey LL65 1DE
☎ 01407 765003 Fax: 01407 765003
e-mail: jwmpinjacs@msn.com
🌐 www.jwmpinjacs.com/co.uk

Commanding a grand view of Holyhead's busy harbour, **Jwmpin Jacs Café Bar** is a stylish place to eat and drink with a clean-cut modern décor and a welcoming atmosphere. There's a superb range of coffees to choose from, and an extensive menu with a distinct Mediterranean element. Everything on the menu is cooked on the premises and local

produce is used wherever possible. There's a good choice of pizzas, baked to order on a fresh thin base; hot grilled paninis freshly prepared on traditional panini bread; Greek salads, tortilla wraps and more. A full takeaway service is available. The café is open every day from 10am to 10pm, bookings are welcome but not essential. With seating on both the ground and first floor, Jwmpin Jacs can accommodate up to 90 customers. Children are welcome and all major credit cards are accepted.

271

Market Street, Holyhead,
Isle of Anglesey LL65 1UW
☎ 01407 763939
e-mail: tommylloyd48@hotmail.co.uk

The Seventy Nine is located in the heart of historic Holyhead and looks down towards the Ferry Terminal and railway station. It used to be called the Cambrian Vaults but everyone locally knew it as The Seventy Nine so the owners finally assumed it as the official name. Mine host, Tommy Lloyd, assisted by bar manager Siobhan, took over here in the summer of 2007.

Open all day, every day for ale, the inn has 2 real ales on tap, one of them a rotating ale, along with a wide selection of other beverages. Food is available every day from noon until 3.30pm and Tommy has plans to also serve food in the evenings. There's a good choice of dishes, all cooked to order and based on fresh local produce. In addition to the regular menu, there's also a daily specials board. The pub has an in-house music system, Sky TV and Sports, and hosts a Quiz every other Wednesday from 9pm. Children are welcome, there's good disabled access, and all major credit cards are accepted.

Valley, Isle of Anglesey LL65 3HH
☎ 01407 740235
e-mail: lloyd@ty-mawr.wanadoo.co.uk
⊕ www.angleseybedandbreakfast.co.uk

Ty Mawr is a large 19th century farmhouse on a 300-acre dairy farm. It is set in a lovely south-facing garden and surrounded by pastureland with uninterrupted views of Snowdonia. The farmhouse is the home of Anne and Richard Lloyd who have lived here since 1970 and have been welcoming bed & breakfast guests since 1987. The house has 2 guest bedrooms, a double and a

twin. The latter has colour TV, a 3-piece suite, hospitality tray and a lovely view. The double also has colour TV, two comfortable armchairs and hospitality tray. In the morning, a fully cooked or continental breakfast can be enjoyed in the beautifully appointed dining room.

Ty Cristion, Bodedern,
Isle of Anglesey LL65 3UB
☎ 01407 741500   Fax: 01407 741500
e-mail: enquiries@angleseyholidays.co.uk
⊕ www.angleseyholidays.co.uk

Located on the outskirts of Bodedern village, **Ty Cristion Holiday Cottages** offer 4 charming properties set in 9 acres of grounds and surrounded by miles of scenic countryside. Attractively furnished and decorated in country style,

the cottages have received a 4-star rating from the Welsh Tourist Board. The largest property can sleep up to 5 people; the smallest sleeps two. Each cottage has its own patio and there's a large grassed play area for children. Open all year round, rentals are available from one night upwards.

33 High Street, Llanerchymedd,
Isle of Anglesey LL71 8EA
☎ 01248 470242

Llanerchymedd is about the most central village on the Isle of Anglesey and stands close to Llyn Alaw, the island's largest lake (actually a man-made reservoir).

The village is also worth seeking out to pay a visit to **The Bull Inn** where Mandi Abrahams is the welcoming host. Mandi actually grew up in a pub, more recently ran a wine bar in Denbighshire before taking over The Bull in the spring of 2007. Already the locals are very fond of her and visitors are beginning to seek the place out from further afield. The inn is open all day, every day, for ale with Marston's Burton Bitter as the regular real ale with a guest rotating ale. Tasty bar snacks are available every lunchtime and evening, and are based on fresh local produce as far as possible. Payment is by cash only.

The Bull is a lively place, especially on Friday and Saturday evenings when there's karaoke twice a month; live music evening once a month and a disco, also once a month. Sky TV and Sports are installed and there's also a pool room. During the lifetime of this edition, Mandi hopes to also offer accommodation and camping spaces, so if you are thinking of staying in this agreeable place, it would be worth giving her a call.

73 TAFARN SNOWDONIA PARC BREW PUB ⃒⃒ ⊨

Waunfawr, Caernarfon, Gwynedd LL55 4AQ
☎ 01286 650218/650409
e-mail: carmen@snowdonia-park.co.uk
⊕ www.snowdonia-park.co.uk

Occupying an idyllic mountain setting on the banks of the River Gwyrfai, 4 miles from the foot of Snowdon, **Tafarn Snowdonia Parc Brew Pub** is a popular venue for families, walkers and climbers with good home cooked food, real ale, and its own micro-brewery. The Snowdonia Park is listed in the *CAMRA Real Ale Guide* and is noted for its delicious real ales which are brewed on the premises by owner Carmen Pierce. Her 'Welsh Highland Bitter' (named after the adjacent railway) and 'Gold Snowdonia' are the regular home brews. She uses the finest malts and hops, together with clear Snowdonia water. Additionally, the bar serves guest ales, Marston's Pedigree and Bitter, 3 decent lagers, cider and Guinness - "and we put real lemon in the gin!" adds Carmen.

The pub was originally built in Victorian times as a house for the station master at Waunfawr Station on the Welsh Highland Railway line. Remarkably, the railway is still operating. The pub provides an excellent location for lunch for those taking the round trip by train from Caernarfon. Customers can watch the narrow gauge steam-hauled locomotives while enjoying lunch or a drink in one of the pub's beer gardens!

You can also dine in the quiet oak panelled dining lounge where the food is mainly home cooked from fresh local produce. The extensive range of delicious wholesome dishes include meat, poultry, fish, pasta, egg and vegetarian choices. Baguettes and hot or cold sandwiches are also available. Incidentally, there is no genetically modified ingredient in any food served on the premises. On Sunday there's a Lunch Special with children's portions available - booking is advisable. The pub has a Family Room, there's a children's menu with plenty of choices, and a children's playground for the younger guests. Dogs are welcome and there's ample parking. Tafarn Snowdonia Parc is open from 11am to 11pm every day, all year. Food is served all day every day from 11am until 8.30pm. The pub is located on the A4085 between Beddgelert and Caernarfon, at the edge of the Snowdonia National Park.

Adjacent to the pub and also beside the river is a small campsite which is open all year for tents, caravans and motor homes. There are electric hook-ups and free facilities including hot showers.

74 NANHORON ARMS HOTEL

Nefyn, Lleyn Peninsula,
Gwynedd LL53 6EA
☎ 01758 720203 Fax: 01758 720203
e-mail: info@nanhoronhotel.com
🌐 www.nanhoronhotel.com

Situated in the centre of the historic town of Nefyn on the stunning Lleyn Peninsula, the **Nanhoron Arms Hotel** is a striking 3-storey white-painted Edwardian building dating back to 1907. Since 1993, it has been owned and run by the Jones family – Melvyn and wife Menna, Linda and Erhard Nierada. They furnish a warm welcome to their guests and their aim is make your visit as comfortable as possible. Visitors can relax with a drink in the stylish modern lounge bar, (a Theakston's XB real ale perhaps) – and then choose from the extensive à la carte menu which includes grills, home-made steak pies, Thai green curry, lasagne and local fresh sea food.

The accommodation comprises 19 en suite bedrooms, all of them equipped with TV and hospitality tray. The hotel also offers facilities for functions, conferences and weddings, and is open to non-residents. From the hotel, it is just a 5-minute walk to Nefyn beach and the immediate area provides a vast choice of activities to choose from. They include golf, sailing and boating, swimming, horse-riding, mountain biking, bird-watching, go-karting or just relaxing amidst some of Wales' most dramatic scenery.

Looking for:

- *Places to Visit?*
- *Places to Stay?*
- *Places to Eat & Drink?*
- *Places to Shop?*

COUNTRY LIVING MAGAZINE RURAL GUIDES

HIDDEN INNS

HIDDEN PLACES

COUNTRY Pubs & Inns

off the **motorway** 3rd edition

www.travelpublishing.co.uk

76 THE LION HOTEL

Tudweilog, Pwllheli, Gwynedd LL53 8ND
☎ 01758 770244

Only a short walk from the beach, **The Lion Hotel** is very much a family-run inn - the Lee family have been dispensing hospitality here for 38 years. This delightful country inn offers a choice of real ales with Purple Moose Glaslyn as one of the favourites. Quality food and a fine list of Malt Whiskeys is served every

lunchtime from noon until 2.30pm, and every evening from 6pm to 9.00pm. The Lion also offers comfortable accommodation in 4 charming en suite rooms. The hotel has a spacious beer garden; children are welcome, and all major credit cards are accepted.

75 WOODLANDS HALL HOTEL

Edern, nr Nefyn, Gwynedd LL53 6JB
☎ 01758 720425 Fax: 01758 720425
e-mail: info@woodlandshall.co.uk
🌐 www.woodlandshall.co.uk

Standing in 7 acres of beautiful grounds, **Woodlands Hall Hotel** is set in the loveliest part of the Lleyn Peninsula, famed for its peaceful sandy beaches where bathing is safe at all times. The hotel is approached by an impressive tree-lined drive leading to the equally impressive main bulding with its attractive conservatory at the front.

A natural port of call for tourists seeking rest and relaxation, the hotel has a well-appointed restaurant serving ample, carefully planned and varied menus. Owners Nick and Nerys Grimes consider good food so important a part of holiday pleasure that they have installed in the kitchens the most modern and hygienic equipment available for the preparation of food. In the stylish Woodlands Restaurant you could enjoy New Zealand Green Lip Mussels or devilled whitebait as your starter; follow that with whole Whitby scampi in natural breadcrumbs, or a steak or a half leg of Welsh lamb delivered to you on a sizzler. To complement your

meal, the hotel boasts a well-stocked cellar with a wide variety of wines.

Less formal dining is available in the Orchard Bar which welcomes families and children and offers an extensive choice of bar meals and daily specials. With both indoor and outdoor play areas, children can thoroughly enjoy their visit while parents sample a well-prepared meal. Food is served every lunchtime (noon until 2.30pm) and evening (6pm to 9pm). If you just fancy a drink, the hotel bar offers a friendly and comfortable welcome with a good choice of cask beers, fine ales and an extensive wine list.

Accommodation at Woodlands comprises 13 bedrooms, all with en-suite bathroom, colour television, direct dial telephone, trouser press and complimentary beverage tray. Rooms are available in single, multiple singles, double and family arrangements.

The hotel also offers facilities for conferences and other functions and can cater for up to 160 people - weddings are a speciality.

Visitors will find plenty to see and do in the area. The stunning beaches of Nefyn and Porthdinllaen are both close by and Morfa Nefyn's famous 27-hole golf course is just one mile from the hotel. Also within easy reach are facilities for sailing, swimming, horse-riding, cycling and walking, or you can just explore the scenic Llyn Peninsula.

276

3 High Street, Abersoch,
Gwynedd LL53 5SG
☎ 01758 713158

After fulfilling a career in nursing, Nina Lewthwaite took over **Oriel Fach Tea Rooms and Licensed Café** in 2004. The bright and attractively furnished premises have colourful paintings adorning the walls and there's a pleasant outdoor area where in good weather customers can enjoy their refreshments al fresco. Nina's enticing menu offers a good choice of home-made treats such as the scones, Bara Brith and wonderful cakes like warm Chocolate and Almond Cake served with cream or ice cream. The menu also offers a Welsh Cream Tea with clotted cream, a range of sandwiches and toasties, and a selection of freshly prepared salads served with French bread. The regular menu is supplemented by a choice of

daily specials, to include seafood as well as casserole of Welsh lamb and

vegetables perhaps. To complement your meal, there's a good selection of hot and cold beverages, and a separate wine list.

The tea rooms are open every day during the high season, from 10am to 5pm; from 11am to 4pm at weekends out of season, plus other days if the town is busy. It is closed on Wednesdays mid-season. Children are always welcome.

Hen Bont Road, Criccieth,
Gwynedd LL52 0DG
☎ 01766 522227

Criccieth Castle, on its commanding headland overlooking Tremadog Bay, is one of those rare castles with a foot firmly in both camps. Criccieth's history is deeply entwined in the medieval conflict between Wales and England. Originally a stronghold of the native Welsh princes, it was later annexed and extended by the English monarch, Edward I.

The core of the castle – a powerful twin-towered gatehouse – is Welsh, built by Llywelyn the Great probably between 1230 and 1240. The castle was taken by Edward's forces in 1283 and extensively refortified. After withstanding further Welsh attack its fate was finally sealed in 1404 when the Welsh leader Owain Glyn Dwr captured and burnt the castle.

78 GLASFRYN COTTAGES

Glasfryn, Pwllheli, Gwynedd LL53 6RD
☎ 01766 810688 Mobile: 07702 876754
e-mail: Helen@beca-tv.com
🌐 www.glasfryn.co.uk

Only 3 miles from Pwllheli with its manifold attractions and set within a 500 acre estate, **Glasfryn Cottages** offer a great choice of self-catering accommodation, all with a 4 or 5-star rating from the Welsh Tourist Board. Glasfryn Parc, located in the heart of the Llyn Peninsula, is Wales' premier activity and adventure centre with numerous activities. Whether you decide to take the challenge of the go-kart circuit or try your hand at archery or ten pin bowling, the park provides everything for the ideal family day.

There are four delightful cottages available, all with beamed ceilings, log fires and all mod cons including a BBQ and picnic tables. 'Glasfryn Fawr' is a beautiful 17th century stone farmhouse which sleeps up to ten people. It is set in park-like gardens with views across farmland to the sea and has a tranquil and welcoming feel. There are 5 bedrooms, including an en suite master bedroom, 3 bathrooms, a spacious drawing room, cosy kids TV room and a fabulous kitchen/diner. The sitting room has a large stone fireplace with a wood burner and is furnished in country house style.

'Garden Cottage' is a charming detached property in a secluded position overlooking an enclosed garden on one side and lovely woodlands on the other. The cottage, which has recently been renovated to a very high standard, is ideal for couples, but can sleep up to 4 adults and 2 children comfortably. The large sitting room with its original terracotta tiled floor is furnished in pretty cottage style and has a wood burner with logs supplied free of charge. Outside, there's a large lawn area which is ideal for badminton and sunbathing.

'Glasfryn Uchaf Cottage ' is ideal for wildlife lovers and gardening enthusiasts as it is surrounded by beautiful gardens, lovely woodlands and is near an outstanding natural 13 acre lake. The cottage has been newly modernised and has 3 bedrooms, a cosy sitting room and a separate kitchen; it can accommodate up to 5 guests.

'Tan y Bryn' is a top quality detached cottage in wild and beautiful surroundings. It has an elevated position with stunning mountain and sea views, has recently been refurbished to a luxury standard and its 3 bedrooms include a master en suite and a kids room with 2 full size bunk beds. Comprehensive details of these outstanding properties can be found on the Glasfryn Cottages website.

80 MYNYDD EDNYFED COUNTRY HOUSE HOTEL

Caernarfon Road, Criccieth,
Gwynedd LL52 0PH
☎ 01766 523269 Fax: 01766 522929
e-mail: myndd-ednyfed@criccieth.net
⊕ www.criccieth.net

The former home of Lloyd George's family in the late 1900s, **Mynydd Ednyfed Country House Hotel** is a 400-year-old country home that has been tastefully refurbished to a high standard, offering both comfort and contemporary style in a stunning location. South-facing, it stands in 7

acres of gardens and woodlands and provides a tranquil retreat with no passing traffic. Throughout the summer months you can enjoy flower-filled gardens, long evening walks and the space to fully unwind. In the winter, enjoy hearty food, roaring log fires and cosy evenings in the comfortable lounge. The hotel's restaurant is open to both residents and non-residents and serves home-made dishes using local produce. There's a fully-stocked bar and an extensive wine list.

For those who wish to keep fit, the old coach house has been converted into a well-equipped gymnasium, or you can play tennis on the all-weather court. After your exertions, ease away your aches and pains in the "OASIS" holistic therapy room. You can have a full hot stone body massage or an aromatherapy facial. Other activities available within easy reach include some fantastic golf courses, shooting, fishing and horse-riding.

81 TIR A MÔR RESTAURANT

1-3 Mona Terrace, Criccieth,
Gwynedd LL52 0HG
☎ 01766 523084

Located in the coastal resort town of Criccieth (Cricieth to the Welsh), the **Tir A Môr Restaurant** is the leading eating place in the area for the discerning diner. It is owned and run by Gwenno (a local lady) and her husband Laurent Hebert who hails from Paris. They have run restaurants in Criccieth since 1993 but took over their current premises in the spring of 2007. They completely refurbished the two-floor restaurant with a bright, eye-catching décor displaying clean, modern lines. Their menu offers an enticing choice of dishes, all of which are based on fresh Welsh produce and are accompanied by vegetables bought in the market that day. Laurent's specialities are the fish dishes, including a fish platter of the day, baked

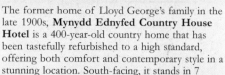

fillet of monkfish and grilled lemon sole with a cider vinegar sauce. The

menu also offers a 12oz Welsh Sirloin Steak, Welsh lamb cutlets, Glamorgan sausages and poultry dishes. Children can have ½ portions of the listed dishes. The restaurant is licensed for diners, open from 6pm to 9.30pm, Tuesday to Saturday, and accepts all major credit cards except Amex and Diners. Such is Tir A Môr's popularity, it is essential to book at all times.

82 PROS KAIRON GUEST HOUSE

23 Marine Terrace, Criccieth,
Gwynedd LL52 0EF

☎ 01766 522453 Fax: 01766 523556
e-mail: kaironhotel.co.uk
🌐 www.kaironhotel.co.uk

The **Pros Kairon Guest House** occupies a superb position on the west side of Criccieth and enjoys impressive views of Cardigan Bay and the nearby 13th century Criccieth Castle. Pros Kairon is Welsh for "Heavenly Place to Stay" and its owners, Janet and Billy Armstrong, hope and believe you will agree. Certainly, the number of repeat bookings indicates that many of their guests are in accord. "As well as welcoming many couples and families" says Janet, "we are also popular with groups of golfers, and with the re-opening of the footpath to Pwllheli we hope to welcome walkers and hikers as well".

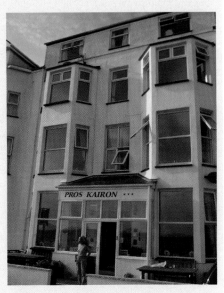

The guest house stands just a few yards from the beach and on a clear day guests may well see the porpoises and dolphins that frequent the bay. Pros Kairon boasts a 4-star rating from the Welsh Tourist Board and four of its 7 rooms command fantastic sea views. All but one of the rooms have en suite facilities; the other has its own private bathroom. There's a mixture of single, double and family rooms. All the accommodation was recently completely refurbished and the rooms have been attractively furnished and decorated. All the rooms are equipped with TV and hospitality tray, and a cot and bedding are available at a small cost. Children are very welcome – babies under one year old stay for free; children up to 15 years old stay at half price. A full Welsh/English breakfast is included in the tariff, and a Continental breakfast is available on order.

Fully licensed, Pros Kairon is an ideal base for exploring the many attractions of the Lleyn Peninsula and Snowdonia with its beautiful mountains ranges and walks. A visit to the Festiniog Railway, which caters for the young and the young at heart, is an absolute must. There are plenty of other attractions – golf, fishing, walking and sailing, or you could visit one of the many historic castles in the surrounding area, starting perhaps with the one on your doorstep – Criccieth Castle which is one of the best preserved in Wales.

83 THE UNION INN

Market Square, Tremadog,
Gwynedd LL49 9RB
☎ 01766 512748

The pretty village of Tremadog, a mile or so north of Porthmadog, takes its name from William Madocks who founded it as an estate village in 1805. In its central Market Square stands **The Union Inn,** a handsome stone building with a very traditional, olde worlde interior.

The brother and sister team of Peta Panter and Martin Batcock arrived here in the early summer of 2007 and have given the old hostelry a new lease of life. Martin worked for many years on the famous Ffestiniog Railway; Peta is an accomplished cook whose menu offers an enticing selection of

home-made dishes based on fresh, locally sourced seasonal produce. Welsh lamb and beef take pride of place but you will also find home-made lasagne and curry, fish dishes and vegetarian options. The regular menu is supplemented by daily specials – local mackerel, perhaps, or a spinach & ricotta cannelloni. To accompany your meal there's a wide choice of beverages available including a locally brewed real ale plus a national real ale. Food is served every day from noon until 2pm, and from 5.45pm to 8.45pm. Children are welcome and major credit cards are accepted.

85 WELSH SLATE MUSEUM

Llanberis, Gwynedd LL55 4TY
☎ 01286 870630 Fax: 01286 871906
e-mail: slate@nmgw.ac.uk

If your idea of a museum is based on glass cases, dusty exhibits and incomprehensible, closely typed labels, then you're in for a pleasant surprise when you visit the **Welsh Slate Museum** in Llanberis. This museum-with-a-difference is not just based at an authentic quarrying workshop. In essence, the museum is the workshop, left just as it was when the workers clocked off for the last time.

The vast Dinorwig Quarry, carved into the slopes of the "mountain that roofed the world", closed for business in 1969. But its doors remained open as the Welsh Slate Museum, the world's only national slate museum. The workmen might have gone, but the museum remains a living place with an authentic working atmosphere. The quarry workshop is still in regular use, brass casting takes place in the foundry, and the blacksmith is kept busy producing tools for the museum as well as quality items for sale in the attractive museum shop. There are demonstrations of slate-splitting, the most delicate and demanding of skills which can reduce a hefty block of slate into wafer-thin thicknesses. And the giant waterwheel - one of the world's largest, which drove machinery through a complicated system of belts and pulleys, continues to turn.

There are new visitor facilities including a shop, and sumptuous new café. The quarry next to the museum now has a working incline - the only one in Britain - showing how slate blocks were transported from top to bottom and there is much improved access to the enormous waterwheel - the largest of its kind on mainland Britain.

Abersoch Road, Llanbedrog, Pwllheli,
Gwynedd LL53 7TH
☎ 01758 740212 Fax: 01758 740257
e-mail: info@glynyweddw.co.uk
🌐 www.glynyweddw.co.uk

Conveniently located on the A499, a few miles southwest of Pwllheli, the **Glyn-y-Weddw Arms** offers outstandingly good food in the beguiling surroundings of a traditional Welsh hostelry. The décor is inviting and has an 'olde worlde' feel, where customers can relax, safe in the knowledge that whatever they require the team will cater for their needs. Owner Martin Cook has recently carried out a complete refurbishment of the inn and also added a new family room. Outside, the pub can seat approximately 130 people, 80 of whom can sit under a unique retractable heated canopy and listen to background music, whilst overlooking the enclosed adventure playground, where children can play safely.

The inn also has a new function room suitable for up to 70 guests. Martin has introduced a new menu offering exclusive in-house meals prepared by head chef Gary Williams who provides an eclectic mix of culinary delights using his knowledge and expertise to create a menu to tantalise your taste buds. Gary's specials include a hearty Braised Steak in a red wine and mushroom sauce, Lamb Shank with gravy, and a Salmon Fillet in a white wine and cream sauce. But the extensive menu also offers a good choice of Welsh beef steaks, fish dishes, curries, a range of pizzas and pasta dishes, along with vegetarian options such as Mushroom Ravioli. Conscious of catering for every taste, the Glyn y Weddw Arms offers smaller portions for the older generation or for those with smaller appetites. Children have their own menu of main meals and sweets. A Carvery is available on Tuesday and Thursday evenings, and on Sundays. On Saturday nights the pub offers a special home-made hot buffet which can range from Chinese, Indian and Mexican to steak and fish nights. There's a snacks menu and a takeaway service for pizzas and ciabattas. Food is served every day from noon until 9pm.

To accompany your meal, there's a choice of Robinson's real ales as well as a full range of other beers, spirits and wines. The inn has ample parking, disabled access is good and there's a disabled toilet and baby changing facility.

Holyhead Road, Betws-y-Coed,
Snowdonia LL24 0BN
☎ 01690 710601
e-mail: stay@bryn-llewelyn.co.uk
🌐 www.bryn-llewelyn.co.uk

In the centre of the picturesque village of Betws-y-Coed, **Bryn Llewelyn Guest House** is an impressive Victorian building of 1880. It's the home of Mick and June Figg who offer 3-star bed & breakfast accommodation all year round. There are 7 guest bedrooms, 5 of which are en suite, the other 2 have private facilities. All are equipped with colour TV, clock/radio alarm and hospitality tray. A traditional full cooked breakfast, using local produce, is included in the tariff (vegetarian option available), and the house has off road parking.

Also available in the nearby village of Trefriw is a 2-bedroomed, 4 star, self-catering cottage.

Castle Square, Harlech, Gwynedd LL46 2YH
☎ 01766 780416
🌐 www.castle-restaurant.co.uk

Located directly opposite Harlech's magnificent castle, the superb **Castle Restaurant** specialises in "traditional dishes from Welsh recipes with a Mediterranean twist". So Madeleine Smith's enticing menu features Welsh Fillet Steak, "Teifi" Salmon Fillet, Minted Welsh Lamb, locally caught Sea Bass, and Celtic Chicken - Chicken Breast stuffed with

Welsh Cheddar & Mustard and wrapped in bacon. The restaurant is fully licensed and booking for evening meals and Sunday lunch is strongly recommended.

Capel Garmon, Llanrwst,
Conwy LL26 0RW
☎ 01690 710271
e-mail: ralton@btconnect.com
🌐 www.whitehorseinnsnowdonia.co.uk

Located in the heart of the Snowdonia National Park, **The White Horse Inn** is an 18th century hostelry of great charm and character. It has a wealth of exposed beams and stonework, and a welcoming olde worlde atmosphere. A Free House the inn is owned and run by Margaret and Bob Alton. They always have a minimum of 2 real ales on tap with Hobgoblin Bitter and Tetleys Cask as the two permanent brews.

The inn is renowned for its good food, based wherever possible on local produce. The chef is particularly noted for her Welsh lamb dishes and sirloin steaks. Diners can enjoy their meals either in the snug Old Cottage Eating Place or, if the weather is kind, outside on the decking. Food is served

Mon - Thurs 6pm to 9pm, Fri and Sat 6pm to 9.30pm. Sunday lunch 12 noon until 2pm, Sunday evening 6pm til 9pm. There is a new menu available in our Cottage Restaurant. If you are planning to stay in this spectacular area, the White Horse has 5 letting bedrooms with a 3-star rating from the Welsh Tourist Board and AA. They all have en suite facilities and TV. The tariff includes a full English or Continental breakfast. From £60 for a double and £40 for a single, 3 for 2 Oct - Jan.

87 THE GWYDYR HOTEL

Betws-y-Coed, North Wales LL24 0AB
☎ 01690 710777
e-mail: gwydyrhotel@btconnect.com
🌐 www.gwydyrhotel.co.uk

Set amidst lush and lovely scenery, **The Gwydyr Hotel** is perfect as a base for exploring Snowdonia and the many sights and attractions of the region. Full of character and atmosphere, the hotel is owned and managed by David and Owen Wainwright, both of whom are very experienced hoteliers. The quality of the hotel is reflected in its recent acquisition of a 3-star rating from the Welsh Tourist Board.

The hotel has a very large Victorian style drawing room, ideal for meeting together after dinner or at the end of your day's activities to sit and relax in comfort. As a special treat, cream teas are served here daily. The lounge bar serves a varied selection of wines, beers, spirits and soft drinks.

The Gwydyr offers a wide choice of meals – breakfast, luncheon and dinner daily – which are served in the elegant and spacious dining room. For lighter appetites, there's an extensive range of bistro meals, served daily between noon and 9pm.

The accommodation is nothing short of superb, with a choice of traditional doubles, singles and family rooms. The large bedrooms are fully equipped with television, radio, telephone, hair dryer, hospitality tray, iron and ironing board facilities, and all have en suite facilities with bath and shower. Children and pets are welcome.

The Gwydyr is particularly popular with people who find their greatest pleasure in fishing. Special fly fishing, spinning and bait fishing holidays for salmon or sea trout are available by the day, week or season along miles of the Rivers Conwy and Lledr.

Under the "Dinorben Hotels" badge, the Wainwright family also owns the Eagles Hotel in Llanrwst, a few miles north of Betws-y-Coed. Both hotels are different but noted for their hospitality, comfort and friendly atmosphere, excellent food, good wine and willing service.

Visitors to Betws-y-Coed will find plenty to see and do in the area. The attractions include the Snowdon Mountain Railway, the beautiful Bodnant Gardens, the fantasy village of Portmeirion, Llechwedd Slate Caverns, Ffestiniog Steam Railway, Sygyn Copper Mines, various Lake Railways, castles at Caernarfon, Conwy, Beaumaris and Penrhyn, the famous Swallow Falls and the delightful Fairy Glen. If you are feeling energetic, you will find easily accessible facilities for walking, climbing, mountain biking, cycling, horse riding, running and sailing.. Or maybe you prefer something a little more sedate such as golf, painting, fishing, photography, country dancing, basket weaving – or even a spot of group singing!

🏛

Harbour Station, Porthmadog,
Gwynedd LL49 9NF
☎ 01766 516024 Fax: 01766 516006
e-mail: enquiries@festrail.co.uk
🌐 www.festrail.co.uk

The world-famous **Ffestiniog Railway** was
originally built to transport slate from the mines to
Porthmadog, where it was transferred to ships for
export and use throughout the world. Like many
other little railways, its original role has been
superseded, but this one has found fame as one of
the country's leading attractions. The world's oldest narrow-gauge passenger-carrying railway, it
runs behind steam locomotives on the 13½-
mile journey from Porthmadog to Blaenau
Ffestiniog; the route climbs 700 feet into
Snowdonia National Park through pastures and
forests, by lakes and waterfalls, round horseshoe
bends and at one point turning back on itself in
a complete spiral.

Calling en route at Minffordd, Penrhyn and
Tan-y-Bwlch, the trip takes just over an hour.
Trains can be hired for private functions,
anniversaries or fine dining evenings, and the
year brings many special events, including trips
on vintage trains using rolling stock dating from
as far back as 1860. The Ffestiniog found itself
at the cutting edge of railway technology in the
1870s: pivoted wheels, or bogie, which gave a

superior ride and allowed coaches to take curves more
smoothly, had appeared in North America in 1873 and it
was on the Ffestiniog that it first came to the UK.

There are shops selling gifts and souvenirs at the
termini and Tan-y-Bwlch. Porthmadog has a café serving
anything from sandwiches and snacks to three-course
meals, and the café at Tan-y-Bwlch is open while the trains
run. Most trains have corridor coaches where refreshments
are sold.

The railway may be little, but it provides a big
experience with a variety of driving programmes, starting
with the more easily handled Penrhyn Lady class
locomotives *Linda, Blanche* or *Taliesin*, leading up to the
ultimate challenge of one of the famous Double Fairlies
hauling 10 carriages. Drivers will enjoy one-to-one personal
tuition
and
work an
eight
hour
shift,

with 14 miles driving and 14 miles firing.
Another course involves operating one of the
oldest steam engines in the sidings at
Minffordd, shunting a rake of slate wagons.

The Ffestiniog Railway is operated and
maintained by volunteers, and help is always
welcome, either working with the railway or
joining the Ffestiniog Railway Society.

High Street, Harlech, Gwynedd LL46 2YA
☎ 01766 780425
e-mail: info@cemlynrestaurant.co.uk
🌐 www.cemlynrestaurant.co.uk

Not many tearooms can boast a terrace with a spectacular view of a medieval castle. **Cemlyn Tea Shop** definitely can since it stands just a few yards from historic Harlech Castle. The views also include the Royal St David's Golf course,

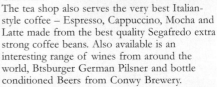

mountains and the sea. Inside, owners Geoff and Jan Cole have fairly recently completely refurbished their tea room and very smart it looks with its linen tablecloths, well-spaced tables, proper comfy chairs and paintings by local artists adorning the walls.

Since it opened in 2000, the tea room has been showered with awards. It has achieved a Tea Council "Award of Excellence" for the past 5 years and were "Runners Up, Top Tea Place UK" in 2004. It is renowned for serving a very wide variety of teas. All of them are loose leafed (not bagged) ranging from the well known Breakfast and Traditional Afternoon, to Indian teas such as Assam, Darjeeling and Nilgiri. Also available are teas from the Far East such as Formosa Oolong, Lapsang Souchong and Keemun as well as black teas, green teas and fragrant teas such as Earl Grey. Ask about their Cemlyn Mix, and teas from Sri Lanka, Africa, China and Japan.

The Tea Shops menu also offers a range of fruit infusions including Apple & Lemon, Kiwi & Strawberry, Blood Orange

and herbal Teas such as Nettle, Peppermint and Camomile. The tea shop also serves the very best Italian-style coffee – Espresso, Cappuccino, Mocha and Latte made from the best quality Segafredo extra strong coffee beans. Also available is an interesting range of wines from around the world, Btsburger German Pilsner and bottle conditioned Beers from Conwy Brewery.

The Coles make all their own food on the premises – from scones and tea cakes to hand-made bread. You can be assured that your Cream Tea will be served with only the very best real Welsh cream, "not that 'squirty stuff' that comes in aerosols". Meals can be enjoyed on the terrace although there are equally good views inside. Well-behaved dogs are welcome on the terrace.

From mid-March to end of October the tea shop is open from 10.30am until 5pm, but closed Mondays and Tuesdays, except for Bank Holiday Mondays. And if you are planning to stay in this historic town, Cemlyn has 2 letting bedrooms located on the first floor, both en suite and one with a 6ft wide King-size bed.

Pen Dref, Harlech, Gwynedd LL46 2SG
☎ 01766 780731 Fax: 01766 781286

Originally built in the late 1700s as an inn, **The Lion Hotel** is a handsome 3-storeyed building in the heart of historic Harlech. Mine hosts are Linda and Eryl who took over the premises in October 2006. Eryl has been in the hospitality business since 2000 and also runs two other public houses in Criccieth.

The pub is open all day, every day, for drinks amongst which are 3 real ales – Flowers, Beddingtons and a guest ale. Food is served every day from noon until 2.30pm, and from 6pm to 9pm. The menu offers a good choice of dishes which are based on locally sourced ingredients. A snack menu is available through the afternoon. Meals can be enjoyed throughout the inn, at tables at the front of the inn, and in the beer garden at the rear.

The Lion also offers comfortable accommodation in 7 guest rooms (3 double en-suite; 1 twin en-suite; 1 single en-suite; 1 single with shared bathroom). Some have bunk beds. Children are welcome; dogs welcome in the bar; all major credit cards are accepted.

93 HARLECH CASTLE 🏛

Harlech Castle, Castle Square, Harlech, Gwynedd LL46 2YH
☎ 01766 780552

Harlech Castle is one of the great castles Edward I built to enforce his rule over the Welsh. Situated high upon a rocky outcrop, its seaward side was defended by sheer cliffs, while a deep moat protected the other sides. It was designed by Master James of St George, who personally supervised its construction, ensuring that the vast fortress was completed in just seven years (1283-1290). The castle is built to a concentric design with an impressive inner curtain wall with huge round towers on the corners, surrounded by an outer perimeter of much lower walls. The inner walls contained domestic buildings, including a great hall, and the more vulnerable east side of the castle was strengthened by a massive gatehouse that contained comfortable residential quarters.

Harlech Castle played a key role in the last great Welsh uprising, led by Owain Glyn Dwr. In 1404, after a long siege, the castle fell to Glyn Dwr, and became his home and headquarters for the next four years. Harlech was finally retaken by the English in 1409, under the command of Harry of Monmouth, prince of Wales – the future King Henry V. Although Glyn Dwr escaped, his family were captured, and the fall of Harlech marked the beginning of the end of the great uprising.

During the Civil War (1642-48), Harlech was the last Royalist stronghold to be lost, its fall signifying the end of the war. Like many other Royalist strongholds the castle was rendered untenable by the victorious Parliamentarians.

94 TREMEIFION HOTEL ⊢ ¶

Soar Road, Talsarnau, Gwynedd LL47 6UH
☎ 01766 770491

For vegetarians and vegans, the recently refurbished **Tremeifion Hotel** has everything, Not only does it serve only vegetarian and vegan food, it also occupies a superb location in the Snowdonia National Park with spectacular views over the river estuary and mountains.  Owners Barbara Heywood, who is a Cordon Vert chef, and Kevin White take pride in serving home-cooked, high quality and interesting food, much of it based on vegetables from their own organic garden. The hotel has 4 comfortable guest bedrooms, all with en suite facilities. Children and dogs are welcome; credit cards accepted.

97 THE BELLE VUE HOTEL ⊢

Marine Parade, Barmouth, Gwynedd LL42 1NA
☎ 01341 280444
⊕ www.belle-vue-hotel.co.uk

Occupying a superb position on the sea front at Barmouth, **The Belle Vue Hotel** is an impressive 4-storey Victorian property which has recently been completely refurbished to a very high standard. The hotel has 19 comfortable guest bedrooms, 17 of which have en suite facilities and 2 share a private bathroom. The rooms are of various sizes and many of them enjoy sea views. Children are welcome and cots and high chairs are available. The tariff includes a generous breakfast and  owners Andy and Virginia have applied for a drinks licence. All major credit cards accepted.

95 TREGWYLAN

Talsarnau, Gwynedd LL47 6YG
☎ 01766 770424

Enjoying unrivalled views of the Snowdonia range and the Lleyn Peninsula, **Tregwylan** is a peaceful and relaxing bed & breakfast establishment. It is ideally located as a central base for discovering the magnificence of Snowdonia to the north and east, while to the west lies the splendour of Portmadoc Bay. When viewed from Tregwylan, the bay leads

the eye to the renowned village of Portmeirion across the estuary. The owner of Tregwylan, Mrs Falmai Edwards, provides her guests with a huge choice at breakfast time with the options of a full Welsh or continental breakfast - or your choice. "We aim to ensure that our guests have a relaxing and comfortable night" she says, "and a hearty start to the morning so that they can thoroughly appreciate their day in this beautiful scenic area". Tregwylan has 5 guest bedrooms, all tastefully decorated and equipped with en suite facilities and hospitality tray.

96 HALFWAY HOUSE

Bontddu, Dolgellau, Gwynedd LL40 2UE
☎ 01341 430635
e-mail: halfway_house_bontddu@talktalk.net
🌐 www.halfwayhousebontddu.co.uk

A fabulous black-and-white half-timbered building, **Halfway House** is as pretty as a picture and is, appropriately, set within an area of outstanding natural beauty and at the heart of a traditional Welsh village. The inn is very much a family business with Davina and Philip, and Davina's mum, Gillian, all involved in the enterprise. Halfway House is ideal for lovers of unaffected, traditional home-cooked food who enjoy an unhurried meal, freshly prepared from local produce wherever possible. Welsh dishes feature prominently in the menu - Lamb Shank, Welsh Black Sirloin steak, and Welsh Faggots, for example. Also on offer are a good choice of fish, pasta and vegetarian dishes, while children have their own, unusually extensive, menu. Daily specials provide further choices. At lunchtimes, light bites such as traditional Welsh Rarebit made with ale, are available along with freshly made sandwiches. On Sundays, the regular menu is supplanted by a Carvery plus vegetarian option. To accompany your meal, there's a good choice of real ales, draught beers, fine wines, spirits and soft drinks. In summer, refreshments can be enjoyed outside in the elevated seating areas. Please note that payment at the Halfway House is cash only.

98 BRYN TEG HOTEL ⊢ ‖

Kings Crescent, Barmouth,
Gwynedd LL42 1RB
☎ 01341 280174 / 280301
Fax: 01341 280174

Set in the heart of Snowdonia National Park, close to the sea and mountains, **Bryn Teg Hotel** offers good food and quality accommodation in an impressive Victorian house where Prime Ministers Gladstone and Lloyd George stayed at different times. Owner Milton Pitcher has been welcoming guests here since 1990 and many of his repeat visitors have become good friends and would go nowhere else. Their appreciative comments in the visitors' book reflect sincere approval of the hospitality they received.

The hotel has a full licence so you can enjoy a drink or two in the atmospheric bar, which is a free house, before moving to the Cornucopia Restaurant which is also open to non-residents. The restaurant serves lunches, afternoon cream teas and appetising evening meals from 6pm onwards with a choice of table d'hôte or à la carte menus. All the meals are prepared on the premises with fresh vegetables. In the morning, the restaurant serves residents with a hearty full English or Continental breakfast.

The quality accommodation comprises 14 guest bedrooms (3 of which are family rooms which can accommodate 5-7 people). All have wash basins and some have en suite facilities. Seven of the rooms have wonderful sea views. The bedrooms are all attractively furnished and decorated with a Victorian theme and are equipped with colour TV and hospitality tray.

99 BRYN MELYN GUEST HOUSE ⊢

Panorama Road, Barmouth,
Gwynedd LL42 1DQ
☎ 01341 280556 Fax: 01341 280342
e-mail: stay@brynmelyn.co.uk
⊕ www.brynmelyn.co.uk

Set on a south-facing hillside and surrounded by its own picturesque grounds, **Bryn Melyn Guest House** commands stunning views of the beautiful Mawddach Estuary, Cadair Range and Cardigan Bay. Just a 10 minute walk from the popular resort of Barmouth, enjoying a pleasant climate and with lots of places of local interest, the house is an ideal place for a restful break. It has a 3-star rating from the Welsh Tourist Board and 8 of its 9 beautifully furnished and decorated rooms have en suite facilities; the ninth has its own private bathroom. All are upstairs and one is family-sized. The tariff includes a hearty breakfast served between 8am and 9.15am either in the dining room or outside on the patio overlooking the bay. Breakfast choices include Full English, vegetarian, porridge and kippers.

In the evening, light snacks and drinks from the lisenced bar are available to residents if required. Bryn Melyn is open throughout the year but at weekends only in November. It is closed over Christmas but open for the New Year. Pets are accepted by arrangement; all major credit cards apart from American Express and Diners are accepted, and there is off road car parking.

The Quay, Barmouth, Gwynedd LL42 1ET
☎ 01341 281126 Fax: 01341 281444
e-mail: davinaalynch@aol.com
⊕ www.pembrokehousebarmouth.co.uk

Occupying a superb position on the quay at Barmouth, **The Anchor Restaurant** commands ravishing views of the Mawddach estuary and the Cader Idris mountain range. These can be enjoyed from tables at the front of the restaurant where you can also watch the world go by. The Anchor's extensive menu offers an enticing choice of appetising and wholesome dishes. Welsh Black beef features prominently but you'll also find fish, poultry, pasta and vegetarian options as well. Main courses include a wonderful Smokey Fisherman's Crumble, Lamb Mignons in a redcurrant and rosemary sauce, a Special Paella and a Mediterranean Vegetable Cannelloni with garlic bread and salad garnish. For lighter appetites, there's a wide selection of hot baked potatoes, home-made burgers, salads, giant baps and sandwiches, and toasties. Amongst the Anchor Specials are a Welsh Ham Melt, a Tuna Melt with Welsh cheddar cheese and the Anchor's Famous Fish and Chips. Kids have their own Happy Meals. The restaurant is fully licensed so you can enjoy a glass of wine, Pimms, bottled beer, cans of bitter, Guinness or cider with your meal. The restaurant is open every day from 9am to 9pm in the summer; from 9am to 5pm out of season. All major credit cards are accepted.

The owners of The Anchor, Davina and Warren Lynch, also own the Knickerbocker's Ice Cream Parlour next door but one to the restaurant. Here you'll find a choice of 25 different flavours of traditional home-made ice creams made with milk and double cream.

Davina and Warren also have 2 luxury self-catering flats, Harbour View and Cader View, situated on the first and second floors of Pembroke House, above the restaurant and ice cream parlour. These stylish and contemporary apartments also enjoy wonderful panoramic views over Barmouth harbour and the Mawddach estuary. This Victorian property has recently been refurbished throughout. Both apartments have 2 bedrooms, a kitchen/diner and bathroom. The master bedrooms are also lounges with a king size bed, LCD TV and Sky channels, and pull out settee bed. Barmouth itself has much to offer. There's a golden sandy Blue Flag beach that stretches for miles and provides beautiful views of the Cader Idris mountain range, Barmouth bridge and the Mawddach estuary. You can take the ferry across the estuary from right outside Pembroke House and catch the narrow gauge steam train for a visit to Fairbourne which also has a safe family beach.

101 CYFNOD CAFÉ & LOCH CAFE

Bala LL23 7SR
☎ 01678 520226

Cyfnod Café is on the town's main street. 'Cyfnod' is Welsh for 'The Times' as this sturdy building once housed a printing works. The premises have been recently refurbished to a very high standard. A major attraction here is the wonderful home cooking with cakes, scones, Welsh cakes and bara brith being freshly baked each day, along with delicious home-made soups. The café is open every day, all year, between 9.30am and 7.30pm. As at the Loch Café, payment is by cash or cheque only.

The **Loch Café**, a former boat house, stands on the foreshore of Llyn Tegid (Lake Bala) which is the largest natural lake in Wales and stretches for five miles. Open every day from Easter to the end of the October, the café offers a good choice of dishes ranging from All Day Breakfasts to jacket potatoes, panini melts and hot or cold sandwiches. There's also a soup of the day, an under-12s selection and a choice of tostidas – toasted continental bread with various fillings. In good weather, there are tables outside where customers can gaze at the ravishing view. Payment is by cash or cheque only.

103 MELIN MELOCH (FORMER WATER MILL)

Bala, Gwynedd LL23 7DP
☎ 01678 520101
e-mail: beryl@melochmill.com
⊕ www.melochmill.com

Melin Meloch has had a chequered history dating back to the 13th century when a mill was built at the junction of the River Dee and Meloch stream. The mill was owned for many centuries by successive princes of Wales but was lost to the English in 1485. It continued as a working mill until the late 1950s and the main building was converted in 1960. The interior is spectacular, its two galleries with oak timbers in abundance. A great fireplace stands at the centre, separating the lounge and dining area where guests are served breakfast. Since 1984 the mill has been the home of Beryl and Richard Fullard who have restored the miller's cottage and the Granary which provide pretty en suite bedrooms with their own front doors to ensure privacy. Richard has also landscaped the lovely gardens, installing ponds and waterfalls, and creating glorious borders in the summer. The mill is close to Bala town and its lake, famous for its rare species of prehistoric fish only found in one other lake in the world. The lake is a centre for both water sports and bird life.

34-36 High Street, Bala LL23 7AG
☎ 01678 520414

The Ship Inn (Y Llong) stands on the main street of Bala and since 2003 has been run by Chris and John Roberts.

Open all day, every day for drinks, the inn stocks a good selection of bitters, lagers and ciders. It also serves food every lunchtime from noon until 4.30pm, and on Friday and Saturday until 8.30pm.

Chris is the accomplished cook and her menu is based on ingredients produced within Wales. Her home-made Lamb & Leek Pie is particularly popular, as are her Sunday roasts.

Sky TV and Sports can be watched in the bar and outside in the small beer garden at the rear. Friday is karaoke evening and on Saturdays there's live music from 9.30pm. Children are welcome. Dogs are also welcome in the bar.

During the lifetime of this edition, Chris and John are hoping to be able to offer accommodation.

Llandderfel, Bala, North Wales LL23 7RA
☎ 01678 530205 Fax: 01678 530723
e-mail: thebryntirioninn@aol.com
⊕ www.bryntirioninn.co.uk

Set in stunning countryside in the village of Llandderfel, close to Bala Lake, **The Bryntirion Inn** is a delightful old hostelry that dates back to 1695. It is owned and run by the cheerful trio of

Martin, Linda and Jenny who met when they worked for the Landmark Trust on Lundy Island. The Trust administers the only pub on the island and the trio eventually decided to branch out on their own.

It was in 2003 that they took over the Bryntirion Inn which is just 4 miles from Bala on the B4401. Their main aim, they say, has been to create a welcoming atmosphere for everyone (including dogs!), whatever their reason for visiting. The happy combination

of a friendly ambience, good food, well-kept ales, a log fire in the winter and a sunny courtyard in the summer has proved to be a great success.

Jenny runs the bar and has a special interest in real ales. The inn always has two brews on tap – Jennings Cumberland Ale and a rotating guest ale. Linda looks after the front of house, and also does the office work. Martin is a qualified chef with more than 20 years experience. His menu is predominantly based on fresh local produce with dishes such as Braised shoulder of Welsh lamb with rosemary gravy, and Welsh black beef, mushroom and ale casserole served in a 'Bryn Bara' featuring prominently on the menu. You'll also find Welsh beef and gammon steaks, as well as tasty fish, poultry and vegetarian dishes. Food is served from noon until 3pm, and from 6pm to 9pm, Monday to Saturday, and from noon until 8pm on Sunday. Booking is recommended on Saturday evenings. Meals can be enjoyed throughout the inn, in the rear courtyard or at tables at the front which command a lovely view.

Once a month, usually on a Tuesday, the inn hosts a pub quiz and there's also a monthly music night.

If you are planning to stay in this scenic area, the inn has a choice of 1 Double/Twin and 1 Double room available, both with en suite facilities and a hearty breakfast is included in the tariff. Children are welcome and all major credit cards apart from American Express and Diners are accepted.

104 CWM HWYLFOD

Cefnddwysarn, Bala, Gwynedd LL23 7LN
☎ 01678 530310
e-mail: cwmhwylfod@tiscali.co.uk
🌐 www.cwmhwylfod.com

In Welsh, **Cwm Hwylfod** means 'Valley of Happiness' and you will surely feel happy at this wonderful 400-year-old farmhouse overlooking the Dee Valley and commanding spectacular views. This traditional

Welsh longhouse, cleverly sited in a dip in the hillside, retains its thick outer walls and wooden inner walls made from ships' timbers. Cwm Hwylfod has three letting bedrooms for bed & breakfast guests. All rooms have tea and coffee making facilities, washbasins with hot and cold water, and, of course, central heating for year-round comfort. There are two bathrooms, and a comfortable residents' lounge with colour television.

HIDDEN PLACES GUIDES

Explore Britain and Ireland with *Hidden Places* guides - a fascinating series of national and local travel guides.

Packed with easy to read information on hundreds of places of interest as well as places to stay, eat and drink.

Available from both high street and internet booksellers

For more information on the full range of *Hidden Places* guides and other titles published by Travel Publishing visit our website on

www.travelpublishing.co.uk
or ask for our leaflet by phoning
01752 276660 or emailing
info@travelpublishing.co.uk

107 CYSGOD Y GARN

Frongoch, nr Bala LL23 7NT
☎ 01678 521457
e-mail: carys@snowdoniafrongoch.co.uk
🌐 www.snowdoniafrongoch.co.uk

Bed & breakfast accommodation in a class of its own is what you will find at **Cysgod Y Garn** in the small village of Frongoch near the popular town of Bala. Surrounded by picturesque gardens and set within a 600-acre working farm which has connections with Abraham Lincoln, this outstanding guest

house boasts a 5-star rating from the Welsh Tourist Board, the highest they award. Built in 1992, it is the home of Carys and Dewi Davies who have beautifully furnished and decorated the house throughout. There are 3 guest bedrooms, all with en suite facilities and one with its own Jacuzzi. No wonder visitors come from around the world to stay here, many of them repeating their visit. A delicious farmhouse breakfast is included in the tariff and evening meals are available by arrangement. The house has off road parking for guests.

106 WHITE LION HOTEL

Cerrigydrudion, Corwen,
North Wales LL21 9SW
☎ 01490 420202
e-mail: whitelionhtl@aol.com

Records show that back in the 1500s there was already an alehouse occupying the site of the **White Lion Hotel.** The present building dates back to the 18th century when it was built as a coaching inn located halfway between Corwen and Llangollen. Today, Carol Broadhurst continues the tradition of hospitality that extends over half a millennium. She took over here in early 2005 and brought a new lease of life to this welcoming old inn with its many attractive features. Scattered around the rooms are lots of brass and copper items, along with other vintage items of interest such as crockery and even a brace of swords.

In the hotel's well-stocked bar you'll find a comprehensive range of beverages, including 2 real ales – JW Lees Bitter which is the permanent brew, and a seasonal Lee's guest ale. The hotel has its own separate restaurant for which Carol is the cook. Her menu offers a good choice of meals for which the majority of the ingredients are sourced locally. Carol's steak and gammon dishes are very popular, as are her home-made curries, steak pie and lasagne. Portions are generous and prices reasonable. Vegetarian and other diets can be catered for (notice may be required). Wednesday is Curry & Pint night with special advantageous prices. Food is served from 7pm to 9pm, every day; also from noon until 2.30pm on Saturday; and from 12.30pm to 3pm on Sunday. At weekends during the season, it is wise to book ahead. Children are welcome; payment is by cash or cheque only. The hotel also has a function room for special events, a beer garden and a children's play area.

If you are planning to stay in this scenic area, the hotel has 10 guest bedrooms, 5 of which have en suite facilities. All rooms are equipped with TV and hospitality tray; hair dryers, iron and ironing board are available on request. The hotel also offers budget accommodation in the form of 2 bunk rooms: one sleeps 5 people, the other up to 10.

The White Lion's location makes it an excellent base for exploring Snowdonia. There's some glorious walking countryside all around, including the new 7-mile trail around Alwen Reservoir. Other amenities within easy reach include fly fishing at Llyn Brenig, just 4 miles away, and Karting at Glan-y-Gors.

Bridge Street, Dolgellau,
Gwynedd LL40 1AU
☎ 01341 422533
e-mail: jostocks9717@hotmail.com
or staginndolgellau@hotmail.co.uk
🌐 www.myspace.com/thestaginn

On its website **The Stag Inn** describes itself as "quite an active pub which sees a diversity of cultures from mountain bikers to gothic students. I also have a large collection of animals (not the customers or staff) ranging from dogs to a guinea pig". It continues "I'm pretty much what you would expect from a pub, got all the usual features; pool table, jukebox, spacious beer garden, good beer and if you're lucky abusive staff (just kidding)! That's a joke for our regulars".

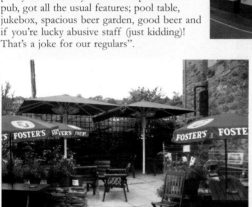

The inn is located in the heart of Dolgellau, within the Snowdonia National Park. Mine hosts are Jo and Geraint and as you might expect from their website, they are a cheerful and friendly pair with a great sense of humour. Their hostelry is open all day, every day for drinks which includes two real ales Banks Original and a rotating guest ale. Jo is in charge of the kitchen and her menu offers a good choice of dishes based on seasonal local produce. Welsh lamb and Welsh Black Beef feature prominently on the menu which also includes a tasty home-made Steak & Guinness Pie. A speciality of the house is its large floured baps with a choice of fillings. All the meats are served with home-made stuffing and gravy. During the winter months, bar snacks are also available and include toasties, sandwiches and burgers. Children have their own choice of meals. Food is served until 9pm and meals can be enjoyed throughout the pub or in the spacious beer garden at the rear. This is also where the petting zoo is, home to rabbits, guinea pigs and a duck. During the winter months, the inn hosts a regular quiz and occasional live music.

With its wandering narrow streets, Dolgellau is a handsome market town, once the county town of Merionethshire. It has as a background the mighty bulk of Cader Idris rising to almost 3000 feet. The town grew up around the River Wnion which is spanned by an elegant 7-arched bridge dating from the early 1600s. It is very much a Welsh town where you can hear the farmers who come into town for market day still speaking Europe's oldest language.

297

109 UNICORN INN 🍴

**Smithfield Square, Dolgellau,
Gwynedd LL40 1ES
☎ 01341 422742**

Located in the centre of the town, the
Unicorn Inn is a fine old 19th century stone
building with an impressive figure of a
unicorn prancing above the entrance. Mine
hosts, Barry and Shirley Jones, have been
here since
1996 and
have made
the
Unicorn
one of
Dolgellau's
most
popular
venues. In
the
evenings they serve a good selection of
favourite pub meals - Liver & Onions, for
example, and also offer a choice of real ales.
There are tables at the front and a patio
garden to the rear; inside, darts and dominoes
are provided.

110 PENMAENUCHAF HALL 🛏 🍴

**Penmaenpool, Dolgellau, Gwynedd LL40 1YB
☎ 01341 422129 Fax: 01341 422787
e-mail: relax@penhall.co.uk
⊕ www.penhall.co.uk**

Built in 1860 as the country residence of a wealthy
cotton magnate, **Penmaenuchaf Hall** is now an
immaculate and stylish country house hotel where
your hosts Mark Watson and Lorraine Fielding and
their staff offer their guests a warm and personal
welcome. In the richly decorated Library, leather sofas,
deep set armchairs, oriental rugs on sea grass, a period
desk and, of course, books, set the scene. The
sumptuously furnished Morning Room enjoys the morning
sun and has outstanding views to the Rhinog mountains
across the Mawddach Estuary. Perfect for relaxing with a
pot of morning coffee or relishing a Welsh Afternoon Tea.
Then there's the grand oak panelled Drawing Room with
its stone arched fireplace, complete with bygone family
coats of arms.

Fine dining is at the heart of the Penmaenuchaf Hall
experience. The Head
Chef and his team
produce "Contemporary British Food" with an emphasis on
flavour, use of local produce and simple, careful presentation.
Home grown herbs, salads and vegetables from the hotel gardens
along with exceptional local suppliers combine to create
imaginative cuisine. The hotel's luxury accommodation consists
of fourteen exquisitely furnished bedrooms, with wonderful
views over the Mawddach Estuary and the mountains beyond.

111 TRAWSFYNYDD HOLIDAY VILLAGE

Bronaber, Trawsfynydd,
Gwynedd LL41 4YB
☎ 01766 540219 / 540555
Fax: 01766 540305
e-mail: staff@logcabinswales.co.uk
🌐 www.logcabins-skiwales.co.uk

Overlooking the Rhinog range of mountains with Cader Idris to the south and Snowdon to the north, **Trawsfynydd Holiday Village** is ideally situated for exploring North and Mid-Wales and the sea is within easy reach. Set within 20 acres of beautiful scenic countryside, many of the privately owned detached Norwegian style log cabins are let through the village's central letting system. The two-bedroomed cabins sleep 4-6 people and the 3-bedroomed cabins sleep 6 - 8. All have well-equipped kitchens, including a cooker, microwave and fridge, and electricity is included in the letting price. The Village has its own shop for basic grocery supplies, papers, fresh milk, bread, and an off licence. Adjacent to the shop is a telephone kiosk and laundry room. Within easy walking distance is the Rhiw Goch Inn which serves good fare at a reasonable price. Just 2 miles from the Village is the renowned Coed-y-Brenin forest which provides some of the best mountain biking to be found anywhere. Other activities within easy reach include golf, canoeing and white water rafting, mountain walks and heritage attractions such as Harlech and Criccieth Castles.

112 Y LLEW COCH - THE RED LION

Dinas Mawddwy, Gwynedd SY20 9JA
☎ 01650 531247
e-mail: berwyhughes@yahoo.co.uk
🌐 www.llewcoch.co.uk

Surrounded by the scenic beauty of southern Snowdonia, **The Red Lion,** or **Y Llew Coch** to use its Welsh name, is a centuries old traditional village inn set in the picture postcard village of Dinas Mawddwy. The inn is full of charm and character, and is renowned for its good value home-cooked food and year round accommodation. It's a family-run business with Beryl Hughes and her son Berwyn as mine hosts. Both were born and bred close to the village and the family also own and run a nearby farm. Food is served every lunchtime, from noon until 2pm, and every evening from 6pm to 9pm. Most of the ingredients used here are sourced locally, notably the lamb from their own farm - the home-made lamb and leek pies are especially popular. Booking is advisable at all times for larger parties. The inn is featured in the CAMRA Good Beer Guide and serves 3 real ales - Worthington, a brew from the Purple Moose at Porthmadog, and a guest ale. Accommodation at the Red Lion comprises 6 comfortable rooms, 4 of which are en suite. All rooms are centrally heated and equipped with TV and hospitality tray.

113 THE RED LION

Maengwyn Street, Machynlleth,
Powys SY20 8AA
☎ 01654 703323
e-mail: curlzz@hotmail.co.uk

Located in the heart of this popular small town, **The Red Lion** is a smart white-painted hostelry with its Welsh name, Y Llew Coch, emblazoned in gold letters above the entrance. Mine hosts at this friendly and welcoming inn are business partners Claire and Jon who arrived here in the autumn of 2006. Claire looks after the front of house while Jon is busy in the kitchen preparing a wide choice of appetising dishes based on locally sourced ingredients. For example, his menu features Tom-Yum Thai-style prawns with a sweet chilli dip amongst the starters. Main courses range from a hearty 14oz gammon steak, through a variety of fish and poultry dishes to salads, burgers and vegetarian dishes like the Mediterranean

Vegetable & Cheese Wellington. Also available are jacket potatoes and filled baguettes. Food is served from 11am to 2.30pm and from 6pm to 8pm, Monday to Saturday, and from noon until 2.30pm on Sunday when only roast meals are served. Two real ales are available - Banks Bitter and a guest brew. The inn hosts live entertainment once a month, and to the rear of the premises is an undercover smoking area, lit and heated.

114 MAENLLWYD GUEST HOUSE

Newtown Road, Machynlleth,
Powys SY20 8EY
☎ 01654 702928 Fax: 01654 702928
e-mail: maenllwydd@btinternet.com
⊕ www.maenllwyd.co.uk

Standing within its own grounds on the edge of the town centre, **Maenllwyd Guest House** is an imposing 3-storey building originally bult as a Manse in the late 1800s. It's the home of Margaret and Nigel Vince who have lived here since 1980 and for nearly all of that time have been providing quality bed & breakfast accommodation. "We are continually striving to update and refurbish" they say, "in order to provide our guests with every comfort." All the rooms are beautifully furnished and decorated, impeccably maintained and thoroughly deserving of their 3-star rating from the AA. The premises have also received a Green Dragon environmental Award. All of the 8 upstairs guest bedrooms have en suite

facilities and are equipped with TV, hair dryer and hospitality tray. Breakfasts at Maenllwyd are really something to look forward to with a good choice and quality ingredients. Guests can also take advantage of the spacious garden where they can sit and enjoy the sunshine. There's also off road parking for approximately 10 cars and safe storage for bikes.

Longbridge Street, Llanidloes,
Powys SY18 6EE
☎ 01686 412270 Fax: 01686 412681
e-mail: geoffhawkins@btconnect.com

Located in the heart of the small market town of Llanidloes, **The Red Lion Hotel** is easy to find with its large, brilliantly red lion standing guard over the portico entrance. Owned and run since 2004 by the Hawkins family – Geoff and Eileen and their son Steven – this traditional style hotel has a relaxing atmosphere which is further enhanced by the huge leather couches provided for drinking in comfort.

The spacious ground floor is divided into a lounge bar, a public bar and restaurant area, and a games room with pool table and other regular pub games. The food served here is honest-to-goodness pub grub at value for money prices. Choose from either the printed menu or from the specials board. With all the dishes, fresh local produce is used wherever possible. Appreciative local diners make the Red Lion their first choice for an excellent Sunday Carvery served from noon until 2pm – booking is essential. During the rest of the week, food is served from noon until 9pm. Real ales on tap include Timothy Taylor Landlord and Adnams Broadside plus two rotating guest ales. The bars are open from 11am to midnight, Monday to Friday, and from 11am to 1am on Saturday and Sunday.

If you are planning to stay in Llanidloes – the exact centre of Wales – the hotel has 9 comfortable guest bedrooms, all with en suite facilities. A hearty breakfast is included in the tariff. The pub has good disabled access and is wheelchair-friendly, but for the rooms it is better to check first. Children are welcome at The Red Lion, all major credit cards are accepted and there's ample parking.

116 THE GREAT OAK CAFÉ

12 Great Oak Street, Llanidloes,
Powys SY18 6BU
☎ 01686 413211

Gerry Collins took over the **Great Oak Café** in the Autumn of 2006 and carried out a complete refurbishment in Spring 2007, around the same time the café acquired

Fairtrade status. The café is well known throughout the area and is highly regarded for the wholesome and appetizing fare on offer, cooked fresh everyday using fresh ingredients from 17 mainly local suppliers. The café serves organic fairtrade coffee made to order, hot chocolates, fairtrade speciality teas, soya milk shakes, organic sparkling cans, ciders and ales. The licensed café provides a venue for local musicians and displays art by local artists.

The dedicated staff of Rosie, Vicky, Suzy and Isla are friendly, charming and efficient. The menu of vegetarian wholefood changes daily and caters for special dietary needs such as vegan, wheat and dairy free, and serves a tasty Soup of the Day such as spicy parsnip and includes dishes such as lasagna, rich leek quiche, Thai or Indian curry or shepherdess pie perhaps, and has an extensive freshly made salad bar.

Then there are the wonderful homemade cakes such as apricot and date flap jacks, coffee and walnut, chocolate and a variety of fruit cakes. The café seats 36 inside, 30 in the rear courtyard and 8 on the pavement tables. Children and nursing mothers are welcome, a baby nappy changer and high chair is available. There is good disabled access and a disabled toilet. The café is open from 9am to 4pm Monday to Saturday with evening and Sunday events advertised as and when, the café is also available for private functions and for outside buffets.

118 WAGGON AND HORSES

Canal Road, Newtown, Powys SY16 2JB
☎ 01686 625790 Fax: 01686 625790
e-mail: njatthewaggon@aol.com

Just a short walk from the town centre, the **Waggon and Horses** is a fine old traditional hostelry, noted for its excellent cuisine, well-kept ales and warm hospitality. Neil and Jackie Roberts have been mine hosts here since 1995 and Neil has

been a chef for some 26 years. In the Garden View Restaurant his enticing menu gives pride of place to Welsh produce with a Welsh Goat's Cheese and braised red onion tart amongst the starters, and Best End of Welsh Lamb and Welsh Black Sirloin as main courses. Other options include a hearty bowl of home-made soup, corn fed chicken breast oven roasted, and a dish based on fresh fish of the day. Food is served

every evening except Wednesday from 7pm to 9pm, and from noon until 2pm Friday to Sunday. On Sundays, only traditional roast meals are served. Booking is essential at weekends.

The well-stocked bar offers 3 real ales to enjoy – Marston's Bitter, Banks's Mild and a rotating guest ale. In good weather, guests can enjoy their refreshments in the spacious and peaceful beer garden at the rear. All major credit cards are accepted apart from American Express.

Llangurig, Llanidloes, Powys SY18 6SG
☎ 01686 440254 Fax: 01686 440337
e-mail: lizanddewi@hotmail.co.uk
🌐 www.bluebell-inn.co.uk

Llangurig is the highest village in mid-Wales and it's here that you'll find the appealing **Blue Bell Inn,** a charming grade 2 listed building dating back to the 1500s and still retaining many of its original features. This friendly hostelry is run by Liz and Dewi Jones, a popular local couple who ran the Llanidloes Rugby Club before taking over here in July 2007.

Liz is an accomplished chef and has made the inn a magnet for lovers of good food. She offers a good variety of bar meals served at both lunch-time and evening as well as an extensive restaurant menu for those with a heartier appetite. This offers a tasty Thai Cod & Prawn Rosti amongst the starters, and a choice of main courses ranging from grills, meat and fish dishes to vegetarian alternatives such as Glamorgan Sausages, Thai Mango Curry and a Five Bean Chilli with rice and chips, all at very reasonable prices. On Sundays, roast dinners are added to the menu. Food is served from noon until 9pm, daily. To accompany your meal, there's a good selection of fine wines, along with a choice of 2 real ales - Bulty Bach and a rotating guest ale.

The Bar area is traditionally furnished with an original fireplace, cosy settle and flagstone floor. The bar stocks a wide range of beers, wines and spirits, as well as seasonal real ales, some of which are brewed in Wales.

For sporting customers, the Blue Bell has a games room with pool table, dart boards, dominoes, cards and fruit machine. Whilst playing, says Liz "why not look at our photo wall with a selection of pictures of our locals, some of which I am sure they would prefer not be seen!"

The Blue Bell also offers Bed and Breakfast accommodation with 9 tastefully decorated and furnished bedrooms available, all of which are equipped with colour television, radio and tea/coffee making facilities. The double, twin and family rooms are all en suite, and the inn also has single bedrooms with washbasins and a communal bathroom adjacent. One of the rooms is on the ground floor. The Inn is child friendly and welcomes families; all major credit cards are accepted.

303

Abermule, Montgomery, Powys SY15 6ND
☎ 01686 630676 Fax: 01686 630676
e-mail: info@abermulehotel.co.uk
⊕ www.abermulehotel.co.uk

The picturesque village of Abermule is set in the Severn Valley surrounded by rolling hills and stunning scenery. The village boasts a primary school, church, community centre, two pubs, a caravan park, village shop and an excellent place to stay, the **Abermule Hotel**. The hotel, which dates back to the mid-1800s, was originally known as the "Railway Hotel". But after the "Great Abermule Train Disaster" of January 26th 1921, which resulted sadly in the death of 17 passengers, including the chairman of Cambrian Railways, it was renamed the "Abermule Hotel" twelve months later.

Guests at the hotel will receive a warm welcome from mine hosts Wendy and Barry Davies who arrived here in December 2006 after some 29 years experience in the hospitality business. Wendy is an accomplished cook whose specialities include Lamb Shank in mint gravy, Steak & Guinness Pie, and various gammon dishes. But her menu also offers a good selection of chicken, fish, pasta and vegetarian dishes. Wendy also does a very good Sunday Carvery with a choice of meats. Food is served every day except Tuesdays and Sunday evenings from noon until 3pm, and from 7pm to 9pm. A selection of Light Bites – jacket potatoes, soup of the day, ploughman's, toasties and such – is also available in the bar. To accompany your meal, an extensive selection of beverages is available including two real ales – Tetleys and Marston's Pedigree.

The hotel also offers accommodation, with 2 en-suite guest bedrooms available. One is a spacious, fully centrally heated room with a double bed, and equipped with colour TV and hospitality tray. It enjoys glorious views of the Welsh hillsides. The other is a family room with two double beds with all the same facilities.

The hotel also caters for touring caravans, campers, cyclists,

anglers, walkers and hikers. Its Caravan and Camping Park is equipped with electric hitch-ups, disabled toilet and a shower room. Other amenities provided by the hotel include a large marquee available for private parties, a large beer garden and patio, a play area and a large floodlit car park at the rear. If you enjoy fishing, the hotel owns the fishing rights to the River Mule which flows past the bottom of the hotel gardens. Walkers can enjoy a pleasant stroll along the towpath of the Montgomery Canal which runs past the outskirts of the village.

119 THE GRO GUEST HOUSE

Pool Road, Newtown, Powys SY16 3AL
☎ 01686 626383
e-mail: mlwilliams@btconnect.com

Set in an acre of its own grounds with superb gardens to front and back, The **Gro Guest House** is an impressive building, parts of which date  back to 1650. Lin and Mick Williams purchased The Gro in 2005 and carried out a major refurbishment. They now offer 4 quality en suite bedrooms, each of which is equipped with TV, hospitality tray, hair dryer, dressing gowns and toiletries. There's also a comfortable residents' lounge and dining room. The Gro is not licensed but guests are welcome to provide their own drinks. Glasses, openers etc. are available in the lounge area..

123 UPPER HOUSE INN

Llandyssil, nr Montgomery,
Powys SY15 6LQ
☎ 01686 668465

Tucked away in the countryside just west of Montgomery, the picturesque little village of Llandyssil is fortunate in still having its own post office, village shop and pub. In fact, all three are part of the **Upper House Inn**, owned and run by Simon James and his mother Margaret. Simon is also the chef and his menu offers all the traditional favourites –  Steak & Kidney Pudding and (Welsh-sourced) steaks, for example, but also less familiar pub fare like the Poached Salmon in a Cream Sauce. Remarkably for a rural inn, the Upper House has a wine list of more than 40 different wines.

121 THE GOAT HOTEL

Llanfair Caereinion, Welshpool,
Powys SY21 0QS
☎ 01938 810428
e-mail: thegoathotel@aol.com
⊕ www.smoothhound.co.uk/hotels/goathotel

Railway enthusiasts will know Llanfair Caereinion as the western terminus of the Welshpool and Llanfair Light Railway, an 8-mile long narrow gauge operation that winds through the valleys of the Sylfaen Brook and Banwy River. Another good reason for visiting this peaceful village is **The Goat**

Hotel, a fine old traditional hostelry with a history going back to 1650. During that time it has served as a court leat, a bed & breakfast and guest house before settling down as an inn some 30 years ago. Since then, for most of the time – 22 years to be precise – the inn has been owned and run by Alyson and Richard Argument, a friendly and welcoming couple who both contribute to cooking the appetising food  on offer. Their menu offers a good choice of main courses, light meals, starters and snacks with pride of place going to home-made dishes based on fresh Welsh produce. In good weather, customers can enjoy their refreshments in the peaceful enclosed patio to the rear of the pub. The Goat also offers comfortable B&B accommodation in 5 guest bedrooms, 3 of which have en suite facilities.

305

122 COTTAGE INN

Pool Road, Montgomery,
Powys SY15 6QT
☎ 01686 668348

The popular and friendly **Cottage Inn** is situated with Montgomery Castle to the rear and Offa's Dyke to the front. The interior has a rustic charm with lots of old horse brasses, open brickwork and a spacious inglenook fireplace. Since 2003, the inn has been owned and run by Linda Wainwright, a welcoming host who is also an accomplished chef who offers an enticing choice of delicious home-made dishes based on fresh, locally sourced produce.

Her very own Steak & Ale Pie and her curries are particularly popular. You can choose from the printed menu or from the daily specials. Linda also lays on an excellent Carvery with a choice of roasts on Sunday lunchtimes. To accompany your meal, the inn offers a wide selection of ales, wines and spirits, including two

real ales – Brains and the locally brewed Duck & Dive. The kitchen is closed on Mondays but open every other day from noon until 2pm, and from 7pm to 9pm during the season. Out of season, food is only served Friday to Sunday but Linda is happy to cater at other times for private bookings. To the rear of the inn is a lovely beer garden, complete with a covered area.

124 THE HORSESHOES INN

Berriew, Welshpool SY21 8AW
☎ 01686 640198

A welcoming traditional hostelry, **The Horseshoes Inn** began life as a coaching inn and smithy in the early 1700s. To the rear is an old lime kiln and within 100 yards, the Montgomery Canal. The Horseshoes is very much a family enterprise with Georgina and Mark Pearce, their son Raymond and daughter Marie all involved. The family took over here in the autumn of 2007 and have given the old inn a new lease of life with local people flooding back and visitors discovering the hospitality, good ales and appetising food. The extensive menu offers something for every taste - grills, old favourites such as Steak & Ale Pie, fish dishes, burgers, curries, pasta and vegetarian choices. Specialities of the house include Beef Wellington, Blackened Cajun Salmon and Welsh

Lamb Cutlets. Supplementing the regular menu are half a dozen or so daily specials. Children have their own choices and Wednesday night is Steak Night when the very reasonable prices include a bottle of red or white house wine. Real ales are also on tap. Incidentally, although the address of the Horseshoes is Berriew, it stands adjacent to the main A483 south of Welshpool.

Berriew, Powys SY21 8PQ
☎ 01686 640 452 Fax: 01686 640 604
e-mail: enquiries@thelionhotelberriew.co.uk
🌐 www.thelionhotelberriew.co.uk

Located in the picturesque village of Berriew and originally built as a coaching inn, **The Lion Hotel & Restaurant** is a charming black-and-white half-timbered building with an interior of exposed beams and wattle and daub adding to the historic

atmosphere. The hotel is owned and run by the mother and daughter team of Beryl and Trudi Jones whose declared aim is to combine fine dining and deeply comfortable facilities with a family atmosphere for all their guests - families, couples, sportsmen and professionals alike. Their passion for food, the exciting seasonal menus and the elegant oak-beamed restaurant have earned The Lion an enviable reputation among discerning diners. The innovative chefs work hard to create new dishes to delight, using local

produce wherever possible, including meat from the local

butcher in the town Welshpool. Good food is also served in the intimate, candlelit bistro and at lunchtime snacks are available in the cosy bar. The Lion's well-appointed bedrooms, many of them professionally designed, provide en suite facilities, television, telephone to reception and hospitality tray. The Superior rooms also have a DVD player while the family suite comprises a double room with a smaller connecting room.

3-4 Main Street, Caersws,
Powys SY17 5EL
☎ 01686 688023

The owners of **The Red Lion,** Jayne and David, ably assisted by daughter Mandy and her husband Jim, provide a warm welcome to their cosy traditional pub

serving up real ales and good food. Genuine fires and other traditional features add to the pub's relaxed ambience. The menu offers old favourites such as home-made pies and chilli, steaks and home-made curry, and on Sundays there's a choice of traditional roasts. Accommodation is available in 2 en suite double bedrooms, available all year round. Fishing and clay pigeon shooting can be arranged for guests.

HIDDEN PLACES GUIDES

Explore Britain and Ireland with *Hidden Places* guides - a fascinating series of national and local travel guides.

Packed with easy to read information on hundreds of places of interest as well as places to stay, eat and drink.

Available from both high street and internet booksellers

For more information on the full range of *Hidden Places* guides and other titles published by Travel Publishing visit our website on

www.travelpublishing.co.uk
or ask for our leaflet by phoning
01752 276660 or emailing
info@travelpublishing.co.uk

127 THE LION HOTEL

Llandinam, Newtown, Powys SY17 5BY
☎ 01686 688233 Fax: 01686 689124
e-mail: lionhotel@yahoo.co.uk

Conveniently located beside the A470 Newtown to Llangurig road in the village of Llandinam, **The Lion Hotel** is a handsome old hostelry that dates back to the early 1800s when it was built as a coaching inn. It still has lots of charm and character with its exposed beams and traditional pub furniture. To the rear, the inn has a spacious beer garden and grounds that run down to the River Severn. Today, The Lion is very much a family-run business with Mary and Peter Randall and their family all involved in the enterprise. They arrived here in the autumn of 2007 and although it is their first venture together they have quickly established a glowing reputation for great hospitality, good food and well-kept ales. The inn has a separate restaurant where Mary and daughter Amanda do the cooking and offer an appetising and very varied menu based on ingredients sourced locally wherever possible. In addition to the regular menu, there are daily specials such as home-made lasagne, or half a roasted

duck in a sticky marmalade sauce. On Sundays, there's a lunchtime Carvery which, like all the food here, is very reasonably priced. Son-in-law Martin offers a well stocked bar and a comprehensive choice of beverages, including one rotating guest real ale which is very popular with the local residents and also the visiting guests.. Food is served from noon until 2pm, and from 6pm to 9pm, every day except Sunday evening. On the third Wednesday of each month, the inn hosts a Pub Quiz and also lays on various types of entertainment from time to time. The Lion also can cater for parties and weddings, please call for more details.

Accommodation at The Lion comprises 4 superb en suite rooms - 2 doubles, 1 twin and 1 family room sleeps up to 5 over 2 rooms - all of them upstairs. The tariff includes a full Welsh breakfast.

Children are welcome at The Lion; all major credit cards apart from American Express and Diners are accepted; and there is good disabled access to the bar and restaurant.

Trefeglwys, nr Caersws, Powys SY17 5PH
☎ 01686 430255
e-mail: doreen.perry@pc-q.net

Standing at the heart of the picturesque village of Trefeglwys, **The Red Lion** is a large and pristine traditional inn complete with original features such as the stonebuilt fireplace and exposed beams. Doreen and Stephen Perry took over here in 2005 and have built up a loyal following for their appetising food and well-kept ales which include 3 real ales – Theakstons XB and two rotating guest brews.

The food on offer features old favourites such as steaks, fish and chips, and lasagne as well as vegetarian choices and a range of bar

snacks. Food is always available up to 9pm when we are open. If the weather is favourable, customers can enjoy their refreshments outside, either in the charming courtyard area at the rear or on the patio at the front. Dogs are especially welcome at The Red Lion with a separate room for them and their owners to eat.

The inn hosts a Quiz once a month, on a Wednesday mid-month, with proceeds going to charity. Card payments are now accepted.

Welshpool, Powys SY21 8RF
☎ 01938 551920
info line: 01938 551944
e-mail: powiscastle@ntrust.org.uk

A mile south of Welshpool off the A483 stands one of the best known landmarks in the area. **Powis Castle** was originally built by Welsh Princes and later became the ancestral home of the Herbert family and then of the Clive family. One of the owners was Edward, son of Clive of India, and the Clive Museum houses a beautiful collection of treasures from India from the famous man's time there. Visitors can also see one of the finest collections of paintings and furniture in Wales.

The Castle is perched on a rock above splendid terraces and gardens both formal and informal. Laid out in 1720 in a style influenced by both French and Italian design, the gardens and terraces retain some splendid original features, including lead urns and statues, an orangery and an aviary.

The woodland, which was landscaped in the 18th century, overlooks the Severn Valley. The Castle is open to visitors from 1 to 5 late March to early November, the gardens from 11 to 6. There's a plant sales area, a shop and a licensed restaurant.

Mount Street, Welshpool,
Powys SY21 7LW
☎ 01938 552531

Completely refurbished in the autumn of 2005, the **Green Dragon** is a popular local standing close to the centre of this bustling market town. Owners Helen and Steve Wright have made sure that the renovations have not impaired the atmosphere of a traditional hostelry, cosy and compact. The inn is open all day, every day for ale, with Greene King IPA as the regular real ale. Throughout the day a selection of bar snacks such as sausage rolls, pies, pasties and sandwiches are available. The inn has two pool tables, hosts karaoke evenings on Sunday and Friday on alternate weeks from 8pm, and also lays on occasional live entertainment evenings. For parties and other special events, the Green Dragon has a small function room available. Another popular amenity here is the hidden rear patio area where customers can sit outside and enjoy Sky Sports and Santana Sports in the comfort of this appealing beer garden.

132 RAVEN INN

Raven Square, Welshpool,
Powys SY21 7LT
☎ 01938 553070 Fax: 01938 553070
e-mail: steve.raveninn@btconnect.com

Located next to the eastern terminus of the Welshpool and Llanfair Light Railway, the **Raven Inn** has been known for almost a decade as one of the best places in the area for dining. Its glowing reputation for good cuisine was earned by its award-winning chef Stephen Griffiths who has now taken over as the licensee of the inn together with business partner Lee Bocking who brings many years of local experience with him.

Thankfully, Stephen continues as Head Chef and his menu offers an extensive choice of appetising dishes. All the ingredients are purchased locally with meat coming from the Irfon Valley Butcher's and Ricki Lloyd's

under the Celtic Pride Brand. You can even find out the name of the farm where the animal came from – just ask! The menu changes according to the season but a typical one would offer the Chef's field mushroom stuffed with a Welsh blue Brie wrapped in Parma Ham, or a large deep-fried onion baggis served with a minty crème fraiche dressing as starters. Amongst the main courses Welsh beef and gammon steak dishes feature prominently, along with dishes such as the chef's home-made balti, a salmon and pepper brochette, and the chef's home-made lasagne. Vegetarians can regale themselves with Glamorgan Welsh vegetarian sausages or the chef's home-made risotto balls. A good selection of salads is also available and there's a separate menu for children. Diners can enjoy their meals throughout the inn or in the eye-catching beer garden to the rear which also has a children's play area. During the summer months food is served from 12 noon until 2:30pm and in the evening from 6pm until 9pm and will change during the winter months to 12noon until 2pm and 6pm until 8.30pm. Such is the popularity of the restaurant, it is essential to book at all times.

Once a month, the Raven hosts themed evenings featuring various national cuisines or particular ingredients such as local Welsh steaks or fresh local fish. And during the winter months OAP lunches are available every Tuesday and Wednesday lunchtimes when the chef creates traditional dishes in smaller portions and at smaller prices. The Raven accepts all major credit cards; has a function room for parties, weddings christenings and so on; and there is ample off road parking.

311

131 WESTWOOD PARK HOTEL ‖ ⊢

Salop Road, Welshpool, Powys SY21 7EA
☎ 01938 553474 Fax: 01938 553474
e-mail: west-wood@btconnect.com

Richard and Diane, my hosts at the **Westwood Park Hotel,** took over here in 2005 and have been gradually refurbishing the stately old premises. In the autumn of 2007 they opened their superb new restaurant

with its brand new state-of-the-art kitchen. In the stylishly furnished and decorated restaurant the tables are covered with crisp white linen tablecloths, gleaming glassware, and quality crockery and cutlery. Richard is himself an

excellent cook but he also employs a head chef. The menu is based on local produce and includes Celtic Pride steaks with fish as a speciality of the house along with Sunday lunch.

Food is served from noon until 2pm, and from 6pm to 9pm. It is strongly recommended that you book ahead at weekends. The hotel has a small parking area for guests at the side of the property and there is a courtyard at the rear, through the wrought iron gates.

The hotel also offers accommodation all year round. There are 7 guest bedrooms, 4 of them with en suite facilities. Children are welcome, all major credit cards are accepted, and there is disabled access to the ground floor only.

133 THE GOLDEN LION HOTEL ‖ ⊢

Offa's Dyke, Four Crosses, Powys SY22 6RB
☎ 01691 830295 Fax: 01691 830295

Standing alongside Offa's Dyke Path and adjacent to the A483 at Four Crosses, **The Golden Lion Hotel** is a fine old hostelry serving real ales, delicious home-cooked food and accommodation. Mine hosts are Rob and Karen Cook Williams - Rob is a professional session guitarist and has installed his own studio within the premises where he will continue to record and teach. In addition

to 5 en suite guest rooms, 5 self-catering cottages and a caravan and camping site are also available.

134 KINGS HEAD ‖ ⊢

Meifod, Oswestry, Powys SY22 6BY
☎ 01938 500171

Dating back to 1748, **The Kings Head** looks as pretty as a picture with its walls clad in creeper. Rob Thomas has owned this welcoming old pub since 1995 and is also the chef. He's passionate about good food, using only quality fresh local produce for his varied menu which ranges from popular pub favourites such as steaks to dishes such as chicken

with Camembert in a Merlot and Redcurrant sauce. The Kings Head also offers comfortable accommodation in 3 attractively furnished and decorated en suite rooms.

135 BRON HEULOG

Waterfall Street, Llanrhaeadr ym Mochnant,
Powys SY10 0JX
☎ 01691 780521
e-mail: diandpeter@bronheulog.co.uk
🌐 www.bronheulog.co.uk

Llanrhaeadr ym Mochnant is in a perfect location, nestling in the picturesque Welsh Berwyn Mountains. If it looks a bit familiar, perhaps you saw the Hugh Grant film *The Englishman who went up a Hill but came down a Mountain* which was filmed around here.

Surrounded by this spectacular countryside is **Bron Heulog,** pronounced Bron hay-log and meaning 'Sunny Bank'. Built in 1861, this beautiful and spacious Victorian house stands in a steeply sloping terraced garden.

The house has stone walls 2 feet thick and many original features are still in place, including the magnificent curved oak staircase, and all the original fireplaces.

Bron Heulog is the home of Diane and Peter Crocker who offer visitors the choice of either B&B or self-catering accommodation. B&B guests stay in the main house where there are 3 attractive guest bedrooms, all en suite and all with original Victorian fireplaces and very high ceilings. Colour TV and tea/coffee-making facilities are provided in all rooms. If you prefer self-catering, Garden Cottage is situated in the grounds of Bron Heulog and is a completely renovated charming Victorian cottage with a conservatory and fully-equipped modern kitchen. The cottage has one double bedroom.

136 HIGHLAND MOORS GUEST HOUSE

Wellington Road, Llandrindod Wells,
Powys LD1 5ND
☎ 01597 825151
e-mail: sue@highlandmoors.co.uk
🌐 www.highlandmoors.co.uk

The impressive 4-storey **Highland Moors Guest House** was built in the 19th century as a luxury spa hotel. In 2003, it was re-opened by a young English and Irish couple in order to restore it to its former glory. Today as a family-

run guest house offering a warm welcome, it has 12 spacious rooms including elegant bays with luxury walk-in shower ensuites, family rooms and guest lounge comfort with real log fire. Excellent breakfasts with local and free range produce. B&B or DB&B on request. Secure off-road parking and lockup. All major credit cards accepted.

137 NEW INN

Newbridge on Wye, Powys LD1 6HY
☎ 01597 860211
e-mail: dave@pigsfolly.co.uk
🌐 www.pigsfolly.co.uk

It may be called the **New Inn** but this former coaching hostelry dates back to the 16th century. It is a delightful whitewashed building with lots of character and stands opposite a statue of an old-time drover, fitting perfectly into the picturesque village of Newbridge on Wye. The pub is owned and run by Dave and Debbie Lang who have been in the hospitality business for many years - in Dave's case, for 57 years. His father and grandfather were also in the same business before him.

Good food is a major priority at the New Inn. The Langs own the butcher's shop next door which sells locally reared meat and makes its own award-winning sausages, pork pies, dry cured ham and bacon and

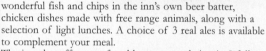

hams, all of which feature on the pub menu. Also on offer is a

wonderful fish and chips in the inn's own beer batter, chicken dishes made with free range animals, along with a selection of light lunches. A choice of 3 real ales is available to complement your meal.

The inn also offers comfortable accommodation in 8 fully en suite rooms, all equipped with TV and hospitality tray. For budget or group visitors, 10 bunkhouse beds are available.

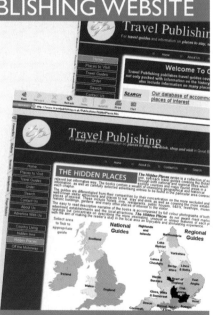

Cross Gates, Llandrindod Wells,
Powys, LD1 6RB
☎ 01597 851238
e-mail:thebuildersarms@btconnect.com

A handsome foursquare stone building dating back to 1821, **The Builders Arms** is a welcoming old hostelry full of charm and character. It's owned and run by the Guest family - David, his wife Tilly and their daughter Chardonnay. David has been a chef for some 12 years so good food is taken very seriously here. In the elegant restaurant with its dark wood furniture, David's menu offers an enticing choice of wholesome and appetising food. Amongst the starters you'll find a home-made soup of the day, Wild Mushroom Brioche and a tasty Antipasto Selection. Main courses range from a Tournedos Rossini or Gressingham Duck Breast to a Seared Salmon Salad and Lamb Noisettes. Vegetarians are well-catered for with dishes such as an oven-baked large field

mushroom filled with leeks and topped with cheesy bread crumbs accompanied by spring onion crushed potatoes and rocket salad. In all the dishes local produce is used wherever possible. Food is served every lunchtime (noon until 2.30 or 3pm), and every evening from 6.30pm to 9.30pm. Because of the restaurant's popularity, booking on Friday and Saturday evenings and for Sunday lunch is strongly recommended. On Sunday lunchtimes, only traditional roasts are served. For the rest of the week, the lunchtime menu offers a selection of hot meals, (including Sausages and Mash made with Francis's of Ludlow home-made sausages), salads, sandwiches, hot baguettes, salads, jacket potatoes and ploughman's. For the afternoon break, the pub offers various home-made cakes to accompany your Cream or Afternoon Tea. Please note that payment is by cheque or cash only.

The Guests have made their pub a lively place, hosting regular Quiz Nights for charity, themed evenings (Spanish, Italian) and even a children's Halloween Party.

The Builders Arms also offers comfortable accommodation in 3 guest bedrooms - 2 doubles and 1 twin - all of which are provided with en suite facilities. Also available is a self-catering cottage to the rear of the premises which sleeps 2 people. It is available all year round and short breaks can be arranged.

Cross Gates village can be found 3 miles north of Llandrindod Wells, at the junction of the A44 and A483.

139 GWYSTRE INN

Gwystre, Llandrindod Wells,
Powys LD1 6RN
☎ 01597 851650

Conveniently located on the main A44 between Rhayader and Cross Gates, the **Gwystre Inn** has a history that stretches back to the 1700s when it stood on a drover's road. Today, mine hosts are Pete and Linda Ramplee, a warm and friendly couple who have made the inn a popular place to eat, drink and stay.

Good food is a major attraction here with extensive à la carte and bar menus offering

dishes based on locally produced ingredients. Roasts are a speciality on Sundays with a choice of 4 different joints. Portions are generous and very reasonably priced. To avoid disappointment, it is wise to book ahead for Friday and Saturday evenings, and for Sunday lunch. Food is served every day from noon until 2.30pm, and from 6pm to 9.30pm. To accompany your meal, there's an extensive choice of beers, wines and spirits, including one real ale - Rev. James. If you are lucky with the weather, you can enjoy your refreshments in the pleasant beer garden with its attractive stream. Inside, you'll find pub games such as darts and coits.

The inn also offers comfortable B&B accommodation in 3 guest double bedrooms, each with full en suite facilities. TV and hospitality tray. All major credit cards are accepted and there's ample off road parking.

316

West Street, Rhayader, Powys LD6 5AF
☎ 01597 810109
e-mail: reservations@élanhotel.co.uk
🌐 www.elan hotel.co.uk

Set in spectacular countryside, nestling on the bank of the River Wye and with the throw of a stone assuring a splash in the Elan Valley lakes, **The Elan Hotel** also commands stunning mountain views. The hotel has a well stocked bar and a relaxing residents' lounge area with Sky Sports TV, video and a wide selection of games if you prefer a quiet day relaxing in the hotel admiring those wonderful mountain views.

The hotel is noted for its good home-cooked food, starting with a breakfast menu that ranges from a full Welsh breakfast to a simple toast and preserves. From 12 noon until 9pm the bar menu is available which offers a wide choice that includes traditional favourites such as Steak & Kidney Pie or Fish and Chips, as well as omelettes, sandwiches, baguettes, paninis, baked potatoes, salads and a Dish of the Day. If you prefer to eat in the restaurant, the enticing menu here offers, amongst the starters, a tasty chicken liver and mushroom pâté with a spiced chutney, Moules Marinieres and a roasted red pepper and mozzarella salad. Local Welsh produce features prominently amongst the main courses with dishes such as Welsh Black Sirloin Steak and Lamb Chops. Fish lovers will surely be tempted by the pan-seared Red Snapper fillet served with buttered new potatoes and a Pernod and herb butter. For vegetarians, the choice includes Baked Italian Aubergine with a side salad or a vegetable stir fry. To accompany your meal, there's a comprehensive selection of beverages including one real ale - more real ales will soon become available. Diners have the choice of eating either in the bar, the restaurant or, weather permitting, in the rear garden with its large patio area.

The hotel also offers quality en suite accommodation with a 5-star rating from the Welsh Tourist Board. There are 10 rooms of varying sizes, all equipped with television and tea/coffee making facilities. Children are always welcome and the hotel staff can make arrangements for cots to be supplied with any hotel room booking.

The Elan Hotel is Wi-fi enabled, so if you need to keep in touch with the office or are always on the go you'll be well catered for! The hotel also has good disabled access; pets are welcome by arrangement, all major credit cards are accepted and there is a large residents' car park.

141 BRYNAFON

South Street, Rhayader, Powys LD6 5BL
☎ 01597 810735 Fax: 01597 810111
e-mail: info@brynafon.co.uk
🌐 www.brynafon.co.uk

Built in 1870, the imposing Victorian Workhouse on the edge of Rhayader has been transformed and is now a beautiful family-run hotel, **Brynafon**. With its creeper-clad walls and 1½ acres of meticulously tended grounds, it

gives no hint of its former miserable purpose. Inside there is a unique water feature where the inmates once did their washing. In the cosy beamed and licensed restaurant where food is served from 8am until 8.30pm, the menu offers a wide choice of appetising dishes. During the day, the choice includes salads, risottos and traditional dishes such as Steak & Guinness Pie. From 5pm, owners Gerry and Linda Wilkinson have introduced what they believe is the first Welsh Tapas Menu in the area. The choices include

Aberaeron Crab Fritters with a sweet chili dressing, and Welsh Duck with a Lavender Oil reduction. From 6pm, the evening menu presents a selection of dishes ranging from Rack of Welsh Lamb to a vegetarian Shropshire Blue Cheese & Walnut Risotto.

The accommodation at Brynafon comprises 20 individually styled bedrooms and family suites, some on the ground floor and all with en suite facilities. Children are welcome and all major credit cards are accepted apart from Amex and Diners.

143 RIVERSIDE LODGE GUEST HOUSE

Elan Valley, Rhyader, Powys LD6 5HL
☎ 01597 810770
e-mail: riversidelodge2@aol.com
🌐 www. riversidelodge.biz

Riverside Lodge Guest House occupies an idyllic location on the bank of the River Elan, the gateway to the lakelands of Wales. Only a mile from Rhyader on the B4518, Riverside is the home of Gill O'Shea and Barry Parsons, a friendly couple who have been welcoming guests to their home since 2003. Gill used to be a Conference Manager; Barry was an engineer. They have 7 guest bedrooms, all attractively furnished and decorated, and most of them

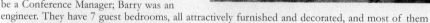

with en suite facilities. All the rooms are on the ground floor. The accommodation has been given a 3-star rating by Visit Wales. The tariff includes a hearty Welsh breakfast based on locally sourced produce. In the afternoon, weather permitting, guests can enjoy afternoon tea in the gardens overlooking the river where, if they are lucky, they may get to see some of the otters who have made it their home. Riverside is open all year; has good disabled access and off road parking, and welcomes children. Payment is by cash or cheque only.

318

Llwynbaedd, Rhayader, Powys LD6 5NT
☎ 01597 811422
e-mail: info@oakwoodlodges.co.uk
🌐 www.oakwoodlodges.co.uk

Set in the beautiful countryside of Mid-Wales, **Oak Wood Lodges** provide quality self-catering holiday accommodation in fully equipped and centrally heated log cabins. They are set in a prominent and commanding position approximately 1000ft above

sea level and enjoy spectacular views across the Elan Valley, a vast nature reserve renowned for the beauty of its lakes, mountains, moors and oak woods.

The lodges are set in 19 acres of land, which also include woodlands of about 3 acres. There are 11 fully equipped lodges available, all of them facing south and with grand views across the valley. From the verandas, red kites may be seen hovering in the sky and at night tawny owls can be heard calling in the woods. The Eagle Owl Lodges have 3 bedrooms and 2 fold-up beds enabling up to 8 people to stay. There's also a bathroom with bath and walk-in shower. The smaller Barn and Tawny Owl Lodges offer 2 bedrooms, a double and a twin, and a shower room. All the lodges have an open plan lounge, dining area and fully equipped kitchen; French windows opening on to the south-facing veranda; full central heating and "Free to Air" satellite television and DVD player. The lodges are available all year round.

Visitors will find plenty to see and do in this lovely part of the country. Bird-watchers will appreciate the Red Kite Feeding Centre and the Mid-Wales Falconry; there's pony trekking in the Cambrian and Black Mountains and in the Brecon Beacons; the River Wye and other beautiful waters of the area provide both fly and coarse fishing. Heritage sites to explore include the abbey ruins at Abbey-cwm-hir, the many castles of Wales, including Powys Castle with its famous Italianate terraces, the Celtica Experience at Machynlleth, and Brecon Cathedral. Other outdoor

activities within easy reach include sailing, canoeing, canal cruising, rally driving, climbing, caving, cycling, mountain and quad biking. Many of the 9 and 18-hole golf courses of the area have spectacular views.

Another way of enjoying the beauty of the Welsh countryside is by travelling on a narrow gauge railway such as the Vale of Rheidol Railway, the Brecon Mountain Railway, the Teifi Valley Railway or the Bala Lake Railway.

144 THE ELAN VALLEY

Elan Valley Visitor Centre, Elan Valley,
Rhayader, Powys LD6 5HP
☎ 01597 810898
e-mail: info@elanvalley.org.uk
⊕ www.elanvalley.org.uk

The Elan Valley is 70 square miles of the Cambrian Mountains in mid-Wales - a special area for wildlife with reservoirs and dams, rivers, woodlands and moorland. There is a well signposted Visitor Centre open from the middle of March to the end of October every day from 10am to 5.30pm which has a wildlife exhibition,

café, shop, toilets, a large car park suitable for coaches and cars and a picnic area beside the River Elan. The Valley has several leafleted walks and many guided walks and wildlife events are led by the team of countryside rangers.

145 MID WALES INN

Pant-y-Dwr, Rhayader, Powys LD6 5LL
☎ 01597 870076
e-mail: andrew.connah@fsmail.net

Set along a designated prime scenic route, the **Mid Wales Inn** is a welcoming place to enjoy great food, drink and accommodation. Mine hosts, Arthur and Andy, took over here in July 2004 and have recently carried out refurbishment to a very high standard. The restaurant here, which specialises in mouth-watering steaks and curries, is so popular that booking is advised at

all times. Real ales on tap include Buckley's which is the regular brew. If you are staying in this lovely part of the country, the inn has 3 well-appointed guest bedrooms, two of which have full en suite facilities.

146 THE RADNORSHIRE ARMS

Beguildy, Powys LD7 1YE
☎ 01547 510634 Fax: 08700 516488
e-mail: p.thompson151@btinternet.com

The Radnorshire Arms has to be one of the prettiest pubs in Wales. Part of the premises dates back to the 1400s and inside, there's a wealth of old beams and horse brasses, and an inglenook fireplace. This appealing old hostelry is owned and run by Peter and Lorraine Thompson who arrived here in 2004. Lorraine is an accomplished cook and her menu offers a good choice that includes old favourites such as a 10oz Welsh Sirloin Steak with peas and fries, as well as less familiar dishes like the Chicken Fillet in a Creamy Stilton Sauce. There are changes made to the menu regularly with meat, fish and vegetarian options always available and children have their own menu. To

accompany your meal there's a comprehensive range of

beverages including house wines and 3 real ales. Food is served from 7pm to 9pm, Tuesday to Saturday, and from noon until 2pm on Sunday. The Radnorshire Arms has been awarded the Cask Marque for service and conditions of real ales the first in the Teme Valley to receive such an award. Please note that payment at the Radnorshire Arms is by cash or cheque only.

Llanshay Lane, Knighton,
Powys LD7 1LW
☎ 01547 520247
e-mail: mail@spaceguarduk.com
🌐 www.spaceguarduk.com

The Spaceguard Centre is a working astronomical observatory that specialises in Near Earth Objects (NEOs), asteroids and comets that could potentially hit the Earth. You might have seen the movies "Deep Impact" and "Armageddon", but the threat of NEOs hitting the earth is more real than most people realise. The Spaceguard Centre offers the opportunity for people to visit and find out about the possibility of a genuine "Deep Impact", and what we can do to stop such an event.

A guided tour takes you around all of the facilities at the Spaceguard Centre, looking at what we do, why we do it and how. We have a fully equipped and unique indoor observatory with a 13-inch telescope capable of tracking NEOs that could be a threat to the Earth. We also have a small

planetarium and Camera Obscura. There are many more fascinating exhibits such as meteorites and samples from impact craters. The Spaceguard Centre is an intriguing place and a great day out for anyone.

Painscastle, Builth Wells, Powys LD2 3JL
☎ 01497 851398
e-mail: chris@outdoor-sport.u-net.com
🌐 www.roastoxinn.com

Located in the picturesque village of Painscastle, southeast of Builth Wells, the **Roast Ox Inn** is a traditional country public house but with the added attraction of a restaurant seating 60 persons, 10 fully en-suite letting rooms and superb conference facilities with full audio-visual equipment.

Although there has been an inn on this site for at least 500 years, the Roast Ox is comparatively recent - an earlier inn was completely destroyed by fire in 1991. The inn retains a number of its original features whilst benefiting from 21st century facilities.

The Roast Ox is well known for its excellent food. "We make no pretence about our food and drink" says

mine host Chris Charters, "only that we use the finest local produce, which our Chef then lovingly prepares. Our Sunday lunches attract great support from the local residents and advance booking is advised". The inn offers a selection of real ales and ciders, and stocks a number of wines along with a very fine range of Malt Whiskies.

Accommodation at the Roast Ox comprises ten comfortable letting rooms each of which is equipped with television and en suite shower room. Conference facilities are also available, including audiovisual presentation aids.

321

Llanfihangel nant Melan, nr New Radnor,
Powys LD8 2TN
☎ 01544 350220
e-mail: redlioninn-midwales.co.uk

Conveniently located on the A44 about 3 miles west of New Radnor, **The Red Lion Inn** is a charming and atmospheric old hostelry with a history stretching back some 400 years. Owners Sandra and John Rathbone arrived here in the summer of 2007 and have already received rave reviews for their food and hospitality, especially from locals. Sandra has been in the hospitality trade for some 25 years and has been together in business with John for the last 6 years. They both take pride in their acclaimed hospitality and the combination of traditional and modern cookery based on local fresh produce has been critical to their success. The inn is recommended in both the *AA Pub Guide* and *AA Britain's Best Country Pubs For Food*. Sandra is the cook and

her most popular dishes include Welsh Black Beef Sirloin Steaks and Organic Salmon. To accompany your meal, there's a well-balanced selection of wines and a choice of 2 real ales, one of which is always from the Woods Brewery. Food is served from noon until 2.30pm, and from 6pm onwards every day except Tuesdays when the pub is closed. In good weather, meals can be enjoyed in the superb beer garden to the rear.

The Red Lion also offers 3-star rated accommodation in 7 warm and comfortable en suite rooms, all with colour television, radio/alarm clock and complimentary tea/coffee tray with biscuits. There are 3 double and 1 twin, and three motel-style rooms, 2 family double and 1 twin. Well-behaved pets are welcome in the 3 chalet rooms whose freedom and privacy make them much favoured by bikers, walkers and riders. This ground floor accommodation is also suitable for less active guests.

Visitors will find plenty to see and do in the area. The Victorian town of Llandrindod Wells, Presteigne with its Judge's Lodging Museum, cosmopolitan Hay-on-Wye, the most famous second-hand book town in the world, and Builth Wells, home to the annual Royal Welsh Show are all within easy reach. Nearby golf courses include Kington - the highest course in England and Wales which has spectacular views; while the River Wye and its tributaries offers good salmon and trout fishing.

150 THE GRIFFIN INN

Llyswen, Brecon, Powys LD3 0UR
☎ 01874 754241 Fax: 01874 754592
e-mail: info@griffin inn-llyswen.co.uk
🌐 www.griffin inn-llyswen.co.uk

Set in the beautiful Brecon Beacons in the heart of Wales, **The Griffin Inn** looks as pretty as a picture with its ivy-clad and partly half-timbered walls. This ancient hostelry dates back to 1467 and was originally a coaching inn. Since it sits on one of the main crossing points in mid-Wales, what is now the junction of the A470 and A479, it must have been a busy and prosperous place.

Inside, original beams and fireplaces are still in place and the rooms abound with charm and character. The Fisherman's Bar, which is decorated with ornaments, pictures and memorabilia relating to angling, you'll find 3 real ales on tap - Rev James and 2 rotating ales. The attractive open plan lounge, which is decorated with a shooting theme, is a great place to relax with a drink and perhaps study the menu for the adjacent 45-seater restaurant. Everything on the menu is home-cooked and 99% of the ingredients sourced from within a 10-mile radius. The Griffin Inn is open from 11am to 11pm during the summer, and serves bar meals at lunchtime with the restaurant open in the evening.

With its central position in the heart of Wales, the Griffin provides an ideal base for exploring this scenic area. The inn has 8 themed guest bedrooms, all attractively furnished and decorated and all with TV, hospitality tray and en suite facilities.

151 THE THREE HORSESHOES

Velindre, Brecon, Powys LD3 0SU
☎ 01497 847304

Standing on an old drover's road, **The Three Horseshoes** was built originally as a farmhouse with parts that date back to the 17th century. It became an alehouse, then a public house and at one time had a smithy at the rear. Today, this charming old hostelry with its exposed beams, adorned with brasses, open fireplace and small-paned windows is well-known locally for its appetising meals which make good use of local produce. Welsh Beef Steaks are particularly popular, as are the Duck Montmorency and the Lamb Shank. For lighter appetites, the bar meals menu offers a choice of traditional pub fare that includes

burgers, jacket potatoes, toasties and baguettes. Food is served every day except Tuesdays from noon until 2pm, and from 6pm to 9pm. It is advisable to book at weekends, especially during the summer. The selection of beverages on offer includes 2 real ales (1 in winter) which rotate and are mainly from local breweries. The pub has a pool and games room and occasionally lays on entertainment. All major credit cards apart from American Express and Diners are accepted, and there is good disabled access.

152 THE TROUT INN

Beulah, Llanwrtyd Wells, Powys LD5 4UU
☎ 01591 620235 Fax: 01591 620235
e-mail: info@thetroutinn.net
🌐 www.thetroutinn.net

Dating back in parts to the late 1700s, **The Trout Inn** is a traditional village inn with a glowing reputation for the quality of its food. Chef Linda Covey's Steak & Ale Pie is particularly popular, as is her Sunday roast lunch - booking ahead is strongly recommended. Linda's husband, Peter, looks after

the well-stocked bar, including the real ales. The Trout also offers comfortable en suite rooms and by the time you read this an extension should be completed offering dormitory/clubroom style accommodation for up to 9 people. All major credit cards accepted apart from Amex and Diners.

153 STONECROFT INN

Dolecoed Road, Llanwrtyd Wells,
Powys LD5 4RA
☎ 01591 610332/610304 Fax: 01591 610304
e-mail: party@stonecroft.co.uk
🌐 www.stonecroft.co.uk

A traditional warm and friendly country pub, **Stonecroft Inn** has a reputation for serving delicious meals and bar snacks with hot food and hot drinks available throughout opening hours. Look out for the Lamb Shank which is one of the inn's tasty specialities, or you might prefer one of the roasts available every day. Families are most welcome here and, if you are lucky with the weather, there's a large riverside garden where you can enjoy your refreshments. There are aviaries here as well as a play fort. Inside, you'll find a games area with pool and darts and the inn regularly hosts quality live music. The inn features in CAMRA's *Good Beer Guide* and always has a minimum of 4 real ales on tap plus a rotating real cider. The inn's owners, Peter and Jane Brown, reckon they provide their customers with more than 200 real ales each year. And in November the inn hosts a Beer Festival at which more than 70 real ales are available to sample.

The inn also offers comfortable accommodation in 6 guest bedrooms, all with en suite facilities. More rooms are available in the adjacent Stonecroft Lodge where self-catering accommodation is available in either private or shared rooms, perfect for backpackers, motor and mountain bikers, families, youth groups and so on. The bedrooms have single and double beds, all made up with fresh linen, including duvets, ready for your arrival. The kitchen is fully equipped with 2 electric cookers, 2 microwaves, kettles, toasters, fridges, freezers, dishwasher and all cutlery, crockery and cooking utensils. The property is centrally heated and has an open fire, satellite TV, DVD and

video in the large L-shaped lounge/dining room. There is also a washing machine and tumble dryer for your use. The Lodge also has a beautiful riverside garden and is just a minute's walk from the town's amenities which include a Doctor's surgery and pharmacy, Tourist Information Centre with internet access and gift shop, a Spar supermarket, a family butcher, petrol and service station, hairdresser's, and cycle shop. About 5 minutes further is Llanwrtyd Wells railway station on the Swansea to Shrewsbury Heart of Wales Line.

154 CARLTON RIVERSIDE RESTAURANT WITH ROOMS 🍴 🛏

Irfon Crescent, Llanwrtyd Wells,
Powys LD5 4ST
☎ 01591 610248
e-mail: info@carltonrestaurant.co.uk
🌐 www.carltonrestaurant.co.uk

The AA's Restaurant of the Year for all of Wales, 2007/8, **Carlton Riverside Restaurant with Rooms** is a quite outstanding establishment which has been showered with many awards. The Welsh Tourist Board awarded it 4 stars and the AA also awarded 4 stars Highly Commended Bed & Breakfast.

The spacious dining room overlooks the River Irfon with views across to the town green. Chef-proprietor Mrs Mary Ann Gilchrist uses only the best fresh produce to create seriously good food. Her menu changes regularly but on a typical day you might find Warm Smoked Eel or Hay-on-Wye air-dried Ham amongst the starters, and Roast Breast of Mallard or a Spinach and Cep Tart as main courses. Then there are

her wonderful puddings Warm Chocolate Brownie with home-made pistachio ice cream, or a Meringue Swan with whipped cream and whinberry coulis. To accompany your meal, the wine list offers more than 80 wines carefully chosen for quality and representing most wine-growing regions of the world.

The guest bedrooms at the Riverside Restaurant are all comfortable and well furnished, provided with en suite facilities, superb pocket-sprung beds, flat screen LCD-TV, hospitality tray and good quality complimentary toiletries.

155 CERDYN VILLA 🛏

Station Road, Llanwrtyd Wells, Powys LD5 4RS
☎ 01591 610635
e-mail: info@cerdynvilla.co.uk
🌐 www.cerdynvilla.co.uk

Just a short walk from the town centre and set in one acre of its own grounds, **Cerdyn Villa** is a handsome Edwardian house built in 1907. It's now the home of John and Bernice Crompton who have been welcoming bed & breakfast guests here since 2005. They have 2 en suite guest rooms available, both attractively furnished and decorated. If you prefer self-catering, they also have a cottage in the grounds which has a 3-star rating from the Welsh Tourist Board. It can sleep up to 3 people and is equipped with Sky TV and Internet access.

156 THE COPPER KETTLE 🍴

103 The Street, Brecon LD3 7LT
☎ 01874 611349

Located in the heart of the town, the popular **Copper Kettle** is a great place to unwind after shopping and enjoy a main meal, snack or just a cup of coffee. The menu offers all day breakfasts, jacket potatoes, sandwiches and baguettes as well as tasty roasts 3 or 4 times a week. There's also a children's menu. During the summer months The Copper Kettle is open every day from 9am to 5pm, in the winter it closes 3.30pm/4pm and is also closed on Sundays.

326

21 The Watton, Brecon LD3 7ED
☎ 01874 611813 Fax: 01874 611813

Originally named after Lord Camden, a local wealthy landowner, the **Camden Arms** enjoys a glowing reputation in the Brecon area for its outstanding food. Marilyn Price is an accomplished chef whose cooking provides a real culinary treat, based as it is primarily on local produce. Especially popular are her home-made Steak & Ale Pie, the Beef Stroganoff and her home-made curries. Vegetarians are unusually well-provided for with a choice that includes a Stilton & Vegetable Crumble, home-made Mushroom Stroganoff and a vegetable curry. Children too have a wider choice than usual with most dishes on the menu available in children's portions.

Marilyn's menu also offers various fish dishes, grills and salads, and the regular menu is supplemented by daily specials.

At Sunday lunchtimes, delicious roasts replace the regular menu. Food is served from noon until 3pm, and from 6.30pm to 9pm, every day of the week. It is essential to book for Friday and Saturday evenings, and for Sunday lunch. Meals can be enjoyed either in the elegant restaurant which seats 25, in the lounge bars or, weather permitting, at picnic tables on the terrace to the rear of the pub. To accompany your meal, there's a wide selection of beverages, including one real ale that changes every month. The restaurant and bars are all wheelchair-friendly and the premises has a disabled toilet and entrance.

The Camden Arms also offers quality accommodation in 2 twin bedrooms on the first floor. They are both en suite and available all year round. The tariff includes a hearty Welsh breakfast. Children are welcome and all major credit cards are accepted.

327

157 PARIS GUEST HOUSE

28 Watton, Brecon, Powys LD3 7EF
☎ 01874 624205
e-mail: enquiries@parisguesthouse,co.uk
⊕ www.parisguesthouse.co.uk

The **Paris Guest House** is run by Dave and Sharon Allen whose aim is to provide a warm and friendly atmosphere. "Being a small business" they say, "we are able to provide the little extras that larger guest houses overlook". The house has 5 en suite guest bedrooms  and is within easy walking distance of all the town's main attractions, excellent scenic walks, the Mon-Brecon canal and the local theatre. Guests also receive a discount on the Dragonfly Boat Trip along the Mon-Brecon Canal. Children are welcome; payment is by cash or cheque only.

160 BRECKNOCK MUSEUM AND ART GALLERY

Captain's Walk, Brecon, Powys LD3 7DS
☎ 01874 624121
⊕ www.powys.gov.uk/museums

Visit the Brecknock Museum and learn more about the history, environment and art of the Brecon Beacons area. Housed in the Old Shire Hall and courtrooms, where you can see a judge and jury try a historic court case, the Museum has a fascinating collection that includes antique lovespoons, fine furniture and paintings, a stage costume that belonged to the opera singer Adelina Patti, Roman standing stones, natural history and the ancient logboat from Llangors Lake. There is also an exciting and varied programme of special exhibitions throughout the year, including Welsh arts and crafts and items from the Museum's extensive collections.

159 THE DROVERS ARMS

Newgate Street, Llanfaes, Brecon,
Powys LD3 8DN
☎ 01874 623377

Just a short walk from the centre of Brecon in the hamlet of Llanfaes, **The Drovers Arms** is a traditional Welsh hostelry with lots of charm and character. Mine hosts, Carolyne and Louise are sisters-in-law who took over here in early 2007 and have quickly made a success of the business. A major part of the appeal is the delicious and wholesome food on offer, all based on locally sourced produce and cooked by Carolyne and Louise. The

menu is displayed on a blackboard and might include a tasty Chicken, Ham and Leek Pie, perhaps, or some succulent Welsh Lamb Chops. Food is served every day from noon until 9pm and to accompany your meal there's a comprehensive range of beverages, including 2/3 real ales from the superb Welsh brewery, Brains. All major credit cards apart from American Express and Diners are accepted. If you enjoy pub quizzes, be sure to drop in on the first Monday of the month when the quiz starts at 8pm. Good disabled access.

Pwllgloyw, Brecon, Powys LD3 9PY
☎ 01874 690282
e-mail: salisbury202@a ol.com

The **Seland Newydd Inn** in the small village
of Pwllgloyw was built as a farmhouse in
1792 and became an inn some 40 years later.
It was then known as the Lord Camden Arms
after a wealthy local landowner but adopted
its present name in 1998. The inn is owned
and run by Paul and Mandy Salisbury who
have made good food a priority. Their menu
is based on locally sourced ingredients and
features dishes such as Glamorgan Sausages, Rack of Welsh Lamb and Anglesey Eggs - a dish
comprising of potatoes, leeks, eggs and Caerphilly cheese sauce. Such is the popularity of the food

here, it is wise to book at all times and is essential for the
Sunday roast lunch. Food is served from 7pm to 9.20pm,
Wednesday to Saturday, and from noon until 12.30pm on
Sunday. Meals can be taken either in the restaurant, the bar
areas or in the spacious beer garden which, rather unusually, is
on the opposite side of the road. During the summer, there are
always 2 real ales on tap with Butty Bach one of the most asked
for. The inn has a pool room and also offers accommodation in
2 double en suite rooms.

HIDDEN PLACES GUIDES

Explore Britain and Ireland with
Hidden Places guides - a fascinating
series of national and local travel
guides.

Packed with easy to read information
on hundreds of places of interest as
well as places to stay, eat and drink.

Available from both high street and
internet booksellers

For more information on the full range
of *Hidden Places* guides and other
titles published by Travel Publishing
visit our website on

www.travelpublishing.co.uk
or ask for our leaflet by phoning
01752 276660 or emailing
info@travelpublishing.co.uk

Brecon Road, Crickhowell, Powys NP8 1DL
☎ 01873 810473

The
charmingly
traditional
White Hart
dates back to
the 16th
century and is
built on the
site of the old
village tollgate. An interesting plaque on the
wall displays the ancient charges - 'A score of
pigs -2d'. The inn is run by Roger and Jackie
Griffiths who arrived in the summer of 2007
and have quickly established a reputation for
their hospitality and good food and ale,
including 3 real ales. Jackie is an accomplished
cook and her menu has a strong Welsh flavour
to it. Sunday lunch at the White Hart offers a
traditional roast only with a choice of meats.
Booking is strongly recommended. In good
weather, refreshments can be enjoyed in the
peaceful beer garden. Children are welcome;
all major credit cards are accepted, and there's
off road car parking.

53 Commercial Street, Ystradgynlais,
Swansea SA9 1LA
☎ 01639 841000
e-mail: info@ynyscedwynarms.co.uk
🌐 www.ynyscedwynarms.co.uk

Set beside the river that runs through the charming village of Ystradgynlais, close to the Dan-yr-Ogof Showcaves and at the gateway to the Brecon Beacons National Park, the **Ynyscedwyn Arms** is a cosy and very tastefully decorated pub with a large restaurant and conservatory extension. Robert Megson took over here at the end of 2006 having recognised the potential of these superb premises. He carried out a major internal refurbishment and the elegant furniture and fittings are a pleasure to behold. Robert employed Kathy Sergeant as manageress and when the restaurant had been completed invited the well-known professional chef Adrian Duffy to create an appetising and enticing menu. It makes good use of fresh Welsh produce with smoked salmon and a warm salad of cockles, laver bread superb! and

smoked bacon amongst the starters; creamed leeks, chive and Caerphilly cheese tartlet as one of the vegetarian alternatives. Amongst the main courses Welsh beef and lamb feature prominently, with Welsh Rump of Lamb served with roast shallots and a garlic and rosemary jus as one of the House Specialities. Everything on the menu is home cooked and even the children's meals are home-made. The fresh vegetables come from Pembrokeshire and the organic cheeses are also Welsh. As all the food is cooked and prepared to order, those with a limited time period are encouraged to phone ahead with their lunch orders. And if you have any food allergies or special requirements, just let the staff know and they will try to accommodate your needs where possible.

To accompany your meal, the well-stocked bar offers a comprehensive choice that includes up to 3 real ales with Buckley's Bitter as the regular brew. The restaurant is open from noon until 2.30pm, and from 6pm to 9.30pm, Tuesday to Sunday. Booking is essential on Friday, Saturday and Sunday.

The inn has a superb beer garden with the river running close by, and also has ample car parking space. All major credit cards are accepted apart from American Express.

If you are planning to stay in this scenic part of the county, the Ynyscedwyn Arms has 5 superb guest bedrooms, all with en suite bathrooms, Sky TV and lots of extra little facilities. The tariff includes an extensive breakfast choice that includes smoked salmon, kippers, hand-cut bacon and more.

Outstanding inn with superb food, real ales, a riverside beer garden and excellent en suite rooms.

High Street, Crickhowell, Powys NP8 1BE
☎ 01873 810362 Fax: 01878 811868
e-mail: info@dragoncrickhowell.co.uk
🌐 www.dragoncrickhowell.co.uk

The Dragon Inn looks very appealing with its pink-washed walls, dormer and bay windows and greenery to the front. It has probably been an inn since 1740 but even then it was re-modelled from an existing building so parts of the fabric probably date from the mid-1600s. The Inn was bought in the summer of 2007 by Ashley Nield, a former journalist. The Inn has a 3-star rating from Visit Wales but, says Ashley, "My goal is to become a 4-star Inn in two years' time". Under the previous owners, the Dragon had developed a reputation as a laid-back, friendly establishment offering excellent food - a reputation that Ashley intends to maintain and develop. He also intends to refurbish significant parts of it without sacrificing any of its charm. A traveller himself, he wants

his hotel to be the kind of place he'd like to stay in when away from home.

Good food is a major priority here. The kitchen is led by head chef Robert Duggan, an Abergavenny man who is largely responsible for the restaurant's excellent reputation. All the meat used has been fattened on the hillsides surrounding Crickhowell and it has only travelled as far as Talgarth, near Brecon, for slaughtering. The fish is delivered fresh every day on a van from Plymouth (supplied by Moby Nick). Local smoked trout, home-made soup served with home-made chunky bread, and mushrooms in local ale and Stilton all feature among the starters. As a main course, how about a steak of Welsh Black beef, Welsh lamb cutlets, or chicken breast stuffed with leeks and Caerphilly cheese? For vegetarians the choice includes Agnolotti Fromagi - pasta filled with 5 cheeses in tomato sauce. Other diets can be catered for given notice. To accompany your meal there's a good selection of wines available by the glass or bottle. For larger parties, the hotel has a private dining/function room that can accommodate up to 30 people.

If you are planning to stay in this unique, small town, the Dragon has 15 guest bedrooms of various sizes, all tastefully decorated and very individual. All rooms are equipped with en suite facilities, television, telephone, hospitality tray, hairdryer, ironing board and iron. The hotel accepts all major credit cards except American Express.

165 GLANGRWYNEY COURT

Crickhowell, Powys NP8 1ES
☎ 01873 811288
e-mail: info@ glancourt.co.uk
⊕ www.glancourt.co.uk

A Grade II listed building, **Glangrwyney Court** occupies a superb location standing in 4 acres of gardens, 33 acres of parkland and 8 acres of woodland running down to the river. Situated within the Brecon Beacons National Park, this fine Georgian house, dating in parts to 1790, enjoys a 5-star rating from both the Welsh Tourist Board and the AA for its bed & breakfast accommodation, and a 4-star rating for its self-catering cottages.

Staying in this modest Georgian mansion with its typically Palladian architecture is a very special experience. During the winter months the log fire beckons and with the honesty bar close by, a comforting drink is readily available. Deep sofas and plenty of reading material complete the picture. In summer, what better than to sit on the patio or lie back in the hammock in the walled garden and sip a glass of

wine. Within the extensive grounds, there are plenty of quiet places to sit and simply enjoy the surroundings. For the energetic the all weather tennis court is available and for those who prefer to take life at a more leisurely pace, how about croquet and boules? Pony trekking, fishing, golf and shooting can be arranged if required, as can cycling including bicycle hire.

The house has 8 guest bedrooms each of which has been individually decorated and offers either en suite or private bathroom facilities. All rooms have TV and hospitality tray, robes as well as fluffy towels, exclusive toiletries, hair dryer, and clock radio, and some rooms have a DVD player - the owners of Glangrwyney Court, Christina and Warwick Jackson have a small library of DVDs, including a choice for children. All the rooms have views over the gardens and parkland. There is a luxury suite in the Garden Courtyard which has a galleried double bedroom, en suite bathroom with bath and shower and also a beautiful sitting room and large full kitchen. It is possible for this to be self catering if requested. In addition there is one double room which is in the Garden Courtyard and which is suitable for those who cannot manage a room on the first floor. Both of these may be viewed by using the link to the Glangrwyney Court self-catering web site.

332

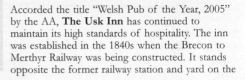

Station Road, Talybont-on-Usk, Brecon,
Powys LD3 7JE
☎ 01874 676251 Fax: 01874 676392
e-mail: stay@uskinn.co.uk
🌐 www.uskinn.co.uk

Accorded the title "Welsh Pub of the Year, 2005" by the AA, **The Usk Inn** has continued to maintain its high standards of hospitality. The inn was established in the 1840s when the Brecon to Merthyr Railway was being constructed. It stands opposite the former railway station and yard on the

edge of the village which itself lies within the Brecon Beacons National Park. Back in 1878, the inn's patrons must have felt in need of another drink when the "Wild Run" of that year spilled the locomotive *Hercules* onto Station Road!

The owners of the Usk Inn, Andrew and Jill Felix, took over here in February 2006 having previously owned the Aberthaw Hotel in Barry. They were dedicated to finding suitable premises in the area to realise their ambition of owning a quality hotel. The Usk currently has a 4-star

rating and they are both determined to retain this prestigious award.

They aim to exceed their guests' expectations, whether in the cosy bar with its armchairs, tub chairs and a sofa, as well as a rather large stack of box games or in the bistro-styled restaurant, which has earned a Rosette for its food, they still insist on using table linen and trendy china. The menu changes regularly according to availability of fresh produce, while the Specials Board features "Some things that never change". Andrew is the chef and specialises in fish dishes such as Cajun spiced Tuna steak with a lime and tomato salsa and served with a

timbale of couscous. The menu also offers a good choice of meat, poultry and, in season, game dishes such as Guinea Fowl wrapped with streaky bacon and presented on a bread and cranberry base served with a blackberry sauce. To complement your meal there's an excellent and extensive choice of wines or, if you prefer, there are 2 real ales on tap.

The bar, with its log fire provides a respite for weary walkers and cyclists and remains open throughout the day. In warmer months, there's plenty of seating in the lovely beer garden fringed by trees.

The inn also offers accommodation in 10 upstairs en suite rooms which have also been awarded 4 stars from the Welsh Tourism Board and the AA.

167 LAKESIDE RESTAURANT ¶¶

Llangorse, Brecon, Powys LD3 7TR
☎ 01874 658170

Llangorse Lake (Llyn Syfaddan) is the largest natural lake in South Wales, some 4 miles in circumference. Located close to the lake, off the B4560, the **Lakeside Restaurant** offers a good choice of wholesome and appetising home-made food. The restaurant has recently been refurbished to a very high standard and is very bright and airy. It seats up to 60 people but there's also seating for a further 40 outside. Bookings are only necessary for large parties. Choose your meal from either the printed menu or from the daily specials board

which might be offering dishes such as Thai Cod and Prawn Fishcakes or a Steak, Ale & Mushroom Suet Pudding. Local produce is used where possible. Lakeside Restaurant is open from Easter to the October school half-term. Daily opening times are from 9.30pm to 5pm on weekdays, and until 6pm at the weekends. During the summer holidays the hours are extended to 9.30pm, Thursday to Sunday. Last order 30 minutes before closing.

The restaurant was recently awarded a Welsh Food Hygiene Award by Powys Council.

169 LA TABERNA - CASA MIGUEL ¶¶

1 New Street, Aberystwyth SY23 2AT
☎ 01970 627677
e-mail: latabernacasamiguel@yahoo.co.uk

Lovers of authentic Spanish food can find the real thing at **La Taberna - Casa Miguel**, located in the heart of Aberystwyth. Owned and run by Miguel de la Rosa and his sons Dany and Miguel, this stylish taberna offers a terrific

choice of scrumptious tapas, paellas and house specialities such as the Fritura de Pescado (a fish medley marinated in lemon and deep fried). La Taberna is open from 6pm onwards, Monday to Saturday, all year round. It seats only 24 people so booking ahead is recommended at all times. Payment is by cash or cheque only.

170 ABERYSTWYTH CLIFF RAILWAY 🏛

Cliff Railway House, Cliff Terrace,
Aberystwyth, Ceredigion SY23 2DN
☎ 01970 617642 Fax: 01970 617642

Aberystwyth Cliff Railway, the only one in Wales, was opened in 1896 and rises 430 feet in its 778 feet of undulating track. It travels at a sedate four miles per hour, and passengers arriving at the summit enjoy superb views over the bay and, inland, to the Cambrian Mountains. The camera obscura is on the summit, along with a gift shop and a café serving afternoon teas and home-cooked snacks. The railway is managed as a charitable trust by Margaret Walters, who was once a driver on it. Trains run every few minutes from 10 to 5 mid-March to early November (10 to 6 in July and August).

168 THE WESTON VAULTS

Thespian Street, Aberystwyth SY23 2JW
☎ 01970 627609
e-mail: weston.vaults@btconnect.com

Just a short walk from the railway station, **The Weston Vaults** is one of the most popular public houses in Aberystwyth. It occupies a striking 3-storey Victorian building with lots of impressive stone decoration and its spacious interior has all the atmosphere you could hope for in a traditional hostelry. Mine hosts, Siân Elin and Phil, took over here in early 2005 and have made it a venue for customers of all ages. As you'd expect of a traditional inn, darts, pool and a juke box all add to the lively atmosphere. Bar food is available throughout the day and includes breakfasts, breakfast snacks, jacket potatoes, burgers, basket meals, sandwiches, home-made pies and other main dishes. Vegetarian alternatives are available and children have their own selection of dishes. On Sundays, succulent roasts are added to the regular menu.

Accommodation at the Weston Vaults comprises 6 upstairs rooms, all with showers. Guests stay on a room only basis but breakfast is available on request. All major credit cards are accepted and there is good disabled access to the bars but not to the rooms.

335

171 DEVIL'S BRIDGE FALLS

Devil's Bridge, Aberystwyth, Ceredigion
☎ 01970 890233

Take a walk along the Nature Trail and see the spectacular 300ft waterfalls and the view of the three bridges which span the breathtaking woodland gorge. The first bridge is reputed to have been built by the Devil but in reality it was built in the 11th century by the monks; the middle bridge was built in 1708, wider than the lower bridge, to take horse drawn vehicles; the top bridge was built in 1901 to cope with modern traffic.

Cross the humped bridge spanning over the Mynach river at the bottom of the waterfalls and begin to ascend the other side of the gorge. Go into Robbers Cave, an old hide-out place next to the waterfall. Alternatively, choose the easier, short walk to view the three bridges and the Devil's Punchbowl. Discover the legend, of how an old lady and her dog outwitted the Devil.

Allow at least half hour for the long walk, (but you can stay longer), 10 mins for the short walk and wear sensible shoes. Not suitable for elderly or disabled due to steps. Open all year.

172 THE GEORGE BORROW HOTEL

Ponterwyd, Aberystwyth, Ceredigion
☎ 01970 890230 Fax: 01970 890587
e-mail: g.borrow-hotel@btconnect.com
🌐 www.thegeorgeborrowhotel.co.uk

Surrounded by beautiful unspoilt countryside, **The George Borrow Hotel** is a characterful old hostelry dating back in parts to the early 1700s. In those days it was a popular watering hole for workers at the nearby silver mines. Today it's a friendly family-run inn with Karen and Rob Atkinson and their daughter Clare all involved in the enterprise. Clare is the accomplished cook, ably assisted by long-serving Anne, a local lady who has worked here for many years. Clare's outstanding food is available from 9am, for breakfast, right through the day until 9pm. Her enticing menu includes old favourites such as grills, battered cod and sausage & mash, along with dishes such as the vegetarian lasagne and an avocado, mozzarella, tomato and basil tart. Drinks available

include 2 real ales, Brains SA and a guest ale. To the rear of the hotel is a spacious beer garden with lovely country views. Friday evening is Bingo night and there's occasional live entertainment. The hotel also offers comfortable accommodation in 9 attractively furnished and decorated en suite rooms. All major credit cards are accepted and there's good disabled access to the bar and restaurant.

336

Goginan, Aberystwyth SY23 3NT
☎ 01970 880650

Located in the village of Goginan, a few miles east of Aberystwyth, **The Druid Inn** enjoys some spectacular views of the unspoilt countryside of the Vale of Rhydol. Mine hosts and owners, Lewis and Lorraine, took over here in spring of 2007 although Lewis had worked here for 5 years before that.

The inn is well known for its excellent food which is served every day from noon until 9.30pm. The extensive menu includes old favourites such as Steak, Ale & Mushroom Pie, or Cod in a real Best Bitter Batter, along with a good choice of home-made pies - these are particularly popular - curries, grills based on Welsh Black beef, and pasta dishes. Vegetarians are well catered for with a choice that includes a potato, cheese and broccoli bake, and a vegetable lasagne. For lighter appetites, there's a selection of basket meals. On Sundays, a traditional roast lunch is served from noon until 3.30pm when the regular menu is again available. Booking is strongly recommended at weekends.

The well-stocked bar provides a comprehensive choice that includes 3 real ales - Banks Bitter, Butty Bach and a guest ale. For additional entertainment, the inn has a separate pool room. Payment at the Druid Inn is by cash or cheque only; there's good disabled access throughout and the inn has its own off road parking.

174 BLACK LION HOTEL

Village Green, Talybont,
Ceredigion SY24 5ER
☎ 01970 832335 Fax: 01970 832335
⊕ www.theblacklionhoteltalybont.co.uk

The Black Lion Hotel stands at the heart of Talybont, facing the village green. It's a fine old building, both inside and out, and the atmosphere is friendly and welcoming. Mine hosts at the Black Lion, Mark and Vicky Joseph, are a young and enthusiastic couple who have the made the hotel a popular venue for locals and visitors alike since they arrived here in the summer of 2007. The hotel is particularly noted for its good food which is served every lunchtime (noon until 2pm) and evening (5pm to closing time). The extensive menu ranges from old favourites like the home-made Steak & Ale Pie to meat dishes made with meat supplied fresh by the local butcher. Also on offer are fish, poultry and salad

dishes, along with a range of curries. Vegetarians have their own menu that includes a home-made Spicy Vegetable Lasagne, and there's also a separate children's menu. Beverages on offer include up to 3 real ales with Hancocks HB as the regular brew. The hotel also has accommodation available in 6 comfortable upstairs en suite rooms. Children are welcome and all major credit cards are accepted.

176 YNYS-HIR RSPB NATURE RESERVE

Derwenlas, Machynlleth,
Powys SY20 8SR
☎ 01654 781265
⊕ www.rspb.org.uk

Ynys-hir reserve mixes the delights of Welsh oak woodland with wet grassland and estuarine salt marshes, stretching along the south side of the magnificent Dyfi estuary in Mid Wales.

A network of short and long nature trails allows you to explore the reserve at your own pace. Spring is a wonderful time to visit the woodland when it is full of birdsong and spring flowers. The full range of typical welsh birds are here – pied flycatchers, redstarts and red kites. Grey herons and little egrets nest in the treetops. Summer brings family flocks of waders, such as lapwings and redshanks, and some very special dragonflies and butterflies.

However, the estuary is at its best for birds in the autumn and winter, when large numbers of ducks and geese feed on the salt marshes and farmland. Rare Greenland white-fronted geese share the marshes with shelducks, pintails and wigeons. Birds of prey are regular too. All can be seen from the shelter of observation hides.

The small visitor centre offers a modest range of sales goods and refreshments. Staff are always happy to provide information and present a series of guided walks all year round.

Due to the hilly terrain, this reserve is not suitable for visitors with restricted mobility. After rain, and particularly during winter, the paths are very muddy. Stout and waterproof footwear is recommended.

175 WHITE LION HOTEL

Talybont Aberystwyth,
Ceredigion SY24 5ER
☎ 01970 832245   Fax: 01970 832658
e-mail: maureen.bumford@btconnect.com
🌐 www.whiteliontalybont.co.uk

With speciality dishes such as Cardigan Bay fresh dressed crab, lobster and trout caught by local fishermen featuring on the menu, it's no wonder that the **White Lion Hotel** in Talybont is a favourite with discerning diners. It's renowned not just for seafood – other popular dishes include home-made chicken curry, locally made faggots, steaks and home-made vegetable curry. All the ingredients are sourced within Wales wherever possible. Such is the fame of the White Lion's cuisine that booking ahead is strongly

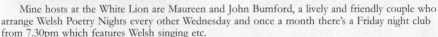

recommended at all times. Food is served every lunchtime from noon until 3pm, and every evening from 6pm to 9pm. Thursday evening is Curry Night when customers can get a curry and a pint for just £6. At Sunday lunchtime a roast is added to the menu.

Devotees of real ales will be pleased to find a choice of 3 brews on tap at the White Lion – Banks Original, Banks Bitter and a rotating guest ale. The hotel has featured in the *Good Beer Guide* for the past 5 years in a row. In good weather you can enjoy your pint either in the spacious beer garden with its children's play area, or a picnic tables to the front of the hotel where you can watch the village life pass by.

Mine hosts at the White Lion are Maureen and John Bumford, a lively and friendly couple who arrange Welsh Poetry Nights every other Wednesday and once a month there's a Friday night club from 7.30pm which features Welsh singing etc.

The hotel, which dates back to the 1800s, also offers comfortable accommodation in 4 attractively furnished and decorated rooms, all of which have en suite facilities. Children are welcome; all major credit cards are accepted and the hotel has its own off road parking.

Church Street, New Quay,
Ceredigion SA45 9NT
☎ 01545 560881 Fax: 01545 560897

The Dolau Inn occupies a superb position less than a hundred yards from the sea shore of this popular resort. The friendly Inn has already proved very popular with visitors and locals alike. It has a terrace to the front which is a real sun trap with picnic tables, colourful parasols – and a fantastic view of the sea. To the rear of the premises is another charming and spacious terrace, this time with a view of cliffs.

The building dates back to the early 1800s, and is run by the mother and son team of Gill and Andrew Thomas who took over here in the spring of 2007 and carried out a major refurbishment which has proved very popular. Due to Gill and Andrews short time here the food menu is currently limited to bar snacks such as freshly made sandwiches, panninis etc, with home made soups and stews available in the winter months. As time goes by, Gill and Andrew intend to extend the menu with more main meals becoming available. Meanwhile, if you just want a tea or coffee, you will still be very welcome. For real ale devotees, the bar has 2 real ales on tap with Hancocks as the regular brew plus a rotating guest ale. Gill and Andrew also have plans to host occasional entertainment events here, please call if you wish to find out more. The Dolau is open all day, everyday throughout the summer months which means you can enjoy the view that little bit more.

179 THE HUNGRY TROUT

2 South John Street, New Quay,
Ceredigion SA45 9NG
☎ 01545 560680
e-mail: thehungrytrout@hotmail.co.uk
🌐 www.thehungrytrout.co.uk

The Hungry Trout enjoys a superb location overlooking Cardigan Bay from which some of the ingredients will have been harvested for chef/ patron Tim Dutnells's superb fish dishes – New Quay Seabass grilled with soy sauce over stir fried pakchoi, perhaps, or the Cardigan Bay Crab, sweetbell pepper and cream cheese tart with a tomato and chilli salsa. Other ingredients, such as the grilled Cardiganshire Rib Eye Steak Bretonne won't have travelled much farther. Fusing creativity, classical simplicity and natural contemporary ingredients, Tim ensures that all fish is dolphin-friendly and cooked fresh to order. Whether your preference be shellfish, lobster, bass, tuna, Dover sole or a traditional meat dish, Tim endeavours to cater to all tastes, including several vegetarian options – "and if it's not on our extensive menu, we'll order it in" says Tim.

He also takes pride in the extensive list of homemade desserts and the Welsh cheese selection The restaurant sits up to 40 people, and features a fully licensed bar offering an extensive wine list with a large selection of brandies, liqueurs and ports. Weather permitting, you can dine outside while watching the dolphins and seals. As well as the à la carte menu, the restaurant offers a traditional Sunday roast, breakfast and lunch menu options. In-house functions for up to 40 people can be catered for, and outdoor catering is also available.

If you are planning to stay in this popular resort, the Hungry Trout has a guest house, situated above the seafood restaurant, which offers visitors two spacious, well-furnished double rooms, with impressive sea views – comfortable, quiet lodgings at reasonable rates. Each room has a sizeable double bed, wardrobe, writing desk, two chairs, a TV, coffee and tea making facilities, and a washbasin. The larger bedroom has an en-suite bathroom (with floor space to sleep two people if so required). A full traditional Welsh breakfast (with a vegetarian option) is also served at the restaurant and included in the tariff. The rooms are only yards from the beach, and all local amenities and attractions are within a 5-10 minute walk. The rest of West/Mid Wales is easily accessible, with Cardigan, Lampeter, Llandysul and Aberystwyth, all typically accessible within a 30-40 minute drive through the beautiful Welsh countryside.

341

178 BLACK LION HOTEL

Glanmor Terrace, New Quay,
Ceredigion SA45 9PT
☎ 01545 560209 Fax: 01545 560585
e-mail: blacklionnewquay@btconnect.com
⊕ www.blacklionnewquay.co.uk

The Black Lion Hotel enjoys superb views overlooking beautiful Cardigan Bay. On clear days Snowdonia is visible and the bottle-nose dolphins can regularly be seen swimming and playing in the bay. The main bar dates back to the late 17th Century, with the hotel added in the early 19th Century, at the same time and built of the same stone as the quay of New Quay. Within the bar is three seperate areas. You can sit overlooking the bay in the small room known as 'Captain Cat's Lookout', soak up the atmosphere in the main bar area or make use of the dining area and 'Dylan's' beyond. There is also a spacious beer garden with children's play area and stunning sea views. Part of the hotel houses a collection of items relating to the great poet Dylan Thomas, who spent much of his time at the Black Lion whilst he was living in New Quay. The hotel rooms are all larger than the average hotel room, most have en-suite facilities and are comfortably furnished. All are equipped with TVs and tea/coffee making facilities and half of the rooms have sea views.

180 FRIENDS COFFEE SHOP

5 Alban Square, Aberaeron,
Ceredigion SA46 0AD
☎ 01545 571122

Friends by name and friendly and welcoming by nature, **Friends Coffee Shop** is a bright and cheerful place occupying the former premises of Aberaeron's Post Office. Owners Diana and Clive, who opened the shop in the summer of 2005 and now have an established clientele for their wholesome menu of salads, tasty filled baguettes and delicatessen items which are also available to take away. Friends is open from 8pm to 6pm, (5pm in summer)every day except Sundays off season. Payment is by cash or cheque only.

HIDDEN PLACES GUIDES

Explore Britain and Ireland with *Hidden Places* guides - a fascinating series of national and local travel guides.

Packed with easy to read information on hundreds of places of interest as well as places to stay, eat and drink.

Available from both high street and internet booksellers

For more information on the full range of *Hidden Places* guides and other titles published by Travel Publishing visit our website on

www.travelpublishing.co.uk
or ask for our leaflet by phoning
01752 276660 or emailing
info@travelpublishing.co.uk

Cross Inn, Llanon, Ceredigion SY23 5NB
☎ 01974 272644
🌐 www.rhos-yr-hafod-inn.co.uk

A delightful village inn which in parts dates back to the early 1800s, **Rhos yr Hafod Inn** is a Free House owned and run by Stephen and Nicola Haines who arrived here at the beginning of 2007. Nicola is a superb cook whose menu offers an enticing choice of dishes which are based on locally sourced ingredients, including organic produce. So you may well find an organic pumpkin soup amongst the starters, and a 12oz horseshoe

gammon steak with chips and a free range egg as a main course. Food is served from 6pm, Tuesday to Sunday, and a Sunday lunch is available from noon until 2pm. Such is the popularity of Nicola's cooking that booking is strongly recommended for Sunday lunch and weekend evenings. The well-stocked bar offers a comprehensive range of beverages including up to 3 real ales with Young's Bitter as the regular brew. Well behaved children are welcome; payment is by cash or cheque only; the inn has good disabled access throughout and there's an attractive beer garden to the rear. There is also off road parking.

High Street, Lampeter,
Ceredigion SA48 7BG
☎ 01570 422172 Fax: 01570 421490
e-mail: blacklion2@sabrain.com

A 17th century former coaching inn, the **Black Lion Hotel** is noted for its excellent food and well-kept brews, including 3 real ales from Brains. The extensive menu offers a good choice of pub favourites such as a grilled cheese and bacon burger, as well as some fantastic steaks made using only the finest quality Welsh beef, salads, pasta and fish dishes. Booking is essential at weekends and for Sunday lunch. The hotel also has 18 guest bedrooms, including 2 family rooms, all tastefully furnished and decorated, and all with en suite facilities.

183 THE CASTLE HOTEL

High Street, Lampeter,
Ceredigion SA48 7BG
☎ 01570 422554

Located in the heart of Lampeter, **The Castle Hotel** is very popular with both locals and visitors alike and there always seems to be a buzz around the place no matter what time of year it is.

In the summer, the exterior of the hotel is decked with a magnificent floral display – the hotel has won the Lampeter in Bloom contest in 2004, 2005 and 2006. It has also won a number of awards from the brewery for it's floral exterior which is always appreciated by passer-by's.

Inside there's a welcoming traditional bar with a large screen TV for Sky Sports which makes it a very popular venue for sports fans. Owners John and Wendy Nicholas have more than 16 years experience in the hotel business and it shows in the expert service and hospitality they and their staff offer.

The hotel's facilities are superb throughout and a major attraction is the separate restaurant serving Wendy's delicious home cooking based on fresh, locally sourced ingredients. Her menu includes a wonderful Steak & Ale Pie, along with seafood dishes, grills, curries, vegetarian dishes and some chef's specials which features a memorable Marinated Breast of Chicken. In addition to your main course there is also a generous choice of tempting side orders from garlic mushrooms to pepper sauce. To accompany your meal there's a selection of well-kept real ales with Brains and Buckley's as the regular brews. If you are staying in the area, the hotel has 9 comfortable guest bedrooms, all with en suite facilities and attractively furnished and decorated. There is an off road car park for visitors and guests. The hotel accepts all major credit cards apart from American Express.

Llangybi, Lampeter, Ceredigion
☎ 01570 493226
e-mail: derekardwyn@ aol.com

A superb country mansion standing in 5 acres of immaculate gardens, **Ardwyn Country House** offers the very best in upmarket bed & breakfast accommodation. The beautiful house was built on a grand scale in 1895 and is now the home of Denise and Derek Manning who have lived here since 2003 and have been welcoming bed & breakfast guests since 2004. The accommodation, which has been awarded a 4-star rating by the Welsh Tourist Board, comprises of 2 double rooms of outstanding quality with furniture, fittings and fixtures all of the highest standard making your stay that extra bit special. Both rooms have their own luxury private bathrooms.

A sumptuous breakfast with silver service is included in the tariff and is served in the elegant dining room overlooking the well kept garden. A crisp white tablecloth drapes the table, Royal Doulton china is used and the menu offers an extensive choice that includes fresh fruit, a Continental breakfast of croissants, cold meat, cheese and preserves, or a pair of succulent kippers. Breakfast is normally served between 8am and 9.30am unless by special arrangement, and may be served outside during the summer if requested. Packed lunches are also available.

If you love to play golf then staying here definately has an advantage. Guests staying at Ardwyn can make use of a special green fee arrangement with the Cilgwyn Golf Club, a pretty 9-hole course that is just a mile away. This special offer includes unlimited use of the golf course and one nights stay for only £50 per person per night. Also features in www.hotelsneargolfcourses.com.

Ffair Rhos, Ystrad Meurig,
Ceredigion SY25 6BP
☎ 01974 831608
🔲 www.teifiinn.co.uk

The Teifi Inn is an appealing old hostelry with a history going back to the 12th century when it was used as a place of refreshment for passing monks. The inn is surrounded by outstanding natural beauty with views over Pontrhydfendigaid and

across the hills and mountains towards Tregaron. Inside, the Teifi Inn is spacious and attractive with a large stone-built open fire and exposed beamwork. There is ample comfortable seating and the well proportioned bar area is always accessible. Friendly staff complement the surroundings and owners Catrin and Mike Arnopp endeavour to make customers old and new feel really welcome.

They took over here in the summer of 2007 and although Mike has been a chef for more than 20 years, this is their first venture together running their own business.

They are very proud of the food they serve here. All products are prepared daily using only the finest and freshest ingredients. Home-made Teifi Inn Fishcakes made with locally caught fish, a home-made soup of the day and dishes such as Oven Baked Field Mushrooms are amongst the appetising starters. For the main courses, top quality Welsh ingredients feature in dishes such as the home-made Welsh Liver Faggots, Welsh Black Beef Steaks, and Ceredigion Welsh Shoulder of Lamb Kebabs. Other dishes include a whole baby chargrilled chicken, fillets of local rainbow trout and a vegetarian roasted vegetable and penne pasta. To accompany your meal, there's a comprehensive selection of beverages that includes 2 real ales. During the summer, food is served from noon until 2pm, and from 6pm to 9pm, Wednesday to Saturday, and from noon until 2pm. Out of season, food is served from 6pm to 9pm, Wednesday to Saturday, plus Saturday and Sunday roast lunch from noon until 2pm. Booking is strongly recommended at all times. Sunday evening is Curry Night only, while on Wednesday evenings there's a special offer of 2 main meals for just £10.

The Teifi Inn is closed on Tuesdays but open every other lunchtime and evening, and during the peak summer period is open all day, Wednesday to Sunday. Children are welcome; all major credit cards are accepted; there's good disabled access throughout and ample off road parking.

Pontrhydfendigaid, Ystrad Meurig,
Ceredigion SY25 6BH
☎ 01974 831232
e-mail: kathsredlion@hotmail.com
⊕ www.redlionbont.co.uk

A former coaching inn dating back to the
mid-1800s, **The Red Lion Hotel** is a fine
old hostelry in the village of
Pontrhydfendigaid (Bridge near the ford of
the Blessed
Virgin). Mine host
at this free house
is Kath Paterson
who took over in
2003. Her inn
offers a good
selection of
home-made
dishes, including
the speciality of the house, Carbonara, and
some wonderful home-made desserts. The
well-stocked bar offers a rotating real ale and
a good selection of draught keg ales. The Red
Lion also offers accommodation in 4 double
en suite rooms. To the rear of the hotel is a
delightful beer garden.

HIDDEN PLACES GUIDES

Explore Britain and Ireland with
Hidden Places guides - a fascinating
series of national and local travel
guides.

Packed with easy to read information
on hundreds of places of interest as
well as places to stay, eat and drink.

Available from both high street and
internet booksellers

For more information on the full range
of *Hidden Places* guides and other
titles published by Travel Publishing
visit our website on

www.travelpublishing.co.uk
or ask for our leaflet by phoning
01752 276660 or emailing
info@travelpublishing.co.uk

Llangeitho, Tregaron, Ceredigion SY25 6TW
☎ 01974 821244
e-mail: ben3horseshoe@aol.com
⊕ www.3horseshoe.net

A cosy traditional hostelry dating back to the
1700s, the **Three Horse Shoe Inn** is very
much the hub of village life in Llangeitho and
is frequented by some wonderful characters.
The pub also has a reputation for good food
and quality beer that draws in locals from
outlying villages as well as holiday-makers.
Owned and run by Jane and Mike Williams
and

their son Jonathan, the pub has 1 or 2 real ales on tap, both
usually coming from Felinfoel Brewery. The excellent food
is sourced locally wherever possible and includes many
home-made dishes. The home-made Beef & Ale Pie is
particularly popular, as is the hearty Sunday roast lunch.
Food is served from 6.00pm to 9-ish, Monday to Saturday,
and from noon until 2pm on Sunday. Payment is by cash or
cheque only. The pub also has its own self-catering
accommodation that sleeps 3-4. The owners are happy to
accommodate pets by prior arrangement and provide bed
linen, towels etc at no extra charge.

347

188 THE NEW INN

Llandewi-Brefi, Tregaron,
Ceredigion SY25 6RS
☎ 01974 298452
e-mail: newinn1@hotmail.com

A fine old traditional inn dating back to the late 1890s, **The New Inn** is a delightful and welcoming hostelry popular with locals and visitors alike. It provides the social centre of this village which acquired national fame as the home of Daffyd, "the only gay in the village", in the TV comedy series *Little Britain*. A major attraction at the New Inn is the excellent home cooking on offer with home-made faggots and curries a speciality. Food is served throughout the day until 9pm and 95% of the ingredients used here are sourced locally. On Sundays between noon and 2pm a traditional roast is served – this is very popular so it is advisable to book ahead. The well-stocked bar provides a wide choice of beverages including one rotating guest real ale. The inn

also offers accommodation all year round with a choice of 2 doubles and 2 singles. The inn is open all day, every day except for Mondays unless it is a Bank Holiday. Children are welcome; there's good disabled access to the bar areas, and the pub has its own off road parking.

Looking for:
- *Places to Visit?*
- *Places to Stay?*
- *Places to Eat & Drink?*
- *Places to Shop?*

COUNTRY LIVING MAGAZINE RURAL GUIDES
HIDDEN INNS
HIDDEN PLACES
COUNTRY Pubs & Inns
off the motorway 3rd edition

www.travelpublishing.co.uk

190 THE GWARCEFEL ARMS

Prengwyn, Llandysul, Ceredigion SA44 4LU
☎ 01559 362720 Fax: 01559 362339
e-mail: gwarcefelarms@aol.com
🌐 www.gwarcefelarms.co.uk

A Free House, **The Gwarcefel Arms** is a friendly and welcoming village inn noted for its real ales – 2 or 3 of them on a rotating basis - and for its good food. The menu offers a good choice of main courses such as steaks, pork, lamb, fish and chicken dishes, as well as home-made Beef Lasagne, Chilli Con Carne and Chicken Balti. Also available are salads, ploughmans, vegetarian and children's meals. In addition to the regular menu, the Chef's Specials are displayed daily on the boards. The home-made desserts are particularly enticing. Food is served every lunchtime and evening.

Ffostrasol, Llandysul, Ceredigion SA44 4SY
☎ 01239 851348

A former coaching inn, **Tafarn Ffostrasol Arms** is owned and run by the brother and sister team of Arthur and Betty Davies. Arthur, a local farmer who has been farming in this area since 1960, has had the property since 1997 and has recently carried out a major makeover whilst still keeping the old hostelry's charm and character. Good food is a priority here and the inn offers a wide choice with something for every palate to enjoy. Amongst the starters you will find a fresh soup of the day, spicy cheese-filled jalapeno served with

cucumber and mint dip, and goat's cheese croquets with apple sauce. Main meals range from old favourites such as home-made Beef & Ale Pie and battered cod, to grills – including a mighty 16oz T-Bone Steak – to chicken, pork, duck and fish dishes, all based on local produce wherever possible. The menu also lists vegetarian options and a children's menu is available.

Food is served from 11.30am to 2.30pm, and from 5.30pm to 9pm, every day. On Sunday lunchtimes Betty takes over the kitchen to cook her famous Sunday roasts – booking ahead is essential. The well-stocked

bar offers a wide choice of beverages, including 2 real ales – Hancocks HB and Brains SA. In good weather, customers can enjoy their drinks in the beer garden. The inn also offers accommodation in the form of 2 self-contained flats located above the main premises. These are available all year round; children are welcome and there's no minimum night stay. This friendly Inn also caters for functions, from day trips to weddings, please call for more details.

349

191 CASTLE CAFÉ & CELLAR BAR

25-26 Quay Street, Cardigan SA43 1HU
☎ 01239 621621 Fax: 01239 621621
e-mail: omgreenhalgh@hotmail.com
🌐 www.middleearthenterprises.co.uk

Located in a quiet lane off Cardigan's main shopping street, the **Castle Café & Cellar Bar** occupies a sturdy stone building more than 200 years old that stands close to the ruins of Cardigan Castle. Owned and run by April and Stephen

Greenhalgh, the café has a cosy cottage-style ambience and offers an enticing menu of home-booked dishes which are based as far as possible on local produce.

One of the most popular dishes – a notable winter warmer but served throughout the year – is cawl, a classic Welsh meat and vegetable stew. But there are plenty of other choices, both on the printed menu and amongst the daily specials. The café is licensed and all major credit cards apart from Diners are accepted. The café is on two floors: upstairs there's seating for 36 in a delightfully atmospheric place with bare stone walls and dark wooden furniture. The fare served here is uncomplicated but hearty food (all prepared on the premises) and drinks, all served by staff who are enthusiastic, eager to please,

friendly and efficient. There is a fixed menu each day that takes advantage of wholesome, fresh local produce wherever possible. There is always a vegetarian option and by prior arrangement, a vegan meal can also be made available.

Downstairs, the Cellar Bar can accommodate up to 60 and it's here that live music is performed five nights a week from 8pm. The music ranges from rock to jazz, from acoustic to folk, from soul to blues. At least four nights a week customers can take part in events such as poetry nights and quizzes. The entry charge of £5 for downstairs includes a plate of food and entry into a raffle.

The café is open from 8.30am each day, until midnight each day except Wednesday when it closes at 4pm, and Sunday when it closes at 3pm. April and Stephen also own Gandalf's Garden just across the road which sells a fascinating variety of unusual gifts and also has an art gallery. They also own nearby Middle Earth which sells everything from earthy fabrics and lovely silks to quirky jewellery, alternative products and ornaments.

Poppit Sands, St Dogmaels,
Pembrokeshire SA43 3LN
☎ 01239 612085
e-mail: webleyhotel@btconnect.com
🌐 www.webleyhotel.com

Croeso is a big word in Wales, in every true sense and here at the **Webley Waterfront Hotel** you are assured of a big warm welcome. Enjoying spectacular views over the River Teifi and out across Poppit Sands Beach and Cardigan Bay beyond the location is inspirational. Owners Sandra

and Simon are welcoming hosts and will endeavour to meet your every request and make your stay truly memorable.

Rooms are comfortably furnished and offer complimentary tea and coffee making facilities and are equipped with new crystal clear LCD TVs with satellite quality reception but it is the beauty and tranquility of the surrounding area that will captivate you in this western outpost of Welsh Wales where the language and culture of 1600 year has shaped the landscape and fascinated visitors as an ancient culture steps forward into a contemporary world.

But the Webley is much, much more... Locally acquiring a reputation for fine dining at affordable prices you will be impressed by the menu that offers a wonderful seasonal mix of fresh seafood, specialities include line caught Cardigan Bay Sea Bass, Dressed Crab or Lobster, Teifi Sewin and fresh meat supplied from local farm including lamb and beef steaks, cheeses (caws) from Cenarth and organic ice cream from Mary's farmhouse, Crymych. The true taste of Wales is reflected in simply prepared dishes that are full of flavour and wholesome goodness.

Meals can be enjoyed in the friendly locals bar with a relaxing pint of real welsh ale or outside in our wonderful beer garden overlooking the waters edge, an area rich in wildlife including numerous sea and land birds and if you are very lucky you may even catch sight of an otter. There is also available a large function room and a smaller lounge where private parties can be arranged. Perfect for special interest groups including golf and walking groups who may consider booking a couple of nights at the Webley and arrange their activities using the hotel as a base.

The Pembrokeshire Coast National Park coastal trail starts just half a mile from the Webley, but there is much more to explore from the Preseli Mountains to the wooded Dyffryn Teifi, Historic Castles, Aberteifi (Cardigan) market town and the old abbey and mill in Llandudoch (St Dogmaels) to mention a few. Also available is a newly refurbished luxurious appointed self-catering appartment, with superb views across the river, a family apartment and 8 berth caravan adjoining the Webley - simply perfect for longer stays and within walking distance of the beach and the local bus that stops right outside.

Cymru yr awyr agored - naws am le - gwlad hyfryd a hynafol - Cymru ein cartref Croeso i bawb.

192 THE HIGHBURY GUEST HOUSE & RESTAURANT

Pendre, Cardigan, Ceredigion SA43 1JU
☎ 01239 613403

The **Highbury Guest House & Restaurant** occupies a splendid late-Victorian villa of 1898 which has been extended by means of a super 3-bayed conservatory overlooking the garden. Highbury is the home of local farmers Angela and Jimmy Wilson who have been welcoming guests here since the spring of 2006. The 3-star accommodation comprises 11 comfortable

rooms, most of them with en suite facilities. Angela is an accomplished cook and the licensed restaurant here offers an appetising selection of dishes based on locally sourced ingredients. The restaurant is open from 7pm to 9pm, Tuesday, Wednesday, Friday and Saturday, and for Sunday lunch.

195 EMLYN CAFÉ

Tanygroes, Cardigan, Ceredigion SA43 2JE
☎ 01239 810143

Family-run by the Evans family, the **Emlyn Café** was actually built by them in the early 1980s. It is located on the A487 and is popular with both locals and passing trade. The menu offers a wide choice starting with a range of breakfasts and continuing with lunches and light bites such as jacket potatoes. Children and vegetarians have their own menus. The Evans family grow their

own vegetables and use local eggs in their dishes. Food is served from 9am to 2.30pm, daily, and from 6pm to 9pm on Friday and Saturday evenings. The café is licensed and is happy to cater for functions.

194 CARTWS CAFÉ

c/o Llanborth Farm, Penbryn Beach, Sarnau, Ceredigion SA44 6QL
☎ 01239 810389
🌐 www.cartwscafe.co.uk

The **Cartws Café** occupies a charming stone building located on land owned by the National Trust which is also a site of special scientific interest and part of the Ceredigion Heritage Coast.
Throughout the summer the café is open every day from 10am until dusk, and offers an extensive selection of meals ranging

from home-made soup of the day, through ploughman's, dressed crab, sandwiches and filled rolls, to delicious home-made cakes. From 7pm the café offers a separate evening menu with dishes such as owner Helen Jones's renowned Thai salmon fishcakes. To find Cartws Café follow the signs off the A487 for Penbryn Beach and you can't miss it. The café is open October 11am - 3pm and Nov & Dec on weekends only.

Llangrannog, Ceredigion SA44 6SL
☎ 01239 654423

Beautifully sited close to the beach and looking out across Cardigan Bay, **The Ship Inn** is located in the picturesque village of Llangrannog, generally regarded as the most appealing village on the Ceredigion coast. It has winding lanes leading to a small beach which is very popular in fine weather.

The inn is a large and pristine pub built of local stone and slate with creamy colour-washed walls. With its wealth of old-world character a charm, the inn provides a welcoming place to enjoy a relaxed drink and to sample the appetising fare produced by chef/patrons Gary and Nicola Ramshaw. Their extensive menu is mouth-watering just to read. Amongst the starters you'll find a home-made traditional Welsh Cawl served with Caerphilly cheese and crusty bread, home-made soup of the day and a tasty Chicken & Sherry Pâté. Main meal possibilities present a difficult choice. Is it to be the home-made ham  & mushroom savoury pancake, the salmon in a home-made lemon dill and prawn sauce, or the home-made Welsh Black Beef curry. If you are looking for something lighter, there's a wide choice of baguettes, jacket potatoes and salads. Vegetarians are well-provided for with a selection of dishes that includes a Stilton & Vegetable Crumble, Vegetable Thai Curry and Three Bean Smokey Chilli. Children have their own mini-menu with choices such as Veggie Teddies, Texas Beefburger and Fish Fingers. Round off your meal with one of the heavenly desserts – 'Lemmony Nice and Moussey', Chocolate Sponge Pudding or a calorie count-busting Black Forest Dream Delight.

Food is served from noon until 2.30pm, and from 6pm to 9pm, every day. On Sundays, there's a choice of five different roasts with all the trimmings for a splendid Sunday lunch. During the summer months, it is wise to book at all times.

To accompany your meal, the bar is well-stocked with a comprehensive range of beverages including 2 real ales – Cwru Bitter as the regular brew plus a rotating ale. Children are welcome at the inn, and all major credit cards are accepted apart from American Express. The Ship has good disabled access and its own off road parking.

353

197 CASTELL MALGWYN HOTEL

Llechryd, Cardigan, Ceredigion SA43 2QA
☎ 01239 682382
e-mail: reception@malgwyn.co.uk
🌐 www.castellmalgwyn.co.uk

Dating back to 1795, the Castell Malgwyn Hotel is a classic Georgian mansion which was built by Sir Benjamin Hammet as his private residence. He loved it so much he declined the honour of becoming Lord Mayor of London so that he could remain at his beloved mansion house. He was fined £1000 for the privilege!

Located in the beautiful Teifi valley, the hotel stands in an 8 acre estate that includes glorious woodland and nearly a mile of private fishing along the Teifi which is renowned for its sea trout and salmon – all of this is at the disposal of the hotel's guests. They can also wander through the

grounds which were once tended by 40 gardeners, or play croquet on the full-size lawn. The hotel itself still retains much of its original Georgian charm and architectural features. Guests can dine in "Lily's", the hotel's renowned restaurant, and savour the local and international first class cuisine prepared by the chef from fresh local produce. And, perhaps, enjoy a fine wine from the carefully selected wine list. Afterwards, relax in the Lounge or Library Bar before mounting the original Georgian staircase to one of the premier en suite rooms, each of which is tastefully decorated in individual styles.

198 PENLLWYNDU INN

Llangoedmor, nr Cardigan SA43 2LY
☎ 01239 682533

Mine host at the **Penllwyndu Inn**, Ryan Williams, knows his premises better than most landlords as it was his first home with his wife Pat – it only became an inn in 1985. Now well-established, the inn serves a selection of real ales – Buckleys Best and a rotating guest brew – keg ales, bitters, cider and stout. Food is always available during opening hours until 9.30pm, with home-made dishes a speciality – lasagne, cottage pie, chilli, soups and so on. The restaurant to the rear seats 30, or you can eat in the bar area and, weather permitting in the secluded beer garden. Booking is strongly recommended for Friday and Saturday evenings. Children are welcome; there's good disabled access, and all major credit cards are accepted.

Windy Hall, Fishguard,
Pembrokeshire SA65 9DP
☎ 01348 872777 Fax: 01348 875630
e-mail: info@tara-hotel.co.uk
🌐 www.tara-hotel.co.uk

Located close to the Stena Ferry Port (Gateway to Southern Ireland) and the Pembrokeshire National Coastal Path, **The Tara Hotel and Restaurant** is a family-run business with Steve and Pam Fensome and their son Jamie all involved in the enterprise.

The building itself dates back to Victorian times and retains some charming features such as the wonderful slate fireplace in the bar area – really snug in the winter months. The whole of the open plan restaurant, bar and lounge area has been designed to create a delightful *'homely'* atmosphere. The restaurant menu is a showcase for traditional Welsh and British recipes, with some Irish influences as well. So do look out for the authentic Welsh Rarebit which contains Welsh beer; the Cawl Abergwaun – the classic beef stew of Wales; the Fish of the Day dish, and the Glamorgan Vegetarian Sausages. Cooks Pam and Jamie endeavour to source their ingredients from local suppliers and producers wherever possible.

The 3-star accommodation at The Tara comprises 7 guest bedrooms, all en-suite and equipped with colour television and hospitality tray. They include two family rooms, the largest of which has commanding views over the bay and ferry port. The hotel welcomes dogs, and there's a private car park.

Market Square, Fishguard,
Pembrokeshire SA65 9HA
☎ 01348 872514
e-mail: dragondai@btinternet.com

Inscribed on the lintel above the entrance to the **Royal Oak Inn** in Fishguard are the words: "Last invasion of Britain Peace Treaty was signed here in 1797". For most of us, the Battle of Hastings in 1066 was the last invasion but, to be precise, it was the last *successful* incursion. The events at Fishguard in 1797 are generally ignored by the history books but they provided the people of west Wales with an exciting few days. A motley force of French troops had been sent by the revolutionary government in Paris in the expectation that the poor country people of Britain would rally to the support of their French liberators. The invasion force of some 1400 troops landed at Llanwnda on February 23rd but the ill-disciplined troops preferred looting to fighting and within two days the invasion had collapsed. The French surrendered to the local militia led by Lord Cawdor and a peace treaty was signed at the Royal Oak on a table that is still on view in the lower restaurant of the pub. A tapestry depicting the events was made to commemorate the bi-centenary in 1997 and can be seen in the town's Visitors Centre.

Today, mine hosts at this historic old inn are Dai and Janet Crowther who arrived here in 2004. Dai is a real ale enthusiast and introduced them to the pub. There are always 3 brews on tap, the Rev James as the regular plus 2 rotating guest ales.

In the first two years after introducing them to the pub, Dai has offered more than 120 different real ales to his customers. Over the May Bank Holiday, the pub hosts a Beer Festival with more than 18 real ales to sample. Over the same period, a Folk Festival is also based here. Dai's wife, Janet, is in charge of the kitchen, aided through the summer months by a chef. Her extensive menu offers a wide choice of dishes based on locally sourced ingredients. There's a particularly good selection of vegetarian options, including The Landlord's Favourite Home-made Vegetable Pie comprising seasonal vegetables cooked in a creamy sauce and with a flaky pastry top. Food is served from noon until 2 pm, and from 6pm to 9pm, and can be enjoyed throughout the pub or in the charming beer garden at the rear. To accompany your meal, as well as the real ales, there's a short but well-chosen wine list.

201 SALUTATION INN

Felindre Farchog, nr Newport, Crymych,
Pembrokeshire SA41 3UY
☎ 01239 820564   Fax: 01239 820355
e-mail: johndenley@aol.com
🌐 www.salutationcountryhotel.co.uk

The village of Felindre Farchog lies within the Pembrokeshire Coast National Park and is well worth seeking out in order to visit a charming old hostelry, the **Salutation Inn.** This ancient 16th century coaching inn is set right on the bank of the river Nevern whose beautiful valley provides guests with a peaceful and relaxing haven away from the pressures of life.

Mine hosts at the Salutation Inn are John and Gwawr Denley who in April 2006 opened their stylish new restaurant called 'Denleys' which is set in beautiful surroundings overlooking the river. It serves delicious food prepared using fresh local produce such as Welsh beef and Preseli lamb. A typical menu might also offer, as a starter, natural smoked haddock topped with Welsh rarebit on a bed of concasse tomatoes. For the main course, how about

Baked Fillet of Sewin (sea trout) served on a bed of asparagus tips with a dill butter sauce, or pan-fried chicken supreme stuffed with Boursin cheese, flamed in Madeira and cream and served on a bed of sautéed Chinese leaves. To round off your meal, there are some glorious desserts, locally-made ice creams, or a selection of Welsh cheeses. For lighter appetites, the bar serves a good selection of tasty snacks. Food is available every lunchtime (12.30pm to 2.30pm) and evening (6.30pm to 9.30pm).

In addition to the restaurant, there's a lounge bar and a locals' bar with pool table. Amongst the comprehensive range of beverages there are between 2 and 4 real ales on tap, with Rev. James and Double Dragon as the regular brews.

The accommodation at the Salutation boasts a 3-star rating from the Wales Tourist Board. There are 8 guest bedrooms, all located on the ground floor and all provided with en suite facilities, television and hospitality tray. They offer the choice of twins, doubles or family rooms.

The hotel provides an ideal base for country leisure activities – including bird watching, fishing and horse riding. The area is also a great location for water sports. Close by is one of the most spectacular sections of the Pembrokeshire Coast Path and there is also excellent walking in the hills around Carn Ingli mountain. Special arrangements can be made for Salutation Inn guests to enjoy a round of golf at the links course near Newport which commands stunning sea views.

357

202 SWN-Y-NANT B&B

Moylegrove, Pembrokeshire SA43 3BW
☎ 01239 881244
e-mail: ludbek@yahoo.com
🌐 www.moylegrove.co.uk

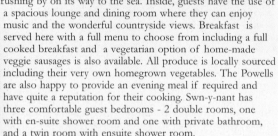

The quiet rural village of Moylegrove enjoys
a scenic location within the Pembrokeshire
Coast National Park, just a 2-minute drive
from the sea at Ceibwr Bay. It's a lovely area
to visit and Brendan and Ludka Powell's
Swn-y-Nant the ideal place to stay at. Swn-y-
nant is Welsh for 'sound of the brook'.
Indeed, a brook does pass close to the house

and from the garden you can hear it rushing by on its way to the sea. Inside, guests have the use of
a spacious lounge and dining room where they can enjoy
music and the wonderful countryside views. Breakfast is
served here with a full menu to choose from including a full
cooked breakfast and a vegetarian option of home-made
veggie sausages is also available. All produce is locally sourced
including their very own homegrown vegetables. The Powells
are also happy to provide an evening meal if required and
have quite a reputation for their cooking. Swn-y-nant has
three comfortable guest bedrooms - 2 double rooms, one
with en-suite shower room and one with private bathroom,
and a twin room with ensuite shower room.

204 THE PENDRE INN

High Street, Cilgerran, nr Cardigan,
Pembrokeshire SA43 2SL
☎ 01239 614223
🌐 www.pendreinn.co.uk

A popular watering-hole on the Cardigan
Heritage Pub Trail, **The Pendre Inn** is a
charming hostelry, parts of which date back
to the 1300s. Its thick stone walls, beamed
ceilings and slate floors all add to the olde
worlde atmosphere. This superb old inn has
been owned and run since October 2004 by
Helen and Jeff Jones, who are friendly and
welcoming hosts. The inn's main bar leads into the cosy snug at one end and there's a separate
lounge/dining room at the other. There is a large Beer Garden to the rear of the inn, with plenty
of bench seating on the enclosed lawned area. No dogs are allowed on the grassed area, however,

they are more than welcome on the patio area which also has
bench seating. The Pendre is well-known for its excellent food,
cooked by Jeff, with home-made dishes a speciality, particularly
the wonderful desserts. As a main course, how about homemade
chilli, or mushroom & Camembert cheese cobbler, or spaghetti
Bolognese? To accompany your meal, the well-stocked bar offers
plenty of choices, including 2/3 real ales with Spitfire as the
regular brew. Another major attraction of the Pendre Inn is its
regular music events and pub quizzes.

Boncath, Pembrokeshire SA37 0JN
☎ 01239 841241 Fax: 01239 841221
e-mail: boncathinn@boncath.com
🌐 www.boncathinn.com

The **Boncath Inn** is a traditional family pub whose owners, Marcus and Sue, are feeling rather pleased with themselves. For the second year running they were selected as the Pembrokeshire Camra Pub of the Year, 2007. It is located in North Pembrokeshire, 5 miles from Cardigan and 3.5 miles from Crymych and the Preseli Hills. The pub takes its name from the village of Boncath, a Welsh word meaning 'Buzzard'.

It is believed that the original building dates back to the 1400s and the owners have retained the features and character of this ancient hostelry where the old and the new co-exist in perfect harmony. It has a large bar room with a dining room attached and an outside seating area. Inside, it exudes a cosy, friendly atmosphere and enjoys a glowing reputation for the quality of the food on offer. It's all home-made and based on local produce whenever possible. The very best fish dishes, grills and steaks are always available, together with speciality dishes such as Orange Duck and Beef Stroganoff. The chefs also offer a selection of vegetarian meals and a choice of menu for the light eater. Food is served from noon until 3pm, and from 6pm to 9pm, Monday to Saturday; and from noon until 2.30pm and from 6pm to 9pm on Sunday. (Sunday is especially popular because of the regular Pub Quiz that starts at 8.30pm). Because of the popularity of the restaurant, booking ahead is strongly recommended. Children are welcome and all major credit cards are accepted.

The Boncath Inn has its own beer cellar where the brews are kept in tip-top condition. "We try to sample all of the best real ales we can find in the UK" says Marcus. "Quite a few excellent real ales we keep as regulars and we generally have four real ales as guests. We believe we have one of the very best selections – certainly in West Wales – but we don't expect you to believe us so we

invite you to come and taste our ales for yourself. Every year at the August Bank Holiday we hold a beer festival, so we can join you in a few!"

The Boncath Inn does not offer accommodation itself, but opposite the inn is a caravan park for up to 5 vehicles. The site is soft standing and provided with showers and toilets.

359

205 GLENDOWER HOTEL

Glendower Square, Goodwick,
Pembrokeshire SA64 0DH
☎ 01348 872873 Fax: 01348 874252
e-mail: glendowerhotel@hotmail.com
⊕ www.glendowerhotel.org.uk

The **Glendower Hotel**, located just a mile or
so northwest of Fishguard and in the heart
of the North Pembrokeshire Coastal National
Park, is a welcoming family-run establishment
which has been owned and run by Bernard
and Noala Jackman since 1985. It has a fine
restaurant, a small bar and comfortable guest bedrooms. The pleasant dining room is also open to
non-residents and offers a varied menu with some unusual dishes. The food is freshly prepared and
home cooked using local produce wherever possible. On Sundays, there is a Carvery for which

booking ahead is essential. The small cosy bar is ideal for a
pre-dinner drink and offers a full range of real ales, beers,
wines, spirits and soft drinks. The accommodation comprises
11 en suite bedrooms of various sizes and all equipped with
colour TV and hospitality tray. Children are welcome and all
major credit cards are accepted. The Glendower Hotel is
ideally located for an overnight stop en route to Ireland, or as
a base for touring Pembrokeshire and Cardiganshire. There
are some fine sandy beaches nearby and the Preseli mountains
are only a short drive away.

206 STONE HALL HOTEL & RESTAURANT

Welsh Hook, Haverfordwest,
Pembrokeshire SA62 5NS
☎ 01348 840212 Fax: 01348 840815
⊕ www.stonehall-mansion.co.uk

Set in 10 acres of outstanding gardens and
woodland near the hamlet of Welsh Hook, **Stone
Hall Hotel & Restaurant** occupies a striking
building, parts of which are 600 years old and
feature
slate-flagged floors and large rough-hewn oak beams. The
house was extended in the 1600s and is notable for its
wood panelling and decorative ceiling. A further extension
was made in mid-Victorian times. The building was
converted to a country hotel in 1984 by owner Martine
Watson - a French lady by birth - who took great care to
preserve all the original features and atmosphere of the
different periods of its history.

The bar and 34-seater restaurant are located in the

oldest part of the
building and there
is a comfortable
residents' lounge and a private dining room. Genuine
French cuisine with extensive à la carte and table d'hôte
menus and a comprehensive wine list are offered. Welsh
produce features prominently with dishes such as Fillet of
prime Welsh beef and Roast Rack of Preseli lamb.

The accommodation at Stone Hall comprises 4
beautifully furnished and decorated guest bedrooms, all
with en suite facilities.

New Street, St Davids,
Pembrokeshire SA62 6SU
☎ 01437 720829
e-mail: city.inn@virgin.net

Just a short walk from the centre of historic St David's, **The City Inn** has been owned and run by Pauline, Gwynneth and Howard since 1995. This popular inn is open every lunchtime and evening and the offerings from the well-stocked bar include

a real ale, Double Dragon, from the Felin Foel Brewery. During the peak season, the inn also offers food in the evening. During this period, a full menu is available and you can also choose from a range of tasty meals from the specials board. The food is wholesome and appetising and based on fresh local produce. The inn has been awarded 3 stars by Visit Wales for its comfortable accommodation available all year round in 11 attractively furnished and decorated rooms, 9 of which have en suite facilities. There's a mixture of different sized rooms and the tariff includes a hearty breakfast. Children are more than welcome and there's

good disabled access to the bar area. The inn also has its own off road parking.

Anchor Drive, High Street, St David's,
Pembrokeshire SA62 6QH
☎ 01437 720876 Fax: 01437 720876
e-mail: enquiries@waterings.co.uk
⊕ www.waterings.co.uk

Located in a quiet relaxing location just a short walk from the city centre and its 800 year old cathedral, **The Waterings** offers 4-star AA and Wales Tourist Board accommodation. The house is set in a large landscaped garden and 5 comfortable well-appointed rooms, all on ground level and set around an attractive sheltered court yard. All rooms have en suite

facilities, TV and hospitality tray. Other amenities include a picnic area and barbecue, a croquet lawn and a 9-hole putting green.

The Close, St Davids, Haverfordwest,
Dyfed SA62 6PE
☎ 01437 720517
⊕ www.cadw.wales.gov.uk

This imposing medieval palace stands in a grassy hollow next to purple-stoned St Davids Cathedral. Even in ruins, the palace – unequalled anywhere else in Wales – still conveys the affluence and power of the medieval church. It is largely the work of the energetic Bishop Henry de Gower (1328-47). No expense was spared in creating a grand residence fit for a major figure of both Church and State. De Gower's palace boasted two complete sets of state rooms ranged around a courtyard, one for his own use, the other for ceremonial entertainment. The palace is richly embellished throughout with lavish stone carvings. Particularly fine are its arcaded parapets – de Gower's trademark – decorated with chequered stonework.

210 EAST HOOK FARMHOUSE

Portfield Gate, Haverfordwest,
Pembrokeshire SA62 3LN
☎ 01437 762211
e-mail: jen.patrick@easthookfarmhouse.co.uk
🌐 www.easthookfarmhouse.co.uk

Offering top quality B&B or self-catering accommodation, **East Hook Farmhouse** stands within a 188-acre working farm with beef and sheep in a gloriously scenic location just a short drive from Haverfordwest. The farmhouse is a Georgian building whose front part dates back to 1760 but with a back part which is much older. It's the home of Jen Patrick and her husband Howard and their two children, Drew and Richard. Jen has lived here since 1997 and has been welcoming B&B guests since 1998, many of whom return to this delightful spot.

B&B guests stay in the main house where there are 6 spacious guest bedrooms, all furnished with antiques or high quality furniture, and all with en suite facilities. There's a family suite consisting of a double with private bathroom, plus a twin en suite. Ground floor bedrooms are also available in the cottage adjacent to the farmhouse.

After a day exploring the Pembrokeshire countryside, guests can relax in the lounge with its comfy leather sofas, or visit one of the good eating places within a 5 mile radius of the farm - recommendations and menus can be found in the bedrooms.

If you prefer self-catering, **East Hook Cottage** is a charming dwelling which was converted from a stone granary and stables in 2005. It has been furnished and decorated to a very high standard which has earned it a 5-star rating from the Welsh Tourist Board. Full of character, the cottage comprises of one upstairs en suite double/twin bedroom, a large lounge, fully fitted kitchen and one ground floor twin/double en suite bedroom. The cottage is perfect for couples or families seeking comfort, peace and quiet. A welcome hamper is provided for arriving guests; parking and spacious gardens are available adjacent to the cottage. Please note that payment is by cash or cheque only.

Visitors to East Hook will find plenty to see and do in the area. The Pembrokeshire Coastal Path is just 4 miles away; boat rides to access and enjoy the nature that Skomer and Stokholm islands have to offer are available just half an hour's drive away, and nearby St David's is notable for its famous cathedral and has more than enough to keep you occupied for a day.

362

Robeston Wathen, Narberth,
Pembrokeshire SA67 8EP
☎ 01834 860778
e-mail: kezffc@yahoo.co.uk

Conveniently located beside the A40 on the edge of Robeston Wathen, **The Bush Inn** is a welcoming family-run hostelry with mine hosts Kerry, Tammy and Ann all involved in the enterprise.

The inn has earned a glowing reputation for the quality of the food served here which is based as far as possible on fresh wholesome local produce. The choice includes locally produced beef steaks expertly grilled, and an extensive selection of salads and chicken, fish and vegetarian dishes. At lunchtime the choice includes a Big Breakfast, ploughman's, jacket potatoes, baguettes and burgers. Children have their very own menu. On Sundays there's a lunchtime carvery from 12 noon with a choice of 3 succulent traditional roasts. Food is served all day everyday from 12 noon to 9.00pm . Because of the popularity of the food, it is advisable to book at weekends.

To accompany your meal, the bar offers a comprehensive choice of beverages including two rotating guest ales. Children are welcome at The Bush; there's good disabled access throughout; and all major credit cards apart from American Express and Diners are accepted.

43 High Street, Narberth,
Pembrokeshire SA67 7AS
☎ 01834 860579   Mob: 07780 697018
e-mail: woodyandwendy@tiscali.com

Located in the heart of Narberth, **The Angel Inn** dates back to the early 1800s though there have been later additions made to the establishment.

Today, the pub is made up of a small, cosy bar and a larger lounge / dining area. It's a friendly and welcoming place thanks to mine hosts Woody and Wendy Wood who took over here in November 2006 after running a social club for some 11 years before that.

They have quickly gathered a glowing reputation for the quality and warmth of their hospitality towards locals and visitors alike. That includes the well-kept ales, three of which are always on tap

with Buckley's Bitter and Rev. James as the two regular brews. The inn is also noted for the great food on offer. Wendy is the cook and her menu gives pride of place to locally grown, farmed and fished fresh Pembrokeshire produce. In addition to the regular menu, Wendy also offers a choice of daily specials.

The Angel is open all day from 10am to closing time, and food is available throughout that time. In good weather, customers can enjoy their refreshments in the pleasant beer garden. And if you are planning to stay in this popular area, the Angel has 8 comfortable letting rooms available, three of which have en suite facilities.

Church Road, Johnston,
Pembrokeshire SA62 3HD
☎ 01437 890080
e-mail: sprkatheri@aol.com

Situated half way between Haverford West
and Milford Haven in the village of Johnston
you will find the **Windsor Hotel,** a striking
white building with a large bay frontage. The
hotel is owned and run by Katherine and
Fred, a friendly couple originally from
Berkshire who extend a warm welcome to all their guests. The hotel's bar area is furnished in
traditional style and stocked with a wide selection of beverages, including 2 real ales – Worthington
and Bass. In the separate restaurant which has seating for up to 65, Linsey the Chef creates some

wonderful home-made dishes with her curries, lasagne and Lamb
and Mint Pie which is especially popular with customers. The
choice also includes an à la carte and grill menu. Local produce is
used wherever possible and there's always a choice of vegetarian
dishes. Food is served from noon until 2pm, and from 6pm to
9pm, daily. Accommodation at the Windsor comprises 5
attractively furnished and decorated rooms, 2 of which have en
suite facilities. A further two en suite rooms are expected to
become available during the lifetime of this book. Children are
welcome and all major credit cards apart from American Express
and Diner's are accepted.

35a Enfield Road, Broad Haven,
Pembrokeshire SA62 3JW
☎ 01437 781152
e-mail: info@thegalleoninn.co.uk
🌐 www.thegalleoninn.co.uk

Ideally located on the stunning Broad Haven
sea front and overlooking a beautiful sandy
beach, **The Galleon Inn** is a traditional pub
serving quality beers and excellent food in a relaxed and happy atmosphere. Mine hosts, Ian and
Jacky Jarvis, offer a warm welcome to all their customers, old and new, in their recently refurbished
bar and restaurant. In the latter, head chef Adam Richards creates appetising dishes based on
locally sourced Pembrokeshire produce. At lunchtime there's a wide choice of traditional dishes

such as steaks, curry, jacket potatoes and filled
baguettes. In the evening, the menu offers treats such as
home-made beef and ale pie, a generous Galleon mixed
grill, along with fish, poultry and vegetarian dishes. The
inn is open every day from 12noon with lunch available
up to 3pm, then evening meals between 6pm and 9pm.
In the bar, real ale enthusiasts will find a choice of 3
brews with Rev. James and Brains SA as the regulars.
Also available is a separate restaurant area which lends
itself to becoming a function room for 30+ covers for
business meetings, small wedding parties, birthdays and
so on.

Burton, Milford Haven,
Pembrokeshire SA73 1NX
☎ 01646 600378   Fax: 01646 602539
e-mail: thejollysailor@f2s.com

The Jolly Sailor occupies a sensational position across the water from Pembroke Dock at the beginning of the Cleddau river system and with a dramatic view of the high bridge that carries the A477 from Pembroke Dock to Milford Haven. It has a large garden right beside the river, set out with picnic

tables and with a children's play area and an aviary. Inside, the dining area also commands superb views across to Pembroke Dock.

Mine hosts, Chris and Michelle Campbell, took over here in the spring of 2005 and have made a great success of this, their first venture into the hospitality business, and have made the inn a magnet for both locals and visitors to the area. Lovers of real ales will be pleased to find 2 brews on tap, Bass and Speckled Hen, along with a comprehensive range of other beverages. For oenophiles there's a well-chosen wine list with selections from around the world.

A major attraction here is the excellent fare on offer. The Jolly Sailor's chefs have put together an extensive menu based on fresh, locally sourced ingredients. The choice ranges from steaks of local Welsh beef, through chicken, fish, pasta and vegetarian dishes, to salads and platters. For those with smaller appetites, there are smaller portions of main menu dishes, jacket potatoes, burgers and sandwiches. Children have their very own menu. The desserts include a delicious home-made apple crumble, or if you prefer a savoury, a mixture of local Welsh cheeses from Pont Mawr Farmhouse Cheeses.

Food is served every day from noon until 2pm, and from 6pm to 9pm. On Sundays, roast dinners are added to the menu. Each day, the regular menu is supplemented by daily specials and there are also special menus for Valentine's Day, St David's Day, Mother's Day, Easter, Father's Day and Christmas parties. Menus can be tailored to individual requirements and buffet meals are also available for parties. All major credit cards are accepted and the inn has good disabled access throughout.

Nolton Haven Farmhouse, Nolton Haven,
Haverfordwest, Pembrokeshire SA62 2NH
☎ 01437 710263   Mob: 07780 697018
e-mail: qualitycottages@noltonhaven.com
🌐 www.noltonhaven.com /
www.noltonhavenqualitycottages.com

Nolton Haven is a quiet hamlet that lies at the centre of the beautiful St Brides Bay coastline with its steep, undulating cliffs and sandy beaches. Lying within the Pembrokeshire Coast National Park and completely unspoiled, it's the perfect place for a peaceful holiday. **Nolton Haven Quality Cottages** has been set up by Jim and Joyce Canton as a joint marketing scheme with cottage owners in and around Nolton Haven to provide prospective holiday-makers with a one-stop shop to provide all the relevant information for arranging an excellent holiday. Properties range from 5-star cottages to caravans, from farmhouse B&Bs to the local hotel. Sample properties include Brooklyn and Beach Cottages with 3 bedrooms sleeping 8 people, "30 yards to the beach, 60 yards to the pub"; Kate's Flat which sleeps 2 people, is 50 yards from the beach and has an entrance reached by an outside stairway; or, for a larger party, Camrose House, a 5-bedroomed Georgian country house set in extensive and secluded grounds which can accommodate up to 14 people. Bed & breakfast establishments include the Mariners Inn beside the beach at Nolton Haven, and Glebe House, the former vicarage in Nolton village.

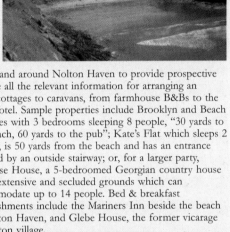

Jim and Joyce let *all* the Welsh Tourist Board 3, 4 and 5-star holiday cottages in Nolton Haven that have a sea view. They and their family live in Nolton Haven and will be on hand to assist you during your stay in any way they can.

The whole of the coastline here is part of the National Park, an area of outstanding natural beauty with a variety of natural amenities available to the holiday-maker, including the Coast Path which extends for more than 160 miles and passes through the haven. There is an abundance of wild life, sea birds, wild flowers and beaches safe for swimming, surfing, boating and fishing. Within a short distance is Newgale, well known for

its surf along 3 miles of golden sands; St David's – the smallest cathedral city in Britain; and nearby are the coastal villages of Little Haven, Broad Haven and Solva which has a particularly beautiful natural harbour.

Interesting places to visit include the Preseli Hills and Cleddau Estuary (both areas of outstanding natural beauty), woollen mills, craft shops, potteries and boat trips to Pembrokeshire's island bird sanctuary.

Main Street, Pembroke,
Pembrokeshire SA71 4LA

☎ 01646 681510 Fax: 01646 622260
e-mail: pembroke.castle@talk21.com
🌐 www.pembrokecastle.co.uk

Looming magnificently above the main street of the town, **Pembroke Castle** is one of Britain's most impressive medieval monuments. It was founded in the 11th century by the Montgomerys, who established the first timber castle on a rocky crag above the River Cleddau.

The stone building which stands today is one of the foremost examples of Norman architecture in the country. It was commenced in the 12th century by Earl William Marshal, and his famous round keep is nearly 80 feet tall with walls 19 feet thick. In 1454 the mighty fortress was held by Earl Jasper Tudor, and the castle is renowned as the birthplace of Jasper's nephew, Henry Tudor, who was to become Henry VII after defeating Richard III at the Battle of Bosworth - thus founding the Tudor dynasty. During the Civil War the castle was held by both the Parliamentarians and the Royalists, and Cromwell travelled there to begin the siege that led to it finally falling under his control. Restoration work in the late 19th century and again in the 1930s has preserved many of the features of the castle that might otherwise have fallen into ruin. The walls, the towers, the turrets, the tunnels and the battlements resound with the history of the centuries, and are an irresistible attraction for lovers of history and for children.

Cosheston, South Pembrokeshire SA72 4UD
☎ 01646 686678 Fax: 01646 684060

Cocheston is an attractive village lying to the northeast of Pembroke and it is here you will find an outstanding hostelry, **The Brewery Inn.** From the outside the inn looks very inviting indeed with its creeper-covered walls and arched windows. The interior is very pleasing too with its natural slate floor, exposed stone walls, settle seating and feature fireplace. This picturesque old building dates back some 400 years when it began life as a coaching inn. Some people have claimed that it is the most picturesque hostelry in the whole county and anyone who sees it usually agrees! But it is not only extremely pretty, it offers the very best in food, drink and convivial company as it is a popular place with locals and visitors alike.

Mine hosts are Melinda and Russell, a friendly and welcoming couple who arrived here in the late summer of 2006. Russell is a professional chef whose menu features an enticing array of appetising dishes, mostly created with locally sourced

ingredients such as Welsh Black Beef and locally caught fish - fish dishes are a speciality of the house, Amongst the starters you'll find a home-made soup of the day and an authentic Welsh Rarebit. For the main course, the choice ranges from a delicious fish and chips with home-made beer batter and home-made tartare sauce, to Cajun Spiced Chicken Breast and a vegetarian Creamy Mushroom, Leek and Thyme Pie. If you prefer a savoury, there's a Welsh cheese board with a selection of the best Welsh cheeses. Food is

served every lunchtime (noon to 2pm), and evening (6pm to 9pm), except for all day Monday and Sunday evening. The restaurant seats 18 but customers can dine throughout the inn. Because of the restaurant's popularity, booking is advisable at all times. All major credit cards are accepted apart from American Express and Diners. For real ale lovers, the bar has 2 real brews on tap, Theakston's Best and a rotating guest ale. A Pub Quiz is held every Wednesday evening from 9.30pm.

If you are planning to stay in this attractive part of the county, the inn has 3 fully equipped self-catering flats available all year round. Each of them can sleep up to 6 people and one has full wheelchair access.

369

219 THE LANTERN LICENSED RESTAURANT AND TEA ROOMS 🍽

Lamphey, Pembroke,
Pembrokeshire SA71 5NW
☎ 01646 672574
e-mail: enquiries@thelanterninlamphey.co.uk
⊕ www.thelanternlamphey.co.uk

The pleasant village of Lamphey, just to the southeast of Pembroke, used to be best known for its ruined Bishop's Palace, but since February 2007 it boasts another major attraction in the form of **The Lantern Licensed Restaurant and Tea Rooms.** Owners Allison and Tim lived in the village for some time before purchasing the restaurant and carrying out a complete refurbishment. The interior white and blue décor, wooden floor and quality furnishings are superb, and the bright, airy setting creates an almost Mediterranean atmosphere.

The quality of the food on offer more than meets the expectations raised by the surroundings. The regular menu offers an extensive choice of dishes, many made to old-fashioned recipes, ranging from a home-made Steak & Ale Pie to vegetarian dishes such as Mushroom & Stilton Tagliatelle and Mushroom Stroganoff. Amongst the starters there's a tasty Ginger & Lemon Grass Chicken Stickler, a home-made soup of the day, and a generous Fish Medley. Choices for the main course include Duck Breast Montmorency, Cod in home-made batter, and a wonderful home-made Chicken, Leek & Ham Pie. The menu also offers a selection of grills, pasta and rice dishes, as well as a variety of salads. In addition to the regular menu, Catch of the Day offers a choice of fish dishes, as well as daily specials – Pork Tenderloin in Madeira Sauce, perhaps. And on Sundays, traditional Sunday lunches are served. All the food is freshly prepared and the chefs try to cater for most dietary requirements. The Lantern is also child-friendly with a special Children's Menu that include a Roast Chicken Dinner and a home-made Spaghetti Bolognese. High chairs, baby beakers,

bowls or bibs for younger visitors are available on request. During the summer, The Lantern is open from 9am to 4pm and 6pm to 9pm, Monday to Saturday, and from noon until 3pm on Sunday. Out of season, it opens from 11am to 3pm, and from 6pm to 9pm, Tuesday to Saturday, and from noon until 3pm on Sunday. The Lantern has a full On Licence so you can, if you wish, pop in for just a beer or a coffee though once you savour the home cooking aroma, you might very well change your mind! The Lantern accepts all major credit cards apart from American Express and Diners; disabled access is good throughout.

Freshwater East, Pembroke,
Pembrokeshire SA71 5LE
☎ 01646 672828   Mob: 07780 697018
e-mail: richardrashley@btinternet.com
🌐 www.freshwaterinn.co.uk

Built in 1912 as the Grotto Country Club,
The **Freshwater Inn** is set in lovely gardens
and enjoys spectacular views along the South
Pembrokeshire Heritage Coast. Since 2004,
the inn has been owned and run by Richard
and Carol, a really friendly and welcoming
couple. Devotees of real ales will be happy
here – at any one time there are 4 of them on
tap with two from the Felin Foel brewery as
the regulars, plus two rotating guest ales. Over the course of one year, Richard hopes to have
offered his customers some 30 different real ales.

Lovers of good food will also be content here.
Richard is the chef and his enticing menu is based as
far as possible on locally sourced ingredients. His fish
and steak dishes are especially popular, but there's also
a wide selection of other dishes such as grills, griddles
and poultry dishes. Choose from either the regular
menu or from the specials board, and there's also a
menu for children and some enticing desserts. For
lighter appetites, the inn offers a wide selection of bar
snacks that includes a traditional pub ploughmans,
jacket potatoes, burgers, hot filled baguettes,
sandwiches, freshly prepared salads and old favourites
such as ham, egg and chips and fish and chips. Food is
served from noon until 2pm, and from 7pm to 9pm,
Monday to Saturday; and from noon until 2pm, and
from 6pm to 9pm on Sundays. During the summer
holidays food is available throughout the day. Booking is essential at weekends and during the
summer season. In good weather, refreshments can be enjoyed in the lovely beer garden which
commands wonderful countryside views. The inn accepts all major credit cards apart from Diners;
and there's ample off road parking.

221 THE STACKPOLE INN

Jason's Corner, Stackpole,
Pembrokeshire SA71 5OF
☎ 01646 672324   Fax: 01646 672716
e-mail: info@stackpoleinn.co.uk
🌐 www.stackpoleinn.co.uk

Set in a beautiful location just south of Pembroke amid scenic countryside and close to the coast, **The Stackpole Inn** from the outside looks like a delightful private house with its creepered walls and sunny, beautifully maintained front garden. This outstanding hostelry was bought by a local couple, Gary and Becky Evans, in the spring of 2007 and they have their hostelry as the premier gastro-pub in the area. The inn's professional chefs have created an enticing menu based on locally sourced ingredients – it has already been awarded the Pembrokeshire Produce Mark. So, amongst the starters you will find Perl Las cheese pots – creamy Welsh blue cheese blended with cream, walnuts and celery and served with crusty bread. As a main course, how about Welsh lamb rack Moroccan style, Welsh Black sirloin steak, or Escalope of local pork? There's always a vegetarian dish of the day, and a choice of desserts that includes local sorbets and ice creams, as well as assorted Welsh cheeses. Food is served every lunchtime from noon until 2pm, and every evening except Sunday from 6.30pm to 9pm. The inn offers a wide choice of beverages including 4 real ales – Rev James, Felin Foel Double Dragon and Best Bitter, plus a guest ale. The inn also offers outstanding accommodation in 4 guest rooms, two of which are on the ground floor. All four rooms have en suite facilities and there is good disabled access throughout the inn. Children are welcome and all major credit cards are accepted apart from American Express and Diners.

222 THE FERRY INN

Pembroke Ferry, Pembroke Dock,
Pembrokeshire SA72 6UD
☎ 01646 682947
e-mail: ferryinn@aol.com

Located close to the old ferry crossing at
Pembroke Ferry, the superb olde worlde
Ferry Inn dates back to 1750 and enjoys
grand river
views. It has
been owned
and run since
2004 by the
Surtees family
– mum
Norma, son
Peter and
daughter
Jayne. A free house, the inn offers 3 real ales
– Bass, Double Dragon and a guest ale, along
with a comprehensive range of other
beverages. The inn is also renowned for its
quality food with fresh fish dishes a speciality
of the house. Food is served every lunchtime
and evening; booking is strongly
recommended at weekends.

223 PEMBROKE DOCK MUSEUM

The Institute, 33 Dimond Street,
Pembroke Dock, Pembrokeshire SA72 6BX
☎ 01646 622246

Pembroke Dock's Gun Tower Museum, in
Front Street, has now reopened. Built in 1851
to repel "unwelcome guests", the imposing
dressed stone tower now welcomes visitors
with open arms. Visitors are offered an
intriguing experience of the life lived by
Queen Victoria's soldiers and marines - who
awaited, in these cramped quarters, the French invasion which never came. Three floors of
colourful models, pictures and full scale displays include life sized soldiers and many authentic
relics. These build up an exciting picture of Pembrokeshire's military heritage.

A splendid panoramic model shows us the town's Royal Dockyard. Here 250 warships were
built, along with five elegant royal yachts. A whole room is devoted to the RAF. During World War
II, Pembroke Dock was the world's largest operational flying boat base.

Important features include an original working roof cannon and the basement magazine, where
20,000 lbs of gunpowder were stored, plus an educational video. Among new exhibits this season
are a majestic 12-foot wingspan model Sunderland flying boat, and a display of authentic World
War IT aircrew uniforms and equipment. Further features are in the pipeline for later this year:
occasional guided tours are given.

A visit to the Gun Tower is a brilliant experience for just a small charge. The museum is open
seven days a week from 10am to 4 pm.

Narberth Road, Tenby,
Pembrokeshire SA70 8HT
☎ 01834 842696
e-mail: info@hoteltenby.com
🌐 www.hoteltenby.com

A friendly, family run hotel with a comprehensive range of facilities, **Hammonds Park Hotel** is located just 500 yards from Tenby's glorious North Beach. As a family hotel it has good facilities to keep children happy so that your stay is as enjoyable as possible. These include cots and high chairs, outdoor and indoor games, a selection of movies, baby listening and a baby sitting service which should be requested in advance. For the grown-ups, there's a Residents Bar stocked with a good selection of wines, spirits and beers from around the world. Bar games are available and tea and coffee are served all day. Residents can also relax in the TV lounge which has a large selection of books and games, unwind in the large garden or on the patio. If you are feeling energetic, the Cardiovascular Gymnasium which is provided with a good range of equipment.

Meals are served in the large, sunny conservatory overlooking the garden. A hearty breakfast is served from 8.30 to 9am, and a vegetarian option is always on offer. Should you be starting out early, just let them know and they will try to accommodate your needs. Evening meals are served between 6pm and 7pm, with a different set menu daily catering for most tastes, A good vegetarian option is always available. Enjoy a glass or a bottle of wine with your meal, chosen from the extensive range of wines from all over the world. A snack menu is available throughout the day for light lunches and meals.

The accommodation at Hammonds Park provides a choice of family, double/twin, and four poster rooms. Most enjoy views over the valley to Caldey Island and the Penally Hills. The rooms are tastefully furnished and decorated, and all have en suite bath and shower, telephone, hair dryer, radio alarm clock, drinks making facilities and television. In the interests of guests, all rooms are non-smoking. All major credit cards are accepted.

Tenby itself offers visitors a host of attractions within easy reach of the hotel. There are 3 award-winning beaches and the old walled town is a delight to wander through. You could take a boat trip to Caldey Island and along the spectacular coast, or try a stretch of the Pembrokeshire Coast Path.

374

225 THE DECK

4 Cambrian Terrace, Saundersfoot,
Pembrokeshire SA69 9ER
☎ 01834 813201
e-mail: rfarrell36@btinternet.com

Mine hosts at **The Deck**, Rebecca and Chris, arrived here in the autumn of 2007 and have quickly made their mark. Chris has been a chef for some 12 years so the food on offer is one very good reason for visiting. His menu is based on local produce and is available from breakfast time until 9pm during the summer months, with shorter hours during the winter. Worthington is the real ale on tap here along with a comprehensive range of other beverages.

226 CROSS INN

Penally, nr Tenby, Pembrokeshire SA70 7PU
☎ 01834 844665
e-mail: johnlangford@fsmail.net

Looking very inviting with its pink-washed walls and colourful flower boxes and baskets, the **Cross Inn** is located in Penally, a charming seaside village

just southwest of Tenby. Mine hosts at this friendly and popular free house are Les and Christine who took over here in 2002. Christine is the cook, together with Andrea, and she has made the inn famous for its good food. Her specialities include fresh fish dishes, lamb shanks and the splendid 3-course Sunday roast lunches. Such is their popularity it is essential to book on Sundays and highly advisable at other times.

Customers can choose either from the extensive printed menu or from the daily specials board. Food is served from noon until 2.30pm, and from 6pm to 8.30pm, every day. Lovers of real ales will be happy at the Cross Inn as there are always three brews on tap – Brains Bitter, Old Speckled Hen and a guest ale. Children are welcome at the Cross Inn; all major credit cards are accepted.

375

227 HUMBLE PIE

5 Lammas Street, Carmarthen,
Carmarthenshire SA31 3AD
☎ 01267 236560

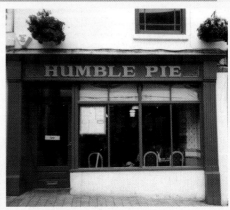

Located in the centre of this market town,
Humble Pie is a light and airy café where
owner Irene Davies, a local lady, offers an
appealing menu of home-cooked food. Her
delicious pies are a speciality of the house but

the menu offers a good and varied choice with
something for everyone. The regular menu is
supplemented by daily specials. The café is open
from 9am to 4.30pm, Monday to Saturday.
Children are welcome; there's good wheelchair
access, and payment is by cash or cheque only.

229 THE NATIONAL BOTANIC GARDEN OF WALES

Middleton Hall, Llanarthne,
Carmarthenshire, Dyfed SA32 8HG
☎ 01558 668768
🌐 www.gardenofwales.org.uk

The No 1 Modern Wonder of Wales boasts the
largest single-span glasshouse in the world and is
set in more than 500 acres of fantastic, unspoilt,
rolling Welsh countryside. The Great Glasshouse is
home to some of the most endangered plants on
the planet from six Mediterranean climate regions – Western Australia, Chile, the Canaries,
California, southern Africa, and the Mediterranean basin.

There is a unique and historic double-walled garden; lakes,
ponds and walks; a theatre; restaurant; shop; gallery; bog garden
and bee garden; Physicians of Myddfai Exhibition and
Apothecaries' Garden; children's farm, children's play area and
discovery centre. Whatever your age, there is something for you
at the most visited
garden in Wales.

Whatever time
of year it is, the
stunning views and
remarkable sights
and smells have to
be experienced to be
believed. But, be
warned, you may not
be able to see and do
it all in a day.

Llanddarog, nr Carmarthen,
Carmarthenshire SA32 8NT
☎ 01267 275395
🌐 www.thebestpubinwales.co.uk

Famous throughout Wales and beyond, **The White Hart Thatched Inn and Brewery** is quite unique. It stands across from the village church and is one of the oldest thatched hostelries in the country dating back to 1371. It is located in the village of

Llanddarog, just off the A48 Swansea to Carmarthen bypass. Inside, ancient oak beamed ceilings, antiques and vintage farm implements, along with a traditional log fire all add to the appeal. It is a beautiful Pub & Restaurant full of character. **Well worth a visit with something for everyone.**

We source local Welsh vegetables, and prepare them freshly in our kitchen. We buy the best potatoes with which we make our own real chips. All meats are fully traceable back to farm and are obtained from a local butcher. Vegetarians are well catered for and

there is also a good childrens' menu. We have a regular large menu and daily specials on the chalk board. Portion sizes are very generous and good value for money. Traditional roast dinners are served daily, along with sandwiches, bar meals, fish, steaks and exotic meats.

Diners can watch their food being prepared and cooked in the open design kitchen. Good disabled facilities and access throughout. On nice sunny days you can relax with a drink and a meal on our flower filled patio or in the child friendly garden at the back, where there is ample parking space.

The Brewery produces amazing beers, lagers and stouts, handcrafted by head brewer Cain using

a secret blend of malted barley and hops together with our own pure water from a 300ft bore hole beneath the White Hart.

This spectacular business has been owned and run by the COLES family since 1994. Geoff and Marcus are the head chefs, Tricia, Cain and Annabelle run front of house with the help of the grandchildren Jessica and Angelica.

To discover more of the history of the White Hart Thatched Inn & Brewery, why not pay us a visit?

230 THE GARDEN CAFÉ

Aberglasney Gardens, Llangathen,
Carmarthenshire SA32 8QH
☎ 01558 668131

Set within the grounds of the award-winning Aberglasney Gardens, **The Garden Café** occupies a charming old stone-built house with flag-stoned floors. The café has been owned and run since the summer of 2006 by Christine and Tony Flack with Christine as the accomplished chef. Her menu, which changes twice a year, offers a good choice of wholesome and appetising food, most of which is based on locally sourced produce. The regular menu is supplemented by occasional specials. The ground floor seats 22, upstairs there are a further 50 covers, and in good weather another 50+ can be accommodated on the terrace which enjoys a delightful view across a small lake. The café is open every day of the year except for Christmas Day. Children are welcome and all major credit cards are accepted apart from American Express, Diners and JCB. After your

meal, why not explore the 9 acres of beautiful gardens which contain six different garden spaces, including three walled gardens. At the heart is a unique fully restored Elizabethan/Jacobean cloister and parapet walk giving wonderful views over the site.

232 TAFARN PANTYDDERWEN

Old School Road, Llangain SA33 5AE
☎ 01267 241560

Hidden away in the countryside south of Carmarthen, the village of Llangain is a popular destination for discerning diners on their way to David and Claire Manning's **Tafarn Pantydderwen**. Since they bought the inn in 1996, the Mannings have established a glowing reputation for the quality of the food on offer here. Claire is a superb cook and her extensive menu makes the most of fresh, seasonal and locally sourced ingredients. All the beef used is locally produced Welsh Black and other dishes with Welsh provenance include Minted Welsh Lamb Steak, Felinfoel faggots and Chicken Cymru - chicken fillet with leeks and a creamy Caerphilly cheese sauce. Vegetarians are well catered for with dishes

such as the Chef's Own Three Bean Chilli and the hom.ne-made Cheese & Broccoli Bake. Children have their own choices which include home-made Chicken Curry and Meatballs & Pasta in Tomato Sauce. The menu also offers a selection of jacket potatoes, basket meals, sandwiches and wraps. Food is served from noon until 2.30pm, and from 6pm to 9.30pm. The well-stocked bar has a comprehensive range of beverages including 2 real ales - Flowers and a guest ale.

378

Banc-y-felin, Carmarthen SA33 5ND
☎ 01267 211341
e-mail:foxandhoundsinn@btconnect.com

Conveniently located just off the A40 midway between Carmarthen and St Clears, the Tafarn yr **Helgwn a'r Cadno / Fox & Hounds Inn** is an ideal family pub with a pretty patio and ample parking. The inn was originally a farm but has been licensed for more than 150 years. Mine hosts are experienced licensees Melvin and Lonwen Thomas who speak both Welsh and English.

Lonwen is an outstanding chef and her menu offers an appetising range of dishes based as far as possible on locally sourced produce. Among her most popular dishes are Duck a l'Orange, Beef Stroganoff, home-made curries, Lamb Shank and home-made pies. Vegetarians are presented with a good choice that includes a Stilton & Almond Bake, Glamorgan Sausage and Spinach & Mushroom Filo Parcel. Customers with light appetites will be pleased with the Light Eaters menu offering dishes such as Cottage Pie on its own and a choice of salads. A traditional roast lunch is served on Sundays - booking in advance is strongly recommended. Food is served every day from noon until 2.30pm, and from 5.30pm to 9pm. The bar has 2 local real ales on tap along with a comprehensive selection of other drinks.

On Bank Holidays and Carnival Day (the first Saturday in July) the inn hosts entertainment. Currently, the inn has no accommodation available but Melvin and Lonwen hope that during the lifetime of this book they will be able to offer quality accommodation.

379

233 THE CARPENTERS ARMS

Broadway, Laugharne,
Carmarthenshire SA33 4NS
☎ 01994 427435

A small town on the estuary of the River Taf, Laugharne is known world-wide as the home of the famous Welsh bard Dylan Thomas for the last four years of his life. He lived in The Boathouse overlooking the estuary and his house has become a literary shrine for thousands of visitors.

Another good reason to visit Laugharne is to visit Susan Jenkins' welcoming hostelry **The Carpenters Arms.** This is very much a child-friendly pub with its very own fully equipped indoor play room complete with bouncy castle, slides and an assortment of play equipment.

Another attraction here is the good food on offer, all based wherever possible on fresh local produce and cooked by Susan herself. Food is served from noon until 3pm, and from 6pm to 9pm daily. Such is the popularity of Susan's wonderful Sunday lunch, booking ahead is essential.

If you are planning to stay in this scenic corner of the county, the Carpenters Arms has 6 attractively furnished and decorated rooms, all with en suite facilities and equipped with television and hospitality tray. The tariff includes a hearty breakfast.

Please note that payment at the Carpenters Arms is by cash or cheque only.

234 BROADWAY COUNTRY HOUSE

Broadway, Laugharne,
Carmarthenshire SA33 4NU
☎ 01994 427969 Fax: 01994 427969
e-mail: enquiries@broadwaycountryhotel.fsnet.co.uk
🌐 www.broadwaycountryhouse.co.uk

Set within 7 acres of woodland and enjoying breathtaking views over Carmarthen Bay and beyond to Devon, **Broadway Country House** is an impressive restored Victorian country retreat on the outskirts of the historical township of Laugharne, famous for Laugharne Castle and more recently, the Welsh poet Dylan Thomas who did much of his writing in the Boat House. The hotel buildings originated 300 years ago, with a new West Wing and Orangery being added in 1914. The recently renovated hotel restaurant is open lunchtime for bar meals and evenings for an à la carte menu. Its famous Sunday Lunch Carvery offers a choice of 3 hand carved meats and a wide selection of vegetables and potatoes along with options for vegetarians

and children. Booking ahead is advisable. Accommodation at Broadway Country House comprises 10 en suite bedrooms, the majority of which enjoy magnificent views. Facilities include colour TV, telephone with internet access and hospitality tray. The hotel is licensed for civil weddings and specialises in catering for these and other functions with a variety of function rooms capable of accommodating up to 140 for a sit down meal, or 180 for a less formal occasion.

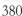

Spring Gardens, Whitland,
Carmarthenshire SA34 0HH
☎ 01994 241329
⊕ www.fishersarms.co.uk

Dating back in parts to the 15th century, the excellent **Fishers Arms** has bags of character and a long pedigree of offering good food, drink and a warm welcome to weary travellers. A huge open fire, exposed beamwork and cosy and comfortable seating add to the pub's charm and relaxed ambience. Owners Steve and Sharon have been here since 2001. Steve looks after the beer and front of house, while Sharon takes care of the cooking. The pub is closed on Mondays and does not serve food on Tuesday lunchtimes, but the rest of the week guests can enjoy lunch or dinner with a range of dishes from fresh sandwiches to hearty favourites such as sausage & chips, steaks, chicken dishes, fish and curries. Two real ales, Double Dragon and Best

Bitter from Felinfoel Brewery are available to complement

your meal. Adjacent to the inn is a scenic camping and caravan site complete with all facilities. The site can accommodate up to 13 tourers, has hard standing pitches and electric hook-ups, and a toilet/shower block fully equipped for the disabled. The site is handy for Oakwood Leisure Park and Folly farm.

Dylan's Walk, Laugharne,
Carmarthenshire SA33 4SD
☎ 01994 427420
⊕ www.dylanthomasboathouse.com

Dylan Thomas, one of the greatest writers of the 20th century, was born in Swansea, although his family roots were in Carmarthenshire. During the last four years of his life he lived at the Boathouse with his wife Caitlin and their children, having fallen in love with the house and Laugharne itself. It was here, under the influence of the water, woods and buildings he could see from his writing shed, that he produced many major pieces of work including *Under Milk Wood*. It is now a heritage centre dedicated to the poet and contains fascinating memorabilia, audio visual presentations, a bookshop and tea room.

Efailwen, Clunderwen, Pembrokeshire/
Carmarthenshire SA66 7UY
☎ 01994 419735

An inscription on the wall outside the popular **Caffi Beca** recalls the events of 1839 when the people of Efailwen rose up and demolished the local toll gates. On the 125th anniversary of that uprising the building that now houses the Caffi Beca was built in a style resembling the old toll house. Today, owner

Robert James offers customers an appetising selection of hot and cold meals based on local produce. Located on the A478, the Caffi Beca is open from 9am to 4.30pm, Monday to Saturday.

239 THE BUNCH OF GRAPES

**Bridge Street, Newcastle Emlyn,
Carmarthenshire SA38 9DU
☎ 01239 711185**

Located close to the old castle in Newcastle Emlyn, **The Bunch of Grapes** is a real gem. Owned and run since the summer of 2007 by Valerie Wylie, this cheerful and attractive 16th century coaching inn is cosy and rustic inside, with open fires, a well-stocked bar with 3 real ales on tap with Courage Directors and Courage Bitter as the regulars. It also has an excellent wine list. The pub features regularly in the *Good Beer Guide,* and was voted 'CAMRA Pub of the Year in 2004'. The inn also has 'Cask Marque' accreditation and so should not be missed by real ale enthusiasts.

The food is outstanding with a range of home-cooked food with dishes to tempt every palate, including daily changing specials and plenty of choice for vegetarians. Booking is advised, especially

for meals in the restaurant and also for the traditional Sunday lunch and Carvery. Food is served from 11am to 10pm every day. The chefs base their dishes on fresh local produce, cooked freshly to order. They host regular food-themed evenings once a week – again, booking ahead is essential. Children are welcome and all major credit cards are accepted.

The inn has a patio area at the front and a lovely secluded garden to the rear where occasional barbecues are held in summer. The Bunch of Grapes is noted for its live entertainment with live bands on Thursday and Saturday evenings.

238 THE THREE HORSESHOES

Cenarth, nr Newcastle Emlyn,
Carmarthenshire SA38 9JL
☎ 01239 710119
e-mail: john-seel@btconnect.com
🌐 www.visitcenarth.co.uk

Located close to Cenarth Falls and Cenarth
Coracle Museum, **The Three Horseshoes** is
a fine old hostelry noted for its excellent food
and real ales. Owners John and Catherine Seel
took over here in December 2005 and have
built up a loyal following. Catherine does most
of the cooking and her appetising menu offers
a wide choice of dishes with her delicious
Seafood Bake the speciality of the house. The
menu includes meals for those with smaller
appetites along with a good selection of
vegetarian dishes. There are 2-3 real ales on
tap with Buckley's Best as the regular brew.

241 EMLYN ARMS HOTEL

Bridge Street, Newcastle Emlyn,
Carmarthenshire SA38 9DU
☎ 01239 710317 Fax: 01239 710792
e-mail: admin@emlynarmshotel.com
☎ www.emlynarmshotel

The delightful **Emlyn Arms Hotel** was built
some 300 years ago as a coaching inn – you
can still drive through the high arch as the
coaches once did to access the stable yard,
now the hotel car park. A listed building, the
hotel has a
cosy bar
with Welsh
ale and
Welsh
spoken, a
comfortable
lounge and
a restaurant
that can

seat up to about 40 diners. The menus range
from 'Snacky' to 'Fancy' and the kitchen team
take pride in producing good food. The 24
guest bedrooms are all en suite and provided
with TV, direct dial phone, hair dryer and
hospitality tray.

240 TEIFI TEA ROOMS/TÉ AR Y TEIFI

Sycamore Street, Newcastle Emlyn,
Carmarthenshire SA38 9AJ
☎ 01239 711356

Newcastle Emlyn is an attractive little market
town surrounded by picturesque scenery. It
has some interesting shops and, best of all, a
top quality place to take tea, the **Teifi
Tearooms** or, in Welsh, Té Ar Y Teifi. Since
2000, the tearooms have been owned and run
by Jill and Susan Lowry who have made this a
place to which customers come back time and
again, and from considerable distances at that.
Everything on the menu here is home-made
and as much as possible the ingredients are

sourced locally. Specialities of the house include a hearty Farmhouse Pâté, tasty home-made soups

and a really delicious mixed pepper & bacon quiche. The regular
menu also offers a tempting selection of Welsh cakes, scones and bara
brith, and is supplemented by a specials board which changes several
times a week. Vegetarian options are available and dietary needs can
be met. The tearooms seat 42 customers inside and in good weather
there's seating for 12 more outside on the pavement-side patio. The
tearooms are open from 9am to 4.30pm, Monday to Saturday;
payment is by cash or cheque only.

Queen Square, Llangadog, SA19 9BW
☎ 01550 777377

Located just off the A40, the pretty little village of Llangadog sits at the foot of Black Mountain. Set right in the heart of the village is the impressive **Castle Hotel,** a 3-storey building that dates back to the early 1800s. Bill and Jane Wright took over here in the summer of 2006 and have given the pub a new lease of life. As one local put it "the place now has a smile on its face". Locals have returned after many years of drinking elsewhere - once again they have their favourite public house back again. Visitors

too are being attracted to the inn to enjoy good food, well-kept ales (including one rotating real ale), and lively company.

The Castle is open all day, every day apart from Wednesdays when it opens at 4.30pm. Food is served every lunchtime and evening, again except for Wednesdays. Choose from either the printed menu or from the specials board. The food is based

on ingredients that have been purchased locally wherever possible. Roasts are added to the menu for Sunday lunches. Enjoy your refreshments either in the pleasant restaurant with its enormous fireplace, or at picnic tables in the peaceful stone-flagged courtyard outside. Children are welcome and dogs too are permitted in the bar area where a plasma TV presents all the major sports events. Apart from American Express and Diners, all major credit cards are accepted. Bill and Jane hope that during the lifetime of this book they will also be able to offer accommodation.

Llanfynydd, Carmarthen,
Carmarthenshire SA32 7TG
☎ 01558 668291
e-mail: hilarycoole@btconnect.com
🌐 www.farmersarmspub.co.uk

Located in the idyllic village of Llanfynydd, the **Farmers Arms** dates back some 300 years and has a real home-from-home atmosphere. It provides visitors in search of a traditional rural setting a superb base from which to explore this beautiful area. A warm welcome is always assured from mine hosts Hilary and Ewan who arrived here in February 2006. They have made this an active community pub with many regular events that both locals and visitors can join in. It hosts a fortnightly Quiz and Crib evenings, a monthly Car Boot sale and a popular Free 4 All Music Night when anyone can come along and play or just listen.

Another major attraction here is the quality food on offer, all of it based on locally sourced produce wherever possible. Amongst the starters are a home-made soup of the day with crusty bread and a

plate of Creamy Garlic Mushrooms. Along with old favourites such as Deep Fried Cod in Beer Batter and a home-made Pie of the Day, the menu also offers dishes such as Chicken Balti & Rice and a vegetarian Aubergine Bake with a Cheddar and Paprika crumble topping. And don't miss out on the delicious desserts such as Bara Brith Whisky & Orange Pudding with vanilla ice cream, or the Llanfynydd Apple Pudding. To accompany your meal there's an extensive choice of beers, wines and spirits, including 2 real ales - Rev James and a rotating guest ale. Food is served from noon to 2pm, and from 6.30pm to around 9.30pm, daily except Mondays when the inn is closed. If you want to sample the hearty Sunday roast lunch, booking ahead is strongly advised.

The inn also offers bed and breakfast accommodation in two well appointed 2 star double and twin rooms which are provided with TV, local information and hospitality. The rooms are ideal for couples, families or business people in search of an intimate retreat, or lovers of walking, cycling, fishing and golfing. The inn has drying facilities for walkers and cyclists and a lockup for bikes. A delicious traditional English breakfast is included in the tariff and evening meals are available if you so wish.

243 THE SALUTATION INN ¶

**33 New Road, Llandeilo,
Carmarthenshire SA19 6DF
☎ 01558 823325**

Built in 1820, **The Salutation Inn** is a former coaching inn that still boasts many original features such as wood floors, real fires and exposed stone walls all adding to the inn's cosy and traditional ambience. In the autumn of 2007 owner David Hughes carried out a major refurbishment that upgraded the facilities while preserving the inn's old time charm. There is now a new restaurant/ brasserie which overlooks the spacious patio and the beer garden beyond.

The inn is open all day, every day, and offers a comprehensive range of beverages including 3 real ales - Thomas Watkins brews, Abbot Ale and regular rotating guest ales. The stylish restaurant serves a full range of wholesome and appetising meals, based wherever possible on locally sourced ingredients. It is open every lunchtime and evening, and early on Saturday mornings for breakfast. The Salutation hosts regular music evenings; has good disabled access and ample parking. Children are welcome and all major credit cards are accepted.

245 THE SALUTATION INN ¶

**Pontargothi, Carmarthen,
Carmarthenshire SA32 7NH
☎ 01267 290336
e-mail: salutation_inn@yahoo.co.uk**

The Salutation Inn is a distinguished place dating back to the 16th century. The wooden floors, exposed beams, thick stone walls and other original features attest to its long history of offering sustenance and welcome to all visitors. Dispensing hospitality today are mine hosts Sue and Kel who took over this small and intimate pub in the spring of 2007. A major priority of theirs is good food and the pub's extensive menu provides plenty of it. It presents a wide choice of grills, meat, poultry and fish dishes plus half a dozen vegetarian options and another half a dozen choices for children. The home-made pies - fish, cottage or steak & Guinness - are especially popular. The regular menu is supplemented by daily specials;

fresh salmon from the Rover Cothi, perhaps, or local game in season. Food is served from noon until 9pm daily, except for Wednesdays in winter when the pub is closed. On Sundays between noon and 3pm, only roasts are served. All major credit cards are accepted. Adjacent to the inn is a secure beer garden with a children's play area.

246 BLACK LION INN

Abergorlech, Carmarthen SA32 7SN
☎ 01558 685271
e-mail: georgerashbrook@hotmail.com
🌐 www.tbla.net

The Black Lion Inn is a real hidden gem. It is tucked away in the small hamlet of Abergorlech. Set on the bank of the River Cothi and flanked by the medieval church the pub itself is almost as old as the church with parts dating back to the 1600s.

Inside, old black beams, stone flagged floors and an inglenook fireplace all add to the considerable charm. Mine hosts at this enchanting old hostelry are George and Louise Rashbrook who bought the pub in the summer of 2006. Since moving in they have put time and effort into making the Inn as welcoming and enjoyable as possible. A mouth watering menu has been introduced providing plenty of hearty homecooked food using fresh, local produce which is proving a real hit with clients old and new. Home made pies, curries and puddings feature for main course, with good old fashioned desserts such as Bread and Butter Pudding, Treacle Tart, Apple and Blackberry Crumble (picked from the garden) and locally sourced dairy ice cream. Sundays offer a 3 course home made lunch and bar snacks.

Food is available for lunch and dinner, except Mondays in the

Winter when the Pub is closed. Booking is necessary in the Summer months for dinner, and is recommended at other times to ensure a cosy spot in the bar or restaurant. Combine your visit to the Inn with a country walk along the Gorlech river in the adjacent forest, or bring your mountain bikes to explore the recently completed trails. A short distance from the Inn is a self contained cottage sleeping 8 to let www.gorlechtrail.com

Llanllwni, Pencader,
Carmarthenshire SA39 9DX
☎ 01559 395633 Mob: 0781 517 3755
e-mail: thetalarddarms@hotmail.com

A very spacious and attractive traditional inn, the **Talardd Arms** has been decorated and furnished to ensure the comfort of guests and the ambience here is always friendly and welcoming. Owner David Walker ran a restaurant for four years before taking over here in January 2005. He has built up a loyal following and is well-recommended locally thanks to the quality of the service, food and drink. David is an experienced chef who creates an enticing range of home-cooked food based on locally sourced ingredients. Steaks and seafood dishes are something of a speciality but you'll also find chicken, gammon, ham, lamb and pork dishes on offer, along with vegetarian choices such as the Cream Cheese & Broccoli Bake, and a

Spinach and Mushroom Lasagne. In addition to the regular menu there are daily specials listed on a blackboard. David also offers a good selection of hot and cold bar meals. Food is served from noon until 2pm and from 6pm to 9pm, Tuesday to Sunday. The inn is closed on Mondays unless it is a Bank Holiday. On Sundays a traditional lunch is served with a choice of roasts and the options of a 1, 2 or 3-course meal. From Wednesday to Friday, a pensioner's lunch is available at a very modest price. The restaurant seats 50 but it is advisable to book ahead, especially at weekends. In the well-stocked bar you'll find a comprehensive range of beverages including 2 real ales – Tetley's and a rotating guest ale. The inn has a pleasant beer garden, ample parking and good disabled access. On Thursday evenings it hosts a Pub Quiz and also holds occasional food-themed evenings. All major credit cards apart from American Express and Diners are accepted. Coach parties are welcome. The inn is conveniently located on the A485 about 12 miles north of Carmarthen.

Llanllwni, Llanybydder SA40 9SQ
☎ 01570 480495
e-mail: belle.vue@virgin.net

Located at Llanllwni on the A485 a short drive southwest of Llanybydder, **Tafarn Belle Vue** is a fine old hostelry dating back to the mid-1700s. It was originally a farmhouse with a smithy, later became an ale house and some time in the 1860s was fully licensed. Today, the premises are owned and run by Andrew and Sue McGill, a couple with vast experience in the catering business who took over here in the autumn of 2006. They quickly established a reputation for outstanding food - they both cook - and people drive many miles to enjoy the experience of dining here.

Customers can either sample the Bar Menu with its extensive choice of appetising dishes, or treat themselves to a meal in the elegant dining room. The menu varies according to season but typical dishes include pan fried Welsh lamb's liver, pink seared tuna with saute fennel and lemon vinaigrette, grilled fillet of beef with butternut bavarois and damson chilli jam. Naturally, dishes based on prime quality Welsh beef feature prominently on the menu and nearby Goetre Farm provides the pork for the Grilled Saddleback Pork, parsnip and Ffos Y Ffin Ale Sausages and potato mash. There's also a selection of pasta dishes, including a home-made chicken pasta with

cheddar, tomato, roast peppers and basil. Children are welcome and smaller portions of dishes on the menu are available for them. In addition to the regular menu, daily specials are also available.

To complement your meal, a comprehensive choice of beverages is stocked in the bar, including an extensive wine list, 1 real ale and 1 real cider. Food is served every day from noon to 2pm, and from 5pm to 9.30pm (from 6pm on Sundays). The restaurant has seating for up to 38 diners but booking ahead is strongly recommended, especially at weekends and for the regular monthly food-themed evenings. The inn also hosts a Pub Quiz on the last Wednesday of the month from 8pm.

Tafarn Belle Vue accepts all major credit cards.

389

249 GLASFRYN GUEST HOUSE

Llanybydder, Carmarthenshire SA40 9TY
☎ 01570 481400 Mob: 07980 576491
e-mail: ron.dubber@btinternet.com
🌐 www.glasfrynguesthouse.co.uk

Built in 1890 as a Vicarage, **Glasfryn Guest House** offers comfortable bed & breakfast accommodation in homely and relaxing atmosphere.

Glasfryn is the home of Ron and Denise Dubber who have been welcoming guests here since 2003. They have retained the character of the house, whilst installing superb en-suite facilities which have been awarded a 4-star rating by the Welsh Tourist Board. Their aim is to ensure your stay with us is pleasant, and relaxing – indeed, a 'home from home'. As an example, babysitting is offered to give parents a break! The house boasts a secluded garden which is a delight. There are 5 guest bedrooms, 2

double and 1 twin, all with en suite facilities, and 2 singles which share a bathroom. Ron and Denise serve a wonderfully hearty breakfast up until 8.30am and can supply an evening meal on request. Special diets can be catered

for. Glasfryn is open throughout the year and guests have unrestricted access. There is ample parking at the rear, motor cycles and cycles can be securely locked away, and fishing tackle, muddy boots and wet clothing can all be taken care of. Payment at Glasfryn is by cash or cheque only.

250 ROBINS ROOST

Cwmann, Lampeter,
Carmarthenshire SA48 8DX
☎ 01570 423839
e-mail: robinsroostbandb@btinternet.com
🌐 www.robinsroostbandb.co.uk

Just a five minute drive from Lampeter along the A485, **Robins Roost** enjoys an isolated and secluded position with wonderful views of unspoilt countryside in every direction. Dating back to 1810, Robins Roost is the home of Liam and Dianne O'Keeffe who have been welcoming bed &

breakfast guests here since 2001.

They have 5 guest bedrooms, all of them with en suite facilities, and all attractively furnished and decorated. One room is on the ground floor and has been completely adapted for the disabled, including a fine walk-in wet room. At breakfast time there's an excellent choice that includes a cooked vegetarian

breakfast. Visitors have waxed lyrical about the breakfasts served here and the fact that they last

them all day. Evening meals are available by arrangement and guests can stay on a dinner, bed & breakfast basis. Children are welcome, payment is by cash only, and there is a small off road car park.

252 THE HARRY WATKINS

2 Millfield Road, Felinfoel, Llanelli,
Carmarthenshire SA14 8HY
☎ 01554 776644
e-mail: rowland@cross1.wanadoo.co.uk

The Harry Watkins used to be known as The Bear but was re-named about 10 years ago in honour of the former captain of Llanelli's Rugby Union team. He played for Wales six times and was known for his great strength. This welcoming and

popular hostelry is well-known for its mouth-watering food and the warm hospitality of mine hosts, Linda and Rowland Cross, both of them local people who took over here in 2004. Linda oversees the kitchen with the help of a professional chef and her menu offers old favourites such as grills, battered cod fillet and curries, as well as popular dishes like the regular Carvery, the Lamb Shank and Beef Bourguinon. Vegetarian options include a tasty Broccoli & Stilton Pasta, and there are separate choices for the under 10s, and for those aged 10 to 14. All main courses and children's meals include one free visit to the Salad Bar. Food is served from 5pm to 8.30pm on Tuesday; noon until 8.30pm, Wednesday to Saturday;

and from noon until 2pm on Sunday for the Carvery only. Because of the popularity of the restaurant, it is wise to book on Friday, Saturday and Sunday. To accompany your meal, there's a comprehensive selection of beverages including 3 real ales - Marston's Pedigree, Banks' Bitter and a rotating guest ale.

The inn is closed on Mondays unless it is a Bank Holiday. On Sunday evening there's regular quiz from 9pm when allcomers are welcome. In good weather, customers can enjoy their refreshment in the patio area, part of which is covered. The inn accepts all major credit cards and has good disabled access.

251 CWMANNE TAVERN

Cwmanne, Lampeter SA48 8DR
☎ 01570 423861

A former coaching inn dating back to 1712, the **Cwmanne Tavern** looks very inviting with its cherry-coloured frontage, window boxes and topiary. Inside, black-and-amber tiles, wooden pew-style seating and other attractive

features all add to the inn's warm and welcoming ambience. In the cosy restaurant, customers can enjoy fine country cooking with a full range of fresh beef, poultry, fish and vegetarian dishes. Three rotating real ales are on tap in the well-stocked bar. The tavern also offers accommodation, a Tuesday quiz and live music on Saturdays. There's a patio to the rear, off road parking and good disabled access.

253 THE NEW LODGE INN

1, Heol-y-Bryn, Pontyberem SA15 5AG
☎ 01269 870679
e-mail: newlodgeinn@tiscali.co.uk

The New Lodge Inn began life as 3 terraced cottages built in the late 1700s and is now a friendly and atmospheric village hostelry. A Free House, the inn has been owned and run by Andrew Prosser since the spring of 2006. Good, home-cooked food is served every weekday evening, apart from Wednesday, and at lunchtime and evenings at the weekend.

There are 2 real ales, Brains SA and a rotating brew, and the pub hosts occasional entertainment, quizzes, karaoke and pool competitions. All major credit cards apart from American Express are accepted.

254 HALF MOON INN

281 Cwmamman Road, Garnant, Ammanford, Carmarthenshire SA18 1LS
☎ 01269 825466 Fax: 01269 822798
e-mail: halfmooninn281@aol.com
🌐 www.halfmooninn281@aol.com

Conveniently located on the A474, east of Ammanford, the **Half Moon Inn** was originally three cottages which were converted into an inn during the early 1800s. The rooms still have a cosy, homely feeling. Mine hosts David and Jean, bought the premises in the summer of 2005 and have carried out many improvements including the addition of 2 superb guest bedrooms, both with en suite facilities, and one with a king size bed. The inn is open all day, every day for ale with rotating real ales from a Welsh brewery always on tap. Currently, the food served is limited to breakfast, sandwiches and rolls which are available throughout the day, but Dave and Jean plan to start serving full lunches shortly. Already, they have introduced live entertainment on Friday and Saturday evenings, as well as a Pub Quiz on Sunday evening starting at 9pm. The inn has a covered patio area which is heated and lit, and provided with colourful parasols. There is a railway line close to the Inn which is subject to a grant from the WDA to set up a steam train line. Subject to the grant it should be in place shortly. Golf enthusiasts will be comforted to know that there are 2 courses nearby, one less than a mile away, the other less than 4 miles.

255 TAFARN-Y-DERI

Ebenezer Road, Llanedi, Pontarddulais,
Swansea SA4 0YT
☎ 01792 883318 Fax: 01792 884318
e-mail: tydereahors @yahoo.co.uk

The outstanding **Tafarn-y-Deri** occupies a spacious building that has had a chequered history having been at various times a Post Office, a village shop and even a slaughterhouse. Even after it became a public house its fortunes were mixed and

when Karen and Wyn Jenkins bought the premises in 1994 its doors had been closed for 4 years after the licensee lost his licence. Karen and Wyn re-licensed it, upgraded its facilities and today preside over one of the most popular hostelries in the area. The pub's quality furnishings and fittings make it seem more like an upmarket hotel rather than a village inn.

Another major attraction here is the quality of the food on offer. Wyn is an accomplished cook who bases her dishes on locally sourced produce. Her specialities include dishes based on Welsh chicken and Welsh beef steaks. The regular menu is supplemented by monthly specials - Seabass Fillets, perhaps, Lamb Hot Pot or a Chicken & Mango Curry. To accompany your meal, the bar stocks a comprehensive range of beverages including 2 real ales - Double Dragon as the regular brew plus a guest ale. Food is served from noon until

2.30pm, and from 5pm to 9.30pm, every day. Booking is strongly recommended at all times. Children are welcome; all major credit cards except American Express are accepted, and there is good disabled access with a ramped entrance and disabled toilets.

Tafarn-y-Deri also offers comfortable en suite accommodation in 4 upstairs rooms. Three of them are twin/doubles, the fourth is a single. All are attractively furnished and decorated, and centrally heated. The tariff includes a hearty breakfast.

1 Gors Road, Burry Port, Llanelli,
Carmarthenshire SA16 0EL
☎ 01554 833224
e-mail: hugh.d@btconnect.com

Conveniently located just across the road from Burry Port's railway station, the **Cornish Arms** is a traditional village pub, handsome and welcoming with a relaxed ambience. Mine hosts, Hugh and Elaine, offer all their guests with a warm welcome

and their capable, friendly staff provide a high standard of service and hospitality. One rotating real ale – usually from a Welsh brewery – is on tap, along with a good selection of lagers, wine, spirits, cider, stout and soft drinks, all served with a smile by bar manager Margaret. A major attraction at the Cornish Arms is the quality of the food on offer. Chef Mike Hewish is also a local fisherman so amongst his specialities are the fresh fish dishes, locally caught Lemon Sole, Plaice and Skate for example. His pièce de résistance is the Seafood Medley which contains sea bass, red gurnard, flounder, salmon, mullet, smoked haddock (poached or grilled), all served in a prawn and cockle sauce. Marvellous! But Mike's extensive menu also

profers a wide choice of grills, poultry dishes, vegetarian options and salads. A selection of burgers is also available. Children have their own menu which, unusually, includes a 6oz Rump Steak. In addition to the regular menu, Mike also offers daily specials – Swordfish with a mushroom and white wine sauce, or local pan-fried Sandy Dabs. Food is served from noon until 3pm and from 6pm to 9.30pm, Tuesday to Saturday, and from noon until 3pm on Sunday when Sunday Roasts only are served. Booking ahead is strongly advised at the weekend; all major credit cards are accepted.

Entertainment at the Cornish Arms includes a regular Pub Quiz on Tuesday evenings from 7.30pm, and there's also live entertainment once a month. The inn has a small and pleasant patio garden and there is good disabled access throughout. Hugh and Elaine hope that very soon they will also be able to offer comfortable en suite guest bedrooms – if you are planning to stay hereabouts, it could be well worth checking with them.

Burry Port itself offers many attractions, not least the lovely marina and the motor racing circuit at nearby Pembrey which is also noted for its Country Park boasting a Blue Flag beach.

257 THE MASONS ARMS ¶

37 Water Street, Kidwelly SA17 5BX
☎ 01554 890298
e-mail: karon@kmcqueen.orangehome.co.uk

The Masons Arms looks very inviting with its thatched roof, colour-washed frontage of pale gold and felingfoel dragon guarding the entrance. Located on the edge of the town centre and with a history going back to 1350, the inn has a good claim to being one of the oldest hostelries in Wales. The interior is just as appealing as the outside. There are open fires in each of the two bars, window seats, lots of interesting bric à brac, paintings and ornamental plates around the walls, and sturdy, traditional style tables and chairs. A family room is tucked away at the back and outside there's a pleasant beer garden. Mine hosts at the Mason Arms are Karon and Stan McQueen and their daughter Nikki who took over here in the summer of 2007. Karon is the cook, offering an appetising menu

based on fresh locally sourced food and available every lunchtime and evening. At Sunday lunchtime roasts only are served and booking ahead is strongly recommended. The two real ales on tap are Double Dragon and Dragon Stout, both from the Felin Foel Brewery. Payment at the Masons Arms is by cash or cheque only. Every Saturday evening the inn hosts entertainment with live music during the summer months.

258 THE PLOUGH AND HARROW ¶

132 Llangyfeltch Road, Brynhyfryd,
Swansea SA5 9LG
☎ 01792 480808

A short drive from junction 46 of the M4, **The Plough and Harrow** is a spacious village pub noted for its award-winning food. Mine hosts Denise and Michael Ismail offer an extensive menu featuring everything from grills and fish dishes to baguettes and jacket potatoes. The home-made vegetarian chilli is particularly delicious. Food is served from noon until 6pm, Monday to Saturday. On Monday and Thursday evenings, there's live entertainment; on Tuesday a Pub Quiz, and on Friday a karaoke.

259 G & T'S BISTRO

602 Mumbles Road, Mumbles,
Swansea SA3 4DL
☎ 01792 367309 Fax: 01792 363115
e-mail: tina.morgan@onetel.net

Facing onto Swansea Bay, **G & T's Bistro** provides a treat for anyone who wants a good meal out with a warm atmosphere and fine cuisine. The bistro is owned and run by Greg and Tina Morgan who took over here in 2003 although Greg has been a professional chef for some 26 years. His menus change frequently but always offer a wide range of English, European and local seafood dishes along with international cuisine and a separate menu for vegetarians. Amongst the starters you may find a Mushroom Mantenel - pan-fried mushrooms, bacon & onions flamed with a port and cream sauce - or a home-made Venison Pâté. The main course menu might offer you various dishes of Welsh beef, Breast of Barbary Duck, or a Leek & Mushroom Crumble. The regular menu is

supplemented by the Chef's Specials listed on the blackboard. Food is served from noon until 2pm, Wednesday to Saturday, and from 6.30pm to 9.30pm,

Tuesday to Saturday, and from noon to 3pm on Sunday. Booking is advisable at all times. All major credit cards are accepted apart from American Express and Diners, and there is good disabled access throughout.

260 TIDES REACH GUEST HOUSE

388 Mumbles Road, Mumbles,
Swansea SA3 5TN
☎ 01792 404877
e-mail: info@tidesreachguesthouse.com
🌐 www.tidesreachguesthouse.com

Tides Reach Guest House is a handsome, 9-bedroom mid-Victorian residence occupying a prime position on the promenade looking out across Swansea Bay and the Mumbles Head. Attractively furnished and decorated throughout, it's the home of Lyn and Mary Hayward who have recently carried out a complete refurbishment of the property. The house is now eco-friendly and they have also created a new family suite which enjoys those grand sea views. Awarded a 4 star rating by the Welsh Tourist Board, the rooms are available all year round. Two of them are on the ground floor and ideal for those who have difficulty with stairs. Guests are served an extra special breakfast each

morning featuring quality local produce along with fresh fruit platters. Tides Reach welcomes well-behaved dogs and accepts all major credit cards. The house is ideally located for exploring the lovely Gower Peninsula and for visitors using public transport there's a bus stop right outside the house.

261 LITTLE HAVEN GUEST HOUSE

Oxwich, Gower, Swansea SA3 1LS
☎ 01792 390940
e-mail: enquiries@littlehavenoxwich.co.uk
🌐 www.littlehavenoxwich.co.uk

Located in the picturesque village of Oxwich, only 11 miles from the bustling city of Swansea, **Little Haven Guest House** is a family-run guest house with a 3-star grading from the Wales Tourist Board. The house occupies an outstanding scenic location

looking down to famous Oxwich Bay. Little Haven is the home of Lorna Lewis who started welcoming bed & breakfast guests some 40 years ago. The house has several twin, double and family rooms, all with en suite facilities, television and hospitality tray. If requested when booking, disabled access and facilities are available. Rooms are available from February to November. The house has a large parking area for guests' cars and boats and all guests

have the use of a heated swimming pool. The B&B tariff is very reasonable and includes a hearty breakfast. The beach at Oxwich Bay is just a short walk away and is excellent for bathing and water sports such as wind-surfing and skiing. It is ranked among the world's 12 best beaches by *Travel* magazine. The village itself boasts a well-stocked General Store, a beautiful 16th century church, a public house and restaurant.

263 THE BRITANNIA INN

Llanmadoc, Swansea SA3 1DB
☎ 01792 386624
e-mail: enquiries@britanniainngower.co.uk
🌐 www.britanniainngower.co.uk

Boasting awe-inspiring views over the Loughor Estuary, **The Britannia Inn** is situated in the picturesque village of Llanmadoc on the North Coast of the famous Gower Peninsula. The inn dates from the 17th century and many of the

original features have been preserved: in the bar there is the original bread oven, while in the restaurant the beams are thought to have come from ships that were 'lanterned' ashore by wreckers. Martin and Lindsay Davies, who took over here in 2006, are both chefs with considerable international experience having travelled and worked in New Zealand, Australia, SE Asia, South Africa and Central America. This experience is reflected in the excellent food that is served in the restaurant. The dishes are based on fresh

local produce with their signature dish being 'cockle, crab and butternut ravioli'. The cosy bar stocks an excellent selection of cask conditioned ales, lagers and stouts.

Along with beer gardens to the front and back, there is also an assortment of rabbits and guinea pigs, a well-stocked aviary with a variety of budgies, parakeets and a parrot, and a duck pond, home to the infamous Elvis and Priscilla! The inn also has two guest bedrooms, both en suite.

262 THE BAY BISTRO & COFFEE HOUSE

Rhossili, Gower, Swansea SA3 1PL
☎ 01792 390519 Fax: 01792 390522
e-mail: suepitton@hotmail.com

With panoramic views over Rhossili Bay you will be assured of a warm and friendly welcome at **The Bay Bistro & Coffee House Rhossili.**

From 10am a Full English breakfast and a wide selection of sandwiches, baguettes, Panini's and salads is available. All our food is prepared fresh on the premises including a fantastic chilli and lasagne. Why not try one of our baked Camembert served with rock salt and rosemary bread or take a look at our daily specials board. If you would prefer to be outside you can always relax on the patio with one of our famous cream tea's. We provide a takeaway service and cater for groups.

In the evening The Bistro is open from 7pm where you will find fresh locally sourced fish including trout, sea bass and mackerel. Or why not try a Welsh Black steak. A great way to finish off your meal is with our home made blackberry and apple crumble or a real welsh cheese board. The Bistro is fully licensed and it is advisable to book as The Bay is a very popular venue.

The Bay is open every day during the summer months from 10am to 5.30pm then re-opens at 7pm for evening meals. Off season The Bay is open every weekend but can still be booked for functions and parties.

All major credit cards are accepted and there is good disabled access throughout.

Next to the Bistro Sue's son Sam runs a surf-hire shop where visitors can hire surf boards, wet suits and other accessories. The shop also stocks gifts and beautiful hand made jewellery. Rhossili itself stands at the western end of the Gower Peninsula and has a fantastic 3 mile stretch of unspoilt beach and many beautiful secluded coves. It is very popular with walkers, bird watchers, surfers and hang gliders. Sunset over The Wormshead was voted the place to go for the most romantic sunset by readers of Country Living Magazine.

Oldwalls, Llanrhidian, Swansea SA3 IHA
☎ 01792 391027
⊕ www.thegreyhoundinnoldwalls.co.uk

The Greyhound Inn is a handsome 19th century traditional roadhouse inn with a cheerful and welcoming atmosphere. Its young and enthusiastic hosts, Chris and Emily, arrived here in the autumn of 2006 although Emily had worked at the pub for some years before taking over with Chris. Emily is an accomplished cook who has made the Greyhound the eating place of choice for many locals and visitors. Her extensive menu ranges from traditional favourites such as home-cooked Ham & Egg or Steak & Ale Pie to fish, poultry, meat, curry and pasta dishes. Amongst the most popular are the locally reared Lamb Shank, locally caught sea bass and the Greyhound Chicken dish with a cheese and leek sauce. For lighter appetites, there's a good selection of baguettes, sandwiches, jacket potatoes, ploughman's and burgers. Vegetarians are well-catered for with dishes such as Shabzi Balti and Broccoli & Stilton Pie, and children under twelve have their own menu or can have smaller portions of some of the pasta dishes. Seasonal desserts are

listed on the blackboard. Food is served every day from noon until 9pm although at Sunday lunchtimes, from noon until 2.30pm, only a choice of roasts or a vegetarian alternative are served. Emily's roasts are much sought after so booking ahead is strongly recommended.

The well-stocked bar offers a choice of 3 or 4 real ales with Bass, Hancock's HB and London Pride as the regular brews.

The Greyhound is the regular meeting place for the local Folk Club which gathers here at 8pm on Sundays and on the third Sunday of each month the club hosts a guest folk singer.

The Greyhound accepts all major credit cards, has good disabled access throughout, and has function and meeting rooms available for hire.

Located at the most westerly tip of the Gower Peninsula, this fine pub is popular with walkers and lovers of nature's beauty as the region provides splendid views along the coast.

399

265 CEDI COTTAGES

Blaen Cedi Farm, Penclawdd,
Swansea SA4 3LX
☎ 01792 851448 Fax: 01792 851448
e-mail: cu@walesgowercottages.co.uk
🌐 www.walesgowercottages.co.uk

Approached by a secluded lane overhung with trees, **Cedi Cottages** are surrounded with fields and enjoy grand estuary views of the Llanrhidian Marshes. The farmhouse and outbuildings are 300 years old and although the majority of the land was sold many years ago, the house and cottages are set in 3 acres of gardens.

The 4 delightful cottages have been renovated to a high standard and have been awarded the top 5-star rating by the Welsh Tourist Board. Each has central heating, full size cooker and fridge, microwave and all the equipment you would expect in 5-star accommodation. There are washing machines and dryers available in the adjoining utility room. The cottages have been lovingly restored with particular attention to décor and furnishings. All linen and towels are supplied and guests are welcomed with fresh flowers and the little extras that make for a special holiday.

One of the cottages, The Stable, has been adapted to allow a wheelchair user to enjoy their holiday without any compromise on the overall aesthetic beauty of the cottage. Beamed high ceilings, stone walls. A spectacular 6ft bed, TV, video, CD player and all the comforts of home make a stay here something to remember.

The Gallery has a 5ft bed on the first floor and takes its name from the beautiful bedroom gallery which was reclaimed from a local chapel. Perhaps because of the gallery, this property has hosted a few honeymoon couples with, perhaps, Romeo and Juliet in mind.

The delightful stone 'Cottage' was originally the cow barn and exudes a cosy atmosphere. It has 2 bedrooms - one single and one double. The fourth property, The Cabin, is set apart from others and has a rustic feel. Set in its own garden it has 2 bedrooms, lounge, kitchen and bathroom with shower. Surrounded by trees and hedges, the only thing to disturb the holiday-maker here is the sound of birdsong.

All the cottages have additional sleeping facilities in the form of a good quality bed settee for the extra child or guest. If these are required, all the additional bedding will be supplied. Owners Marion and Jeffrey Walters also offer free use of the spacious hot tub and the surrounding deck. Garden equipment is provided for all guests and they can also hire bicycles and helmets at a very reasonable rate.

266 SHEPHERDS COUNTRY INN ⫙ ⊢

18 Heol Myddfai, Felindre,
Swansea SA5 7ND
☎ 01792 794715
e-mail: joanne@shepherdsinn.co.uk
⊕ www.shepherdsinn.co.uk

Shepherds Country Inn is a fabulous country pub and well worth seeking out for its superb food, drink and accommodation. Everything on the menu and specials board is home-made using the freshest ingredients and includes tasty steaks and traditional favourites. The lunchtime menu features Welsh produce in such dishes as Welsh Gammon Ham with a creamy parsley sauce, and traditional Welsh recipe faggots with gravy. Also on offer are local speciality sausages, salads and children's meals. The evening menu offers succulent Welsh steaks, Welsh Lamb Chops, fish and vegetarian dishes and children's meals. The choice of drinks to accompany your meal includes 3 choices of real ales. A Free House, the inn has a cosy, homely feel and

looks more like a family home from outside. There's a covered porch area

at the front and a handsome beer garden complete with children's area to the rear. The accommodation comprises 3 recently refurbished rooms, all tastefully furnished and decorated. The inn is run by the husband and wife team of Rob and Joanne Davies who have a wealth of experience having run some of London's landmark pubs in the past.

267 LA CUCINA ⫙

47 New Road, Skewen, Neath SA10 6EP
☎ 01792 323004
⊕ www.lacucinaskewen.co.uk

Located on the main street in Skewen, close to junction 43 of the M4 and about a mile west of Neath, **La Cucina** is a popular eating place selling a huge variety of wholesome and appetising food. The choice ranges from café classics such as Ham, Egg & Chips, Chicken Curry or Cods, Peas & Chips to salads and pizzas. There are 20 different kinds of filled jacket potatoes, including a delicious Chicken Tikka with a yoghurt and mint dressing, and an extensive selection of omelettes, sandwiches, baguettes, paninis and wraps. A traditional cooked breakfast is served all day and every day along with "Breakfast in Bread" - baguettes, paninis or sandwiches filled with traditional breakfast items If you just want a light snack, the menu offers either egg, bean, tomatoes, mushrooms or cheese

on toast. Children

have their own choice of meals and sandwiches. Drinks available include various teas and coffees, several chocolate drinks, cold drinks, milk shakes and frappuccinos. The café is on two floors, seating 13 downstairs and 27 upstairs. At present La Cucina is open from 9am to 4pm, but during 2008 owners Robert and Alison Smith plan to stay open longer, including Sunday lunchtimes and some evenings. Payment at La Cucina is by cash or cheque only. The café has good disabled access and a disabled toilet.

268 DULAIS ROCK INN   ¶ ⊢

Aberdulais Road, Neath SA10 8EY
☎ 01639 644611
e-mail: radfordandy77@aol.com
🌐 www.DulaisRock.com

Located on the outskirts of Neath and adjacent to the famous National Trust owned Aberdulais Falls, the **Dulais Rock Inn** dates back to the times of Oliver Cromwell but has recently been regenerated with an exciting and innovative refurbishment. The bars each have their own distinct atmosphere, with antique wood, leather furniture and real open fires, and offering traditional home cooked food, with chefs special boards available from 12pm and an afternoon bar menu with a difference. Mine hosts at the Dulais Rock, Andy and Nanette Radford, who have some 15 years experience in the hospitality business, have made good food their top priority. The new 50-seater restaurant provides the benchmark of service and standards at the Dulais Rock and gives customers

the ultimate in dining experience. It has a modern old traditional style and Andy's expertise as the chef has quickly attracted recognition with its inclusion in Dining Out in Wales's Top 150 Restaurants in Wales. All Andy's dishes are fresh and produced on the premises using the best local ingredients available. There is a lunch to early evening menu available until 7pm which offers hearty favourites such as beer battered cod, home-made beef in ale pie, and home-made lasagne, along with lighter fare such as a pot of mussels, a mushroom topped muffin, jacket potatoes and freshly baked filled baguettes or pita bread. The restaurant is open from 12.00pm until 9pm seven days a week with a menu that offers enticing dishes such as Coriander, Lime & Mango Chicken; Rosemary Lamb Shank; grills and pasta dishes, as well as vegetarian alternatives such as a Bean Chilli Casserole. Last orders for the restaurant are at 9.00pm.

On Thursday evenings the bar hosts a quiz and on Friday evenings there is occasional live entertainment. A highlight of the year is the real ale Beer Festival held during the summer. The accommodation at the Dulais Rock maintains the same high standards that are evident throughout the hotel. The 3 guest bedrooms, all doubles, have been built into the roof space of the original old mill and are furnished and decorated to a very high standard. The tariff includes the Inn's own breakfast menu including a full English.

The Dulai Rock welcomes children; all major credit cards are accepted; there is good disabled access to the bars and restaurant; and the hotel has ample off road parking.

269 BISHOPS CAFÉ BISTRO

27 Herbert Street, Pontardawe,
Swansea SA8 4EB
☎ 01792 869711

In a quiet corner of Pontardawe is the delightful Bishops Cafe Bistro. Taking its name from the owner, Julie Bishop, this is a rare find. A sandwich shop that can offer a real choice in fresh and tasty fillings. The range is excellent and the prices very reasonable, whether you decide to take away or enjoy your sandwich inside. The sit down menu starts the day with light refreshments such as hot toast or tea cakes with jam or marmalade served until 11.30am.

Then there's usually a choice of two home-made soups served with a french stick, a range of baked potatoes with various hot or cold fillings and a selection of home-made meals such as Chilli con Carne and tender pieces of Lamb in a Minted Gravy. The dining area is bright and colourful and the open kitchen means you can see your food being prepared. To round off your lunch, or to

accompany your coffee, there is a divine selection of wicked desserts. Everything on the menu is prepared here with fruit and vegetables freshly delivered each day. Bishops is open from 9am to 3pm, Monday to Friday; payment is by cash or cheque only.

HIDDEN PLACES GUIDES

Explore Britain and Ireland with *Hidden Places* guides - a fascinating series of national and local travel guides.

Packed with easy to read information on hundreds of places of interest as well as places to stay, eat and drink.

Available from both high street and internet booksellers

For more information on the full range of *Hidden Places* guides and other titles published by Travel Publishing visit our website on

www.travelpublishing.co.uk
or ask for our leaflet by phoning
01752 276660 or emailing
info@travelpublishing.co.uk

271 TREGIB ARMS

39 Cwmgarw Road, Brynamman,
Ammanford, Carmarthenshire SA18 1BY
☎ 01269 823290
e-mail: info@thetregibarms,co.uk
⊕ www.thetregibarms.co.uk

Surrounded by the foothills of the Black Mountains, the **Tregib Arms** is a warm and welcoming inn serving wholesome home-made food. Owners Jay and Jacqui Joseph lived in the village for some years before taking over here in October 2007. In addition to the bar food which is available from noon until 9pm each day, the inn serves an excellent real ale, Cwrw Braf, which is brewed by Tomas Watkins. The inn has a pool table and hosts a quiz every Sunday evening. The accommodation here comprises 3 spacious and attractively decorated rooms, 2 of which are en suite, the third has its own private bathroom.

Alltwen Hill, Alltwen,
Pontardawe SA8 3BP
☎ 01792 863320

Formerly known as the Pen-yr-Allt Hotel, the **Celtic Lodge Inn** stands on the outskirts of Pontardawe, just a short distance from junction 45

of the M4. Recently acquired by partners Macmillan Laverty, Joe Wasson and John Joyce, who have a real passion for the hotel and catering industry with a wealth of experience between them. The inn offers fine ales and comfortable accommodation.

Although the Inn does not currently serve food the owners are planning

to change that by offering a hearty menu in the near future. The inn has a full on licence and is open every lunchtime and evening every day of the week. It has a well-stocked bar and is currently serving one real ale, which is the popular Bass, but the partners plan to add others to the list.

The accommodation, which is available all year round, comprises of 6 attractively furnished and decorated bedrooms each with en suite and all of which are upstairs. Every bedroom is equipped with colour TV and hospitality tray.

272 CROSS INN HOTEL

Main Road, Cross Inn, Llantrisant,
Pontyclun, Rhondda Cynon Taff CF72 8AZ
☎ 01443 223431
e-mail: thecrossinnhotel@aol.com

The village of Cross Inn is just a very short drive from Llantrisant and it's here you will find the picturesque **Cross Inn Hotel** which dates from the late 1800s and stands just across the road from the railway line. Mine hosts, Martin and Cheryl Williams, were born and bred in the area and have been Stewards at the local rugby club since 2005. They took over here in the autumn of 2007 and have build up a loyal local following with word quickly spreading outside the immediate area. The inn is open all day, every day, and currently serves food only from noon until 3pm but Martin and Cheryl plan to start providing food in the evenings as well in the near future.

They already have weekly Curry and Steak Nights. Cheryl and a local lady are the cooks and they base their dishes on locally sourced produce wherever possible. Such is the fame of their Sunday lunches that booking ahead is a necessity. To accompany your meal, the bar offers a comprehensive choice that includes 4 real ales: Hancocks HB, Spitfire and Brains Bitter are the regulars, plus a rotating guest ale. Please note that payment is by cash or cheque only.

Looking for:
- *Places to Visit?*
- *Places to Stay?*
- *Places to Eat & Drink?*
- *Places to Shop?*

273 MISKIN HOTEL

Miskin Road, Trealaw, Tonypandy,
Rhondda CF40 2QN
☎ 01443 430058

The Hargest family have owned and run the **Miskin Hotel** for 26 years and have acquired an enviable reputation for great hospitality, good wholesome food and excellent en suite accommodation. The extensive menu is based on fresh Welsh produce and is served Monday to Thursday evenings from 6.30pm

to 9pm. Friday to Sunday, a snacks menu is available. On Fridays, a live singer entertains from, from 8.30pm; on Saturday from 9pm, and on Sundays there's a Quiz from 8.30pm. Payment at the Miskin is by cash or cheque only.

405

274 THE PRINCE OF WALES

21 High Street, Treorchy,
Rhondda Cynon Taff CF42 6AA
☎ 01443 773121
e-mail: princeofwales@unicornbox.co.uk

Treorchy became one of the best known mining towns in the world because of the international fame of the Treorchy Male Choir which is the oldest in Wales. Located on the main street in this busy little town is **The Prince of Wales,** a lively and popular hostelry which Janet and Darren Hale took over in the summer of 2007. This fine old traditional inn is noted for its well-kept draught brews which include Carling, Strongbow and Worthington Creamflow. The inn also serves quality pub grub based as far as possible on local produce. The three chefs offer a varied menu with something for every palate. Food is served from noon until 2.15pm, Tuesday to Saturday, and

there's a traditional roast at Sunday lunchtime. Wednesday evening is Curry Night from 7pm to 9.15pm, all year round except over the Christmas period. There's also live entertainment on Thursday and Saturday evenings from 9.15pm, and a live artist entertains on Sunday afternoon once a month. Children are welcome; payment is by cash only; and there's good disabled access throughout.

276 JEFFREYS ARMS HOTEL

Jeffrey Street, Caegarw, Mountain Ash,
Rhondda Cynon Taff CF45 4AD
☎ 01443 475930

Located just off the A4059 at Mountain Ash, the **Jeffreys Arms Hotel** is a welcoming family-run hostelry where David and Sandra Lock and their family took over in the summer of 2007. They are experienced hosts and quickly put the inn back on the map again after a rather difficult period. It is now firmly established as a place where good food and well-kept ales can be guaranteed. Phil is the professional chef and specialises in wholesome and appetising home-cooked food. His menu offers a versatile choice of dishes, all freshly prepared from fresh, quality ingredients. Food is served from 6pm to 9pm on Tuesday, from noon until 2pm and from 6pm to 9pm, Wednesday to Friday; from noon until 9pm on

Saturday; and from noon until 4pm on Sunday. Phil's Sunday roasts are very popular so it's a very good idea to book ahead. A rotating real ale is on tap. The Lock family also run the nearby Cefnpennar Inn at Cefnpennar which they have owned since 1991. Sandra is the cook here and has a well-established reputation for providing top quality dishes.

275 THE DUNRAVEN HOTEL

13 Dunraven Street, Treherbert,
Mid-Glamorgan CF42 5BG
☎ 01443 778222
e-mail: dunravenhotel@btconnect.com

Located in the village of Treherbert at the head of the Rhondda Valley, **The Dunraven Hotel** has been dispensing hospitality for almost a century and a half. Its spacious rooms, wood-panelled walls and quality furnishings present the appearance of a rather grand country house rather than a village hostelry. Nick and Ruth Watson took over at this fine old traditional establishment in 2003 and have made the hotel a popular venue for locals and visitors alike.

The bar is open all day, every day, with John Smith and Worthington Creamflow among the most popular brews. The hotel is noted for its excellent food which is served every lunchtime and evening. The menu offers a good variety of dishes based on local produce, freshly prepared and served in generous portions. At Sunday lunchtime the regular menu is replaced by traditional roasts and booking is strongly recommended. In good weather, refreshments can be enjoyed on the terrace in the peaceful beer garden.

The hotel's accommodation comprises 9 comfortable rooms of various sizes. There is also good disabled access to the ground floor.

277 PEPPERS RESTAURANT

27 Cannon Street, Aberdare CF44 7AP
☎ 01685 884011

Located in the heart of Aberdare, the popular **Peppers Restaurant** has been owned and run by the same family for 20 years. Elaine and Jim Bradley, and Elaine's mum Joan Evans, are all involved in the enterprise. Elaine, with the aid of two chefs, is in charge of the kitchen and her menu offers a varied choice of home-cooked dishes that includes an All Day Breakfast, home-made pies, jacket potatoes and other light meals. The menu also offers fish, meat and salad dishes, and is supplemented by daily specials. Fresh, seasonal produce is used, and roast lunches are available every day. Booking for Sunday lunchtime is strongly advised. Don't miss out on the wonderful tarts and cakes such as Butterscotch and

Walnut, and Chocolate Fudge. Food is served from 9am to 5.30pm, Monday to Saturday, and from 11.30am to 3.30pm on Sunday. Peppers is licensed and the bar offers a good choice of beers, lagers and spirits, with house wine available by the glass or small bottle. Children are welcome at Peppers, there's good wheelchair access; payment is by cash or cheque only.

279 THE OLD WHITE HORSE

12 High Street, Pontneddfechan,
Neath SA11 5MP
☎ 01639 721219
e-mail: anthonymorgan.unicornboxco.uk

Hidden away in the village of Pontneddfechan in the Vale of Neath, the **Old White Horse Inn** is a fine old hostelry noted for its excellent food and well-kept ales. Mine hosts are Tony and Clare, a local couple who took over here in the summer of 2007. Their delightful inn dates back to the early 1800s and has an enticing olde worlde atmosphere with its exposed beams and a log fire in the bar area. Clare is an outstanding chef and her menu offers a varied choice of dishes with something to suit every palate. Home-made soup and Atlantic prawn cocktail feature amongst the starters while the main courses range from home-cooked 'Cow Pie', through grills and curries to lighter options such as jacket potatoes and filled baguettes. Vegetarians and children have their own options and in addition to the

regular menu, Clare also dreams up some daily specials. Food is served from noon until 9pm, Wednesday to Sunday. To complement your meal, the bar stocks a wide range of beverages including 2 real ales, Brains 8A and a guest brew. The inn is closed on Monday evenings, but open all day for the rest of the week; payment is by cash or cheque only. Also available is an adjacent Bunkhouse that sleeps up to 8 people.

278 WELSH HARP INN

Trecynon, Aberdare,
Mid-Glamorgan CF44 8LU
☎ 01685 872450
e-mail: dj@welshharpinn.freeserve.co.uk
🌐 www.welsh-harp.co.uk

Located opposite picturesque Aberdare Park, the **Welsh Harp Inn** is a family business that has been run on traditional lines for 50 years. David and Janet Fowler introduced catering over 30 years ago and have never looked back, building up a reputation for fine food and unique dishes, whilst utilising fresh, local produce whenever possible. Customers travel from far afield to enjoy their unusual and original recipes, or to refresh memories of their old established dishes.

The restaurant area seats a comfortable 40 and has recently been refurbished, along with the lounge, in the Art Deco / Nouveau styles. The kitchen crew comprises the chef, David, who creates the menus as well as many original recipes, Janet who organises the restaurant when David's cooking and the cooking when David is not. Second chef Alison has been with them for many years and together with Nick, the Maitre de, responsible for the comprehensive wine list and organising staff out front, form a tight knit team.

Mike meanwhile controls the Bar and Lounge areas and the general running of the liquid side of the business. A fine selection of wines, at reasonable prices, together with Beers, Lagers and a large varied selection of bottled Beer from around the globe.

Every six weeks or so the Welsh Harp create a different menu to ensure an interesting and varied menu is always available. Special Gourmet Evenings are a regular occurrence, which entails a complete evening of three specialy prepared courses, followed by a selection of cheeses, a glass of port and concluding with freshly made coffee, all for a set price. "These nights are always a pleasure to create menus for" says David, "as there seems to be many people who enjoy a taste of unusual and varied cuisine whilst enjoying an evening with like minded folk". At a recent evening, customers were given a choice of 3 options from 3 courses. For a starter you could have had thin slices of home cured Salt Beef on a bed of Penne lightly coated in a Walnut cream sauce and garnished with chopped pickled Walnuts. As a main course, how about Seared Sea Bass on a nest of sauteed Bok Choi and Spring Onion floating in Champagne Sauce. And for dessert, perhaps Green Apple Mousse, apples softened in butter, layered between dark chocolate and apple mousse and encircled with Giaconda sponge atop a delicate Cinnamon Sauce. Definitely a meal to remember.

Sunday lunches are a sell out and with their own home cooked roasts, fresh vegetables and Janets Gravy, prior booking is essential. The Welsh Harp has been awarded a Food Hygiene Certificate by the Environmental Services. For more information visit their website.

280 TY NEWYDD COUNTRY HOTEL

Penderyn Road, Hirwaun,
Mid-Glamorgan CF44 9SX
☎ 01685 813433 Fax: 01685 813139
e-mail: relax@ tynewyddcountryhotel.co.uk
🌐 www.tynewyddcountryhotel.co.uk

The outstanding **Ty Newydd Country Hotel** is set at the end of a lengthy drive off the A4059 on the edge of the Brecon Beacons National Park. The house was originally built by the coal baron, William Llewellyn, the uncle of Olympic show jumping gold medallist Sir Harry Llewellyn, who trained his horse Foxhunter here. The detached property was constructed in the 1930s in the neo-Georgian style; the bedroom wings and function rooms were added in 1989 and 1991 and more recently, conservatory extensions have also been added to the side and rear of the building.

Today, this privately-run and very special hotel provides every modern convenience for today's discerning guests whilst retaining the character and style of a fine Georgian country house. It boasts an excellent restaurant, log fires, a welcoming bar and lovely gardens with magnificent views of the Beacons and Neath Valley.

The hotel is renowned for its excellent cuisine and friendly service. In the delightful George Restaurant the lunchtime and evening menus feature a traditional selection of home-made dishes using the freshest fish, local game, meats and locally sourced seasonal produce. Children have their own unusually varied menu.

The residents bar has three quarter height oak panelling and the residents lounge has an open log fire and an adjoining art gallery featuring the work of local artists.

At the day's end, residents can retire to the splendid comfort of one of the 28 beautifully appointed bedrooms. There are room sizes and styles to suit everyone, from standard rooms to spacious family room and luxuriously appointed superior rooms. There are four poster beds, Jacuzzi baths big enough to share, and rooms with fantastic views. Most rooms feature an en suite bathroom with bath and/or power shower; colour television; radio alarm; direct dial telephone; complimentary broadband access; hair dryer; trouser press; hospitality tray and the latest books and magazines. The hotel welcomes wheelchair users and has three ground floor bedrooms with extra wide doors, ramps, handrails and low switches to make your stay comfortable.

With its elegant ambience, excellent facilities and lovely gardens, the hotel is particularly popular as a quality choice for conferences and weddings hosting, on average, 100 weddings per year.

Church Road, Penderyn,
nr Aberdare CF44 9JR
☎ 01685 811914 Fax: 01685 811914

The popular **Red Lion Inn** stands opposite the ancient church in the village of Penderyn and it's believed that the masons building the church in around 1120 were housed in what is now the Red Lion. The inn has been owned and run since 1978 by the James family - Keith and Beryl, their daughter Natalie and son Leighton. Together they have made the inn the hub of village life and currently are planning to create workshops to house local crafts people plus an information centre within the inn's grounds. The Red Lion is open every evening and Saturday and Sunday lunchtimes with longer opening hours in the summer and on Bank Holidays. Beer lovers will be delighted to find up to 12 brews to enjoy including

ones from the local Rhymney Brewery, Tomas Watkins and Brains Breweries. A selection of snacks is also available. During the lifetime of this book, the family hopes to be offering accommodation on a bed & breakfast or self-catering basis.

120 Hoel West Plas, Coity, Bridgend CF35 6BH
☎ **01656 653192**
e-mail: thesixbellsinn@aol.com

Located directly opposite the historic 12th century Coity Castle, The **Six Bells** inn is a welcoming family-run hostelry with Brian and Caroline Stiles and their son Ted all involved in the enterprise. The pub occupies a striking building with a half-

timbered upper storey and a decking area to the rear which is ideal for those al fresco moments.

The Six Bells is noted for its excellent food and has recently introduced a new menu offering a superb selection of freshly prepared, home-made dishes including Daily Specials and Sunday Roasts. Ted is the chef and his extensive menu ranges from traditional favourites like Fish & Chips, Chilli con Carne and home-made Steak and Ale Pie, to less familiar dishes such as the Salmon Kyoto, Spinach & Stilton Stuffed Chicken and a vegetarian home-made Leek & Mushroom Crumble. Or you might be tempted by the

Six Bells Feast for two, an appetising medley of chicken wings, chunky beer-battered chips, breaded mushrooms, onion rings, spring rolls, scampi and garlic bread. The menu also features a tasty selection of grills and salads. Portions are generous and the prices provide remarkable value for money. And don't miss out on the wonderful desserts such as the home-made Apple & Blackberry Pie or Rhubarb & Ginger Crumble. Food is served from noon until 3pm and from 6pm to 9pm, Monday to Friday; from noon until 9pm on Saturday, and from noon until 4pm on Sunday - on Sundays a traditional roast dinner is available. On Wednesday and Friday lunchtimes, a special 'Seniors' 2-course meal is available.

To accompany your meal, the well-stocked bar stocks a comprehensive range of beverages including a range of quality cask conditioned ales, premium lagers and wines. There are 3 real ales on tap, Hancocks HB, Worthington and Wadsworth 6X.

Children and dogs are welcome at the Six Bells; payment is by cash or cheque only; and there is good disabled access throughout. The inn is open from noon until 11pm, Monday to Saturday, and from noon until 10.30pm on Sunday.

Mary Street, Porthcawl CF36 3YA
☎ 01656 783510

Located just a short walk from the sea front and the town centre, **Seaways Hotel** is an impressive stone building with lofty bay windows and spacious rooms. Owners Judith and Colin Price took over here in the winter of 2007 and have been busy bringing the premises up to their own high standards. For holiday makers, the hotel offers a comfortable base from which to explore the many beauties of the area. Of the 16 attractively

furnished and decorated guest bedrooms, 10 have en suite facilities and there's a mixture of different sized rooms from single to family. All rooms available all year round and are equipped with colour television, direct dial telephone, radio and room call system, and hospitality tray.

Breakfast is served to both residents and non-residents from 7am to 9am; lunches from noon to 2.30pm with a good selection of bar meals; and in the evening the restaurant offers an extensive menu and wine list. Judith is an accomplished chef and her menu provides an appetising choice of home-cooked dishes based on the freshest and best of locally sourced ingredients. The hotel has two luxurious bars open throughout the day where the friendly atmosphere provides the perfect ambience for an enjoyable evening. Currently, just one real ale, Bass, is available but the Prices intend to add to this number. The hotel has good disabled access to the bars and restaurant; all major credit cards are accepted apart from American Express and Diners; and there is free street car parking between 6pm and 8am.

Visitors staying at Seaways will find plenty to see and do in the area. Activities available within easy reach include golf, mini golf, bowls, fishing trips from the harbour, many sandy beaches and the outdoor attractions of Margam Park Country Park. Places of interest just a short journey away include St Fagan's Folk Museum, the Day yr Ogof Caves, Cardiff and Caerphilly Castles, and the Afan Argoed Welsh Miners Museum.

The Square, Porthcawl,
Mid-Glamorgan CF36 3BW
☎ 01656 783380
e-mail: salthouseonthesquare@tiscali.co.uk

Located on the seafront at Porthcawl, the recently refurbished **Salthouse on the Square** offers two different kinds of dining experiences. The bar menu is available from 9.30am when a selection of breakfasts is served. At noon, the menu is extended to offer a good choice of lite bites and filled breads, Goat's Cheese Bruschetta, for example, and appetising main courses such as slow roasted Shoulder of Welsh Lamb, locally caught hake in beer batter and steaks. All the beef used by head chef Stuart Bevan is matured for a minimum of 21 days. The steaks are char-grilled to your liking and served with chunky chips or creamed potatoes, grilled tomatoes, flat cap mushrooms and a choice of sauces. Vegetarians are well-catered for with dishes such as Herb Risotto, Saffron Noodle Broth and Pesto Penne Pasta.

In addition to this appetising fare, owners Emma and Malcolm

Griffiths have created the Sodium Restaurant to provide fine dining for the discriminating customer. Of all the food served, 95% is made on the premises, including bread and ice cream. The menu changes seasonally but typical dishes include a smooth Artichoke Veloute, a Mosaic of Ham Hock and Foie Gras, or pan-fried Cornish Hake amongst the starters. As main courses, there's Fillet of Welsh Black Beef, Roast Line Caught Local Seabass, and a Plum Tomatoes & Greek Feta Tart. And for dessert, how about home-made Ice Cream & Sorbets, Raspberry & Passion Fruit Delice, or white Chocolate & Bailey's Torte. To accompany your meal, the bar stocks a wide range of beverages including 3 real ales with Brains SA as the regular brew, plus two rotating guest ales. The restaurant is open from 6.30pm to 9.30pm, Monday to Saturday, and seats 30. Bookings are advisable, especially at weekends.

Salthouse on the Square welcomes children until 9pm, later if they are dining, and is also disabled friendly with a ramp access and disabled toilets, as well as baby-changing facilities. The restaurant also arranges entertainment of various kinds on Thursdays from 8pm. All major credit cards are accepted apart from American Express and Diners.

The Esplanade, Porthcawl CF36 3YR
☎ 01656 782004

The Pier Café occupies a superb position on the Esplanade at Porthcawl looking out to sea. This quality tea room and café is owned and run by business partners Esther Phillips and Andrea Clarke, together with Esther's mum, Kath. Through their charm, hospitality and culinary skills they have made this one of the most popular eating places in the area. Their days starts at 8am with a breakfast menu that ranges from a mighty Pier Breakfast to lighter bites such as fried eggs or baked beans and egg on toast, along with Breakfast Sarnies. From 11.30am a selection of light bites is served including jacket potatoes, baguettes, sandwiches, rolls, wraps and paninis. Hearty salads are also available. Everything is freshly made to order and the ingredients are, wherever possible, sourced within Wales. Particularly popular at the café are the wonderful home-made pies and cakes, along with scones, assorted muffins and toasted

teacakes. During the winter months the café closes between 4.30pm and 5pm but during the season is open until late every day of the week. The café can seat 70 customers inside with space for a further 50 on the outside patio. Please note that payment at The Pier is by cash only.

HIDDEN PLACES GUIDES

Explore Britain and Ireland with *Hidden Places* guides - a fascinating series of national and local travel guides.

Packed with easy to read information on hundreds of places of interest as well as places to stay, eat and drink.

Available from both high street and internet booksellers

For more information on the full range of *Hidden Places* guides and other titles published by Travel Publishing visit our website on

www.travelpublishing.co.uk
or ask for our leaflet by phoning
01752 276660 or emailing
info@travelpublishing.co.uk

Penarth, South Glamorgan CF64 5UY
☎ 02920 701678

Set within the park. **Cosmeston Medieval Village** is a Heritage project that is unique in Britain. The reconstructed **14th Century** village is on its original site and consists of medieval buildings. gardens, rare breeds and a small yet fascinating museum. Special events are held throughout the year including jousting.

combat, archery and medieval crafts. There is a small admission charge to the village. Cosmeston Lakes Country Park has free car parking for 350 cars at the entrance with reserved spaces for disabled visitors. The visitor centre houses an information/reception area with gift shop. display area. toilets and restaurant.

287 THE SIX BELLS

Penmark, Vale of Glamorgan CF62 3BP
☎ 01446 710229
⊕ www.sixbellspenmark.co.uk

The tiny hamlet of Penmark is found just over a mile from Cardiff International Airport and is well worth seeking out to pay a visit to **The Six Bells**, a spacious, convivial and welcoming place where Allan Roberts is the friendly host. The expansive floor space is divided into three areas - the public bar with

its log fire, the lounge/restaurant and the spacious and attractive function suite. The whole of the premises were completely refurbished in the winter of 2007. The inn is open every lunchtime and evening and the well-stocked bar offers a comprehensive choice of beverages, including 3 real ales. Children are welcome; there's good disabled access throughout, and all major credit cards are accepted.

288 THE BEACH CAFÉ

Llantwit Major,
Vale of Glamorgan CF61 1RF
☎ 01446 792665
e-mail: davehoskins@hotmail.com

Standing just a few yards from the beach at Llantwit Major, **The Beach Café** has been owned and run by the same family for more than 40 years. Today, Maria and David continue the family tradition of providing quality food throughout the day and giving a warm welcome to all their customers. The day starts with a selection of breakfasts served from 9am to 11.45am, followed by a full menu of delicious home-cooked food based on Welsh produce. The regular menu is always supplemented by a choice of daily specials. The café, which has featured in the S4C television programme *Y Pris*, is open every day of the year except Christmas Day from 9am until 10pm in summer, and from 9am to 5pm out of season. In

addition to the 65-seat restaurant, in good weather customers can

also take advantage of the outside patio overlooking the beach. The café also sells takeaway foods and ice creams along with confectionery, souvenirs and beach toys. Maria and David are also happy to take bookings for functions and parties. The café has good disabled access throughout.

416

Monknash, nr Cowbridge,
Vale of Glamorgan CF71 7QQ
☎ 01656 890209
e-mail: info@theploughmonknash.com
⊕ www.theploughmonknash.com

Just a short walk from the seafront, **The Plough and Harrow** is a real gem with a superb olde worlde interior with real fires and ancient beams decked with brasses and vintage pottery. In the restaurant a fascinating collection of rugby memorabilia adorns the walls. Mine host Gareth

Davies took over here in the summer of 2007 having been manager for the previous 18 months. He presides over a bar where lovers of fine ales will be delighted to find themselves presented with a choice of 9 cask ales with Bass and Hereford Pale Ale as the regular brews. There's also a choice of 12 traditional ciders, most of them brewed in Wales. The pub is noted too for the quality of its food which is prepared by a professional chef. A bar menu is available at both lunchtimes and in the evenings when an à la carte menu is also available. The varied choice includes dishes such as Diced Venison cooked in port and cranberries, Spanish-style Paella, and vegetarian alternatives such as Wild Mushroom brandy puff pastry strudel. Such is the popularity of the restaurant that booking ahead at weekends is highly advisable.

Ewenny Road, St Bride's Major, nr Bridgend,
Vale of Glamorgan CF32 0SA
☎ 01656 880285
⊕ www.stbridesmajor.com

The Fox & Hounds is a family run local village pub at the heart of St Brides Major. The landlord is Mark Lewis, a local man who recognised that St Brides Major needed its local village pub back. Gone are the days when it was a restaurant, and back are the traditional values of a true village local. The two bar areas offer a slightly different experience depending on your preference. The lower bar boasts a traditional ambience with a wood burning stove and comfortable sofa area for a relaxing and cosy time by the fire. This area is accompanied by tables to enable socialising with friends or a place to sit down and enjoy a freshly cooked meal from the quality menu. The top bar

lends itself to a more contemporary atmosphere whilst respecting the values of a traditional village pub. The pool table, quiz machine, juke box and darts board provide an invitation for a friendly competition or a more relaxed game to pass the time, perhaps whilst enjoying one of the 3 real ales on tap - Hancocks HB and Bass, and a rotating guest ale.

291 EWENNY FARM GUEST HOUSE

Ewenny Cross, Ewenny, Bridgend,
Vale of Glamorgan CF35 5AX
☎ 01656 658438 Fax: 01656 655565
🌐 www.ewennyfarm-guesthouse.co.uk

Set in 2½ acres of lovely grounds but just 10 minutes from junction 35 of the M4, **Ewenny Farm Guest House** offers top of the range 4-star accommodation in a friendly relaxed atmosphere. This is very much a family-run business with Howard Jennings, his son Mark and daughter-in-law Claire all involved in the enterprise. They have been welcoming bed & breakfast guests here since 1998 with many of their customers paying repeat visits. The house has 8 well-appointed bedrooms, all of them with high quality double beds, en suite facilities, remote colour TV, direct dial telephone, radio and hospitality tray. Comfort is of paramount importance for all guests at Ewenny Farm, so each room is very spacious and equipped with easy chairs. There are also stunning views of the surrounding grounds and countryside. There is no extra charge for single occupancy and special rates available for long stays. The house has a large secure car park available to all guests. The tariff includes a hearty breakfast, served from 7am to 8.30pm and although the Jennings do not provide evening meals there are plenty of good eating establishments nearby.

Visitors to Ewenny Farm will find plenty to see and do in the area. Ewenny Priory, dating back to 1141, is one of the finest fortified religious houses in Britain and the nearby Ewenny Pottery, founded in 1610, has been in the same family ever since. It is believed to be the oldest working pottery in Wales. Ogmore Castle and its famous Stepping Stones should not be missed, while golfers will want to face the challenge presented by the course at Southerndown Golf Club. The

maestro Henry Cotton described the first hole here as one of the most difficult opening holes he'd encountered. This downland links championship course has wonderful rolling fairways and fast greens. At high tide the beach is totally useless but at other times this is a huge sandy beach. It's great for the kids with lots of rock pools and fossils - though keep away from the cliffs as they can fall at any time. Nearby are the remains of Dunraven Castle. About 30 years ago the castle was demolished by the Earl of Dunraven in a fit of pique because the local council wouldn't let him develop it.

Church Road, Llanblethian, Cowbridge,
Vale of Glamorgan CF71 7JF
☎ 01446 772995

A fine old traditional village hostelry, **The Cross Inn** is family-run by the Jones family who arrived here in the autumn of 2007. Good wholesome food is a priority here with an appetising choice available every lunchtime and evening, except Sunday evening. The lunchtime menu offers a choice of light bites (including Welsh rarebit, naturally), baguettes and salads. The main menu has a good selection of grills, jacket potatoes, burgers and old favourites such as Steak & Ale Pie, Scampi, and Cod in beer batter. In addition to the regular menu, daily specials are also available. Food is served from noon to 2.30pm, and from 6.30pm to 9.30pm, Monday to Saturday, and from noon until 4.30pm on Sunday. On Sundays only traditional roasts and a

vegetarian alternative are served and it is advisable to

book ahead for this meal. Real ales are on tap with Hancocks HB as the regular brew plus a guest ale. Children are welcome; there's good disabled access throughout; all major credit cards are accepted apart from American Express and Diners; and the inn has its own off road parking.

295 TECHNIQUEST SCIENCE DISCOVERY CENTRE 🏛

Stuart Street, Cardiff,
South Glamorgan CF10 5BW
☎ 02920 475475
e-mail: catherine@techniquest.org
🌐 www.techniquest.org

Techniquest Science Discovery Centre located in Cardiff Bay has over 150 hands on interactive exhibits, covering all aspects of science. Family show in the Science Theatre cover topics from Slime to Superhero's and run during school holidays and at weekends. Visitors can also visit the Planetarium which has a choice of an under 7s or an over 7s show and both are followed by a tour of the stars.

Cowbridge Road, Aberthin, Cowbridge,
Vale of Glamorgan CF71 7HB
☎ 01446 773429

About a mile north of Aberthin on the A4222 is the **Farmers Arms,** a fine old hostelry dating back to the early 1800s. Mine host is Michael Pugh, a qualified chef who took over here in 2003. His appetising cooking is what attracts discerning diners from all over the area. There are separate menus for lunch and dinner. Between noon and 2pm, Tuesday to Friday and until 2.30pm on Saturday the menu offers a good choice of dishes ranging from freshly prepared soup served with hot French bread or cheeseburger to main courses such as Jumbo Battered Cod and Hot Chicken Salad. In the evenings, from 6pm to around 9pm (9.30pm on Saturday), a more extensive menu offers old favourites such as Ham 'n' Eggs or Chicken Curry as well as interesting dishes such as the starter Sticks of Fire - crisp pastry sticks filled with chicken, shredded white

cabbage, chives, diced water chestnuts and chilli, deep fried and served with a chilli relish dip. For the main course, the choice includes a selection of char-grilled dishes - Caribbean Chicken Stir Fry, perhaps - to the hearty Farmers Arms Combos. One of these, the Farmer's Surf and Turf presents you with a 10oz rump steak served with two butterfly whole tail prawns and three whole tail scampi. Vegetarian options include a Mushroom & Cashew Nut Stroganoff and a Spicy Vegetable Curry "served with a poppadom and 'arf 'n' arf pilau or boiled rice". Children have their own menu featuring dishes such as Chicken Nuggets or Fishasaurus. There's a separate menu for Sunday lunch with a choice of 4 different roasts. Small and children's portions of the main course are available. The dining area seats up to 60 people but such is the popularity of Michael's cooking that it is advisable to book ahead at all times. To accompany your meal the bar stocks a comprehensive range of beverages including a minimum of 2 real ales with Hobgoblin and Wadsworth 6X as the regular brews.

In good weather customers at the Farmers Arms can enjoy their refreshments in the outdoor covered patio area which has a stream running alongside. All major credit cards are accepted apart from American Express; the inn has good disabled access throughout and there's ample off road parking space.

294 THE BUSH

St Hilary, Cowbridge,
Vale of Glamorgan CF71 7DP
☎ 01446 772745
e-mail: artizan.leisure@virgin.net
🌐 www.artizanleisure.com

Inns don't come any more picturesque than **The Bush** in the village of St Hilary near Cowbridge. With its low-slung thatched roof, bay windows and roaring log fires, it's an absolute delight. The food is very good too with chef Kurt Fleming dedicated

to creating varied and interesting dishes based on honest-to-goodness Welsh produce. Kurt believes that the quality and integrity of his food should be something special - prepared with passion and served with relaxed, friendly informality. The menu changes weekly but typically include popular dishes like the traditional Welsh faggots served with buttered mash and garden peas, or the Glamorgan sausages, pan fried Penclawdd laver bread with bacon and, of course, Welsh rarebit on crusty bread with local bacon. But the menu also offers a good selection of steaks, fish and poultry dishes. Vegetarians have

an unusually wide choice with dishes such as fresh local asparagus and Welsh brie baked in puff pastry, and a Welsh Stilton, walnut and pear salad with a crème fraiche dressing. In addition to the regular menu, at lunchtime a light lunch menu is available with dishes such as sliced mushrooms in a cream sauce with garlic and herbs served on toasted ciabatta, burgers, ploughman's, freshly baked baguettes and seasonal salads. To complete your meal, choose from a selection of freshly prepared home made desserts or from the range of organic artisan cheeses from Neal's Yard served with home made chutney.

Food is served every lunchtime from noon until 2.30pm (3pm on Sunday), and Monday to Saturday evenings from 6.30pm to 9.30pm. To accompany your meal, quality real ales (3 of them) and beers are on tap, together with a progressive, interesting, varied and well priced wine list - many of which are available by the glass. Booking is strongly recommended and essential at weekends. Children are welcome; there's good disabled access throughout and all major credit cards are accepted apart from American Express and Diners.

Church Road, St Brides Wentllooge,
Newport NP10 8SN
☎ 01633 680807

The village of St Brides Wentllooge is located just off the B4239 southwest of Newport and close to the mouth of the River Severn. It's well worth seeking out in order to enjoy the quality food and drink on offer at the **Church House Inn** which is found just a few hundred yards from the village's 13th century church. Mine hosts, Gary and Sharon, took over here in the summer of 2007, bringing with them a wealth of experience in the hospitality business. Sharon is an outstanding cook and her menus offer something for every palate. Her Sunday Carvery, when there are 3 different roasts served, is particularly popular, so much so that booking is essential. To accompany your meal, there's a comprehensive selection of beverages available,

including 2 real ales - Brains Bitter and Brains SA. The inn is child-friendly with a play area in the excellent beer garden where during the summer months there's also a bouncy castle. Once a month, the inn holds a themed evening and there's also occasional entertainment. The inn has good disabled access throughout; all major credit cards except American Express and Diners are accepted.

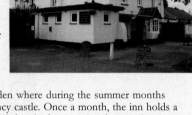

297 THE WHEATSHEAF INN

The Square, Magor,
Monmouthshire NP26 3HN
☎ 01633 880608 Fax: 01633 889282
e-mail: wheatsheafinn @msn.com

Offering the very best in accommodation, food and drink, **The Wheatsheaf Inn** dates in part to the 14th century and was formerly known as the Princess of Wales. A complete refurbishment was carried out in the autumn of 2007 which has

upgraded the inn's facilities while retaining all its charm and character. Mine hosts at the Wheatsheaf are Clare and Dave Hennah who took over here in 2001 but have some 13 years experience of the hospitality business. Clare is in charge of the kitchen and her expertise has made the inn well known for its excellent home-cooked food. Particularly popular are her famous Wheatsheaf Curry, homemade lasagne and Steak & Ale Pie. The menu also offers a good choice of grills with a mixed grill made to satisfy those with the most hearty of appetites, 5oz rump, 6oz gammon, 2 lamb cutlets & a pork sausage served with onion rings, and mushrooms. For those with lighter appetites, the Snack Menu offers a selection of dishes including an all day breakfast,

burgers, jacket potatoes and sandwiches/ciabattas. On weekdays, from noon until 5pm, there's a Meal Deal menu with a variety of dishes at very reasonable prices. On Sunday lunchtimes, roasts are added to the regular menus. Food is served from noon until 9.30pm, Monday to Saturday, and from noon until 3pm on Sunday. Booking ahead is strongly recommended on Friday, Saturday and Sunday. In good weather, you can enjoy your meal outside in the beer garden where there is a dining area with heating. To accompany your meal, a full range of beverages is available including 4 real ales - Flowers is the regular brew, the other 3 rotate and many come from small micro-breweries.

The Wheatsheaf also offers quality accommodation in 6 attractively furnished and well-appointed rooms, all of which have en suite facilities and are available all year round. The inn has good disabled access and toilet; children are welcome and there's ample off road parking.

Magor Road, Llanmartin,
South Wales NP18 2EB
☎ 01633 413382
🌐 www.theoldbarn-llanmartin.co.uk or
🌐 www.theoldbarn-llanmartin.com

The hamlet of Llanmartin is tucked away in the South Wales countryside just a short distance from the A48. Apart from the glorious scenery, the major attraction here is **The Old Barn Country Inn & Restaurant** which is an absolute must for anyone who appreciates outstanding food prepared from top quality ingredients and beautifully presented. Owners Jackie and Phil Moore took over this Free House in 2004 and have maintained a superlative standard not just with the restaurant but also in the lounge.

The menus change regularly to make the best of seasonal produce. The Lite Bite menu offers amongst the starters dishes such as grilled goat's cheese served on mixed leaves, chef's soup of the day, and Mexican nachos with salsa cheese and jalapeno peppers. Main courses include old favourites such as traditional fish & chips, or steak and guinness pie, along with grilled breast of chicken Cajun style and a supreme of poached salmon with a sweet chili sauce and salad. Also available is a selection of salads and tortilla wraps.

The main menu is a gastronome's delight. As a starter, how about mushrooms in a sauce of port and Stilton, finished with cream and served with French bread? For the main course, there's an extensive choice of grills, fish, poultry, pasta and salad dishes, Vegetarians are well catered for with an unusually wide selection of meals written on the blackboard. The main menu is available from noon until 2.30pm and 6pm to 9.30pm, Monday to Thursday; from noon until 9.30pm on Friday and Saturday; and from noon until 8pm on Sunday. The Lite Bite menu is served from noon until 2.30pm and from 6pm to 7pm, daily and all day Friday and Saturday. Meals can be enjoyed in the 50-seater restaurant, but alfresco dining is also available for up to 30 diners on the patio which is heated, lit and can be fully covered.

The Old Barn will be able to offer 4 star en suite accommodation from July 2008. One of the rooms is a suite; 8 of the rooms are on the ground floor, some rooms can be interconnecting, and some are disabled friendly. Children are welcome; all major credit cards are accepted apart from American Express and Diners; and there's plenty of off road parking.

299 THE LORD NELSON INN

Commercial Street, Nelson, Treharris,
Mid-Glamorgan CF46 6ND
☎ 01443 451116

A charming stone-built hostelry, **The Lord Nelson Inn** has a history that goes back to the late 1500s. Owned and run by Kelvin Rees since the spring of 2006, this fine old traditional inn has a glowing reputation for its well-kept real ales and its excellent food. There are 2 real ales on tap, Brains SA and Rev. James, along with a

comprehensive range of other beverages. The varied menu on offer, based on locally sourced ingredients, includes amongst the starters spicy Thai fish cakes, and breaded Camembert filled with cranberries in a rich sweet sauce. For the main course, the choice ranges from grills and curries to fish dishes, from freshly boiled Glamorgan ham to freshly prepared Welsh faggots served with mushy peas and buttered mash with a rich onion gravy. A daily choice of vegetarian options is available on request, children have their own menu and daily specials are listed on the chalkboards. Food is served from noon until 2pm, and from 6pm to 9pm, Monday to Saturday; and from noon until 3pm on Sunday. If you are planning to stay in Nelson, the inn has 6 standard rooms available - 3 doubles and 3 family rooms. Children are welcome and all major credit cards are accepted.

Pontllanfraith, Gwent NP12 2HT
☎ 01495 220255
🌐 www.halfway-house.co.uk

Tucked away in the hillside of Pontllanfraith near Blackwood, **The Halfway House** really is a hidden treasure. A country pub oozing with tradition, style and good old-fashioned values, this

has been made probably the most popular destination for miles around by the welcoming mine host, Graham Pugh.

The inn offers an extensive selection of real ales to complement the tantalising home-cooked food, based on local produce, and prepared by professional chefs, which is served every day. The extensive menu includes a succulent 8oz Fillet Steak, freshly prepared Salmon Escalope with a sweet chilli sauce, traditional lamb Shank served in red wine and rosemary sauce, and the inn's own Indian Curry - a hot chicken curry. Vegetarians are well-catered with dishes that include a Bourguinonne served with rice and a rich red wine sauce containing courgettes, mushrooms, onions, celery and carrots topped with herb dumplings.

The inn's fish dishes are always popular, especially the Sea Food Penne - king prawns, cod, salmon and monkfish in a three cheese white wine and cream sauce served on a bed of pasta with garlic bread. Food is available every lunchtime from noon until 2pm (3.30pm on Sunday) and in the evening from 6pm to 9pm, (9.30pm on Saturday and Sunday). Such is the popularity of the food served here that booking is advisable at all times. In good weather, refreshments can be enjoyed in the large garden where customers can enjoy an al fresco evening in the lovely covered dining area and perhaps take a stroll through the orchard.

At the end of a great evening, what better way to finish the day than to stay in one of the Halfway House's beautifully appointed and newly refurbished rooms. All of these en suite double rooms have a 3-star rating and are equipped with flat screen TV, hospitality tray and all that you would require on a luxury stay away, not forgetting the far-reaching views of the countryside.

The Halfway House welcomes children and accepts all major credit cards.

301 | THE ROCK TAVERN

Tredegar Road, Blackwood,
Gwent NP12 1DD
☎ 01495 223441

When Paul and Jennifer Taylor took over **The Rock Tavern** (formerly the Rock Inn) it had fallen on difficult days and had actually closed down. Fortunately, with their 12 years experience in the trade, they knew what needed to be done and they set about transforming the place completely, revitalising the kitchen and re-introducing real ales. They re-opened in July 2007 and since then have gone from strength to strength.

The current real ales - London Pride as the regular, plus a guest brew - will be added to over time. Quality food is served every lunchtime and evening. At lunchtime (noon to 2.30pm) old favourites such as home-cooked ham, egg and chips, sausages and mash, and gammon steak, are supplemented by a selection of baguettes and jacket potatoes. In the evenings (6.15pm to 9.30pm) the more extensive menu offers dishes such as hot cheese-filled jalapenos or venison pâté among the starters, and grills, poultry, fish and vegetarian choices as main courses. Popular dishes include the lamb shank in mint and onion gravy, and the duck in black cherry

Kirsch sauce. At Sunday lunchtimes, the kitchen offers a choice of 4 different roasts - it is essential to book ahead for this meal and also for Friday and Saturday evenings. The inn is closed on Sunday evenings but open all day on Friday and Saturday. In good weather, refreshments can be enjoyed on the decked and covered area at the rear of the inn.

Currently, the Rock Tavern has 5 large guest bedrooms, all upstairs and all with en suite facilities. A sixth will soon be added. The B&B tariff includes a continental breakfast. The inn accepts all major credit cards except American Express and Diners and there is ample off road parking.

427

302 OPEN HEARTH INN ¶¶

Wern Road, Sebastopal, Pontypool,
Torfaen NP4 5DR
☎ 01495 763752 Fax: 01495 757453
e-mail: theopenhearth@btinternet.com

The **Open Hearth Inn** occupies a lovely position alongside the Brecon and Monmouthshire Canal in the village of Sebastopol, just a short drive south of Pontypool. This friendly and welcoming hostelry is very much a family affair with Don and Angela Jones, their son Phillip and daughters Cheryl and Lyndsey all actively involved in the business. The

inn is popular with lovers of real ales as if offers no fewer than 6 brews with Deuchars as the regular plus 5 rotating guest ales. Even more are on offer at the Beer Festivals hosted by the inn three or four times a year.

Quality food is another major attraction here. Cheryl is an accomplished cook and her extensive menu offers a choice ranging from a 16oz Mixed Grill, through traditional home-made pub meals, through fish dishes and vegetarian meals to a

selection of children's meals. That's just the regular menu, there are also daily specials. Food is served from noon until 9pm, Monday to Saturday, and from noon until 3pm on Sunday. Booking is essential at the weekends. Meals can be enjoyed either in the lounge, the 22-seater dining room, the 50-seater downstairs restaurant or, weather permitting, outside either on the decked area or at picnic tables beside the canal.

303 THE CROSS KEYS INN ¶¶ ⊢━

55 Five Locks Road, Pontnewydd,
Cwmbran NP44 1BT
☎ 01633 861545

A popular place with walkers, cyclists, pleasure boaters and bird watchers, the **Cross Keys** stands by the Monmouthshire & Brecon Canal a short drive north of Cwmbran. Leaseholders Chris and Sian Davies, here since the summer of 2002, have a

warm welcome for one and all, and in the bright, inviting bar a good range of drinks is dispensed, to enjoy either inside or out in the large beer garden by the canal. Food is served every day between 11 in the morning and 9.30 in the evening, and the printed menu and specials board offer a good range of generously served, reasonably priced dishes prepared by Sian and the cook Sue. All the old favourites are there - Cottage Pie, Liver & Onions,

and Steak & Ale Pie, along with an extensive choice of meat, poultry, fish and vegetarian dishes. Booking is advisable for Sunday lunch - when only roasts are served - and for parties of 10 or more. The area round the Cross Keys offers a wide variety of attractions for the visitor, and the inn's three guest bedrooms - one of them a family room - are available all year round.

428

304 THE LITTLE CROWN INN

Eiled Road, Wainfelin, Pontypool NP4 6DR
☎ 01495 763148 Fax: 01495 758211
e-mail: ajms229@aol.com

Hidden away in the village of Wainfelin, a short drive from Pontypool off the A4043, **The Little Crown Inn** is a fine old traditional hostelry which has been recently totally refurbished by owners Alison and Gus Gregory. The refurbishment has, if anything, enhanced the traditional character of this beautiful village inn. It is open all day, every day, and lovers of real ales will be pleased to know that there's always a choice of 3 rotating brews to enjoy. Another major attraction is the quality of the food on offer - honest-to-goodness home cooking and cooked to order. For Sunday lunch there are delicious roast dinners on offer, together with all the trimmings. Food is served

every lunchtime and evening except for Sunday evening. Children are welcome and all major credit cards are accepted. In good weather, customers can take advantage of the lovely beer garden with its lawns, patio area, picnic tables, barbecue and children's play area. The inn is disabled friendly with a ramp and disabled toilet, and there's a newly-created off road car park.

305 SPRINGFIELDS GUEST HOUSE

371 Llantarnam Road, Llantarnam, Cwmbran, Torfaen NP44 3BN
☎ 01633 482509
e-mail: Springfields@webster.uk.net
🌐 www. springfieldsguesthouse.com

If you plan to stay in this part of South Wales and are looking for comfortable bed & breakfast accommodation, **Springfields Guest House** could be just the place. It has a 3-star rating from Visit Wales and owners Theresa and Trevor have worked hard to create a genuine 'home-from-home' atmosphere. There are 9 guest bedrooms in this spacious Edwardian property, 4 of which are on the ground floor. Currently, 4 of the rooms have en suite facilities but during the lifetime of this guide, 2 more rooms will also be equipped. Breakfast at Springfields is definitely rather special with a menu that includes a full Welsh breakfast, eggs cooked in any way you want, kippers, smoked haddock and porridge. For the

younger visitors, cots, chairs, books and bears are available as well as family rooms with hide and seek corners. A large park with swans and swings is just two minutes drive away, and there are many attractions for the whole family to enjoy just a stone's throw away. Springfields also has a separate annex available which Theresa and Trevor call The Pantry. A local joiner has created a quality interior with features such as specially carved bed head boards.

306 BRITISH CONSTITUTION INN

41 Commercial Road, Talywain,
Pontypool NP4 7HT
☎ 01495 772768
e-mail: jh.robinson@btinternet.com

Mine hosts at the **British Constitution Inn,** Julie and Neville, only arrived here in the spring of 2007 and although it is their first venture they already have a success on their hands. Julie's Sunday lunches are especially popular, so much so that booking is strongly advised. During the lifetime of this book, Julie and Neville aim to extend their food service and also to offer accommodation. The inn has strong connections with rugby's 'Famous Pontypool Front Row' - the back room is named after them and sporting memorabilia abounds. Entertainment includes karaoke on Fridays, live music on Saturday, and Sky Sports.

307 MYNYDD LODGE GUEST HOUSE

Tillery Road, Cwmtillery NP13 1JN
☎ 01495 321052
e-mail: mynyddlodge@aol.com
⊕ www.abertillery.biz

A former Zion Chapel built in 1850, **Mynydd Lodge Guest House** was converted and stylishly refurbished with great flair by owners Nell and Lisa Coughlin. It now offers comfortable bed & breakfast accommodation in 9 guest bedrooms, 2 of them on the ground floor and all of them equipped with en suite facilities. Guests are welcome to stay on either a bed & breakfast, or

dinner, bed & breakfast basis. Evening meals are available from 5.30pm to 9.30pm; breakfast times are flexible.
Children are welcome and all major credit cards are accepted.

308 THE BRIDGEND INN

8 King Street, Brynmawr,
Gwent NP23 4RE
☎ 01495 310721

Cosy and welcoming, **The Bridgend Inn** began life as cottages built in the late 1600s which were later converted to create this fine traditional inn. The Smith family - Ashley, Graham and Rebecca arrived here in the summer of 2007 and have completely

refurbished the inn in traditional style and to a very high standard. This is a popular place for dining, with appetising and varied food served every lunchtime and evening, apart from Sunday evening. Children are welcome; all major credit cards are accepted.

Market Square, Brynmawr, Blaenau,
Gwent NP23 4AJ
☎ 01495 312430

Located in the heart of the town, **The Talisman** occupies a handsome late-Victorian building and has a very traditional and welcoming atmosphere. Sandra and David Williams have owned the inn since 1988 and have made The Talisman a popular venue for both townspeople and visitors. It is particularly noted for its outstanding food which is based on local produce and freshly prepared. At lunchtime (11.30am to 2pm), there's a fairly limited menu of dishes at very reasonable prices - Cumberland Sausage, for example, or a Club Steak Baguette. In the evening (7pm to 9.30pm) a much more extensive menu is available

that includes main meals such as home-made Beef Pie, grills, curries and vegetarian options like the Mushroom and Cheese Bake. For lighter appetites, there's a good selection of snacks, jacket potatoes, omelettes and salads. Meals can be enjoyed either in the upstairs dining room or in the bar areas. To accompany your meal, the bar stocks a comprehensive range of beverages including one real ale, Bass. Children are welcome at the Talisman, and there's good disabled access as well as a disabled toilet. Please note that the Talisman is closed on Sundays and that payment is by cash or cheque only.

Merthyr Road, Princetown,
Tredegar NP22 3AE
☎ 01685 844441
e-mail: johnrichardswcu@aol.com
🌐 www.princeofwales.me.uk

Located just a short distance off the 'Heads of the Valleys' road (A465), the **Prince of Wales Inn** is a superb country hostelry offering the very best in hospitality, food, ale and accommodation. Keri and John Richards have been here since the spring of 2005 and have made this Free House one of the most popular eating places in the area. Keri is an

outstanding cook and her extensive menu offers something for every palate. All the ingredients are sourced within Wales and along with old favourites such as steaks, curries and fish dishes you'll also find wild boar, venison and swordfish poached in a white wine sauce. These meals are all cooked to order and served in the elegant restaurant with its crisp white tablecloths. You can also eat in the bar with its centrally

located real fire. Here the choice includes steaks, home-made faggots, and plaice and chips. Food is

served every day from noon until 9pm. The inn also offers 3-star quality bed & breakfast in 2 comfortable ground floor rooms, both with en suite facilities. All major credit cards are accepted and there is good disabled access throughout.

431

311 CROWN INN

Nontybwch, Ashvale, Tredegar, Blaenau,
Gwent NP22 4AQ
☎ 01495 722176
e-mail: thecrowninn@btinternet.com

A fine old traditional country pub, **The Crown Inn** started life in the late 1700s as a coaching inn. Steve and Wendy Gunter took over here in the summer of 2007 and although it is their first venture in the hospitality business they have made a great success of the enterprise. An important element in that success has been the quality of the food on offer in the restaurant here. The menu offers a wide and varied choice of dishes, all freshly prepared by professional chefs using local produce wherever possible. The regular menu is supplemented by daily specials and during the week there's a special pensioners' lunch at value-for-money prices. Food is served from noon until 3pm, and from 6pm to 9pm, every day. In the bar,

the comprehensive range of beverages includes popular ales such as Carling, John Smith's Smooth, Brains Smooth and Fosters. In good weather, refreshments can be enjoyed in the peaceful beer garden. Please note that payment at the Crown is by cash or cheque only. Children are welcome and there's good disabled access throughout.

313 CHEPSTOW CASTLE

Castle Car Park, Bridge Street, Chepstow,
Gwent NP16 5EY
☎ 01291 624065

Chepstow Castle is set high upon cliffs above the River Wye, where it guarded the main river crossing from Southern England into Wales. It was one of the first stone castles in the country, built within a few years of the Battle of Hastings (1066), for William fitz Osbern, who had been made Earl of Hereford by William the Conqueror.

The castle was further developed during the first half of the 13th century by the Marshall family, and then later that century by Roger Bigod III, with more modifications made during the Tudor period. During the Civil War (1642-48) it was twice besieged and fell to Parliamentary cannon. After the war, the defences of the castle were reinforced and remodelled for the use of cannon and muskets. The castle was used as military barracks and as a detention centre for political prisoners, most notably housing Henry Marten who spent 20 years in captivity in the tower that now bears his name. The castle finally fell into disuse after 1690 when the remaining troops from the garrison were withdrawn.

Lone Lane, Penallt,
Monmouthshire NP25 4AJ
☎ 01600 712615
e-mail:theboatpenallt.co.uk
🌐 www.theboatpenallt.co.uk

Occupying a superb position on the bank of the River Wye looking across to Gloucestershire, **The Boat Inn** is a traditional Welsh pub with the unusual feature of being built against a solid rock face. Also rather uncommon is the fact that while the inn is in Wales, its car park is in England. Access via the old Rail Bridge. Business partners Ben Freeman and Shaleen Goodman took over the inn in the autumn of 2006 and they made this very olde worlde hostelry a popular venue, especially with walkers and

cyclists, The inn is open every lunchtime and evening, and all day on Saturday and Sunday. Wholesome and appetising food is served every lunchtime (noon until 2.30pm) and evening (7pm to 9pm) except Sunday nights. The menu offers something for every taste but why not try the speciality dish Pan Haggerty? Lovers of real ales will be very happy at the Boat. In summer, there are up to 8 brews served straight from cask (4 in winter), along with lagers, stout and no fewer than 10 traditional ciders & perry to sample. Because of their customers' interest in real

ales, Ben and Shaleen are planning to host a beer festival in 2008. And if you like country fruit wines, the bar stocks 25 of them in all. In summer, customers can enjoy their refreshments in the attractive gardens with waterfalls. Boats can moor here and on the first Sunday in September, a Raft Race is held on the river while live music entertains participants and watchers. Entertainment at the Boat is another major attraction with live music every Tuesday and Thursday from 9pm. The inn welcomes children and dogs; please note that payment is by cash or cheque only.

314 THE BRIDGE INN

Bridge Street, Chepstow, Gwent NP16 5EZ
☎ 01291 625622

Picturesquely sited close to Chepstow's elegant 5-arched cast iron bridge, **The Bridge Inn** is a fine old traditional town hostelry with a cosy, friendly atmosphere encouraged by mine hosts, Alan and Karen. The inn has a delightful riverside beer garden that looks out across the Wye to England on

the other bank. Inside, the comfortable bar with its log fire is well-stocked with a good selection of real ales, lagers, spirits and fine wines. The regular real ale is Brains with two other guest ales in rotation. The Inn has ample off street parking for patrons. Chepstow itself is a delightful old market town with an impressive and well-preserved Norman castle and a fine racecourse where the Welsh Grand National is run.

315 CALDICOT CASTLE

Church Road, Caldicot,
Monmouthshire NP26 4HU
☎ 01291 420241 Fax: 01291 435094
e-mail:
caldicotcastle@monmouthshire.gov.uk
🌐 www.caldicotcastle.co.uk

Visit **Caldicot Castle** in its beautiful setting of tranquil gardens and a wooded country park. Founded by the Normans, developed in royal hands as a stronghold in the Middle Ages and restored as a Victorian family home, the castle has a romantic and colourful history. Find out more with an audio tour, explore the medieval towers and take in the breathtaking views from the battlements. Enjoy a leisurely game of chess or drafts, using giant playing pieces, visit the Children's Activity Station or relax in the gardens and grounds. Events take place throughout the season. Open Daily March to October.

HIDDEN PLACES GUIDES

Explore Britain and Ireland with *Hidden Places* guides - a fascinating series of national and local travel guides.

Packed with easy to read information on hundreds of places of interest as well as places to stay, eat and drink.

Available from both high street and internet booksellers

For more information on the full range of *Hidden Places* guides and other titles published by Travel Publishing visit our website on

www.travelpublishing.co.uk
or ask for our leaflet by phoning
01752 276660 or emailing
info@travelpublishing.co.uk

64 Church Road, Caldicot,
Gwent NP26 4HW
☎ 01291 420509

Taking its name from the well-preserved Caldicot Castle just a few yards away, **The Castle Inn** is a handsome 17th century stone-built inn that presents a charming and cheerful exterior to the world. Inside, the atmosphere is warm and welcoming. After careful and sensitive restoration, the inn is a happy marriage of traditional and modern comforts. Mine hosts, Stephen and Judith Gribble, took over here in 2004 and since then have gathered an impressive array of awards. The *Morning Advertiser* acclaimed The Castle as both the Best Pub in Wales 2007 and also the Regional Family Pub of the Year 2007. And for the past three years in succession, it has received an award from the local council for the Best Garden in the Area.

A major factor in the Castle's success is the outstanding quality of the food served here. The extensive menu offers home-made soup, fresh creamy garlic mushrooms and home-made Thai salmon fishcakes amongst the starters. For the main course,

there's a difficult choice between the fresh fish dishes, the various steak options, pasta dishes and the range of old pub favourites like the 18oz Mixed Grill, home-made Chicken Curry or whole tail scampi. Early Bird diners have their own menu that includes dishes such as haddock in a home-made crispy beer batter, steaks and omelettes. In addition to the regular menu, there are daily Chef's Specials - Ostrich Steak, perhaps, or Wild Boar Fillet. Other specialities of the house include steaks and home-made steak & ale pie. Portions are generous and the prices very reasonable. Food is served from noon until 3pm, and from 5.30pm to 9pm, Monday to Saturday, and from noon until 5.30pm on Sunday. The Sunday menu is confined to roasts plus vegetarian and fish alternatives. Such is the popularity of the food here, it's a good idea to book ahead at all times. To accompany your meal, there's a comprehensive choice of beverages including 2 real ales - IPA and a guest ale.

Children are very welcome at the Castle. Outside in the large beer garden, there's a spacious play area with a Wild West fort. From time to time, the Castle hosts live entertainment on Saturday evenings, and there's also a Pub Quiz every other Sunday.

317 THE NORTHGATE INN

**Caerwent, nr Chepstow,
Monmouthshire NP26 5NZ
☎ 01291 425292**

Set back from the main A48 between Newport and Chepstow, the **Northgate Inn** is a handsome white-painted building dating back some 60 years. It takes its name from the adjacent ruins of the North Gate of the Roman city of Venta Silurum. Well furnished and smartly decorated, the inn has been in the capable hands of Viv and Chris Dure since 2003. It enjoys a glowing reputation for the quality of the food on offer. Along with old pub favourites such as Cottage Pie, ham, egg and chips, and battered cod, the menu offers a good choice of steaks, curries, chicken and vegetarian dishes. Food is served every lunchtime (noon until 3pm) and evening (6pm to 9pm), except for Sunday evening and all day Monday. The Sunday

roast lunch is particularly popular so booking ahead is strongly recommended. To accompany your meal, there's a choice of 2 real ales - the regular Theakston's XB and a guest ale - as well as a comprehensive selection of other drinks. If the weather is kind, refreshments can be enjoyed in the pleasant beer garden which also provides access to the North Gate ruins.

319 THE SOMERSET ARMS

**Victoria Street, Abergavenny,
Monmouthshire NP7 5DT
☎ 01873 852158**

Just a short walk from the town centre, **The Somerset Arms** is a popular hostelry, well-known locally for its range of draught ales - Carling, Worthington Creamflow and Strongbow. At lunchtime (noon until 2pm) a variety of bar snacks are available but the evening menu is just chicken - but

chicken grilled on the Rotisserie minutes before you eat it and served with home-made chips and your choice from a huge range of sauces. A vegetarian home-made lasagne is also available. Bookings only. On Thursdays the inn holds an open darts competition, and on Sunday, a quiz. Accommodation in 2 en suite rooms is also available.

320 CRUMBS CAFÉ

**5 Market Street, Abergavenny,
Monmouthshire NP7 5SD
☎ 01873 852614**

Located in the heart of Abergavenny, **Crumbs Café** will appeal to all those who love good old-fashioned home cooking. The café is owned by Helen Barrett-West who does the cooking and is assisted by her mother Susan. Among the most popular choices here are

faggots, gammon, minute steak and fish dishes, all prepared from locally sourced ingredients. In addition to the regular menu, there are also daily specials. In addition to the hot meals, there are some delicious home-made cakes and pies. Crumbs is open from 7.30am to 4pm, Monday to Saturday. Payment is by cash or cheque only.

Gwehelog, nr Usk,
Monmouthshire NP15 1RB
☎ 01291 672381
e-mail: stuart.savage@btconnect.com

A distinctive old building, **The Hall Inn** is a delightful pub that has associations with the Chartist movement of the mid-1800s. Today, life at this olde worlde hostelry is altogether less revolutionary. The interior is very traditional, with flagstone floors, heavy oak beams and roaring open fires. Cosy and comfortable, the inn has two bars with a separate lounge area that provides just the right ambience for a relaxing drink. As a free house, there is always a fine choice of real ales on tap here with Brains SA and Brains Bitter as the regular brews together with a rotating guest ale. The pub is also the meeting, and playing venue for the local darts club. Mine host, Stuart Savidge,

who has been here since 2000, and renowned chef Stewart McCracken pride themselves on serving some of the best food to be found in the area. Everything is prepared to order from locally sourced ingredients. All steaks are cut to order and fish is delivered 4 times a week. The menu, which features many local specialities, is supplemented by a constantly changing list of daily specials. The regular menu offers appetising dishes such as the salmonn cod & leek fish cake among the starters, along with baked goat's cheese with basil pesto and mussels with onion and garlic cream. For your main course, how about prime Welsh sirloin steak or braised skirt of beef on horseradish and parsley mashed potato with a red wine and redcurrant sauce? Home-made puddings are something of a speciality here with old favourites like the bread and butter pudding with double cream vying for your attention with dishes such as fresh baked apple pie and a melt-in-the-mouth raspberry Pavlova. A note on the menu urges vegetarians, if they are struggling to find something they like, to have a word with the chef - "He is very adaptable and will strive to please!" food is served every lunchtime and evening, except Sunday evening and all day Monday unless it is a Bank Holiday. Booking ahead is strongly recommended at weekends. The inn also offers comfortable quality accommodation in 3 double rooms, all with en suite accommodation.

321 THE HARDWICK

Old Raglan Road, Abergavenny,
Monmouthshire NP7 9AA

☎ 01873 854220 Fax: 01873 854623

e-mail: info@thehardwick.co.uk

🌐 www.thehardwick.co.uk

Standing on the outskirts of Abergavenny and with scenic views of open countryside, **The Hardwick** is a fine old inn noted for its excellent food and well-kept real ales. This is very much a family-owned and run business with Stephen and Joanna Terry and their daughters Olivia and Phoebe all involved in the enterprise. Although this is their first venture all together in the hospitality trade, Stephen has some 22 years experience in the business.

Providing top quality food is a major priority at the Hardwick and gastronomes will be in their element here. Professional chefs bring imagination and flair to creating menus that are fresh and exciting. The menus change regularly but on a typical day you might find amongst the starters Fresh Perroche Goat's Cheese from Neals Yard Creamery, Dorstone near Hereford served with roasted golden and candy beetroot, romaine, dandelion and capers; or a Carpaccio of

Rare Roast Herefordshire Beef on rocket with anchovy, garlic & rosemary dressing. The main courses show similar inventiveness - Oxtail & Kidney Casserole with Guinness and a parsley and horseradish dumpling, for example, or slow-cooked shoulder and pan fried neck of local lamb with chick peas cooked with cumin, viola aubergine fritter, chilli and parsley salsa, lamb juices and extra virgin olive oil. Vegetarians too can escape the usually limited choice of over-familiar dishes. At the Hardwick they can treat themselves to dishes such as Penne Pasta with Scottish Girolle

Mushrooms, broad beans, buffalo mozzarella, rocket, capers, pine nuts and Parmesan. To accompany your meal, there's a comprehensive range of beverages including wine half-bottle carafe or glass, and 2 rotating guest real ales. Meals are served in the 60-seat restaurant every lunchtime from noon until 3pm, and in the evening from 6.30pm to 10pm, except on Sunday evening and all day Monday unless it is a Bank Holiday when the restaurant is open for lunch. Children are welcome and all major credit cards apart from American Express and Diners are accepted.

As we go to press, the Terry family are initiating a major refurbishment of the inn. When completed, this will provide a larger restaurant, new toilets - including disabled toilets - and also 8 guest bedrooms, 5 of which will be on the ground floor and all of which will have en suite facilities. Another new amenity will be a terraced hot tub with views along the valley.

322 THE LION INN

Merthyr Road, Govilon, nr Abergavenny,
Monmouthshire NP7 9PT
☎ 01873 830404
e-mail: jeljebs@gmail.com

A handsome old building dating back to 1780, **The Lion Inn** is a delightful village inn which mine hosts, Jane and Bernie Long, have made the social hub of the village. The inn is also noted for its quality food and well-tended ales, including 2 real ales. Jane is an outstanding cook and her regular menu offers a good selection of dishes based on local produce. These include curries, steaks and, when available, a venison casserole. The regular menu is supplemented by daily specials - aubergine & walnut bake, perhaps, or a delicious ale-battered cod and chips. The kitchen also offers a choice of light bites - soup, jacket potatoes, paninis and more. Food is served from 7pm to 9pm, Tuesday, Thursday and Friday; and from noon until 3pm, and from 7pm to 9pm on Saturday and Sunday. During the summer months, these hours are extended. Children are welcome, and dogs are permitted in the bar area.

Once a month, The Lion hosts a pub quiz on Sunday from 8pm; there's a karaoke once a month on Saturday from 8.30pm; and also occasional live entertainment. The pub has a beer garden with a children's play area and a covered smoking area with large umbrella, heating and lighting. The Lion also offers accommodation in 3 comfortable standard rooms.

323 THE NAVIGATION INN

51 Main Road, Gilwern,
Monmouthshire NP7 0AU
☎ 01873 832015

Standing beside the Monmouthshire and Brecon Canal, **The Navigation Inn** is a fine old traditional hostelry with a very relaxed and welcoming atmosphere and with boat moorings. Siôn and Jess Driscoll took over here in the summer of 2007 and their enthusiasm and commitment have brought new life to this venerable inn. Siôn is a local boy and also an accomplished cook. His menu is based as far as possible on ingredients sourced locally with organic and Fairtrade produce also strongly featured. Food is served every lunchtime (noon until 3pm) and evening (6pm to 9pm), and at Sunday lunchtime there's a choice of delicious roasts. Booking at weekends is strongly recommended. On Tuesdays, there's a '2 courses for the price of one' offer, while Wednesday is Curry Night when you get your meal and

a pint at a special price. To accompany your food, there's an extensive choice of beverages, including one rotating real ale. In good weather, you can enjoy your refreshments in the large canalside beer garden. The Navigation has regular entertainment with a Pub Quiz on Tuesday evenings and live music - jazz, blues or folk - every other Sunday afternoon from 3pm. The Driscolls hope that soon they will also be offering accommodation. Dogs are welcome.

324 ROCK & FOUNTAIN HOTEL

Clydach North, Abergavenny,
Monmouthshire NP7 0LL
☎ 01873 830393
e-mail: archer@rockandfountain.co.uk
🌐 www.rockandfountain.co.uk

Not many establishments can boast that they have a natural mountain stream running through their restaurant, but the **Rock & Fountain Hotel** does

indeed have one. This picturesque inn with its whitewashed walls and abundance of flowers in hanging baskets and troughs, is located in the Clydach Gorge within the Brecon Beacons National Park. It's a family owned and family run inn with Emma and Ryan Jowitt, and Emma's mum and dad, Sue and Stephen, all actively involved.

The hotel is noted for its excellent food which is served every evening and Sunday lunchtime - such is the restaurant's reputation that booking is strongly recommended on Friday, Saturday and Sunday. The bar serves one real ale - Wadworth's 6X - along with a full range of other beverages.

The Rock & Fountain is also well-known for its Saturday night live entertainment with a variety of different kinds of music. If you are planning to stay in this scenic part of the country, the hotel has 7 well-appointed rooms, including a family suite and 2 family rooms, one of which can sleep 5 people. Most rooms command a spectacular view over the beautiful Clydach Gorge.

Tourist Information Centres

ABERAERON
The Quay, Aberaeron, Ceredigion SA46 0BT
Tel: 01545 570602 Fax: 01545 571534
e-mail: aberaerontic@ceredigion.gov.uk

ABERDULAIS FALLS
The National Trust, Aberdulais Falls,
Rhondda, Cynon, Taff SA10 8EU
Tel: 01639 636674 Fax: 01639 645069
e-mail: aberdulais@nationaltrust.org.uk

ABERDYFI
The Wharf Gardens, Aberdyfi, Gwynedd LL35 0ED
Tel: 01654 767321 Fax: 01654 767321
e-mail: tic.aberdyfi@eryri-npa.gov.uk

ABERGAVENNY
Swan Meadow, Monmouth Road, Abergavenny,
Monmouthshire NP7 5HL
Tel: 01873 853254 Fax: 01873 853254
e-mail: abergavennyic@breconbeacons.org

ABERYSTWYTH
Terrace Road, Aberystwyth, Ceredigion SY23 2AG
Tel: 01970 612125 Fax: 01970 612125
e-mail: aberystwythtic@ceredigion.gov.uk

BALA
Pensarn Road, Bala, Gwynedd LL23 7SR
Tel: 01678 521021 Fax: 01678 521021
e-mail: bala.tic@gwynedd.gov.uk

BANGOR
Town Hall, Deiniol Road, Bangor, Gwynedd LL57 2RE
Tel: 01248 352786 Fax: 01248 352786
e-mail: bangor.tic@gwynedd.gov.uk

BARMOUTH
The Station, Station Road, Barmouth,
Gwynedd LL42 1LU
Tel: 01341 280787 Fax: 01341 280787
e-mail: barmouth.tic@gwynedd.gov.uk

BARRY ISLAND
The Promenade, The Triangle, Barry Island,
Vale Of Glamorgan CF62 5TQ
Tel: 01446 747171 Fax: 01446 747171
e-mail: barrytic@valeofglamorgan.gov.uk

BEDDGELERT
Canolfan Hebog, Beddgelert, Gwynedd LL55 4YD
Tel: 01766 890615 Fax: 01766 890615
e-mail: tic.beddgelert@eryri-npa.gov.uk

BETWS Y COED
Royal Oak Stables, Betws y Coed, Gwynedd LL24 0AH
Tel: 01690 710426 Fax: 01690 710665
e-mail: tic.byc@eryri-npa.gov.uk

BLAENAU FFESTINIOG
Unit 3, High Street, Blaenau Ffestiniog,
Gwynedd LL41 3ES
Tel: 01766 830360 Fax: 01766 830360
e-mail: tic.blaenau@eryri-npa.gov.uk

BLAENAVON
Blaenavon Ironworks, North Street, Blaenavon,
Torfaen NP4 9RQ
Tel: 01495 792615 Fax: 01495 792615
e-mail: blaenavon.ironworks@btopenworld.com

BORTH
Cambrian Terrace, Borth, Ceredigion SY24 5HY
Tel: 01970 871174 Fax: 01970 871365
e-mail: borthtic@ceredigion.gov.uk

BRECON
Cattle Market Car park, Brecon, Powys LD3 9DA
Tel: 01874 622485 Fax: 01874 625256
e-mail: brectic@powys.gov.uk

BRIDGEND
Bridgend Designer Outlet, The Derwen,
Bridgend CF32 9SU
Tel: 01656 654906 Fax: 01656 646523
e-mail: bridgendtic@bridgend.gov.uk

BUILTH WELLS
The Groe Car Park, Builth Wells, Powys LD2 3BL
Tel: 01982 553307 Fax: 01982 553841
e-mail: builtic@powys.gov.uk

CAERLEON
5 High Street, Caerleon, Newport NP18 1AE
Tel: 01633 422656 Fax: 01633 422656
e-mail: caerleon.tic@newport.gov.uk

CAERNARFON
Oriel Pendeitsh, Castle Street, Caernarfon,
Gwynedd LL55 1ES
Tel: 01286 672232 Fax: 01286 676476
e-mail: caernarfon.tic@gwynedd.gov.uk

CAERPHILLY
The Twyn, Caerphilly CF83 1JL
Tel: 029 2088 0011 Fax: 029 2086 0811
e-mail: tourism@caerphilly.gov.uk

CARDIFF
The Old Library, The Hayes, Cardiff CF10 1AH
Tel: 08701 211 258 Fax: 029 2023 2058
e-mail: visitor@cardiff.gov.uk

CARDIGAN
Theatr Mwldan, Bath House Road, Cardigan,
Ceredigion SA43 1JY
Tel: 01239 613230 Fax: 01239 614853
e-mail: cardigantic@ceredigion.gov.uk

CARMARTHEN
113 Lammas Street, Carmarthen,
Carmarthenshire SA31 3AQ
Tel: 01267 231557 Fax: 01267 221901
e-mail: carmarthentic@carmarthenshire.gov.uk

CHEPSTOW
Castle Car Park, Bridge Street, Chepstow,
Monmouthshire NP16 5EY
Tel: 01291 623772 Fax: 01291 628004
e-mail: chepstow.tic@monmouthshire.gov.uk

CONWY
Castle Buildings, Conwy, Conwy LL32 8LD
Tel: 01492 592248 Fax: 01492 573545
e-mail: conwytic@conwy.gov.uk

DOLGELLAU
Ty Meirion, Eldon Square, Dolgellau,
Gwynedd LL40 1PU
Tel: 01341 422888 Fax: 01341 422576
e-mail: tic.dolgellau@eryri-npa.gov.uk

FISHGUARD HARBOUR
Ocean Lab, The Parrog, Fishguard Harbour,
Pembrokeshire SA64 0DE
Tel: 01348 872037 Fax: 01348 872528
e-mail: fishguardharbour.tic@pembrokeshire.gov.uk

FISHGUARD TOWN
Town Hall, Market Square, Fishguard Town,
Pembrokeshire SA65 9HA
Tel: 01437 776636 Fax: 01384 875582
e-mail: fishguard.tic@pembrokeshire.gov.uk

HARLECH
Llys y Graig, High Street, Harlech, Gwynedd LL46 2YE
Tel: 01766 780658 Fax: 01766 780658
e-mail: tic.harlech@eryri-npa.gov.uk

HAVERFORDWEST
Old Bridge, Haverfordwest, Pembrokeshire SA61 2EZ
Tel: 01437 763110 Fax: 01437 767738
e-mail: haverfordwest.tic@pembrokeshire.gov.uk

HOLYHEAD
Stena Line, Terminal 1, Holyhead,
Isle Of Anglesey LL65 1DQ
Tel: 01407 762622 Fax: 01407 761462
e-mail: holyhead@nwtic.com

KNIGHTON
Offa's Dyke Centre, West Street, Knighton,
Powys LD7 1EN
Tel: 01547 529424 Fax: 01547 529242
e-mail: oda@offasdyke.demon.co.uk

LAKE VYRNWY
Unit 2, Vyrnwy Craft Workshops, Lake Vyrnwy,
Powys SY10 0LY
Tel: 01691 870346 Fax: 01691 870697
e-mail: laktic@powys.gov.uk

LLANBERIS
41b High Street, Llanberis, Gwynedd LL55 4EU
Tel: 01286 870765 Fax: 01286 871924
e-mail: llanberis.tic@gwynedd.gov.uk

LLANDOVERY
Heritage Centre, Kings Road, Llandovery,
Carmarthenshire SA20 0AW
Tel: 01550 720693 Fax: 01550 720693
e-mail: llandovery.ic@breconbeacons.org

LLANDRINDOD WELLS
Auto Palace, Temple Street, Llandrindod Wells,
Powys LD1 5HU
Tel: 01597 822600 Fax: 01597 829164
e-mail: llandtic@powys.gov.uk

LLANDUDNO
Library Building, Mostyn Street, Llandudno,
Conwy LL30 2RP
Tel: 01492 876413 Fax: 01492 872722
e-mail: llandudnotic@conwy.gov.uk

LLANELLI
Millennium Coastal Park Visitor Centre, North Dock,
Llanelli, Carmarthenshire SA15 2LF
Tel: 01554 777744 Fax: 01554 757825
e-mail: DiscoveryCentre@carmarthenshire.gov.uk

LLANFAIRPWLLGWYNGYLL
Station Site, Llanfairpwllgwyngyll,
Isle Of Anglesey LL61 5UJ
Tel: 01248 713177 Fax: 01248 715711
e-mail: llanfairpwll@nwtic.com

LLANGOLLEN
Y Chapel, Castle Street, Llangollen,
Denbighshire LL20 8NU
Tel: 01978 860828 Fax: 01978 861563
e-mail: llangollen@nwtic.com

MACHYNLLETH
Royal House, Penrallt Street, Machynlleth,
Powys SY20 8AG
Tel: 01654 702401 Fax: 01654 703675
e-mail: mactic@powys.gov.uk

MERTHYR TYDFIL
14a Glebeland Street, Merthyr Tydfil CF47 8AU
Tel: 01685 379884 Fax: 01685 379884
e-mail: tic@merthyr.gov.uk

MILFORD HAVEN
94 Charles Street, Milford Haven,
Pembrokeshire SA73 2HL
Tel: 01646 690866 Fax: 01646 690655
e-mail: milford.tic@pembrokeshire.gov.uk

MOLD
Library Museum & Art Gallery, Earl Road, Mold,
Flintshire CH7 1AP
Tel: 01352 759331 Fax: 01352 759331
e-mail: mold@nwtic.com

MONMOUTH
Shire Hall, Agincourt Square, Monmouth,
Monmouthshire NP25 3DY
Tel: 01600 713899 Fax: 01600 772794
e-mail: monmouth.tic@monmouthshire.gov.uk

MUMBLES
The Methodist Church, Mumbles Road, Mumbles,
Swansea SA3 4BU
Tel: 01792 361302 Fax: 01792 363392
e-mail: info@mumblestic.co.uk

NEW QUAY
Church Street, New Quay, Ceredigion SA45 9NZ
Tel: 01545 560865 Fax: 01545 561360
e-mail: newquaytic@ceredigion.gov.uk

NEWPORT
Museum & Art Gallery, John Frost Square,
Newport NP20 1PA
Tel: 01633 842962 Fax: 01633 222615
e-mail: newport.tic@newport.gov.uk

NEWPORT (PEMBS)
2 Bank Cottages, Long Street, Newport (pembs),
Pembrokeshire SA42 0TN
Tel: 01239 820912 Fax: 01239 821258
e-mail: NewportTIC@Pembrokeshirecoast.org.uk

NEWTOWN
The Park, Back Lane, Newtown, Powys SY16 2NH
Tel: 01686 625580 Fax: 01686 610066
e-mail: newtic@powys.gov.uk

OSWESTRY TOWN
The Heritage Centre, 2 Church Terrace, Oswestry Town,
Powys SY11 2TE
Tel: 01691 662753 Fax: 01691 657811
e-mail: ot@oswestry-welshborders.org.uk

OSWESTRY MILE END
Mile End Services, Oswestry Mile End, Powys SY11 4JA
Tel: 01691 662488 Fax: 01691 662883
e-mail: tic@oswestry-bc.gov.uk

PEMBROKE
Visitor Centre, Commons Road, Pembroke,
Pembrokeshire SA71 6TW
Tel: 01646 622388
e-mail: pembroke.tic@pembrokeshire.gov.uk

PORTHCAWL
Old Police Station, John Street, Porthcawl, Bridgend
CF36 3DT
Tel: 01656 786639 Fax: 01656 782387
e-mail: porthcawltic@bridgend.gov.uk

PORTHMADOG
High Street, Porthmadog, Gwynedd LL49 9LD
Tel: 01766 512981 Fax: 01766 515312
e-mail: porthmadog.tic@gwynedd.gov.uk

PRESTEIGNE
The Judge's Lodging, Broad Street, Presteigne,
Powys LD8 2AD
Tel: 01544 260650 Fax: 01544 260652
e-mail: presteignetic@powys.gov.uk

PWLLHELI
Min y Don, Station Square, Pwllheli,
Gwynedd LL53 5HG
Tel: 01758 613000 Fax: 01758 613000
e-mail: pwllheli.tic@gwynedd.gov.uk

RHAYADER
The Leisure Centre, North Street, Rhayader,
Powys LD6 5BU
Tel: 01597 810591
e-mail: rhayader.tic@powys.gov.uk

RHYL
Rhyl Childrens Village, West Parade, Rhyl,
Denbighshire LL18 1HZ
Tel: 01745 355068 Fax: 01745 342255
e-mail: rhyl.tic@denbighshire.gov.uk

SAUNDERSFOOT
The Barbecue, Harbour Car Park, Saundersfoot,
Pembrokeshire SA69 9HE
Tel: 01834 813672 Fax: 01834 813673
e-mail: saundersfoot.tic@pembrokeshire.gov.uk

ST DAVIDS
1 High Street, St Davids, Pembrokeshire SA62 6SA
Tel: 01437 720392
e-mail: enquiries@stdavids.pembrokeshirecoast.org.uk

SWANSEA
Plymouth Street, Swansea SA1 3QG
Tel: 01792 468321 Fax: 01792 464602
e-mail: tourism@swansea.gov.uk

TENBY
Unit 2, The Gateway Complex, Tenby,
Pembrokeshire SA70 7LT
Tel: 01834 842402 Fax: 01834 845439
e-mail: tenby.tic@pembrokeshire.gov.uk

TYWYN
High Street, Tywyn, Gwynedd LL36 9AD
Tel: 01654 710070 Fax: 01654 710070
e-mail: tywyn.tic@gwynedd.gov.uk

WREXHAM
Lambpit Street, Wrexham LL11 1WN
Tel: 01978 292015 Fax: 01978 292467
e-mail: tic@wrexham.gov.uk

Towns, Villages and Places of Interest

TRAVEL PUBLISHING ORDER FORM

To order any of our publications just fill in the payment details below and complete the order form. For orders of less than 4 copies please add £1.00 per book for postage and packing. Orders over 4 copies are P & P free.

Name:

Address:

Tel no:

Please Complete Either:

I enclose a cheque for £ _____ made payable to Travel Publishing Ltd

Or:

Card No: _____ Expiry Date: _____

Signature:

Please either send, telephone, fax or e-mail your order to:

Travel Publishing Ltd, 64-66 Ebrington Street, Plymouth, Devon PL4 9AQ

Tel: 01752 276660   Fax: 01752 276699   e-mail: info@travelpublishing.co.uk

	Price	Quantity		Price	Quantity
HIDDEN PLACES REGIONAL TITLES			**COUNTRY PUBS AND INNS**		
Comwall	£8.99	....	Cornwall	£5.99	....
Devon	£8.99	....	Devon	£7.99	....
Dorset, Hants & Isle of Wight	£8.99	....	Sussex	£5.99	....
East Anglia	£8.99	....	Wales	£8.99	....
Lake District & Cumbria	£8.99	....	Yorkshire	£7.99	....
Northumberland & Durham	£8.99	....	**COUNTRY LIVING RURAL GUIDES**		
Peak District and Derbyshire	£8.99	....			
Yorkshire	£8.99	....	East Anglia	£10.99	....
HIDDEN PLACES NATIONAL TITLES			Heart of England	£10.99	....
			Ireland	£11.99	....
England	£11.99	....	North East	£10.99	....
Ireland	£11.99	....	North West	£10.99	....
Scotland	£11.99	....	Scotland	£11.99	....
Wales	£11.99	....	South of England	£10.99	....
HIDDEN INNS TITLES			South East of England	£10.99	....
			Wales	£11.99	....
East Anglia	£7.99	....	West Country	£10.99	....
Heart of England	£7.99	....			
South	£7.99	....			
South East	£7.99	....	**TOTAL QUANTITY:**		
West Country	£7.99	....			
OTHER TITLES			**POST & PACKING:**		
Off the Motorway	£11.99	....	**TOTAL VALUE:**		
Garden Centres & Nurseries	£11.99	....			

READER REACTION FORM

The *Travel Publishing* research team would like to receive reader's comments on any visitor attractions or places reviewed in the book and also recommendations for suitable entries to be included in the next edition. This will help ensure that the *Country Living series of Guides* continues to provide its readers with useful information on the more interesting, unusual or unique features of each attraction or place ensuring that their visit to the local area is an enjoyable and stimulating experience. To provide your comments or recommendations would you please complete the forms below and overleaf as indicated and send to:

The Research Department, Travel Publishing Ltd,
64-66 Ebrington Street, Plymouth, Devon PL4 9AQ

Your Name:

Your Address:

Your Telephone Number:

Please tick as appropriate:

Comments ☐   Recommendation ☐

Name of Establishment:

Address:

Telephone Number:

Name of Contact:

READER REACTION FORM

COMMENT OR REASON FOR RECOMMENDATION:

....

....

....

....

....

....

....

....

....

....

....

....

....

....

....

....

....

....

....

....

Index of Advertisers

455

INDEX OF ADVERTISERS

456

INDEX OF ADVERTISERS

PLACES OF INTEREST